New

EUROPE'S LARGEST OUTDOOR SCREEN:

THE EXPERIENCE IS EVEN MORE UNIQUE

48. festival internazionale del film Locarno. 3-13 August 1995

MANFRED DURNIOK PRODUKTION FÜR FILM UND FERNSEHEN

International Motion Picture
and Television Productions,
Co-Productions and Film Distribution.
Hausotterstraße 36, D-13409 Berlin,
Germany, Phone (030) 491 80 45
Telex 1-81 717 Dufi D
Fax (030) 491 40 66

EDITED BY PETER COWIE

VARIETY

INTERNATIONAL

FILM GUIDE

1995

LONDON
HAMLYN

HOLLYWOOD
SAMUEL FRENCH TRADE

HOW CAN YOU CELEBRATE
YOUR 75th ANNIVERSARY AND
FEEL NEWLY BORN?

It's quite simple - at least for AB Svensk Filmindustri, SF!

On December 27, 1994, we will celebrate our 75th anniversary.

Needless to say, we intend to mark the event! Not by looking back but by looking ahead. SF has seldom been so busy with future plans. We are thinking in new directions, doing old things in a new way and learning all the time. Just like a new born child.

We are in the process of building Sweden's and Europe's best multiplex. Right in the heart of Stockholm, facing one of the city's most popular squares, Hötorget. This 14-screen multiplex will astound Stockholmers and radically change entertainment in Stockholm.

An entirely new studio facility - the most modern in Europe - is to be constructed in the southern part of Stockholm. With two new studios for feature films and TV productions.

A creative center will be added to this studio. Through our own efforts and in cooperation with others, this facility in Kungens Kurva will simmer with creativity and supply our market with all types of programs.

We are setting up our own TV production unit, with its roots in true SF tradition, presenting exciting and entertaining programs for all ages. All types of expertise will be utilized and our company will be involved in new forms of distribution such as CD-discs, digital TV channels, distribution via telecommunications networks, and the new satellite revolution with hundreds of channels, in addition to current activities. Not because we are a technology-based company, but simply because we want to reach our audience everywhere.

We will work across borders through various forms of joint ventures, both in Scandinavia and Europe.

Consequently, there is little time for reminiscing. Although we are keenly aware of our origins, our future progress is of much greater interest.

Hence, the future will be a highly exciting time for SF, marked by activities which will reflect our dedication and ambition to move forward.

LENNART WIKLUND
PRESIDENT & CEO

AB SVENSK FILMINDUSTRI. Södermälarstrand 27 • S-117 88 Stockholm, Sweden. Tel. +46 8 658 75 00

CONTENTS

Editor: Peter Cowie
Consulting Editor: Derek Elley
Assistant Editor: Steve Pemberton
New York Liaison: Fred Lombardi
Advertising Co-ordination: Zoë Hoenig
Cover Design: Stefan Dreja
Book Design: John Harmer
Photo Consultants: The Kobal Collection

WORLD SURVEY

Editorial and Business Offices:
Variety
34-35 Newman Street,
London W1P 3PD
Tel: (071) 637 3663
Fax: (071) 580 5559

ISBN 0 600 58516 6
British Library Cataloging in Publication Data
Variety International Film Guide 1995
1. Cowie, Peter
011.37

U.S. Library of Congress Catalog Card No: 64-1706
Copyright © 1994 by Reed U.S. Publishing Ltd
Photoset by Avonset, Midsomer Norton, Bath
Printed and bound in Great Britain by Cromwell Press Ltd

CONTENTS

INTERNATIONAL LIAISON

Africa: Jean Michel Frodon,
        Mohammed Rouda,
        Thérèse-Marie
        Deffontaines
Argentina: Alberto Tabbia
Asia: Jean Radvanyi,
        Rashmi Doraiswamy
Australia: David Stratton
Austria: Susanna Pyrker
Belgium: Patrick
Duynslaegher
Brazil: Luis Arbex
Bulgaria: Ivan Stoyanovich
Canada: Gerald Pratley
Chile: Hans Ehrmann
Croatia: Tomislav Kurelec
Czech Republic: Eva Zaoralová
Denmark: Ebbe Iversen
Egypt: Fawzi Soliman
Far East: Derek Elley
Finland: Matti Apunen
France: Michel Ciment
Germany: Jack Kindred
Greece: Yannis
Bacoyannopoulos
Hungary: Derek Elley
Iceland: Gísli Einarsson
India: Uma da Cunha
Indonesia: Marselli Sumarno
Iran: Jamal Omid
Ireland: Michael Dwyer
Israel: Dan Fainaru
Italy: Lorenzo Codelli
Japan: Frank Segers
Latvia: Andris Rozenbergs
Lithuania: Grazina Arlickaite

Luxembourg: Jean-Pierre
Thilges
Malaysia: Baharudin A. Latif
Mexico: Tomás Pérez Turrent
Netherlands: Pieter van Lierop
New Zealand: Phil Wakefield
Norway: Trond Olav
Svendsen
Pakistan: Aijaz Gul
Philippines: Agustin Sotto
Poland: Wanda Wertenstein
Puerto Rico: José Artemio
Torres
Russia: Andrew Horton
Serbia & Montenegro:
        Goran Gocić
Slovakia: Hana Cielová
Slovenia: Milan Ljubić
South Africa: Martin Botha
Spain: Peter Besas
Sri Lanka: Amarnath
Jayatilaka
Sweden: Jannike Åhlund
Switzerland: Christoph Egger
Syria: Rafik Atassi
Turkey: Atilla Dorsay
U.K.: George Perry
U.S.A.: William Wolf
Zimbabwe: Judy Kendall

UNITED INTERNATIONAL PICTURES
A *Paramount* • Metro Goldwyn Mayer • **UNIVERSAL** COMPANY

DISTRIBUTORS OF

JUNIOR

THE WAR

MILK MONEY

STAR TREK-GENERATIONS

TANK GIRL

WATERWORLD

GOLDEN EYE

UIP HOUSE, 45 BEADON ROAD HAMMERSMITH LONDON W6 0EG
TELEPHONE: 081 741 9041 FAX: 081 748 8990

Bruce Willis and Maria de Madeiros in Quentin Tarantino's PULP FICTION

Brad Pitt and Julia Ormond in Ed Zwick's LEGENDS OF THE FALL
photo: Kerry Hayes/TriStar

NEW AND COMING

Harriet Andersson and Inger Lise Winjevoll in Berit Nesheim's BEYOND THE SKY

Top left: Victoria Abril in Pedro Almodóvar's KIKA (photo: Jean Marie Leroy). Above: Irène Jacob in TROIS COULEURS ROUGE

NEW AND COMING

Above: Seema Biswas in Shekhar Kapur's THE BANDIT QUEEN. Below: Winona Ryder in Gillian Armstrong's LITTLE WOMEN   photo: Joseph Lederer/Columbia

Gong Li in Zhang Yimou's TO LIVE

Cel from Nick Park's Academy Award-winning THE WRONG TROUSERS, from Aardman Animations

Tom Hanks in Robert Zemeckis's FORREST GUMP

photo: Paramount

HOLLYWOOD

Made in Hollywood, edited on

Lightworks

Mrs Doubtfire
Editor - Raja Gosnell
Director - Chris Columbus

Pulp Fiction
Editor - Sally Menke
Director - Quentin Tarantino

Clear & Present Danger
Editor -Neil Travis ACE
Director - Philip Noyce

Speed
Editor - John Wright, ACE
Director - Jan De Bont

Waterworld
Editor - Peter Boyle
Director - Kevin Reynolds

Brave Heart
Editor - Steve Rosenblum
Director - Mel Gibson

Immortal Beloved
Editor -Dan Rae
Director - Bernard Rose

The Pelican Brief
Editor - Tom Rolf, ACE & Trudy Ship
Director - Alan Pakula

Blown Away
Editor - Tim Wellburn
Director - Stephen Hopkins

Heaven & Earth
Editor - David Brenner & Sally Menke
Director - Oliver Stone

Highlander III: The Magician
Editor - Yves Langlois
Director - Andrew Mohrahan

Six Degrees of Separation
Editor - Peter Honess
Director - Fred Schepisi

LIGHTWORKS

Lightworks Editing Systems Ltd
31-32 Soho Square
London W1V GAP
UK
Tel: 00 44 (71) 494 3084
Fax: 00 44 (71) 437 3570

Lightworks USA
6762 Lexington Avenue
Suite no.2
Hollywood
CA 90038 USA
Tel: (1) 213 465 2002
Fax: (1) 213 463 1209

Lightworks USA
133 5th Avenue
6th Floor
New York
NY 10003 USA
Tel: (1) 212 677 9775
Fax: (1) 212 677 9773

Awards sweep for SCHINDLER'S LIST

U.S. Academy Awards: 1994

Best Film: *Schindler's List.*
Best Direction: Steven Spielberg for *Schindler's List.*
Best Actor: Tom Hanks for *Philadelphia.*
Best Actress: Holly Hunter for *The Piano.*
Best Supporting Actor: Tommy Lee Jones for *The Fugitive.*
Best Supporting Actress: Anna Paquin for *The Piano.*
Best Original Screenplay: Jane Campion for *The Piano.*
Best Adapted Screenplay: Steven Zaillian for *Schindler's List.*
Best Cinematography: Janusz Kaminski for *Schindler's List.*
Best Costume Design: Gabriella Pescucci for *The Age of Innocence*
Best Art Direction: Allan Starski, Ewa Braun for *Schindler's List.*
Best Editing: Michael Kahn for *Schindler's List.*
Best Original Score: John Williams for *Schindler's List.*
Best Original Song: "Streets of Philadelphia" from *Philadelphia*. Music and Lyrics by Bruce Springsteen.
Best Sound: Gary Summers, Gary Rydstrom, Shawn Murphy, Ron Judkins for *Jurassic Park.*
Best Make-Up: Greg Cannom, Ve Neill, Yolanda Toussieng for *Mrs. Doubtfire.*
Best Visual Effects: Dennis Muren, Stan Winston, Phil Tippett, Michael Lantieri for *Jurassic Park.*
Best Sound-Effects Editing: Gary Rydstrom, Richard Hymns for *Jurassic Park.*
Best Foreign Language Film: *Belle Epoque* (Spain)
Best Documentary Feature: *I Am a Promise: The Children of Santon Elementary School.*
Best Documentary Short: *Defending Our Lives.*
Best Animated Short: *The Wrong Trousers.*

Best Live-Action Short: *Black Rider.*
Jean Hersholt Humanitarian Award: Paul Newman.
Honorary Academy Award: Deborah Kerr.

British Academy of Film and Television Arts Awards 1994

Best Film: *Schindler's List.*
Best British Film: *Shadowlands.*
Best Direction: Steven Spielberg for *Schindler's List.*
Best Actor: Anthony Hopkins for *The Remains of the Day.*
Best Actress: Holly Hunter for *The Piano.*
Best Supporting Actor: Ralph Fiennes for *Schindler's List.*
Best Supporting Actress: Miriam Margoyles for *The Age of Innocence.*
Best Original Screenplay: Danny Rubin, Harold Ramis for *Groundhog Day.*
Best Adapted Screenplay: Steven Zaillian for *Schindler's List.*
Best Original Film Music: John Williams for *Schindler's List.*
Best Foreign-Language Film: *Farewell My Concubine* (China).
Best Short Film: *Franz Kafka's It's a Wonderful Life.*
Best Short Animated Film: *The Wrong Trousers.*
Fellowship Award: Michael Grade.
Michael Balcon Award: Ken Loach.
Special Awards: Sir Richard Attenborough, Thora Hird.

European Film Awards: 1993

Best Film: *Urga* (Russia).
Best Young Film: *Orlando* (U.K.)
Best Actor: Daniel Auteuil for *Un cœur en hiver* (France).
Best Actress: Maia Morgenstern for *Balanta* (Romania).
European Achievement of the Year: Nik Powell, Stephen Wooley for *The Crying Game.*
European Film Academy Lifetime Achievement Award : Michelangelo Antonioni.
European Film Academy Award of Merit: Erika Gregor, Ulrich Gregor, Naum Kleiman.
Best Documentary: *Det sociala arvet* (Sweden).
FIPRESCI Award: *Benny's Video* (Austria).

French César Academy Awards: 1994

Best Film: *Smoking/No Smoking*.
Best Foreign Film: *The Piano* (Australia /France).
Best Director: Alain Resnais for *Smoking/No Smoking*.
Best Actor: Pierre Arditi for *Smoking/No Smoking*.
Best Actress: Juliette Binoche for *Bleu*.
Best Supporting Actor: Fabrice Luchini for *Tout ça pour ça*.
Best Supporting Actress: Valérie Lemercier for *Les visiteurs*.
Most Promising Young Actor: Olivier Martinez for *Un deux trois soleil*.
Most Promising Young Actress: Valéria Bruni-Tedeschi for *Les gens normaux n'ont rien d'exceptionnel*.
Best First Film: Tran An Hung for *L'odeur de la papaye verte*.
Best Screenplay: J-P Bacri, Agnès Jaoui for *Smoking/No Smoking*.
Best Cinematography: Yves Angelo for *Germinal*.
Best Editing: Jacques Witta for *Bleu*.
Best Original Score: Khaled for *Un deux trois soleil*.
Best Sets: Jacques Saulnier for *Smoking/No Smoking*.
Best Sound: Jean-Claude Laureux, William Flageollet for *Bleu*.
Best Costumes: Sylvie Gautrelet, Caroline de Vivaise, Bernadette Villard for *Germinal*.
Best Short: *Gueule d'atmosphère*.

Italian Donatello Awards 1994

Best Film: *Dear Diary (Caro diario)*
Best Director: Carlo Verdone for *Perdiamoci di Vista*.
Best Producer: Aurelio De Laurentiis for *For Love, Only for Love*.
Best Actor: Giulio Scarpati for *Law of Courage*.
Best Actress: Asia Argento for *Perdiamoci di Vista*.
Best Supporting Actor: Alessandro Haber for *For Love, Only for Love*.
Best Supporting Actress: Monica Scattini for *Sentimental Maniacs*.

Best Screenplay: Giovanni Veronesi, Ugo Chiti for *For Love, Only for Love*.
Best Cinematography: (shared) Bruno Cascio for *Father and Son*; Dante Spinotti for *The Secret of the Old Woods*.
Best Music: Nicola Piovani for *Dear Diary*.
Best Art Direction: Antonello Geleng for *Dellamorte Dellamore*.
Best Costumes: Piero Tosi for *Sparrow*.
Best Editing: Carlo Valerio for *Father and Son*.
Best Sound: Tullio Morganti for *Sud*.
Best First Film: (*shared*) Francesco Martinotti for *Abyssinia*; Leone Pompucci for *Mille Bolle Blu*; Simona Izzo for *Sentimental Maniacs*.
Best Foreign Film: *In the Name of the Father* (U.K.).

Independent Spirit Awards of Independent Feature Project/West 1994

Best Film: *Short Cuts*.
Best Foreign Film: *The Piano* (Australia/France).
Best Director: Robert Altman for *Short Cuts*.
Best Actor: Jeff Bridges for *American Heart*.
Best Actress: Ashley Judd for *Ruby in Paradise*.
Best Supporting Actor: Christopher Lloyd for *Twenty Bucks*.
Best Supporting Actress: Lili Taylor for *Household Saints*.
Best Screenplay: Robert Altman, Frank Barhydt for *Short Cuts*.
Best First Feature; *El Mariachi* (Colombia).
Best Cinematography: Lisa Rinzler for *Menace II Society*.

Juliette Binoche: best actress award for TROIS COULEURS: BLEU

Par son soutien financier
et ses investissements,
la SOGIC appuie
L'INDUSTRIE QUÉBÉCOISE
DU CINÉMA
et contribue à la promotion
et à la diffusion de ses produits
sur les marchés extérieurs.

Through its financial
assistance and its investments,
SOGIC supports
THE QUÉBEC FILM INDUSTRY
and helps promote and
distribute its products on the
international market.

Exportation

Production

Diffusion

Événements

Et bien
d'autres
formes de
soutien
financier...

Société générale des industries culturelles Québec
1755, boul. René-Lévesque Est, bureau 200,
Montréal (Québec) H2K 4P6
Téléphone : (514) 873-7768 Télécopieur : (514) 873-4388

DIRECTORS
of the year

Jane Campion

by David Stratton

Jane Campion's women may, at first glance, seem disfunctional. However, on closer inspection they are far stronger than we might have supposed. Kay (Karen Colson) in *Sweetie* is frightened of trees and incredibly superstitious, but her fears and superstitions are proved, eventually, to be far from groundless. Janet Frame (played by various actresses, ultimately by Kerry Fox) in *An Angel at My Table*, undergoes horrific treatment for her supposed schizophrenia, but survives and triumphs as a brilliantly gifted and independent writer. Ada McGrath (Holly Hunter) in *The Piano* has made a decision not to speak yet through her beloved piano, and her feisty daughter, she is able to determine the course of her life in colonial New Zealand.

These women, and others to be found in Campion's films (Sweetie herself, for instance) are strikingly original creations, totally unstereotypical and strangely, hauntingly romantic. Jane Campion's vision is as astonishing as it is original. In a short career which has embraced only two feature films actually made for the cinema (both *Two Friends* and *An Angel at My Table* were produced for television), Campion has distinguished herself by being the first woman to win the coveted Cannes Palme d'Or, as well as only the second woman ever nominated for an Academy Award for direction (in a vintage year, she missed out to Steven Spielberg); and yet she's astonishingly modest and even shy about her work.

JANE CAMPION was born in New Zealand on April 30, 1954; both her parents were in show business, her father a theatre director and her mother an actress. However, she was initially more interested in the plastic arts, and studied painting and sculpture, obtaining a diploma in anthropology. In 1977 she arrived in Sydney to complete her studies, and soon after her arrival attended the Sydney Film Festival in the hope of meeting interesting people. She was so fascinated by the wide range of international cinema she saw during the two weeks of the festival that she determined to make films herself which one day might be good enough to participate in the event.

On the strength of an 8mm short film,

Tissues, she was accepted into the Australian Film Television and Radio School in Sydney and during her period there she made a series of striking short films which eventually brought her to international attention. The first of these was the quirky road movie *Peel* (1982), which made an impact at the 1983 Sydney Film Festival and which won the Palme d'Or for Best Short Film at Cannes three years later; and yet, Campion has recalled that some key members of the Film School establishment, far from encouraging her, were unenthusiastic ("They thought I was arrogant," she says, "and when they saw the first cut of *Peel* they told me not to bother to finish it.") Her other Film School shorts, *A Girl's Own Story* (1983) and *Passionless Moments* (1984) were equally striking; the first two were photographed by fellow student Sally Bongers; the third by Campion herself in collaboration with another student, Alex Proyas, whose first Hollywood film, *The Crow*, was released in 1994.

Campion's short films were seen by a Sydney producer, Jan Chapman, who at the time was working for ABC Television. She approached Campion, and they decided to work together on a telemovie based on a script by Helen Garner. The result was *Two Friends* (1986) which was eventually screened at many international film festivals, including Cannes. Like the Harold Pinter screenplay, *Betrayal*, the story is told backwards; it begins in July and ends the previous October. The teenage friends are Louise (Emma Coles) and Kelly (Kris Bidenko); Louise is the steady, serious one who's better able to cope with life than her

neurotic friend, who leaves home after one of her father's friends makes a pass at her. Campion charts the disintegration of the friendship with compassion and a quirky sense of humour.

Love and Romance, Sex and Family

Campion's first cinema feature was *Sweetie* (1989). "I didn't want to ape the kind of films made by other people," she says. "I wanted to invent my own. I decided to make a film about love and romance, sex and family. I wanted to provoke, but at the same time to touch people."

The film involves two sisters and their parents, but the structure is far from conventional. The younger sister, Kay, is introduced and established well before her hated sibling, Dawn (Genevieve Lemon), better known as Sweetie, appears on the scene. The parents of these strange daughters appear later still. Says Campion: "The characters of Kay and her boyfriend, Louis (Tom Lycos) came first; then Sweetie emerged and started taking over. She just grew." The central character is Kay, however, who believes in fate and romance, but who isn't very successful in the latter department.

Sally Bongers, who shot Campion's first two short films, photographed *Sweetie*. "When I saw the first cut of the film," says Campion, "I thought it had been made by Martians!"

Sweetie was selected to compete in the 1989 Cannes Film Festival, but received, to put it mildly, a mixed reaction. It's unquestionably a challenging film, which seems to have outraged and offended some people for its depiction of this offbeat family and for the strangely depressing sexual scenes. Campion was hissed and booed by some sections of the Cannes audience, although some key critics and festival programmers recognised the unusual new talent on display.

Campion immediately embarked on her next project, a three-part television mini-series based on the autobiographies of New Zealand author Janet Frame. Shot on

Genevieve Lemon and Michael Lake in SWEETIE

Janet Frame with the actresses who played her in AN ANGEL AT MY TABLE: Karen Ferguson, Alexia Fox, and Kerry Fox

photo: Kobal Collection

16mm by Stuart Dryburgh (who would later be cinematographer on *The Piano*), *An Angel at My Table* depicts the childhood and youth of Frame, who was diagnosed as a schizophrenic and who underwent shock therapy in the 1950's.

At first, Campion was reluctant to have the film screened at festivals, and turned down an invitation from Cannes. As she pointed out, the film was shot and framed for television, and she had no confidence that it would work on a large screen. However, she was persuaded to present it, on 16mm and in three separate parts (with three sets of credits) at the Sydney Film Festival; the standing ovation she received there convinced her the film had a theatrical future. It was successfully blown up to 35mm, and received its international premiere at Venice, where it won a major award.

Even in the relatively conventional childhood scenes of the first section, Campion's singular view of humanity is clearly apparent, so that what might, in lesser hands, have been familiar material becomes quirky, pungent and original. The later hospital scenes are utterly harrowing and, in the last part of the film (with Janet

touchingly portrayed by Kerry Fox), the journey of this remarkable writer reaches a kind of fulfilment far from home.

Campion had written her next film, which became *The Piano*, even before *Sweetie*, and she alone is responsible for the Bronte-esque screenplay which is set in 19th-century New Zealand. Once again we have an apparently handicapped female protagonist, though in this case Ada McGrath's inability to speak is a self-imposed one. A Scottish widow, she travels to the other side of the world with her two most treasured possessions, her daughter, Fiona, and her grand piano, to marry Stewart, an articulate colonialist she has never met but who believes that, because God loves dumb creatures, then so should he, literally.

Yet again, Campion's astonishing vision transcends what could have been a familiar triangular relationship between Ada, Stewart and Baines, the man who pays her to teach him to play the piano, lessons which become gradually more erotic, and more fulfilling for Ada, as they proceed.

With a relatively modest budget provided by the French company CiBy 2000 (after development money from Australian government sources), Campion was able to cast whoever she wanted in the film. Her choice of Holly Hunter as Ada proved to be a masterstroke; Hunter's astonishingly expressive face, often framed in the black bonnets worn at the time, and her sensuality in the remarkably erotic love scenes ensure that this is her finest performance, richly deserving of the Oscar and other awards she's won. Hardly less effective is Harvey Keitel, cast against type as the ardent, illiterate Baines, while Sam Neill, in the difficult role of the rigid Stewart, is also excellent. One of the most impressive characters in the film, though, is that of little Fiona, and in this role Campion cast a local New Zealand girl, Ana Paquin, who had never acted before, extracting from her one of the best performances a child has ever given on the screen, and earning yet another Oscar into the bargain.

This passionate tale of female emancipation, with its almost revolutionary scenes of sexuality and one terrifying moment of violence, sparked a chord with audiences around the world: it was launched in Cannes, where it shared the Palme d'Or with Chen Kaige's *Farewell My Concubine*, went on to sweep the pool at the Australian Film Awards, and has, at the time of writing, grossed $US120 million worldwide.

One of the most memorable moments in the film comes when Ada, after being attacked by Stewart, slowly sinks into the mud, her crinoline dress billowing around her like a deflated balloon; but this, like so many other beautiful moments in the film, was improvised on the set, when experiments with a slow-motion camera revealed this moment of tactile pain and beauty.

Also crucial to the success of the film is Michael Nyman's score, which has become immensely popular on its own account around the world. Evoking the Scottish music of Ada's background, it's a haunting score, and the fact that Hunter, herself an accomplished pianist, was able to play the music herself in the film adds an extra dimension of authenticity. Campion has admitted that, after the astonishing reaction to *The Piano*, she approaches her next project, an adaptation of Henry James' *Portrait of a Lady*, to star Nicole Kidman, with some misgivings. It has, in any event, been put on hold while she awaits the birth of her second baby (her first died, tragically, soon after he was born in June, 1993).

Jane Campion once wrote a note to this writer in which she described herself as "a very difficult, reluctant Aussie directress". It's an interesting description on all levels. She may be difficult, sometimes, with the press, but by all accounts those who've worked with her are bowled over by her talent and personality. Reluctant? An interesting self-description. Notable, too, is the fact that, after 17 years in Australia, she sees herself as an "Aussie", not a "Kiwi", director/directress.

Harvey Keitel and Holly Hunter in THE PIANO   *photo: Kobal Collection*

Campion's oblique vision of the world, and especially of women, her fascination for the dark side of romance, and above all her perverse sense of humour, make her unique among film-makers in the 1990's. In her 40th year, she has a long and exciting career ahead of her.

Campion Filmography

Campion's short films include: *Peel* (1982), *A Girl's Own Story* (1983) and *Passionless Moments* (1984).

1986
TWO FRIENDS

Script: Helen Garner. Direction: JC. Photography: Julian Penney. Editing: Bill Russo. Production Designer: Janet Patterson. Players: Emma Coles (*Louise*), Kris Bidenki (*Kelly*), Kris McQuade (*Janet, Louise's mother*), Debra May (*Chris, Kelly's mother*), Peter Hehir (*Malcolm*), Tony Barry (*Charlie*), Steve Bisley (*Kevin*), Kerry Dwyer (*Alison*), Stephen Leeder (*Jim*), Sean Travers (*Matthew*). Produced by Jan Chapman for the ABC. 76 mins.

1989
SWEETIE

Script: JC, Gerard Lee. Direction: JC. Photography: Sally Bongers. Music: Martin Armiger. Editing: Veronica Heussler. Production Designer: Peter Harris. Players: Genevieve Lemon (*Dawn [Sweetie]*), Karen Colston (*Kay*), Tom Lycos (*Louis*), Jon Darling (*Gordon*), Dorothy Barry (*Flo*), Michael Lake (*Bob*), Andre Pataczek (*Clayton*). Produced by John Maynard for Arenafilm. 97 mins.

1990
AN ANGEL AT MY TABLE

Script: Laura Jones, based on the autobiographies of Janet Frame. Direction: JC. Photography: Stuart Dryburgh. Music: Don McGlashan. Editing: Veronika Haussler. Production Designer: Grant Major. Players: Kerry Fox (*Adult Janet*), Alexia Keogh (*Young Janet*), Karen Fergusson (*Teenage Janet*), Iris Churn (*Mum*), Jessie Mune (*Baby Janet*), K. J. Wilson (*Dad*), Melina Bernbecker (*Myrtle*), Andrew Binns (*Bruddle*), Glynis Angell (*Isabel*). Produced by Bridget Ikin for Hibiscus Films. 150 mins (theatrical version).

1993
THE PIANO

Script and Direction: JC. Photography: Stuart Dryburgh. Music: Michael Nyman. Editing: Veronika Jenet. Production Designer: Andrew McAlpine. Players: Holly Hunter (*Ada McGrath*), Harvey Keitel (*George Baines*), Sam Neill (*Stewart*), Ana Paquin (Fiona McGrath), Kerry Walker (*Aunt Morag*), Genevieve Lemon (*Nessie*). Produced by Jan Chapman for Jan Chapman Productions and CIBY 2000. 120 mins.

1994-1995
PORTRAIT OF A LADY

(In production)

Clint Eastwood

by Richard Combs

Clint Eastwood's arrival as a director – the critical accolades and Oscars for Best Film and Best Director that greeted *Unforgiven* – has been long and hard in coming. It has, of course, had a considerable obstacle to overcome: Eastwood's status as one of the most successful movie stars of all time.

It is not simply that before *Unforgiven* Eastwood was denied all recognition as a director. His earliest films, *Play Misty for Me* and *High Plains Drifter*, were generally perceived as promising, and in 1976 *The Outlaw Josey Wales* was clearly a landmark Western in a decade that produced some strong competition in the genre. By the time he came to make *Bird* and *White Hunter, Black Heart*, two films that seemed particularly addressed to the European following he had attracted, Eastwood had fully proven himself.

The problem has been that, as his stature has grown behind the camera, it has been matched, checked and neutralised by his monolithic presence in front of it. Perhaps Eastwood has been too casual about indulging the macho image in those films he hasn't bothered to direct, the straight-forward action movies with which he still intersperses his more ambitious, personal projects. These include two knockabout slug-fests in which he co-starred with an orang-utan and four Dirty Harry sequels. By contrast, when he directs himself, Eastwood has done his best to mock, undermine and even to wish away – by turning him into a ghost – the very model of macho manhood he has come to stand for.

Even this distinction is not easy to make. Eastwood didn't direct *Tightrope*, the film which most explicitly attacks the Dirty Harry ethos (directed by its writer, Richard Tuggle, who also wrote the best of the Eastwood-Don Siegel collaborations, *Escape from Alcatraz*). On the other hand, Eastwood *did* direct two of the most unashamedly brutal of his latterday cop movies: the third Dirty Harry sequel, *Sudden Impact*, and *The Rookie*, which manages to be a shallow imitation of a Dirty Harry sequel.

Perhaps it's truer to say that Eastwood is *always* looking askance at his own acting persona. The fascinating thing about that persona is the degree of negativity it has contained, as if its creator had shaped it out of ambivalence and self-mockery verging on self-loathing. Eastwood seems to look upon his screen self with the eye of a director, even when he is not directing, or even before he began to direct.

The ambivalence is just as evident in the orang-utan films (*Every Which Way But Loose* and *Any Which Way You Can*), only played for burlesque rather than the modulated irony of Eastwood's remarkable series of self-critiques, from *The Outlaw Josey Wales* through *The Gauntlet* to *Unforgiven*. What distinguishes the best Eastwood is not how negatively he views himself, but what is then positively opened up in the other roles and in the film as a whole.

CLINTON EASTWOOD JNR was born in San Francisco on May 5, 1930 and his childhood was spent in the shadow of the Depression as his father travelled up and down California in search of work. The discipline and economy evident in his film-making style, and the running of his own

Don Siegel, an Eastwood mentor, appeared with the director in Eastwood's PLAY MISTY FOR ME
Photo: Universal/The Kobal Collection

production company, Malpaso, perhaps has its origins here. It's the beginning of the Eastwood negativity, defining himself by what he is not: he is not profligate or self-indulgent in front of the camera or behind it. Negativity is enshrined, too, in that name: Malpaso means "bad step" in Spanish, which is what Eastwood's manager told him he was taking when, in 1964, he agreed to act in an Italian remake of a Japanese film shot in Spain.

Bit-part Apprenticeship

Before Sergio Leone, and box-office success as the "Man with No Name", beckoned, Eastwood underwent the usual discouraging apprenticeship of bit-part roles. After army service, he was to study business administration in Los Angeles, but was persuaded to take a screen test at Universal. A fledgling career of appear-ances in films like *Revenge of the Creature* (1955), *The First Travelling Saleslady* (1955) and *Lafayette Escadrille* (1958) followed.

His first success came in the television series *Rawhide*, where he played the trail boss "ramrod", Rowdy Yates, from 1959 to 1966. During a schedule break, he took up Leone's offer to appear as the nameless, virtually voiceless, cigarillo-chewing hero of *A Fistful of Dollars* (1964). Eastwood's three Spaghetti Westerns with Leone established his persona as an actor, but they might also be evidence of his first work as (almost) a director. He has claimed "authorship" of the Man with No Name's distinctive wardrobe, and took a hand in paring the scripts away to their expressive minimum.

By the time he returned to the States, to attempt to reincarnate his Spaghetti role in an American Western (*Hang 'em High*, 1968), Eastwood had his mind set on another career: "Working on the European scene sort of inspired me to get back into directing." He had already made an unsuccessful bid to direct episodes of *Rawhide*, and he now took an option on a property, *Play Misty for Me*, three years before he was allowed to direct it in 1971. In the meantime, he had the good fortune to be given Don Siegel as his director on the film *Coogan's Bluff* (1968) that was intended to establish him as an American star.

Siegel's style of film-making, so crisp and economical that it becomes strangely elliptical, semi-surrealist in its fragmentary realism, suited Eastwood's temperament. Similarly, Siegel's line in anti-heroes fitted with the way Eastwood was developing, directing, his own anti-persona. Leone and Siegel have been anointed Eastwood's mentors – reasonable, perhaps, though it may be more that he has assimilated their influence to his own ambivalent-negative kind of myth-making.

Their names often cropped up in reviews of Eastwood's first two films as director: *Play Misty for Me*, a psychological thriller about a DJ (Eastwood) whose casual pick-up of a fan (Jessica Walter) leads to a murderously obsessive relationship; and *High Plains Drifter* (1972), a baroque Western in which the sins of a whole town are avenged by a stranger (Eastwood) who,

humanly speaking, might not be all there. But Eastwood has resisted the suggestion that *Drifter* is mere imitation Leone – "I didn't shoot it like he does; I used a different style" – and despite the imagery of hellfire and damnation, it's clear that what Eastwood has in mind for this benighted community is redemption.

Assimilating the Bleakness

The themes become clearer in his next Western, *The Outlaw Josey Wales*. Where Leone's films take place in a West that is a permanent desert, and its ruling forces are greed and dynastic ambition, *Josey Wales* tries both to assimilate this bleakness and to develop beyond it. The film actually shows how the Man with No Name got that way: Josey (Eastwood) is initially a farmer, who is turned into a homeless wanderer, bent only on revenge, when his family is destroyed in the bitter border skirmishing of the Civil War. Humanity is restored to the character, and the possibility of renewal for the nation (and for the Western), when he becomes reluctant shepherd to a motley group of pilgrims.

The Gauntlet (1977) was a fascinating attempt to do in an urban context – or to do for Dirty Harry – what *Josey Wales* does for the Man with No Name. Here the maverick macho cop has become a drunken, rather stupid incompetent, whose arrogance and defensiveness must be broken down – courtesy of the belligerent female prisoner

Chief Dan George with Eastwood in THE OUTLAW JOSEY WALES

photo: Kobal Collection

Forest Whitaker in BIRD

photo: Warner Bros.

Clint Eastwood dispensing death . . .
photo: Warners/The Kobal Collection

. . . with guns and dynamite in PALE RIDER
photo: Warners/The Kobal Collection

(Sondra Locke) he is escorting – before his redemption is possible in a finale whose extravagant religious symbolism is aptly suggested by the title. Both these films, stylistically and thematically, were major advances for Eastwood, demonstrations of how much he could do by, as it were, treating himself so badly.

Two subsequent films, *Bronco Billy* (1980) and *Honkytonk Man* (1982), seem to take this deconstruction further while adding real self-confession to the picture. Two studies of failed heroes – the impresario of a Wild West show and a would-be Country and Western singer – they connect with Eastwood's own family history in their background of hard economic times. Both were generally well received, partly for this reason, and one commentator, Norman Mailer, claimed *Honkytonk Man* as Eastwood's masterpiece. But both in a way have turned the negative Eastwood hero into a dead end; sentimental "little heroes" who can only be redeemed in sentimental gestures.

Pictures of Others

More rewarding has been the way Eastwood has escaped that negative self-picture through pictures of others – a different kind of negativity, perhaps. The series begins, unpromisingly, with the first film he directed in which he did not act, *Breezy* (1973), the soap opera-ish tale of a May-December romance (Kay Lenz and William Holden, respectively). Masterly,

though, is *Bird* (1988), about self-destructive jazzman Charlie Parker (Forest Whitaker). Everything here is shades of black, and negativity has become an anarchy that is the source of emotional confusion and musical genius. Something of the same equation is worked through, with less definitive and satisfying results, in Eastwood's direction of himself as another kind of film-maker, John Huston in all but name, in *White Hunter, Black Heart* (1990).

Eastwood's two most recent films have reworked his ambivalence about his own supremely successful screen persona with a confidence that in one is magisterial, and in the other puzzling. *Unforgiven* (1992) is about cycles of death and violence, though it doesn't so much preach that violence is bad as demonstrate that there is no such thing as a single act of violence, a containable pain. Its vehicle, an unredeemed, unresolvable ex-gunslinger,

Boy Mathias Chuma and Clint Eastwood in WHITE HUNTER, BLACK HEART
photo: Warners/The Kobal Collection

William Munny (Eastwood), is the enigmatic proof that there is no truth that is unequivocal, no myth without its element of possibility.

For *A Perfect World* (1993), Eastwood exiled himself so far to the boundaries of the plot – about an escaped convict (Kevin Costner) trying to reclaim his life – that his character seemed ready to explode in frustration. This may be Eastwood's most generous film, insisting that we look not at him but at how Costner redeems an imperfect past by becoming parent to his diminutive hostage. Or it may be his most self-abnegating, the last line spoken by his Texan lawman being a triple whammy of negativism: "I don't know nothing. Not one damn thing." Or it may be both, forced together in this strangely expansive "little film" that is as bitter as it is sentimental. On reflection, it may prove to be one of Eastwood's richest.

Eastwood Filmography

1971
PLAY MISTY FOR ME

Script: Jo Heims, Dean Riesner. Story: Jo Heims. Direction: CE. Photography (Technicolor): Bruce Surtees. Music: Dee Barton. Editing: Carl Pingitore. Production Design: Alexander Golitzen. Players: Clint Eastwood (*Dave Garland*), Jessica Walter (*Evelyn Draper*), Donna Mills (*Tobie Williams*), John Larch (*Sgt. McCallum*), Jack Ging (*Frank Dewan*), Irene Harvey (*Madge Brenner*), James McEachin (*Al Monte*), Clarice Taylor (*Birdie*), Donald Siegel (*Murphy*), Duke Everts (*Jay Jay*), Tim Frawley (*Deputy Sheriff*). Production: Malpaso, for Universal. 102 mins.

1972
HIGH PLAINS DRIFTER

Script: Ernest Tidyman. Direction: CE. Photography (Technicolor, Panavision): Bruce Surtees. Music: Dee Barton. Editing: Ferris Webster. Production Design: Henry Bumstead. Players: CE (*The Stranger*), Verna Bloom (*Sarah Belding*), Mariana Hill (*Callie Travers*), Mitchell Ryan (*Dave Drake*), Jack Ging (*Morgan Allen*), Stefan Gierasch (*Mayor Jason Hobart*), Ted Hartley (*Lewis Belding*), Billy Curtis (*Mordecai*), Geoffrey Lewis (*Stacey Bridges*), Scott Walter (*Bill Borders*), Walter Barnes (*Sheriff Sam Shaw*), Paul Brinegar (*Lutie Naylor*), Richard Bull (*Asa Goodwin*), Anthony James (*Cole Carlin*). Production: Malpaso, for Universal. 105 mins.

1973
BREEZY

Script: Jo Heims. Direction: CE. Photography (Technicolor): Frank Stanley. Music: Michel Legrand. Editing: Ferris Webster. Production Design: Alexander Golitzen. Players: William Holden (*Frank Harmon*), Kay Lenz (*Breezy*), Roger C. Carmel (*Bob Henderson*), Marj Dusay (*Betty Tobin*), Joan Hotchkid (*Paula Harmon*), Jamie Smith Jackson (*Marcy*), Norman Bartold (*Man in Car*), Lynn Borden (*Overnight Date*), Shelley Morrison (*Nancy Henderson*), Dennis Olivieri (*Bruno*), Eugene Peterson (*Charlie*), Lew Brown (*Police Officer*), Richard Bull (*Doctor*). Production: Malpaso, for Universal. 107 mins.

1975
THE EIGER SANCTION

Script: Warren B. Murphy, Hal Dresner, Rod Whitaker. Based on the novel by Trevanian. Direction: CE. Photography (Technicolor, Panavision): Frank Stanley. Music: John Williams. Editing: Ferris Webster. Production Design: George Webb (US), Aurelio Crugnola (Switzerland). Players: CE (*Jonathan Hemlock*), George Kennedy (*Ben Bowman*), Vonetta McGee (*Jemima Brown*), Jack Cassidy (*Miles Mellough*), Heidi Bruhl (*Anna Montaigne*), Thayer David (*Dragon*), Reiner Schoene (*Freytag*), Michael Grimm (*Meyer*), Gregory Walcott (*Pope*). Production: Malpaso, for Universal. 125 mins.

1976
THE OUTLAW JOSEY WALES

Script: Phil Kaufman, Sonia Chernus. Based on the novel *Gone to Texas* by Forrest Carter. Direction: CE. Photography (DeLuxe Color, Panavision): Bruce Surtees. Music: Jerry Fielding. Editing: Ferris Webster. Production Design: Tambi Larsen. Players: CE (*Josey Wales*), Chief Dan George (*Lone Watie*), Sondra Locke (*Laura Lee*), Bill McKinney (*Terrill*), John Vernon (*Fletcher*), Paula Trueman (*Grandma Sarah*), Sam Bottoms (*Jamie*), Geraldine Keams (*Little Moonlight*), Woodrow Parfrey (*Carpetbagger*), Joyce Jameson (*Rose*), Sheb Wooley (*Travis Cobb*), Royal Dano (*Ten Spot*), Matt Clark (*Kelly*), Will Sampson (*Ten Bears*), William O'Connell (*Sim Carstairs*). Production: Malpaso, for Warner Bros. 134 mins.

1977
THE GAUNTLET

Script: Michael Butler, Dennis Shryack. Direction: CE.

Photography (DeLuxe Color, Panavision): Rexford Metz. Music: Jerry Fielding. Editing: Ferris Webster, Joel Cox. Production Design: Allen E. Smith. Players: CE (*Ben Shockley*), Sondra Locke (*Gus Mally*), Pat Hingle (*Josephson*), William Prince (*Blakelock*), Bill McKinney (*Constable*), Michael Cavanaugh (*Feyderspiel*), Carole Cook (*Waitress*), Mara Corday (*Jail Matron*), Douglas McGrath (*Bookie*), Jeff Morris (*Desk Sergeant*), Carver Barnes (*Bus Driver*), Mildred J. Brion (*Old Lady on Bus*). Production: Malpaso, for Warner Bros. 109 mins.

1980
BRONCO BILLY

Script: Dennis Hackin. Direction: CE. Photography (DeLuxe Color): David Worth. Music/Songs: Steve Dorff, Snuff Garrett, J. Durrill, C. Crofford, M. Brown, G. Harju, L. Hebstritt. Editing: Ferris Webster, Joel Cox. Production Design: Gene Lourie. Players: CE (*"Bronco Billy" McCoy*), Sondra Locke (*Antoinette Lily*), Geoffrey Lewis (*John Arlington*), Scatman Crothers (*"Doc" Lynch*). Bill McKinney (*"Lefty" LeBow*). Sam Bottoms (*Leonard James*), Dan Vadis (*Chief Big Eagle*), Woodrow Parfrey (*Dr. Canterbury*). Production: Warner Bros. 116 mins.

1982
FIREFOX

Script: Alex Lasker, Wendell Wellman. Based on the novel by Craig Thomas. Direction: CE. Photography (DeLuxe Color, Panavision): Bruce Surtees. Music: Maurice Jarre. Editing: Ferris Webster, Ron Spang. Production Design: John Graysmark, Elayne Ceder. Players: CE (*Mitchell Gant*), Freddie Jones (*Kenneth Aubrey*), David Huffman (*Buckholz*), Warren Clarke (*Pavel Upenskoy*), Ronald Lacey (*Smelovsky*), Kenneth Colley (*Colonel Kontarsky*), Klaus Löwitsch (*General Vladimirov*), Nigel·

Hawthorne (*Pyotr Baranovich*), Stefan Schnabel (*First Secretary*), Thomas Hill (*General Brown*). Production: Warner Bros. 136 mins.

1982
HONKYTONK MAN

Script: Clancy Carlile. Based on his own novel. Direction: CE. Photography (Technicolor): Bruce Surtees. Music Supervision: Snuff Garrett. Editing: Ferris Webster, Michael Kelly, Joel Cox. Production Design: Edward Carfagno. Players: CE (*Red Stovall*), Kyle Eastwood (*Whit*), John McIntire (*Grandpa*), Alexa Kenin (*Marlene*), Verna Bloom (*Emmy*), Matt Clark (*Virgil*), Barry Corbin (*Derwood Arnspriger*), Jerry Hardin (*Snuffy*), Tim Thomerson (*Highway Patrolman*), Macon McCalman (*Doctor Hines*), Joe Regalbuto (*Henry Axle*). Production: Warner Bros. 123 mins.

1983
SUDDEN IMPACT

Script: Joseph C. Stinson. Story: Earl E. Smith, Charles B. Pierce. Based on characters created by Harry Julian Fink, R.M. Fink. Direction: CE. Photography (Technicolor): Bruce Surtees. Music: Lalo Schifrin. Editing: Joel Cox. Production Design: Edward Carfagno. Players: CE (*Harry Callahan*), Sondra Locke (*Jennifer Spencer*), Pat Hingle (*Chief Jannings*), Bradford Dillman (*Captain Briggs*), Paul Drake (*Micky*), Audrie J. Neenan (*Ray Parkins*), Jack Thibeau (*Kruger*), Michael Currie (*Lt. Donnelly*), Albert Popwell (*Horace King*), Mark Keyloun (*Officer Bennett*). Kevyn Major Howard (*Hawkins*), Bette Ford (*Leah*). Production: Warner Bros. 117 mins.

1985
PALE RIDER

Script: Michael Butler, Dennis Shyrack. Direction: CE. Photography (Technicolor,

Panavision): Bruce Surtees. Music: Lennie Niehaus. Editing: Joel Cox. Production Design: Edward Carfagno. Players: CE (*Preacher*), Michael Moriarty (*Hull Barret*), Carrie Snodgress (*Sarah Wheeler*), Christopher Penn (*Josh LaHood*), Richard Dysart (*Coy LaHood*), Sydney Penny (*Megan Wheeler*), Richard Kiel (*Club*), Doug McGrath (*Spider Conway*), John Russell (*Marshal Stockburn*), Charles Hallahan (*McGill*), Marvin J. McIntyre (*Jagou*), Fran Ryan (*Ma Blankenship*), Richard Hamilton (*Jed Blankenship*). Production: Malpaso, for Warner Bros. 116 mins.

1986
HEARTBREAK RIDGE

Script: James Carabatsos. Direction: CE. Photography (Technicolor): Jack N. Green. Music: Lennie Niehaus. Editing: Joel Cox. Production Design: Edward Carfagno. Players: CE (*Sergeant Thomas Highway*), Marsha Mason (*Aggie*), Everett McGill (*Major Powers*), Moses Gunn (*Sergeant Webster*), Eileen Heckart (*Little Mary*), Bo Svenson (*Roy Jennings*), Boyd Gaines (*Lieutenant Ring*), Mario Van Peebles (*"Stitch" Jones*), Arlen Dean Snyder (*Master Sergeant Choozoo*), Vincent Irizarry (*Fragetti*), Ramon Franco (*Aponte*), Peter Kock (*"Swede"*), Richard Venture (*Colonel Meyers*). Production: Malpaso, for Warner Bros. 130 mins.

1988
BIRD

Script: Joel Oliansky. Direction: CE. Photography (Technicolor): Jack N. Green. Music Supervision: Lennie Niehaus. Editing: Joel Cox. Production Design: Edward C. Carfagno. Players: Forest Whitaker (*Charlie "Yardbird" Parker*), Diane Venora (*Chan Richardson*), Michael Zelniker (*Red Rodney*), Samuel E. Wright (*Dizzy Gillespie*), Keith David (*Buster Franklin*), Michael

Gene Hackman and Frances Fisher in a typically sombre composition from UNFORGIVEN

photo: Warners/The Kobal Collection

McGuire (*Brewster*), James Handy (*Esteves*), Damon Whitaker (*Young Bird*), Morgan Nagler (*Kim*), Arlen Dean Snyder (*Dr. Heath*), Sam Robards (*Moscowitz*). Production: Malpaso, for Warner Bros. 160 mins.

1990
WHITE HUNTER, BLACK HEART

Script: Peter Viertel, James Bridges, Burt Kennedy. Based on the novel by Peter Viertel. Photography (Technicolor): Jack N. Green. Music: Lennie Niehaus. Editing: Joel Cox. Production Design: John Graysmark. Players: CE (*John Wilson*), Jeff Fahey (*Pete Verrill*), Charlotte Cornwell (*Miss Wilding*), Norman Lumsden (*Butler George*), George Dzundza (*Paul Landers*), Edward Tudor Pole (*Reissar*), Marisa Berenson (*Kay Gibson*), Richard Vanstone (*Phil Duncan*), Jamie Koss (*Mrs. Duncan*), Mel Martin (*Margaret MacGregor*), Boy Mathias Chuma (*Kivu*). Production: Malpaso/Rastar, for Warner Bros. 112 mins.

1990
THE ROOKIE

Script: Boaz Yakin, Scott Spiegel. Direction: CE. Photography (Technicolor): Jack N. Green. Music: Lennie Niehaus. Editing: Joel Cox. Production Design: Judy Cammer. Players: CE (*Nick Pulovski*), Charlie Sheen (*David Ackerman*), Raul Julia (*Strom*), Sonia Braga (*Liesl*), Tom Skerritt (*Eugene Ackerman*), Lara Flynn Boyle (*Sarah*), Pepe Serna (*Lieutenant Roy Garcia*), Marco Rodriguez (*Loco*), Pete Randall (*Cruz*), Donna Mitchell (*Laura Ackerman*), Xander Berkeley (*Blackwell*), Tony Plana (*Morales*), David Sherrill (*Max*). Production: Malpaso, for Warner Bros. 121 mins.

1992
UNFORGIVEN

Script: David Webb Peoples. Direction: CE. Photography (Technicolor, Panavision): Jack N. Green. Music: Lennie Niehaus. Editing: Joel Cox. Production Design: Henry Bumstead. Players: CE (*Bill Munny*), Gene Hackman (*Little Bill Daggett*), Morgan Freeman (*Ned Logan*), Richard Harris (*English Bob*), Jaimz Woolvett (*"The Schofield Kid"*), Saul Rubinek (*W.W. Beauchamp*), Frances Fisher (*Strawberry Alice*), Anna Thompson (*Delilah Fitzgerald*), David Mucci (*Quick Mike*), Rob Campbell (*Davey Bunting*), Anthony James (*Skinny Dubois*), Tara Dawn Frederick (*Little Sue*), Beverley Elliott (*Silky*), Shane Meier (*Will Munny*), Aline Lavas-seur (*Penny Munny*). Production: Malpaso, for Warner Bros. 131 mins.

1993
A PERFECT WORLD

Script: John Lee Hancock. Direction: CE. Photography (Color, Panavision): Jack N. Green. Music: Lennie Niehaus. Editing: Joel Cox. Production Design: Henry Bumstead. Players: CE (*Red Garnet*), Kevin Costner (*Butch Haynes*), Laura Dern (*Sally Gerber*), T.J. Lowther (*Phillip Perry*), Keith Szarabajka (*Terry Pugh*), Leo Burmester (*Tom Adler*), Paul Hewitt (*Dick Suttle*), Bradley Whitford (*Bobby Lee*). Production: Malpaso, for Warner Bros. 138 mins.

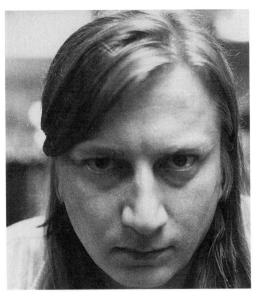

Aki Kaurismäki

Mika Kaurismäki

The Kaurismäki Brothers

by Peter Cowie

The achievement of Aki and Mika Kaurismäki has defied commercial reality. Their films, made for the most part in Finland (but also in France, Germany, Britain, and Brazil), attract modest numbers of spectators. Their fans, however, are ferociously loyal, applauding their latest exploits whether it be at the Berlin Forum of Young Cinema, or in Paris, or in Manhattan.

MIKA KAURISMÄKI was born on September 21, 1955, in Orimattila (Finland); his younger brother AKI was born on April 4, 1957, in Helsinki. Mika attended the Film School in Munich from 1977 to 1981, and established Villealfa Film Productions with his brother in 1980.

"Me and my brother, we wanted to open the windows to Europe and make European films, of course with a Finnish touch," says Mika. "I wanted to avoid the Finnish clichés, you know, the lakes and the forests."

Their films are neither the first nor the best made in Finland. The Kaurismäkis' love-hate relationship with their native land colours the texture of their work, and also obscures both the heritage of Finnish cinema and the talent of Finnish film-makers outside their orbit.

They do, however, deserve credit for promoting the gifts of a new generation of Finnish directors. Christian Lindblad, Veikko Aaltonen, and Pauli Pentti have all been supported by Villealfa, the production company established by the brothers and which is, of course, a tribute to Jean-Luc Godard's *Alphaville*.

The Godard reference runs like a bass line throughout Aki and Mika's work. One can sense in every frame of their films a nostalgia for the 1960's, with its mood of love and anarchy. They may lack Godard's piercing intellect, and his gift for establishing a dialectic between his characters and the society in which they move, but they swagger through life with the same devotion to grunge, tobacco and liquor, transforming sophomore humour into a virtue as they go. Like Godard, the Kaurismäkis adore the atmosphere and nihilism of American pulp-fiction B and Z-movies. *Calamari Union* and *Helsinki Napoli – All Night Long* echo the work of Samuel Fuller, Robert Aldrich, and Joseph Pevney as much as they do the novels of Erich Maria Remarque.

Matti Pellonpää and Pirkko Hämäläinen in THE WORTHLESS

A more subtle influence on the brothers derives from the bohemian traditions of Finland and Hungary, linked by common linguistic (Fenno-Ugrian roots). Restless wanderers both, Mika and Aki seem happier respectively on location in the Amazon forest or growing wine in Portugal than in the grey chill of a Finnish autumn.

More Than Twenty Features

Their joint output runs to more than twenty features in less than fifteen years. Some of these have been tossed off without much forethought; others have germinated over many a season. If they were to die tomorrow, the world would probably cherish the following films: *Crime and Punishment, Shadows in Paradise, Hamlet Goes Business,* and *The Match Factory Girl* (from Aki); and *The Worthless, Rosso, Amazon,* and *Tigrero* (from Mika). Their other features contain few themes that are not better articulated in the titles listed above, and indeed none of their films has enjoyed the kind of art-house popularity so familiar to Pedro Almodóvar, Krzysztof Kieślowski or – a closer parallel – Rainer Werner Fassbinder.

Mika was early drawn to production matters as well as to directing his own films. Aki wrote terse, rhetorical dialogue, and fancied himself as an actor. Their medium-length films (*The Saimaa Gesture, The Liar*) aroused a flutter of enthusiasm in Finnish film circles, but it was *The Worthless* (*Arvottomat*, 1982) that established them as a force for the future. It breathed what Mika Kaurismäki termed "the melancholy of cheap cafeterias" and in the words of Helena Ylänen (a prominent Finnish critic and advocate of the brothers' talent), "*The Worthless* is an ironic and philosophical getaway story vibrating with a beauty that eliminates all gloom and self-pity." Its small-time gangsters order Calvados in a coffee shop (an impossibility under Finnish licensing laws, so all the more poignant for that), and seek always to escape from the concrete claustrophobia of the big city.

The heroine of *The Worthless* is a quiet, traditional "broad", a blonde who in form and personality has appeared in most of the Kaurismäki pictures. Women in Mika's world are warm, sensual home-makers; Aki's girls are plain, timid, and curiously endearing in the face of male inhibition or exploitation.

Markku Toikka in CRIME AND PUNISHMENT

Aki's first film as director, *Crime and Punishment (Rikos ja rangaistus*, 1983), remains among his most accomplished, and yet eluded the questing gaze of festival programmers, as did his next solo effort, *Calamari Union* (1985). These two features staked out the extremes of his universe: *Crime and Punishment* with its rigorous, almost Bressonian interaction between word and image, and the absurdist fantasy of *Calamari Union*, a pock-marked odyssey from one end of Helsinki to the other, with time out aplenty in bars and subway stations.

Shadows in Paradise (Varjoja paratiisissa, 1986) did acquire international kudos to some degree, and audiences in Finland and abroad responded to the deadpan acting of Matti Pellonpää and Kati Outinen as a garbage-truck driver and a supermarket checkout girl reaching tentatively for each other's affections in a crass, consumerist world. Aki's storylines are always implausible; his characters hover tremulously above reality, oblivious to moral codes and the common courtesies of life. Something in the spaniel stare of his actors, however, cuts straight to the quick, and elicits chuckles of affection as well as amusement from a sympathetic audience.

Mika, meanwhile, had directed *The Clan – The Tale of the Frogs (Klaani*, 1984), a bleak, outrageous study of a band of criminals scrounging an existence somewhere in the Helsinki "green belt", and *Rosso* (1985), the most underrated film of the period in Finland. Completed in 15 days on a shoestring budget (just seven in the crew, with Aki as camera operator), *Rosso* tracks the destiny of an Italian hoodlum (Kari Väänänen, a favourite Kaurismäki actor) assigned to kill an enemy of the Mafia. Restrained even in its humour, the film yearns for a lost innocence, a paradise that must surely lie just beyond the high-rise buildings and the gouged-out earthworks "created" by modern society.

Cult Following

Although Aki was by now attracting a cult following outside Finland, and no longer collaborated with his brother on individual films, common themes persisted in the work of both men. Tongue-in-cheek comedy conceals a fundamental insecurity in the characters played by such Kaurismäki stable-mates as Kari Väänänen, Matti Pellonpää, Kati Outinen, and Esko Nikkari. Crime is provoked by social abuse and injustice. The "conditions" by which the community signifies its disapproval of the individual – unemployment, imprisonment, poverty –

Mika Kaurismäki (left) with Kari Väänänen and Markku Halme on location for THE CLAN

Kari Väänänen in ROSSO

Matti Pellonpää and Kati Outinen in SHADOWS IN PARADISE

recur in films as disparate as Mika's *Paper Star* (*Paperitähti*, 1989), and Aki's *Ariel* (1988), and *The Match Factory Girl* (*Tulitikkutehtaan*, 1990). The brothers' affection for the road movie genre colours *Helsinki Napoli – All Night Long* (1987), *Amazon* (1991), *Zombie and the Ghost Train* (1991), *Leningrad Cowboys Go America* (1989) and its lethargic sequel, *Leningrad Cowboys Meet Moses* (1993).

Everyone is a loser in the land of the Kaurismäkis, whether it be the Robert Davi character in *Amazon* or Kati Outinen's rejected daughter in *The Match Factory Girl*, Pirkko Hämäläinen's doomed model in *Paper Star*, or the hapless Mimi in *La Vie de Bohème* (1992).

With no fewer than four films signed by the brothers being presented in the space of three months at Berlin and Cannes 1994, the danger of staleness and repetition loomed. The Kaurismäkis have become a phenomenon on a cottage scale, each new film more significant as an event than as an

artistic success. A documentary as pedestrian as *Total Balalaika Show* (1994) will attract an initial audience because it is "directed" by Aki.

Despite this prolific output, however, each brother has retained something of his old sparkle. Mika's *Tigrero – A Film That Was Never Made* (1994) set up a dialogue between Sam Fuller and Jim Jarmusch as Fuller returns to the Amazonian rain forest to visit a location for a film cancelled by

Aki Kaurismäki with Kari Väänänen on the set for CALAMARI UNION

Vesa Vierikko and Kati Outinen in THE MATCH FACTORY GIRL

Fox in the 1950's. Awkward in its opening minutes, *Tigrero* slowly exerts a beguiling spell, until Fuller's long-vanished project starts to re-form before one's eyes. Mika's direction is vigilant yet discreet, slipping beyond the boundaries of the talking-heads documentary and communicating the frustration and fantasy of a renegade auteur like Fuller.

Aki for his part returned to form with *Take Care of Your Scarf, Tatiana!* (*Pidä huivista kiinni, Tatjana*, 1994), a mere hour's worth of wry nostalgia for a 1960's that never was. Two taciturn men career through the countryside of southern Finland in a battered Volga. At the Russian border they pick up two women trying to hitch a ride. Reino (Matti Pellonpää) exemplifies the

satirical vein in Aki's work, downing pint after pint of vodka in cafeterias where such behaviour would be forbidden even in contemporary Finland. Timo Salminen's black-and-white cinematography coaxes a sombre beauty from the small hotels and the industrial skylines.

The jury is still out on this charismatic duo. Will they ever be able to describe women as anything other than sexual ciphers? Can they achieve sufficient mastery of technique to transcend the essentially trivial, comic-sheet concerns of their characters? Can they attract the major distributors of foreign films in the United States such as Miramax and Sony Classics? One thing is certain: they have flung a pebble into the still waters of Nordic cinema, marking their surface for a long time to come, and they have won many friends in the process.

Kirsi Tykkyläinen and Kati Outinen in TAKE CARE OF YOUR SCARF, TATIANA!

Kaurismäki Filmography

Note: Aki Kaurismäki has also directed the following short films: *Rocky VI* (8 mins, 1986), *Thru the Wire* (6 mins, 1987), *Those Were the Days* (5 mins, 1992), and *These Boots* (5 mins, 1992). Mika Kaurismäki directed *Jackpot 2* (35 mins, 1982).

1981
SAIMAA-ILMIÖ (The Saimaa Gesture)
Direction: MK. Photography:

Lasse Naukkarinen, Timo Salminen, Toni Sulzbeck, Olli Varja. Music: Eppu Normaali, Juice Leskinen & Slam, Hassisen Kone. Editing: Antti Kari. Produced by AK, MK, for Villealfa Film Productions. 125 mins.

VALEHTELIJA (The Liar)
Script: AK, Pauli Pentti. Direction: MK. Photography: Toni Sulzbeck, Kay Gauditz, Olli Varja. Music: Lasse Keso. Editing: Antti Kari.

Players: AK (*Ville Alfa*), Pirkko Hämäläinen (*Tuula*), Juuso Hirvikangas (*Juuso*), Lars Lindberg (*Ville's brother*), Esa Sirkkunen (*Olli*), Jukka Järvalä (*Man in bar*), Mikko Mattila (*Hemingway's friend*), Matti Pellonpää (*Chandler's friend*), Maija Heiskanen, Taina Nyström, Eija Vilpas, Tony Sulzbeck, Juhani Tommola, Juice Leskinen & Slam. Production: MK and Hochschüle für Fernsehen und Film (Munich). 52 mins.

1982
ARVOTTOMAT (The Worthless)

Script: AK, MK. Direction: MK. Photography: Timo Salminen. Music: Anssi Tikanmäki. Editing: Antti Kari. Production Design: AK, Heikkio Ukkonen, Timo Eränkö. Players: Matti Pellonpää (*Manne*), Pirkko Hämäläinen (*Veera*), Juuso Hirvikangas (*Harri*), Esko Nikkari (*Hagström*), Asmo Hurula (*Väyry*), Jorma Markkula (*Mitja*), AK (*Ville Alfa*), Aino Seppo (*Tiina*), Pehr-Olof Sirén (*Art-buyer*), Ari Piispa (*Vasili*), Veijo Piskonen (*Terrorist*), Veikko Aaltonen (*Juippi*), Elina Kivihalme (*Anna-Kaarina*), Aarre Karén, Kauko Laurinainen, Harri Hyttinen, Langri Jr., Tuija Vuolle, Aila Pervonen, Eija Vilpas, Rauli Badding Somerjoki & The Agents, Rauli-Sakari & Karhukopla. Produced by MK for Villealfa Film Productions. 105 mins.

1983
RIKOS JA RANGAISTUS (Crime and Punishment)

Script: AK, Pauli Pentti, from the novel by Fyodor Dostoievsky. Direction: AK. Photography: Timo Salminen. Music: Shostakovich, Schubert. Editing: Veikko Aaltonen. Production Design: Matti Jaaranen. Players: Markku Toikka (*Antti Rahikainen*), Aino Seppo (*Eeva Laakso*), Esko Nikkari (*Inspector Snellman*), Matti Pellonpää (*Nikander*), Harri Marstio (*Singer*), Pedro's Heavy Gentlemen, Kari Sorvali (*Sormunen*), Pentti Auer (*Kari Honkanen*), Asmo Hurula (*Bar-tender*), Risto Aaltonen (*Painter*), Tarja Keinänen (*Mrs. Pennanen*), Tiina Pirhonen (*Maid*). Produced by MK for Villealfa Film Productions. 93 mins.

1984
KLAANI – TARINA SAMMAKOITTEN SUVUSTA (The Clan – The Tale of the Frogs)

Script: MK, AK, based on the novel by Tauno Kaukonen. Direction. MK. Photography: Timo Salminen. Music: Anssi

Tikanmäki. Editing: MK, Raija Talvio. Production Design: Matti Jaaranen. Players: Markku Halme (*Alexander the Great Frog*), Minna Soisalo (*Miriam Andersson*), Lasse Pöysti (*Bristlehead*), Juhani Niemelä (*Samuel Frog*), Kari Väänänen (*Levi Frog*), Antti Litja (*Benjamin Frog*), Mikko Majanlahti (*Birger Andersson*), Sakari Rouvinen (*Robert Andersson*), Tuija Vuolle (*Ulla Frog*), Soli Labbart (*Grandma Sarah*), Ville Salminen (*Grandpa Alexander*), Eila Halonen (*Rachel*), Matti Pellonpää (*Ritsari*), Veijo Pasanen (*Priest*), Hannu Lauri (*Banker*), Sampo Saaristo-Nuotio (*Alexander when young*), Jorma Markkula, Esko Nikkari, Matti Viironen (*Inspectors*). Produced by Jaakko Talaskivi, Anssi Mänttäri for Villealfa Film Productions. 95 mins.

1985
ROSSO

Script: MK, Kari Väänänen. Monologues: AK, Dante Alighieri. Direction: MK. Photography: Timo Salminen. Music: Marco Cuccinatta. Editing: Raija Talvio. Players: Kari Väänänen (*Rosso*), Martti Syrjä (*Martti*), Leena Harjupatana (*Marja*), Mirja Oksanen (*Girl*), Maija-Liisa Majanlahti (*Bank cashier*), Orazio Anelli (*Boss*), Arli Fiila (*Father*), Liisa Kalliomaa (*Mother*), Marco Cuccinatta & Co. (*Orchestra*), Langri Jr. (*Arms dealer*). Produced by MK for Villealfa Film Productions. 78 mins.

CALAMARI UNION

Script and Direction: AK. Photography: Timo Salminen. Music: Casablanca Vox et al. Editing: AK, Raija Talvio. Players: Matti Pellonpää (*Frank*), Puntti Valtonen (*Frank*), Pirkka-Pekka Petelius (*Frank*), Kari Väänänen (*Frank*), Asmo Hurula (*Frank*), Pertti Sveholm (*Frank*), Kari Heiskanen (*Frank*), Martti Syrjä (*Frank*), Mikko Syrjä (*Frank*), Markku Toikka (*Pekka*), Timo

Eränkö (*Frank*), Pate Mustajärvi (*Frank*), Saku Kuosmanen (*Frank*), Mato Valtonen (*Frank*), Hande Nurmio, Dave Lindholm, Pirkko Hämäläinen, Mari Rantasila, Sanna Fransman. Produced by AK for Villealfa Film Productions. 80 mins.

1986
VARJOJA PARATIISISSA (Shadows in Paradise)

Script and Direction: AK. Photography: Timo Salminen. Editing: Raija Talvio. Production Design: Pertti Hilkamo. Players: Matti Pellonpää (*Nikander*), Kati Outinen (*Ilona*), Saku Kuosmanen (*Melartin*), Esko Nikkari (*Workmate*), Kylli Köngäs (*Girlfriend*), Pella Laiho (*Shop Steward*), Jukka-Pekka Palo (*Third man*), Svante Korkeakoski (*Policeman*), Mari Rantasila (*Nikander's sister*), Safka (*Pianist*), Antti Ortamo (*Second pianist*), Mato Valtonen (*Pelle*), Sakke Järvenpää (*Staffan*), Ulla Kuosmanen (*Melartin's wife*), Neka Haapanen (*Cook*), Riikka Kuosmanen. Produced by AK for Villealfa Film Productions. 76 mins.

1987
HAMLET LIIKEMAAILMASSA (Hamlet Goes Business)

Script and Direction: AK. Photography: Timo Salminen. Editing: Raija Talvio. Production Design: Pertti Hilkamo. Players: Pirkka-Pekka Petelius (*Hamlet*), Kati Outinen (*Ophelia*), Elina Salo (*Gertrude*), Esko Salminen (*Klaus*), Esko Nikkari (*Polonius*), Kari Väänänen (*Lauri*), Hannu Valtonen (*Simo*), Mari Rantasila (*Helena*), Turo Pajala (*Rosen-crantz*), Aake Kallala (*Guilden-stern*), Pentti Auer (*Father*), Matti Pellonpää (*Guard*). Produced by AK for Villealfa Film Productions. 86 mins.

HELSINKI NAPOLI – ALL NIGHT LONG

Script: MK, Richard Reitinger. Direction: MK. Photography:

Helge Weindler. Music: Jacques Zwart. Editing: Helga Borsche. Production Design: Olaf Schiefner. Players: Kari Väänänen (*Alex*), Roberta Manfredi (*Stella*), Jean-Pierre Castaldi (*Igor*), Margi Clarke (*Mara*), Nino Manfredi (*Opa*), Samuel Fuller (*Boss*), Eddie Constantine (*Old gangster*), Saku Kuosmanen (*Young gangster*), Melanie Robeson (*Lilli*), Katharina Thalbach (*Co-worker*), Harry Baer (*First man*), Gerd Jochum (*Second man*), Wim Wenders (*Attendant*), Werner Masten (*Bar-keeper*), Jim Jarmusch (*Bar-keeper*), Remo Remotti, Ugo Fagarezzi, Carlo Hafzalla (*Neopolitans*). Produced by MK for Villealfa Film Productions/Francis von Büren for Mediactuel. 94 mins.

1988
ARIEL

Script and Direction: AK. Photography: Timo Salminen. Editing: Raija Talvio. Production Design: Risto Karhula. Players: Turo Pajala (*Raisto Kasurinen*), Susanna Haavisto (*Irmeli*), Matti Pellonpää (*Mikkonen*), Eetu Hilkama (*Riku*), Erkki Pajala (*Miner*), Matti Jaaranen (*Mugger*), Hannu Viholainen (*Accomplice*), Jorma Markkula (*Tallyman*), Tarja Keinänen (*Woman in the harbour*), Kauko Laalo (*Night hostel warden*), Esko Nikkari (*Car dealer*), Esko Salminen (*Crook*), Eino Kuusela, Jyrki Olsonen, Marja Packalen, Mikko Remes, Tomi Salmela, Reijo Marin, Heikki Salomaa, Veikko Uusimäki, Hannu Kivisalo, Pekka Wilen. Produced by AK for Villealfa Film Productions. 73 mins.

1989
PAPERITÄHTI (Paper Star)

Script: Antti Lindqvist, MK from an original idea by MK. Direction: MK. Photography: Timo Salminen. Music: Anssi Tikanmäki. Editing: Veikko Aaltonen. Production Design: Risto Karhula. Players: Pirkko

Hämäläinen (*Anna Kelanen*), Kari Väänänen (*Ilja Kulovaara*), Hannu Lauri (*Ulf Tallgren*), Matti Rasila (*Taukka*), Minna Soisalo (*Assi*), Soli Labbart (*Sörkan Ruusu*), Tomi Salmela (*Detective*), Mirja Oksanen (*Miss Wet T-shirt*), Tiina Björkman, Mauri Sumén, Peter Lindholm. Produced by MK for Villealfa Film Productions/Klas Olofsson, Katinka Faragó for the Swedish Film Institute. 86 mins.

LENINGRAD COWBOYS GO AMERICA

Script and Direction: AK. Photography: Timo Salminen. Music: Leningrad Cowboys. Editing: Raija Talvio. Players: Leningrad Cowboys, Nicky Tesco, Matti Pellonpää, Kari Väänänen. Produced by AK for Villealfa Film Productions/Klas Olofsson, Katinka Faragó for the Swedish Film Institute. 82 mins.

1990
TULITIKKUTEHTAAN TYTTÖ (The Match Factory Girl)

Script and Direction: AK. Photography: Timo Salminen. Editing: AK. Production Design: Risto Karhula. Players: Kato Outinen (*Iris*), Elina Salo (*Mother*), Esko Nikkari (*Stepfather*), Vesa Vierikko (*Man*), Reijo Taipale (*Singer*), Silu Seppälä (*Brother*), Outi Mäenpää (*Workmate*), Marja Packalén (*Doctor*), Richard Reitinger (*Man in the bar*), Helga Viljanen (*Office employee*), Kurt Siilas, Ismo Keinänen (*Policemen*), Klaus Heydemann (*Worker*). Produced by AK for Villealfa Film Productions/Klaus Olofsson, Katinka Faragó for the Swedish Film Institute, in association with Esselte Video AB and Finnkino Oy. 70 mins.

I HIRED A CONTRACT KILLER

Script and Direction: AK. Photography: Timo Salminen. Music: Billie Holiday, Joe Strummer and the Astro-Physicians. Editing: AK.

Production Design: Mark Lavis. Players: Jean-Pierre Léaud (*Henri*), Margi Clarke (*Margaret*), Kenneth Colley (*The Killer*), Nicky Tesco (*Pete*), Joe Strummer (*Guitarist*), Serge Reggiani (*Vic*). Produced by AK for Villealfa Film Productions/Swedish Film Institute, in association with Finnkino (Helsinki), Esselte Video (Stockholm), Megamania (Helsinki), Pandora Films (Frankfurt), Pyramide Films (Paris), Channel Four Television (London). 80 mins.

1991
AMAZON

Script: MK, Richard Reitinger. Direction: MK. Photography: Timo Salminen. Music: Nana Vasconcelos. Editing: Michael Chandler. Production Design: Tony de Castro. Players: Robert Davi (*Dan*), Rae Dawn Chong (*Paola*), Kari Väänänen (*Kari*), Minno Sovio (*Nina*), Aili Sovio (*Lea*), Rui Polonah (*Julio Cesar*). Produced by Pentti Kouri, MK for Villealfa Film Productions Oy/Noema Pictures in association with Sky Light Cinema Foto Arte Ltda (Brazil). 94 mins.

ZOMBIE JA KUMMITUSJUNA (Zombie and the Ghost Train)

Script: MK, based on a story by MK, Pauli Pentti, and Sakke Järvenpää. Direction: MK. Photography: Olli Varja. Music: Mauri Sumén. Editing: MK. Production Design: Kari Laine. Players: Silu Seppälä (*Zombie*), Marjo Leinonen (*Marjo*), Matti Pellonpää (*Harri*), Vieno Saaristo (*Mother*), Juhani Niemelä (*Father*), Sakke Järvenpää, Mato Valtonen, Mauri Sumén, Jyri Närvänen, Jarmo Haapanen (*Mulefukkers*), Jussi Rinne, Matti Viholainen, Roger Nieminen (*The Ghost Train*), Marko Rauhala (*Barber*), Kauko Laurikainen (*Doctor*), Heikki Skippari (*Policeman*), Juho Rastas (*Old man*). Produced by MK for Marianne Films Oy/Villealfa Film Productions Oy. 88 mins.

1992
LA VIE DE BOHEME

Script and Direction: AK. Photography: Timo Salminen. Music: Damia, Little Willie John, Sacy Sand, Moulodji, Mauri Sumén, Serge Reggiani, Tchaikovsky, Georg Ots, The Fake Trashmen, Toshitake Shinohara. Editing: Veikko Aaltonen. Production Design: John Ebden. Players: Matti Pellonpää (*Rodolfo*), Evelyne Didi (*Mimi*), André Wilms (*Marcel*), Kari Väänänen (*Schaunard*), Christine Murillo (*Musette*), Jean-Pierre Léaud (*Blancheron*), Laika (*Baudelaire*), Carlos Salfgado (*Barman*), Alexis Nitzer (*Henri Bernard*), Sylvie van den Elsen (*Mme. Bernard*), Gilles Charmant (*Hugo*), Dominique Marcas (*Lady in second-hand shop*), Samuel Fuller (*Gassot*), Jean-Paul Wenzel (*Francis*), Louis Malle (*Gentleman*). Produced by AK for Sputnik Oy (Helsinki)/Pyramide Production – Films A2 (Paris)/Swedish Film Institute (Stockholm)/Pandora Film (Frankfurt). 100 mins.

1993
THE LAST BORDER

Script: MK, Pia Tikka. Direction: MK. Photography: Timo Salminen. Music: Anssi Tikanmäki. Editing: MK. Production Design: John Ebden. Players: Jolyon Baker (*Jake*), Jürgen Prochnow (*Duke*), Fanny Bastien (*Doaiva*), Kari Väänänen (*Borka*), Matti Pellonpää (*Dimitri*), Soli Labbart (*Old Woman*), Esko Salminen (*Jake's father*), Arvid Dahl (*Young Jake*), Clas-Ove Bruun (*Skunk*), Jussi Lampi (*Rabbit*), Juice Leskinen (*Bartender*), Jochen Nickel, Tixa Juka (*Beggars*), Andrew Krasne (*Officer*), Mato Valtonen (*Drunkard*). Executive Producers: Willy Bär, Klas Olofsson. Produced by MK for Last Border Productions/Connexion Film/Sandrews/MC4. 90 mins.

Jim Jarmusch and Samuel Fuller in Rio for TIGRERO

1994
LENINGRAD COWBOYS MEET MOSES

Script: AK, from a story by Sakke Järvenpää, AK, and Mato Valtonen. Direction: AK. Photography: Timo Salminen. Music: Mauri Sumén. Editing: AK. Production Design: John Ebden. Players: Matti Pellonpää (*Moses/Vladimir*), Kari Väänänen (*The Mute*), André Wilms (*Lazar/Johnson/Elijah*), Nicky Tesco (*American cousin*), Jacques Blanc (*Owner of bingo parlour*), Mme Helie (*Bingo hostess*), Kirsi Tykkyläinen (*Singer of Babylon*), Twist-Twist Erkinharju, Ben Granfelt, Sakke Järvenpää, Jore Marjaranta, Ekke Niiva, Lyle Närvänen, Pemo Ojala, Silu Seppälä, Mauri Sumén, Mato Valtonen (*Leningrad Cowboys*). Produced by AK for Sputnik Oy (Helsinki)/Pandora Film (Frankfurt)/Pyramide Production – La Sept Cinéma. 92 mins.

TOTAL BALALAIKA SHOW

Direction: AK. Photography: Heikki Ortamo. Editing: Timo Linnasalo. Music Recording: Heikki Savolainen. Produced by AK for Sputnik Oy. 52 mins. Documentary featuring Leningrad Cowboys and the Alexandrov Red Army Chorus and Dance Ensemble.

TIGRERO – A FILM THAT WAS NEVER MADE

Script and Direction: MK. Photography: Jacques Cheuiche. Music: Nana Vasconcelos, Chuck Jonkey, The Karajá. Editing: MK. Players: Samuel Fuller, Jim Jarmusch, The Karajá Indians (*Themselves*). Produced by MK for Marianna Films/Premiere (Hamburg)/YLE/TV1 (Helsinki)/Sky Light Cinema/Mira Set (Rio de Janeiro)/Lichtblick (Cologne). 75 mins.

PIDÄ HUIVISTA KIINNI, TATIANA (Take Care of Your Scarf, Tatiana!)

Script: AK, Sakke Järvenpää. Direction: AK. Photography: Timo Salminen. Music: Tchaikovsky, etc. Editing: AK. Production Design: Kari Laine, Markku Patila, Jukka Salmi. Players: Matti Pellonpää (*Reino*), Mato Valtonen (*Valto*), Kati Outinen (*Tatiana*), Kirsi Tykkyläinen (*Klaudia*), Elina Salo (*Hotel receptionist*), Irma Junniläinen (*Valto's mother*), Veikko Lavi (*Vepe*), Pertti Husu (*Pepe*). Produced by AK for Sputnik Oy (Helsinki)/Pandora Film (Frankfurt). 62 mins.

In preparation:
BEYOND THE LAW

Direction: MK. Produced by Oak Island Films (New York).

Ken Loach

by Steven Gaydos

A1994 *New York Times* "Film View" piece by Caryn James offered a series of short profiles on contemporary British and Irish film-makers headlined "If You Can't Tell a Figgis from a Newell," the point being that it's all too easy to mix up the U.K. auteurs, since "the profiles of the directors remain fuzzy". The directors in question included (besides Mikes Figgis, Newell and Leigh), Jim Sheridan, Neil Jordan, Stephen Frears and Ken Loach. This was perhaps the only time in his long TV and film career that the unrepentant social gadfly Ken Loach was ever labelled "fuzzy".

The maker of gritty, engaging working class social/political dramas like *Family Life, Hidden Agenda, Riff-Raff, Raining Stones, Ladybird, Ladybird,* fuzzy? Thorny, outspoken, strident, progressive, militant, humanist, documentarian, left-wing, anti-Thatcherite, maybe, but "fuzzy" never.

Loach's best films are toughminded, socially conscious portraits of Britain's lower and middle classes. But what makes him one of international cinema's most lauded and respected film-makers isn't just political correctness, even if it does seem that Loach's profile rises precipitously at a moment when the Tories' sunset appears to draw nearer. He has influenced virtually all of his fellow British directors mentioned

in the James piece by remaining true to his naturalistic film roots, by combining a stunning technical proficiency with a master's touch for performances and by staying the course of his political beliefs, especially during the Thatcherite 1980's when, as Loach pungently phrased it, in one interview (in typically unfuzzy terms), "the rats rose to the surface".

KENNETH (now "Ken") LOACH was born on June 17, 1936, in Nuneaton, England. Loach studied law and acting at Oxford, before taking the BBC's directors course. This led to a BBC television directing career that took off while Loach was still in his twenties. In 1965 he won the British TV Guild's Director of the Year Award and his TV film *Cathy Come Home* garnered him more awards in 1966, the year he began collaborating with producer Tony Garnett on a highly regarded series of 75-minute original teleplays. Setting the tone early for his entire career, these were usually social dramas, and often experimented with a mix of fiction and documentary techniques.

Growing Interest in Psychology

Loach's scorching honesty and relentless probing into political issues was complemented by a growing interest in psychology, especially as articulated by maverick psychologist R. D. Laing. With TV dramas like *In Two Minds*, a case history of a schizophrenic girl, and *Cathy Come Home*, his prize-winning look at England's housing problems, Loach took a resolutely activist approach to film-making without becoming a mere polemicist. In addition to the obvious risks – witness Oliver Stone and Spike Lee – holding to ideals that cut left of comfortable liberalism is not the easiest path to success in film or television.

But Loach and Garnett settled in and established a long, rewarding partnership that produced a bounty of television dramas and led to the formation of their own production outfit, Kestrel Films Ltd.

Loach's first theatrical feature, *Poor Cow* (1968), has its admirers, although the

Bill Dean, Sandy Ratcliffe, and Grace Cave in FAMILY LIFE

director himself is not among them. Focusing on the romantic entanglements of an English working-class *ménage à trois*, Loach blamed what he considered the film's artistic failings on his "making every mistake you could make", including working with the wrong producer, a crew made up of too many "old features' sweats", and "allow(ing) actors to dictate". The film is perhaps not the disaster Loach terms it, with solid performances from Carol White and Terence Stamp, and a sweet, sunny score by 1960's pop troubadour Donovan.

Loach's point about working with the right producer and crew was made on his next feature. The first film from Kestrel, *Kes* (1970) immediately put Loach and producer Tony Garnett on the theatrical map. One of its many fans was Polish director Krzysztof Kieślowski, who drew from Loach's work a quality that transcended what one critic dismissed as Loach's talent as an "effective polemicist". In fact, Kieślowski credits Loach with the ability to "escape from ... literalism" a feat he says occurs "once in 10,000 times", and "a miracle" that he credits Orson Welles with achieving "once", Fellini and

Bergman "a few times" and Loach with *Kes*. It's an accomplishment Kieślowski says he himself "will never achieve".

Kieślowski's enthusiasm for the film was a widely shared sentiment at the time. In notes for the 1969 London Film Festival, John Gillett compared it to Truffaut's *The 400 Blows*, calling it "brilliant ... sad, funny and disturbing", while noting its "verisimilitude" and "inner realism".

After the made-for-television feature, *In Black and White* (1970), another project Loach feels doesn't represent his best work, the British director made his second landmark film in 1972, *Family Life*, again in partnership with producer Garnett. Derived from the aforementioned production of David Mercer's *In Two Minds*, which they had done for the "Wednesday Play" series for the BBC, *Family Life* was an emotionally powerful examination of the social roots of a young girl's madness. Among its many virtues, actress Sandy Ratcliff gave an unforgettable performance as the troubled youth, caught in a suffocating dysfunctional family, and the gritty drama remains a key reference point for an entire generation of film-makers. The film's documentary-like veracity and authenticity also helped *Family Life* develop a following among professional psychologists, and the video version has become a valued teaching aid.

Loach's next four films could be called his "middle" period if there were any organising principle beyond a director constantly in search of production funding.

David Bradley and Colin Welland in KES
photo: Michael Barnett

Frances Dormand and Brian Cox in HIDDEN AGENDA
photo: Hemdale/Kobal Collection

Loach has said that he considered himself "lucky" each time a film was commissioned, but if he wasn't entirely in control of his professional fate, he certainly maintains a clear vision of how well he accomplished his goal each time out. One might guess these weren't his happiest years professionally, because only two of the films earned him respect.

Young Lives Facing Dead Ends

Though Loach's next film, *Black Jack* (1979), scored a Cannes Critics Award, and solid critical praise, the period adventure picture rates lowly on Loach's own list of films, and he's clearly more pleased with *Looks and Smiles* (1981), an urban drama about young lives facing dead ends. Like three other Loach films, *Looks and Smiles* was brilliantly photographed in black-and-white by Chris Menges. Not to slight the distinguished work of Loach's other cinematographers, but their partnership was as central to the development of Loach's art as the Kestrel team of Loach and producer Garnett, and Loach's extraordinary ability to shoot lyrical, forceful dramas using very small crews and available light grew through this teaming.

Fatherland (also known in the U.S. as *Singing the Blues in Red*, 1986) is dismissed by Loach as a film that "should have been better". Loach feared its mix of East-West politics and a complex narrative "(wasn't) ... going to work" in the final form, a fear that he says "was borne out".

Though more of a traditional "thriller" than Loach was accustomed to tackling, *Hidden Agenda* (1990) proved something of a watershed film for Loach, and he has been working steadily since the scorching IRA drama won a Cannes Jury Prize and introduced Loach to a new generation of film audiences. A taut, suspenseful detective story shot on the streets of Northern Ireland, the film boasts terrific performances by Brian Cox and Americans Brad Dourif and Frances McDormand.

With *Riff-Raff* in 1991, Loach began perhaps the most fruitful and consistently sure-handed period of his entire career. Winner of the European Film of the Year Award, *Riff-Raff* is a raucous, lively study of construction workers who are denied any rights, and who begin, as their class anger grows, to lose all of their fears, and they begin to rebel. The film re-established Loach's connection to working class England, and announced that his political convictions, like his film-making, had only matured over the decades, not softened or grown "fuzzy".

The 1993 Cannes Jury Prize winner, *Raining Stones*, is a parabolic masterpiece. Detailing the struggles of a decent working man trying to afford a Communion dress for his daughter, the tale is told as simply and elegantly as the best of De Sica.

Ladybird, Ladybird (1994) picked up a prize at the Berlin Fest, and makes for a stunning, if sullen, companion to the lighter spirited *Raining Stones*. A brutal and unrelenting portrait of spousal abuse and single motherhood, it shows that Loach has returned to the gut-wrenching dramatics of *Family Life*, a film that announced his commitments and intentions 22 years ago.

A recent *Film Comment* profile dubbed him "Britain's best-kept secret", a distinction somewhat contradicted by the article's later mention of his four Cannes Festival Critics' awards. But the truth is, midway through the 1990's Ken Loach is both a secret and a long-established master film-maker. Unlike many other British directors at work today, Loach has never achieved a breakaway commercial success, even in art-house terms. Hence the "secret".

Praise from Kieślowski

As for his reputation inside professional and critical circles, one of his contemporaries expresses it best. In his autobiographical book, *Kieślowski on Kieślowski*, the Polish master film-maker says of Loach's *Kes*: "I always thought that I'd never be able to do anything like that [*Kes*] in my life ... not due to lack of money or because I didn't have sufficient imagination, intelligence ... talent. ... I never wanted to be anybody's assistant but ... if ... Ken Loach were to ask me, then I'd willingly make him coffee ... so I could see how he does it all. The same applied to Orson Welles, or Fellini, and sometimes Bergman."

Kieślowski's appreciation of Loach's achievements is shared by a freshly burgeoning Loach cult. The critical praise for *Hidden Agenda* and *Riff-Raff* (1991) led to more praise, and the solid world box-office performance of *Raining Stones*. Yet more

Crissy Rock in LADYBIRD, LADYBIRD
photo: Parallax Productions

plaudits greeted *Ladybird, Ladybird*, which has gained Loach his widest U.K. release to date, as well as a prestigious spot on the North America release chart of the Samuel Goldwyn Co.

As Loach's newest film *Land and Freedom* rolls through the production process, the 58-year-old veteran of nearly 30 TV programmes and a dozen films is finding production funding for his often troubling and bleak pictures much less of "a struggle" as he has termed it, and it's his "secret" that looks ready for retirement, not the creatively thriving film-maker.

Still from Loach's RAINING STONES

photo: Kobal Collection

Loach Filmography

Loach's television work continued into the 1980's, and the film-maker lists three of his television projects: *Cathy Come Home* (1966), *The Gamekeeper* (1980) and *Which Side Are You On?* (1984) among his own "preferred list of films", while excluding three of his features: *Poor Cow*, *Black Jack* and *Fatherland*.

1968
POOR COW

Script: Nell Dunn, KL, based on the novel by Dunn. Direction: KL. Photography: Brian Probyn. Editing: Roy Watts. Music: Donovan. Art Director: Bernard Sarron. Players: Carol White (*Joy*), Terence Stamp (*Dave*), John Bindon (*Tom*), Kate Williams (*Beryl*), Queenie Watts (*Aunt Emm*). Produced by Joseph Janni. A National General Pictures release. 104 mins.

1970
KES

Script: Barry Hines, KL, Tony Garnett, from Hines's book "A Kestrel for a Knave." Direction: KL. Photography: Chris Menges. Editing: Roy Watts. Music: John Cameron. Production Design: William McCrow. Players: David Bradley (*Billy*), Colin Welland (*Mr. Farthing*), Lynne Perrie (*Mrs. Casper*), Freddie Fletcher (*Jud*), Brian Glover (*Mr. Sugden*), Bob Bowes (*Mr. Gryce*). Produced by Tony Garnett, for Kestrel Films. A United Artists release. 107 mins.

1970
IN BLACK AND WHITE

Script: Direction: KL Photography: TK. Editing: TK. Music: TK. Production Design: TK. Music: TK. Production Design: TK. Costumes: TK. Players: TK.

1972
FAMILY LIFE (also released as Wednesday's Child)

Script: David Mercer, from his teleplay "In Two Minds". Direction: KL. Photography: Charles Stewart. Editing: Roy Watts. Music: Marc Wilkinson. Production Design: William McCrow. Players: Sandy Ratcliff (*Janice*), Bill Dean (*Mr. Baildon*), Grace Cave (*Mrs. Baildon*), Malcolm Tierney (*Tim*), Hilary Martyn (*Barbara*), Michael Riddall (*Dr. Donaldson*), Alan MacNaughton (*Mr. Carswell*). Produced by Tony Garnett for Kestrel Films. Released by Anglo/EMI. 108 mins.

1979
BLACK JACK

Script: KL, from the novel by Leon Garfield. Direction: KL. Photography: Chris Menges. Editing: Bill Shapter. Music: Bob Pegg. Production Design: Martin Johnson. Costumes: Sally Nieper. Players: Jean Franvel (*Black Jack*), Stephen Hirst (*Tolly*), Louise Cooper (*Belle*), Andrew Bennett (*Hatch*), Packie Byrne (*Dr. Carmody*), Pat Wallis (*Mrs. Gorgandy*). Produced by Tony Garnett for Kestrel Films. 106 mins.

1981
LOOKS AND SMILES

Script: Barry Hines. Direction: KL. Photography: Chris Menges. Editing: Steve Singleton. Music: Mark Wilkinson. Production Design: Martin Johnson. Costumes: Gwenda Evans. Players: Graham Green (*Mick*), Carolyn Nicholson (*Karen*), Tony Pitts (*Alan*), Phil Askham (*Mick's Dad*), Cilla Mason (*Karen's Ma*). Produced by Tony Garnett for Kestrel Films. Executive Producer: Irving Teitelbaum. Black Lion Films, MK2 Productions. An MK2 release. 104 mins.

1986
FATHERLAND

Script: Trevor Griffith. Direction: KL. Photography: Chris Menges. Editing: Jonathan Morris. Music: Christian Kunert and Gerulf Pannach. Production Design: Martin Johnson. Costumes: Antji Peterson. Players: Gerulf Pannach (*Klaus Dritteman*), Fabienne Babe (*Emma de Baen*), Sighert Steiner (*Father*), Christian Rose (*Lucy Bernstein*). Produced by Raymond Day. A Film Four/MK2/Classart presentation of a Kestrel II production. Executive Producer: Irving Teitelbaum. 110 mins.

1990
HIDDEN AGENDA

Script: Jim Allen. Direction: KL. Photography: Clive Tickner. Editing: Jonathan Morris. Music: Stewart Copeland. Production Design: Martin Johnson. Costumes: Daphne Dare. Players: Frances McDormand (*Ingrid*), Brian Cox (*Kerrigan*), Brad Dourif (*Paul*), Mai Zetterling (*Moa*), Bernard Archard (*Sir Robert Neil*), John Benfield (*Maxwell*), Bernard Bloch (*Henri*), Michelle Fairley (*Teresa Doyle*). Produced by Eric Fellner for Hemdale Films Corporation. 107 mins.

1991
RIFF-RAFF

Script: Bill Jesse. Direction: KL. Photography: Barry Ackroyd. Editing: Jonathan Morris. Music: Stewart Copeland. Production Design: Martin Johnson. Costumes: Wendy Knowles. Players: Ricky Tomlinson (*Larry*), Robert Carlyle (*Stevie*), Emer McCourt (*Susie*), Jimmy Coleman (*Shem*), George Moss (*Mo*), Willie Ross (*Gus Siddon*). Produced by Sally Hibbin for Parallax Pictures Ltd. and Film Four International. 92 mins.

1993
RAINING STONES

Script: Jim Allen. Direction: KL. Photography: Barry Ackroyd. Editing: Jonathan Morris. Music: Stewart Copeland. Production Design: Martin Johnson. Art Director: Fergus Clegg. Costumes: Anne Sinclair. Players: Bruce Jones (*Bob*), Julie Brown (*Anne*), Ricky Tomlinson (*Tommy*), Tom Hickey (*Father Barry*), Gemma Phoenix (*Coleen*), Jonathan James (*Tansey*), Mike Fallon (*Jimmy*). Produced by Sally Hibbin for Parallax Productions and Channel Four, a Film Four International release. 90 mins.

1994
LADYBIRD, LADYBIRD

Script: Rona Munro. Direction: KL. Photography: Barry Ackroyd. Editing: Jonathan Morris. Music: George Fenton. Production Design: Martin Johnson. Costumes: Wendy Knowles. Players: Crissy Rock (*Magie*), Vladimir Vega (*Jorge*), Sandie La Velle (*Mairead*), Mauricio Venegas (*Adrian*), Ray Winstone (*Simon*), Clare Perkins (*Jill*), Jason Stracey (*Sean*), Luke Brown (*Mickey*), Lily Farrell (*Serena*). Produced by Sally Hibbin for Parallax Pictures Ltd. and Film Four International. 102 mins.

LAND AND FREEDOM

Script: Jim Allen. Direction: KL. Photography: TK. Production Design: Martin Johnson. Costumes: Ana Alvagonzalez (Spain), Daphne Dare (Liverpool). Players: Ian Hart (*David*), Rosana Pastor (*Blanca*), Tom Gilroy (*Lawrence*), Frederick Pierrot (*Bernard*), Eoin McCarthy (*Coogan*), Mark Martinez (*Vidal*), Iciar Bollain (*Mayte*). Produced by Rebecca O'Brien for Parallax Pictures Ltd., Messidor Films, ReadMovies Dritte Produktionen with the participation of British Screen, support of BIM, Diaphana, European Co-Production Fund, Eurimages, TVE, Canal Plus (Spain), BBC and Filmstiftung Nordrhein-West-falen.

Quentin Tarantino

by Derek Elley

Quentin Tarantino's movies are bubblegum for the brain. In arguably the most explosive opening shots in English-speaking cinema since Nicolas Roeg rearranged the board in the early 1970's, Tarantino has directed at least one classic (*Reservoir Dogs*), written a near-classic (*True Romance*), and managed to beat the "sophomore jinx" (and walk off with the Cannes Palme d'Or) with his second feature, *Pulp Fiction*. At the age of thirty he has a following that is even stronger in Europe than in his native America.

Tarantino is the original video-age movie nerd who has managed to put his obsessions on film. His movies pulsate with references to and borrowings from anything from Hongkong crime movies to Hollywood programmers of the 1940's and 1950's. A pulp buff who learnt his vocabulary from TV, working in a video store, and comic books, he is in direct contrast to a parallel generation who learnt theory at film school and then set out to make art movies for the world.

However, what sets him apart from other junk-food, MTV-age directors is his subjugation of images to words, of technique to content. Tarantino is first and foremost an actor's writer-director and, though his sensibilities are based in the visceral emotions of popular American drama, his delight in the rhythms and subtleties of dialogue is probably the main reason for his enormous cult following in Europe. Just as the French New Wave 30 years earlier challenged an inflexible, ossified mainstream industry, so Tarantino and his like thumb their noses at the self-censoring correctness of mainstream

Tim Roth and Harvey Keitel in RESERVOIR DOGS

American cinema, currently going through its most conservative period since the 1950's. If there is an American New Wave of the 1990's, Tarantino is its Godard.

His two features, and two filmed scripts (*True Romance*; *Natural Born Killers*), should be seen as only the opening volleys in a career that would seem to have reached its limit on present subject-matter. He himself has said he now wants to do something different. Only once before has IFG saluted a director after only two features (Krzysztof Kieślowski in 1981); we were prescient then, and there's every reason to believe we won't be eating our words when Tarantino turns forty.

QUENTIN TARANTINO was born in 1964, in Tennessee and grew up in Los Angeles where he moved when very young. He began as an actor in local theatre productions and TV series like *The Golden Girls* (playing an Elvis impersonator) and counts James Best and Allen Garfield (with whom he studied for three years) among his drama tutors. While

working as an order clerk in Video Archives, in Manhattan Beach, Southern California, he turned to scriptwriting and managed to sell *True Romance*, written in 1986, to a studio. However, the script remained "in development", and it was not until *Reservoir Dogs*, which Tarantino penned during three weeks in October 1990, that his career suddenly moved up a gear.

Love of Classic Heist Movies

According to Tarantino, the idea for *Dogs* came from his love of classic heist movies like *The Asphalt Jungle*, *Rififi*, *The Killing*, *The Thomas Crown Affair* and *Topkapi* – but to turn the expected around by looking at what happened to the characters *after* the crime. Desperate to break into film-making, and having enrolled in the Director's Workshop at Robert Redford's Sundance Institute, Tarantino originally planned to shoot it on 16mm with $30,000 he and a producer friend, Lawrence Bender, had raised. Tarantino was to play one character (Mr. Pink) and Bender another (Nice Guy Eddie), with other roles taken by friends.

Just before they were about to start shooting, the duo had a stroke of luck. Bender had shown the script to one of his acting coaches, Lily Parker, who had sent it to Harvey Keitel, whom she knew through the Actors Studio in New York. Keitel read it, immediately called to say he wanted to meet the writer, and a deal was struck whereby Tarantino would direct and Keitel personally put up some money to get the $1.5 million project off the ground.

Keitel was also instrumental in bringing Tarantino to New York to cast for actors, but even when the film started shooting it was not fully financed. The result premiered at the Sundance Festival, Park City, Utah, in January 1992 and was released the following October by Miramax. In North America it grossed only a paltry $3 million over the next six months; but in the meantime, it had already become a hotly requested item on the international festival circuit, with

Tarantino established in one bound as a director to watch.

In Tarantino's words: "Part of the problem with movies recently is that you pretty much know what's gonna happen before it happens. What I like to do is use that against you psychologically – you turn left and I turn right – not just for gamesmanship but to be an interesting storyteller."

Bizarre Group

From the word go, *Dogs* is Tarantino's credo writ large. Starting with a seven-minute sequence of a bizarre group of characters chatting around a breakfast table in a restaurant, the film screams self-assurance in every frame. The audience is kept in the dark as to who these men are; but from their ripe language, dark suits, tough-guy attitudes and air of physical menace, it is clear they aren't priests.

The lightly comic conversation has an unreal character, ranging from a dissection

Uma Thurman in the diner sequence of PULP FICTION

Writer-director Quentin Tarantino (left) on location for
RESERVOIR DOGS

of what Madonna's song "Like a Virgin" really means to the ethics of tipping waitresses and the U.S. minimum wage. The screen blacks out, a disc-jockey voice announces "K-Billy's Super Sounds of the '70's," and to a sassy beat and slow-motion shots of the group striding across a parking lot in dark glasses, the film is off.

Immediately, Tarantino springs the first of several surprises, cutting to a shocking scene of one of them (Tim Roth) screaming in blood-drenched pain from a stomach wound while another (Harvey Keitel) attempts to calm him while driving a speeding car. A crime has gone wrong and, as the various characters reassemble at a deserted warehouse, it gradually becomes clear that one of them has betrayed his colleagues.

In almost literary style, Tarantino's script switches back and forth between initial meetings with the crime boss (veteran Lawrence Tierney), initial panic just after the jewellery store theft itself, real-time developments at the warehouse – including a horrifying sequence of one hood (Michael Madsen) casually torturing a trussed-up cop – and, after the stoolie has been revealed to the audience, scenes of him infiltrating the gang. The ending is swift and violent, with a subliminal burst of gunplay that takes repeated viewings to unravel.

At every level throughout the film, Tarantino keeps the audience on its toes, not simply by time-juggling and plot twists but also by taking familiar elements and slightly moving the goalposts. Though the proceedings are deadly serious, each gang member is assigned an alias (Mr. Brown, Mr. Pink, Mr. White, etc) that reduces them almost to characters in a game of Cluedo; though the action is set in the present, everyone wears black suits and ties that are closer to a Jean-Pierre Melville film of the 1950's or 1960's, even as the music is made up of bubblegum hits of the 1970's; though none of the protagonists is at all educated, many (and especially Steve Buscemi's Mr. Pink) talk in a florid, almost literary style that's completely at odds with their background; and though the movie is essentially dialogue-driven, and for the most part set in interiors, Tarantino consciously chooses to shoot the whole thing in 'scope.

In the true spirit of pulp, where imitation is the sincerest form of admiration rather than copyright theft, the film is a treasure trove of references. In its jump cuts and fragmented style, the film recalls early Godard (Tarantino's production company, A Band Apart, is even named after one of Godard's early movies), and in its spare visual style recalls Melville movies like *Second Breath* or *The Samurai*. The colour-coded aliases of the hoods is a direct snitch from *The Taking of Pelham One Two Three*, the gunplay recalls John Woo's *A Better Tomorrow* and *The Killer*, and several elements in the plot are drawn straight from a segment of Ringo Lam's 1987 gangster movie, *City on Fire*.

Overflowing with Wild Characters

After getting *Dogs* off the ground, Tarantino happened to meet director Tony Scott, who suggested he retrieve the script of *True Romance*. After originally thinking of just producing, Scott ended up directing the picture which, though slightly changed from Tarantino's original script and given a technical gloss treatment at odds with its creator's sparer directing style, is recognisably a Tarantino movie in content and preoccupations.

The main characters, film-obsessed nerd Clarence (Christian Slater) and hooker-with-a-heart Alabama (Patricia Arquette, in a role briefly referred to by Keitel in *Dogs*), are modern versions of lovers on the run in B-movies of the 1940's and 1950's like Joseph H. Lewis' *Gun Crazy* (1949). Here, the love birds escape from dreary Detroit to sunny Los Angeles with a suitcase of cocaine accidentally stolen from a courier for the Mob.

The film overflows with wild characters (Gary Oldman as a psychotic white rastafarian; Christopher Walken as a ruthless Mafia Don; Saul Rubinek as a caricature Hollywood producer, modelled on Joel Silver), over-the-top cartoon violence (Arquette beaten up in her hotel room; the final three-way shootout in a Beverly Hills hotel), and wonderful dialogue set-pieces (Dennis Hopper explaining to Walken how Sicilians are descended from African "niggers") that are pure Tarantino in demolishing accepted norms of "taste" and delighting in the raw romanticism of frontier America.

Though Slater's character died from an eye wound in Taratino's original script, the film's celebration of pulp fiction values remains intact, despite the happy ending. (Other changes, forced on the film by the U.S. ratings board, are restored in the 120-minute "director's cut" released theatrically outside America and within the U.S. on laserdisc.)

While Oliver Stone turned to rewriting and directing another of Tarantino's earlier scripts, *Natural Born Killers*, a bloody tale of two serial murderers, Tarantino himself embarked on his ambitious second feature, *Pulp Fiction*, originally intended as three stories with different directors.

The finished movie, a giant 2¼-hour kaleidoscope that premiered at Cannes in May 1994, plays on and then pulls out the rug from under the feet of those expecting just another rerun of *Reservoir Dogs* or *True Romance*. On the surface, there are several similarities: one pair of characters, hitmen played by John Travolta and Samuel L. Jackson, recall the hoods of *Dogs* with their black suits and philosophical exchanges on

Bruce Willis in PULP FICTION
photo: Linda R. Chen

anything from European fast food to the existence of God; the script's black humour, long dialogue sequences, time-play cross-cutting, characters on the edge (Bruce Willis' 1940's B-movie boxer on the run), and casual gun-play all inhabit Tarantino's familiar world of white-trash characters raised to an unreal, almost literary level. And the film's setpiece, in a massive 1950's-influenced diner, further disorients the viewer with off-centre cultural references.

It soon becomes clear, however, that Tarantino is after bigger fish here, with an elaborate game plan that only starts to swim into focus after the first hour. Very slowly, the three separate stories start to click together, anchored by the central characters of Travolta and Jackson and propelled by the latter's Road to Damascus conversion that God exists even for a humble hitman.

Guns and Gas-guzzling Chevies

It's a lunatic proposition that comes from taking an early scene, in which Travolta explains some of the cultural differences between Europe and America, and slowly building on Jackson's realisation that there's more to life than his own narrowly prescribed world of guns and gas-guzzling Chevies. If Jackson attains some kind of peace with himself at the end, and manages to pass on his wisdom to tyro hoods Tim Roth and Amanda Plummer (whose stick-up of a diner bookends the whole movie), other characters also manage to shake off their past through casual acts of good will – notably Willis' buzz-cut boxer, who saves arch-enemy Ving Rhames from a fate worse than death in a spooky cellar.

Though the film is over-leisurely during its first hour, featuring a dead-end story of Travolta minding Rhames's druggie wife (Uma Thurman) that's slow to catch fire, the latter half fully rewards its audience's patience, starting with an hilarious, shaggy-dog monologue by Christopher Walken whose place in the jigsaw only becomes clear later on. If *Pulp Fiction* bears any relation to *Reservoir Dogs*, it is on an emotional plane – spending more time with a similar set of characters and finding out where the trail leads. Just as Claude Chabrol (another pulp enthusiast) once stated he always like to follow a story one reel beyond its obvious ending, in *Pulp Fiction* Tarantino goes a good two or three. And if that leaves audiences still thinking when they leave the theatre, then so much the better.

Tarantino Filmography

As well as in his own films Reservoir Dogs and Pulp Fiction, Tarantino's acting appearances include Jean-Luc Godard's King Lear (1987) and Rory Kelly's Come Sleep with Me (1994). He was one of three executive producers on fellow Video Archives alumnus Roger Avary's Killing Zoe (1994). As of summer 1994, he was planning to direct a segment of the portmanteau feature Four Rooms, and play Johnny Destiny in Rafal Zielinski's Destiny Turns on the Radio. He has written the screenplay for True Romance (1993) and the story for Natural Born Killers (1994).

1992
RESERVOIR DOGS

Script and Direction: QT. Photography ('scope): Andrzej Sekula. Editing: Sally Menke. Music supervision: Karyn Rachtman. Production Design: David Wasco. Players: Harvey Keitel (*Mr. White/Larry*), Tim Roth (*Mr. Orange/Freddy*), Michael Madsen (*Mr. Blonde/Vic Vega*), Chris Penn (*Nice Guy Eddie*), Steve Buscemi (*Mr. Pink*), Lawrence Tierney (*Joe Cabot*), Eddie Bunker (*Mr. Blue*), QT (*Mr. Brown*), Kirk Baltz (*Marvin Nash, the cop*). Produced by Lawrence Bender for Live America. 105 mins.

1994
PULP FICTION

Script and Direction: QT, from stories by QT and Roger Avary. Photography ('scope): Andrzej Sekula. Editing: Sally Menke. Music supervision: Karyn Rachtman. Production Design: David Wasco. Players: John Travolta (*Vincent Vega*), Samuel L. Jackson (*Jules*), Uma Thurman (*Mia*), Harvey Keitel (*The Wolf*), Tim Roth (*Pumpkin*), Amanda Plummer (*Honey Boney*), Maria de Madeiros (*Fabienne*), Ving Rhames (*Marsellus Wallace*), Eric Stoltz (*Lance*), Rosanna Arquette (*Jody*), Christopher Walken (*Koons*), Bruce Willis (*Butch*), QT (*Jimmie*). Produced by Lawrence Bender for *A Band Apart* and Jersey Films. 154 mins.

John Travolta and Samuel L. Jackson in PULP FICTION

BOOK REVIEWS

David Bordwell continues his distinguished career with **The Cinema of Eisenstein** (Harvard University Press, Cambridge and London), which should revive the flagging fortunes of this path-breaking director with a new generation of film buffs. Bordwell has a firm grasp of the Russian master's theories of film technique, and of course Eisenstein and semantics are almost synonymous. Bordwell's style is articulate and never patronising, and his frame enlargements are crystal-sharp compared with those in most books.

Produced with all the magnificence that one has come to expect from Harry N. Abrams (New York and London), **Ingmar Bergman, Film and Stage** should reach a public beyond those film buffs who may regard the Swedish master with a jaded eye. Robert Emmet Long writes enthusiastically about the Swede's stage work, and devotes a section to each of the films. He has the courage to criticise when he feels like it, and he has clearly read all the available literature on Bergman. But it is the 200-odd illustrations that set this book apart as a gift item.

Another successful book from the same house anticipates the cinema's centenary with a bang. Robert Sklar's **Film, An International History of the Medium** (Harry N. Abrams, New York: Thames & Hudson, London) is a thinking buff's coffee-table book, splendidly illustrated as well as aesthetic and thematic developments, although it's a pity that he could find no room to mention masterworks like *Apocalypse Now*, *Chimes at Midnight* or *Five Easy Pieces*.

Almost as lavish in presentation, George Perry's **Sunset Boulevard, from Movie to Musical** (Pavilion Books, London) may be intended as a companion to the Andrew Lloyd Webber musical but may live for its meticulous reconstruction of Billy Wilder's 1950 jewel in the film noir crown, enhanced with several nostalgic duotone illustrations of the way Sunset Boulevard was in that power heyday.

The fourth edition of Roy Pickard's **The Oscar Movies** (Studio Vista, London) includes some 600 films that have won Academy Awards since 1929. Even more useful is the appendix of nominees (although a random listing of 200 "Films That Weren't Nominated" has a trivia ring to it).

The Marx Brothers industry roll on. Latest to come off the assembly line is **Groucho Marx and Other Short Stories and Tall Tales,** Edited by Robert S. Bader (Faber and Faber, Boston and London). It's a delicious ragbag of droll observations and provocations, including letters to *Variety,* odd pieces for *The New Yorker, Collier's Redbook* and other magazines, spread over half a century from the early 1920's to Groucho's death.

The least expected gem of the reading year is the late Tony Richardson's memoir, **Long Distance Runner** (Faber and Faber, London and Boston). Discovered by his family on the day of his death, the manuscript paints a portrait of a man equally gifted in theatre and cinema, a director at the cutting edge of the renaissance in British culture in the late 1950's and early 1960's, and a maverick in private as well as public life, someone who recognised his own weaknesses and looked them straight in the eye.

Although his career has been spotty at best, Hollywood producer Robert Evans reveals a fine mind and a self-critical awareness, in **The Kid Stays in the Picture** (Hyperion, New York; Aurum Press, London). This extraordinary, titillating memoir moves like an express train from the 1950's to the 1990's.

Raw-nerved Recollections

Tony Curtis, **The Autobiography** (Heinemann, London) reached the bestseller lists in Britain, and offers a clever admixture of raw-nerved recollections by Curtis and useful comments on the films by Barry Paris. Few Hollywood stars have chronicled their addictions so candidly as Curtis in this memoir.

Two unusual books have come from the British Film Institute this year. Derek Threadgall's **Shepperton Studios, An Independent View** (BFI Publishing, London) examines the topsy-turvy history of the British studio outside London where Sir Alexander Korda and British Lion once held court. *Shadowlands* and *Judge Dredd* are among films shot recently on the stages of Shepperton.

Also from the BFI, two further entries in the miniseries devoted to individual classic films, **Boudu Saved from Drowning,** by Richard Boston and **It's a Gift** by Simon Louvish. Boston's knowledge of French culture places the Renoir film in a three-dimensional perspective, while Louvish delves rewardingly into Fields's antecedents as a stage comic.

The deification of Michael Powell in recent years has tended to stifle the memory of his colleague and screenwriter, Emeric Pressburger. Now his grandson, Kevin Macdonald, has written a commendable, humane biography, **Emeric Pressburger, The Life and Death of a Screenwriter** (Faber and Faber, London and Boston), including extracts from scripts, and a myriad details about the frustration of fine-tuning a film during its formative phase. Faber has also issued the screenplay for **The Life and Death of Colonel Blimp,** by Powell and Pressburger, edited by Ian Christie.

In a year when *Trois Couleurs: Rouge* was far and away the outstanding picture, **Kieślowski on Kieślowski,** edited by Danusia Stok (Faber and Faber, London and Boston), offers cat-nip to all admirers of this Polish director. Kieślowski talks at length about his childhood, life in Poland, and the themes of each of his films. The sheer physical difficulty of making movies, and solving day to day problems on set or on location, marks every page of this creative memoir.

Amid all the euphoria surrounding Steven Spielberg, Darren Slade and Nigel Watson have produced an engaging little booklet entitled **Supernatural Spielberg** (Valis Books, London). The emphasis is on the director's use of supernatural themes and beliefs, and covers the films that Spielberg has produced as well as the familiar classics.

The bright-green memory of Orson Welles is well served in a sumptuous boxed set of two volumes: **Orson Welles, Una España Immortal,** by Esteve Riambau and **Orson Welles, España como Obsessión,** by Juan Cobos (Filmoteca Española, Madrid). The text (in Spanish focuses primarily on Welles's "Spanish" films, and the pictures, are superb, in particular those from *Chimes at Midnight*, on which Cobos served as assistant director.

French Books of Note

From across the Channel, several interesting new works have appeared in French in the past year. **Le Cinéma Soviétique,** by Marcel Martin (L'Age d'Homme, Paris) deals authoritatively with the turbulent, rapidly changing period between 1955 and 1992, and shows that from Khruschev to Gorbachev, the Soviet cinema churned out much dross but also numerous masterworks, from *The Cranes Are Flying* to *Taxi Blues*.

Le Cinéma Coréen, edited by Adriano Aprà (Centre Georges Pompidou, Paris) is the latest volume in Jean Loup Passek's Cinéma/Pluriel series, including pioneering material, fact, and comment about the burgeoning Korean film. Another, more arcane entry is **Naples et le Cinéma** (Centre Georges Pompidou, Paris), although it discusses films by De Sica, Rossellini and Pasolini among others, and persuades us that Naples is not so much a place as a way of life.

Editions Actes Sud have teamed with the Institut Lumière in Lyon to launch a new paperback series of quality texts on the cinema. All the emphasis falls on the text, rather than on stills, and Bertrand Tavernier kicks off the enterprise with a meaty tome on **Amis Américains.** These interviews with American directors of the older (or even deceased) generation are full of plums, and make perfect bedside reading.

So do **Joseph Losey, L'Oeil du Maître,** edited by Michel Ciment (Actes Sud, Arles), and **Paolo et Vittorio Taviani, Entretien au pluriel,** edited by Jean A. Gili (Actes Sud, Arles). The Losey book is a juicy ragbag of letters, script snippets and comments, and autobiographical essays by the late director.

On the reference front, the Finnish national filmography moves majestically towards the halfway point – with four volumes out of a projected ten now available. Tomes 3 and 4 (covering the years 1942 to 1952) cover every feature film made in Finland, with comprehensive discussions and descriptions of each, plus full credits and related data. All in Finnish, alas, but there is a useful introduction in English, with translation of the technical terms. and all in all, **Suomen Kansallis Filomografia** (VAPK/Finnish Film Archive, Helsinki) is essential for major libraries and archives.

Finally, a commendation for Humphrey Burton's **Leonard Bernstein** (Faber and Faber, London and Boston). As a biography of the protean musician, the book is already compelling, but film buffs should consult it for primary source material on musicals like *West Side Story* and *On the Town,* not forgetting Bernstein's work as a Hollywood composer for *On the Waterfront,* or the revelation that the handsome young maestro was courted by Hollywood in the war years as a potential star.

Peter Cowie

Introduction

When I launched *International Film Guide* in the winter of 1963, one of my fundamental aims was to celebrate the art-houses where readers could expect to view quality films in excellent conditions.

Times have changed for movie buffs since the 1960's. The art-house concept has all but vanished. Two things have replaced it: an ever-burgeoning network of festivals —and the laser disc.

We believe that watching films on laser represents the closest experience to theatrical viewing that you can achieve in the home. Most companies try harder when it comes to laser. They offer original 'scope or widescreen ratio transfers; they provide original theatrical trailers, voice-over commentaries by the director, technicians, or members of the cast, and additional materials and memorabilia from screenplays to out-takes.

The near-perfect resolution (especially in the PAL format) is not the only advantage. Laser discs can communicate sound at an extraordinarily sophisticated level, creating for the eye as well as the ear an illusion of depth to the image. Dolby Surround and Pro-Logic speaker arrangements bring special effects into the home screening-room. And not just for recent releases. Who can fail to flinch when Regan's devil yells defiance through the rear speakers as Max von Sydow arrives at the house in *The Exorcist?*

Indeed, the past yields almost as much pleasure as the present where laser discs are concerned. Too many mainstream companies pursue a haphazard release policy, failing to recognise the film buff's hunger for sparkling reissues of classic films. And "classic" need not be restricted to foreign-language movies. Lovingly struck versions of *Vertigo, El Cid,* and *Personal Best* remain on collectors' crave lists, and our features by Derek Elley and Sedgwick Clark track the highlights of the 1993-1994 release schedule on PAL and NTSC.

Statistics paint a frustrating picture of the state of laser. The U.S. has a healthy "installed base" of players (1.2 million) but sales of discs have now levelled out. The U.K. boasts a pathetic 18,000 players and with so few machines around it's not surprising that even superb PAL transfers like *Basic Instinct* only sell a thousand or two. But the persistence of Pioneer, Columbia TriStar, and Tartan is by degrees improving the situation, and 1994's

Sleeve for Criterion's superb SPARTACUS disc

Cliffhanger and *In the Line of Fire* are alone worth the price of admission.

To make it easier for U.K. and U.S. readers to locate sources of laser discs, we include a directory of stores and mail order shops, which will be expanded and amended in each edition. Plus a guide to the magazines and newsletters that cover the subject.

Peter Cowie

U.S. and NTSC round-up

by Sedgwick Clark

After a decade of false starts, technical bumbling, and half-hearted transfers, the video industry at last appeared ready in the early 1990's to commit itself to the smaller but quality-conscious laser disc audience. Glossy brochures filled with newly-released information, accompanied by fervent manifestos trumpeting "The Laser Advantage", were distributed in major video stores. The price of laser hardware came down. And then, say some, the worldwide recession simply went on too long. Now, promoters of new technologies are declaring LD to be an obsolete format.

"It's a horrifying, bad rumour that has snowballed out of proportion due to the CDI and CD-ROM technologies on the way," insists George Feltenstein, Senior Vice-President/General Manager of MGM/UA Home Video and one of the format's most passionate and productive champions. "It will be four or five years before five-inch discs can achieve the quality of LD. We will certainly continue releasing discs, and when the new technology comes along we will transfer our efforts there," he adds. Feltenstein has earned his quality credentials by over-seeing the release of practically all the major films in the MGM library and systematically replacing inferior discs from the medium's early years with new transfers from fresh sources. Around 1990, MGM/UA was releasing fifteen LDs a

month, but by mid-1994 the total had fallen to two or three. "It is a fact that recent films sell better than classic films," he continues. "We have suffered a tremendous setback because the retailers have stopped supporting classic product. They will order *Chopper Chicks from Hell*, which does sell well, but not *The Great Waltz*, which has a smaller audience. We have 200 titles I would like to release, but it's not feasible right now. Nobody in the industry really expected LD to compete with tape; I always hoped for 20 to 25% of the market, but that hasn't happened."

Obviously, the mass audience wants a quickie rather than a first-rate home-video experience. But commitment to film as an art form is hardly necessary to recognise the benefits of LD for casual enjoyment. The format's vastly superior image – 60% better resolution over videocassette – is instantly apparent. Laser also provides greater sonic crunch, a necessary element in showing off a fancy home-video system. The split-second equivalent of tape's cumbersome fast forward and rewind, random access, the ability to freeze frame or deconstruct the latest celluloid example of gore and devastation – these all point to LD as the sexy way to view film in the home.

Criterion Becomes State-of-the-Art

Perhaps the medium would have flourished if the major companies had promoted it adequately in the sunny economic climate of 1984, when the Voyager Company inaugurated its new "Criterion Collection" with *Citizen Kane* and *King Kong*. At that time the majors viewed LD as simply another format rather than an opportunity to give the consumer a different, heightened film experience. The same grainy, monochromatic, low-contrast, panned-and-scanned TV prints used for videocassette were the rule in those days, and they looked even more objectionable in the blinding light of laser clarity. The sallow, splattered image of *Lawrence of Arabia's* first LD on RCA/Columbia, for instance, never fails to appal when viewed today against the restored version on

LASER DISC – NOTHING BRINGS YOU CLOSER.

Jurassic Park – the greatest movie for 65 million years – is now available on Laser Disc.

And this is just the beginning.

Forthcoming releases include The Firm, Addams Family Values and the epic Schindler's List to name but a few. Or choose from over 100 great films already available including Dances with Wolves, Cliffhanger, Basic Instinct and Terminator 2.

For more information on Laser Disc and details of retail outlets, please call our Laser Link line on 0753 789 635.

THE
ULTIMATE
CUT

*Pioneer's TERMINATOR 2: JUDGMENT DAY, voted
the all-time top LD   photo: Kobal Collection*

Criterion, RCA/Columbia, and Columbia/
TriStar (each slightly different but using
the same director-approved transfer).
Voyager changed all that: its Criterion
transfers were state-of-the-art, from the
best available elements at that time, and
included such supplementary materials as
production photos, trailers, script excerpts,
short stories, documentaries, outtakes,
audio essays by noted critics, commentaries by the directors – and, most
importantly, letterboxing of widescreen
films. Moreover, each release was accompanied by extensive notes, complete
production credits and cast were duly
listed, and chapter stops were added for
easy access to individual scenes. Voyager's
persistence in concentrating on a small but
elite audience of serious film buffs has
produced the classiest catalogue in the
industry.

One of the format's hottest trends –
opulent reissues transferred from superior
generational sources and studded with
extras – is only one example of how
Voyager transformed LD. MGM/UA's
latest release (its third, and the Criterion
makes four) of *The Wizard of Oz*, this time
dubbed **The Ultimate Oz**, offers seven
hours of supplementary audio material,
including actual recording sessions of the
songs (retakes and all), a "Making of ... "
documentary, test footage, deleted scenes,
publicity materials, and the shooting
script, which enables one to chart all the
scenes deleted over the years. Returning to
the original nitrate negatives this time,

MGM/UA's new THX transfer has
provided colour so rich, so beautiful, so
true that tears come to the eyes of this
veteran *Oz* watcher; only the unfocussed
"sepia" black-and-white sequences are
disappointing.

Fox Video's monolithic nine-disc, 13-
pound-heavy, $250 list, CAV, THX package
entitled **The Star Wars Trilogy The
Definitive Edition** provides enough extras
to keep a working videophile busy until
the Shoemaker-Levy 9 comet arrives. Hard
on the heels of the *Trilogy* and also in its
fourth incarnation, is Pioneer Special
Edition's **T2 Special Edition**, offering 15
minutes of "restored" footage from an
earlier cut – another hot, and controversial,
trend – and an extensive step-by-step
explanation of the special effects. Fox's
"Limited Commemorative Edition" of **The
African Queen** includes not only a fine
new transfer but also Katharine Hepburn's
memoir of the filming. Fox also scheduled
new THX transfers of Rodgers and
Hammerstein's *Oklahoma, South Pacific* and
The Sound of Music (and one hopes that
many more of the company's discs will be
refurbished from better elements, as well).

Gems Transferred

The old RCA/Columbia catalogue was
infamous for its orange complexions and
washed-out colour – a label to avoid like
the plague. While many discs remain in the
bins at a reduced price to trap the unwary,
help has arrived. Sony purchased
Columbia Pictures, changed the name of its
home video arm to Columbia TriStar, and
in the spring of 1994 began releasing brand
new transfers of its considerable, hitherto
misrepresented gems. David Lean's **The
Bridge on the River Kwai** (letterboxed at
last) and Fred Zinnemann's **From Here to
Eternity** are huge improvements, with Elia
Kazan's **On the Waterfront** and Robert
Rossen's **All the King's Men** less impressive only because their first disc releases
were not as dreadful. Source material for
Frank Capra's **It Happened One Night**
and **You Can't Take It With You** is in sad
shape, but the new transfer of the former is
far superior to the slapdash initial disc, and

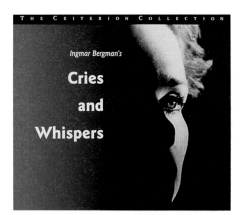

Criterion have released several Bergmans on LD

the latter (in its first disc incarnation) is mostly clear, with fine contrast. The discs are now chapter stopped and lack only Criterion-like cast and production credits. Among innumerable remastered disc editions to anticipate if this commitment to quality is sustained are **The Jolson Story** and **Jolson Sings Again**, whose gorgeous Technicolor was grossly falsified by the old discs.

Universal apparently took greater care in preserving its films, and MCA/Universal Home Video's LD releases have been of notably high quality as far back as the mid-1980's. (Exceptions are many of the Hitchcock colour films, which are badly in need of careful restoration.) The detail, clarity, and contrast in the studio's classic 1930's and 1940's black-and-white horror flicks (Bela Lugosi's **Dracula**, in particular) have been eye-openers to those acquainted only with television prints.

Another Criterion favourite : Powell and Pressburger

Genre fans were treated to a bonanza in 1993-94 with several duo and box sets. "The Mummy Collection", contained the four quasi-sequels to Boris Karloff's 1933 *The Mummy* (**The Mummy's Hand, Tomb, Ghost,** and **Curse**). A two-disc set of **House of Frankenstein** and **House of Dracula** almost completed another series; still to come is **The Ghost of Frankenstein**, which could have been handily boxed with the two *Houses* and the already endisced *Frankenstein Meets the Wolfman*. In the genre's waning days, Universal subjected its noble monsters to Abbott and Costello, and the four films (**A&C Meet Frankenstein, Dr. Jekyll and Mr. Hyde, The Mummy**, and **The Invisible Man**) are gathered in a second box set, featuring a new transfer of the first and best of this series, **Frankenstein**. The 1950's brought an entirely new brand of horror, dominated by interplanetary aliens and giant insects. Yet another three-disc box set, "The Golden Age of Science Fiction Thrillers!" gathers together **It Came from Outer Space, Tarantula, The Mole People**, and **The Deadly Mantis**. Finally, another two-disc set completes the Creature series with **Revenge of the Creature** and **The Creature Walks Among Us**. Transfers are uniformly excellent; source elements nearly always impeccable. And at last MCA is chaptering its LDs.

High quality notwithstanding, some LD buyers wonder if the companies are deliberately releasing inferior transfers to pave the way for new and improved versions. "Director's Cut", "Restored Version", "New Remastered Edition", "THX", "Surround Stereo Remix", are increasingly familiar come-ons for the latest retreads. The improvements of classic favourites are obvious and welcome, but the pocketbook is leery. The 1956 sci-fi classic **Forbidden Planet** received its fourth LD treatment midyear from MGM/UA, this time in CAV widescreen and 1983 panned and scanned efforts, as well as Criterion's 1989 widescreen version (a "must" for its extras). My enthusiasm for this film now retails to the tune of over $230, but I'm sure there's still room for "The Ultimate Id". It should be interesting to see how many new and improved incarnations of *Jurassic Park* turn up over the next few years, in the wake of this autumn's CAV and CLV mega-release.

Letterboxing Offers Hope

Is laser disc a dying format? Hollywood didn't get where it is today by favouring enlightened taste. Moreover, the American public at large is so accustomed to faded TV prints and bad reception that even a smeary tape image is evidently acceptable. But Disney and Paramount have begun letterboxing recently, and one hopes that the refurbished LDs of George Pal's **The War of the Worlds** and **When Worlds Collide** indicate that Paramount will follow Disney in a full-scale programme of remastering (**Shane, To Catch a Thief, One-Eyed Jacks,** please?) Also, Warner Home Video has lifted its moratorium on older films with its letterboxed **All the President's Men** and a handful of John Wayne oaters.

The industry finally appears to have targetted the laser disc audience: male, in his forties or fifties, with grown children. He prefers action, horror and sci-fi, musicals and epics, but not the classic Bette Davis tear-jerkers and their ilk. He insists upon quality and is willing to pay for it, especially the big deluxe re-releases with loads of extras. With LD hardware continuing to come down in price, perhaps now is the time for an aggressive marketing campaign to show the American home videophile just what he's missing.

SOMETHING MISSING?

Write to us if you require a back issue of *International Film Guide*. Many years are still available (from 1968 onwards), and each copy costs £12.00 including post and packing.

Variety, 34-35 Newman
Street, London W1P 3PD

The Criterion Collection

A survey by Peter Cowie

For the film buff or institution (film schools in particular) taking the plunge into the wondrous realms of laser disc, the Criterion Collection offers the best means of establishing a cinémathèque in the living-room.

A majority of the Criterion releases comprise not only the actual film, transferred and/or restored with meticulous attention to detail, grading, and subtitling, but also a wealth of additional material – a director or critic commenting throughout the film on the analogue soundtrack, a documentary on the making of the picture, talking-head interviews with cast and crew, production stills, original trailers, even storyboards and bibliographies.

From Europe, some of the more impressive entries in the Criterion Collection are as follows:

Ashes and Diamonds (Wajda, 1958);

Soft Skin (*La Peau douce*, Truffaut, 1964);

Andrei Rublev (Tarkovsky, 1966 – uncut version);

L'Avventura (Antonioni, 1960 – two versions, CLV, and CAV, with an extremely lucid, articulate commentary by Gene Youngblood);

Children of Paradise (*Les enfants du paradis*, Carné, 1945 – with an interview with Carné you can hear in either French or English);

Cries and Whispers (*Viskningar och rop*, Bergman, 1973), released with subtitles or, on analogue, a pretty commendable American dubbed track;

Other Bergman titles available at Criterion: *The Silence, Winter Light, Through a Glass Darkly, Smiles of a Summer Night, The Seventh Seal* (with commentary by yours truly), and *Wild Strawberries*;

Antonioni's L'AVVENTURA, restored to its full glory on laser by Voyager/Criterion   *photo: The Kobal Collection*

Damage (Malle, 1991 – with one of the finest of all director commentaries);

Repulsion (Polanski, 1965 – with both Polanski and Catherine Deneuve talking about the film);

The Lacemaker (Goretta, 1977 – no extra features but all credit for giving the laser treatment to a rare masterpiece);

Lola Montès (Ophüls, 1955 – again, no extra features but the best "print" you are ever likely to see of this majestic folly);

Several carefully-restored Michael Powell films: *The Red Shoes, Peeping Tom, The Tales of Hoffmann, I Know Where I'm Going, 49th Parallel, Black Narcissus,* and *The Life and Death of Colonel Blimp.*

   From Japan, the selection is even more mouth-watering:

Ugetsu (Mizoguchi, 1953 – excellent print, with intriguing interview with cinematographer Kazuo Miyagawa, plus production stills showing how some of the most difficult sequences were shot);

Seven Samurai (Kurosawa, 1954 – a superlative transfer of the original, 203-minute version that looks as sparkling as the day it left the labs forty years ago);

Other Kurosawa titles available at Criterion are *Sanjuro, The Hidden Fortress, Ikiru, Rashomon, Red Beard, Yojimbo,* and *Throne of Blood;*

Kwaidan (Kobayashi, 1964, including the fourth story, and in original 'scope ratio);

Osaka Elegy (Mizogushi, 1936);

Tokyo Olympiad (Ichikawa, 1965 – again, the full, original 'scope print: 170 mins.);

Floating Weeds (Ozu, 1959);

The Makioka Sisters (Ichikawa, 1983);

The Burmese Harp (Ichikawa, 1956).

   Yet Criterion by no means restricts its activities to plundering the vaults at Janus

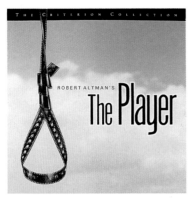

Altman has fared well, with THE PLAYER given the Criterion treatment in the States ...

... and also released in sparkling PAL by Pioneer in Europe

Films, source of most of the quality foreign material. Indeed many LD buffs would agree that the company has outclassed some of the major studios with its restorations and transfers of major titles, not to mention its supplementary tidbits.

Prime examples of this expertise and devotion are: *The Magnificent Ambersons* (Welles, 1942), with commentary by Robert Carringer, plus extracts from the storyboard, the entire shooting script, silent film and radio treatments of the Ambersons story, etc.);

The Silence of the Lambs (Demme, 1991 – the most widely trumpeted of all Criterion discs, justifiably so in view of the articulate comments by Demme, Jodie Foster, Anthony Hopkins, and screenwriter Ted Tally, not forgetting THX mastering, and a host of goodies such as storyboards, deleted scenes, and a complete filmography of the genre);

Bram Stoker's Dracula (Coppola, 1991). The Columbia TriStar PAL disc is state-of-the-art, but with Criterion you get Coppola and son Roman chatting away on analogue;

Lawrence of Arabia (Lean, 1962). Extras include behind-the-scenes production footage, and a featurette on the making of the film;

Raging Bull (Scorsese, 1980 – plus commentary by the director, and editor Thelma Schoonmaker);

Robinson Crusoe on Mars (Haskin, 1964 – a really fine effort, with commentaries by star Paul Mantee and screenwriter Ib Melchior, and a clutch of extras such as blueprints and artist sketches, front-of-house colour stills, etc.).

Peter Cowie

U.K. and PAL round-up

After hobbling along for years as the laser disc market's eternal stillborn, Europe's PAL industry finally showed signs of commitment and real growth during 1993. Collectors forced for years to buy overpriced NTSC imports (most of which produce compromised results on non-multi-standard monitors) finally found a sizable number of LD releases tailormade to their native technology.

Any Euro collector outside France will remember the first thrill of viewing a top-class PAL-sourced LD on PAL equipment. Was it Pioneer's *Terminator 2*, state-of-the-art back in 1992? Or the same company's four-hour *Dances with Wolves* in 1993? Or Columbia/TriStar's *Last Action Hero* in 1994? Though the format has its drawbacks (slightly speeded-up running time; generally harder, colder colours), at its best the PAL LD experience can beat NTSC any time in needle-sharp clarity, depth of imagery and all-round viewing experience.

But there are still major doubts as to whether it will ever develop the critical mass to take off as a self-sustaining market, providing collectors with a real alternative to costly NTSC imports.

Compared with four million players in Japan, two million in the rest of Asia (which also has a healthy LD rental market), and one million in the U.S., Europe has some 400,000 players (up from 50,000 back in 1989). Some 250,000 of those are in France (ironically, the one major market that is SECAM rather than PAL, though the difference is purely one of colour system, not number of scanlines); the U.K. is still almost virgin territory, with a paltry 20,000.

According to figures from the Dutch-based European Laser Disc Association, set up in 1990 to promote the medium, PAL disc sales hit 2.3 million in 1993. Some 110,000 players were sold that year and by the end of 1994 Europe's installed base should total half a million.

Pioneer Leading the Way

Without the efforts of a single company, Pioneer, on both the software and hardware sides of the market, laser might never have reached European shores as an affordable, non-professional item. The company adopts a European outlook to the LD market, rather than a purely U.K. one, and now encodes multilingual teletext subtitles on some of its discs to benefit from economies of scale. Its movie catalogue now has some 70 titles.

But prices for PAL discs are still high in Europe, on a strict exchange-rate comparison with dollar prices for U.S. equivalents. In the U.K., a two-disc set (and some single-disc arthouse titles) retails at around £35 ($52); single-disc movies can vary in price from £24-28 ($36-42) for new, vanilla-packaged U.S. movies to £35 ($52) for arthouse issues. In mainland Europe they are even more expensive.

Pioneer's European marketing chief Guy Warren says that, with the present size of the PAL market, £24 is the lowest profit-

This scene from BASIC INSTINCT has a crystalline sharpness in LD, especially in PAL from Pioneer

making price possible for a single-disc release. For a double-disc release, including some CAV, £39 is realistic, though this can come down to £35 if "blockbustered" (like *Terminator 2*). At £20 retail, a company is basically only breaking even, he says.

To its credit, and as a further market stimulus, in early '94 Pioneer unloaded some older, pan-and-scanned titles like *Johnny Handsome, Field of Dreams* and *Last Exit to Brooklyn* at a bargain of £13.99.

As the biggest issuer in the PAL market, Pioneer (now under increasing pressure from its Japanese owners, hit by local recession, to maximise profits) has been trying to be all things to all people – appeasing the buff/collectors market, trying to extend the reach of laser (amid a rolling Euro-consumer recession) with popular new titles, and attempting to keep up a regular flow of releases to instil confidence in the market. Not surprisingly, it has often been caught between a rock and a hard place.

There is still no proof, and even less likelihood, that laser will ever become more than a niche market in Europe, especially in countries like the U.K. which has a mature, decade-old videotape market and a take-it-or-leave-it attitude toward cinema in general. By issuing titles like *Housesitter, City Slickers, Honeymoon in Vegas* and *Wayne's World*, Pioneer simply alienated its core LD market (by appearing to waste issues on titles in which buffs have little interest), without attracting mass consumers. The latter, despite attempts at education through ads, still perceive laser as a format that requires vast expense on hardware and masses of technical know-how.

With run-of-the-mill PAL videos now hitting new hights in technical shoddiness (blurred images, appalling lack of colour range), Pioneer's popular titles could have made a small score; but many have been less than ideal (an over-dark *Patriot Games*, a pan-and-scanned *The Lover*, a grubby-looking *Death Becomes Her*) and often dull-hued compared with their NTSC counterparts. With the F/X-heavy *Death Becomes Her*, which could have crossed over to buffs with a CAV version, Pioneer put out the entire disc in CLV.

At their best, however, the company's releases offer the ultimate in home entertainment, especially when played on a system hooked up to a Dolby Pro-Logic Surround set-up. Titles like *Basic Instinct* go from strength to strength on repeated home viewing, while theatrically borderline movies like *Last Action Hero* and *Sliver* seem far more satisfying, with the former's effects track not so overwhelming and the latter featuring a wonderfully subtle surround dub (far better than on its VHS video).

However, errors of judgment in title selection and the like still reinforce the impression that much of the PAL LD industry is being run by people who do not quite understand its audience. It still has no equivalent to MGM/UA's George Feltenstein or the guys at Criterion.

Pioneer's classic label, Pioneer Cinema, has so far been well-meaning but flawed. The Selznick classic, *Portrait of Jennie*, was handsomely packaged, with a colour poster and two lobby cards, but the transfer was over-contrasty (and not in a true black-and-white), no extra material (not even the original trailer) was included, and nowhere on the sleeve was it mentioned that the LD included the final sequence in Technicolor (of prime buying interest to buffs).

Pioneer's Warren says quality, not price, is the key to the PAL LD market. At a not-too-high, but by no means come-on price of £30 ($45), *Jennie* represents poor value. At £50 ($75), the two-disc *Ossessione* is right off the scale. Future titles in the series, that already includes *Confidential Report/Mr. Arkadin, Duel in the Sun, La Ronde, Knife in the Water* and *Spellbound* (with tinted final gun flash), include Siodmak's *The Spiral Staircase* and Peckinpah's *Junior Bonner* (widescreen).

Specialist Labels Emerge

Among specialist issuers, Metro Tartan has been most warmly welcomed by collectors. Following an earlier heap of medium-vintage issues, attractively priced (starting at £20 ($30), well-letterboxed, in fine transfers and with good sleeve-notes – *McCabe & Mrs Miller*, *The Arrangement*, *Inside Daisy Clover*, *Finian's Rainbow* (with the third side of CAV), and *The Double Life of Veronique* – the company has continued with newer items like *Jamon, Jamon* (though a tad over-saturated), *Matador*, and *Law of Desire*. Its only black mark so far has been *Cinema Paradiso*, released in its short international version.

Encore Entertainment, which bowed in in February 1994 with *Howards End* and licenses titles from Electric Pictures' arthouse catalogue (*Delicatessen*, *Orlando*, *Leon the Pig Farmer*), has come in at the higher single-disc price of £35 ($52), with no extras and, in the case of *Henry ... Portrait of a Serial Killer*, a version still trimmed by the British Board of Film Classification (BBFC), the U.K.'s censor, though not by as much as the VHS tape. Encore founder Stephen Haines says it plans to release around 15 titles by the end of the year and has just signed a deal with Columbia/Tri-Star to license selected titles (*The Young Americans*, *Red Rock West*, *Posse*).

The growing nanny-state hand of the U.K. censor, which insists on "classifying" even NTSC imports, has driven a whole number of them underground, including *Reservoir Dogs*, *The Exorcist*, and *Apocalypse Now*. Tower Records, one of London's few big stockings of LDs, was heavily fined in 1993 for stocking some NTSC imports without BBFC-approved stickers.

Bureaucratic petty-mindedness of this kind, in a fragile still growing market, is the last thing laser needs in the U.K. But the street runs both ways. After sensibly leading the way for years in dual-standard machines – without which laser would never have caught on in Europe – in summer 1994 Pioneer was joining other companies like Encore in considering

Columbia TriStar released A FEW GOOD MEN on laser in the U.K. before cassettes reached the stores

action in the U.K. against NTSC importers of titles already licensed for PAL.

This particular grumble by the PAL LD industry has been going on for some time. For example, when Pioneer eventually issued its technically splendid, reasonably-priced *Basic Instinct* (uncut, with a few extras), it found sales hit by impatient collectors having already shelled out for the high-priced NTSC edition.

The real villain is industry holdback agreements affecting windows between theatrical and sell-through, plus ridiculous thinking that brackets laser with video and sees it as a threat to theatrical (thus barring any LD advertising while a film is still in initial release).

A recent U.S. study that found laser actually encouraged viewers to re-experience a title theatrically seems to have had little effect on the Luddite mentality of the U.K.'s distribution and exhibition sectors.

Though Pioneer has dipped its toe into sketchy special editions (*Dirty Dancing*, *Basic Instinct*), the truth is that the PAL feature film catalogue is still dismally small and selective, with none of the in-depth NTSC special editions (of both old and new showpieces) that LD collectors crave.

Columbia/TriStar, which doesn't have Pioneer's problem of having to acquire licences to titles and remain at the mercy of the licensor's video-release plans, has led the ways in getting PAL discs out fast. It has so far published *Dracula*, *A Few Good*

Men, Groundhog Day, The Age of Innocence and *My Girl 2* prior to their U.K. video release and in 1994 issued *Last Action Hero* (in an excellent, partly CAV version) and *Philadelphia* even prior to the NTSC LD. Quality is generally high, though some look as if they stem from NTSC, rather than original PAL, transfers to telecine.

However, Columbia/TriStar's enterprising attitude only extends to big, commercial titles; beyond those, the company has taken a cautious, often hot-cold attitude to the PAL market. At one point during the past year, the company was cancelling more than it was putting out (including *Hero* and *Nowhere to Run*, reckoning the market had already been used up by NTSC); for less popular titles it now has agreements with smaller issuers like Encore and LaserDisc Distribution, the latter of which can afford to do a smaller number of pressings (c. 500) because it has its own plant.

Pioneer's big chance to get major publicity for laser will come in November '94, when it is set to release both CLV and CAV versions of *Jurassic Park* on the same day as the U.K. sell-through video. If it can persuade collectors to hold off pre-ordering the NTSC version, the company expects European sales to top 100,000 (a new record).

The move is a direct result of its new deal with CIC Video for Paramount and Universal product. Pioneer says it plans to release 25 new and back titles from the CIC catalogue, though some may be delayed in mainland Europe because of Philips' previous licensing deal with CIC. Pioneer also has a licensing deal with U.K. distributor First Independent.

Real growth in the PAL market, however, will depend on companies like Pioneer following Columbia's lead in closely matching NTSC release dates and also making LDs available prior to rental/sell-through on video. The latter would hardly affect the cassette market but provide a big boost for LD. A further major boost would be Warner and Disney climbing off the fence and entering the PAL LD market.

Even allowing for present rates of development and the non-emergence of some other format in an already consumer-baffling market, most people in the industry see VideoCD displacing LDs in the West only ten years down the line. By then, even PAL laserdisc collectors may be serviced by an industry that really understands their needs and hunger, and produces software worthy of the format's technical supremacy.

Derek Elley

IFG's NTSC LD CHOICE, 1993-94

The Ultimate Oz (MGM/UA)
Comments in a time-tested classic, looking and sounding better than ever, lovingly outfitted with matchless extras.

The Art of Conducting: Great Conductors of the Past (Teldec)
Fascinating historical footage and commentary, judiciously adapted from the award-winning BBC documentary to allow even more extended musical excerpts than before.

Ben-Hur (MGM/UA)
Another fine package, with Miklós Rózsa's glorious score superbly reproduced in stereo and isolated on a separate track.

The Bridge on the River Kwai (Columbia TriStar)
Letterboxed and with accurate colour at last.

Forbidden Planet (MGM/UA)
The fourth try's the charm, colourwise, with a more menacing Monster from the Id and shimmering "electronic tonalities" than ever.

Richard III (Voyager)
Worth waiting for and carefully transferred, as all of this company's work is.

The Gold Rush (FoxVideo)
Not the original cut, but the finale to an important series, transferred from Chaplin's own, mostly pristine copies.

The War of the Worlds (Paramount)
Not a great film, but a beautiful transfer and a hopeful sign that a laggardly company is finally taking the preservation of its films seriously.

Two English Girls (Voyager)
Truffaut's underrated 1971 film was heavily

cut by its U.S. distributor but is now properly restored.

The Connery Collection (MGM/UA)
The first three Connery Bond films, with *From Russia With Love* and *Goldfinger* transferred from an earlier generation than all previous releases, including the Criterions; colour could be stronger, but the image is cleaner and details are sharper.

BEST NTSC LASERDISCS

The Laser Disc Newsletter, the indispensable review of laserdiscs in the U.S., publishes an Annual Consumer Poll in which readers select their preferences in several categories. Herewith "The Ten Best Discs of All Time," as recorded in the February 1994 issue:

Terminator 2: Judgment Day (Live Home Video)
The Abyss Revised Version (MGM/UA)
The Star Wars Trilogy (FoxVideo)
The Ultimate Oz (MGM/UA)
Apocalypse Now (Paramount)
Alien (FoxVideo)
Spartacus (Voyager)
Aliens (FoxVideo)
Fantasia (Disney)
Bram Stoker's Dracula (Voyager)

The *Newsletter's* indefatigable editor and publisher, Douglas Pratt, notes that the first four "dominated consumer preferences in almost every category" and that they "mak[e] the year a watershed for boxed laser disc collector's packages in the American laser disc market" – S.C.

IFG's PAL LASERDISC CHOICE: 1993-94

Basic Instinct (Pioneer)
Last Action Hero (Columbia/TriStar)
Sliver (Pioneer)
In the Line of Fire (Columbia/TriStar)
Cliffhanger (Pioneer)
Universal Soldier (Pioneer)
Scent of a Woman (Pioneer)
Jamon, Jamon (Metro Tartan)
Dirty Dancing (Pioneer)
Orlando (Encore)

Above selection is based on technical quality, presentation and programme content, not on the films' relative artistic worth.

Guide to Sources

If you have been a LaserDisc collector for some time, you will appreciate that being a member of an enthusiasts' community (in the U.K. at least) can sometimes be frustrating. Comments such as "supply and demand" and "Laser what?" can only be met with little more than polite contempt. The continual struggle with local record stores, hi-fi dealers and other prospective outlets, however, seem to be coming part of the neanderthal past.

During the compilation of this list I was pleasantly surprised to see what amounts to a phenomenal growth in recent years. From just a few specialists in the late 1980s, you can now order LD's over the counter at any "Our Price" outlet. Nationwide chains such as HMV, Virgin, and Tower Records, now sell both British (PAL) and American (NTSC) discs, and can also order almost anything you require. Many of the once Hi-Fi only specialists are now home cinema centres, and supply not only the equipment, but also offer a wide selection of discs. Many conversations with dealers have also shown increased awareness and knowledge of the format and what it has to offer. Almost all outlets listed will happily order any title not in stock and usually supply within a few days. With publications such as the *Laser Video File*, we now have a vast catalogue from which to choose.

Sedgwick Clark taps the latest version of THE WIZARD OF OZ *as the best release of the past year in the States*
photo: Kobal Collection

I hope this list will be helpful to existing LD owners and invaluable to those who may be about to join the ever increasing market. Unless otherwise stated, all shops sell PAL (European) and NTSC (U.S.A. and Japan) discs, although all Japanese discs are sourced through the United States.

Richard Sayce

Laserdisc Outlets – U.K.

H=Shops selling laserdisc players

M=Shops offering Mail Order

S=Shops offering Special Order

Technosound
7 Granville Square, Willen. Local Centre, Milton Keynes, Bucks. MK15 9JL. Tel: (0908) 604949

H M S produces own informative newsletter

The Hi-Fi Company
42 Cowgate, Peterborough, Cambs. PE1 1NA. Tel: (0733) 341755

H M S large stockist of box sets

Video Box Office
19-23 Manasty Road, Orton Southgate, Peterborough, Cambs. PE2 0UP. Tel: (0733) 233464

M S

Aston Audio Limited
4 West Street, Alderley Edge, Cheshire SK9 7EG. Tel: (0625) 582704

H M S Classical disc and karaoke specialist

Peter Foulkes
122 High Street, Colchester, Essex CO1 1SZ. Tel: (0206) 767428

H M S

Classic Sound & Vision
Unit 19, The Royals, Southend-on-Sea, Essex SS1 1DQ. Tel: (0702) 461634

H M S Good selection of Japanese titles

20/20 Audio Visual
Unit 205, Lakeside Centre, West Thurrock, Essex RM16 1ZQ. Tel: (0708) 891818

H M S A/V specialist with three demonstration rooms. Over 5,000 discs in stock. From U.K., U.S.A. and Japan

Now That's Hi-Fi
24 Arundel Way, Portsmouth, Hants. PO1 1NY. Tel: (0705) 811230

H M S

Gladden LaserDisc Entertainment
166 Pixmore Way, Letchworth, Herts. Tel: (0462) 483847

M S

W. Darby
6 Market Place, St. Albans, Herts. AL3 5DG. Tel: (0727) 851596

H M S European LaserDisc specialist

Hi-Fi City
15 Charter Place, Watford, Herts. WD1 2RS. Tel: (0923) 226129

H M S

Esprit LaserDisc
Esprit House, Railway Sidings, Meopham, Kent DA13 0LT. Tel: (0474) 567900

M S

Ainleys Music & Video
10-12 Haymarket, Leicester, Leics. LE1 3GD. Tel: (0533) 620618

H M S

The Cinema Store
46 Monmouth Street, London. Tel: (071) 379 7839

M S Good current NTSC titles at reasonable prices

Laser Club International
14 Bute Street, London SW7 3EX. Tel: (071) 581 9882

M S

HQ Electronics
Yaohan Plaza, 399 Edgware Road, London NW9. Tel: (081) 200 0009

H M S Probably the largest karaoke and Japanese LD selection in the country, plus they rent!!

Active Laser Distribution
133 Tottenham Lane, Crouch End, London N8 9BJ. Tel: (081) 340 7775

M S Free Mail Order club with big discounts for members

Hi-Spek Electronics
344 Regents Park Road, Finchley, London N3 2LJ. Tel: (081) 349 1166

H M S Japanese and European stockists

The Laser Empire
185 Dawes Road, Fulham, London SW6 7QP. Tel: (071) 386 9666

M S

Covent Garden Records
84 Charing Cross Road, London WC2H 0JA. Tel: (071) 379 7635

M S One of the original stores, they still offer one of the best selections of all types of disc and the latest releases at competitive prices

SRS Laser World
56-58 Regent Street, London W1R 5PJ. Tel: (071) 287 2458

H M S Pioneer retail outlet carrying every available PAL title

The Laser Disc Shop
15 Needham Road, London W11 2RP. Tel: (071) 243 3142

M S Unusual music titles plus large stocks of all types of disc

Bruce Campbell
8 Dewhurst Road, London W14 0ET. Tel: (071) 603 4833.

M S Mail Order only service. Competitive prices.

Inner City Laser
PO Box 3599, London N22 4ST. Tel: (081) 889 3177

M S Efficient Mail Order only service. Extremely good prices on all discs

Digital Home Theatre
71 Seaview Road, Liscard, Wallasey, Merseyside L45 4QW. Tel: (051) 630 7198

H M S One of the few who rent discs. Also has a Laser club and produces own newsletter

Thames Valley Laser
9 Crown Walk Shopping Centre, Bicester, Oxon. OX6 7HY. Tel: (0869) 320550

H M S

Moving Pictures
PO Box 67, Lichfield, Staffs. WS14 9HR. Tel: (0543) 432397

M S Mail Order discounts

The Laser Library
PO Box 145, Ipswich, Suffolk IP8 4LQ. Tel: (0473) 658155

M S Probably the first Mail Order club. Offers discs on approval; second-hand available

Croydon Laser Vision
35 Lower Addiscombe Road, Croydon, Surrey CR0 6PQ. Tel: (081) 688 5551

M S Karaoke and second-hand in stock

Sovereign Disc Club
40 High Street, Weybridge, Surrey KT13 8AB. Tel: (0932) 820287

M S For annual fee members receive a whole host of goodies and discounts on all discs

Zebra
18 Brighton Road, South Croydon, Surrey CR2 6AA. Tel: (081) 688 2491

H M S

The LaserDisc Centre
318 Seaside, Eastbourne, East Sussex BN22 7RH. Tel: (0323) 640911

H M S Over 3,000 titles in stock

Reddingtons Rare Records
17 Cannon Street, Birmingham, W. Midlands B2 5EN. Tel: (021) 643 2017

M S Second-hand and part exchange

Sounds Expensive
12 Regent Street, Rugby, Warks. Tel: (0788) 540772

H S Laserdisc and Home Cinema including state of the art THX Surround Sound

Club 50/50
PO Box 1277, Chippenham, Wilts SN15 3YZ. Tel: (0249) 445400

M S Free post and packing plus an updated monthly list

Yorcom
9 Davy Gate Centre, Davy Gate, York, N. Yorks. YO1 2SU. Tel: (0904) 641862

H M S

The Movie Boulevard
5 Cherry Tree Walk, Leeds, W. Yorks. LS2 7EB. Tel: (0532) 422888

H M S Produces own monthly magazine of over 1,000 titles

Music 'n Movies
30-32 Church Crescent, Dumfries DG1 1JD. Tel: (0387) 57751

M S

The Video Disc Club
11 North Street, Ratho, Newbridge, Edinburgh, Lothian EH28 8RD. Tel: (031) 333 1075

M S Large supplier and supporter of PAL discs

System Design
Princes Square, 48 Buchanan Street, Glasgow, Strathclyde
G1 3JN. Tel: (041) 248 4801

H M S

C. Wilcock Video Libraries
1-3 Mold Street, Buckley, Clywd CH7 2AE. Tel: (0244)
550331

S

Quinns
Castell Close, Phoenix Way, Enterprise Park, Swansea,
Glams. SA7 9EH. Tel: (0792) 773644

H S

Hi-Fi Western Limited
52 Cambrian Road, Newport, Gwent NP9 4AB. Tel: (0633)
262790

H S

L.R.G. Sound & Vision
171-175 Albertridge Road, Belfast, Co. Down BT5 4PS.
Tel: (0232) 451381

H S

Video Centre
Hillgrove Street, St. Helier, Jersey, Channel Islands

S

The following multiple chain stores all sell laserdiscs and a quick
phone call will tell you which branch is closest to you.

HMV Head Office
Tel: (071) 439 2112

M S

Virgin Megastore
Head Office Tel: (071) 221 5155

M S

Tower Records
Head Office Tel: (071) 938 3625

M S

Radford Hi-Fi
Tel: (0225) 446245

H M S

*HARD TARGET, one of the many action thrillers released
by Pioneer on LD in PAL*

Paul Roberts Hi-Fi
Tel: (0272) 250760

H M S

Music & Video Club
Tel: (0628) 477701

S Discounts for club members

Fenway Television
Tel: (0638) 663166

H M S

Hamlets
Tel: (061) 428 6367

H M S

Sevenoaks Hi-Fi
Head Office Tel: (0732) 459555

H M S

Primetime
Head Office Tel: (071) 631 1932

Rental service

Bill Hutchinson Limited
Tel: (061) 839 8800

H M S

U.S. Outlets

Laser Blazer
2518 Overland Ave., Los Angeles, California 90064.
Tel: (310) 558 8356. Fax: (310) 558 3255

M S

Ken Crane's
15251 Beach Boulevard, Westminster, California 92683.
Tel: (714) 892 2283. Fax: (714) 892 8369

Huge stocks and mouth-watering sales

Laser Craze
329 Newbury Street, Boston, Massachusetts 02115.
Tel: (617) 267 3311. Fax: (617) 267 2271

Laserland
200 Glen Cove Road, Carle Place, NY 11514.

Tel: (516) 746 3147

Discs available for both purchase and rental

Sight and Sound

27 Jones Road, Waltham, Massachusetts 02154. Tel: (617) 894 8633

Specialists in imported animation and French films

Laser Video West

11701 Wilshire Boulevard, Los Angeles, California 90025. Tel: (310) 479 4069. Fax: (310) 479 4870

Discount prices. Domestic and foreign orders welcomed

Transpacific Laser

11730 NE Fargo Street, Portland, Oregon 97220. Tel: (503) 684 3250. Fax: (503) 256 8498

Imported discs from Japan

Ceba Video

PO Box 44411, Fort Washington, Maryland 20749. Tel: (301) 292 6670

Specialising in second-hand discs

Disc and Dat

420 Forest Avenue, Staten Island, NY 10301. Tel: (800) 231 6941

Over 1,000 second-hand discs

Dallas Digital Discs (Videoquest)

5934 Royal Lane, Suite 128, Dallas, Texas 75230. Tel: (214) 987 4744. Fax: (214) 987 3544

Laserdisc Enterprises

2516 Cobb Parkway, Smyrna, Georgia 30080. Tel: (404) 955 8909

Same day shipping. Discounts on some titles

Starship Industries

605 Utterbank Store Road, Great Falls, Virginia 22066. Tel: (703) 450 5780. Fax: (703) 430 6657.

M "No time limit" disc warranty with all purchases

Publications Covering LaserDisc

EMPIRE

42 Great Portland Street, London W1N 5AH. Films, Films, Films.

HI-FI NEWS & RECORD REVIEW

Link House, Dingwall Avenue, Croydon, Surrey CR9 2TA. Predominantly Hardware with new product information and technology insights, monthly.

HOME ENTERTAINMENT

19 Bolsover Street, London W1P 7HJ. A must for laserdisc enthusiasts; monthly disc reviews, hardware updates, amusing and informative. Excellent.

LASERDISC REVIEW

PO Box 526, London SW10 9AB. Bi-monthly, edited and published by Hil Parr. Disc and equipment reviews. A hive of information.

PREMIERE

16-19 Great Titchfield Street, London W1. Dealing with the latest in the film industry.

SATELLITE & VIDEO TODAY

19F St Charles Square, North Kensington, London W10 63F. Monthly technology bible.

SATELLITE TIMES

23 Mitcham Lane, London SW16 6LQ. Extra-terrestrial home entertainment.

VIDEO HOME ENTERTAINMENT

Strandgate, 18-20 York Buildings, London WC2. A look at home movie variations.

VIEW

10A City View, 463 Bethnal Green Road, London E2.

WHAT HI-FI?

38-42 Hampton Road, Teddington, Middx TW11 0JE. The biggest hi-fi magazine now branching out into home cinema with regular and informative hardware and software reports. Monthly.

WHAT VIDEO

57-59 Rochester Place, London NW1 9JE.

E.L.D.A.

Waalresweg 17, 5554 Ha Valkenswaard, The Netherlands.

LASERVIEW

3A Oak Road, Fairfield, NJ 07004 U.S.A. Would seem to have a review on every disc released each month.

LASERDISC NEWSLETTER

P.O. Box 420, East Rockaway, NY 11518-0420. Tel: (516) 594 9304. The single most detailed and passionate of all LD publications. Well worth a subscription at $50 for twelve issues by airmail.

LASER CLASSICS

12122 Aero Drive, Garden Grove, California 92641. Tel: (714) 530 3543. Review publication $24 for 12 issues domestic; $45 foreign.

LASERDISC GAZETTE

Road 2, Box 654-LDN, Harpers Ferry, West Virginia 25425. Monthly journal $20 for 12 issues domestic; $35 foreign.

THE CINEMA LASER

P.O. Box 198, Commack, NY 11725-0198. $10 for 4 issues; $20 foreign.

Irène Jacob in THE DOUBLE LIFE OF VERONIQUE

POLISH CINEMA NOW

In the tenth of our annual close-up scrutinies of national cinema, we focus on Poland, celebrated in the past year for both *Schindler's List* and the glorious trilogy by Kieślowski. **WANDA WERTEN-STEIN** looks back in this first article over the years of transition in Polish cinema.

Five years ago, after the historic compromise of the Round Table and the landslide victory of Solidarity candidates in the semi-democratic elections of June 1989, Poland began its return to democracy, which was sealed by *really* free parliamentary elections in November 1991. But changes in the system and national economy began immediately with prime minister Tadeusz Mazowiecki's government. The long and difficult transformation towards a free market economy had begun.

Changes in Polish cinema began too. Proposed by the Association of Polish Film-makers, Juliusz Burski (previously script manager of the Film Group "Perspektywa") became President of the Committee for Cinema and was given the rank of Vice-Minister of Culture. He initiated the first steps towards privatisation of film distribution and exhibition. The film "Units" (a Polish invention) like Wajda's "X" or Zanussi's "Tor", which helped Polish cinema of the late 1970's and early 1980's to be more independent than in the neighbouring countries and were imitated by some of them (e.g. Hungary and the U.S.S.R.), were soon transformed into independent Film Studios and became fully-fledged producers.

After Burski's untimely death in September 1990 his programme and ideas were continued and developed by his successor Waldemar Dąbrowski, a young, intelligent, resourceful organiser who had proved his capabilities as manager of one of Warsaw's theatres. In his four years in office he devoted all his energies to helping and securing the existence and development of the Polish film industry and film culture – with the result that film production, distribution of important and valuable films and cultural events fared better than could be expected in the very difficult general financial conditions of the transformation period.

The three agencies founded in 1991 fully proved their value. The Script Agency gives subsidies for project development, and between November 1993 and April 1994 it supported 25 projects. It also offers grants for subject research. The Production Agency can grant up to 70% of production costs of a film on the basis of its budget, eventual co-producers' participation and promised or signed distribution deals. Since Poland joined Eurimages in September 1991, 18 films co-produced by Polish producers have received their support: in 1991 – 1; in 1992 – 6; in 1993 – 7; in 1994 – 4. The Agency also funds certain documentary, animated and educational films. The Distribution Agency supports the exhibition of some Polish and foreign films with grants for publicity expenses

and production of prints. These sums are reimbursable to the Agency from box-office results.

New Legislation Urgently Needed

In the new situation, with no restrictions (censorship having been abolished in June 1990) and free access for foreign capital, new legislation is urgently needed and a new law on cinema is in preparation to replace the very unsatisfactory one of 1987 (based on the principles of the former regime and enacted towards the end of martial law). Until now most regulations that help the functioning of Polish film industry today were introduced under the old law.

To give an idea of the Polish film scene, we can sketch its principal features. The **Committee for Cinema** and its president represent the interests of Polish cinema at home and abroad, supervise the various sections of the film industry, channel State monies to film institutions, agencies and foundations and through them to production, distribution, film studios, festivals and other cultural film events, to the National Film Library and the State Films, Television and Theatre School in Łodź, the Film Museum in Łodź and the Film Poster Museum in Warsaw.

State and private producers (some created ad hoc for a single project) are entitled on an equal basis to receive financial support for specific film projects. On the same principle, private or still State-owned distribution firms receive grants for publicity expenses and print production of specific films. Among the most active State-owned producers are **Film Studio TOR, Film Studio PERSPEKTYWA, Film Studio ZODIAK** and **Karol Irzykowski Film Studio** (for young film-makers). The most important private production company to date is Heritage Films Ltd., co-producer of Steven Spielberg's *Schindler's List* and Costa-Gavras's *Minor Apocalypse*. Some 30-40% of Polish feature films are made for, co-produced with, or produced by Polish Television, most of them screened in the cinemas.

As with film production, central distribution and exploitation, State organs have been dissolved; the remaining State-owned, privatised or new, private distribution firms function independently; some 8.5% of cinemas are run by State distributors, 30% are rented to private exhibitors, and some 60% belong to local administrations. All exhibitors are completely free in the choice of films they show.

Film Art Foundation is an important feature of Polish cultural life – it runs art cinemas nationwide, organises the annual Warsaw Film Festival, and other special film events.

The **National Film Library** guards in its archives the national and world film patrimony, gives all interested access to its rich library of film books and publications; offers help to researchers in all aspects of film art, screens old and new films in its own cinema, and special seasons of new foreign films (these together with the respective embassies).

The **State Film, Television and Theatre School in Łodź**, founded in 1948, is still the mother of Polish cinema and Polish film-makers. Young talents follow the old masters and practically everyone who counts in our cinema was a student. To quote just a few names: Andrzej Munk, Andrzej Wajda, Roman Polański, Wojciech Marczewski, Krzysztof Kieślowski, Krzysztof Zanussi, Jerzy Skolimowski – directors; Witold Adamek, Sławomir Idziak, Edward Kłosiński, Witold Sobociński and his son Piotr, Witold Stok, Jerzy Wójcik, Jarosław Żamojda, Jerzy Zieliński – cameramen; and the animation genius Zbigniew Rybczyński (Academy Award 1983 for animated short film).

The state **Film Polski** Agency organises the promotion of Polish films abroad, publishes and distributes publicity materials, helps contacts between Polish and foreign film producers and distributors, and promotes and services the participation of Polish films in world film festivals.

Huge Growth in Video Consumption

To see the situation in the film market in its

Escape by train in 300 MILES TO HEAVEN, directed by Maciej Dejczer

POLISH TELEVISION

The biggest producer of feature films in Poland and Central Europe.

Produces 150 hours of features annually.

Made the debuts of Poland's new generation of film directors:

Jan Jakub Kolski
Johnny the Aquarius, Cannes, Certain Regard '94

Dorota Kedzierzawska
The Crows, Cannes, Quinzaine des Realisateurs '94

Filip Zylber
A Farewell to Maria, New York, The Human Rights Festival '94

SMALL SCREEN ■ BIG CINEMATOGRAPHY

Telewizja Polska S.A. Film Production Department
17 Woronicza Street, 00-999 Warsaw, Poland
Ph. (48 22) 47 81 67 Ph/Fax (48 22) 43 48 33

correct perspective, two paradoxically contrasting factors must be taken into account. First and foremost is the drastic impoverishment of the broad masses as a result of the change of the system towards a free market economy and secondly the huge growth in the number of video-recorders in private homes (not forgetting countless legal and pirate video-cassettes in circulation).

In the last year of the old regime (1988) the country had some 1,600 cinemas, 10% less than in 1987. In 1992 the number fell to 933 and in 1993 to 755. Correspondingly, audiences declined from over 85 million in 1988 to 13.7 million in 1993. While in 1988 31% of the viewers saw Polish films, in 1993 they amounted to only 10% (1,318,272 admissions). In 1988 the first on the list of top grossing films (*Crocodile Dundee*) attracted 2.4 million viewers and a Polish film with 1.8 million was sixth (*The Bow of Eves*); in 1993 *Jurassic Park* had 2.4 million viewers and no Polish film was in the top ten. Of the 158 films first shown on Polish screens in 1993 – 90 were American, 32 Polish (14 of them co-produced with foreign companies), 26 were European (2 co-produced with Poland) and 10 from non-European countries excluding the United States. On the weekend of July 15-17, 1994, the 37 Warsaw art and regular cinemas were screening 55 recent and older films; of these 37 were American, 9 European, 3 British, 1 Australian, 2 New Zealand, 1 Mexican, 1 Russian and 1 Polish. Three foreign films were made by Polish directors; by Agnieszka Holland, Yurek Bogayewicz, and Krzysztof Kieślowski. A summer weekend is not, of course, really typical because most of the cinema-going public is out of town. Those who remain prefer to stay at home after the heat of the day and watch television. So the exhibitors must try to attract them by showing the most popular American films – some of them great and some, well, not so great.

The discriminating public sees the world's most interesting films at the annual **Warsaw Film Festival**, flooding the cinemas where the films are shown from 9 or 10 a.m. to midnight or later. In 1993 the Festival showed 68 foreign and 6 new Polish films by 48 foreign and 8 Polish directors. Other important cultural events include "weeks" of national films from a particular country, such as the very successful week of French films in the spring of 1994.

Three competitive film festivals, the **Festival of Polish Feature Films** in **Gdynia** (earlier in Gdańsk), the **Festival of Polish and East-Central European Films** in **Łagów**, and the **International Festival of Short Films** in **Kraków** are a long tradition. The **First International Festival of the Art of Cinematography, CAMERIMAGE** in Torún was initiated and organised by a group of enthusiasts from the Copernicus city in November 1993. Its success was beyond all expectations – attended by many of the world's greatest directors of photography – including Vittorio Storaro (who was President of the Jury, Sven Nykvist (awarded the Life Achievement Prize), Victor Kemper (President of A.S.C.) and the representatives of the British, German, Italian and French associations. It promises to become one of the great world international festivals. It makes us remember that cinema is a visual art.

The Importance of Co-Productions

Thanks to the institutions mentioned earlier, co-productions and/or services to foreign crews working in Poland seem to have coped better with the economic hardships of the transformation period than distribution and exhibition. In the late 1970's and 1980's the average production of feature films was between 30 and 40 films. In 1990 it was 22, in 1991 – 25, in 1992 – 26, and in 1993-94 – 56. It is significant that before 1989 all films were produced by State producers (called at the time "groups" or "units"). In 1989 only 2 films were co-produced with Polish Television and 2 with foreign companies. In 1992, 50% of the films were international co-productions and 29% were made by private producers. In 1993 private producers were responsible for 38% of the films and over 30% were international co-productions. In 1994 the ratio was: private producers 44%, co-productions 52%. About 60-70% of theatrically distributed films are made with, for, or by Polish Television.

With no barriers to international

Still from Pasikowski's PIGS

contacts, co-productions or services to foreign productions became an important factor in the economy of Polish cinema. And the professional level and efficiency of the artists and technicians has gained the growing appreciation of world film-makers and producers. After shooting *Schindler's List* Steven Spielberg told Kraków television that he was amazed and enchanted by the devotion and efficiency of his Polish crew and that this being his twelfth feature film, he had never dealt with such a fast-working and very welol-organised production. And his Polish co-producer Lew Rywin said that Spielberg's crew left more money in Poland than is budgeted for the country's entire feature film production! Spielberg's director of photography, incidentally, was Janusz Kamiński (a Pole living and working in the United States); his production designer was Allan Starski and his set director Ewa Braun (both Polish), both Academy Award 1994 winners.

Wave after Wave

The first Polish films to attract international attention were two testimonies to the horrors of Nazi occupation – Wanda Jakubowska's Auschwitz drama *The Last Stage* (*Ostani etap*, 1947) and Aleksander Ford's *Border Street* (*Ulica Graniczna*) on the tragedy of the Warsaw ghetto. Ten years later a batch of young new directors came out with films that became known as "the Polish School". Those directors (Andrzej Munk, Andrzej Wajda, Wojciech Has, Jerzy Kawalerowicz, the writer-director Tadeusz Konwicki, the writer Jerzy Stefan Stawiński) were founders of the new Polish cinema.

The next wave, dubbed "moral anxiety", came in the late 1970's with its protest against the regime using metaphorical images of failure, demoralisation and injustice. Led by Krzysztof Zanussi and backed by Wajda in his famous "X" Unit the new "moral anxiety" directors are today established international names – to quote the best known: Feliks Falk, Agnieszka Holland, Krzysztof Kieślowski, Wojciech Marczewski, Janusz Kijowski, Janusz Zaorski, Edward Żebrowski and Jerzy Domaradzki. And the outsiders who debuted between the two "waves" are Roman Polański, Jerzy Skolimowski, Marek Piwowski and Andrzej Żuławski.

Philippe Volter in Kieślowski's THE DOUBLE LIFE OF VERONIQUE

Krystyna Janda in Ryszard Bugajski's long-banned INTERROGATION

"The Truth is Brutal"

Towards the end of the old regime Krzysztof Zanussi told his colleagues at a meeting in 1988: "The truth is brutal; it will never be for us as easy to make films as it was for Ford or Jakubowska. That kind of paradise is gone forever." Zanussi's warning proved to be too pessimistic. The past five years proved that films could be made but the real difficulty was to make them find their way to the public. Ideas, not money, posed the major problem. What could move the public when so many excellent American films helped them forget the hardships of the day? The success of Agnieszka Holland's German-produced *Europa, Europa* (1990) was a striking surprise. What would the public expect from the national production?

It would be difficult to show some dominant thematic or stylistic tendencies of the films of 1989-1994. It seems better to try to see what the directors of the most important films of the period had to say to their public.

1989 – Maciej Dejczer makes his debut with *300 Miles to Heaven (300 mil do nieba)*, a story of two young boys escaping, still under the rule of martial law, to Sweden hiding in the undercarriage of a lorry. He wins the 1990 Felix Award for first feature.

The national masterpiece, Adam Mickiewicz's (1798-1855) powerful romantic drama *Forefathers' Eve* is adapted for the screen by Tadeusz Konwicki – some of its scenes and dialogue sounding strangely contemporary. (When the play was produced in the Warsaw National Theatre in 1968 it was banned soon after its premiere on the pretext that the public read too much into the poet's words and reacted accordingly – against the regime; the ban was followed by a huge campaign against intellectual circles, students and – particularly – Jews.) Konwicki called his film *Lava (Lawa)*.

Krzysztof Kieślowski was continuing his *Decalogue* series; the first two films – *A Short Film About Killing* (5th Commandment) and *A Short Film About Love* (6th Commandment) – were shown theatrically in 1988.

1990 – Wojciech Marczewski's *Escape from Liberty Cinema (Ucieczka z kina Wolność)*, inspired by a sequence from Woody Allen's *The Purple Rose of Cairo*, was

Still from Wojciech Marczewski's ESCAPE FROM LIBERTY CINEMA

a tragicomedy about a film censor's examination of conscience; and the historical fact is that at the end of the film's production, censorship in Poland was indeed abolished.

Wajda's *Korczak* was a tribute to the memory of the great Jewish doctor and educator who was forced by the occupation authorities to move his orphanage into the Warsaw ghetto, tried to spare his children the ghetto's horrors and hunger and, when the ghetto was abolished, led his charges, preceded by the Polish national flag carried by one of the boys, to the train that was to drive them to the gas chambers at Treblinka. Some foreign protests against the film (especially in France) manifested total insensitivity to its dramatic defence of human dignity in extremis.

1991 – Another film on the fate of Polish Jews during the Nazi occupation, Jan Łomnicki's *Only This Forest (Jeszcze tylko ten las)* shows an old servant who must lead the small daughter of her employer out of the Warsaw ghetto and take her to the safety of her native village. They fail, due to an unwitting lapse by the child. This deeply moving story was beautifully acted by Danuta Szaflarska as the old woman.

Racial problems delicately alluded to in the peaceful atmosphere of the countryside, the air of xenophobia, of curiosity and mistrust of the inhabitants towards the gypsy tribe who set their camp on the outskirts of their village form the background of a nascent teenage love in *Devils, Devils (Diabły, diabły)*, the first feature by Dorota Kędzierzawska, already winner of various national and international awards for her short films.

The revelation of a new talent also came with *Kroll*, the first feature by 32-year-old Władysław Pasikowski; an ugly vision of the world very well told.

The great film of 1991 was of course Krzysztof Kieślowski's Polish-French *The Double Life of Véronique (Podwójne życie Weroniki)* portraying the parallel lives of two girls, one Polish, the other French, born on the same day, with Irène Jacob playing both.

1992 – Krzysztof Zanussi's British-Polish *The Silent Touch (Dotknięcie ręki)*, with Max von Sydow, Lothaire Bluteau and Sarah Miles, probing into the mysteries of artistic creation; Andrzej Wajda returning to his early themes of war and Polish Underground Army in *The Horsehair Ring*

Still from Jan Łomnicki's ONLY THIS FOREST

(Pierścionek z orłem w koronie); war and suffering again in *All That Really Matters (Wszystko co najważniejsze)* by Robert Gliński, based on the memories of Ola Wat, deported like innumerable Polish citizens from Lwow to the bare plains of Kazakhstan after the undeclared Soviet invasion of East Poland in September 1939, following the secret Ribbentrop-Molotov pact) invited serious reflection on human nature and fate. And Pasikowski again thrilled his admirers with *Pigs (Psy)* describing the gang fights among former Security agents.

1993 – The heyday of Kieślowski. The

Still from Tadeusz Konwicki's A TALE OF ADAM MICKIEWICZ'S "FOREFATHERS' EVE"

Still from Wajda's THE HORSEHAIR RING

first of his Polish-French-Swiss produced trilogy, *Three Colours: Blue,* bathing in the glory of Golden Lions at Venice (for Kieślowski and his director of photography Sławomir Idziak) opened in October. The other two soon followed – *Three Colours: White* in February 1994 and *Three Colours: Red* in May.

But not only Kieślowski. Based on the stories of Maria Kuncewicz, Andrzej Barański's *Two Moons (Dwa księżyyce)* shows in beautifully structured, loosely interconnected episodes, the ancient picturesque Kazimierz on the river Vistula where, before the war, painters and writers used to come for their summer holidays. A fine gallery of characters interpreted by excellent actors. A contemporary provincial town forms the site of a short romance between the visiting great actor (played by Daniel Olbrychski) and teenage music student, played in her fascinating debut by Maria Seweryn, the daughter of Krystyna Janda and Andrzej Seweryn in *The Sequence of Feelings (Kolejność uczuć),* a sympathetic comedy with satirical overtones written and directed by Rydosław Piwowarski.

With his *Johnny the Aquarius (Jancio Wodnik)* Jan Jakub Kolski confirms the promise of his earlier *Funeral of a Potato (Pogrzeb kartofla,* 1990) and *Pograbek* (1992). Firmly anchored in the authenticity of village life, this tale of a man who can summon rain in times of drought and believes in his healing gifts is rich both in satire and metaphor.

The as yet unreleased Kolski film, *Miraculous Place (Cudowne miejsce)* is said to be in the same vein.

Another promising newcomer is Filip Zylber. His *Farewell to Maria (Pożegnanie z Maria)* based on the prose of Tadeusz Borowski, reconstructs, using the framework of a wedding party, the Nazi terror in occupied Warsaw. Zylber admires the purity and readiness for sacrifice of young members of the underground Home Army and the tragedy of Jewish fugitives from the ghetto.

Two fake documentaries satirised the attitudes of the Warsaw man-in-the-street: Maria Zmarz-Koczanowicz's *Edge of the World (Kraj świata)* set on the eve of the former system's collapse and Piotr Szulkin's *Meat (Mięso)* on the viewpoints typical of the long years of PRL (the popular code for the old system, actually the acronym for Polish People's Republic).

Finally, Kazimierz Kutz's *Death as a Slice of Bread (Smierć jak kromka chleba)* is a serious, honest and deeply moving recreation of the events after the declaration of martial law in December 1981, when the striking miners of the Wujek coalmine were massacred by the riot police.

Urgent Need

Let's sum up the past five years. Films were and are made – some great, some not so good, some bad, even very bad. The general feeling is, however, that they do not respond to the expectations of the public. Some of the best can be seen as part of the cosmopolitan European cinema, some – popular with the public – are rather poor imitations of American thrillers, and only rare exceptions can be seen as reflecting Polish problems, customs, culture and tradition. The attempts of new directors like Dejczer, Kędzierzawska, Kolski, Zmarz-Koczanowicz, Grzegorzek give hope for an original, revelatory, universal but characteristic Polish cinema. There is an urgent need for new philosophies. Janusz Kijowski wrote in *Kino* this year of the need for: "a cinema that isn't shy to refer to its own cultural sources and aesthetic models, open to the world at large but presenting it in its own way."

Juliette Binoche in Kieslowski's TROIS COULEURS: BLEU

POLAND AND FILM CO-PRODUCTION: NOT ONLY *SCHINDLER'S LIST*

"To my dedicated crew –

All of you placed your lives and bared your souls so that *Schindler's List* would ring true to those courageous enough to look.

I will forever be in your debt.

Steven"

Those words were addressed to Heritage Films and its chief Lew Rywin, one of the outstanding Polish film producers, as well as to all the Polish crew who had worked on the Oscar-winning *Schindler's List*. As you remember the Polish team of set decorators Allan Starski and Ewa Braun have received the Oscars too. But the most important thing is that Polish film-makers have started to believe they are capable of working with anybody – even the most famous directors in the world.

After the dramatic change of 1989, Poland, similarly to other post-communist countries, has changed the system of management and financing her film production. To re-create – after 50 years of its non-existence – the institution of private film producer was very difficult, but badly needed: the state could repay only the 30% of production costs. In the space of a few years more than 180 film companies were established. The majority of them are ready to supply highly specialised services, but there are a few that can organise complete production of full-length feature film. Polish film-makers have ample experience in collaborating with foreign partners in the production of their projects.

Steven Spielberg on location in Poland in 1993 for SCHINDLER'S LIST

photo: Universal/David James

Last year's national film festival in Gdynia featured seven films co-produced with foreign partners. Some of them were made with traditional partners, like Russia (*Beautiful Lady* by Jerzy Hoffman), Germany (*The Stranger Must Fly* by Wiesław Saniewski), or Hungary (*Better Be Rich and Beautiful* by Filip Bajon), but others were prepared in collaboration with new ones – Canada (*Memento Found in a Hunched Back* by Janusz Kidawa-błoński), Norway (*Colossus* by Witold Leszcyński) and the United States (*The Gospel According to Harry* by Lech J. Majewski). That kind of activity is maintained and brings satisfying results.

Services Available to Foreign Producers

But it is services supplied to foreign producers which open the greatest opportunities for Polish cinematography. Virtually all domestic film companies were prepared to collaborate with film-makers from abroad. They offer Polish film studios, interesting locations as well as the talent of established Polish experts. Ask, for example, the crew of TNT movie *Frankenstein* by David Wickers; their Polish co-producer was MM Potocka Production. Lew Rywin's Heritage Films participated in the production of *La petite apocalypse* by Costa Gavras as well as in the making of other French and American films. And, of course, we cannot forget the internationally acclaimed films by Krzysztof Kieślowski – *The Double Life of Véronique* and *Three Colours*. All of them

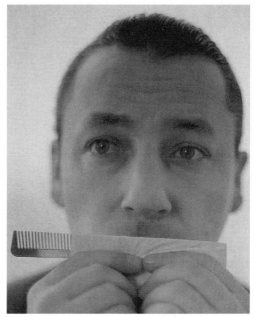

Zbigniew Zamachowski in Kieślowski's TROIS COULEURS: BLANC

were produced or co-produced by "Tor" Film Studio, managed by Krzysztof Zanussi, in collaboration with Marin Karmitz's MK2.

"These films highlight Poland's return to the European cinema," some people maintain. I believe – as Kieślowski said during the first Felix ceremony – that "Poland is a part of Europe" and the international collaboration in the field of film-making should testify to that fact.

Konrad J. Zarebski

BLEU, the first in Kieślowski's trilogy, TROIS COULEURS

Irène Jacob in THE DOUBLE LIFE OF VERONIQUE

POLISH TV

Polish Television – hitherto a "state", now a "public" outlet, has been an important film producer for over twenty years. Under socialism, television was a source of political and ideological propaganda while at the same time it granted considerable creative freedom to Poland's best cinema artists. It also shelved some of Poland's most distinguished pictures about war and holocaust; Andrzej Brzozowski's *By the Railway* and Stanisław Różyewicz's *In the Joint*, made in 1963-65, were not broadcast for a long time.

Several Polish directors worked in television. In the 1960's Krzysztof Zanussi made his series of parabolical stories, in the mood of Rohmer's "Contes moraux". Among them was *Behind the Wall* (1969), one of Zanussi's best films ever, for which he wrote the script with Edward Żebrowski who also directed for television. Wajda made his film *The Birch Wood* in 1970 for television and then, at the end of the 1970's a hugely popular TV series called *Years Pass, Days Pass*. That family saga was interpreted in 1979 as a prophecy of the vast social and political changes to come.

In the 1970's the streets of Poland were deserted every time a Polish film was on TV. Until today, the light adventure films of those years (for example, Andrzej Konic's series *A Stake Higher Than Life* about a Polish spy in the Nazi police).

Then came the ambitious "cinema of moral concern" movement started in television in the 1970's with a cycle entitled "Family Situations". Directors like Agnieszka Holland, Zbigniew Kamiński and Radosław Piwowarski made their debut in this context. It was the time when another Polish director, Stanisław Morgenstern made a TV series.

Krzysztof Kieślowski entered TV with his *Personnel* which was awarded the Grand Prix of the Mannheim Film Festival in 1974. In the mid-1980's Kieślowski worked in television again making *Decalogue*.

Main Investor in Cinema

Nowdays, in view of the decreasing numbers of cinema audiences, television is

Still from Kieślowski's A SHORT FILM ABOUT KILLING

becoming the main investor in the Polish film business. "This is where the future of cinema is being built," says Mirosław Bork, the director of Film Department in Polish Public Television. "Today Television's spending exceed state financing of films y at least five times."

Television produces around fifteen features annually and several other programmes, like TV series and soap-operas, which altogether total about 150 hours of annual production.

Television has been modernising its facilities. Today it has at its disposal labs which match European standards as well as two sound-stages. A technique allowing the switch from photosensitive negatives (blue prints) to electronic systems (the so called "wet gate") is about to be introduced. Getting ready for broadcasting in High Definition, television has purchased Super 16 cameras.

Television is the main organiser of co-productions, attracting partners from the West for such international enterprises as *Wizard* – a big TV series shot in Australia, or *Erotic Tales* – a twelve-episode series made by various European directors (Janusz Majewski in Poland). The latest initiative is a series dedicated to European women entitled *She*.

It is hard to separate a feature from a TV film today. The well-being of Polish film-makers largely depends on the input of public television. We are now in the process of creating one coherent system. Television is the future of the cinema.

Tadeusz Sobolewski

Directors

ANDRZEJ WAJDA

Born in 1926, has a secure position in the history of Polish cinema. One of the most interesting personalities on the European art scene of the postwar era, Wajda witnessed the transformation of several of his films into cult pictures. Today, continuous references, parodies and re-interpretations of Wajda's main themes are still commonplace.

Andrzej Wajda graduated from the Academy of Arts in Kraków where he had studied painting, and he later completed his education as a film director in the Łódź Film School. He debuted with a series of war pictures: *A Generation* (1954), *Kanal* (1956) – which won the Golden Palm in Cannes 1957 – and *Ashes and Diamonds* 61958). For *Ashes and Diamonds* he discovered Poland's James Dean figure, Zbyszek Cybulski, and their mutual inspiration lasted for years – until Cybulski's tragic death in 1967.

In the 1960's Wajda made several of his unforgettable literary adaptations of the classics of neo-romanticism: *Ashes* (1965), *The Wedding* (1972) and *Promised Land* (1974). Yet it was his shipyard sagas: *Man of Marble* (1976) and *Man of Iron* – Golden Palm in Cannes 1981 – that made the strongest appeal on the Solidarity generation.

The auteur of *Danton* (1982) and *Korczak* (1990), Wajda is brilliant and unique in capturing the accidental character of history which creates and devours its heroes.

Andrzej Wajda

Krzysztof Zanussi

KRZYSZTOF ZANUSSI

Born 1939, graduated from physics at Warsaw University, philosophy at the Jagiellonian University in Kraków and film direction at the Łódź Film School in 1966. A rigorous intellectual, extremely precise and analytic, he brought into the Polish cinema a different tradition. His films usually offer little plot and only a thin conflict but impress with the psychological, philosophical and lyrical depths they explore. His art is often identified with the movement of "the cinema of moral concern" and indeed conscience, responsibility and guilt are his main themes. From 1981-84 Zanussi worked exclusively abroad and has since then been working mainly in co-productions as head of the "Tor" Studio.

Among his best-known pictures are: *The Structure of Crystals* (1969), *Family Life* (1970), *Illumination* (1973), *The Balance-Sheet* (1974), *Camouflage* (1976), *The Constant Factor* (1980) and the most recent one, *The Silent Touch* (1992), with Max von Sydow and Sarah Miles.

KRZYSZTOF KIEŚLOWSKI

Born 1941, graduated from the Łódź Film School in 1969. He made several documentaries and short features at the onset of his career, and then debuted with a feature called *Personnel* (1975) for which he won the Grand Prix of the Film Festival in Mannheim. He then made several films based on his own scripts: *Peace*

(1976, premiered in 1980), *The Scar* (1975), *Camera Buff* (1979) and *Coincidence*. During the martial law court hearings of the workers who participated in the strikes of 1990, Kieślowski met the lawyer, Krzysztof Piesiewicz, who became his screenwriter. *A Short Film About Killing* (1988) was their first spectacular success and began Kieślowski's international career. He then made together with Krzysztof Piesiewicz a series of ten episodes (including *A Short Film About Killing* and *A Short Film About Love*) entitled *The Decalogue*. As an already well-established artist he made *The Double Life of Véronique* in co-production with France and then the trilogy *Three Colours – Blue* (Golden Lion in Venice, 1993); *White* (Silver Bear in Berlin, 1994) and *Red* (1994).

On several occasions Kieślowski has announced that the trilogy could be his last films.

Krzysztof Kieślowski

AGNIESZKA HOLLAND

Born in 1948, graduated from the Prague Film School in 1971. She began her career working with Zanussi on his film *Illumination* and then worked as a scriptwriter with Andrzej Wajda in the Unit X – a production studio set up by him. She debuted with the film *An Evening with Abdon* in 1975. In the 1970's she made *Provincial Actors* (1979), *Fever* (1980) and *Woman Alone* (1981), films in which she boldly examined the hypocrisy, conformity and deviousness in institutional life. In the prevailing atmosphere of mediocrity, Holland revealed the overwhelming syndrome of Polish helplessness. She brilliantly portrayed grotesque people leading lives of desperation. In 1990 she made *Europa, Europa*, a drama with a much wider viewpoint, treating the accidents of history which give individuals and nations the puppet roles. *Olivier Olivier* (1991), made in France, is a contemporary tale of mistaken identity, a story of frustrated dreams and desires. Agnieszka Holland's latest film, *The Secret Garden*, is by far the best version of this classic children's story. It has established Holland's place as one of the best female directors of today.

WŁADYSŁAW PASIKOWSKI

Born 1959, is one of the most interesting directors of younger generation. After graduating from the Łódź Film School in 1989 he made his first feature film *Kroll* telling the story of a young soldier who after a series of brutal attacks from his colleagues escapes from the army. He tries to go back to his old life but finds nobody is waiting for him. Set in contemporary surroundings, *Kroll* pictures a tough and merciless world peopled by unscrupulous individuals. But Pasikowski's dark humour found a better manifestation in his next film and Poland's long-awaited domestic commercial success, *Pigs*. This story of secret service officials who get involved in mafia dealings in Poland's new-born capitalism touches upon an intriguing aspect of the new order. *Pigs 2*, an overtly commercial sequel, might be but an episode preceding this talented

Cinematographers

SŁAWOMIR IDZIAK

Born 1945, graduated from the Łódź Film School in 1969. He debuted as a director of photography with several documentaries and animated shorts. Early in his career he established a long-term co-operation with Krzysztof Zanussi, working with him on such productions as *The Balance-Sheet* (1974), *The Contract* (1980), *The Constant Factor* (1980), *Man from a Far Country* (1981) and others.

He directed photography for Krzysztof Kieślowski's *The Scar* (1976) and twelve years later he met with Kieślowski again on the set of *A Short Film About Killing*. The contribution of Idziak's photography to the success of Kieślowski's films is especially visible in the very latest pictures by this director: *The Double Life of Véronique* and *Three Colours: Blue* (for which Idziak was awarded in Venice in 1993).

Sławomir Idziak has recently gone back to his earlier experiences as a film director. In 1992 he wrote the script and directed *Enak* starring Irène Jacob.

JERZY ZIELIŃSKI

Born 1950, graduated from the Łódź Film School in 1974. He started his career working as a director of photography for Filip Bajon: on *Aria for an Athlete* (Bajon's directorial debut) for which he was awarded at the Polish Film Festival in Gdańsk in 1979, on *Children on Strike* (1980) and on *Daimler-Benz Limousine* (1981). In the 1980's he worked as a cameraman on Jacek Koprowicz's *Destiny*, Wojciech Wiszniewski's *Elementary Book* (for which Zielinski got an award at the Short Film Festival in Kraków in 1981) and for Wojciech Marczreski's *Shivers* (1981) and *Escape from Liberty Cinema* (1990).

Screenwriters

CEZARY HARASIMOWICZ

Born 1955, graduated from the Łódź Film School in 1985. So far, eight Polish films were based on

Sławomir Idziak

his screenplays, among others, *300 Miles to Heaven* (1989), directed by Maciej Dejczer, for which Harasimowicz was nominated for Felix as the Best Screenwriter of the Year. The film *State of Fear* based on his script got the main award at Karlovy Vary Film Festival in 1990. His script for *Seychelles* (1992) got the Jury Award as well as the Audience Award at the Paris Film Festival. He was the co-author of the filmic adaptation of *The Beautiful Mrs. Seidenman*, produced by Arthur Cohn. From 1989 to 1993 he worked as the head of development for a private film production company. This year he was awarded the Hartley-Merrill prize for the best script by RKO Pictures.

Composers

ZBIGNIEW PREISNER

Born 1955, graduated from history at the Jagiellonian University in Krákow. Only during his studies did he become interested in music. In the late 1970's, as a self-taught composer, he started working for several theatres in Kraków and the legendary artistic cabaret "Piwnica pod Baranami". Zygmunt Konieczny, at that time one of the most popular Polish composers helped to promote this young talent and in 1982 Preisner wrote his first score for a feature film: *Battlefields*, dir. by Antoni Krauze. He was then noticed by Krzysztof Kieślowski with whom he has co-operated on a regular basis since 1984. He wrote the scores of *Decalogue* (1987-88), *The Double Life of Véronique* and *Three Colours* (1993-94).

He also works in close co-operation with Agnieszka Holland. He composed the music for *Europa, Europa* and *Olivier Olivier* as well as *The Secret Garden*. He has been awarded by the Los Angeles film critics in 1991 (for his music to *Europa, Europa*), 1992 (for *Damage*, dir. Louis Malle) and in 1993 (for *Three Colours: Blue*).

His compositions, recorded on CDs, became world famous and are already "classics", including the captivating motif of *The Double Life of Véronique*.

WOJCIECH KILAR

Born 1932; graduated from the Katowice Conservatoire in 1955. He performed for several years as a pianist and composed various contemporary classical music. As a composer of film music he is the author of over 120 scores. Kilar co-operated on regular basis with Kazimierz Kutz (wrote the scores for *The Salt of Black Earth* (1969), *The Beads of One Rosary* (1979)

and others), Stanisław Rózewicz (*The Romantic* (1970), *Glass Ball* (1972) and others), Krzysztof Zanussi (*Structure of Crystals* (1969), *Illumination* (1973), *Spiral* (1978), *The Constant Factor* (1980) and others). He wrote the score for Andrzej Wajda's *Promised Land* (1974) and Paul Grimault's *Le Roi et l'oiseau*. His recent achievements include the score for Francis Ford Coppola's *Bram Stoker's Dracula* (1992).

Wojciech Kilar

Actors

JANUSZ GAJOS

Born 1939. He applied to Drama Schools for four years before finally being accepted into the Łódź Film School which he completed in 1965. His talent, self-will and persistence allowed him to become one of the most popular as well as highly respected figures in the history of Polish cinema. Compelled to fight against the image of an unconcerned playboy he created in one of his first roles – a popular TV series – he went through periods of popular success as well as total obscurity. In the series *A Man in His Forties* (1976) he revealed fine comic gifts. For his performance in *Millionaire* (1977), Gajos won the Best Actor Award at the Polish Film Festival in Gdańsk and was recognised for his great ability for psychological analysis of the character he plays. From 1979 to 1981 he appeared in Andrzej Wadja's *The Conductor* and *Man of Iron*, he was a newspaper editor in Janusz Kijowski's *Kung-fu* and a worker in Filip Bajon's *Daimler-Benz Limousine*. However, his most stunning performance and the decisive breakthrough in his career, was the role of a TV star – a man destroyed by Stalinism and ruined by illness – in *The Little Pendulum* (1981) by Filip Bajon for which Gajos won his second Best Actor Award at the Gdańsk Film Festival.

In 1981 he played a secret policeman who tortures his prisoners in Ryszard Bugajski's *Interrogation*. The film was shelved for years and not premiered until 1989. His next great performance was the role of a censor in Wojciech Marczewski's *Escape from Liberty Cinema* (1990) for which (together with his performance in *Interrogation*) he received the prize of the Gdańsk Film Festival for the third time, once again becoming one of the most admired personalities of Polish cinema.

DANIEL OLBRYCHSKI

Born 1945, Daniel Olbrychski was only 18 years old when he first appeared in a feature film, Janusz Nasfeter's *Wounded in the Forest* (1963). When director Jerzy Hoffman offered him the main role in his costume film, *Colonel Wołodyjowski* (1968), Olbrychski was already a well-known actor with films like Andrzej Wajda's *Ashes* (1965) and *Everything for Sale*

Daniel Olbrychski

(1968) under his belt. Olbrychski's performance in Hoffman's adaptation of the novel on seventeenth-century Poland, his candid and passionate manner, brought him immediate nationwide fame and tremendous popularity. Jerzy Hoffman made the next part of Sienkiewicz's trilogy into a film in 1974 (*Deluge*) and once again it proved to be a great success. But Olbrychski left no time for labels performing in several contemporary productions by such directors as Krzysztof Zanussi, Kazimierz Kutz and Andrzej Wajda. In 1970 Olbrychski starred in what many consider the greatest performance of his career, Andrzej Wajda's *Landscape after the Battle*, playing a frustrated intellectual in a prisoner-of-war camp. He then played the lead in Andrzej Wajda's *The Wedding* (1972), *Land of Promise* (1975) and *The Maids of Wilko* (1978), Zanussi's *Man from a Far Country* (1981), Kieślowski's *Decalogue* (3, 1988), Filip Bajon's *Children on Strike 1901* (1980) and *White Visiting Card* (1986), Piotr Szulkin's *Ga, Ga, Glory the Heroes* (1985) and featured in over 25 foreign productions. In Poland he several times played himself, quite understandably, as he has become a living legend of Polish cinema.

BOGUSŁAW LINDA

Born 1952. A graduate of the Theatre School in Kraków, Bogusław Linda is the most charismatic figure to be seen in Polish films. As one critic said: "Every time he appears on the screen the story acquires new dimension and relationships between the characters become more pronounced." Unsettling and frighteningly real, he is equally convincing as a self-denying hero and as a cunning villain.

After making an appearance in Feliks Falk's parabolic story of a dance leader, *Top Dog* (1977), Linda brilliantly established his credentials in Agnieszka Holland's *Fever* (1980). Soon the centre of attention, Linda had the chance to work with Andrzej Wajda (*Man of Iron* (1981) and Wojciech Marczewski (*Shivers* (1981)). He then went back to work with Wajda in his 1982 production, *Danton*. He was a star of Krzysztof Kieślowski's *Coincidence* (1981) and Janusz Zaorski's *Mother of the Kings* (1982). He worked with Jacek Bromski (*Funeral Ceremony*, 1983) and Filip Bajon (*Magnate*, 1986). Several years later, his work with Bromski resulted in one of Poland's best police movies, *Kill Me Cop* (1987). Linda's recent popularity is owed to his roles in Wladyslaw Pasikowski's films *Kroll* (1991) and *Pigs* (1992) in which he plays an amoral anti-hero, quite fitting for Poland's new reality. Bogusław Linda made a debut as a director with a 1992 production *The Seychelles*.

JACEK BŁAWUT

Born 1950, graduated from the Photography Dept. at the Łódź Film School. He started in the late 1970's, directing photography for several shorts. He then directed seven documentaries before moving on to features. After working as a cameraman on Marek Koterski's *Inner Life* (1987) and *Porno* (1989), Jerzy Domaradzki's *The Arch of Eros* (1987) and Krzysztof Kieślowski's *Decalogue* (1988), Jacek Bławut made his directorial debut, *The Abnormal*, in 1990. A story of unsettling authenticity, *The Abnormal* was quite an event on the Polish film scene and the film won numerous awards in Poland (at the Gdańsk Film Festival and the Don Quixote Award of the Polish Federation of Film Clubs) as well as abroad (two awards at Mannheim 1991, Frankfurt 1991 and the Jury Award at San Sebastian 1992). "Such a humane and beautiful film," said Andrzej Wajda about *The Abnormal*, "has not been made in this country for a long time, maybe not since (Zanussi's) *Structure of Crystal*." Jacek Bławut's career is worth watching as the most mature and valuable achievements of this unique personality are almost certainly still to come.

PIOTR SOBOCIŃSKI

Born 1958, is a graduate of the Łódź Film School, Photography Dept. While still studying he worked on several documentaries, the most significant was *The Rat-catcher* 1994 (dir. Andrzej Czarnecki), a prize-winner at the Kraków Short Film Festival. In 1983 he was director of photography for Krzysztof Lang's feature debut, *Draw*. He then co-operated with director Filip Bajon on *The Magnate* (1986), *White Visiting Card*, (TV series, 1986), *The Ball at Koluszky Junction* (1989) and *Pension Sonenschein* (1990) as well as with Tadeusz Konwicki on *Lava* (1987) and Krzysztof Kieślowski on *Decalogue* (1988 – as the only cameraman to shoot more than one episode). Since 1989 Sobocinski has been working a lot in Germany on numerous films and TV productions with the director Werner Masten. In 1993 he was the director of photography for Krzysztof Kieślowski's *Three Colours: Red*.

JERZY SATANOWSKI

Born 1947, graduated from Polish Philology Dept. at Poznań University. He is a self-taught composer and author of scores for 30 films, over 200 theatrical plays and innumerable popular songs performed by Polish actors, like Krystyna Janda and Zbigniew Zamachowski. He received an individual award at the Gdańsk Film Festival for the music to Andrzej Domalik's film *Upstairs, Downstairs* (1989). He wrote the score for the following main prize-winners of the Festival in Gdańsk: *Woman in a Hat* (dir. Stanisław Różyewicz, 1985), *Siekierezada* (dir. Witold Leszczyński, 1986), *Interrogation* (dir. Ryszard Bugajski 1982, awarded in 1989 and 1990), *All That Really Matters* (dir. Robert Gliński, 1992) and Wojciech Marczewski's *Escape from Liberty Cinema* (1989 – nomination for Felix '91 for the Best Supporting Actor), Krzysztof Kieślowski's *Decalogue* (1989, episode ten), Bogusław Linda's *The Seychelles* (1989) and Jacek Gąsiorowski's *Yes, Yes* (1991). He also played in Filip Bajon's *The Ball at Koluszky Junction* (1988) and *Sauna* (1992), Andrzej Wajda's *Korczak* (1989) and Jerzy Skolimowski's *Ferdydurke* (1991). His so far most impressive achievement is however the leading role in Krzysztof Kieślowski's *Three Colours: White* (1993), awarded at the Berlin Film Festival in 1994). Playing an impotent husband of a French beauty (Julie Delpy), Zamachowski was profoundly human in his powerlessness and misfortune. With a lot of talents still to be discovered Zbigniew Zamachowski is Poland's great pride as well as great hope.

CEZARY PAZURA

Graduated from the Warsaw Drama School in 1986. He made his film debut in a 24-episode TV series, *Borderland on Fire* (1985-90). This Slav-looking, agile actor has performed in about 30 films but his genuine leading role is still to come. He made his name delivering masterly episodes and brilliant secondary roles with the kind of presence that glues a film together and without which the integrity of the story would be lost. His popularity is mainly due to his performance in Władysław Pasikowski's commercially successful features: *Kroll* (1989) and *Pigs* (1992) but also worth mentioning are Jan Łomnicki's *The Great Betrayal* (1992), Juliusz Machulski's *Squadron* (1992), Konrad Szołajski's *Man of ...* (1993), Łukasz Wylężałek's *The Bash* (1993) and Marek Piwowski's *The Kidnapping of Agata* (1993). In 1992 Pazura played a secret policeman in Andrzej Wajda's *Horse Hair Ring*. This role, well structured and performed with an obvious touch of inspiration shows the versatile talent of this actor. Pazura's self-discipline, his nervous manner and expressive body language contribute to an indeed brilliant performance. He should now be getting ready for a solo role which will secure Pazura the kind of lasting fame he rightly deserves.

Filmographies compiled by Monika Pietkiewicz

Polish Actresses

Krystyna Janda

Agnieszka Wagner

Maria Seweryn

Grazyna Szapołowska

Film Authorities and Semi-Governmental Bodies

State Committee of Cinematography
ul. Krakowskie Przedmieście 21/23
00-071 Warszawa
Tel: (48 22) 26 34 49
Fax: (48 22) 26 27 40

Film Production Agency
ul. Puławska 61
02-595 Warszawa
Tel: (48 22) 45 40 41
Fax: (48 22) 45 55 86

Script Agency
ul. Chełmska 21
00-724 Warszawa
Tel: (48 22) 41 12 11, ext. 265, 344

Film Distribution Agency
ul. Trebacka 3
00-74 Warszawa
Tel: (48 2) 635 20 38
Fax: (48 2) 635 15 43

Film Polski
ul. Mazowiecka 6/8
00-048 Warszawa
Tel: (48 22) 26 84 55, 26 09 49
Fax: (48 22) 27 57 84

State Funded Production Houses

(in alphabetical order)

Film Studio DOM
Tel./Fax: (48 22) 45 50 65

Film Studio KADR
Tel./Fax: (48 22) 45 49 23

Film Studio OKO
Tel./Fax: (48 22) 45 55 81

Film Studio PERSPEKTYWA
Tel./Fax: (48 22) 45 54 94

Film Studio PROFIL
Tel./Fax: (48 22) 45 49 86

Film Studio TOR
Tel./Fax: (48 22) 45 53 03

Film Studio ZEBRA
Tel./Fax: (48 22) 45 54 84

Film Studio ZODIAK
Tel./Fax: (48 22) 45 20 47
ul. Puławska 61
02-595 Warszawa

Karol Irzykowski Studio
ul. Mazowiecka 11
00-052 Warszawa
Tel: (48 22) 27 66 53
Fax: (48 22) 26 73 57

Television

Poltel International
(Polish State TV – Dept. of Film Acquisition and Sales)
ul. Woronicza 17
00-950 Warszawa
Tel: (48 22) 47 61 39, 47 67 73
Fax: (48 22) 44 02 06

Film Production Department
(Polish State TV)
ul. Woronicza 17
00-950 Warszawa
Tel: (48 22) 43 48 33

Polsat
(Polish television with a national broadcasting licence)
Head Office and Advertising Office:
ul. Andersa 5
Tel: (48 2) 635 43 91
Fax: (48 2) 635 43 23

Telewizja Kraków
ul. Krzemionki 30
30-955 Krakow
Tel: (48 12) 66 75 22
Fax: (48 12) 66 15 43

Producers

Aqua-Gemini
ul. Hauke-Bosaka 1/2
01-540 Warszawa
Tel: (48 22) 33 67 58

Ant Studio
ul. Traugutta 8
90-107 {A209}odź
Tel: (48 42) 33 27 69
Fax: (48 42) 36 53 88

Apple Film Productions Ltd.
Plac Konstyucji 3/10

00-647 Warszawa
Tel/Fax: (22) 29 07 54

Crackfilm
ul. Czarnowiejska 49/6
30-049 Krákow
Tel: (48 12) 33 74 94
Tel/Fax: (48 2) 33 22 28

Ekran Bis
ul. Łakowa 29
90-554 Łodź
Tel: (48 42) 37 25 77
Fax: (48 42) 36 20 46

Eureka Films
ul. Fabryczna 27/27
00-446 Warszawa
Tel/Fax: (48 22) 29 41 10

Euromedia Ltd.
ul. Niepodległości 120/13
02-577 Warszawa
Tel/Fax: (48 22) 49 45 32

Fero-Film
ul. Jabłeczna 17/1
50-539 Wroclaw
Tel/Fax: (48 71) 63 62 86

Filmcontract Ltd.
ul. Chełmska 21
00-724 Warszawa
Tel/Fax: (48 22) 41 65 91

Focus Producers Co. Ltd.
ul. Ryżowa 42
02-495 Warszawa
Tel: (48 2) 662 75 86
Fax: (48 2) 662 70 83

Gambit Productions
ul. Przemysłowa 7
02-496 Warszawa
Tel/Fax: (2) 667 45 96

Heritage Films
ul. Marszałkowska 2/6
00-581 Warszawa
Tel: (2) 625 26 01, 625 25 53
Fax: (2) 625 26 93

Indeks
ul. Targowa 61/63
90-323 Łodź
Tel: (48 42) 74 94 94
Fax: (48 42) 74 81 39

Mavo Film & TV Production
ul. Rydygiera 3

Tel: (48 22) 39, 78, 87, 39, 77, 49
Fax: (48 22) 39 94 11

Michał Szczerbic Films
ul. Chełmska 21
00-724 Warszawa
Tel: (48 22) 40 59 35
Fax: (48 22) 40 50 56

Solopan
Krakowskie Przedmieście 21/23
00-071 Warszawa
Tel: (48 2) 635 19 27
Tel/Fax: (48 2) 635 00 44

MN Film Productions
ul. Chełmska 21
00-724 Warszawa
Tel/Fax: (48 2) 644 34 00

Montevideo Co., Ltd.
ul. Powstańców ñlóskich 28/30
53-333 Wrocław
Tel: (48 71) 67 09 80
Fax: (48 71) 67 07 35

Periscope Ltd.
al. Wojska Polskiego 29/95
01-515 Warszawa
Tel: (48 22) 39 42 91

Pleograf Ltd.
pl. Mirowski 18
00-138 Warszawa
Tel: (48 22) 20, 51, 26, 24 85 14
Fax: (48 22) 20 83 42

Potocka
ul. Puzonistów 4
02-876 Warszawa
Tel: (48 2) 643 95 56, 643 95 57
Fax: (48 2) 643 95 53

Profilm
ul. Wały Piastowskie 1
80-958 Gdańsk
Tel: (48 58) 37 43 78, 37 46 85
Fax: (48 58) 37 46 37

Saco Film Ltd.
ul. Ułańska 41 a
52-213 Wrocław
Tel: (48 71) 68 70 27
Tel/Fax: (48 71) 21 92 47

Video Studio Gdansk
ul. Grodska 20
80-841 Gdańsk
Tel: (48 58) 31 55 24, 31 63 44
Fax: (48 58) 31 92 11

Visa Film International
ul. Krakowskie Przedmieście 79, #205
00-079 Warszawa
Tel: (48 2) 635 52 76
Fax: (48 2) 26 85 05

Distributors

Black Cat
ul. Magnoliowa 2
20-208 Lublin
Tel/Fax: (48 81) 77 46 54

Fundacja Sztuki Filmowej
ul. Andersa 1
Warszawa
Tel: (48 22) 31 16 36
Fax: (48 22) 635 20 01

Iti Cinema
ul. Marszałowska 138
00-004 Warszawa
Tel: (48 22) 26 98 62, 27 96, 83
Fax: (48 22) 26 85 52

Mlodziezowa Akademia Filmowa
ul. Marszałkowska 28
00-639 Warszawa
Tel: (48 2) 621 78 28
Tel/Fax: (48 2) 628 96 98

Silesia-Film
ul. Kosciuszki 88
40-519 Katowice
Tel: (48 32) 51 45 88
Tel/Fax: (48 32) 51 22 84

Solopan Film Centrum
ul. Krakowskie Przedmieście 21/23
00-071 Warszawa
Tel: (48 2) 635 19 27
Tel/Fax: (48 2) 635 00 44

Syrena Entertainment Group
ul. Marszałkowska 115
00-102 Warszawa
Tel: (48 22) 27 52 04, 27 35 00
Fax: (48 22) 27 56 48

Video and TV Distributors

Arathos
ul. Lakowa 29
90-554 Łodź
Tel: (48 42) 36 25 92, 37 68 38
Fax: (48 42) 36 04 87

Artvision
al. Jerozolimskie 125/127, office 611
01-017 Warszawa
Tel: (48 2) 628 93 15
Fax: (48 22) 46 72 39

Best Film
ul. Twarda 16a
00-105 Warszawa
Tel: (48 22) 20 12 01, ext. 42, 43

Boom Film
Os. Piastów 12c
Kraków
Tel/Fax: (48 12) 48 68 02

IMP – International Movie Productions Poland
ul. Hoza 66/68
00-950 Warszawa
Tel: (48 2) 628 70 91
Tel/Fax: (48 2) 628 76 91

Imperial Entertainment
ul. Kolska 12
01-045 Warszawa
Tel: (48 22) 38 73 00, 38 71 70
Fax: (48 22) 38 73 02

Iti Home Video
ul. Kłobucka 23
02-699 Warszawa
Tel: (48 22) 47 20 52, 47 15 52
Fax: (48 22) 43 05 85

NVC – Neptun Video Centre
ul. Nowogrodzka 31
00-511 Warszawa
Tel: (48 22) 29 00 52

Poltel Home Video
ul. Woronicza 17
00-950 Warszawa
Tel: (48 22) 47 67 16, 43 42 43
Fax: (48 22) 27 00 21

Vision
ul. Rydygiera 7
Tel: (48 22) 39 07 53
Fax: (48 22) 39 13 67

Market Research Services

Graffiti Info
ul. Krasinskiego 34
Kraków
Tel: (48 12) 22 14 32
Fax: (48 12) 22 77 67

WORLD SURVEY

ARGENTINA — Alberto Tabbia

By late May 1994, the Argentine film industry was shaken up as never before as two different projects for a long-delayed film law were being discussed in Congress. It is not easy to convey for foreign readers a situation where film people were in basic agreement but vociferously opposed, mostly on questions of personal mistrust and bureaucratic procedure.

A text for a new film law, adapted to the present market situation, had already been around for almost two years, sponsored by the Instituto Nacional de Cinematografia. Its main innovation was to create a new source of revenues for film finance, taxing TV channels and video publishing and rental. (In Argentina, contrary to Western European countries, TV is not supposed to co-produce cinema, and the prices it pays for films are ludicrous.) After a long period of backstage lobbying against it by TV and video people, the text finally made it to the first chamber of Congress, only to be shortcircuited there by another proposal, liberating TV channels from any obligation to the film industry and taxing only the less well-defended video industry.

This second proposal also asks for the funds to be collected, as every other tax, by the internal revenue office, which is to forward them immediately to the Instituto. The previous text proposed to create an independent fiscal body under the Instituto's jurisdiction. In a country where newspapers seem to give more space to cases of corruption than to other current events, where indeed corruption is supposed to be second only to Italy, this elicited from film people suspicions of eventual mismanagement by the Instituto officials. The option they faced was one between a less brilliant increase in funding but with a supposedly transparent administration, and on the other hand a substantial regular increase (yet to be accepted by TV channels, ready to enter an all-out legal battle) but subject to a would-be

TOP TEN GROSSING FILMS IN ARGENTINA: 1993

Jurassic Park
Tango Feroz
The Bodyguard
Aladdin
Scent of a Woman
Indecent Proposal
Como agua para chocolate
The Crying Game
The Fugitive
Bram Stoker's Dracula

Alfredo Alcón in EL AMANTE DE LAS PELÍCULAS MUDAS, directed by Pablo Torre

Eusebio Poncela and Miguel Angel Solá in UNA SOMBRA YA PRONTO SERÁS, directed by Héctor Olivera

discretional management ...

By May 20 the very active directors' association had split in two, the issue being the demand by some of their members for the departure of the Instituto's head, Guido Parisier, allegedly not supportive of a film law in Congress, needed whatever the project, after the chances of his own one, empowering the Instituto to collect the new taxes, started looking like a losing bet.

Far from such simultaneously serious and farcical comings and goings, there is the not insignificant question of recent Argentine films, a meagre crop and one of the least satisfying in years. An interesting trend is to shoot away from Buenos Aires, in provinces so far ignored by mostly urban film-makers. Another seems to strive for an imaginative grasp of the present social upheavals, after the failure of naturalism to convey the present-day chaos. It is a pity that, whatever the widely different degrees of ambition in the projects, and of talent in the film-makers involved, the results have proven modest at best.

ALBERTO TABBIA is an Argentine film critic and cultural journalist. He co-edited the film series *Flashback* and is a regular contributor to the main Buenos Aires and Montevideo dailies, their literary supplements and other magazines as well.

Recent and Forthcoming Films

CONVIVENCIA (Living Together)

Script: C. Galettini, Luisa Irene Ickowicz, based on the play by Oscar Viale. Dir: Carlos Galettini. Phot: Félix Monti. Music: Oscar Kreimer. Players: José Sacristán, Luis Brandoni, Cecilia Dopazo, Betiana Blum, Victor Laplace. 93 mins.

Two friends, bachelors reaching fifty, have spent their weekends together for twenty-five years, at a run-down house on the Paraná river delta – a boyish-dreams labyrinth of streams and overwhelming vegetation just an hour away from the centre of Buenos Aires. During a storm, a girl misses her boat back to the city and asks for shelter. A bittersweet comedy and a rueful probing of romantic illusions and personal loyalties submitted to the passing of the years.

AMIGOMÍO

Script and Dir: Jeanine Meerapfel, Alcides Chiesa, adapted freely from a book by Pablo Bergel. Phot: Victor González. Music: Osvaldo Montes. Shot in Buenos Aires, in northern Argentina, in Bolivia and Ecuador. Players: Daniel Kuzniecka, Mario Adorf, Diego Mesaglio. 114 mins.

Unemployed and freshly separated from his wife, a young father learns to discover his son during a journey. Leaving the Europeanised surface of Buenos Aires, they go deeper and further into the (to their urban eyes) disconcerting and awesome realities of Latin America.

UNA SOMBRA YA PRONTO SERÁS (Soon to be a Ghost)

Script: Osvaldo Soriano, H. Olivera, based on the novel by Soriano. Dir: Héctor Olivera. Phot: Félix Monti. Music: Osvaldo Montes. 105 mins.

A bunch of zany characters meet and part in this sort of circular road movie. The mixture of metaphysics and social observation results in a humorous, occasionally weird oddity. A new collaboration between the director-producer and the writer of *No habrá más penas ni olvido (Dirty Little War)*, Berlin Film Festival Silver Bear of 1984.

EL AMANTE DE LAS PELÍCULAS MUDAS (A Lover from Silent Movies)

Script and Dir: Pablo Torre, based on his own novel. Phot: Marcelo Iaccarino. Music: Luis Maria Serra. Players: Alfredo Alcón, Carola Reyna, Laura Novoa, Marta González, Gerardo Romano. 92 mins.

A camp fantasy set in Hollywood in 1926, at the time of Valentino's death. A penniless Argentine immigrant suddenly has a chance of occupy the vacant throne of the idol... The first feature by Leopoldo Torre Nilsson's younger son.

HIJO DEL RÍO (Son of the River)

Script: Ciro. Cappellari, Jose Luis Ubertalli. Dir: C. Cappellari. Phot: Roger Heereman, C. Cappellari. Players: Juan Ramón López, Gabriel Mario Tureo, Luisa Calcumil, Norman Briski. Shot in Buenos Aires and in the province of Salta. 100 mins.

An 18-year-old Indian from the north of Argentina leaves his aboriginal reserve for Buenos Aires. In a shanty town he soon gets mixed up with other youngsters performing hold-ups for and under the protection of a gang of corrupt policemen.

HASTA DONDE LLEGAN TUS OJOS (As Far as Your Eyes Can Reach)

Script: Diana and Silvio Fischbein, Clara Voltes. Dir: Silvio Fischbein. Phot: Carlos Torlaschi. Music: José and Fernando Isella. Players: Arturo Bonín, Inda Ledesma, Emilio Bardi, Isabel Quinteros. 92 mins.

A very mixed bunch of impoverished middle-class as well as marginal characters squat a building once occupied by the construction company that swindled them out of their savings. A comedy trying to enliven its social criticism with grotesque and outlandish touches.

FUEGO GRIS (Grey Fire)

Script: Pablo César, Gustave Viau. Dir: P. César. Phot: Jose Treja. Music and songs: Luis Alberto Spinetta. Players: María Victoria d'Antonio, Cristina Benegas, Arturo Bonín, Alejo García Pintos, Leonardo Sbaraglia. 90 mins.

An Alice-in-Horrorland variation. After a "heavy folk" concert, a heroine named Milena falls through a trap into a netherworld of robots and nightmarish landscapes. The film chronicles her search for a way out.

CON EL ALMA (With All My Soul)

Script: Gerardo Vallejo, Oscar Balducci, Eva Piwowarski, Héctor Olmos. Dir: G. Vallejo. Phot: Héctor Collodoro. Music: Chango Farías Góz. Players: Alfredo Alcón, Lito Cruz, Gerardo Vallejo, Eva Piwawarski, Juan Palomino. 86 mins.

Veering between fantasy and fact, a film director's conjuring of the dead pro-jectionist of his native village's now closed cinema. In turn, Don Quixote, Martín Fierro and other fictional heroes materialise in a portentous soul-searching allegory of Argentine history.

Producers

Argentina Sono Film
Lavalle 1973/75
1051 Buenos Aires
Tel: 49-0216/17/18/19
Fax: 541-814 4063

Gea Cinematográfica, S.A.
Pacheo de Melo 2141
1126 Buenos Aires
Tel: 803-7779/3421
Telex: 19051 Geaci Ar

Jorge Estrada Mora Producciones
Reconquista 609
1003 Buenos Aires
Fax: 541-311 4498

Oscar Kramer Producciones
Libertad 1213 2'
1012 Buenos Aires
Tel: 41-6801
Fax: 804-1296

Mandala Films
Carlos Pellegrini 739 10' B
Buenos Aires
Tel: 322-8194
Fax: 322-8631

Distributors

Distrifilms S.A.
Lavalle 1860
1051 Buenos Aires
Tel: 45-6347, 40-3438

Eurocine S.A.
Tucumán 1968
1050 Buenos Aires
Tel: 40-3731, 40-3631
Fax: 541-49 0547

Filmarte S.R.L.
Ayacucho 595
1026 Buenos Aires
Tel: 40-3662, 45-9945
Fax: 476-1739

Transeuropa Cinematográfica S.A.
Ayacucho 580/86
1026 Buenos Aires
Tel: 49-2219/2553/3417
Fax: 541-11-1191

Transmundo Films S.A.
Ayacucho 492
1026 Buenos Aires
Tel: 953-3384/4219
Fax: 541-112479

United International Pictures S.R.L.
Ayacucho 520
1026 Buenos Aires
Tel: 49-0261/64
Fax: 541-111303

Warner Bros
Tucumán 1938
1050 Buenos Aires
Tel: 45-6094/97
Fax: 541-111191

Useful Addresses

Instituto Nacional de Cinematografia
Lima 319
1073 Buenos Aires
Tel: 37-9091
Fax: 541-112559

AUSTRALIA — David Stratton

1993-94 has been another year of achievement for the Australian cinema, which has continued to make its mark internationally even if box-office returns at home and, more importantly, returns to film producers from those receipts, leave a lot to be desired.

There was no outstanding film like last year's *The Piano*, but that was to be expected. On the other hand, a number of interesting film-makers, including Rolf De Heer, John Duigan, Bill Bennett and Stephan Elliott confirmed their talents, and there were a significant number of successful debut features.

Perhaps the year's biggest surprise was **Bad Boy Bubby**, Rolf De Heer's fourth feature (after *Tail of a Tiger, Incident at Raven's Gate* and *Dingo*), which received plenty of attention last year in Venice, winning several awards. Wildly ambitious and provocative, the film stars newcomer Nicholas Hope in a story carrying resonances of both Truffaut's *The Wild Child* and Herzog's *Kaspar Hauser*.

Bubby has been kept in one grubby room by his overweight, alcoholic mother (Claire Benito) since birth; now he's over thirty and knows nothing of the outside world – his only experience of sex is with his mother. But his long-lost father, a priest, returns one day unexpectedly, and Bubby's world is thrown out of whack; when both his parents are killed, Bubby leaves his prison and ventures into the outside world, soaking up information, speech patterns and social attitudes from the people he meets along the way.

A challenging film containing something to offend just about every section of the community, *Bubby* was filmed in 'Scope by a huge team of prominent cinematog-raphers (who bring a different "look" to the protagonist's various encounters) and employs an innovative and intricate sound system, devised by Jim Currie. A film about innocence, and the pollution and decay of contemporary life, this is an astonishing achievement but, despite the Venice accolades, may prove too daunting for wide acceptance; although it was snapped up by Australia's largest distributor, this important film remains, at the time of writing, unreleased in Australia nine months after the publicity it generated in Italy.

John Duigan is very well established as one of Australia's most interesting and personal directors; his semi-autobio-graphical films, *The Year My Voice Broke* and *Flirting* struck a particular chord with Australian audiences. He had wanted to make a film about the controversial artist and writer Norman Lindsay, who scandalised stuffy Australian society earlier this century with his provocative, and to some eyes occasionally blasphemous, paintings and drawings, which frequently featured voluptuous nudes. In the event, though, Duigan's Lindsay film, **Sirens**, emerges as a comedy of manners and more, another Australian film to look back questioningly at the country's traditional links with Britain. Hugh Grant is an Oxford-educated cleric, newly arrived in Australia with his prim wife, Tara Fitzgerald; they are sent by the Bishop of Sydney to Lindsay's Blue Mountains home in an attempt to persuade the artist to withdraw from an exhibition an etching which offends the church; but the strait-laced English couple soon find themselves in a tender trap, seduced by Lindsay's models, or sirens (one of them played by the spectacular model, Elle MacPherson). So the film winds up being not a study of Lindsay (charmingly played by Sam Neill)

Sam Neill and Hugh Grant in SIRENS   *photo: Robert McFarlane*

but of the now dated controversies he stirred and, at the same time, an exploration of female emancipation (it's surely no accident that the English couple are named Campion).

Tense Dissection of Marriage

Another film about a displaced couple from Europe, and one of the most interesting debuts of the year, is Pauline Chan's **Traps**. Vietnamese-born Chan, whose excellent student short films (notably *The Face Between the Door and the Floor*) have been widely seen internationally, returned to her native country to make this challenging story, set in the early 1950's, just before the Communist insurgency that toppled French rule in what was then Indo-China. The couple (Saskia Reeves and Robert Reynolds) arrive at a French-controlled rubber plantation to write a promotional piece for the company that owns the place. Their already strained marriage is further taxed by the events which take place in this faraway place, and especially by the

friendship the wife forms with the strange daughter (beautifully played by Jacqueline McKenzie) of the plantation manager (Sami Frey). The film develops into a tense dissection of the marriage and is climaxed by a gripping sequence in which the two women are captured by Communist rebels, yet Chan remains unable to create a totally satisfying experience, perhaps because the transfer of the action of Kate Grenville's original book, "Dreamhouse", from Tuscany to Vietnam is flawed at best.

A more popular first feature is like to be P.J. Hogan's **Muriel's Wedding**, which scored a success at the Directors' Fortnight in Cannes. This is an abrasively accurate, if slightly cruel comedy about a plain, plump but very romantic young woman (delightfully played by Toni Collette) who has been browbeaten for years by other members of her family, including her awful father (Bill Hunter), a small-time politician. Muriel just wants to be a bride, and her journey to reach this goal is a heady mixture of hilarity and pain. As her best friend who is cruelly stricken with cancer, Rachel Griffiths gives an astonishing performance.

Hogan (no relation to the *Crocodile Dundee* Hogan) is an important new talent.

Another crowd-pleaser which combines fun with a message was chosen for the Un Certain Regard section in Cannes. This is Stephan Elliott's second feature (after *Frauds*), **The Adventures of Priscilla, Queen of the Desert**, which is about three drag queens, a trans-sexual and two gays, who travel from Sydney through the outback in a battered bus called Priscilla to perform at a casino in Alice Springs. Terence Stamp is quite wonderful as the trans-sexual, a touching portrayal of a crabby, slightly bitter middle-aged dame whose latent masculinity occasionally bursts through her elegant exterior, while Hugo Weaving and Guy Pearce are fun as her partners. Elliott is shaping up as an original and exciting film-maker.

There's a curious connection between this film and Ann Turner's latest, **Dallas Doll**, which draws heavily (though without acknowledgement) on Pier Paolo Pasolini's *Teorema*, which starred Stamp as a bi-sexual stranger who seduced every member of a bourgeois family. In Turner's feature, her third after the interesting *Celia* and the generally disappointing *Hammers over the Anvil*, the Stamp character is played by Sandra Bernhard, a golf pro brought to Australia to advise on the establishment of a golf club for Japanese tourists and who stays with a "normal" family. Soon she has seduced the teenage son, led his father into adultery, and introduced his mother (a fine performance from Victoria Longley) into the joys of gay sex; the only family member not involved with the outsider is a teenage daughter who's more interested in UFOs, and Turner suggests there's a link between the UFOs and Bernhard. There are some great ideas in *Dallas Doll*, which has the potential of becoming a cult success; but ultimately it's frustratingly unresolved.

Rather Woolly Cox

Also disappointing is the latest film from the prolific Paul Cox, **Exile**, which competed for Australia at Berlin. Set in the last century, this is a rather woolly, Robinson Crusoe-like tale in which a young man (morosely played by Aden Young) is abandoned on an island as a punishment for stealing sheep (he needed the money to marry girlfriend Claudia Karvan) and who is joined in his exile by a sweet, simple girl (Beth Champion). Cox makes rather heavy weather of this modest story, which is weighed down with mystic allusions, including Norman Kaye's ghostly priest.

Bill Bennett, who specialises in low-budget features and documentaries, made a comeback with the lively **Spider and Rose**, a widescreen road movie involving a crotchety old woman (Ruth Cracknell) and a bitter young ambulance driver (Simon Bossell). It sounds like familiar material, but Bennett makes it both touching and funny, without resorting to sentimentality, and his direction is extremely inventive. A most pleasant surprise.

Equally delightful is **The Sum of Us**, based on a successful stage play by Australian expatriate (and former director of such films as *The Clinic*), David Stevens, which deals with a widower (Jack Thompson) who is proudly accepting of the fact that his son (Russell Crowe) is gay. Kevin Dowling, who directed the U.S. stage production, co-directs the film with cinematographer Geoff Burton, and the result is a very likeable, warm-hearted production which is marred only by the retention of annoying theatrical conventions, like having the characters talk directly to the audience.

Also likeable is Donald Crombie's **Rough Diamonds**, a lightweight family film about a woman (Angie Milliken) who, together with her teenage daughter, escapes a bad marriage in the city and finds romance (with Jason Donovan) and a new life in the country.

On an altogether different scale, Paul Hogan returned to the big screen after the debacle of *Almost an Angel*, with a spoof western, **Lightning Jack**, made entirely in America and directed by Australian Simon Wincer. Hogan's own screenplay is painfully thin and relies heavily on the actor's own charm and personality (cf *Maverick*, in which another Aussie, Mel Gibson, gives a similarly narcissistic performance). *Jack* wasn't quite the box-office blockbuster Hogan was hoping for. But at least it was better than another genre effort, the very weak **Police Rescue**, a weedy spinoff of an excellent and popular TV series.

Ultra-Low Budget

Several ultra-low budget films made their mark during the year. Chris Kennedy's **This Won't Hurt a Bit** is a modest charmer about an Aussie dentist on the loose in England. Susan Lambert's **Talk** is a well-scripted observational drama about 24 hours in the life of two thirty-something women friends (Victoria Longley, Angie Milliken, both in top form) who discuss their sex lives and obsessions with passion. Incorporated fantasy scenes add nothing to the film, though. **The Roly Poly Man**, by Bill Young, is an amiable private-eye-cum-

horror pic in which a bumbling private eye (Paul Chubb) investigates a series of deaths in which the victims' heads have exploded, and romances a woman who works in a morgue. **Body Melt**, by Philip Brophy, emulates New Zealander Peter Jackson in the low-life gore-pic stakes, with a bizarre story about a mad doctor who's invented a new kind of vitamin which proves to have ghastly side effects. And **Les and Rory**, made without government assistance by young writer-director Dean Murphy in the provincial city of Albury-Wodonga, deserves an A for effort but seems hardly a convincing portrait of contemporary teenagers.

Alongside this healthy feature film lineup is an equally healthy short film and documentary culture (documentaries can still achieve first-run release in some cinemas in Melbourne and Sydney), and the long-established film festivals in those cities, as well as the newcomer in Brisbane, continue to flourish.

Jacqueline McKenzie and Sami Frey in TRAPS   *photo: Elise Lockwood*

Of course, Hollywood films still dominate the country's cinemas, but the best of international and independent American cinema can also be found, and the SBS television network screens a wide variety of international cinema past and present. All in all, for the film lover, Australia in the 1990's isn't at all a bad place to be.

DAVID STRATTON was Director of the Sydney Film Festival (1966-1983) and divides his time between writing for *Variety* and *The Australian,* and presenting movies on the S.B.S. TV network in Australia.

Finance

The best in the world – that's how its many admirers describe Australia's support system for film, TV drama and documentaries.

Some producers and talent agents believe the seeds of the new era of adventurous film-making, typified by such 1994 Cannes clicks as *Muriel's Wedding* and *The Adventures of Priscilla: Queen of the Desert,* were sown by the multi-tiered system of government support.

The Australian Film Finance Corporation (FFC), the Australian Film Commission and the state film bodies give writers and producers a multiplicity of sources for development coin, equity investment and marketing assistance.

"It's much easier for budding writers and directors to get films made here because of the excellent support system," says the Willliam Morris Agency's Sydney rep Anthony Williams, whose clients include Paul J. Hogan and Jocelyn Moorhouse.

For budding film-makers and actors, there are first-rate government-sponsored training institutions, led by the Australian Film, Television and Radio School, and the National Institute of Dramatic Art.

A handful of producers, including Phillip Emanuel, continue to tap the 10BA tax incentives (providing 100% write-off in the year the film is made). But the first port of call for most is the FFC, which invested in the majority of the 20 new Aussie films offered at Cannes. However, the bulk of the funding for *Priscilla* and *Muriel's Wedding* came from foreign sources – respectively, Polygram Int. and CiBy 2000.

The federal government allocated $A57 million to the FFC in 1993-94. That reduces to $A54 million in 1994-95 and $A50 million the following year. Beyond that, the agency's future and funding is contingent

(continued on page 101)

Recent Films

THE ADVENTURES OF PRISCILLA, QUEEN OF THE DESERT

Script and Dir: Stephan Elliott. Phot: Brian J. Breheny. Players: Terence Stamp, Hugo Weaving, Guy Pearce, Bill Hunter, Sarah Chadwick, Mark Holmes. Prod: Al Clark, Michael Hamlyn, for Latent Image-Specific Films.

BAD BOY BUBBY

Script and Dir: Rolf De Heer. Phot: Ian Jones (and 30 others). Players: Nicholas Hope, Claire Benito, Ralph Cotterill, Carmel Johnson. Prod: Domenico Procacci, Giorgio Draskovic, De Heer, for Bubby P/L-Fandango Productions.

BODY MELT

Script: Philip Brophy, Rod Bishop. Dir: Philip Brophy. Phot: Ray Argall. Players: Gerard Kennedy, Andrew Daddo, Ian Smith, Vince Gil, Regina Gaigalas, Maurie Annese. Prod: Bishop, Daniel Scharf, for Dumb Films.

DALLAS DOLL

Script and Dir: Ann Turner. Phot: Paul Murphy. Players: Sandra Bernhard, Victoria Longley, Frank Gallacher, Jake Blundell, Rose Byrne. Prod: Ross Matthews, for Dallas Doll Prods.

ENCOUNTERS

Script and Dir: Murray Fahey. Phot: Peter Borosh. Players: Kate Raison, Martin Sacks, Martin Vaughan, Tiana Fahey-Leigh. Prod: Fahey, for Winfalz International.

EXILE

Script and Dir: Paul Cox. Phot:

Nino Martinetti. Players: Aden Young, Beth Champion, Claudia Karvan, David Field, Norman Kaye, Chris Haywood. Prod: Paul Cox, Santhana Naidu, for Illumination Films.

LIGHTNING JACK

Script: Paul Hogan. Dir: Simon Wincer. Phot: David Eggby. Players: Paul Hogan, Cuba Gooding Jr., Beverly D'Angelo, Kamala Dawson, Pat Hingle. Prod: Paul Hogan, Wincer, Greg Coote, for Lightning Ridge-Village Roadshow Productions.

MURIEL'S WEDDING

Script and Dir: P.J. Hogan. Phot: Martin McGrath. Players: Toni Collette, Bill Hunter, Rachel Griffiths, Jeanie Drynan. Prod: Lynda House, Jocelyn Moorhouse, for House and Moorhouse Films/CIBY 2000.

POLICE RESCUE

Script: Debra Oswald. Dir: Michael Carson. Phot: Russell Bacon. Players: Gary Sweet, Zoe Carides, Sonia Todd, Steve Bastoni, John Clayton. Prod: Sandra Levy, John Edwards, for ABC-UIP.

THE ROLY POLY MAN

Script: Kym Goldsworthy. Dir: Bill Young. Phot: Brian J. Breheny. Players: Paul Chubb, Les Foxcroft, Susan Lyons, Zoe Bertram, Frank Whitten. Prod: Peter Green, for Total Film & Television.

ROUGH DIAMONDS

Script: Donald Crombie, Christopher Lee. Dir: Donald Crombie. Phot: John Stokes. Players: Jason Donovan, Angie Milliken, Peter Phelps, Jocelyn Gabriel, Hayley Toomey, Jeff Truman. Prod: Damien Parer, for Forest Home Films.

SIRENS

Script and Dir: John Duigan. Phot: Geoff Burton. Players: Hugh Grant, Tara Fitzgerald, Sam Neill, Elle MacPherson, Portia de Rossi, Kate Fischer, Pamela Rabe. Prod: Sue Milliken, for Samson Productions-Sarah Radclyffe Productions.

SPIDER & ROSE

Script and Dir: Bill Bennett. Phot: Andrew Lesnie. Players: Ruth Cracknell, Simon Bossell, Max Cullen, Lewis FitzGerald, Jennifer Cluff, Tina Bursill, Beth Champion. Prod: Lyn McCarthy, Graeme Tubbenhauer, for Dendy Films.

THE SUM OF US

Script: David Stevens. Dirs: Geoff Burton, Kevin Dowling. Phot: Burton. Players: Jack Thompson, Russell Crowe, John Polson, Deborah Kennedy. Prod: Hal McElroy, for Southern Star Prods.

TALK

Script: Jan Cornell. Dir: Susan Lambert. Phot: Ron Hagen. Players: Victoria Longley, Angie Milliken, Richard Roxburgh, Jacqueline McKenzie. Prod: Megan McMurchy, for Suitcase Films.

THIS WON'T HURT A BIT

Script and Dir: Chris Kennedy. Phot: Marc Spicer. Players: Greig Pickhaver, Jacqueline McKenzie, Maggie King, Patrick Blackwell. Prod: Kennedy, for Oilrag Productions.

TRAPS

Script: Pauline Chan, Robert Carter. Dir: Pauline Chan. Phot: Kevin Haywood. Players: Saskia Reeves, Robert Reynolds, Sami Frey, Jacqueline McKenzie. Prod: Jim McElroy, for Ayer Productions.

Forthcoming Films

COUNTRY LIFE

Script and Dir: Michael Blakemore. Phot: Steven Windon. Players: Sam Neill, Greta Scacchi, John Hargreaves, Kerry Fox. Prod: Robin Dalton, for Dalton Films.

EBBTIDE

Script: Bob Ellis, Peter Goldsworthy. Dir: Craig Lahiff. Phot: Steve Arnold. Players: Harry Hamlin, Judy McIntosh, John Waters, Susan Lyons, John Gregg, Frankie J. Holden. Prod: Lahiff, Helen Leake, Paul Davies, for Genesis Films.

EPSILON

Script and Dir: Rolf De Heer. Players: Ulli Birve, Syd Brisbane. Prod: Domenico Procacci, De Heer, for Psilon-Fandango.

EVERY NIGHT ... EVERY NIGHT

Script: Alkinos Tsilimidos, Ray Mooney. Dir: Alkinos Tsilimidos. Phot: Toby Oliver. Players: David Field, Bill Hunter, Robert Morgan, Phil Motherwell, Jim Daly. Prod: Alkinos Tsilimidos, for Lanigan Productions.

THE FINAL STAGE

Script and Dir: Frank Howson. Phot: John Wheeler. Players: Adrian Wright, Abigail, Michael Lake, Tommy Dysart. Prod: Howson, for Boulevard Films.

GINO

Script: Vince Sorrenti, Larry Buttrose. Dir: Jackie McKimmie. Phot: Ellery Ryan. Players: Nicholas Bufalo, Zoe Carides, Bruno Lawrence, Rose Clemente. Prod: Ross Matthews, for Southern Star.

HOTEL SORRENTO

Script: Richard Franklin, Peter Fitzpatrick. Dir: Franklin. Phot: Geoff Burton. Players: Joan Plowright, Tara Morice, Caroline Goodall, Caroline Gilmer, John Hargreaves, Ray Barrett. Prod: Franklin, for Bayside Pictures.

THE LIFE OF HARRY DARE

Script: Gerald Thompson. Dir: Aleksi Vellis. Phot: Geoff Hall. Players: John Moore, Gordon Weetra, Aaron Wilton, Billy Trott, Bobbi-Jean Henry. Prod: Terry Charatsis, for Infinity Pictures.

LUCKY BREAK

Script and Dir: Ben Lewin. Phot: Vince Monton. Players: Gia Carides, Anthony LaPaglia, Rebecca Gibney, Jacek Koman, Maryanne Fahey, Robyn Nevin. Prod: Bob Weis, for Generation Films.

NAPOLEON

Script: Mario Andreachhio, Michael Bourchier, Steven J. Spears. Dir: Andreacchio. Phot: Roger Dowling. Prod: Andreacchio, Bourchier, Naonori Kawamura, for Film Australia/ Furry Feature Films/Herald Ace.

SPEED

Script and Dir: Geoffrey Wright. Phot: Ron Hagen. Players: Aden Young, Tara Morice, Ben Mendelsohn, Nadine Garner. Prod: Daniel Scharf, for Daniel Scharf Productions.

THAT EYE, THE SKY

Script: John Ruane, Jim Barton. Dir: Ruane. Phot: Ellery Ryan. Players: Peter Coyote, Lisa Harrow, Jamie Croft, Mark Fairall, Amanda Douge. Prod: Peter Beilby, Grainne Marmon, for Entertainment Media.

TUNNEL VISION

Script and Dir: Clive Fleury. Phot: Paul Murphy. Players: Patsy

Australian Film Award for Harvey Keitel in THE PIANO

Kensit, Robert Reynolds, Rebecca Rigg. Prod: Phillip Avalon, for Avalon Films.

VACANT POSSESSION

Script and Dir: Margot Nash. Phot: Dion Beebe. Players: Pamela Rabe, John Stanton, Toni Scanlon, Linden Wilkenson. Prod: John Winter, for Wintertime Films.

AUSTRALIAN FILM AWARDS 1993

Best Film: *The Piano* (dir: Jane Campion; prod: Jan Chapman)
Best Director: Jane Campion (*The Piano*)
Best Actor: Harvey Keitel (*The Piano*)
Best Actress: Holly Hunter (*The Piano*)
Best Supporting Actor: David Ngoombujarra (*Blackfellas*)
Best Supporting Actress: Judy Davis (*On My Own*)
Best Original Screenplay: Jane

Campion (*The Piano*)
Best Adapted Screenplay: James Ricketson (*Blackfellas*)
Best Photography: Stuart Dryburgh (*The Piano*)
Best Editing: Veronika Jenet (*The Piano*)
Best Music: Michael Nyman (*The Piano*)
Best Production Design: Andrew McAlpine (*The Piano*)
Best Costumes: Janet Patterson (*The Piano*)
Best Sound: Lee Smith, Tony Johnson, Gethin Creagh, Peter Townsend, Annabelle Sheehan (*The Piano*)
Best Documentary: *Exile and the Kingdom* (Frank Rijavec) and *For All The World To See* (Pat Fiske)
Best Short Fiction: *Mr. Electric* (Stuart McDonald)
Best Animation: *The Darra Dogs* (Dennis Tupicoff)
Best Foreign Film: *The Crying Game*
Byron Kennedy Award: Matt Butler, Evanne Chesson, Adrian Martin, Gary Warner
Raymond Longford Award: Sue Milliken

TOP TEN GROSSING FILMS IN AUSTRALIA: 1993

	million $A
Jurassic Park	31.7
The Bodyguard	18.2
Aladdin	17.6
Sister Act	13.6
The Fugitive	11.7
Cliffhanger	10.4
Sleepless in Seattle	10.4
Indecent Proposal	10.3
The Piano	9.2
The Firm	8.6

(continued from page 98)

on a Department of Arts review which was due to start in the latter half of 1994. The Communications and Arts Minister Michael Lee has reaffirmed the government's commitment to assisting the film industry.

At the time of writing, in fiscal 1993-94 the FFC committed investment totalling $A27.1 million in 10 feature films. The recipients included *Epsilon*, Rolf de Heer's follow-up to *Bad Boy Bubby*; Michael Rymer's *Angel Baby*; Alan Madden's *Mushrooms*; Richard Franklin's *Hotel Sorrento* and Clive Fleury's *Tunnel Vision*.

Paul Hogan used division 10B of the Tax Act (100% write-off over two years) to raise $A36 million for *Lightning Jack*. That route is costly and time-consuming and isn't likely to be widely travelled.

The Australian box-office climate could not be warmer or more hospitable both for mass-appeal and arthouse pics. In 1993 admissions and box-office receipts set another record – the sixth consecutive year of growth.

Takings totalled $A369 million, up 15% on 1992, and admissions topped 52.7 million, a 16% gain. The box-office cake in 1993 was twice the size of 1987.

All three major chains, Greater Union, Village Roadshow and Hoyts, are adding screens, as are indie exhibitors. Much of the growth in the indie sector is in arthouses operated by the likes of Palace Entertainment, Ronin and Dendy. Indeed, indie theatres' share of the national box-office has rocketed from about 8% in 1988 to 25% in 1993. Yet indie distributors accounted for a slender 4.7% of Australian box-office receipts last year, with the rest carved up by the majors including Village Roadshow.   Don Groves

Producers

Village Roadshow Pictures
G.P.O. Box 1411M
Melbourne 3001
Tel: 667 6666
Fax: 663 1972*

Barron Films
7/85 Forrest Street
Cottesloe 6011
Tel: (09) 385 1551
Fax: (09) 385 2299

David Hannay Prods.
P.O. Box 291
Broadway 2007
Tel: 211 2022
Fax: 212 2350

Kennedy Miller
30 Orwell Street
Kings Cross 2011
Tel: 357 2322
Fax: 356 3162

Meridian Films
117 Rouse Street
Port Melbourne 3207
Tel: 646 4025
Fax: 646 6336*

Palm Beach Pictures
P.O. Box 409
Paddington 2021
Tel: 331 1088
Fax: 360 1746

Southern Star Entertainment
Level 10
8 West Street
North Sydney 2060
Tel: 957 2788
Fax: 925 0849

Anthony Buckley Prods.
27A Johnston Crescent
Lane Cove 2066
Tel: 428 2344
Fax: 427 0247

Colosimo Film Production
22 Hanover Street
Fitzroy 3065
Tel: 417 1241*
Fax: 416 1779

Entertainment Media
157 Eastern Road
South Melbourne 3205
Tel: 690 1044
Fax: 696 2533*

Film Australia
Eton Road
Lindfield
Tel: 413 8777
Fax: 416 5672

Generation Films
111 Nott Street
Port Melbourne 3207
Tel: 646 1033*
Fax: 646 2158

Illumination Films
1 Victoria Avenue
Albert Park 3205
Tel: 690 5266*
Fax: 696 5625

Phillip Emanuel Prods.
24 Herbert Street
Artamon 2064
Tel: 901 4400
Fax: 901 4356

Rosen Harper Entertainment
163 Brougham Street
Wooloomooloo 2011
Tel: 357 4955
Fax: 358 5842

Daniel Scharf Prods.
117 Wellington Street
Windsor 3181
Tel: 509 8320*
Fax: 509 4170

Serious Entertainment
P.O. Box 600
North Sydney 2059
Tel: 957 5375
Fax: 955 8600

Smiley Films
33 Riley Street
Wooloomooloo 2011
Tel: 361 4164
Fax: 332 3427

House & Moorhouse Films
3 Elm Grove
Richmond 3121
Tel: 428 7812
Fax: 428 6884*

Distributors

Beyond Films
53-55 Brisbane Street
Surry Hills 2010
Tel: 281 1266
Fax: 281 1153

Roadshow Film Distributors
G.P.O. Box 1411M
Melbourne 3001
Tel: 667 6666
Fax: 663 1972

Hoyts Distribution
P.O. Box C353
Clarence St. P.O.
Sydney 2000
Tel: 261 7777
Fax: 283 2191

New Vision Films
254 Bay Street
Port Melbourne 3207
Tel: 646 5555*
Fax: 646 2411

Ronin Films
15-19 Boundary Street
Rushcutters Bay 2011
Tel: 361 4255
Fax: 361 4962

Palace Entertainment Corp.
233 Whitehorse Road
Balwyn 3103
Tel: 817 6421*
Fax: 817 4921

Dendy Films
19 Martin Place

Sydney 2000
Tel: 233 8166
Fax: 232 3841

Premium Films
92 Bay Street
Port Melbourne 3207
Tel: 645 1612*
Fax: 645 1591

REP Films
4/21 Chandos Street
St Leonards 2065
Tel: 438 3377
Fax: 439 1827

Sharmill Films
4/20 Toorak Road
South Yarra 3141*
Tel: 826 9077
Fax: 826 1935

Hayden Film Distribution
380 Military Road
Cremorne 2090
Tel: 908 1799
Fax: 908 4238

Southern Star Film Sales
Level 10
8 West Street
North Sydney 2060
Tel: 957 2788
Fax: 925 0849
*=for Melbourne

Useful Addresses

Australian Film Finance Corp.
G.P.O. Box 3886
Sydney 2001
Tel: 268 2555
Fax: 264 2663

Australian Film Commission
150 William Street
Wooloomooloo 2011
Tel: 951 6444
Fax: 959 6403

Screen West
420 Hay Street
Subiaco 6008
Tel: 09 382 2500
Fax: 09 381 2848

AUSTRIA

Susanna
Pyrker

With attendances of 750,000, Steven Spielberg's dinosaur adventure *Jurassic Park* was the uncontested top earner of the Austrian movie year 1993, followed by several other U.S.-made hits that grossed considerably more at the box-office than in previous years. In Vienna alone, the increase in ticket sales was more than 23%, much to the relief of a business that has seen practically nothing but setbacks ever since the mid-1980's.

Cinemas Dying and the Multiplex Factor

The Austrian cinema scene has changed fundamentally in the past few years. While the cinema as such has been under siege, a far-reaching structural change for high-quality theatres is under way at the same time. In 1990 Austria still had 290 theatres with 399 screens and 85,351 seats. At the beginning of 1994 there were only 260 theatres with 391 screens and 71,914 seats left. Between 1990 and 1994 Austria thus lost 30 businesses, 8 theatres and 13,437 seats.

Simultaneously, a link-up between the two leading chains in Austria, "Constantin" and "Kiba", led to a market concentration that gave them control over no less than 70% of the Austrian movie theatres. This is also exerting a notable effect on film releases in Austria, since Constantin, which had been specialising in independent European films before, can now present more U.S. mainstream pro-ductions, formerly monopolised by the Kiba group, on its screens. Thus U.S. productions are increasingly blocking up the Austrian market.

As a first joint project, Constantin and Kiba realised the rebuilding of the tradition-honoured "Apollo" movie house into a multiplex cinema with seven theatres to seat 1,400 people. It is expected to attract half a million moviegoers per year and is the first of four multiplex projects that are in planning in and around the capital city of Vienna for the coming years.

The lack of adequate movie theatres for non-American productions made the Constantin group for the first time enter into a co-operation with small Austrian distributors such as the "Filmladen". As the most important supplier of the independent programme cinemas, the "Filmladen" releases up to 25 films per year, among them Austrian productions such as the successful black comedy *India* (1993).

Successful Austrian Films

Of the 18 Austrian productions that came out in 1993, only two were successful at the box-office: Reinhard Schwabenitzky's sar-castically playful emancipation comedy *Leave Your Husband, Lady,* starring Elfi Eschke (attendance: 90,000) and *India,* directed by Paul Harather, a perspicacious and sentimental insight into the Austrian soul with the Vienna cabaret entertainers Josef Hader and Alfred Dorfer (attendance: 160,000). *India* was even suggested for the 1993 Oscar as best foreign film, but did not receive an official nomination.

With few exceptions, Austrian films are having rather short-lived runs in domestic movie theatres. They stand a better chance in many European festivals; however, the real big events in Berlin, Cannes and Venice seem to be off limits to films made in Austria.

Of all the Austrian productions that came out in 1993 besides the successful *India* and *Leave Your Husband, Lady,* Götz

Still from INDIEN

Spielmann's **The Neighbour** (*Der Nachbar*) and Ulrich Seidl's dramatised documentary **Losses To Be Expected** (*Mit Verlust ist zu rechnen*) deserve attention; both films also received artistic recognition at international festivals. The most interesting documentaries of the year were Helmut Grasser's **The Campaigners**, a study of electioneers in a right-wing political party in Austria, and **James Ellroy**, Reinhard Jud's filmic portrait of the American thriller writer.

The children's film, *Holidays with Silvester* (*Ferien mit Silvester*, directed by Bernd Neuburger) and Michael Haneke's *Benny's Video* continued their 1992 success throughout this past year. Both films made the breakthrough to cinemas all over Europe and were awarded numerous prizes. *Benny's Video* received a nomination for a 1993 European Film Award.

Film Festivals in Austria

Though not particularly rich, the Austrian film harvest of the 1992/93 season was presented by no less than three domestic festivals. On the one side, the independent "Austrian Film Days" under the direction of Reinhard Pyrker took place again in June in Wels, Upper Austria; on the other, the Vienna film festival "Viennale" in October featured premières of Austrian films, and finally, a government-subsidised unspooling of Austrian productions was held for the first time in December in Salzburg.

In late 1993, the "Viennale", Austria's largest film festival, was divided as the two managers failed to agree on a programme line. After some public controversy, their responsibilities were split up; in the future, the main event in October will take place under the sole direction of Wolfgang Aichberger, while co-director, Horwath, will be responsible for a series of "specials" throughout the year.

At the end of 1993, Axel Corti died; he was one of Austria's best-known directors. His greatest successes were mainly TV productions such as the émigré trilogy *Whither and Back* (*Wohin and zurück*) with its much-praised third part *Welcome in Vienna*. Corti's films for the cinema were not as successful; *The King's Whore* with Timothy Dalton remained his biggest international project.

In March 1994, the director Margareta Heinrich took her own life; she was only 43 years old. This committed film-maker had won success with documentaries on

Still from TOTSCHWEIGEN

TOP TEN GROSSING FILMS IN AUSTRIA: 1993

	Attendance
Jurassic Park	750,000
The Bodyguard	670,000
Sister Act	490,000
Hot Shots 2	460,000
Home Alone 2	440,000
Ein unmoralisches Angebot	440,000
Beauty and the Beast	390,000
Made in America	300,000
Sommersby	290,000
Sliver	250,000

Nicaragua as well as with features such as *Happy Eyes (Ihr glücklichen Augen)*. The final project she was working on was the documentary *The Shroud of Silence (Totschweigen)*.

SUSANNA PYRKER lives as a free-lance journalist in Vienna. She works for the Austrian News Agency APA and others and is a regular contributor to the German film journal "Filmecho-Filmwoche".

Recent and Forthcoming Films

INDIEN (India)

Script: Paul Harather, Josef Hader, Alfred Dorfer. Dir: Paul Harather. Phot: Hans Selikovsky. Players: Josef Hader, Alfred Dorfer. Prod: Dor-Film Vienna. 86 mins.

A repulsive member of the petty bourgeoisie and a careerist who has been touched by the yuppie Zeitgeist, tour the provinces as inspectors of restaurants and hotels. Their initial hostility evolves into a friendship which, in the end, endures even the intensive care unit.

DIE WAHLKÄMPFER (The Campaigners)

Script: Helmut Grasser, Hubert Canaval. Dir: Helmut Grasser. Phot: Peter Zeitlinger, Othmar Schmiderer. Prod: Allegro-Film Vienna. 118 mins.

A documentary about electioneers in the sinister political milieu of the Austrian right-wing party FPÖ which caused much

debate among critics for its uncritical style of presentation.

TOTSCHWEIGEN (The Shroud of Silence)

Script and Dir: Margareta Heinrich, Eduard Erne. Phot: Hermann Dunzendorfer. Prod: Extra-Film Vienna. 90 mins.

Ten days before the end of the Second World War 180 Jewish forced labourers were shot in the small Austrian village of Rechnitz. And even today the search for their corpses causes turmoil and fears in the community.

HÖHENANGST (Fear of Heights)

Script: Houchang Allahyari, Reinhard Jud, Tom Allahyari. Dir: Houchang Allahyari. Phot: Helmut Pirnat. Players: Fritz Karl, Dolores Schmidinger, Leon Askin. Prod: Epo-Film Vienna.

From the brutal, but easy-to-see-through subculture of the prison, Mario is thrust into the anonymity and temptations of

Vienna. He flees from the big city, only to find himself confronted with the rules and regulations of a village community.

JAMES ELLROY (James Ellroy)

Script: Reinhard Jud, Wolfgang Lehner. Dir: Reinhard Jud. Phot: Wolfgang Lehner. Players: James Ellroy, Bill Moseley. Prod: Fischer-Film Linz. 90 mins.

Trauma, ego, reality. James Ellroy: the eye of the novelist.

VOR LAUTER FEIGHEIT GIBT ES KEIN ERBARMEN (No Mercy from Cowards)

Script and Dir: Andreas Gruber. Phot: Hermann Dunzendorfer. Prod: Provinz Film International Wels. 100 mins.

A feature film about the breakout of prisoners from the Mauthausen concentration camp in the year 1945 and about how relentlessly the fugitives were hounded by the local population.

Producers

Allegro Film
Krummgasse 1a
1030 Vienna
Tel: (1) 712 50 36
Fax: (1) 712 50 36-20

Dor Film
Neulerchenfelder Straße 12
1160 Vienna
Tel: (1) 402 21 38
Fax: (1) 402 21 39

Epo Film
Ziernfeldgasse 9a
8010 Graz
Tel: (316) 37556
Fax: (316) 37556-75

Extrafilm
Große Neugasse 44
1040 Vienna
Tel: (1) 562 56 03
Fax: (1) 587 27 43

Lotus Film
Hietzinger Kai 169
1130 Vienna
Tel: (1) 876 26 42
Fax: (1) 876 26 45

MR-Film
Paracelsusgasse 9
1030 Vienna
Tel: (1) 712 32 53
Fax: (1) 712 32 53-32

Odelga Film
Landhausgasse 2/37
1010 Vienna
Tel: (1) 535 04 33
Fax: (1) 532 84 96

Satel Film
Kirchgasse 19
1070 Vienna
Tel: (1) 523 76 74
Fax: (1) 526 43 28

Schönbrunn Film
Neubaugasse 1
1070 Vienna
Tel: (1) 93 22 65
Fax: (1) 93 96 58

Star Film
Konstanze Weber-Gasse 3
5020 Salzburg
Fax: (662) 25 96 92

Terra Film
Lienfeldergasse 37
1160 Vienna
Tel: (1) 45 80 96
Fax: (1) 45 47 60

Thalia Film
Schliessmanngasse 4
1130 Vienna
Tel: (1) 877 65 66
Fax: (1) 876 52 87

Wega Film
Hägelingasse 13
1140 Vienna
Tel: (1) 982 57 42
Fax: (1) 982 58 33

Distributors

Buena Vista
Hermanngasse 18
1070 Vienna
Tel: (1) 526 94 67
Fax: (1) 526 94 68-5

Centifox
Neubaugasse 35
1070 Vienna
Tel: (1) 93 26 29
Fax: (1) 526 72 97

Columbia Tri-Star
Wallgasse 21
1060 Vienna
Tel: (1) 597 15 15
Fax: (1) 597 15 16

Constantin
Siebensterngasse 37
1070 Vienna
Tel: (1) 52128-0
Fax: (1) 52128-60

Einhorn Film
(also Filmwelt)
Raiffeisenstraße 34
6700 Bludenz
Tel: (5552) 67034
Fax: (5552) 63674-6

Filmhaus Stöbergasse
Stöbergasse 11-15
1050 Vienna
Tel: (1) 545 32 44-21
Fax: (1) 545 32 44-24

Filmladen
Mariahilferstraße 58

1070 Vienna
Tel: (1) 523 43 62
Fax: (1) 526 47 49

Smile Film
(also Cineart)
Lange Gasse 52
1080 Vienna
Tel: (1) 43 67 10
Fax: (1) 408 98 43

Stadtkino Verleih
Vogelweidplatz 14
1150 Vienna
Tel: (1) 98100-336
Fax: (1) 98100-376

Top Film
(also Kinowelt)
Lindengasse 56
1070 Vienna
Tel: (1) 526 19 19
Fax: (1) 526 19 18

UIP
Neubaugasse 1
1070 Vienna
Tel: (1) 523 46 31
Fax: (1) 526 75 48

Warner Bros
Zieglergasse 10
1070 Vienna
Tel: (1) 93 86 26
Fax: (1) 523 94 62

Useful Addresses

Austrian Film Commission
Stiftgasse 6
1070 Vienna
Tel: (1) 526 33 23
Fax: (1) 526 68 01

Bundesministerium für Unterricht und Kunst
(Ministry of Education and Arts)
Freyung 1
1014 Vienna
Tel: (1) 53120-2314
Fax: (1) 53120-2215

Cine Austria
(National Tourist Office/Location Office)
Margaretenstraße 1
1040 Vienna
Tel: (1) 58866-210
Fax: (1) 58866-20

Dachverband der Filmschaffenden
(Federation of Film Trade Associations)
(including Screenwriters, Directors, Cinematographers, Editors, Art Directors, Sound Engineers, Actors)
Pilgramgasse 22/53
1050 Vienna
Tel/Fax: (1) 587 81 14

Fachberband der Audiovisions- und Filmindustrie Österreichs
(Association of Audiovisual and Film Industry)
Wiedner Hauptstraße 63
1045 Vienna
Tel: (1) 50105-3010
Fax: (1) 50206-276

Österreichische Gesellschaft für Filmwissenschaft, Kommunikation und Medienforschung
(Austrian Society of Film Sciences,

Communications and Media Research)
Rauhensteingasse 5
1010 Vienna
Tel: (1) 512 99 36
Fax: (1) 513 53 30

Österreichisches Film Büro
(Austrian Film Office)
Columbusgasse 2
1100 Vienna
Tel: (1) 604 01 26
Fax: (1) 602 07 95

Österreichisches Filminstitut
(Austrian Film Fund)
Stiftgasse 6
1070 Vienna
Tel: (1) 526 97 30
Fax: (1) 526 97 30-440

VAM-Verwertungsgesellschaft Audiovisuelle Medien
(Collecting Society for Producers)
Neubaugasse 25

1070 Vienna
Tel: (1) 526 43 01
Fax: (1) 526 43 02-3

VDFS-Verwertungsgesellschaft Filmschaffende
(Collecting Society for Directors, Cinematographers, Editors, etc.)
Bösendorferstraße 4
1010 Vienna
Tel: (1) 505 96 24
Fax: (1) 504 48 95

Wiener Filmfinanzierungsfonds
(Vienna Film Fund)
Stiftgasse 6
1070 Vienna
Tel: (1) 526 50 88
Fax: (1) 526 50 88-20

BELGIUM

Patrick Duynslaegher

This was definitely not a vintage year for Belgian cinema. While a handful of locally reputed directors offered disappointing new films, the few newcomers could hardly be called promising. Flemish cinema certainly didn't produce a new *Daens* and neither did the French-speaking Walloon cinema deliver a work that could compete with *C'est arrivé près de chez vous* (*Man Bites Dog*). Not one new film made a strong impression. The most talked about event in Flemish cinema was, in fact, a television series, *Mother, What's the Meaning of Life?*, a fine social drama directed by Guido Henderickx. The most exciting film from Walloon was more than thirty years old: *Déjà s'envoie la fleur maigre* (1960). Hardly distributed when the film was made, the reissue of this exceptional neorealistic document was long overdue. Paul Meyer, who never got to make another film, describes the arrival of a new Italian

family in the Borinage coal mining region. The black-and-white cinematography has a distinctive, unobtrusive poetic style, the images have a looseness and immediacy and the whole film is of considerable historical interest.

Although it may not herald the birth of a genuine film-maker, **La Vie sexuelle des Belges** was in many ways the most promising among the first features. Jan Bucquoy is already a notoriously provocative artist, widely known as curator of the Belgian Academy of Underpants. His first film venture is quite mild compared to his well-publicised attacks on all things holy and royal. Bucquoy chronicles some thirty years – from the early 1950's to the late 1970's – in the life of Jan, a Flemish working-class lad. The best scenes cover his childhood and youth in a sharply and cruelly observed repressed Flemish household, dominated by a stingy mother. His sexual initiation on a camping site in the popular seaside resort of Blankenberge is hilarious and Bucquoy certainly makes the most of a ridiculous cheap budget (his film was privately financed except from some post-production money from the French-speaking community).

The film runs out of steam when the would-be-writer lands in 1960's Brussels. To our naïve provincial hero the Belgian capital looks like a paradise for sexual experiments and political activism. One moment he experiences free love, the next he learns how to fabricate a Molotov cocktail. Alas, even the 1960's don't last forever and without ever writing his great novel, Jan falls for the trappings of petty bourgeois life.

Already acclaimed for his short films, Marc-Henri Wajnberg made his feature debut with the colourful, richly atmospheric but dramatic undernourished **Just Friends**. The background for this tale of friendship, love and artistic ambition is the Antwerp art-scene of the end of the 1950's. At the centre: a talented tenor saxophonist (Josse De Pauw), who dreams of crossing the ocean and making it in that Mecca of Jazz, New York. In the meantime he has to adjust himself to a less exciting existence and unworthy commercial jobs; he must also make up his mind concerning the two women in his life (both belonging to another man). As a mood piece with a beautifully modulated soundtrack full of bebop and big band music, *Just Friends* delivers. Wajnberg is less successful when his melancholy film tries to incorporate the more tragic undercurrents of bohemian life (the heroin-addicted musician, for example).

Standing Ovation at Cannes

Lighting cameraman Charlie Van Damme has worked for Alain Resnais and Agnès Varda, but is best known for his long association with Belgian helmer André Delvaux. **Le Joueur de Violon**, his first attempt at direction, was an official entry in Cannes, where it was badly received by

the press but got a standing ovation at the gala presentation. It's the story of a classical violinist who, for reasons left frustratingly unclear, runs away from the gilded world of concert halls, cuts himself off from everyone and literally descends into the underworld – the Parisian metro where he leads the existence of a beggar. French actor Richard Berry impressively creates the illusion of playing the violin as a great virtuoso (it's really maestro Gidon Kremer on the immaculate soundtrack). Unfortunately this technical challenge gets lost in a woolly, free floating existential drama that doesn't move us one iota. Van Damme also builds his film to a mystical musical apotheosis that's rather difficult to swallow.

Ad Fundum, another first feature, begins with an intriguing premise – a college rite of passage that involves a lot of drinking and humiliation and goes terribly awry. Director Erik Van Looy demonstrates an impressive technical knowledge throughout but is hampered by a truly ridiculous script. One can also doubt the necessity of this kind of product favoured by a new generation of cynical, commercially oriented local talent. It's a Flemish imitation of second-rate Hollywood youth fare.

After an absence of twelve years from the screens, Paul Collet made his come-back with the dubious Aids-revenge fable **Close**. The less said about this self-proclaimed philosophical thriller, the better. With **Le Moulin de Daudet**, Samy Pavel offers an evocation of the life and work of Alphonse Daudet, the nineteenth-century author of sentimental tales of provincial life in the south of France. The film shares Daudet's passionate and sensuous impressionistic description of Provence, but the mix of biographical fragments and re-enactments of Daudet's short stories doesn't gel.

An even sadder affair is **L'Ordre du jour**. The highly talented Michel Khleifi was born in Palestine but has been based in Brussels since the early 1970's. After two remarkable films about rituals and conflicts in the Middle East, Khleifi goes wide of the mark. *L'Ordre du jour* is a heavy-handed satirical take on European bureaucracy. Kafkaesque cliches abound. The hero, Martin K.(!) is a civil servant at the Ministry of Public Works. In order to survive the pointless red tape and suffocating work atmosphere, he escapes in his dreams, staged by Khleifi as silly surrealistic fantasies. Right from scene one the film goes remorselessly to pieces.

Ritual and Dance

Finally two experimental art films of highly dissimilar quality. Veteran documentary film-maker Frans Buyens based **Tango Tango** on a stage performance by a theatre company for mentally handicapped people. The actors perform all kinds of symbolic rituals, centred on a funeral. We catch a glimpse of their dreams and longings (a fat girl poses as a diva; a boy imagines himself as a karate champion) but the film is so artificially stylised that even the expressive actors don't come through. Buyens, never a great stylist, has made some bizarre choices that handicap his film. Due to the elimination of all natural sound, the filmgoer is even more cut off from the performance and the rituals are even more dominated by the over-insistent nagging tango score.

The best Belgian film of the year was made by the internationally renowned choreographer Anne Teresa De Keersmaeker. **Achterland** is, of course, based on her most famous dance piece, but it's a real cinematic interpretation of her work. The stage is bare of props other than a line of functional Bauhaus chairs and small platforms that get moved around by

Still from Anne Teresa De Keersmaeker's
ACHTERLAND

the actors/stagehands. On stage is also the violinist Irvine Ardetti playing three solo violin sonatas by the Belgian composer Eugène Ysaye, or pianist Rolf Hind who plays piano *études* by Hungarian composer Gyorgy Ligeti. Eight dancers leap and roll through elaborate moves. The five women wear business suits and high heels or strike pin-up poses. Although they rebound from the floor as soon as they fling themselves to the ground, they seem to have more weighted movement than the three men who weave in and out of the repetitive dance cycles with extraordinary lightness and freedom in their bodies. The contrasts are extreme, exhilarating and surprisingly playful. Through hypnotic camerawork, extraordinarily precise black-and-white photography, brilliant editing and sound effects, De Keersmaeker explores even further the complex and enigmatic body language and the constantly changing spatial configurations of her original choreography.

PATRICK DUYNSLAEGHER is film critic for the leading Belgian weekly magazine, *Knack*. His articles have appeared in *Variety*, *Sight and Sound*, and other periodicals. Co-author of a book on André Delvaux.

Recent and Forthcoming Films

SUITE 16

Script: Lise Mayer and Charles Higson. Dir: Dominique Deruddere. Phot: Jean François Robin. Players: Pete Postlethwaite, Antonie Kamerling, Geraldine Pailhas.

Prod: Corsan Productions-Paul Breuls/Theorema Films-Frank Bak.

HEY STRANGER

Script: Sophie Simon and Peter Woditsch. Dir: Peter Woditsch.

Phot: Elfi Mikesch. Players: Vincent Rouche, Bénédicte Loyen, Hanna Schygulla, William Hickey, Julien Schoenaerts. Prod: Alert Films and Sophimages, Alfred Hürmer and Sophie Schoukens.

TAXANDRIA

Script: Frank Daniel, Raoul Servais and Alain Robbe-Grillet. Dir: Raoul Servais. Phot: Walther Van den ende and Gilberto Azevedo. Players: Armin Mueller-Stahl, Andrew Sachs, Richard Kattan, Cris Campion, Julien Schoenaerts, Katia Studt. Prod: Iblis Films, Bibo TV & Film, Les Productions Dussart.

BLENDED

Script and Dir: Mathieu Kassovitz. Phot: Pierre Aim. Players: Mathieu Kassovitz, Julie Maudouech, Hubert Kounde. Prod: Nomad Films. Christophe Rosignon, Jacques de Clercq, Dimitri de Clercq, Boudjema Dahmane.

THE SORROW OF BELGIUM

Script: Hugo Claus, based on his novel. Dir: Claude Goretta. Phot: Dominique Brenguier. Players: Marianne Basler, Rik Van Uffelen, Mathias Engelbeen, Marisa Berenson, Rüdiger Vogler. Prod: Kunst & Kino. Jan Van Raemdonck.

COMME UN AIR DE RETOUR

Script and Dir: Loredana Bianconi. Phot: Michel Baudour, Pierre Gordower. Players: Sarah Balthazart, Marie-Ange Dutheil, Pascal Greggory, Dora Van Der Groen. Prod: Paradise Films, ZDF, RTBF.

FARINELLI

Script: Gérard and Andrée Corbiau. Dir: Gérard Corbiau. Phot: Walther Van Den Ende. Players: Stefano Dionisi, Enrico Lo Verso, Elsa Zylberstein, Jeroen Krabbé, Caroline Cellier, Marianne Basler. Prod: Vera Belmont, Maria Theresa Gaeta, Dominique Janne.

ILHEU DE CONTENDA

Script: Leão Lopes and Jose Fanha. Dir: Leão Lopes. Phot:

João Lourenço, Camacho Costa, Pedro Wilson. Prod: Vermedia and Saga Film.

LOIN DES BARBARES

Script: Liria Bégéja and Philippe Barassat. Dir: Liria Bégéja. Phot: Patrick Blossier. Players: Dominique Blanc, Timo Flloko, Ronald Guttman, Sulejman Pitarka. Prod: Michèle Ray-Gavras. K.G. Productions (France), Urania Films (Italy), Prima Vista (Belgium).

LA PARTIE D'ECHECS

Script and Dir: Yves Hanchar. Phot: Denis Lenoir and Rémon Fromont. Players: Olivier Maes, Pierre Richard, Christian Maillet, Catherine Deneuve, James Wilby, Denis Lavant. Prod: Anne-Dominique Toussaint, Pascal Judelewicz.

SOUVENIRS D'ANVERS

Script: Didier Daeninckx. Dir: Marc Lobet. Phot: Michel Baudour. Players: Patrick Catalifo, Karen Van Parys, Valérie Leboutte, François Beukelaers. Prod: Jerome Minet, Maurice Brover, Hubert Toint.

THREE SHAKE A LEG STEPS TO HEAVEN

Script: Frank Feitler and Andy Bausch. Dir: Andy Bausch. Phot: Klaus Peter Weber and Kai Brauss. Players: Udo Kier, Désirée Nosbusch, Eddie Constantine, Richy Müller. Prod: Jani Thiltges, Paul Thiltges, Paul Kieffer, Gerhard Von Richthofen, Luc Dardenne.

Producers

Les Films de la Drève
Rue de la Victoire 175
1060 Brussels
Tel: 02/537.88.94

Kunst en Kino
Avenue Louise 32/4
1050 Brussels
Tel: 02/511.63.41
Fax: 02/512.68.74

Corsan Productions
J.De Hasquestraat 7
2000 Antwerpen
Tel: 03/234.25.18
Fax: 03/226.21.58

Independent Productions
Sphere Business Park
Doornveld 1 Box 42
1731 Zellik
Tel: 02/463.11.30
Fax: 02/466.94.60

Emotion Pictures
Volaardestraat 250
9200 Dendermonde
Tel: 052/41.37.83

Distributors

Alternative Films
Place Coligny 10
1030 Brussels
Tel: 02/242.19.30
Fax: 02/242.01.80

Belga Films
Rue Royale 241
1210 Brussels
Tel: 02/217.83.19
Fax: 02/217.43.65

Buena Vista International
Avenue E.Plasky 157
Tel: 02/737.17.11
Fax: 02/737.17.97

Cinélibre
Chaussée de Haecht 270
1030 Brussels
Tel: 02/245.87.00
Fax: 02/216.25.75

Columbia TriStar/Fox
Rue Souveraine 38
1050 Brussels
Tel: 02/512.39.14
Fax: 02/514.19.75

CNC
Chaussée de Haecht 60
1030 Brussels
Tel: 02/217.94.41
Fax: 02/217.94.59

Independent Film Distribution
Sphere Business Park
Doornveld 1 Box 42
1731 Zellik

Tel: 02/463.11.30
Fax: 02/466.94.60

Progrès Films
Rue Royale 243
1210 Brussels
Tel: 02/218.09.60
Fax: 02/218.43.54

UIP
Rue Royale 288
1030 Brussels
Tel: 02/218.52.06
Fax: 02/218.79.33

Warner Bros.
Boulevard Brand Whitlock 42
1200 Brussels
Tel: 02/735.42.42
Fax: 02/735.49.19

Concorde Film
Terhulpsesteenweg 130
1050 Brussels
Tel: 02/675.20.50
Fax: 02/675.30.76

Classic Films
Visserij 110
9000 Gent
Tel: 09/233.67.97

Liberty Films
Rue de Praetere 14
1050 Brussels
Tel: 02/644.00.08
Fax: 02/644.38.97

Movie Max
Verlatstraat 10
2000 Antwerp
Tel: 03/248.74.73
Fax: 03/238.44.27

Useful Addresses

Flanders Image
Handelskaai, 18 box 2
1000 Brussels
Tel: 02/219.32.22
Fax: 02/219.34.02

Wallonie Bruxelles Image
Boulevard Adolphe Max 13
1000 Brussels
Tel: 02/223.23.04
Fax: 02/218.34.24

Ministry of the Flemish Community
Koloniënstraat 29-31
1000 Brussels
Tel: 02/510.34.11
Fax: 02/510.36.51

Communauté Française de Belgique
Boulevard Léopold II, 44
1080 Brussels
Tel: 02/413.22.21
Fax: 02/413.20.68

Decatron
(technological support and general contractor in multiplex theatres)
Kampioenschapslaan 1
1020 Brussels
Tel: 02/478.31.97
Fax: 02/478.33.85

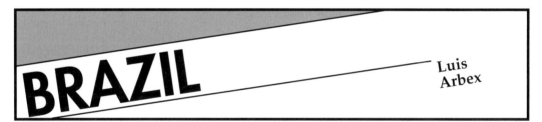

BRAZIL

Luis Arbex

This industry has finally been reborn from the ashes – the former impeached government having eliminated the basis of domestic movie making, which suffered the most violent economic censorship in its history. The new Ministry of Culture has distributed US$13 million to resume production. Twelve new films are about to be screened and many more are in progress. A seminar bringing together Brazilian and American independent producers (Grund, Scahmus, Stark, Tope and Araki) traced the aesthetics, marketing, budgets and ideal modelling of a successful film pointing out the ways to be followed.

Leon Cakoff's 18th São Paulo International Film Festival remains remarkable each year thanks to the talented Cakoff's excellent choice. Two hundred highlights of world cinema were screened with the aid of the State Secretary of Culture and the British Council. An unique non-competitive event in our history.

Public attendance dropped 2.5% and admissions increased by 2.43%. Box-office grosses dropped to US$112.5 million. The number of cinemas is 146; 282 multiplexes opened at shopping centres; and the average ticket price went up to US$1.95 (source: Consórcio Severiano Ribeiro & Marcondes).

DR. LUIS ARBEX won a scholarship in the U.S. for postgraduate medical training and remained there for eight years. Now retired, he dedicates his time to cinema research and travelling as a genuine movie buff.

Recent Films

BUCCANEER SOUL (Alma Corsária)

Script, Dir, Phot: Carlos Reichenbach. Players: Bertrand Duarte, Jandir Ferrari, Andréa Richa, Mariana de Moraes. Prod: Donald Ranvaud/Serene Prods. 116 mins.

Torres and Xavier, childhood friends, celebrate the publication of their joint collection of poems in a bar, inviting their publisher and his girlfriend, a potential suicide among others. A flashback to 1957 describes the beginning of their friendship. Xavier is introduced to the secrets of a lower-middle class district, moves to the coast in 1959, has his first physical and sentimental experience with a sensual woman. As the farce progresses, humorous situations arise involving the failed suicide and the newly-arrived prophet who introduces a flash-back of memories of 1968 — political upheavals, drugs, the encounter with the activist Oscar, an intense romance with the lovely "warrior" Eliana. End of the party: the editor's girl is drunk, and the failed suicide is trying to take advantage of the situation when a charming angel appears in the form of a woman looking for Torres, who finally embraces his destiny.

LAMARCA

Script: Sérgio Rezende, Alfredo Oroz. Dir: Sérgio Rezende. Players: Paulo Betti, Carla Camurati, José de Abreu, Deborah Evelyn. Prod: Riofilme. 125 mins.

Carlos Lamarca (1937-1971), the sharp-shooting army captain at odds with the country's course in 1964, joins the armed opposition's group against military dictatorship. He deserts and steals seventy rifles. Living underground, he gets involved in assaults and kidnappings (the Swiss ambassador), undermining the régime and stirring up the press. After sending his family away to Cuba, he falls in love with a guerrilla girl, but she kills herself when trapped by the army. An informer leads the soldiers to the captain's hiding-place ...

THE THIRD BORDER OF THE RIVER (A Terceira Margem do Rio)

Andréa Richa and Bertrand Duarte in ALMA CORSÁRIA
photo: Alexandre de Oliviera

Script and Dir: Nelson Pereira dos Santos. Phot: Guimarães Rosa. Players: Ilya São Paulo, Sonja Saurin, Barbara Brandt, Jofre Soares. 115 mins.

Clever interweaving of four different "magic realist" stories.

SAVAGE CAPITALISM (Capitalismo Selvagem)

Script: André Klotzel, Djalma Batista. Dir: Klotzel. Players: Fernanda Torres, José Mayer, Marisa Orth, Marcelo Tass.

A female reporter is writing the story of a mining manager and his enterprise. She discovers that he is the only survivor of a slaughtered Indian village. Recognising his origin they start a love affair that will convert him, but events conspire to destroy their relationship.

VACANCY FOR GENTEEL LADIES (Vagas Para Moças de Fino Trato)

Script: Alcione Araujo. Dir: Paulo Thiago. Players: Norma Bengell, Lucélia Santos, Maria Zilda Bethlem, Paulo Cesar Pereio. Prod: Riofilmes.

Comedy about a piano teacher and two girl pupils.

THE CURSE OF SANPAKU (A Maldição de Sanpaku)

Script: Sérgio Rezende, José Joffily, Paul Helm. Dir: Joffily. Players: Felipe Camargo, Patrícia

Pillar, Roberto Bomtempo, Sérgio Britto.

After working for years for a precious-stone smuggler, a youth scores by stealing a valuable emerald. Pursued by a gang he takes refuge in a schoolmate's home ...

THE GOSPEL ACCORDING TO THE OPPRESSED (Cristo Procurado)

Dir: Anim. Background: Rui de Oliveira. Prod: Denoy de Oliveira for Palmares/Beca/Lestepe.

Ironic parable about the reappearance of Christ in a big Latin-American city.

ONCE UPON A TIME ... (Era Uma Vez ...)

Script and Dir: Arturo Uranga. Players: Eduardo Felipe, Rodrigo Penna, Anna Cotrim, Oberdan Junior.

Fairy tale about three youngsters who set out into the world like wandering knights looking for adventure, and a girl-thief joins them along the way.

ATLANTIS OCEAN

Script and Dir: Francisco de Paula. Phot: Adib Lufti. Players: Nuno Leal Maia, Dercy Gonçalves, Antonio Abujamra. Prod: Naive Productions.

HEAR THIS SONG (Veja Esta Canção)

TOP TEN GROSSING FILMS IN BRAZIL: 1993

	Rentals (millions of cruzeiros)
Jurassic Park	9,769
Indecent Proposal	4,561
Aladdin	4,300
Scent of a Woman	3,214
Bram Stoker's Dracula	2,042
The Bodyguard	2,042
A Few Good Men	1,665
The Last of the Mohicans	1,615
Dennis the Menace	1,263
Sliver	1,164

Script: Carlos Diegues, Rosane Svartman, Fabiana Egrejas, Walter Lime Jr, Miguel Faria Jr, Euclydes Martinho. Dir: Carlos Diegues. Players: Debora Bloch, Pedro Cardoso, Leon Goes, Carla Alexandar. Prod: Mapa/Banco Nacional/TV Cultura. 110 mins.

Inspired by four songs written by Gil, Ben Jor, Caetano Veloso and Chico Buarque, this portmanteau film is the first joint venture with TV.

Distributors

Look Filmes
c/o Denise Jancar
Rua Felix Sousa
71 - Campo Belo
São Paulo 04612-080
Tel: (011) 536-9366
Fax: (011) 61-2121

ALVORADA
Av. Ipiranga
318 - São Paulo
Tel: (011) 288-8226
Fax: (011) 239-3982

Paris Filmes
Av. Pacaembu
1702 - São Paulo
Tel: (011) 864-3155
Fax: (011) 872-4498

F. J. Lucas
Av. São João
1588 - São Paulo
Tel: (011) 220-5622

Fax: (011) 222-8679

Pandora (C.A.C.A.V.)
Rua Nebraska
335 - São Paulo - 045 60-010
Tel: (011) 530-0839
Fax: (011) 530-0839

Belas Artes Cinematográficas Ltda
Rua do Triunfo
34 - São Paulo
Tel: (011) 221-3080
Fax: (011) 220 6062˙

United International Pictures
Av. São João
799 - São Paulo - 010 35 100
Tel: (011) 222 1411
Fax: (011) 220 7439

Columbia TriStar Films of Brasil Inc.
Rua do Triunfo
134/5° - São Paulo - 01212 903
Tel: (011) 200 4022
Fax: (011) 221 7423

Fox Filmes do Brasil
Av. São João
802 - Conj. 11 - São Paulo - 01036 000
Tel: (011) 222 1411
Fax: (011) 220 7439

Warner Bros.
Rua Conselheiro Crispiniano
217 Conj. 62 - São Paulo
Tel: (011) 221 7455
Fax: (011) 221 7811

Top Tape
Pça da República, 146,
7° andar - 01045 000 - Sãop Paulo
Tel: (011) 257 6300

Pandora Filmes
Films do Estação
Rua Augusta
1475 - São Paulo
Tel: (011) 288 6780

Norma Bengell in VAGAS PARA MOCAS DE FINO TRATO

BULGARIA

Ivan Stoyanovich

Everybody feels confident that the way to modern film production lies in privatisation, the fast transition of interests towards authors. Under the copyright Law of August 1, 1993, Bulgarian film-makers have the rights to a movie, which are controlled by the producer and performing studio respectively, if the authors grant their rights for production and distribution to it.

This is the policy of action now of the newly founded associations of independent producers and distributors who have the free choice of working fully or partially with state capital, their own private funds, or with foreign producers and distributors as well as on the basis of domestic and external co-productions. The National Film Centre with the Ministry of Culture is the main co-ordinating body, organising commissions of art and economic specialists for the different genres, who approve or disprove of projects by secret ballot.

The State, respectively the Ministry of Culture, the Film Centre and the commissions, are not involved with capital investments, co-productions or orders on the part of foreign producers, commissioners and distributors who get into direct contact with the authors, producers and studios that have aroused their interests.

The practical implementation of this promising reform, however, still meets with considerable obstacles: a government and parliament composed in their majority of retrograde legislators who hinder the process of private initiative and degrade the nation's cultural needs; the mistrust of foreign investors concerning the Bulgarian industry as such given today's economic and political situation including the film industry: the hard process of reorientation of authors and producers, both private and state, inheriting a false and clumsy bureaucratic system, and last but not least, the impoverished Bulgarian state continuing in vain to try to cope with inflation, the rising dollar, the prices of food, not to mention capital investments in the art of the cinema still needing a crutch to help it stagger into the post-Communist era. It's naive to believe that if an average feature film here already costs some 16,000,000 Levs (in mid 1994 that means nearly three million dollars) , a feature film can ever be made by the Bulgarian director, hand in hand with the Bulgarian producer, even with some state subsidies.

And yet, as though from Pandora's box, Bulgarian films do emerge, some of which even venture beyond the borders of the country. It is a hopeful sign that the toughness of the Bulgarian directors, the energy of the studios and the National Film Centre, along with the assessment of the western managers are reviving the Bulgarian cinema. Not just the feature film, but also the documentary and especially animation.

This hope has its proof in such films as Rangel Vulchanov's **Fatal Tenderness,** supported by French capital - an absurd and picturesque philosophic look at death and love; French funds also supported Peter Popzlatev's **Something in the Air** - love and death again but this time in the convention range of Alain Robbe Grillet. Both works will be embarking on a tour of Europe and America. Producer Plament Maslarov, with a team of young directors, scriptwriters and cameramen (Christian Nachev, Christian Simeonov, Emil Tanev and Georgi Todorov) shot the Bulgarian-French production **The Frontier** - a brave, even cruel criticism of violence in the Bulgarian army of the recent past. Another

Still from DISASTROUS TENDERNESS, with Lydia Deleva

sharp criticism of the Communist past had its premiere in 1994 - director Evgeni Mihailov's **Canary Season**, a tragic personal account of family members morally crushed by the Bolshevik system. I wish to emphasise that these films also had their premieres abroad, in Vienna, Berlin, the U.S.A. and Hungary, and the responses were pretty good.

Re-make of The Goat Horn

The new version of **The Goat Horn** has also been completed, helped by French capital and produced by Nikolai Volev. The plot developing during the Ottoman oppression times acquires entirely new dimensions in Volev's eyes: the divine sense of goodness incorporated in man and the purity of love rise against the dogmas of creed and vendetta.

A more superficial solution is offered by Nidal Algafari's guest performance in **La Donna e Mobile** and Angel Toshev's **Pantoudi**

Italian capital has helped the current filming of **Love Dreams** from the story by Stefan Zweig, directed by Ivan Nichev - a promising artistic drama set in the 1920's.

Before the end of 1994 we expect **The Black Swallow** by Georgi Dyulgerov, Hristo Hristov's **Sulamit**, Lyudmil Kirkov's **A Nameless Band II**, the **Late Full Moon** by Eduard Zahariev - all of them well-known, talented directors revealing a broad range of thematic and narrative preferences.

There are also completed co-productions, orders and services with numerous foreign companies such as **The Investigation of Commissar Catani** - the sixth series in Angelo Zemella's **Octopus,** Thierry Laillon's **Hommes de nuit**, Andreas Pantzi's **The Slaughter of the Cock** (a Cyprus, Italian and Greek co-production) and **Bird of Prey** from Sneak Review Productions and BM5 Bulgarian Productions. There is little reason to call all this an upsurge but in any case there is some light in the tunnel of the grave overall economic crisis in Bulgaria - it shows the cinema has a chance to dig its own tunnel!

IVAN STOYANOVICH has been a film critic for 35 years and has numerous publications and books to his credit. Also author of a series of literary works, plays and scripts. For 32 years he has been the Editor-in-Chief of the Bulgarian Films Magazine, and for the past 2 years of the Intercine Magazine. In 1992 he was cultural director of the Bulgarian National Television and in 1993–94 he became Managing Director of Animation Film Studio "Sofia".

Albena Ivanova and Ivailo Tzvetkov in LOVE DREAMS

Georgi Dyulgerov, director of THE BLACK SWALLOW

TOP TEN GROSSING FILMS IN BULGARIA: First Quarter of 1994

Basic Instinct
Mrs Doubtfire
Robin Hood: Men in Tights
Striking Distance
Cliffhanger
Demolition Man
Undercover Blues
Fatal Instinct
Dennis the Menace
The Addams Family 2

Forthcoming Films

LYUBOVNI SUNISHTA (Love Dreams)

Script from Stefen Zweig. Prod, Script and Dir: Ivan Nichev.

CHERNATA LYASTOVITSA (The Black Swallow).

Prod: Radiovision Ltd. Script: Georgi Dyulgerov and Svetoslav Ovcharov. Phot: Atanas Yanakiev. Players: Ivailo Hristov, Tsvetan Angelov. *A drama involving gypsy characters, appealing against family and civil feud.*

SULAMIT.

Prod: ET Slaval-7. Script: Vladimir Daverov. Dir: Hristo Hristov. *The life and death of the historically famous actress Rosa Herskovic.*

ORKESTUR BEZ IME II (A Nameless Band II).

Prod: ET META BM 4. Script:

Stanislav Stratiev. Dir: Lyudmil Kirkov.

ZAKUSNIALO PULNOLUNIE (Late Full Moon)

Prod: ET PLAMEN. Script and Dir: Eduard Zahariev. *A modern psychological drama.*

TRAK-TRAK (Tap-Tap).

Prod: Import-Commerce-Export. Script and Dir: Iliya Kostov. *An amusing adventure story.*

Useful Addresses

Ministry of Culture
17 A.Stamboliiski Blvd
Sofia 1000
Tel: 86111
Fax: 877339
International Relations:
Tel: 802430

National Film Centre
2a Dondukov Str.,
Sofia 1000
Tel. 883831
Fax: 873626

Bulgarian National Film Library
36 Gurko Street
Sofia 1000
Tel: 359 2 876004

Union of Bulgarian Film-makers
37 Exarch Joseph Street
Sofia 1000
Tel: 359 2 878956
International Relations:
Tel: 359 2 882860

Boyana Film Studio
16 Boyana Films
Sofia
Tel: 359 2 596056, 597159
Fax: 359 2 593115
Telex: 22367

Vreme Film Studio
9 Zaimov Street
Sofia 1000
Tel: 359 2 442823

Ekran Studio
7 Gavril Genov Street
Sofia 1000
Tel: 359 2 883833, 870871

Animation Film Studio Sofia
1616 Sofia
Kinocenter Boyana
Tel: 595061, 58131/580
Fax: 597165

CAMBODIA — Fred Marshall

No country in the world has more landmines buried in its soil than Cambodia, and no country has so many amputees per capita as this tragic land. A recent Canadian documentary about landmines and their victims in Cambodia, was made by the NFBC.

The **10th Dancer**, a highlight of last year's Hawaii International Film Festival, is a stirring profile of an instructor and dancer in Cambodia's Royal Ballet School. It is a joint venture between the BBC and Australia's Channel 9.

The Saw Wheel, made in Pnomh Penh last year, features Dr. Haing Ngor (Oscar-winner for *The Killing Fields*) and a prominent actress of the 1970's, Dy Saveth. The budget was $500,000. Saveth is the sister of Haing Ngor, and the film is a contemporary story of love and money, Cambodian-style. It offers an insight into their occidental culture, and was written and directed by Jennifer Tien, a Cambodian-born American.

Another recent Cambodian release is **This Is My Mother** (*A nee mae Chan*), a melodrama, shot in colour and similar to Thai cinema in tone. It involves an elderly woman and her surviving family. *This Is My Mother* stars the daughter-in-law of Hun Sen, the Prime Minister who also served as producer of the picture.

Slick, Slow, but Stunning

Rithy Panh returned to his native country and with the assistance of the Cambodian National Film Centre in Pnom Penh, took his crew and equipment through the region, filming exteriors. The result is **People of the Rice Fields** (*Neak Sri*), a slow, slick but stunning debut film of one hundred minutes in colour, which illustrates the symbiotic relationship between rice and human beings with only passing acknowledgement to recent politics. It may not match *The Scent of the Green Papaya* or *The White Page*, but it has created an awareness of artistic sensitivity in these troubled times in Cambodia.

Various foreign film-makers have visited the region recently, among them Ron Fricke and Mark Magidson (*Koyaanisqatsi, Chronos*), who shot scenes in Cambodia for their new release, *Baraka*.

FRED MARSHALL is an American film-maker who has lived in southeast Asia for many years and is a familiar figure on the festival circuit.

Telefilm

Canada

Telefilm Canada,
a major partner
in the Canadian
film and television
industry

Telefilm Canada, involved
at every stage of Canadian film
and television production.

Canadian Broadcast Program
Development Fund

Feature Film Fund

Feature Film Distribution Fund

Versioning Assistance Fund

Canadian Production Marketing
Assistance Fund

Industrial and Professional
Development Fund

Special Production Fund

Production Revenue Sharing
Program

Canadian Film and Video Festivals
Grants Fund

Official Co-productions

Canadian Participation in
International Film Events

Closed Captioning for the
Hearing Impaired

Foreign Launch Fund

Scriptwriting Assistance Program

Head Office
Tour de la Banque Nationale
600 de la Gauchetière Street West
14th Floor
Montréal, Quebec
H3B 4L8
Telephone: (514) 283-6363
Fax: (514) 283-8212

Los Angeles
9350 Wilshire Boulevard
Suite 400
Beverly Hills, California 90212
U.S.A.
Telephone: (310) 859-0268
Fax: (310) 276-4741

Other offices
Halifax
Toronto
Vancouver

London
Paris

℮ Telefilm Canada

CANADA

Gerald Pratley

This was the year when more travellers than ever crowded the Yellow Brick Road, now renamed in the interest of being PC, the Information Highway, which in turn, is now referred to as the "hypeway". The Canadian searchers going south, anxiously looking for production deals in film and television, pass the Americans coming north to play an even larger role in their domination and direction of the market here, and to swell the tide of location shooting. There are no thunderstorms, however, to impede the traffic. The sun is continually shining these days and everyone is smiling on their way to the Stock Exchange. A visitor alighting on the glittering road adorned with satellite dishes and boxes, optic fibres, digital cables, and integrated computer and communication networks, all pouring forth American programming and movies, might well wonder what has been happening during the past twelve months.

Appearances are deceptive. The main cinemas may be filled with Hollywood films and the TV screens may be predominantly American, but the media tell a different story. A person has only to pick up newspapers and magazines and turn on the radio and TV to discover that all is well with the film industry. Under the title CANADIAN PRODUCTION the headlines tell the story: "A crafty generation of Canadian producers, steeled by bitter experiences during the failed 1970's movie boom, is carving out a lucrative role in US television." (*Report on Business*) "Skyvision Entertainment Scoops F/X series" (*CP*). This we learn, means that Canada's great brewery, John Labatt, the company which brought us *RoboCop: The Series* (d. Paul Lynch) will now film 22 episodes of *F/X* this year with Brian Dennehy and Bryan Brown. "*Tekwar* is here. William Shatner, with his Hollywood players, will make the new series here for Atlantis" (*The Sun*). "Alliance's top billing unchallenged at home" (*The Globe and Mail*), telling us that it will make the $30m *Johnny Mnemonic* with Keanu Reeves, Ice T and the great Dolph Lundgren. Further, Alliance will produce three films for Universal in the first multipicture Canada-U.S. deal! Flying in from Hollywood is another contender in the Canadian Film category, none other than *Lonesome Dove: The Series*, to be filmed in Calgary. And we are still anxiously awaiting the first of the series of Canadian-made movies taken from Harlequin Romances!

One Minute Items

In our cinemas the only glimpse of Canadian history we see are one minute items shown with the adverts, sponsored by the CFB Foundation and the Post Office.

Still from FOR THE MOMENT, *released by Malofilm*

Mia Kirshner in Atom Egoyan's EXOTICA   *photo: Johnnie Eisen/Alliance*

The latest depicts Sam Steele, legendary figure of the North West Mounted Police, seeing off an American prospector who insists on bringing his guns into the country. No one is making a film about Steele. But Paragon has made *Sodbusters* with Kris Kristofferson and the $39m *Wyatt Earp* with Kevin Costner! And it was Paragon who led the parade of companies on the trip to the stock market – after its second offering it sold off some 38% of its shares.

Alliance Communications, which during its lifetime has received more than $6m in public funding, was the next to go, raising $34m with one third of its shares. Then Montréal's Cinar Films went public, selling off 36.7% of its total shares; this 2.5m share offering raised $13.5m. They were followed by Malofilm, Atlantis and Imax. The latter "Big Picture" Corporation has been sold to the U.S. company WGIM Acquisition, who merged Imax with Douglas Trumbull's high-tech company. Trumbull calls the deal "a unique marriage creating exciting productions that cannot be duplicated on any other system". The Imax principals,

Graeme Ferguson, Robert Kerr, Bill Shaw and Roman Kroitor, who founded the company, will remain with the new group "as consultants".

Hot on the heels of these travellers comes Seagram of Montréal, now anxious to raise its 15% stake in Time-Warner by mounting a $20b takeover bid! Edgar Bronfman Jr., now chief executive of the company, has taken some of the cash flow from its du Pont holding to finance his fascination with the movies. However, he has drawn fire from Seagram shareholders and Wall Street investors who fear the $6 billion company will be overwhelmed in the cut-throat entertainment world at a time when Seagram's main business, liquor and beverage, is generating disappointing returns. Good news from Cineplex Odeon Corp.: four years ago the company was almost bankrupt. Allan Karp and his team have turned the company around and made a profit of $969,000 on a cash flow of $36.6m and a $380m refinancing package from the banks.

The number of titles, production deals

and financial manipulations announced with the U.S. networks and studios would fill a great many pages in the IFG. On the one hand, this flood of activity is seen as a bold move on the part of producers to explore investment initiatives here and in the U.S., France and the U.K., and to become less reliant on government loans and subsidies; this public money calls for them to show something of Canada on the screen, which they are greatly reluctant to do. It could be argued that with private money they can do what they like and if they are successful in pursuing profits and lining pockets it is entirely their own business. This will strengthen the U.S. in its resolve to get the Canadian government to drop all subsidies to film and TV, and the other "cultural industries", under the conditions of NAFTA, being able to point out that our production companies are raising their own funds.

Being responsible to shareholders, however, means paying dividends, and if difficulties arise in doing so, dancing to the requirements of the networks and the speciality channels will undoubtedly result in lowering the already mediocre standards of TV programming.

Why fight to make films and pro- grammes Canadian when it is so much easier to be American? Richard Borchiver, president of Paragon, defends this movement: "It's going to allow us to invest in non-Canadian content shows. If we are not in this we'll be little service companies for the rest of our lives." Imagine the future: they will become big service companies, in which well-trained, well- paid technicians, and the like will be slaves to the American production mills. ...

Québec is Different

The genuinely indigenous TV-film-series **Filles de Caleb (Emilie)** and **Blanche** (both directed by Jean Beaudin) – the story of a nurse who wanted to become a doctor in Montréal of the 1920's – has not only averaged over more than three million viewers a week (making it the most watched series in Québec television

history) it is also extremely popular in France and has been sold to over 50 countries.

Beaudin's latest series **Shehaweh**, also with Marina Orsini, has too, found millions of viewers in that province and has sold well abroad. This time the setting is seventeenth-century Lower Canada and the subject the harrowing life of a young Iroquois woman, brutally abducted from her village and taken to the settlement of Ville Marie – later the city of Montréal. Not only this, but Montréal producer Marie- Josée Raymond has embarked on an ambi- tious series in which Mazo de la Roche's very British-Canadian *Jalna (Whiteoaks)* novels are being filmed in French for the network France-2. Among the French and Québec cast is the lovely Danielle Darrieux, now the matriarch of French cinema. According to her "the French love *Jalna* and know all the characters by heart. We would sit around and talk about them by the hour."

In Memoriam

John Candy, the likeable, affable, kind and generous comedian, died of a heart attack while on location in Durango, Mexico, acting in *Wagons East*. He was 43. He made his name in the SCTV Canadian TV comedy series, the result being a call to Hollywood where his many films brought him a large following. He was immensely popular throughout Canada, and the country mourned his passing. The shock of his death brought Toronto to a standstill; his funeral service was televised and the media paid tribute to him in pages of testimony and with hours of programming on his life and work. His first film as a director, *Hostage for the Day* (U.S. filmed in Toronto), was shown a week later. Francis Mankiewicz, without doubt our finest film- maker (*Les Bons Debarras, Conspiracy of Silence*), a quiet and gentle man, the consummate artist, died of cancer in Montréal. He was 49. "All my films," he once said, "are rooted in a specific reality, in something I'm familiar with. I think Canadians can best understand themselves by telling their own stories intensely and truthfully. Every time we try to compete by stepping out of our own reality we fail." And Gordon Sparling, who began telling our smaller stories back in the 1930's with the Canadian Cameo series and worked on *Carry On Sergeant!* with Bruce Bairnsfather in 1928, died in Kingston, Ontario, aged 93. Only La Cinémathèque Québécoise noted his passing and paid tribute to him.

Headlines

Canadian Film Sector Pleased with GATT. The industry breathes a sigh of relief over the exclusion of entertainment from world trade agreement. Said Robert Lantos: "It clearly proclaims that nations are protecting their culture and the highways on which it travels. It's the outcome we've been hoping for." *500-channel TV Dooms Canadian Content Rule.* Keith Spicer, head of the CRTC, told CBC listeners that "We see our content rules withering away. We can't keep the Americans out. What we can do is provide better Canadian shows." *U.S. Films Take 80% of Québec Box-office.* In urging exhibitors to give more time to Québec films, Roger Frappier said, "I think our films should have access to the best screens at the best possible times of the year." *Canadian TV's Beasts of Burden have gone: E.N.G. and Street Legal, Canadian stories written to the American formula, have ended.* "Compared to American shows they were nothing to be ashamed of," said the *Globe and Mail.* "Compared to the BBC's *Between the Lines* they needed a ton of work." A series about hospital life is planned for later this year.

Changes and Takeovers

Rogers Communications (cable, etc) has paid over $3 billion for Maclean Hunter Ltd. (publishing, cable, TV, FUND for screenwriting) and will "invest $13.5m in film production ... " in the light of the Paramount-Viacom merger, Investment Canada will review its effect on Paramount's Famous Players cinema circuit and on Ginn, the educational publishing house also owned by Paramount. As if to forestall any government action (which is unlikely) Viacom has rushed in

with a plan to invest $5m in Canadian production ... the Festival of Festivals' name has been changed by its Board to the Toronto International Film Festival. ...

John Grierson cannot rest in peace it seems. A play, *Public Lies*, by Robert Fothergill pillories him for his patriotic passions, among other matters. At least he hasn't been forgotten as many once influential individuals are these days. ... Yves Simoneau, always a follower of U.S. movies, has found a home in LA and made three excellent films: *Cruel Doubt* (NBC 1992), *Mother's Boys* (Miramax/Dimensions)(CBS 1993) and *Amelia Earhart* (Turner Pictures 1994), an exceptionally fine film with Diane Keaton, and screenplay by the Canadian, Anna Sandor.

Telefilm

Telefilm provides government funding – primarily through loans and equity investment – for development, production and distribution of films and TV programmes. Executive director, Pierre DesRoches (who left Telefilm in the spring) said of the past year that "we have tried to reconfirm our cultural responsibility, particularly in the light of GATT, NAFTA, and their cultural exemptions. Changes in the production of film and TV from international trade agreements to the impending 500-channel universe means that indigenous productions must become even more original and distinctively Canadian, while at the same time striving to compete more successfully on the international market."

Despite financial restraints Telefilm is budgeted this year at $152m including $122.3m in funds from Parliament and $20m in projected revenues together with $8.5m carried over from last year. This is divided into $24.5m for feature production, $65m for the broadcast fund and $13m for the distribution fund. DesRoches said Telefilm remains committed to Canadian films but acknowledged that despite some improvement box-office receipts remain poor, especially for English-track productions. "Nevertheless, we must continue; a

Adèle Gray and Michael Stevens in THE RETURN OF TOMMY TRICKER, the fifteenth in Rock Demers's "Tales for All" series   *photo: Jean Demers*

country without films to show to its people is not a country; it's just a geographic place." No one has been better as Telefilm's Executive Director; DesRoches will be missed, and hard to replace.

The NFB: 55th Anniversary Year

Speaking at a special anniversary press conference the Government Film Commissioner, Joan Pennefather, said: "The NFB's capacity to adapt to change has been severely tested and we have met the challenges. Responding to reductions to our Parliamentary appropriation we have reduced our permanent workforce by 13.7% through retirements and voluntary departures. We have scaled down our administration, established new distribution partnerships, eliminating certain costs, and doing more with less to deal with a cut to our overall budget of almost $7m." This

reduced last year's budget of $81.2m to $74.8m. "In making these changes," said Pennefather, "our primary goal has been to maintain and if possible increase our funds for production. Our major reason for being is to make films. ... "

Among the more than 40 films in production are: *Animation* from Oscar-winner John Weldon (*Scant Sanity*), and from Oscar-nominees Richard Condie (*Playroom*) and Ishu Patel (*The Tibetan Book of the Dead*). Documentaries cover such current subjects as the future of the family (Bill MacGillivray's *For Generations to Come*), the failure of some ambitious city planning projects (Bay Weyman's *Return to Regent's Park*), troubled teens seeking to rebuild their lives (Jeremiah Hayes's *Our Words*) and the cultural fate of aboriginal communities (Hugh Brody's *The Washing of Tears*). Also, *by Woman's Hand*, a film by

Still from LOUIS 19

Pepita Ferrari and Erna Buffie about a little-known group of 1920's women artists, *Baseball Girls*, Lois Siegel's affectionate history of women's participation in baseball and softball, and *Third Gender*, Margaret Westcott's exploration of lesbian history around the world.

The Atlantic and Pacific coasts are the settings for four dramatic features: *Double Happiness* (d. Mina Shum), the film industry itself in *Paint Cans* (d. Paul Donovan), two visions of the future, *Cyberteens in Love* (d. Brett Dowler) and *Anchor Zone* (d. Andrée Pelletier). History and prehistory alike have inspired the directors of *Canada Remembers*, Terry Filgate's four-part series on the 50th anniversary of the end of the Second World War), *Summer of '67*, Donald Winkler's encounters with members of the 'sixties generation, and *Marco Polo*, Roger Hart's tale of the Canadian ship that was once the fastest in the world. Many of the NFB's films are made in collaboration or in association with leading producers and broadcasters – NHK Japan, Stornoway Productions, CBC, A&E, Sphinx Productions, PBS and Tamarack Productions.

In Montréal (reports *Canadian Press*) it's a far cry from the days when a National Film Board projectionist would travel from town to town showing scratchy films on a temperamental projector. At the CineRobotheque, the new VFB viewing

centre in Montréal, movie buffs can lean back in a swivel chair outfitted with stereo speakers and order up a film on a computerised selector. Not some splotchy fifth-generation videocassette copy, but a state-of-the-art videodisc. And taking orders inside a glass booth is a dream bureaucrat: an obedient robot that retrieves the discs, plays them and returns them to their proper slot. "The public will have access to NFB films that have rarely been seen – and in less than a minute," says Pierre Ducharme, director of the NFB Montréal centre. Ducharme says that in two years, the centre will use fibre optics to deliver the same service across Canada. And fibre-optics technology could soon bring NFB's library to the fingertips of anyone who has a phone, a computer and a TV monitor. The federal agency estimates that all 9,000 films in its library will be transferred to videodisc by 1995. So far, 753 films are available for viewing at the CineRobotheque, from award-winners like Claude Jutra's *Mon Oncle Antoine* to the marvellous animated works of Norman McLaren.

"What we're doing," says Ducharme, "is giving back to the Canadian public 54 years of NFB movies that they've helped to

Macha Grenon and Gianpaolo Bini in THE MYTH OF THE MALE ORGASM

produce." The new NFB centre on St-Denis Street also boasts a 142-seat cinema and 20-seat video theatre designed for group viewing. In addition to operating film and video centres in eight cities, the NFB will increase the number of access points in Canada – now numbering more than 400 – for its films and videos, and develop and enhanced, interactive communications link with customers and audiences, using computer networks, and improving and expanding the services now provided by a national 1-800 number. Grierson would probably be pleased to see this activity – 55 years later.

Recent Films

ADRIFT

Script: Graham Flashner, Ed Gernon, Terry Gerretsen. Dir: Christian Dugay. Players: Kenneth Welsh, Kate Jackson, Bruce Greenwood, Kelly Rowan. Prod and Dist: Atlantis. 90 mins.

A dead steal from Australia's *Dead Calm*, all at sea and washed up with nowhere to go!

APRIL ONE

Script and Dir: Murray Battle. Players: Steven Shellen, Djanet Sears, David Strathairn, Gordon Clapp, Pierre Curzi, Wayne Robson. Prod: Primedia. Dist: Astral. 90 mins.

The High Commissioner for the Bahamas in Ottawa is taken hostage by a former prisoner. He politely requests the use of an empty firehall in Ottawa to be used as a shelter for women as the price for her freedom. This event actually happened; it makes a quiet, psychologically interesting, sometimes flawed and inappropriately scored, documentary-based story told without sensationalism or violence.

BECAUSE WHY

Script and Dir: Arto Paragamian. Players: Riley, Doru Bandol, Martine Rochon, Heather Mathieson, Victor Knight, Hank Hum. Prod and Dist: Aska Film International. 110 mins.

A first film comedy about a wanderer who returns to Montréal to live out a series of disappointments, meeting eccentric characters everywhere he turns. Sophisticated, wry, and human-istic, touched by a poetic vision and a delightful absurdity, the fragility of the whole is frequently beset with tedium and repetition. Michael Riley as the classic clown holds it together.

LA BETE DE FOIRE

Script and Dir: Isabelle Hayeur. Players: Linda Roy, David La Haye, Grigori Hlady. Prod: Martin Paul-Hus. Dist: Cinema Libre. 70 mins.

An impossible puzzle picture for most audiences about a woman who lives in a cage within her apartment and only leaves when her lover is gone. In between she has strange dreams and nightmares – as obscure to the film-maker perhaps as they are to her characters.

BOULEVARD

Script: Rae Dawn Chong. Dir: Penelope Buitenhuis. Players: Rae Dawn Chong, Kari Wuhrer, Joel Bissonnette, Lou Diamond Phillips. Prod and Dist: Norstar. 96 mins.

Prostitutes on Yonge Street; the innocent one, the knowing pack, the vicious pimp, the foul-mouthed detective, a sleazy box-office brew descending into a frightening pit of sex, blood and violence.

THE BURNING SEASON

Script: Annette Cohen, Harvey Crossland. Dir: Crossland. Players: Akesh Gill, Ayub Khan Din, Omi Puri, Habib Tanvir, Uttara Bgokev, Pankaj Kapoor. Prod: Primedia Pictures/Siren Films. Dist: Astral Films. 103 mins.

Set in Canada and India. A young Indo-Canadian woman is living out an arranged and loveless marriage in the home of her wealthy and traditional in-laws. She falls in love with her teacher, an Indian man, and returns with him to his village where she becomes shunned and tormented by traditions and practices unfamiliar to her. Potentially fascinating, the script fails to live up to the subject,

the actors are lost, an interesting situation becomes the boring season. Vic Sarin's photography is up to his usual standard and struggles against an over-blown score.

BUST A MOVE

Script and Dir: Julian Grant. Players: Francine Paul, Pra, Michael Bederman, Jacen Braithwaite, Venetia Marie, Kirk Cooper, Marja Leena Roberts. Prod: JFDI Films. Dist: Libra Films. 90 mins.

A first film made on a shoestring without government funding, this is a likeable, down-to-earth and natural comedy-drama about young people with ambitions caught up in the delinquency of their Toronto housing estate.

CADILLAC GIRLS

Script: Peter Behrens. Dir: Nicholas Kendall. Players: Jennifer Dale, Mia Kirshner, Gregory Harrison, Adam Beach. Prod: Imagex/Orca/NFB/Movie Network. Dist: Cineplex Odeon. 105 mins.

A banal mother-and-daughter conflict set in an unbelievable Nova Scotia town, the whole being drenched in Americana. Foolish, trivial and predictable.

C'ETAIT LE 12 DU 12 ET CHILI AVAIT LES BLUES (Chili's Blues)

Script: Jose Frechette. Dir: Charles Biname. Players: Roy Dupuis, Lucie Laurier, Joelle Morin, Juli Deslauriers, Fanny Lauzier, Marie-Josée Bergeron. Prod: Les Productions du Cerf. Dist: Alliance. 100 mins.

A group of passengers is waiting in the railway station for a snowbound train.

Some get to know each other. This is a familiar plot device, but what follows is certainly different, a curiously affecting reprise of the 1960's with melodies from the juke box providing an ironic counterpart to the emotional problems of young students. One, on the verge of suicide, finds release in a brief encounter with a travelling salesman. Uneven at times, but naturally played, funny, nostalgic and appealing.

COYOTE

Script: Michel Michaud (from his novel), Richard Sadler, Louise-Anne Bouchard. Dir: Richard Ciupka. Players: Mitsou Gelinas, Patrick Labbe, Thierry Magnier, Jean-Claude Dreyfuss, François Massicotte, Claude Legault. Prod: Les Films Stock International. Dist: Alliance Vivafilm. 99 mins.

Another first film – a story of young love in somewhat puzzling terms concerning two young lovers attempting to make their own world among dreams and despair. Different and deceptively quaint.

CRACK ME UP

Script: Bachar Chbib, Daphne Kastner, Maryse Wilder. Dir: Chbib. Players: Daphne Kastner, Tim Brazil, Mary Crosby, David Charles. Prod and Dist: Oneira Pictures. 76 mins.

This is yet another of Chbib's LA set and filmed low-budget sex-comedies, this one concerning an innocent, modern cowboy with a mission: to make the world a more loving and funny place with sex and more sex.

DEUX ACTRICES (Two Can Play)

Script, Dir and Ed: Micheline Lanctot. Players: Pascale Bussières, Pascale Paroissien, François Delisle, Louise Traverse, Suzanne Garceau. Prod: Stopfilm/NFB. Dist: Max Films. 94 mins.

An observant and affecting study of a woman who finds a stranger at her door claiming to be her long-lost sister. Highly emotional, unconventional and honest, the fervent and volatile relationship between the two is tempered by the inclusion of video tape sequences showing the two actresses discussing their lives and the roles they are playing. A small, inexpensive film of power, integrity and passion.

DIGGER

Script: Rodney Gibbons. Dir: Robert Turner. Players: Adam Hann-Byrd, Joshua Jackson, Leslie Nielsen, Olympia Dukakis, Timothy Bottoms, Barbara Wilson. Prod: Circle Northwood-WIC Western International Communications. Dist: Norstar. 95 mins.

Disappointing tale of a young boy trying to come to terms with his parents' disintegrating marriage. Supposedly Canadian but conceived as American, the Vancouver scenery is the only authentic element in this sentimental and bathetic brew.

DUE SOUTH

Players: Paul Gross, David Marciano, Wendel Meldrum, Gordon Pinsent, Ken Pogue, Charles Shamata. Prod: Alliance/CBS/CTV. Dist: Alliance. 120 mins.

A policeman with with RCMP goes to Chicago to catch the man who murdered his father, and becomes friendly with a local policeman assigned to work with him. A hands-across-the-border hybrid conceived in the interests of "lessening the risk" co-productions, this is filled with inept cartoon characters and silly situations – from Chicago to the Yukon.

EXOTICA

Script and Dir: Atom Egoyan. Players: Arsinee Khanjian, Mia Kirshner, Bruce Greenwood, Don McKellar, Elias Koteas, Sarah Polley, Victor Garber, Calvin Green. Prod: Ego Arts. Dist: Alliance. 90 mins. (Canada's entry in competition, Cannes 1994, and the recipient of the FIRPRESCI Critics Award.)

The director has a more coherent narrative in this bizarre mix of sex, sin and guilt than in his previous films. Running among the lurking sub-plots is a tax collector who has lost his daughter and who seeks solace in a hall of sex with a young girl resembling her. Cold, superficial and flat with cardboard characters, but titillating and saleable.

FOR THE MOMENT

Script and Dir: Aaron Kim Johnston. Players: Russell Crowe, Christianne Hirt, Wanda

Cannon, Scott Kraft, Peter Outerbridge, Sara McMillan. Prod: John Aaron Features. Dist: Malofilm. 120 mins.

An appealing, nostalgic wartime romance set in Manitoba in 1942 during the time of the famed British Commonwealth Air Training Plan, made up of little dramas involving local women and visiting airmen. One, an Australian, falls in love with a married woman. Familiar, unsurprising, sometimes strained in its conflicts, it poignantly represents a principled past, is well-acted, and looks and sounds Canadian in a most recognisable way.

HARVEST

Script: Malcolm MacRury. Dir: Michael Scott. Players: Ted Shackelford, Ron White, Rebecca Jenkins, Ken Pogue. Prod: Alliance/The Family Channel. Dist: Alliance. 90 mins.

Manitoba is "Anywhere Rural in the U.S." in this reasonably authentic story of a family farm in distress, winding its way along the road to a predictably simplistic outcome.

HENRY AND VERLIN

Script and Dir: Gary Ledbetter. Players: Gary Farmer, Keegan Macintosh, Robert Joh, Margot Kidder, Nancy Beatty, Eric Peterson, Joan Orenstein, Wilfred Bray, David Cronenberg. Prod: Opeongo Films. Dist: Malofilm. 87 mins.

A countryside tale about the friendship between a mute boy and his uncle, a giant Indian man with a child-like mind. A special bond forms between the two outcasts, but the neighbours question their relationship resulting in tragedy. Based on true incidents in the life of the writer, this is oddly affecting, natural and honest in the telling.

JACK OF HEARTS

Script: Namir Khan, Cynthia Roberts. Dir: Roberts. Players: Andrew Scorer, Kirsten Johnson, Valerie Buhagiar. Prod and Dist: BBW Motion Pictures. 92 mins.

A crumbling household made up of a very strange family and friends is concerned about a father attempting to prolong his life with anti-rejection drugs administered by Doctor Mustapha! It might well leave most audiences feeling decidedly strange, particularly as no ending is forthcoming.

KABLOONAK (Nanook)

Script: Claude Massot, Sebastien Regnier. Dir: Massot. Players: Dance, Adamie Quasiak Inukpuk, Georges Claisse, Matthew Saviakjuk-Jaw, Natar Ungalaq. Prod: France/Canada/Russia, Ima Films, UGC Images. Dist: UGC. 105 mins.

An impressive and captivating depiction of Robert Flaherty's trip to the Arctic in 1922 to film his now classic, *Nanook of the North*. Charles Dance plays Flaherty with a sensitive understanding and the Inuit people play themselves, with Nanook being uncannily believable. Never has the Arctic been photographed with such drama and beauty; a sense of Flaherty's visual poetry is everywhere present. This is only the third (among many) of Canada's co-productions to benefit this country – the first being *Black Robe*; the second, *Map of the Human Heart*.

KANADA

Script and Dir: Mike Hoolboom. Players: Babs Chula, Gabrielle Rose. Prod: MH Productions. Dist: Cinema Esperanáa. 65 mins.

A satire in the experimental manner foreseeing Canada engaged in a long-running civil war. A hit-and-miss proposition.

THE LIFEFORCE EXPERIMENT (Breakthrough)

Script: Mike Hodges and Gerard MacDonald, based on the novella "Breakthrough" by Daphne du Maurier. Dir: Piers Haggard. Players: Donald Sutherland, Mimi Kuzyk, Corin Nemec, Vlasta Vrana. Prod: Filmline International/Screen Partners/USA Pictures/Sci-Fi Channel. Dist: Filmline. 120 mins.

A CIA agent is sent to the outer reaches of Newfoundland (actually Nova Scotia) to find out what a mysterious scientist is up to in trying to harness life's magnetic flux – whatever that might be! It doesn't save the film from being extremely tiresome.

LILLY

Script and Dir: David Marcoux. Players: Shelly Hong, Deanne Judson, Shirley Cui. Prod and Dist: Psychosomatic Productions. 105 mins.

From the "camera never moves long take" school of film-making comes this little drama of an Asian girl who works in her family's dry-cleaning shop and becomes a suspect in murder.

LOUIS 19, LE ROI DES ONDES (King of the Airwaves)

Script: Emile Gaudreault, Sylvie Bouchard, Michel Michaud. Dir: Michel Poulette. Players: Martin Drainville, Agathe de la Fontaine, Dominique Michel, Patricia Tulsane, Gilbert Lachance, Jean L'Italien. Prod: Les Films Stock International. Dist: Malofilm. 93 mins.

A highly successful and consistently amusing Québec comedy about a dull everyman who spends his leisure time watching popular television, and then becomes a media celebrity when every minute of his life is shown on TV as a result of winning a contest. Going from frontscreen to backscreen, from outside to inside, provides a lighthearted opportunity to make fun of television's

power to misrepresent so much of what it feeds to its passive audience.

LOVE & HUMAN REMAINS

Script: Brad Fraser, based on his play *Unidentified Human Remains and the True Nature of Love*, and listed in last year's IFG as *The True Nature of Love*. Dir: Denys Arcand. Players: Thomas Gibson, Ruth Marshall, Cameron Bancroft, Mia Kirshner, Joanne Vannicola, Matthew Ferguson, Rick Roberts. Prod: Max Films/Atlantis. Dist: Max Films. 99 mins.

This re-edited version (after the original was not accepted at Cannes) is a hybrid of film and theatre providing larger-than-life portraits of young people at loss with contemporary society. Sex and murder abound as Arcand cleverly combines comedy and rage in this sometimes shallow and confusing foray into the "realities of big city life".

MATUSALEM

Script and Dir: Roger Cantin. Players: Marc Labrèche, Emile Proulx-Cloutier, Steve Gendron, Jessica Barker, Marie-France Monette. Prod: Les Films Vision 4. Dist: Allegro Films. 82 mins.

Michelle Little and Garwin Sanford in THE PERFECT MAN

An appealing fable for family audiences about the ghost of an eighteenth-century gentleman who returns to earth every half-century to enlist the help of a schoolboy in an unfinished quest. Good humoured and imaginative.

M. BUTTERFLY

Script: David Henry Hwang, based on his play. Dir: David Cronenberg. Players: Jeremy Irons, John Lone, Ian Richardson, Anabel Leventon. Prod: Geffen Pictures. Dist: Warner Bros. 100 mins.

The far-fetched premise that a French diplomat in China during the 1960's conducted an 18-year affair with a native man he always thought was a woman simply cannot be believed on film – not the way Cronenberg tells it. And in choosing a British actor to play the Frenchman and John Lone to play Song Liling, disbelief becomes even greater. There is no emotion or understanding of any kind between them to suggest that this relationship was possible.

MON AMIE MAX

Script: Jefferson Lewis. Dir: Michel Brault. Players: Geneviève Bujold, Marthe Keller, Rita Lafontaine. Prod: Les Productions du Verseau/Lazennec/NFB. Dist: C/FP. 107 mins.

A slow-moving story of a middle-aged classical pianist, Marie-Alexandrine, who returns to Québec City after a 25-year absence to renew and old friendship with a woman, who is also a pianist, and to find a long-lost son. An extended flashback shows us their younger years and how life begins to go wrong. The characters are hardly credible or appealing.

MOUVEMENTS DU DESIR (Desire in Motion)

Script and Dir: Léa Pool. Players: Valerie Kaprisky, Jean-François Pichette, Jolianna L'Allier-Matteau, Willima Jacques, Matthew MacKay, Elyse Guilbaut. Prod: Cinémaginaire/Catpics/NFB. Dist: Alliance. 94 mins.

The setting is Via Rail's Trans Continental train from Montréal to Vancouver. The scenery is magnificent, the film much less so. A woman with a young daughter is suffering the emotional pangs of a broken marriage – her husband left her for a man. She meets a fellow passenger who has emotional pains from a father who left his mother. Both suffer nightmares giving the director an opportunity for surreal inserts. In the lifeless train they meet and fall in love: a cheerless, adolescent excursion into sexual fantasies swamped by a sticky score. The sound effects and photography (Pierre Mignot) in the Lean tradition are brilliant. The train keeps moving, the narrative is an unreal journey into nowhere.

THE MYTH OF THE MALE ORGASM

Script: John Hamilton, David Reckziegel. Dir: Hamilton. Players: Bruce Dinsmore, Miranda de Pencier, Mark Camacho, Burke Lawrence, Ruth Marshall. Prod: Telescene Communications. Dist: C/FP. 90 mins.

Three young professional men, who live together in Montréal and delight in chasing women as sex objects, attend a sociological survey conducted by women to determine men's feelings about them. Excessively talkative – some words are well said, but mostly it is sheer silliness.

PARIS, FRANCE

Script: Tom Walmsley. Dir: Gerard Ciccoritti. Players: Leslie Hope, Peter Outerbridge, Victor Ertmanis, Dan Left, Raoul Trujillo. Prod: Lightshow Communications. Dist: Alliance. 112 mins.

A relentless tale of sexual perversion among the so-called literati involving a young novelist, her failed publisher-husband who believes that John Lennon is calling from the grave, and a stranger who lives for sex. This is a shallow film about unpleasant, unlikeable and foolish characters, a descent into bad taste.

THE PERFECT MAN

Script: Wendy Hill-Tout, Lynda Shorten. Dir: Hill-Tout. Players: Michelle Little, Garwin Sanford, Phyllis Diller, Brian Jensen, Janice Ungaro. Prod: Midnite Cafe Productions. Dist: Alliance. 94 mins.

A lightweight comedy-romance about a painter whose life lacks that "something extra" until she meets the handsome owner of a gallery. Love, family and living together are the motivating considerations, simply put and played.

LES POTS CASSES

Script: Gilles Desjardins. Dir: François Bouvier. Players: Gilbert Sicotte, Marie Tifo, Marc Messier, Louise Deslières, Jean-Marc Parent. Prod: Les Productions du lundi matin. Dist: Allegro Films. 90 mins.

A tidy psychological thriller in which a successful author of horror stories writes one in which she kills her husband. Afraid that her premonitions will come true she burns the manuscript and flees – from life and her husband. Once she has found herself again, she returns to him and a new reality.

RACE FOR FREEDOM – THE UNDERGROUND RAILROAD

Script: Diana Braithwaite, Nancy Trites Bodkin, Peter Mohan. Dir: Don McBrearty. Players: Michael Riley, Courtney B. Vance, Janet Bailey, Dawn Lewis, Ron White. Prod: Atlantis/United Image Entertainment/The Family Channel/Black Entertainment/CTV. Dist: Atlantis. 120 mins.

In 1850 the U.S. proclaimed the Fugitive Slave Act under which runaway slaves could be captured in the free states of the north. To escape, over 3,000 trekked to Ontario using designated places to hide on their journey. This story of four of them lacks a sense of historical reality and while sentimentality is minimal the result is a modest drama.

RELATIVE FEAR

Script: Kurt Wimmer. Dir: George Mihalka. Players: Darlanne Fluegel, James Brolin, M. Emmett Walsh, Denise Crosby, Matthew Dupuis. Prod: Allegro. Dist: Norstar. 90 mins.

From autism to Alzheimers a feeble variation of the Bad Seed set in an American city and played by a mostly American cast. A young boy is obsessed by TV's The Crime Channel and those who taunt him die mysteriously. False notes predominate in yet another weak attempt at horror.

THE RETURN OF TOMMY TRICKER (Le retour des aventuriers du timbre perdu) (Tales For All No. 15)

Script and Dir: Michael Rubbo. Players: Michael Stevens, Joshawa Mathers, Heather Goodsell, Adele Gray, Tommy Pierre Tutangata. Prod and Dist: Les Productions La Fête. 100 mins.

Tommy and his friends are determined to free the mysterious lad held prisoner on Canada's famous Bluenose stamp, a journey taking them as far away as the Cook Islands. Lots of adventures, laughs and obstacles to overcome. A worthy addition to Rock Demers's delightful series.

LE SEXE DES ETOILES (Sex and the Stars)

Script: Monique Proulx. Dir: Paule Baillargeon. Players: Marianne Mercier, Denis Mercier, Tobie Pelletier, Sylvie Drapeau, Luc Picard. Prod: Constellation Inc. Dist: C/FP. 100 mins.

A well-intended but slow and heavy-handed piece of romanticism concerning the emotional dilemma of a young girl whose father comes back into her life as a woman.

SILENT WITNESS

Script: Paris Qualles. Dir: Bruce Pittman. Players: Amir Jamal Williams, Mia Corf, Clark Johnson. Prod: Power Picture Corp. Dist: EPS. 90 mins.

A young boy is the only witness to a gang murder, and the murderers, including his brother, know he saw them. A convincing treatment of a familiar situation.

SMALL PLEASURES

Script and Dir: Keith Lock Qi Guang. Players: Lily Zhang, Reimonna Sheng, Phillip Mackenzie. Prod and Dist: Wondrous Light Inc. 85 mins.

A likeable first feature set in Toronto's Chinatown concerning the difficulties and delights of a family from Beijing coming to terms with a new society.

TWO BROTHERS, A GIRL AND A GUN

Script: William Hornecker, Grant Dryden. Dir: Hornecker. Players: Shaun Johnson, Kim Hogan, David Everhart. Prod: Black Market Motion Pictures. Dist: Cineplex Odeon. 93 mins.

A forgettable, low-budget, unoriginal first film setting the violent American road movie in Alberta, where a stud in black leather jacket and his lost and lonely girlfriend are on the run from the police.

LE VOLEUR DE CAMERA (The Camera Thief)

Script and Dir: Claude Fortin. Players: Fortin, Madeleine Belair, Jacinthe Marceau, Johanne Goulet, Regin Boivin. Prod: Vue des VC. Dist: Cinema Libre. 106 mins.

An imaginative and original film questioning the nature of film-making and those who control the rapidly developing world of media communications. The director plays an aspiring videographer who comes to learn his craft, makes a film and turns the tables on the system. Set against a lively Montréal background the events include a witty working-class version of Arcand's *Decline of the American Empire*.

ZERO PATIENCE

Script and Dir: John Greyson. Players: John Robinson, Normand Fauteux, Dianne Heatherington. Prod: Zero Patience. Dist: Cineplex Odeon. 100 mins.

A superficial and muddled musical-comedy worked around AIDS and the controversial "Patient Zero" theory which holds that a French-Canadian airline steward first brought the disease to North America. He is joined in the film, for no good reason, by a badly-played Sir Richard Burton. The high jinks are mostly unattractive, and what the film is supposed to be saying about the subject in question is hard to discern.

Box-Office Statistics

Latest information from *Statistics Canada* (1991): 723 cinemas (742 in 1990) of which 620 were regular cinemas (633) and 103 were drive-ins (109). Receipts from admissions (excluding taxes) $380.4m ($439.4m) of which regular cinemas accounted for $367.3m ($424.8m). Amusement taxes decreased to $22.9m ($27.2m). Paid admissions: $69.2m ($76.3m). Note: the number of cinemas is misleading as most are multiplexes including approx. 2,500 screens.

Distributors

Allegro Films Inc
2187 Larivere St
Montréal Qué
H2K 1P5
M4W 3C7
Tel: (514) 529-0320
Fax: (514) 529-0328

Alliance Releasing
920 Yonge Street
Suite 500
Toronto, Ontario
M4W 3C7
Tel: (416) 967-1174
Fax: (416) 960-0971

Alliance Vivafilm
355 Place Royale
3e étage
Montréal (Québec)
H2Y 2V3
Tel: (514) 844-3132
Fax: (514) 284-2340

Astral Communications
2100 rue Ste-Catherine ouest
Bureau 900
Montréal (Québec)
H3H 2T3
Tel: (514) 939-5000
Fax: (514) 939-1515
also at:
181 Bay St., Ste. 101
P.O. Box 787
Toronto, Ontario
M5J 2T3
Tel: (416) 956-2000
Fax: (416) 956-2020

Atlantis Releasing Inc.
Cinevillage
65 Heward Avenue
Toronto, Ontario
M4M 2T5
Tel: (416) 462-0016
Fax: (416) 462-0254

Canadian Filmmakers Distribution Centre
67A Portland Street
Toronto, Ontario
M5V 2M9
Tel: (416) 593-8661
Fax: (416) 593-8661

Canadian Filmmakers Distribution West
1131 Howe Street
Suite 100
Vancouver, British Columbia
V6Z 2L7
Tel: (604) 684 3014

CBC Enterprises-TV Program Sales
250 Front Street West
Toronto, Ontario
M5V 3G5
Tel: (416) 205-3311

C/FP Distribution Ltd
146 Bloor Street W.
Suite 204
Toronto, Ontario
M5S 1P3
Tel: (416) 944-0104
Fax: (416) 944-2212

Cinar Films Inc
1207, rue St André
Montréal, Québec
H2L 3S8
Tel: (514) 843-7070
Fax: (514) 843-7080

Cineplex Odeon Films Canada
1303 Yonge Street
Toronto, Ontario
M4T 2Y9
Tel: (416) 323-6600
Fax: (416) 323-4711

Cinema Esperanca Int. Inc.
96 Spadina Avenue
Suite 301
Toronto, Ontario
M5V 2J6
Tel: (416) 865-1225
Fax: (416) 865-9223

Cinéma Libre
4067 Boulevard Saint-Laurent
Bureau 403
Montréal (Québec)
H2W 1Y7
Tel: (514) 849-7888
Fax: (514) 849-1231

Cinema Plus International Inc.
154 Avenue Laurier ouest
Bureau 300
Montréal (Québec)
H2T 2N7
Tel: (514) 270-6170
Fax: (514) 270-6988

Ciné 360 Inc.
810 Châtelaine
Laval, Québec
H7W 4H9
Tel: (514) 686-1940
Fax: (514) 688-9443

Cinevideo Plus Inc.
2100 rue Ste-Catherine ouest
Bureau 810
Montréal (Québec)
H3H 2Y3
Tel: (514) 937-7986
Fax: (514) 937-8332

Creative Exposure Ltd
2236 Queen Street E
Toronto, Ontario
M4E 1G2
Tel: (416) 690-0775
Fax: (416) 690-0775

Ellis Enterprises
1231 Yonge Street
Suite 201
Toronto, Ontario
M4T 2T8
Tel: (416) 924-2186
Fax: (416) 924-6115

Les Films du Crépuscule Inc.
55 Ouest Mont-Royal
Bureau 202
Montréal (Québec)
H2T 2S5
Tel: (514) 849-2477
Fax: (514) 849-5859

Films Transit Inc.
402, rue Notre-Dame E
3e étage
Montréal (Québec)
H2Y 1C8
Tel: (514) 844-3358
Fax: (514) 844-7298

Imax Corporation
45 Charles Street East
Toronto, Ontario
M4Y 1S2
Tel: (416) 960-8509
Fax: (416) 960-8596

Jasmine Tea Films Inc.
83 Rameau Drive
Unit 5, Willowdale
Ontario M2H 1T6
Tel: (415) 493 3584
Fax: (415) 495 9117

Lapointe Films International Inc.
450 rue Isabey
Saint-Laurent (Québec)
H4T 1V3
Tel: (514) 521-7884
Fax: (514) 524-6435

Libra Films
96 Spadina Avenue
Suite 302
Toronto, Ontario
M5V 2J6
Tel: (416) 203-2171
Fax: (416) 203-2173

Malofilm Distribution Inc.
3575 Boulevard St-Laurent
Bureau 650
Montréal (Québec)
H2X 2T7
Tel: (514) 844-4555
Fax: (514) 844-1471
also at:
2221 Yonge Street
Suite 100
Toronto, Ontario
M4S 2B4
Tel: (416) 480-0453
Fax: (416) 480-0501

Nelvana Limited
32 Atlantic Avenue
Toronto, Ontario
MGK 1X8
Tel: (416) 588-5571
Fax: (416) 588-5588

Norstar Releasing Inc.
86 Bloor Street W.
4th Floor
Toronto, Ontario
M5S 1M5
Tel: (416) 961-6278
Fax: (416) 961-5608

Paragon International
119 Spadina Ave
Ste 900
Toronto, Ont
M5V 2L1
Tel: (416) 595-6300
Fax: (416) 977-0489

Prima Films Inc.
1594 boul. Saint-Joseph E.
Montréal (Québec)
H2J 1M7
Tel: (514) 521-1189
Fax: (514) 521-2918

Productions La Fête Inc.
225, rue Roy E.
Bureau 203
Montréal (Québec)
H2W 1M5
Tel: (514) 848-0417
Fax: (514) 848-0064

Sullivan Films Distribution Inc.
16 Clarence Square
Toronto, Ontario

M5V 1H1
Tel: (416) 597-0029
Telex: 06-218692
Fax: (416) 597-0320

THA Media Distributors
1100 Homer Street
Vancouver, British Columbia
V6B 2X6
Tel: (604) 687-4215
Fax: (604) 688-8349

Winnipeg Film Group
304-100 Arthur Street
Winnipeg, Manitoba
R38 1H3
Tel: (204) 942-6795
Fax: (204) 942-1555

Useful Address

Telefilm Canada
Tour de la Banque Nationale
600, rue de la Gauchetière Ouest
14 étage
Montréal (Québec)
H3B 4L2
Tel: (514) 283-6363
Telex: 055-60998
Fax: (514) 283-8212
22 Kingly Court
London
W1R 5LE
Tel: (44-71) 437-5308
Fax: (44-71) 734-8586

CHILE
Hans Ehrmann

Chile's film centennial is not far behind the rest of the world: on August 25, 1896 an audience of 150 saw a group of films of less than one minute each, in an exhibition organised by Julio Prá, a resident Frenchman. They included *Baby's Soup* and *The Wall*.

The first locally-shot material, three minutes on exercises by the local fire brigade, was exhibited in Valparaiso (May 1902) and other documentaries followed until the first narrative film, *Manuel Rodriguez*, opened in September 1910. A contemporary review was quite enthusiastic, but did mention flaws such as soldiers shooting time and again without reloading their rifles.

All this and much more can be found in the recently published *Cine Mudo Chileno (Chilean Silent Cinema)*, a first-rate piece of research by Eliana Jara Donoso, made particularly difficult by the fact that of close to one hundred silent films shot in Chile, only one feature, the 1925 **The Hussar of Death** (*El Húsar de la muerte*) survives. A similar fate befell nearly all the early documentaries.

In those far-off days, the publicity slogan for a locally made film read: "It's so good it doesn't seem Chilean." That kind of inferiority complex belongs to the past, although local production has certainly had its ups and downs.

Although 1993 only provided three features (one in 16mm), the State Bank loans to Cine Chile (a company formed by 28 local directors and producers) helped finance the two commercial releases. More are expected in 1994 but, in spite of low costs (an average of $600,000), with barely 120 cinemas in the country, even a big hit is unlikely to recoup its investment locally. The bottom line will inevitably depend on international sales which, to put it mildly, may sometimes be unavailable.

Up and Down Reception

When a picture is an out and out local flop, both at the box-office and with the critics, its prospects are even worse, as was the case of Leo Kocking's **Total Delivery** (*Entrega Total*) a sort of road movie that couldn't read traffic signs, lost its way, and produced less than eight thousand

TOP TEN GROSSING FILMS IN SANTIAGO: 1993

	Attendance
Jurassic Park	388,000
The Bodyguard	311,000
Aladdin	218,000
Indecent Proposal	171,000
Home Alone 2	162,000
L'Amant	131,000
Bram Stoker's Dracula	121,000
Scent of a Woman	107,000
The Fugitive	91,000
A Few Good Men	87,000
(Santiago spectators correspond to approximately 65% of the country's total.)	

spectators, plus scathing reviews in Santiago.

On the other hand Gustavo Graef-Marino's **Johnny Cien Pesos** was well received locally (85,000 spectators) and invited to the Sundance Festival, the New Directors series at Moma in N.Y. and over a dozen other festivals. Based on a real event in 1990 downtown Santiago, it deals with the bungled assault on an illegal money exchange with a video store front. Five men and a woman are held hostage for hours while police surround the premises, crowds mill around the building and television covers and sensationalises the scene.

As soon as the four punks and Johnny, a 17-year-old schoolboy (Armando Araiza), break into the money exchange, their inexperience is obvious and their attempt to replace brain by brawn proves unsuccessful. Clumsiness is not limited to them. Officials, worried about the government's image at home and abroad, also fumble.

Johnny's high school teacher basks in the limelight when TV comes to visit; his mother first defends then disowns him. Tensions rise among the hoodlums and hostages, holed up in the besieged apartment and an unexpected relationship develops between the schoolboy and Gloria (Patricia Rivera), secretary and the owner's mistress at the money exchange. The actual newsreel footage of the crowded streets, when police finally carted

off the delinquents is well blended with the fictional images.

The film's plusses lie in its irony and the way it pokes fun at Chilean mores, from judges and ministers, to television and those who try to bask in its limelight. No-one seems able to do anything efficiently

The year's third item was Cristián Sánchez's 16mm **The Wish's Fulfilment** (*El cumplimiento del deseo*), a labour of love seven years in the making, that falls somewhere between Ruiz and Rohmer, but failed to find even a limited audience among local film buffs.

Attendances Still Meagre

In Chile, as just about everywhere else, *Jurassic Park* was the key to the year's box-office. Its 388,000 Santiago spectators were unequalled since 1979 when *Doña Flor and Her Two Husbands* attracted 420,000.

The dinosaurs obviously affected the year's filmgoing statistics. Santiago spectators (65% of the country's total) had been diminishing from a weekly 137,000 in 1988 to 73,500 in 1992. This makes even the dino-induced 1993 increase of 0.54% (to 73,896) look good.

Tickets are expensive by local living standards, at $5.75 in the posher uptown districts and $3.45 downtown. This is confirmed by the fact that over a third of the audience picks Wednesdays, when tickets are half-price, for its filmgoing.

Over the last decade several houses have been refurbished and turned into duplexes, but the first specially-built mall multiplex was only inaugurated in September 1993. This sixplex, decorated in garish Las Vegas chic, is jointly owned on a 50/50 basis by Texas exhibitors Cinemark and Conate, the Daire's father and son company. Located in a densely populated district it has been very successful, attracting approximately 15% of Santiago's audiences.

Conate now controls 29 of Santiago's 50 screens, including all its first-run houses.

Of the remaining 21, 16 cover the soft core, action and/or double bill areas, and there are also five art-houses.

Further multiplexes at other malls have been in the planning stage for considerable time but, until some of these materialise in districts bereft of cinemas since the former neighbourhood houses closed down, much improvement cannot be expected in cinema-going habits

HANS EHRMANN has been a Variety correspondent for over thirty years. He is a columnist and critic on Santiago's daily *La Nación*.

Useful Addresses

Cine Chile
Moneda 1140, ofic. 703
Santiago
Tel: 56 2 646 4796 or 6722832
Fax: 56 2 696 2165

Oficina de Difusion de la Cinematografia Chilena
Villavicencio 352
Santiago
Tel: 56 2 632 6565 or 632 6607
Fax: 56 2 632 6389

Chile Films
(studio, lab, distributor and exhibitor)
La Capitania 1200
Santiago
Tel: 56 2 220 4086
Fax: 56 2 211 9826

Filmocentro
(production)
Jorge Washington 302
Ñuñoa
Santiago
Tel: 56 2 204 2058
Fax: 56 2 225 5234

Asociacion de Productores de Cine y TV
Irarrázabel 4280
Tel: 56 2 226 3308 or 226 3355

Viña Del Mar Film Festival
Villavicencia 352
Santiago
Tel: 56 2 632 2892
Fax: 56 2 632 6389

Laboratorio Cinevisión
República de Israel 1057
Santiago
Tel & Fax: 56 2 274 0038

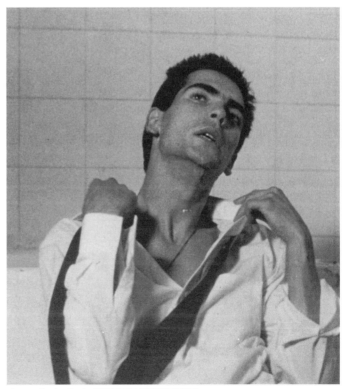

Armando Araíza in JOHNNY CIEN PESOS

CHINA — Derek Elley

Despite the worst intentions of politicians at home, and a tough economic climate for the domestic industry, mainland Chinese film-makers maintained a strong presence on the international stage during 1993-94. However, following draconian new guidelines on co-productions which came into force in early 1994, there are now real fears among the industry that the era of high-profile movies could temporarily be over.

The atmosphere began to sour as long ago as spring 1993, following the appearance of Tian Zhuangzhuang's *The Blue Kite (Lan fengzheng)* in the Cannes Quinzaine in May without Peking's approval. Things got worse when the Locarno festival went ahead and showed Zhang Yuan's *Beijing Bastards (Beijing zazhong)*, despite Peking's protests and its withdrawal of Liu Liaomiao's *An Innocent Babbler (Dazui zi)*. (Liu's film was subsequently shown at Venice in September, though the director herself had to arrange transportation of the print.)

To add to Peking's public loss of face, even the usually diplomatic Tokyo festival screened *The Blue Kite* and *Beijing Bastards* in September, triggering a walkout by the official Chinese delegation.

Meanwhile, Peking had taken a second look at Chen Kaige's Cannes Palme d'Or winner *Farewell to My Concubine (Bawang bie ji)* and decided it needed cutting prior to mainland release. Following single screenings in Shanghai and Peking in late July, Chen's film was finally released in China in September after trims by the director. (Ironically, the international version was cut far more heavily – at the urging of its distributor Miramax – for commercial reasons. Retitled *Farewell My Concubine*, it now runs 156 mins, compared to 170 mins at its Cannes showing.)

Peking's displeasure basically boiled down to lack of control over foreign funded co-productions, the negatives of which were held outside the country. Despite the fact that it is these films that have raised China's profile internationally, and provided badly needed income for local studios, official retaliation was swift. In late October, both Zhang and Tian were blacklisted from working in the country, with the former forced to suspend shooting on his new film after ten days.

Draconian Rulings Trap New Films

Mainland productions continued to seep out, however, with two low-budget independents, **Red Beads** (*Xuan lian*) by He Yi (pen name for He Jianjun) and Wang Xiaoshuai's **The Days** (*Dongchunde rizi*) hitting the festival circuit in November.

Next came Peking's most draconian rulings: from January 1, 1994, all co-productions would have to be processed on the mainland, before they could be exported, and from March it was decided that they would have to be passed by Peking's censors as well.

With his usual consummate timing, Zhang Yimou's Taiwan-via-Hongkong financed **To Live** (*Huozhe*) just sneaked out for post-production in Japan in time; but other movies found themselves trapped inside the country, with shooting on actor Jiang Wen's directorial debut, *In the Heat of the Sun (Yangguang canlande rizi)*, financed out of Hongkong and Taiwan, even affected. (The movie deals with childhood during the Cultural Revolution.) Offshore production companies like Hsü Feng's Tomson Films and Chiu Fu-sheng's Era International (financiers of Chen Kaige and Zhang Yimou) started to re-evaluate future projects.

Still from RED FIRECRACKER, GREEN FIRECRACKER

The list of mainland film-makers banned from working with the country's laboratories, equipment rental companies, and 16 studios includes, in addition to Zhang Yuan and Tian Zhuangzhuang, directors Wang Xiaoshuai, He Yi, Wu Wenguang (director of several sensitive video documentaries), and Dai Lin.

Though Zhang Yimou's *To Live* took part in the Cannes Competition in 1994 (winning a deserved Best Actor prize for Ge You), Zhang himself did not attend the festival, returning to Peking after doing pre-festival publicity in Paris. His tip of the hat to the Chinese authorities was widely interpreted as an insurance policy for being allowed to make his next film, *Shanghai Triad*, financed by French sources, but shooting hit troubles in September.

Reaction among Hongkong and Taiwan film-makers, who have been working in droves on the mainland during the past three years, has been official anger and a desire to explore alternative possibilities in Taiwan, South Korea and Singapore. However, with the boom in exotically-locationed costume pictures on the wane in Hongkong, China's studios could see a drastic fall in co-production income if the new rulings stay in place.

Gleam of Hope

The replacement in May 1994 of arch-conservative Ai Zhisheng, Minister of radio, TV and film, with Sun Jiazheng, deputy party secretary of Jiangsu province, raises a gleam of hope that the new rulings will be shortlived. In practice, they are simply another of the government's periodic warnings to both locals and foreigners not to overstep the line, and may well quietly be forgotten after a period of face-saving.

The above developments are doubly ironic during a year (1993) dubbed "the year of co-productions" – some 53, according to official figures. In fact, most were financed by Hongkong or Taiwan sources, with local studios supplying labour and facilities in exchange for domestic distribution rights. But with studios now having to pay their own way (in theory), such income has become vital; another lucrative source of income is selling off their annual allocation of chuangbiao (local production allocations). Foreign co-productions, also technically subject to studio quotas, are to be limited to 26 a year, according to official pronouncements.

Local statistics for 1993 make bleak reading: domestic film production fell by 50% (in terms of movies screened); attendances fell by 60%; box-office grosses fell by 35%, and rentals by 40%. In major centres, however, like Peking, Shanghai and Jiangsu, grosses rose on a year-on-year basis, thanks to a few popular titles.

With exhibition suffering from competition from other forms of entertainment, like karaoke, KTV (videotheques), pirated videos, and the like, the market is wide open for U.S. blockbusters to perk cinemagoing. After years of talks, and the authorities' resistance to rental deals, it now looks as if the U.S. majors will finally get through the distribution door in the near future.

That, however, could spell further doom and gloom for the local industry, already struggling to adapt to private financing and audiences' rejection of the same tired old product. Local co-productions between studios and a variety of private sources are now the rule rather than the exception, but the whole sector – from production through to exhibition – is in desperate need of major long-term investment.

UCI Joint Venture

In May 1994, it was announced that the Malaysian-Hongkong-Singaporean-Chinese joint venture SMI Leisure & Entertainment (SMILE) is to build some 60 screens at 12-15 sites over the next 18 months at a cost of $60 million. The cinemas will be managed by western

exhibitor UCI, owned by Paramount and Universal. This follows the classic formula of foreign capital partnering with local sources to bring modern plexing to underdeveloped territories.

According to official figures, some 150 films are planned for 1994, but there are major doubts as to whether this figure will be reached.

Zhang Yimou's **To Live** was undoubtedly the most eagerly-awaited film of the year, though reaction was mixed at its initial Cannes screening. Based on a novel by New Wave writer Yu Hua, the film is a long-limbed panorama of one family's travails across thirty years of Chinese history, from the 1940's to the early 1970's, taking in the Second World War, the setting up of the PRC in 1949, the Cultural Revolution, and the like. Ge You, as the indolent gambler who learns to survive anything that history can throw at him, brings a marvellous irony to the central role; Gong Li, as his wife, is lower key but solid. But in retreading ground already covered by *Concubine* and *Blue Kite*, and adopting a distanced, uninvolving style, Zhang's film fails to break ground in the same way as in *Raise the Red Lantern* and *The Story of Qiuju*.

Huang Jianxin, meanwhile, goes from strength to strength since his return from Australia, following *Stand Up, Don't Bend Over* (see IFG 1994) with two totally contrasted works. **The Wooden Man's Bride** (*Wu kui*), financed by Taiwan's Long Sheng International, is a powerful period tale of love and revenge, set in remote northwest China during the 1920's, that has the inevitability of Greek tragedy, directed with painterly flourishes. His subsequent **Back to Back, Face to Face** (*Bei kao bei, lian dui lian*), financed from Hongkong, is completely the opposite stylistically, with low-key direction that never calls attention to itself. The film marks a return to the warm but black-humoured style of *Stand Up*, following the tangled office politics in a city's cultural bureau as a deputy head tries every trick in the book to become director.

Still from BACK TO BACK, FACE TO FACE

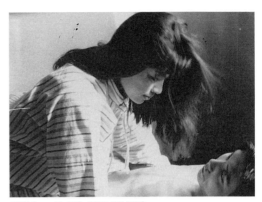

Still from He Yi's RED BEADS

Another Hongkong-financed production, **Red Firecracker, Green Firecracker** (*Paoda shuang deng*), saw young director He Ping more than fulfilling the promise of his previous Leone-like *Swordsman in Double-Flag Town*. An elemental tale about the proscribed love between a female owner of a firecracker factory and an itinerant artist, the film has a mythic flavour and enhanced by spectacular use of landscape and finely judged direction that often attains an almost operatic intensity. Not on the same level, but ambitious all the same, is Wu Ziu's **Sparkling Fox** (*Huo hu*) – financed by Hongkong's Simpson Productions, which also funded *Back to Back* – a kind of *Hell in the Pacific* tale of two feuding men (a hunter, and a town-dweller) in the snow-covered wilds of the northeast.

Other notable works of the past year include Zhang Xiaowen's slick, stylised, blackly witty **Lie-Detector** (*Cehuang qi*), about a philandering husband haunted by the ghost of the wife he's murdered, and Yin Li's delicate, photogenic peasant melo-drama **The Story of Xinghua** (*Xinghua sanyue tian*), about a barren young wife and her gross, money-grabbing bully of a husband.

On the independent front, Zhang Yuan's highly-touted **Beijing Bastards** turned out to be a muddled, often tedious look at aimless, modern youth that, while capturing a contemporary mood, fails to turn it into compelling cinema, ending up as confused and aimless as its subjects. More stylised but much better overall were two low-budget, black-and-white productions:

He Yi's **Red Beads**, an offbeat study of the shy love affair between a sanatorium orderly and a mad girl, and Wang Xiaoshuai's **The Days**, an almost 1960's European look at a young couple whose marriage is slowly falling apart. Both announce potentially interesting talents.

Plenty of New Films to Come

The coming year should see plenty of new movies, with most names engaged on productions. Li Shaohong's *Rouge* (*Hongfen*), originally to have been financed by Taiwan's Chiu Fu-sheng but now locally funded, is a drama centred on a prostitute in the early Republic. Zhou Xiaowen has made *Ermo* (*Er mo*), about a married woman's romance in a bleak northern village. Liu Miaomiao, made head of Ningxia Studio in 1993, has shot *Family Scandal* (*Jiachou*), a 1920's melodrama. And young director Huang Jun has directed the contemporary relationships comedy, *Living with You* (*Yu ni tongzhu*).

Both He Yi and Zhang Yuan have received finance from the Rotterdam Festival's Huub Bals Fund for their new pictures – He's *Postman* got $35,000 in postproduction money and Zhang's *East Palace West Palace* (*Dong gong xi gong*), about homosexuals in modern China, got script development finance. The fund previously contributed to Zhang's *Beijing Bastards*.

Huang Shuqin, after censorship travails over the film *La Peintre* (*Hua hun*), starring

Gong Li as a well-known Paris-based artist, turned to TV with the series *Journey Without a Stop*. As of summer 1994, Wu Ziniu was planning to film *The Nanking Massacre* (*Nanjing da tusha*) at the end of the year, with Taiwan funding. Veteran director Xie Jin, following the rustic drama *An Old Man and His Dog*, co-produced through his own company, Hengtong, was planning several projects with Taiwan sources. In February 1994, even exiled director Wu Tianming finally returned from California to China after five years to plan production of a new film, *Green Card* (*Lu ka*).

The first Shanghai International Film Festival finally took place in October 1993, with an undistinguished lineup of films in competition, a smattering of western celebrities, and less-than-perfect arrangements. The current plan is to alternate the event with the new Zhuhai festival (held June 13-19, 1994), a less ambitious affair but with real cash prizes for film-makers. However, Taiwan's participation at the latter "cross-straits" event was minimised by Taipei's bitterness over the Qiandao Lake tourist massacre in March, and only Hou Hsiao-hsien's *The Puppetmaster* took part. Beneath the rhetoric about the three Chinese territories growing closer, old tensions still linger.

The 13th Golden Rooster Awards

The awards were made in Guangzhou on November 23, 1993, alongside those of the 16th Hundred Flowers Awards (voted by readers of the monthly magazine *Popular Cinema*). Both were for films released in 1992. The main awards were as follows:

Best Film: *The Story of Quiju*.
Best Director: Xia Gang *(Letting Go)*.
Best Script: Wang Xingdong *(Scientist Jiang Zhuying)*.
Best Actor: Ge You *(Letting Go)*.
Best Actress: Gong Li *(The Story of Qiuju)*.
Best Supporting Actor: Wei Zongwan *(San Mao Joins the Army)*.
Best Supporting Actress: Zhang Liwei *(The Beginning of Life)*.

Best Photography: Li Chensheng *(Divorce)*.
Best Art Direction: Jin Shanwu, Lu Qi, Zhao Jun *(Imperial Concubine Yang)*.
Best Editing: Zhang Xiaodong *(Stand Up, Don't Bend Over)*.
Best Music: no award.
Best Sound: Zhan Xin *(A Confucius Family)*.
Best Documentary: Skyline.
Best Children's Film: San Mao Joins the Army.
Best Director's First Work: no award.
Best Costume Design: Li Jianqun *(Imperial Concubine Yang)*.
Best Make-up: Yin Lihua, Shen Dongsheng *(San Mao Joins the Army)*.
Special Jury Prize: animated film *Desert Wind*.

The 16th Hundred Flowers Awards

Best Films: Raise the Red Lantern, The Story of Qiuju, Imperial Concubine Yang.
Best Actor: Gu Yue *(The Story of Mao Zedong)*.
Best Actress: Gong Li *(Raise the Red Lantern)*.
Best Supporting Actor: Feng Gong *(Stand Up, Don't Bend Over)*.
Best Supporting Actress: Chen Xiaoyi *(Divorce)*.
First Zhuhai International Film Festival
The following prizes were awarded on June 19, 1994:
Best Film: *Back to Back, Face to Face* (H.K./China).
Best Director: Yee Tung-shing *(C'Est La Vie, Mon Chéri)* (H.K.).
Best Actor: Wu Zhenhua *(Back to Back, Face to Face)*.
Best Actress: Anita Yuen *(C'Est La Vie, Mon Chéri)*.
Best Script: *Back to Back, Face to Face*.
Best Photography: *Red Firecracker, Green Firecracker* (H.K./China).
Best Music: no award.
Best Art Direction: *Crime Story* (H.K.).
Best Sound: *The Puppetmaster* (Taiwan).
Special Jury Prize: *Country Teachers* (China).

DEREK ELLEY has been associated with IFG for more than 20 years, during which time he has written extensively on East Asian cinema. An associate editor of Variety, he is also editor of the annual Variety Movie Guide. He is currently completing A Handbook of Chinese Cinema.

Recent and Forthcoming Films

YANGGUANG CANLANDE RIZI (In the Heat of the Sun)

Script and Dir: Jiang Wen, from Wang Shuo's novel. Exec. prod: Liu Xiaoqing, Jiang Wen. Players: Jiang Wen, Xia Yu, Ning Jing, Tao Hong, Siqin Gaowa, Wang Xueqi. Prod: Dragon Film Intl. (H.K.)/Hsieh Ho Films (Taiwan).

LAOREN YU GOU (An Old Man and His Dog)

Script: Li Huai, from Zhang Xianliang's novel *Xing laohan he gou de gushi*. Dir: Xie Jin. Players: Siqin Gaowa, Xie Tian, Gao Baocheng. Prod: Hengtong Film, Peking Studio.

HUO HU (Sparkling Fox)

Script: Wu Ziniu, Wang Chunbo. Dir: Wu Ziniu. Players: Gong Hanlin, Tu Men, Sharen Gaowa. Prod: Simpson (H.K.)/Changchun Studio (China).

PAODA SHUANG DENG (Red Firecracker, Green Firecracker)

Script: Da Ying, from Feng Jicai's novel. Dir: He Ping. Players: Ning Jing, Wu Gang, Zhao Xiarui, Gao Yang. Prod: Yung & Associate (H.K.)/Xi'an Studio, Beijing Salon Films (China).

WU KUI (A Wooden Man's Bride)

Script: Yang Zhengguang, from Jia Ping'ao's novel. Dir: Huang Jianxin. Players: Chang Shih, Wang Lan, Wang Yumei, Kao Ming-chun, Ku Pao-ming. Prod: Long Shong (Taiwan)/Xi'an Studio (China).

FENG YUE (Temptress Moon)

Dir: Chen Kaige. Players: Wang Ying, Leslie Cheung, Chang Ting, Hsiao Han-ju, Jiang Kun. Prod: Tomson Films (H.K.).

EAST PALACE WEST PALACE

Dir: Zhang Yuan.

POSTMAN

Script: He Jianjun, You Ni. Dir: He Jianjun. Players: Fang Yuanzheng, Liang Danni, Pu Quanxin, Huang Xing. Prod: United Frontline.

DA CHONGZHUANG (The Offence)

Script and Dir: Zhang Xiaomin. Players: Zhang Xiaomin, Jie Rui, Zhai Yuguo. Prod: Xi'an Studio.

BAI LU YUAN

Dir: Xie Jin, from Chen Zhong-tou's novel. Prod: Hengtong Film.

JIACHOU (Family Scandal)

Script: Le Meidong, Zhang Yanji, from Ji Ning's novel *Dang pu*. Dir: Liu Miaomiao, Cui Xiaoqin. Players: Wang Zhiwen, Li Wannian. Prod: Ningxia Studio, Peking Youth Studio.

BEI LIE PAI BANG

Dir: Huang Jun.

WU ZHAI (The Foggy House)

Script: Li Pingfen. Dir: Huang Jianzhong. Line prod: Hu Mei. Players: Zhu Shimao, Chen Hong, Song Chunli. Prod: Peking Studio, Pacific Culture Entertainment.

ER MO (Ermo)

Script: Xu Baoqi. Dir: Zhou Xiaowen. Players: Liu Peiqi, Ailiya.

YU NI TONGZHU (Living with You)

Script: Xu Jianhai, Huang Jun. Dir: Huang Jun. Players: Zhang Guangbei, Ma Ling, Chen Wei. Prod: Fujian Studio.

HONGFEN (Rouge)

Script: Ni Zhen, Li Shaohong. Dir: Li Shaohong. Players: Wang Ji, He Saifei, Wang Zhiwen. Prod: Peking Studio, and others.

YUE LUO YU CHANG HE

Dir: Xie Tieli. Prod: Peking Studio.

DIAGULUDE YAOLAN (Cradle on Wheels)

Script: Chen Jianyu. Dir: Mi Jiashan. Players: Wang Xueqi, Gai Lili, Liang Tian, Ding Jiali. Prod: Emei Studio.

NUREN HUA (Woman, Flower)

Dir: Wang Jin. Players: Jin Chaoying, Yuan Li. Prod: Pearl River Studio.

BEI KAO BEI, LIAN DUI LIAN (Back to Back, Face to Face)

Script: Huang Xin, Sun Yuan, from Liu Xinglong's novel *Qiu feng zuile*. Dir: Huang Jianxin. Players: Niu Zhenhua, Lei Gesheng, Li Qiang, Ju Hao, Liu Guoxiang. Prod: Simpson (H.K.)/Xi'an Studio.

CROATIA

Tomislav
Kurelec

Today's situation in Croatian cinema can be briefly described as a national production that has an impressive past and that will probably have a bright future. The problem is a present which is practically non-existent, especially in the field of feature films.

The values of the past most acknowledged abroad are the animation (the famous Zagreb school of animation) and also the documentaries and other kind of short films which won a lot of international prizes. But even the feature films which didn't achieve the same success in the more intense competition in their category have made a name for a number of talented directors, cameramen, actors and other artists.

It seems that the same amount of talent or maybe even more may be possessed by the new up-and-coming generation of young cineastes, emerging in recent years from the Academy of Dramatic Arts (which includes theatre, cinema and television) in Zagreb. They are the future hope for Croatian cinema. They have made (in co-production with Croatian Television) some very interesting short films and one of the most promising among them, Hrvoje Hribar, is the director of a highly unusual and original TV-movie *Croatian Cathedrals*, about a young art critic whose essay about the national sacred art was stolen by the editor who doesn't care for art or ideals but is concerned only with profit. Hribar has succeeded in communicating through this movie an unconventional and very convincing image of the sensibility of a young generation.

But Hribar and his colleagues have only just begun to confront the main problem of Croatian cinema – the lack of money. This shortage is understandable to a certain degree, because the war in Croatia has not really ended and the problems with the defence of the country, the huge damage inflicted by Serbian aggression and the occupation of a quarter of Croatian territory, and above all half a million refugees have used up the state's funds and budget. But the majority of artists (and not only film directors) views the matter in another light, thinking that even in this situation they deserve a better treatment, owing to the fact that Croats have preserved their national identity during the centuries under foreign domination in the first place through art, culture and language. It seems that this point of view is also close to the former film director and producer Slobodan Praljak, who became a general during this war. He is now working for the ministry of defence and is trying to find a way to aid film production with the resources of his department, without controlling the author's choice of themes or ways of interpretation. But many people did not welcome this idea, fearing that it marks the first step towards the state's control of the arts.

Only Two Features Released

In the meantime the production of features has narrowly survived. From mid-1993 to mid-1994 only two new features have been screened. Probably the best Croatian film of the 1990's, **Countess Dora**, by Zvonimir Berković, had its premiere in July 1993 at the national film festival in Pula and won the "Big Golden Arena" (Grand Prix). It took nearly a year for us to see the next film – **The Price of Life** by Bogdan Žižić. That also means that the festival in Pula will not be held this year.

Even *Countess Dora* was shot some four years before the war. Berković had a lot of problems to complete this masterpiece. But this veteran is probably used to complications, because *Countess Dora* is only the fourth feature he has been able to make, although two of the former three – *Rondo* (1966) and *The Premeditated Love Letters* (1985) – had outstanding values, which deserve a place in any anthology of the Croatian cinema. The same high level is achieved by Berković in *Countess Dora*, a fictional love story involving a real person – the aristocrat Dora Pejačević, one of the first women composers in Europe. She was solitary and introvert, her biography doesn't yield too much material for a film, but she wrote some beautiful music, which is the only trace of her feelings. Former music critic Berković invented a lover for her – the cabaret master who fancies film. The movie is set in the 1920's and the first third is devoted to the beginning of the love affair. Then the director concentrates more on his male protagonist showing how this giddy-brained womaniser gradually fell in love with Dora and also with serious film directing. With much nuance and precision in his own idiosyncratic style, Berković integrates the story and the sentiments of the protagonists with Dora's music and the nostalgic evocation of Zagreb's atmosphere of the 1920's, achieving also a complexity of meaning, especially in the relationship between the reality and the illusion, and also between life and art.

The Price of Life, the fifth film by another veteran, Bogdan Žižić, did not enjoy the same success. Even though his first two features – *The House* (1975) and *Don't Lean Out* (1977) – have both won the Grand Prix at festival in Pula, Žižić is probably better as a director of short films (with many international prizes to his credit). During the war Žižić was one of the busiest directors making documentaries for Croatian television. This experience gave him the idea for his new feature about the Croat who escaped from a Serbian concentration camp, but is captured by an elderly Serbian peasant to work for him as a slave on penalty of death (by denunciation to the camp authorities). But as dramatic as the story was, the movie is not too convincing, because of flaws in the screenplay. Apart from that it seems that

Still from COUNTESS DORA

Žižić as a documentarist believes that the themes and events are the most important things in a film, but in features this conviction includes the danger that the characters become illustrations of ideas and not real people.

So, two films made by veterans in a season which has established the youngest generation of film-makers but which also poses the question, what is going on with everyone else? And there are at least ten very mature and intriguing directors. In the present situation this is maybe too much for a country like Croatia. Nevertheless their talents, furnished with some more money and far better organisation, can provide Croatia with a very interesting cinema.

TOMISLAV KURELEC has been a film critic since 1965. He has also directed five shorts and some hundred TV programmes.

Recent and Forthcoming Films

KONTESA DORA (Countess Dora)

Script and Dir: Zvonimir Berković. Phot: Goran Trbuljak. Players: Rade Šerbedžija, Alma Prica, Zdravka Krstulović, Tonko Lonza, Ksenija Pajić, Božidar Boban, Helena Buljan, Irena Alferova. Prod: Croatia Film, Croatian Television.

VUKOVAR SE VRAĆA KUĆI (Vukovar Is Coming Home)

Script: Pavao Pavličić. Dir: Branko Schmidt. Phot: Goran Trbuljak. Players: Sanja Marin, Goran Navojec, Horst Janson, Fabijan Šovagović, Mustafa Nadarević, Žarko Potočnjak, Ivo Gregurević. Prod: Croatian Television, Telereport GmbH (Germany).

CIJENA ŽIVOTA (The Price of Life)

Script: Fabijan Šovagović, Bogdan Žižić. Dir: Bogdan Žižić. Phot: Goran Trbuljak. Players: Slavko Juraga, Barbara Vicković, Ico Tomljenović, Goran Grgić. Prod: Graphis, Jadran Film.

GOSPA (Our Lady)

Script: Ivan Aralica, Paul Gronseth. Dir: Jakov Sedlar. Phot: Vjekoslav Vrdoljak. Players: Martin Sheen, Morgan Fairchild, Michael York. Prod: Wayne Films (New York)/Marianfilm (Toronto)/Jadran Film.

CZECH REPUBLIC
Eva Zaoralová

At the end of 1993, a new law finally put paid to the state monopoly on film matters, and gave the green light for the privatisation of the industry. Although this privatisation had already taken effect in the production and distribution sectors, most theatres still remained in the hands of the municipalities as before.

With some 1,400 screens, the Czech Republic is still one of those countries where the number of screens in proportion to the population is above the European average. However, during the first six months of 1994, attendances shrunk by 28% compared to the same period the previous year. This abrupt fall is due in particular to a new TV channel, owned by the first private TV company, Nova, which has shown a large number of films and this, in turn, has had a negative impact on the video market.

In 1993, Czech theatres screened 165 new films, of which 75% were American, and only 14 Czech titles were released. Still, at least two or three Czech pictures made the 'Top Ten' in terms of tickets sold. For example, in spring 1994 a remarkable comedy, **Accumulator** (*Akumulátor*) by the young Jan Svěrák, actually topped the charts, followed closely by two other domestic films, **The Immortal Aunt** (*Nesmrtelná teta*), a fairy story by Zdeněk Zelenka, and **Angel Eyes** (*Andělské oči*), a comedy by Dušan Klein based on a book by Hrabal.

Czech TV the Most Prolific Producer

Production remains pretty much as it was last year: grants can be given producers by an independent commission on the basis of a screenplay. The resources of the Ministry of Culture's National Film Fund are drawn exclusively from a tax on each ticket sold, which limits the amount disposable and of course the number of projects that can receive aid. Moreover, the subsidy never exceeds 30% of a picture's budget.

Still, 16 features were shot in 1993, and more or less the same number is forecast for 1994. Although Barrandov Studios, the largest producer under the old state system, has virtually abandoned film production in favour of other activities (services for foreign producers, etc.), certain film production companies are quite vigorous.

Czech TV has recently become one of the most significant producers, having financed or co-financed five films in 1993, among them Karel Kachyňa's **The Cow** (*Kráva*), which earned the prize for best domestic film at the National Film Festival in Pilsen in 1994, and the top award at the Festival of Strasbourg. In 1994, Czech TV has already produced Jiří Věrčák's **Saturnin** and Zuzana Hojdová's **The Sandcastle** (*Zámek z písku*).

Several foreign directors are shooting their new films in co-production with Czech partners, among them the Bosnian, Emir Kusturica, and the Croat, Lordan Zafranović. One of the most interesting projects of the year will be **The Too Noisy Solitude** (*Příliš hlučná samota*), a first film by the Franco-Czech director Věra Caisová, from the novel by Bohumil Hrabal, starring Philippe Noiret.

A New "New Wave"?

Since the 1960's, the distinction between the "old" cinema and the new has never been so pronounced. Those who used to irritate the public with their advanced film language (Jaromil Jireš, Drahomíra Vihanová) seem old-fashioned to those young critics who prefer the cinema of their pals, Jan Hřebejk, Jan Svěrák, Vladimír Michálek, Irena Pavlásková, and Milan Šteindler. Svěrák's *Accumulator*, an ironic transposition of Hollywood themes to a Czech universe, risks becoming a cult movie, like **Big Beat** (*Šakalí léta*), a look back at the 1950's to the beat of banned music, or **America** (*Amerika*), a first film by Vladimír Michálek, loosely inspired by a Kafka novel, interpreted in a spirit of ironic eclecticism. The rejection of symbolism and humanist reflection, so close to those who were thirty-something in the 1960's, is so strong among young people today that one can speak of a conflict of "postmodernism" v. "modernism".

Between these two extremes lies the cinema of Zdeněk Tyc, already known for *Vojtěch Called Orfelin*, (1991), who in his second film, **The Razor's Edge** (*Žiletky*) reveals his links with the lyricism of the Czech and Slovak new wave.

If Drahomíra Vihanová in her second feature, **The Fortress** (*Pevnost*), made 25 years after her first, banned film, *A Lost*

Sunday (*Zabitá nedele*), evokes this lyrical mood with nostalgia, Karel Kachyna, more eclectic and more pragmatic, seems able to adapt to the new mood in *The Cow*, while still clinging to his vision of art and the world. The same applies to Jiří Menzel, with his **Extraordinary Adventures of Private Conkin** (*Život a neobyčejná dobrodružství vokáka Ivan Čonkina*).

Where Can We See European Films?

Even if the domination of the local market by the American majors is an established fact, the big international distributors are still not satisfied with their revenues. This is why Guild abandoned its base in the Czech Republic in 1994, and was immediately replaced by a new, small, wholly Czech company – Falcon. The strongest distributors remain Lucernafilm (representing UIP and Fox), Gemini Films (Warner Bros. and Columbia TriStar), and Intersonic (a Slovak company also covering the Czech Republic).

To survive, all these companies try to release as many films as possible, in order to allow themselves the occasional luxury of buying a European film (even if they almost always fail at the box-office).

Fortunately, the cultural centres of Poland, Hungary, France, Italy, and the Goethe Institute are very active; and in April 1994 EFDO came to Prague to help stage some "European Film Days." A group of young executives has founded Czech Film Promotion in order to highlight Czech cinema abroad and to represent local producers at an international level.

Another organisation, the Karlovy Vary Film Festival Foundation, was established in 1993, under the aegis of the Ministry of Culture, in order to continue the tradition of the Karlovy Vary event each and every year into the future.

EVA ZAORALOVÁ (Hepernová) is a Czech film critic and Editor of the magazine *Film a Doba*. She is author of many essays and two books and taught film history at FAMU in Prague for ten years.

PEVNOST
(The Fortress)

Script: Alexander Kliment, Drahomírá Vihanová, from a novel by Kliment. Direction: Drahomíra Vihanová. Photography: Jiří Macák. Music: Jiří Stivín. Editing: Drahomíra Vihanová, Martin Čihák. Players: György Cserhalmi, Miroslav Donutil, Zuzana Kocúriková, Josef Kemr. Produced by K.F./Synergia Film, in association with CNC (Paris).

It is the 1980's. The regime is on its knees but still clings to power. Evald, an intellectual who is forbidden from carrying out his profession, arrives at a certain village to examine the water sources. He set himself up in a caravan close to the local castle, an inaccessible and rather sinister place, inhabited by soldiers. Nobody knows what they are overseeing. Even if the commander of the fortress tries to win Evald's confidence, an entire universe separates the two men – one of whom must perish ...

Vihanová (born in 1930) made her first film, *A Lost Sunday*, in 1968-69. It ended up in the cupboards of civil servants who judged it to be dangerous on account of its "existential pessimism". The director was silenced for too many years, although she managed to become one of the best documentarists of the 1980's. Since the "velvet revolution" she has been struggling to raise money for her second feature. *The Fortress*, conceived in black-and-white, uses the allegorical language of the 1960's, even if the story takes place in a more recent past. "The conflict between despotic and rigid power, and an individual aspiring to liberty remains eternal," emphasises Vihanová. The well-known György Cserhalmi, a key actor for Miklós Jancsó, acts magnificently as Evald.

Eva Zaoralová

Recent and Forthcoming Films

AKUMULÁTOR 1 (Accumulator 1)

Script: J. Slovák, Zdenek Svěrák. Dir: Svěrák. Phot: F.A. Brabec. Players: Petr Forman, Edita Brychta, Zdeněk Svěrák, Marian Labuda, Bolek Polívka. Prod: Heureka Production PF/Luxor/Pro Heureka Film.

AMERIKA (America)

Script: V. Michálek, Martin Duba, based on the novel from F. Kafka. Dir: Vladimír Michálek. Phot: Martin Duba. Players: Martin Dejdar, Jiří Lábus, Oldřich Kaiser, Jiří Schmitzer, Tomáš Vorel. Prod: Simply Cinema/Czech Television.

ANDĚLSKÉ OČI (Angel Eyes)

Script: Václav Nývlt, D. Klein, based on the novels of Bohumil Hrabal. Dir: Dušan Klein. Phot: Josef Vaniš. Players: Josef Abrhám, Viktor Preiss, Pavel Zedníček, Pavel Kříž, Zlata Adamovská, Markéta Hrubešová. Prod: Czech Television/Heureka Production PF.

DIKY ZA KAŽDÉ NOVÉ RÁND (I Thank You for Each New Morning)

Script: Halina Pawlowská. Dir: Milan Šeindler. Phot: Jiří Krejčík. Players: Franciszek Piecska, Ivana Chýlková, Miroslav Etzler, Barbora Hrzánová, Tereza Brodská, Karel Heřmánek. Prod: Česká filmová společnost/Czech Film Society/Czech Television/Ekoagrobanka/Mazda.

HELIMADOE (Helimadoe)

Script: Václav Šašek, based on the novel by Jaroslav Havlíček. Dir: Jaromil Jireš. Phot: Petr Polák. Players: Josef Somr, Jana Dolanská, Lucie Zedníčková, Zuzana Bydžovská, Ljuba Krbová, Jakub Marek. Prod: Czech Television.

KRÁVA (The Cow)

Script: Karel Čabrádek, K. Kachyňa. Dir: Karel Kachyňa. Phot: Petr Hojda. Players: Radek Holub, Alena Mihulová. Prod: Czech Television.

LEKCE FAUST (Faust)

Script and Dir: Jan Švankmajer. Phot: Svatopluk Malý. Animation: Bedřich Glaser. Marionettes: Jiří Bláha. Players: Petr Čepek, Jan Kraus. Prod: Athanor, Prague/

CNC/Fonds Eco (France)/BBC Bristol (UK)/Pandora Film (Ger-many)/Heart of Europe (Czech Rep.)/Lumen Films (France)/Konick Films (UK).

NESMRTELNÁ TETA (The Immortal Aunt)

Script and Dir: Zdeněk Zelenka. Phot: Viktor Růžička. Players: Jiřina Bohdalová, Filip Blažek, Barbora Bobulová, Jaromír Hanzlík, Petr Kostka. Prod: BONTON, Agrobanka/Czech Television/Visual Connection/Rencar/GMS.

SATURNIN (Saturnin)

Script: Magdalena Vágnerová, Jiří Věrčák, based on the novel from Zdeněk Jirotka. Dir: Jiří Věrčák. Phot: Josef Špelda. Players: Oldřich Vízner, Ondřej Havelka, Milan Lasica, Lucie Zedníčková, Jana Synková. Prod: Jupiter Film/Czech Television.

ŠAKALÍ LÉTA (Big Beat)

Script: Petr Jarchovský, J. Hřebejk, based on the novel by Petr Šabach. Dir: Jan Hřebejk. Phot: Jan Malíř. Players: Jakub Špalek, Martin Dejdar, Josef Abrhám, Sylva Tománková, Jitka Asterová, Jan Semotán. Prod: NOVA – Independent Television Comp./Polytechna, Space Films.

ŽILETKY (Blades)

Script and Dir: Zdeněk Tyc. Phot: Marek Jícha. Players: Filip Topol, Markéta Hrubešová, Iva Janžurová, Tomáš Hanák. Prod: Ajeto Film 1, Ministry of Culture of the Czech Republic/Czech Television/ArtCam International/Fondation GAN/CNC.

Producers

AB Barrandov a.s.
Kříženeckého nám. 322
152 53 Praha 5
Tel: 42-2/24 51 07 01
Fax: 42-2/24 51 06 28

Ateliéry ZLIN a.s.
Filmová 174
761 79 Zlín
Tel: 967/527 400
Fax: 067/527 510

BONTON Films a.s.*
Severozápadní UV/39
141 00 Praha 4
Tel: 42-2/748 907
Fax: 42-2/765 750

Etamp Film Production s.r.o.*
U továren 261
102 00 Praha Ú
Tel: 42-2/705 257
Fax: 42-2/706 077

Febio, Ltd.
Růžová ul. 13
110 00 Praha 1
Tel: 42-2/2421 39 33
Fax: 42-2/2421 42 54

Heureka Film s.r.o.
Litevská 8
100 05 Praha 10
Tel: 42-2/742 558
Fax: 42-2/743 413

Heureka Productions s.r.o.
Vaníčkova 2
160 17 Praha 6
Tel: 42-2/527 418
Fax: 42-2/354 772

KF a.s.*
Jindřiška 34
112 07 Praha 1
Tel: 42-2/2421 24 10
Fax: 42-2/6445 111

Mirrorfilm
Na poříčí 14
110 00 Praha 1
Tel: 42-2/2481 09 66
Fax: 42-2/2481 06 32

Space Films s.r.o.
Korlovo nám. 19
120 00 Praha 2

Tel: 42-2/2491 30 43
Fax: 42-2/2491 30 45

VaC – Vachler ART Comp.
Na Žertvách 40
180 00 Praha 8
Tel: 42-2/68 32 600
*also distributor

Distributors

Lucernafilm a.s.
Národní tř. 28
111 21 Praha 1
Tel: 42-2/2422 67 63
Fax: 42-2/2422 52 63

Filmexport Prague
Na Moráni 5
128 00 Praha 2
Tel: 42-2/24 91 52 39
Fax: 42-2/29 33 12

Falcon
V jámě 5
111 40 Praha 1
Tel: 42-2/24 21 57 38
Fax: 42-2/24 22 63 8

Gemini Film s.r.o.
V Jámě 1
110 00 Praha 1
Tel: 42-2/24 16 24 71
Fax: 42-2/24 22 65 62

Intersonic Taunus Prod. Ltd.
Staré Grunty 34
842 25 Bratislava
Tel: 42-7/72 10 05
Fax: 42-7/72 20 70

Useful Addresses

Film Department of the Ministry of Culture
Valdstejnská 12
110 00 Praha 1
Tel: 42-2/513 23 38, 513 24 78
Fax: 42-2/53 70 55

National Film Archive/Film Institute/Národni tr. 40
110 00 Praha 1
Tel: 42-2/24 22 71 37, 24 22 73 11
Fax: 42-2/24 22 77 44

DENMARK

Ebbe
Iversen

Today it is not possible to produce a Danish feature film entirely with private funds. All films are financially supported by the governmental Danish Film Institute (DFI), and more and more films are made as co-productions with other countries, especially the Scandinavian nations.

Nevertheless, the Danish film community is – as always – complaining that the funding is insufficient. Eleven Danish feature films opened last year, but according to people in the film business an annual production of at least 20 feature films is necessary to ensure continuity and quality. At a meeting in April 1994 it was suggested by all the major Danish film trade organisations that the DFI should be allocated an extra DKK 100 million for film production and DKK 50 million for film promotion. It is unlikely, however, that a political majority in the Danish parliament (Folketinget) will support this suggestion.

As it is now, state funding of film production is distributed by three consultants at the DFI – Hans Hansen, Jørgen Ljungdahl and Per Nielsen, the latter dealing exclusively with films for children. Each of them works with an annual budget of DKK 16 million, which covers two feature films at the most. It is the consultants' task to support films of artistic merit, but it is also possible to receive a subsidy from the DFI via the so-called fifty-fifty arrangement, whereby producers are automatically allocated half their production expenses – up to DKK 3.5 million – provided backers put up the rest.

Progress has, however, been made. The two national Danish TV channels – Danmarks Radio and TV 2 – have been allocated an extra DKK 45 million annually for the production of fiction, and although the money may be used for TV series, it is hoped that a substantial amount will be invested in Danish feature films to open in the cinemas and later be shown on TV. An additional DKK 24 million, to be channelled via both the DFI and the National Film Board of Denmark, which deals with short films and documentaries, has been allocated for the production of short feature films.

Continuing Decline in Seats

The number of cinemas in Denmark is still decreasing. In 1980 there were 329 with a total of 112,219 seats; today there are only 166 with 51,492 seats. 1993 was not, however, a bad year for Danish cinemas. Compared to the previous year attendance rose from 8,648,000 to 10,222,000, and the number of tickets sold for Danish films rose from 1,591,000 to 1,763,000. Thus, domestic films enjoyed a market share of 17.2%, which is quite high in a European context.

The major cinematic media event in Denmark in 1993 was the opening of Academy Award and Palme d'Or winner Bille August's **House of the Spirits** (*Åndernes hus*) with Jeremy Irons, Meryl Streep and Glenn Close in the main roles. The film – which is based on Isabel Allende's best-selling novel, and is basically a German production, financed by Bernd Eichinger in Munich – got a lukewarm reception from most Danish critics, and was later butchered by the British critics, but it was a huge commercial success in Denmark.

Bille August is now planning to make a film about the American painter Georgia O'Keefe, possibly with Michelle Pfeiffer in the lead, and a film based on Danish writer Peter Høeg's internationally acclaimed

novel *Frøken Smillas fornemmelse for sne* –
the British title of the novel is *Miss Smilla's
Feeling for Snow*, whereas the American title
is *Smilla's Sense of Snow*.

Another big domestic success in the
Danish cinemas was first-time director Ole
Bornedal's thriller **Nightwatch** (*Natte-
vagten*), which was presented in the
Semaine de la Critique at the 1994 Cannes
Film Festival. It is not a flawless film, but it
is made with admirable professional confidence, and in its best scenes it is
genuinely spooky and scary. Ole Bornedal
is definitely a promising new talent –
which is much needed in Danish films, as
producers generally prefer to invest in
middle-aged or older directors because of
their experience.

One of the main parts in **Nightwatch** is
played by the brightest young female star
in Danish cinema, Sofie Gråbøl. She also
has a main part – and plays it very
touchingly – in Anders Refn's new film
Black Harvest (*Sort høst*), the working title
of which was *In the Bosom of the Family*,

Ole Ernst in BLACK HARVEST

which tells the tragic story of a wealthy
landowner ruining himself and his family
through drinking, gambling and forni-
cating. The film – based on a novel by the
cynical writer Gustav Wied (1858-1914) – is
a handsome and visually attractive period
piece with a gloomy vision of life.

Respectful, Stale and Stiff

Director, actor and writer Erik Clausen
gave a respectful, but far too stale and stiff
description of the leading Danish composer Carl Nielsen's childhood and youth
at the end of the 19th century in **Carl – My
Childhood Symphony** (*Min fynske
barndom*) – it is much more rewarding to
read Carl Nielsen's wonderful autobiography, on which the film is based –
while Helle Ryslinge, also well known
outside Denmark for the vital and funny
Cœurs Flambés, disappointed most people
with her **Carlo & Ester** about two old
people, a widow and a married man,
falling in love to the great indignation of
their families and friends. A decent and
sincere film, but far too obvious in its
arguments.

Eddie Thomas Petersen, whose first film
was *Spring Tide*, made a gentle and
attractive romantic comedy **Red Roses and
Parsley** (*Roser og persille*), but Susanne Bier
chose the wrong script for her second
feature film, **It Stays in the Family** (*Det
bli'r i familien*), which tells a very contrived
story about a chef, who discovers that he is
adopted, and travels with his biological
mother in search of his father.

Anne Wivel made a long and interesting,
but far too talkative documentary called
Søren Kierkegaard about the Danish
philosopher, and Flemming Quist Møller
and Søren Fjelmark created a funny, well-
crafted animated film called **Jungle Jack**
(*Jungledyret*).

Veteran director and Academy Award
winner (for *Babette's Feast*) Gabriel Axel
finally managed to make the film he had
been dreaming of for years, **Prince of
Jutland** (*Prinsen af Jylland*). It is based on a
tale by Danish historian Saxo Grammaticus

Sofie Gråbøl and Philip Zandén in BLACK HARVEST

(who died in approximately 1220), which also inspired Shakespeare to write *Hamlet*. It is thus the story of a young prince avenging the murder of his father, the king. *Prince of Jutland* is a Dutch-French-Danish-English co-production shot in English with Christian Bale playing the prince, Gabriel Byrne the evil king and Helen Mirren the queen. It had its world premiere in Paris in spring 1994 and by summer 1994 had not yet opened in Denmark, which is no wonder, as it is the sort of respectful and utterly stolid film that makes audiences yawn. Not a bad film, just boring.

Experienced director Jørgen Leth – who now lives in Haiti – made the documentary **Michael Laudrup** (*Michael Laudrup – En fodboldspiller*) about the likeable Danish soccer star and his career with FC Barcelona. Two Danish films had their world premiere at the 1994 Cannes Film Festival. **The Wedding Photographer** (*Bryllupsfotografen*) about a famous war photographer, who tries (but fails) to start a new and more peaceful life in his native provincial town in Denmark is ambitious

without quite reaching its philosophical goals, but the film is interesting as an example of Scandinavian co-operation – the script is by Norwegian Dag Solstad, the director is Swedish Johan Bergenstråhle, and the first-time producer is Danish Peter Nørgård, who has founded a company called Such Much Movies.

The other new Danish film in Cannes was **The Daughter of the Puma** (*Pumaens datter*), also directed by a Swede – Ulf Hultberg – and shot in southern Mexico. It tells a story inspired by Nobel Peace Prize winner Rigoberta Menchu about a young Indian woman from Guatemala, who tries to find her missing brother after a military massacre has taken place in their village. Mexican Indians play the parts, and the simple and semi-documentary film is worth showing on television, but will not draw crowds to the cinemas.

Coming up is a new long animated film by veteran Jannik Hastrup, **The Secret Weapon** (*Det hemmelige våben*), and a new film by another veteran, Henning Carlsen –

TOP TEN GROSSING FILMS IN DENMARK: 1993

Jurassic Park
The Bodyguard
Stolen Spring (Det forsømte forår)
Hot Shots! Part Deux
Aladdin
Fish Out of Water (De frigjorte)
Home Alone 2
Indecent Proposal
The House of the Spirits
Crumb at a Gallop (Krummerne II – Stekkels Krumme)

his first for more than ten years. It is called **Pan** and based on a novel by Norwegian writer and Nobel Prize receiver Knut Hamsun (previously filmed by among others Swedish director Bo Widerberg), and was shot in the summer of 1994 in northern Norway with Sofie Gråbøl in one of the main parts.

Young director Jesper W. Nielsen, who has made very promising short films, is going to make his first feature film, **The**

Last Viking (*Den sidste viking*) in Estonia and Latvia. It deals with war and love among the Vikings and has Swedish actors Per Oscarsson and Marika Lagercrantz (who was in *Black Harvest*) in the cast.

Bo Widerberg is also directing again. His new film is called **And All Things Fair** (*Lust och fägring stor*, Swedish title) and is produced by Danish Per Holst. The story takes place during the Second World War and deals with a 15-year-old boy – played by the director's son Johan Widerberg – who has an affair with his teacher, portrayed by Marika Lagercrantz. The film's budget is DKK 18.8 million.

Carsten Sønder, whose first film was **Pretty Boy** (*Smukke dreng*) about a young male prostitute's tough life in Copenhagen, will direct **Wonderful World** (*Vidunderlige verden*) about 35-year-old Hannah – played by the fine stage actress Charlotte Sieling, who also provided the idea for the film – who falls in love with a much younger

Still from Johan Bergenståhle's THE WEDDING PHOTOGRAPHER   *photo: Ole Kragh-Jacobsen*

man. Female director Kirsten Stenbæk, who has not made feature films for about twenty years, comes back with the romantic comedy **Love at First Desperate Glance** (*Kærlighed ved første desperate blik*), and finally the DFI has invested DKK 3.5 million in Finnish director Pekka Lehto's satirical comedy **Bottoms Up** (original title) – a Finnish-Danish-Russian co-production – which once again will give us a chance of seeing Sofie Gråbøl on the screen.

EBBE IVERSEN has been a professional journalist since 1966. He has been film critic of "Berlingske Tidende" since 1973, and is a former co-editor of the magazine, "Kosmorama".

National Film Board of Denmark

A number of documentary films from Statens Filmcentral (National Film Board of Denmark) had an international apeal in 1993-94. Jørgen Leth, who has previously made films about the heroes of bicycle races, has created a film about the Danish footballer, **Michael Laudrup,** while he was one of the stars of F.C. Barcelona. The feature-length documentary, which had a cinema release in Denmark and was sold on cassette in Barcelona, focuses on the artistic qualities of the play, on how Laudrup moves when he does not have the ball, on the game as a light and playful, and not a powerful performance.

Arne Treholt – the Man and His Destiny by Morten Henriksen is also a portrait, which focuses on psychology. Treholt, a Norwegian diplomat who was sent to prison in 1984 for espionage in favour of the U.S.S.R., was on the front page of the newspapers in the Nordic countries for a number of years. In his opinion he was wrongfully convicted, a point of view which is reflected in the film. For 82 minutes the film makes the man tell his story, not to give the audience a possibility of evaluating his guilt, but to illustrate what happens to a man who is in prison for eight years and is exposed to a treatment which has marked him for the rest of his life. The story of how Arne Treholt managed a cold

war treatment also had a Danish cinema release and the Norwegian premiere took place in connection with the Haugesund Festival in August 1993.

The most ambitious portrait, however, was made by female director Anne Wivel, who in her 165-minutes long documentary film about **Søren Kierkegaard** makes a number of Danes gathered in a high school speak on the texts of the world-famous philosopher and writer. The film, shot on 35mm, follows these conversations, the expressions of the speaking and listening people in a form which could be called an anti-film – and yet so informative and inspiring. Surprisingly, the film was shown for six weeks in Danish cinemas and is destined to have a wide international distribution.

Lars Movin, journalist and video director, has already sparked international interest in his **The Misfits – 30 Years of Fluxus,** an 80-minute investigation of the history and idea behind this art movement, including people like Nam June Paik, Yoko Ono, Jonas Mekas and Ben Vautier, as has Jon Bang Carlsen with his experimental and poetic personal story **Life Will Be Lived – Letters from a Mother,** which is based on letters which the director's mother wrote to his son in the U.S.A. from the rough and beautiful landscapes of Northern Jutland, the roots of Jon Bang Carlsen, so often described in his earlier works.

Like Jon Bang Carlsen, Lars Johansson, director of **Traveller's Tale,** travels from Denmark through Poland and Romania to the Black Sea. The film – 75 minutes long – is a journey in remembrance where the director mixes film and video shootings in a medley of fiction and documentary, a

Still from Jørgen Leth's profile of MICHAEL LAUDRUP

NATIONAL FILM BOARD
OF DENMARK

27, VESTERGADE
DK-1456 COPENHAGEN K
DENMARK

PHONE: (+45) 3313 2686
TELEFAX: (+45) 3313 0203

form which made many Danish reviewers describe the film as innovative within the classic documentary film world.

Talk like Whales by Vibeke Vogel is in the same way a film that mixes genres in its description of the whales – intelligent, gentle and sympathetic animals – so that the categories video art, cinematic essay and documentarism blend and merge.

As usual the production company Film-forsyningen made new, international children's films, a genre which the Nordic countries are still developing. The so-called Tegnedrengene, Anders Sørensen and Per Tønnes Nielsen, continued their adventurous stories in animating **The World History** – in 52 minutes. And using the pixillation style, female director Liller Møller presented **Morten's Beach Ball,** a charming story for the youngest.

Also for children, Thomas Vinterberg – one of the most promising talents of Danish film – made **The Boy Who Walked Backwards,** a moving, Truffaut-like story about a boy's experience of his brother's death.

Tue Steen Müller

Producers

ASA Film Production ApS
Mosedalvej
DK-2500 Valby
Tel: 3618 8200
Fax: 3116 8502

Crone Film Produktion A/S
Blomstervænget 52
DK-2800 Lyngby
Tel: 4587 2700
Fax: 4587 2705

Dagmar Film Produktion ApS
Puggaardsgade 15
DK-1573 København V
Tel: 3393 9291
Fax: 3393 8373

Danish Film Studio
Blomstervænget 52
DK-2800 Lyngby
Tel: 4587 2700
Fax: 4587 2705
Telex: 37798 (studio dk)

Domino Film & TV Production
Guldbergsgade 29 F
DK-2200 København N

Tel: 3536 0909
Fax: 3536 0904

Film & Lyd Produktion A/S
Bredgade 63A
DK-1260 København K
Tel: 3312 1050
Fax: 3312 1093

Film-Cooperativet Danmark 1983 ApS
Bymandsgade 3
DK-2791 Dragør
Tel: 3253 5631
Fax: 3253 6852

Fortuna Film
Vordingborgvej 90
DK-4681 Herføge
Tel: 5367 6446
Fax: 5367 6484

Grasten Film, Regner
Lykkevej 6
DK-2920 Charlottenlund
Twl: 3163 4424
Fax: 3163 4823

Holst Film A/S, Per
Rentemestervej 82

DK-2400 København NV
Tel: 3888 7800
Fax: 3888 7878

Høyberg Film & Video ApS
Ryesgade 106
DK-2100 København Ø
Tel: 3543 4322
Fax: 3142 4299

Lense-Møller Film ApS, Lise
Fortunvej 56
DK-2920 Charlottenlund
Tel: 3164 2284
Fax: 3164 2269

Locomotion Kofod Schiller Film A/S
Nannasgade 28
DK-2200 København N
Tel: 3183 8900
Fax: 3582 1737

Madsen, Kenneth Filmproduktion A/S
Guldbergsgade 29 F
DK-2200 København N
Tel: 3536 0036
Fax: 3536 0011

Metronome Productions A/S
Søndermarksvej 16
DK-2500 Valby

Nordisk Film Production A/S
Mosedalvej
DK-2500 Valby
Tel: 3630 1033
Fax: 3116 8502

Obel Film, ApS
A.N. Hansens Allé 23
DK-2900 Hellerup
Tel: 3161 0666
Fax: 3161 0667
or
Norgesvej 25
DK-9480 Løkken
Tel: 9899 1353
Fax: 9899 2036

Panorama Film International Ltd,
The Old Mill, London Road, Hook,
Hants AG27 9EH England
Tel: (44) 256766-868
Fax: (44) 256768-747

Penta Film
Strandgade 4 B
DK-1401 København K
Tel: 3296 6230
Fax: 3296 0014

Ravn Film og Media Aps
Mosedalvej 11 B
DK-2500 Valby
Tel: 3645 5800
Fax: 3645 0808

Superfilm Productions
Forbindelssvej 5
DK-2100 København Ø
Tel: 3142 4611
Fax: 3142 4611

Vestergaard Film, Jørgen
Gadekøret 24, Sennels
DK 7700, Thisted
Tel: 9798 50020
Fax: 9798 5020

Victoria Film
Blomstervænget 52
DK-2800 Lyngby
Tel: 4587 2500
Fax: 4587 2505

Zentropa Entertainments ApS
Ryesgade 106, st.
DK-2100 København Ø
Tel: 3142 4233
Fax: 3142 429

Distributors

AB Collection
Hirsemarken 3
DK-3520 Farum
Tel: 4499 6200
Fax: 4295 1786

Camera Film
Mikkel Bryggers Gade 8
DK-1460 København K
Tel: 3313 6112
Fax: 3315 0882

Cinnamon Film ApS
Brandts passage 15
DK-5000 Odense C
Tel: 6612 1716
Fax: 6612 8082

Constantin Film ApS
Skelbækgade 1
DK-1717 København V
Tel: 3325 2424
Fax: 3325 0707

Egmont Audio Visual A/S
Skelbækgade 1
DK-1717 København V
Tel: 3325 4000
Fax: 3325 4002

20th Century Fox
Skelbækgade 1, 3.
DK-1717 København V
Tel: 3325 4000
Fax: 3325 4002

Gloria Film
Vesterbrogade 149
DK-1620 København V
Tel: 3327 0022
Fax: 3327 0099

Kommunefilm
Baltoppen
DK-2750 Ballerup
Tel: 4265 6262
Fax: 4477 2708

Nordisk Film Distribution A/S
Skelbækgade 1
DK-1717 København V
Tel: 3123 2488
Fax: 3123 0488

Scala Film
Centrumpladsen
DK-5700 Svendborg
Tel: 6221 8866
Fax: 6221 0821

UIP – United International Pictures
Hauchsvej 13
DK-1825 Frederiksberg C
Tel: 3131 2330
Fax: 3123 3420

Warner & Metronome ApS
Søndermarksvej 16
DK-2500 Valby
Tel: 3146 8822
Fax: 3644 0604

Useful Addresses

Danish Film Institute
Store Søndervoldstræde 4
DK-1419 København K
Tel: 3157 6500
Fax: 3157 6700
Tlx: 31465 dfilm dk

Danish Film Institute Workshop
Vesterbrogade 24
DK-1620 København V
Tel: 3124 1624
Fax: 3124 4419

National Film Board of Denmark
Statens Filmcentral
Vestergade 27
DK-1456 København K
Tel: 3313 2686
Fax: 3313 0203

The Danish Film Studio
Blomstervænget 52
DK-2800 Lyngby
Tel: 4587 2700
Fax: 4587 2705

Risby Studios
Ledøjevej 1
DK-2620 Albertslund
Tel: 4262 9646

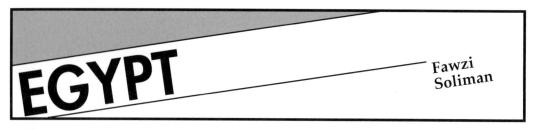

EGYPT

Fawzi Soliman

The problem of privatisation of Egyptian cinema – referred to in IFG 1994 – caused a lot of debate. The state actually established a holding company involving tourism, housing and cinema. Cinema assets such as studios – among them Studio Misr, the oldest in the Arab World (1935) – laboratories, and theatres were offered for sale. Those who backed privatisation asserted that this would improve production proficiency. It was expected that the process of privatisation would be totally accomplished by the end of 1996. Nevertheless many warned against privatisation on the assumption that it would hand over this effective mass media to reactionary or commercial bodies.

In April 1994, a conference, called by the Cultural Development Fund and *Al Ahram* newspaper, was held under the auspices of the Prime Minister to discuss the future of the Egyptian cinema. The conference was concluded by the Minister of Culture's declaration that all cinema assets would remain owned by the state. It was unanimously acknowledged that this would be necessary in order to upgrade the culture of the masses in a country still predominantly illiterate. Besides the Misr company of distribution and cinema houses (affiliated to the Ministry of Culture) decided to finance some films by up to 60% of their production budget. Part of this contribution would be in the form of technical services in studios and labs.

Censorship

The problem of censorship was raised by many critics and writers. They condemn its restrictions, narrow-mindedness and obstruction of free expression and democracy. Scriptwriters complained that censorship confines their freedom to deal with real social problems in such time of crucial changes.

The Minister of Culture responded by establishing a Higher Council of Censorship comprising a number of intellectuals, specialists in the fields of politics, law, mass media and (of course) cinema. Its function is to put forward strategies for enlightened censorship.

It is worth mentioning that a court has this year passed a verdict allowing the screening of a film which was banned 11 years ago, namely *Five Doors (Khamsa Bab)* which is an adaptation of *Irma La Douce* by Billy Wilder. The film scored a great success!

Fresh Wind

Out of the 53 films shown in 1993, eight are by new directors. Some of them aspired to create different cinematic styles in presenting the realities of society, but the majority of films are straightforward in their commercial appeal.

One of the newcomers is Tarek El Telmissany – a successful director of photography for ten years – who makes his directing debut with **Laughters, Games, Seriousness and Love**. He tries to initiate a narrative style far removed from the traditional one. The film deals with moral issues, with a human perspective, in depicting the atmosphere of Egyptian society in 1968 – the year of student unrest and following the military defeat of 1967. Here we see young men torn apart socially and psychologically, looking for a new world away from their school, where they cannot overcome the burdens and restrictions imposed by family and society. We observe the loss of dreams, rebellious spirit, and of imagination.

Mercedes, written and directed by Yusri Nasralla, is considered by critics as a true representative of the New Egyptian

Still from MERCEDES

Still from LAND OF DREAMS

Cinema. It does not involve a style of narrative, but a series of situations with long effective scenes. The worries of Egypt in the 1990's are reconstructed from a subjective view point. A panorama of the frustrations, the sense of loss provoked by the downfall of he big dreams, extremism, escape into drug addiction and football mania. Although it did badly at the box-office it reaped most of the major awards at the annual Film Society festival. It has also been awarded the second prize at Khrebka Film Festival in Morocco, and a special mention by the Egyptian Association of Film Critics (also a special award of merit from the magazine *Nouvel Observateur*), was screened at such festivals as Locarno, Toronto and Dublin.

Dream of America

Emigration to the U.S.A., a dreamland to many an Egyptian youth, has become widespread in the last two decades. In some of the films of the 1970's and 1980's this issue was referred to. But recently three films dealt with the problems as a main topic: **America Shikia Bika**, by Khairy Beshara, **Land of Dreams**, by Daoud Abdel Sayed, and **The Visit of the President**, by Monier Rady.

In *America Skika Bika*, a group of people belonging to the petit bourgeoisie are united by the dream of escaping poverty by emigrating to the U.S.A. One of them, for example, is a cobbler whose idol is Sylvester Stallone; others include a retired nightclub dancer, a country tailor, a bum, and an ailing young girl. The man who

arranged the journey to Romania for them turns out to be a swindler. He is supposed to get their American visas for them, but he disappears, leaving them to face alienation, hunger, cold and death. They are convinced that emigration is nothing but a mirage. The songs in the film comment on the incidents. *America Skika Bika* was shot outdoors in streets, forests, railway stations and airports. All in all, some good co-operation with Romanian technicians.

We turn from the emigration of the poor to the emigration of the well-off in *Land of Dreams*, where we find characters representing the bourgeoisie. A mother in her fifties is urged by her son and daughter to emigrate to the States to pave the way for their own emigration; they yearn for more luxury. She hesitates for fear of alienation, of missing her neighbours, and the life she is accustomed to. All the events take place in one night. She ends up with the conviction that the real land of dreams is the land you belong to, where you achieve fulfilment.

The film's intense narrative style gives life to every tiny detail. It was selected by the Association of Egyptian Film Critics as the best film of the year.

The third film is *Visit of the President*, directed by Moneir Radi, adapted from a novel by Yousef El Kaeed. The inhabitants of a poor village expect a visit by the American President. There is a mood of carnival, and everybody is looking forward to the rich rewards to come. But the train does not stop at the village in which the

Still from THE CAPTAIN

viewer witnesses the rise and the fall of the American dream!

A Daring Act

At a time when this country is marked by a wave of terrorism including attempts on the lives of the Ministers of Information and interior and later the Prime Minister himself, and the death of innocent victims, including children, in the streets, the production of such a film as **The Terrorist** was a daring act. It was written by Lenin El Ramly (an eminent playwright) and stars

Still from THE TERRORIST

Adel Emam, the most outstanding actor of the moment. Right from the start of the film, there are clear indications of what is actually happening in Egypt. A bearded man with a grim face breaks into a jewellery shop, burns video clubs and shoots at a tourist bus.

The cinemas where the film was screened were guarded by the police and attracted unprecedented takings. Extremists stormed a cinema showing the film in Tripoli-Lebanon, and used force to prevent the showing of the film. In Jordan the Minister of Information – under pressure from fundamentalists – banned the film after two weeks of huge success. *The Times* of London referred to these events, and European television stations showed crowds in front of the Egyptian cinemas.

The 1993 Cairo International Film Festival

For the second time, holding the Cairo International Film Festival in December was a challenge. The 1992 event took place after an earthquake and acts of terrorism in Upper Egypt. Then in 1993 some serious acts of terrorism occurred just a few days before the opening.

Two actors from the popular American TV series, *The Bold and the Beautiful*, came for the opening: Terri Ann Linn or "Christine" and Daniel Mc Vic or "Clark". Out of 19 films in competition, the Palestinian film *Curfew*, co-produced with Holland, won the Golden Pyramid for best film. The Special Prize of the Jury and Best Actress Prize went to the Russian film *You Are My Only Love*, directed by Dimitri Asktrakhn. Best Director went to Nabiel El-Maleh, whose Syrian film *The Extra* deals with two frustrated lovers.

FAWZI SOLIMAN is Vice-President of the Egyptian Film Critics Association, and a frequent member of the FIPRESCI jury at international film festivals. A member of the Higher Committee of the Cairo International Film Festival, he contributes articles to magazines and newspapers in Egypt and the Arab world. He has edited and translated books on the cinema.

TOP TEN GROSSING FILMS IN EGYPT: 1993

Jurassic Park
The Bodyguard
Home Alone 2
Metal Storm 3D (shown 1983 without 3D)
Cliffhanger
The Fugitive
Teenage Ninja Turtles III
Universal Soldier
Batman Returns
The Last Action Hero

Recent Films

DEHK, WA LAIP WA GAD WA HOB (Laughter, Games, Seriousness and Love)

Script: Magdy Ahmad Aly. Dir: Tarek El Telmissany. Phot: Kamal Abdel Aziz. Players: Amr Diab, Yusra, Omar Sharif. Prod: Tayf for Prod.

ZEYARAT EL SAYED EL RAIS (The Visit of the President)

Script: Bashir El Deek, Ahmed Metwalli. Dir: Mounir Rady. Phot: Maher Rady. Players: Mahmoud Abdel Aziz, Nagah El Mougy, Ahmed Rateb. Prod: Rady Colour Prod Co, Nawal Str, Agouza, Cairo. Tel & Fax: 3933909.

MERCEDES

Script and Dir: Yusri Nasralla. Players: Yusra, Zaki Fateen Abdel Wahab, Abla Kamel, Seif El Din. Prod: Ramsis Marzouk for Misr International.

DISCO DISCO

Script: Abdel Hay Adib. Dir: Inas El Deghedy. Phot: Mohsen Nasr. Players: Naglaa Fathi, Mahmoud Hemeda, Salah Zulfakkar. Prod: Misr El Arabia Films.

A woman director of a private school confronts corruption – represented in a wealthy man who has a spoiled son. When her brother is lured by addiction, she takes a serious decision against the rich, powerful man. The film won the top prize for best production at the National Film Festival, as well as best actress and best screenplay awards.

KHALTABITA (Mixed Up)

Script and Dir: Medhat El Sebaiy. Phot: Saeed El Shimy. Players: Mahmoud Abdel Aziz, Hussein El Sherbini, Mona Al Said. Prod: Hollywood El Arab, 13 Dokki Str. Tel: 3496160.

Like the hero of Kafka's *The Trial*, the protagonist does not know what crime he is accused of, now a normal individual faces the authorities. The film is a fantasy, designed to condemn corruption and political oppression.

AL IRHABY (The Terrorist)

Script: Lenin El Ramly. Dir: Nader Galal. Players: Adel Emam, Ahmed Rateb, Madiha Yusri, Hanan Shawki. Prod: Pop Art.

A militant terrorist, fleeing the police, is knocked down by a bourgeois girl driving her car. She takes him home to look after him. The atmosphere of her tolerant family begins to influence him, his fundamentalist thoughts disappear, and

he starts to reconsider his ideas – too late ...

AL MUHAGER (The Emigrant)

Script: Youssef Chahine and R. Sabban. Dir: Youssef Chahine. Phot: Ramses Marzouk. Players: Yusra, Mahmoud Hemeda, Safia El Emary, Khaled El Nabqwy, Michael Piccoli. Prod: Misr International.

Chahine takes his inspiration from the story of Joseph in the Bible, showing him with a will strong enough to overcome challenges. Being a co-production with France, it has a much larger budget than any Egyptian film has enjoyed.

Useful Addresses

National Film Centre
City of Arts
Al Ahram Avenue
Giza (Cairo)
Tel: 5854807
Fax: 5854701

Cultural Development Fund
Gezira
Cairo
Tel: 3404234. 3939686

Chamber of Film Industry
33 Oraby St
Cairo
Tel: 741677
Fax: 751583

Producers/ Distributors

Sphinx Film
2 Behlar (Kasr El Nil St)
Cairo
Tel: 3920702-9
Fax: 3920710

Al-Alamia for T.V. & Cinema
20 Emad El Din St
Cairo
Tel: 770359
Fax: 770029

Misr International
35 Champollion St
Cairo
Tel: 5788038
Fax: 5788033

Al Ahram for Cinema & Video
1 Abu El Karamat Square
Mohandessen
Cairo
Tel: 3464328
Fax: 3470286

Misr El Arabia
12 Soliman El Halaby Str
Cairo
Tel: 753953
Fax: 5748358

Tamido
95, Mohamed Farid St
Nozha
Heliopolis
Cairo
Tel: 2470461
Fax: 2471203

Top Art Film
3B Soliman El Halaby Str
Tel: 5752234, 5744911

Tayf for Prod. & Dist.
Nasr City
9 Yousef Abbas Str.
Tel: 606634
Fax: 3401166

FINLAND — Matti Apunen

There's good news and there's bad news, as far as Finnish cinema is concerned.

The good news is represented by the fact that the downward spiral in Finnish attendances seems to be over. Admission figures are up on last year, so there is still hope for exhibitors.

In the megabuck class, Finland scrupulously emulated the international pattern. Universal's *Jurassic Park* trampled records beneath its massive feet, of course: the new first weekend attendance record is 64,561. Renny Harlin's *Cliffhanger* fell to second place, despite Harlin's Finnish origin and the huge publicity generated by his love affairs and wedding festivities. Poor old *Last Action Hero* was rudely dumped to 28th place in the box-office race.

One of the happy surprises of 1993 was the perhaps not wholly unexpected success of Jane Campion's *The Piano*. The film has been seen by almost 200,000 Finns, and it again proved that the Finnish market is mature and hot for adult-oriented, ripe, full-bodied and semi-dry art house movies. *The Piano* repeated and doubled the success of Alain Corneau's *Tous les matins du monde* and Kieślowski's *The Double Life of Véronique*. It is pretty easy to predict that Kieślowski's *Blue* will be this year's Finnish art house steamroller.

The total number of admissions climbed to 5.75 million, which was a bit less than expected, but anyway 6.54% more than in 1992. In general, the Finnish market is clearly going to extremes: a fewer number of foreign films has been distributed but their market share has been steadily growing. The geographic polarisation of the market will definitely be emphasised in the near future: Finland's market leader, Finnkino, has presented a plan to open a new multiplex in the heart of Helsinki. The new complex would consist of 14 cinemas and is estimated to siphon off about 10% of all cinemagoers in Finland.

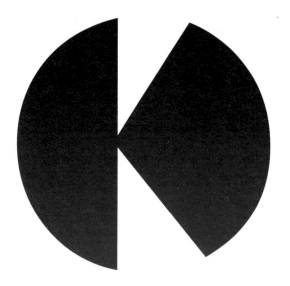

Still from Veikko Aaltonen's OUR FATHER (aka PATER NOSTER)

Esko Salminen on the trail in PLAY IT ALL, directed by Matti Kassila

No Laughing Matter for Comedies

The *bad* news is that Finnish films are doing even worse than before. The share of domestic films out of all tickets sold plummeted from 10.9% to 6.3% – a figure that can only be described as pitiful. The number of domestic productions has been pretty stable in recent years, i.e. between 8 and 13 films a year.

At international festivals Finnish films made the rounds successfully in 1993 and attracted some 30 awards, but on the domestic market people were not too impressed with this success. The most alarming single feature is that domestic farces, cheap and absolutely unintelligent comedies, are waning in popularity, and with them the backbone of Finnish film production is more or less broken.

The Finnish box-office champ for many, many successive years, Uuno Turhapuro, is now out of the national Top Ten, and in some big cities even out of the Top Twenty: admissions to the latest *Turhapuro* movie shrunk to 123,000 from the former standard level of 250,000-350,000.

The Finnish Film Foundation, the state-backed support organisation, has purposefully tried to support popular films, even brain-dead comedies and action films but this policy has not yielded the greatest returns. Turhapuro's clones and successors have all proved disappointing, and the formula of making films around popular TV comedy characters has provoked more yawning than laughter.

Even Spede Pasanen, the Goldfinger of Finnish producers, failed. Pasanen produced an action thriller called **The Romanov Stones**, but the debut film of young Aleksi Mäkelä turned out to be a cheap, semi-violent imitation of American buddy movies, and the expected great migration to the cinemas turned out to be just another great – migraine.

Moomin and Other Round Figures

The year 1993 saw the comeback of two renowned veterans, Matti Kassila and Åke Lindman. Kassila announced his retirement a few years ago, but he returned to direct a stylish crime film, **Play It All**. Åke Lindman has had a remarkable career in television, but he hasn't directed a feature film since the early 1960's. Lindman adapted the acclaimed police novel by Matti Yrjänä Joensuu called **Harjunpää and the Trouble-Makers**, and he also got favourable reviews in the press. *Harjunpää* is an everyday police story, realistic and almost too laconic, with little glory and plenty of prosaic troubles.

If kids could vote, the new President of Finland would not be Martti Ahtisaari but his amazing look-alike, the Moomin, a fantasy character created by novelist Tove Jansson in the 1940's. The dough-faced, pot-bellied Moomin is a phenomenon that has driven Finnish families to the brink of madness: Moomins are simply everywhere between TV and cereals. They scored in cinemas too: the animated film **Moomin and the Comet** came seventh in last year's

TOP TEN GROSSING FILMS IN FINLAND: 1993

	Attendance
Jurassic Park	444,654
Cliffhanger	336,343
The Bodyguard (1992)	178,911 (243,276)
The Firm	173,633
The Fugitive	171,404
Indecent Proposal	170,068
Moomin and the Comet (Japanese-Dutch)	166,738
Hot Shots: Part Deux	166,279
Beauty and the Beast	143,758
Sliver	128,127

Top Ten at the box-office. The film is a Dutch-Japanese-Finnish co-production, in which Japanese animators have preserved relatively well the charming atmosphere of the original Moomin books.

A prophet has no honour in his own country, not least in Finland. Aki Kaurismäki's **Leningrad Cowboys Meet Moses** did not meet its audience: all the international popularity of the band did not help this film, which was seen only by some 6,000 people – a poor figure even in Finland.

The same applies to Veikko Aaltonen. In spite of seven(!) awards at international film festivals for his *Prodigal Son* and some excellent reviews in the international press, Aaltonen is still practically unknown in his own country. *The Prodigal Son* was followed by **Our Father**, a powerful black-and-white rural drama that reunited the talents of Aaltonen and scriptwriter Iiro Kuttner. *Our Father*, again, earned rave reviews, but the audience neglected it as relentlessly as before. Aaltonen's film was this year's major winner at the Jussi ceremonies, the annual Finnish Film Awards, but this surely is cold comfort if the audience stays away.

The other Jussi winner was **Land of Happiness** by Markku Pölönen, a film also deeply rustic in tone but otherwise rather different from *Our Father*. Pölönen's light, fresh and optimistic approach results in one of the most promising new features in the last decade. Young Peter Lindholm also showed his talent in his modern thriller **Anita**.

Meanwhile in Berlin ...

Aki Kaurismäki, the foremost Finnish film-maker, announced that he will retire from film-making – a mere two hours after a similar announcement by Krzysztof Kieślowski. This can mean more bad news for Finland, if it is news at all. Kaurismäki may just be buying peace and privacy after a few exhausting years; privacy in which he can reorientate. I for one would not like to see *Leningrad Cowboys Meet Moses* as Kaurismäki's celluloid last will and testament.

MATTI APUNEN is film critic for the Tampere-based morning newspaper *Aamulehti*.

ONNEN MAA (Land of Happiness)

Script and Direction: Markku Pölönen. Photography: Kari Sohlberg. Players: Pertti Koivula, Katariina Kaitue, Anja Pohjola, Veikko Tiitinen. Produced by Dada-Filmi.

Land of Happiness is a film nobody expected to do anything. It is a sympathetic minia-ture painting of life somewhere in the Finnish countryside in the 1960's. But suddenly, in Helsinki, people were queueing to see this little bagatelle smelling of fresh hay and cowshit. When it was shown on television, it was seen by one fifth of the population, over a million Finns.

A city boy returns to his roots for one hot summer. He falls in love with the dairy girl, and spends the summer dreaming of her, chasing her and losing her.

Pölönen uses a great deal of Finnish tango as a musical comment. The tango, as we know, is the indoor equivalent of cross country skiing: serious and concentrated people moving slowly in wide circles, their feet hissing on the wooden floor. Pölönen doesn't mock these people, but approaches them rather with a certain respect. *Land of Happiness* does not try to hide what it is, a package made up of utter nostalgia and a little silliness.

Pölönen has a touch that is different from what Finnish films are usually famous for. He is not melancholy or gloomy, neither sarcastic nor witty – *Land of Happiness* is simply light and optimistic and it shows Pölönen's affection for the people he is depicting – a rare gift these days.
Matti Apunen

Recent and Forthcoming Films

PIDÄ HUIVISTA KIINI, TATJANA (Take Care of Your Scarf, Tatjana)

Dir: Aki Kaurismäki. Phot: Timo Salminen. Players: Matti Pellonpää, Kirsi Tykkyläinen, Mato Valtonen, Kati Outinen. Prod: Sputnik Films.

LENINGRAD COWBOYS MEET MOSES

Dir: Aki Kaurismäki. Phot: Timo Salminen. Players: Matti Pellonpää, Sakke Järvenpää, Mato Valtonen. Prod: Sputnik Films.

KAIKKI PELISSÄ (Play It All)

Dir: Matti Kassila. Phot: Henrik Paersch. Players: Esko Salminen, Satu Silvo, Hannele Lauri.

HARJUNPÄÄ JA KIUSAN-TEKIJÄT (Harjunpää and the Trouble-Makers)

Dir: Åke Lindman. Script: Åke Lindman, Esko Salervo. Phot: Pertti Mutanen. Players: Kari Heiskanen, Riitta Havukainen, Mats Långbacka. Prod: Åke Lindman Film Productions/Jörn Donner Film Productions.

ROMANOVIN KIVET (The Romanov Stones)

Dir: Aleksi Mäkelä. Script: Kalle

Chydenius, Aleksi Mäkelä, Santeri Kinnunen. Phot: Ilkka Ruuhijärvi. Players: Samuli Edelman, Santeri Kinnunen, Stig Fransman. Prod: Spede-Tuotanto.

ISÄ MEIDÄN (Our Father ...)

Dir: Veikko Aaltonen. Script: Veikko Aaltonen, Iiro Küttner. Phot: Olavi Tuomi. Players: Hannu Kivioja, Martti Katajisto, Elina Hurme. Prod: Villealfa Filmproductions.

THE LAST BORDER

Dir: Mika Kaurismäki. Script: Mika Kaurismäki, Pia Tikka. Phot: Timo Salminen. Players: Jolyon Baker, Jürgen Prochnow, Fanny Bastien, Kari Väänänen, Matti Pellonpää.

ANITA

Dir: Peter Lindholm. Script: Olli-Pekka Parvianinen. Phot: Kjell Lagerroos. Players: Liisa Mustonen, Pirkka-Pekka Petelius, Taneli Mäkelä. Prod: Fantasia-filmi.

KASVOTON MIES (The Man Without a Face)

Dir: Lauri Törhönen. Script: Perti Takatalo. Players: Tom Pöysti, Jonna Järnefelt. Prod: Jörn Donner Productions.

Producers

Dada-Filmi
Kolmas linja 5
SF-00530 Helsinki
Tel: (0) 73 77 88
Fax: (0) 73 07 34

Fantasiafilmi
Metsäpurontie 16
SF-00630 Helsinki
Tel: (0) 754 31 33

Filminor
Lönnrotinkatu 35 D 46
SF-00180 Helsinki
Tel: (0) 60 70 33
Fax: (0) 60 76 45

Filmiryhmä Oy
Vyökatu 8
SF-00160 Helsinki
Tel: (0) 17 10 55
Fax: 66 26 02

Jörn Donner Productions
Pohjoisranta 12
SF-00170 Helsinki
Tel: (0) 135 60 60
Fax: (0) 135 75 68

Kinofinlandia
Rahapajankatu 1 F 33
SF-00160 Helsinki
Tel & Fax: (0) 17 09 01

Kinotuotanto Oy
Katajanokankatu 6

SF-00160 Helsinki
Tel: (0) 66 32 17

Reppufilmi Oy
Nervanderinkatu 12 B
SF-0010 Helsinki
Tel: (0) 49 83 78
Fax: 49 84 59

Spede-yhtiöt
Ilmalankatu 2
SF-00240 Helsinki
Tel: (0) 14 16 33

**Villealfa Filmproductions
Oy/Sputnik Films/Marianna
Films**
Uudenmaankatu 13 D
SF-00100 Helsinki
Tel: (0) 60 28 11
Fax: 60 22 92

Distributors

Cinema Mondo
Museokatu 44
00100 Helsinki
Tel: (0) 49 48 27

Finnkino Oy
Kaisaniemenkatu 2 B
SF-00100 Helsinki
Tel: (0) 13 11 91
Telex: 1001658
Fax: 13 11 93 00

Kinoscreen
Katajanokankatu 6
SF-00100 Helsinki
Tel: (0) 66 37 17

Miofilm Oy
Torpantie 36
SF-90230 Oulu
Tel: (81) 22 86 60
Telex: 32300 urfil sf

United Pictures Finland
Kaisaniemenkatu 1 C 98
SF-00100 Helsinki
Tel: (0) 66 21 66
Fax: (0) 66 50 05

Urania Film Oy/Ltd
Torpantie 36
90230 Oulu
Tel: (81) 22 86 60

Warner Bros Finland Oy
Kaisaniemenkatu 1 B a
SF-00100 Helsinki
Tel: (0) 63 82 88
Fax: 63 81 61

Useful Addresses

**Central Organisation of Finnish
Film Producers**
Katajanokankatu 6
SF-00160 Helsinki
Tel: (0) 66 32 17

Finnish Film Foundation
Kanavakatu 12
SF-00160 Helsinki
Tel: (0) 17 77 27
Fax: 17 71 13
Telex: 125032

**Finnish Cinema Association
Finnish Film Chamber**
Kaisaniemenkatu 3 B
SF-00100 Helsinki
Tel: (0) 63 55 06

FRANCE — Michel Ciment

It was with relief that the French public opinion and film industry received the news that in the final round of the GATT negotiations, culture – and henceforth cinema – would not be included in the general agreement. It was feared that the very elaborate system of financial help and subsidies provided by the *Fonds de soutien* (fuelled by a tax levied on every ticket at the box-office) would be dismantled.

This debate dominated the French political, cultural and economic scene for some months with almost unanimous agreement among all the political parties, generally at loggerheads on every topic. A petition signed by a great number of current film-makers and under the patronage of Pedro Almodóvar, Bernardo Bertolucci, Stephen Frears and Wim Wenders (none of them French) showed that the issue concerned most of the real artists in Europe. But it is true that the French political establishment was the spearhead of an action to protect national cinema against an American hegemony of the world market.

There seem to be two major reasons for this attitude: firstly, French cinema is the most lively in Europe, both in quantity and quality (thanks in a large part to the protective measures mentioned above) and when you are alive you have more strength for your survival than, say, the Dutch film industry. Secondly, there has been a tradition of state patronage in the arts which the republic has taken over from the kings. André Malraux, the future minister of culture, ended in 1946 his *Esquisse d'un psychologie du cinéma* with this sentence: "Beside, cinema is an industry ..." The idea that cinema cannot be entirely dominated by market forces and that many worthy films have been made without enjoying commercial success has always been prevalent in the national consciousness. The conviction too that if so many major film-makers – who started in the 1950's – Godard, Rivette, Rohmer, Chabrol, Varda, Resnais, Marker, Deville, etc have managed to continue producing a substantial body of work was partly due to the favourable atmosphere surrounding cinema in France – including the economic facilities.

Overwhelming U.S. Totals

The worry over the GATT discussion was also made acute by the overwhelming presence of Hollywood film at the box-office; eight films out of the top ten grossers being American with one British and one French sneaking into the list (see box). If the French cinema kept the same share of the market in 1993 (39.6% as against 34.9% in 1992) it was mostly due to the enormous success of *Les Visiteurs* (more than 13 million seats). The appeal of American films is also stimulated by the exhibition strategy. If 359 films (as against 381 in 1992) were released in 1993 including 133 French films, 126 American and 100 from the rest of the world, only 24 out of these 133 French films opened in more than 20 theatres in Paris and its suburbs (18%) whereas 64 out of the 126 American films (51%) had the same opening. Strikingly, 64 French films opened in less than five theatres which reveals a serious problem. Obviously many of these titles (some of high quality) have difficulty finding a strong enough distributor, cinema exhibitors and consequently an audience ...

On the whole 1993 proved a good year for exhibitors with an increase of 15.6% in attendance (133 million) with a spectacular jump in the provinces (+19% as against 4.5% in Paris). The recent strategy has been to open multiplex cinemas on the outskirts of big cities (ten, including Toulon and Avignon) to attract customers who had lost the habit of going to the movies. The number of screens shows a remarkable stability: 4,397 (as against 4,402 in 1992). The ever active Centre National de la Cinématographie (CNC) is developing a strategy of exhibition (with the collaboration of the industry) focusing on towns of less than 30,000 inhabitants, 72% of the projects aiming at creating or improving screens in those areas.

Production Steady

Production has shown signs of stability with 152 films in the year (against 106 in Italy and 63 in Germany) although this figure includes 15 films made in Eastern Europe where the French involvement is primarily financial. There are also 70 international co-productions (with 15 from the Eurofund) with France as a majority partner (15 with Italy, 14 with Switzerland, 9 with Belgium and Germany).

The role of France in international production was evident in Cannes when many of the entries in competition from Mexico, Russia, Romania, Iran and Italy particularly were financed by French backers. The role of television is more and more important with the risk of imposing a certain "average taste" for prime-time viewing (69 films were made with the help of TV and 96 were pre-sold to the cable programme Canal +). Gaumont (4 films with a total investment of 202 mf), CiBy 2000 (5 films for 206 mf) and MK2 (4 films with 104 mf) were the main producing companies this year. The economic crisis made itself felt by the decrease in the production of big budget films (two notable exceptions being *La Reine Margot* and *Germinal* both for Renn Productions) and a lowering of the average price per film. However, the fact that 61 films were first or second features is an encouraging sign of vitality and of a renewal of talents.

Indeed, a number of extremely interesting first films was one of the main characteristics of the season and in many cases due to women directors. **Petits**

arrangements avec les morts by Pascale Ferran won the Caméra d'or at the Cannes Film Festival. While a sandcastle is being built and then destroyed on a beach, three vacationers recall their memories, each of them having encountered the problem of death. Pascale Ferran weaves these tales together with sensitivity and a strikingly original manner. Laurence Ferreira Barbosa in **Les gens normaux n'ont rien d'exceptionnel** manages to create a dynamic and funny film about a girl abandoned by her boyfriend, who suffers from a breakdown and enters a mental hospital. She then through her sheer vitality decides to help the inmates, and in so doing finds a new belief in life. Superbly acted by Valeria Bruni Tedeschi the film is at once moving and entertaining.

Agnès Merlet in **Le fils du requin** returns to the lyrical and poetic realism of a director like Jean Vigo in evoking the rebellion of two youths in the bleak landscape of the North of France. Marion Vernoux in **Personne ne m'aime** has chosen an aggressive tone to portray ageing women (Bernadette Lafont, Bulle Ogier) on a spree. The satire is sometimes facile, but she loves her characters and reveals a sense of satire if too undisciplined.

Their male counterparts are comparatively tamer directors but – talented too. Pierre Salvadori in **Cible émouvante** portrays a hired hand (Jean Rochefort) who falls in love with his victim, a classical situation but treated in an absurdist tone and with a real sense of the ambiguity of feelings. More straightforward, **Faut-il aimer Mathilde?** by Edwin Baily is essentially a very sensitive portrait of an ordinary woman (but with an extraordinary actress in Dominique Blanc) who can't make up her mind about the man she wants to live with. Set in the working class of northern France the film has a warm feeling to it which recalls a forgotten tradition of "proletarian" subjects (Duvivier, Renoir).

Métisse by young actor Mathieu Kassovitz is a comedy about a mulatto girl with two lovers, a *She's Gotta Have It* French-style, with the director giving the best performance. One finds him also playing next to Jean-Louis Trintignant in Jacques Audiard's (son of Michel Audiard and a screenwriter in his own right for Claude Miller among others) **Regarde les hommes tomber**. It's a striking debut in the film noir genre, consisting of two parallel stories, one with Jean Yanne forlorn and depressed, abandoning his wife to find the men who have murdered a young friend of his, and the other about those very killers (Kassovitz and Trintignant) who will finally end up on his track. Beautifully written and acted, the film is in strong contrast, with its literary and stylist approach, to the taste for realism of most beginners.

Fruitful Marriage of TV and Cinema

The best of this realistic trend was to be found in a fruitful collaboration between cinema and television (Arte, the cultural channel): **Tous les garçons et les filles de leur âge**, a series of nine films spanning the last thirty years (three films per decade) and each evoking the adolescence of the various directors. André Téchiné in **Les roseaux sauvages** sets his story at the time of the Algerian war (early 1960's), Olivier Assayas (*L'eau froide*) in the early 1970's, a time of open rebellion against the family, Patricia Mazuy (*Travolta et moi*) in the mid-1970's and Cedric Kahn (*Trop de bonheur*) in the early 1980's. Five more are to come. They all share a sequence with the dance and music of the time and as expected all deal with amorous relationships. But it is fascinating to observe the variety of talents, the difference in atmosphere, the area where the action takes place from the South of France to the suburbs of Paris. The very active Assayas had released only a few months before **Une nouvelle vie**, in which he confronts two generations in a freewheeling style that seems to catch, through the circular movements of the cameras, the confused states of mind of the characters.

Eric Rochant, also a young film-maker, tried in his third film to break away from the dominant trend of the "slice of life". His **Les Patriotes** is a film on the Mossad, the Israeli secret service, with a sure command of narration and acting but which fails to give the genre a new perspective and style. Toni Marshall for her second feature, **Pas très catholique**, breaks away from the complacency of her debut film and, though following the pattern of a classical comedy, traces the portrait of a female private eye (magnificently embodied by Anémone) who is at a loss with her life and accidentally meets her boy, now eighteen, whom she has not seen since she left his father when he was a child.

Major Names Active and Successful

As usual the major French film directors have been mostly active with more or less success. Jacques Rivette's **Jeanne la pucelle**, an almost six-hour film about the life of Joan of Arc (in two parts, *The Battle* and *The Prison*, though there are battles in the second part too) received as expected a tremendous critical acclaim but did poorly at the box-office in spite of Sandrine Bonnaire's genuine performance. The film lacked rhythm and invention, Rivette being ill at ease with a straightforward narrative. Jean Luc Godard in **Hélàs pour moi** was, on the contrary, pushing the limits of his idiosyncratic style, the beauty of sound and image contrasting with the esoteric meaning of the tale with Depardieu stranded on a hieroglyphic shore. In **L'enfer**, Claude Chabrol used an old script written by Clouzot for a film which was started but never completed, and made it his own; a new study of jealousy in the French provinces. François Cluzet, an innkeeper, is obsessively suspicious of his wife (Emmanuelle Béart) to the point of insanity. Chabrol sometimes belabours his situation, but the film has its moments and fine performances. Michel Deville's **Aux petits bonheurs** is also very much in the line of this film director's taste for the game of love and chance. A woman (Anémone) returns twenty years later to a country house where she had her first love affair. Among the guests strong relationships start to develop, reactivated by her presence. As usual Deville elaborates his conceits with an expert hand for dialogue and acting.

Sabine Azéma and Pierre Arditi star in SMOKING and NO SMOKING, by Alain Resnais

In the wake of *J'entends plus la guitare*, Philippe Garrel confirms his new maturity in **La Naissance de l'amour**, a very sensitive portrayal of middle-aged men and women played among others by Lou Castel and a surprising Jean-Pierre Léaud. Bertrand Blier failed to renew his inspiration with **Un deux trois soleil**, an attempt to convey an imaginary and stylised version of the suburbs of Marseilles with their population of North African and black immigrants – a bold endeavour which fails to blend the dreamlike quality of some scenes with the realistic context of the situation. However, Blier has been one of the strongest personalities in the last two decades of French cinema and his influence has been pervasive, as three successful recent films testify.

Funny and Intelligent Fable

Grosse fatigue, the second feature by Michel Blanc (Best Screenplay at the Cannes Festival) draws in part on an original idea by Bertrand Blier. It is a funny and intelligent fable about the star syndrome, Michel Blanc and everybody around him playing themselves until we (as well as the protagonist) discover the existence of his double. Both hilarious and frightening, *Grosse fatigue* is a clever self-portrait where the actor betrays his own anguish and doubts. Claude Miller's **Le Sourire** marks a radical change in this director's career, particularly as it succeeds the rather stilted *L'accompagnatrice*. Jean-Pierre Marielle plays a doctor in a grotesque style, a man obsessed by death who falls in love with a young woman

Irène Jacob posing for the poster in Kieślowski's TROIS COULEURS: ROUGE

about to perform half-naked in a local fair. The film mixes buffoonery and pathos, sex and poetry, with a boldness of style that will irritate some but seduce others with its true originality.

Le parfum d'Yvonne, by Patrice Leconte, gives another astonishing role to Jean-Pierre Marielle, who plays a flamboyant homosexual on a French lake near Switzerland at the time of the Algerian war. He keeps company with a mysterious and beautiful young girl who fascinates a young deserter. Adapted from a novel by Patrick Modiano, Leconte's story has the sensuality and charm that are linked to some remembrance of things past. The past – but a distant one – is also the subject of Bertrand Tavernier's **La fille de d'Artagnan**, an episode of the Musketeers' life never written by Dumas but invented by Riccardo Freda (who initially was to direct the film) and out of which Tavernier has concocted a delightful screenplay full of jokes and incidents. Sophie Marceau is sprightly and athletic (horse riding and fencing) as the daughter of d'Artagnan, while the ageing Musketeers (Noiret as the benevolent father, Sami Frey as Aramis) meditate on the passage of the years.

But it's a real novel by Dumas, **La Reine Margot**, set during the protestant and catholic war and the climax of the St. Bartholomew night in the sixteenth century that has inspired Patrice Chereau, the well-known theatre director. Leaning more towards Christopher Marlowe (Chereau once staged *Massacre in Paris*) than towards Dumas, the film is an ambitious attempt to create a chaotic and

passionate world of lust, incestuous lovers and blood-thirst. It fails to succeed completely due to a confused script and some permanently high-pitched direction. *La Reine Margot* is part of the big-budget production slate established by Claude Berri's company to rival American block-busters. The producer-director's **Germinal** was the other huge undertaking of the year, far more successful commercially (at least on the home market) if much more classical in its *mise en scène*.

Highpoints of the Year

The two most stunning efforts of the year have certainly been Krzysztof Kieślowski's trilogy **Blue, White** and **Red** and Alain Resnais's twin movies **Smoking/No Smoking**. Kieślowski's variations on liberty, equality and fraternity, the second one only being a Polish film, make sense only when one has seen the ensemble. Then one realises the various tonalities, the moral ambiguities, and the philosophical undertones that link the three parts. *Red* appears as the crowning achievement of the trilogy, a supreme example of the director's mastery at playing with various narrative threads which exemplify the role of chance. Curiously enough fraternity, rather than liberty and equality, seems to be possible as a young woman (Irène Jacob), full of love for others, establishes a relationship with a sceptical judge (Jean-Louis Trintignant in one of his best roles) who is prisoner of his own misanthropy.

Resnais's latest films reveal once more his taste for the theatre quite apart from his authentic boldness. The theatricality that is ever more present in his work finds a marvellous opportunity to express itself with his brilliant adaptation of Alan Ayckbourn's eight plays *Intimate Exchanges*. Nine roles are played by two outstanding comedians, Sabine Azéma and Pierre Arditi, exemplifying Resnais's and Ayckbourn's view of life as a series of crossroads and possible choices. The extraordinary aesthetic achievement (from Jacques Saulnier's sets to Renato Berta's photography) of these films, their playful use of language, the wit and humour of the

TOP TEN GROSSING FILMS IN FRANCE: August 1993-June 1994

	Attendance
Aladdin	1,504,183
Jurassic Park	1,252,180
Mrs. Doubtfire	997,081
The Fugitive	982,106
Four Weddings and a Funeral	758,691
Germinal	744,146
Manhattan Murder Mystery	720,150
Philadelphia	630,623
A Perfect World	610,718
Cliffhanger	582,475
Note: these figures are for the greater Paris area only.	

acting, should not hide some deeper feelings of loss and melancholy.

After these towering accomplishments in film direction and reordering of reality, a swing of the pendulum brings us back to two remarkable documentary essays. **Starting Over**, which marks American director Robert Kramer's return to Vietnam twenty-five year after his first visit, a dispassionate look at the state of the country, and **Veillée d'armes**, Marcel Ophuls's two-part film on war correspondents in Sarajevo. As usual Ophuls uses the interview technique to offer a medi- tation on the most complex of issues: this time the nature of information and how it is communicated to us. The director has never been freer (talking to the camera, inserting clips from old films) more ironical and more intimate than in this film, a dazzling exercise in intelligence as well as a protest against all manipulations.

MICHEL CIMENT is one of the key figures behind the well-known French magazine Postif, and the author of numerous books on film, including the award-winning studies of Kubrick, Losey, Rosi, Kazan, and Boorman.

Recent and Forthcoming Films

L'AFFAIRE

Script: Sergio Gobbi, Victor Arnold. Dir: Sergio Gobbi. Phot: J.F. Gondre. Players: Robert Hossein, Bruno Wolkowitch, F. Murray Abraham, Anna Falchi. Prod: Flach/Film Auramax.

ALICE ET ELSA

Script: Diane Kurys, Antoine Lacombiez. Dir: Diane Kurys. Phot: Fabio Conversi. Players: Anne Parillaud, Béatrice Dalle, Alain Chabat, Bernard Verley, Marie Guillard. Prod: Passion Production.

LES AMOUREUX

Script: Cathérine Corsini,

Pascale Breton. Dir: Cathérine Corsini. Phot: Ivan Kozelka. Players: Nathalie Richard, Pascal Cervo, Olaf Lubaszenko, Loic Maquin. Prod: Rezo Films/M6 Films.

LES ANGES GARDIENS

Script: Christian Clavier, Jean-Marie Poiré. Dir: Jean-Marie Poiré. Players: Gérard Depardieu, Christian Clavier. Prod: Alter Films.

L'ANNÉE JULIETTE

Script: Philippe de Guay, Jean-Louis Richard, Brigitte Rouan. Dir: Philippe de Guay. Phot: Pierre Novion. Player: Fabrice

Luchini. Prod: Les Prods Lazennec.

L'APPAT

Script and Dir: Bertrand Tavernier. Phot: Alain Choquart. Players: Marie Gillain, Richard Berry, Olivier Sitruk, Bruno Putzulu. Prod: Hachette Première.

CASQUE BLEU

Script: Gérard Jugnot, Philippe Lopes Curval. Dir: Gérard Jugnot. Phot: Gérard de Battista. Players: Gérard Jugnot, Victoria Abril, Jean-Pierre Cassel, Valérie Lemercier, Roland Marchisio. Prod: CIBY 2000.

LA CITÉ DE LA PEUR

Script: Dominique Farrugia, Chantal Lauby, Alain Chabat. Dir: Alain Berberian. Phot: Laurent Dailland. Players: Chantal Lauby, Alain Chabat, Dominque Farrugia, Gerard Darmon. Prod: Canal +/Téléma.

LA CITÉ DES ENFANTS PERDUS

Script and Dir: Jean-Pierre Jeunet, Marc Caro. Phot: Darius Khondi. Players: Ron Perlman, Dominique Pinon, Daniel Emilfork, Jean-Claude Dreyfus, Judith Vittet. Prod: Constellation Production.

CONSENTEMENT MUTUEL

Script: Philippe Delannoy, Bernard Stora. Dir: Bernard Stora. Phot: Romain Winding. Players: Anne Brochet, Richard Berry. Prod: Les Prods Lazennec.

LA CRI DU CŒUR

Script: Robert Gardner, Idrissa Ouedraogo, Jacques Achoti. Dir: Idrissa Ouedraogo. Phot: Jean Monsigny. Players: Saïd Diarra, Félicité Wouassi, Alex Descas, Richard Bohringer, Clémentine Célarié. Prod: Sophie Salbot/CEC Rhône-Alpes/Les Films de l'Avenir.

DAISY ET MONA

Script and Dir: Claude d'Anna. Phot: Denis Clerval. Players: Marina Golovine, Lilah Dadi, Dina Gauzi, Valérie Baurenns, Caroline Behr. Prod: Alain Queffélean/A.K. Productions.

L'EAU FROIDE

Script and Dir: Olivier Assayas. Phot: Denis Lenoir. Players: Virginie Ledoyen, Cyprien Fouquet, Laszlo Szabo, Jean-Pierre Darroussin. Prod: IMA Films.

ELISA

Script: Fabrice Carazo, Jean Becker. Dir: Jean Becker. Phot: Etienne Becker. Players: Vanessa Paradis, Gérard Depardieu. Prod: Christian Fechner/Solo Productions.

ELLES NE PENSENT QU'À ÇA

Script: Charlotte Dubreuil, Georges Wolinski. Dir: Charlotte Dubreuil. Phot: Carlo Varini. Players: Claudia Cardinale, Carole Laure, Heinz Bennent, Roland Blanche. Prod: Flach Film/France 2.

EN COMPAGNIE D'ANTONIN ARTAUD

Script: Gérard Mordillat, Jérôme Prieur. Dir: Gérard Mordillat. Phot: François Catonne. Players: Sami Frey, Marc Barbe, Julie Jezequl, Valérie Jeannet. Prod: Archipel 33/Laura Prods./La Sept-Arte.

L'ENFER

Script: Henri-Georges Clouzot, José-André Lacour. Dir: Claude Chabrol. Phot: Bernard Zitzermann. Players: Emmanuelle Béart, François Cluzet, Marc Lavoine, Mario David. Prod: MK2.

LES FAUSSAIRES

Script: Pierre Chosson, Olivier Dazat, Frédéric Blum. Dir; Frédéric Blum. Phot: Bernard Lutic. Players: Gérard Jugnot, Jean-Marc Barr, Claude Piéplu, Viktor Lazlo, François Perrot. Prod: Adélaïde Productions /Lumière.

LA FILLE DE D'ARTAGNAN

Script: Riccardo Freda, Bertrand Tavernier, Eric Poindron, Michel Leviant, Jean Cosmos. Dir: Bertrand Tavernier. Phot: Patrick Blossier. Players: Philippe Noiret, Sophie Marceau, Sami Frey, Nils Tavernier, Claude Rich. Prod: CIBY 2000/Little Bear.

LES FRERES GRAVET

Script and Dir: René Féret. Players: Jean-François Stévenin, Robin Renucci, Jaques Bonnaffé, Pierre-Loup Rajot, Seymour Cassel. Prod: Les Films Alyne.

LE GRAND BLANC DE LAMBARENE

Script and Dir: Bassek Ba Kobhio. Players: André Wilms, Marisa Berenson, Alex Descas, Anne-Marie Pisani, Elizabeth Bourgine. Prod: L.N. Production.

GRANDE PETITE

Script and Dir: Sophie Fillières. Phot: Benoît Delhomme. Players: Judith Godreche, Hugues Quester, Emmanuel Salinger, Philippe Demarle. Prod: Paris New York Prods.

GROSSE FATIGUE

Script and Dir: Michel Blanc. Phot: Eduardo Serra. Players: Michel Blanc, Carole Bouquet, Philippe Noiret, Josiane Balasko, Marie Anne Chazel. Prod: Gaumont.

LE HUSSARD SUR LE TOIT

Dir: Jean-Paul Rappeneau. Players: Juliette Binoche, Olivier Martinez. Prod: Hachette Première.

J'AI PAS SOMMEIL

Script: Claire Denis, Jean-Pol Fargeau. Dir: Claire Denis. Photo: Agnès Godard. Players: Katherina Golubeva, Richard Coucet, Line Renaud, Alex Descas, Béatrice Dalle. Prod: Arena Film.

DEATH AND THE MAIDEN

Script: Ariel Dorfman, Rafael Yglesias. Dir: Roman Polanski. Phot: Tonio Delli Colli. Players: Sigourney Weaver, Ben Kingsley, Stuart Wilson. Prod: Electra Film/Flach Films.

LA MACHINE

Script and Dir: François Dupeyron. Phot: Dietrich

Lohmann. Players: Gérard Depardieu, Nathalie Baye, Didier Bourdon. Prod: Hachette Première/DD Productions.

MARIE DE NAZARETH

Script: Jean Delannoy, Jaques Douyau. Dir: Jean Delannoy. Phot: Claude Agnosti. Players: Myriam Muller, Didier Bienaime, Laurence Cortadellas, Eric Jakobiak. Prod: Azur Films.

LES MILLES

Script and Dir: Sébastien Grall. Players: Jean-Pierre Marielle, Ticky Holgado, Rudiger Vogler. Prod: Blue Films.

MINA TANNENBAUM

Script and Dir: Martine Dugowson. Phot: Eric Zaouali. Players: Romane Bohringer, Elsa Zylberstein, Florence Thomassin, Nils Tavernier. Prod: Ima Films/UGC Images.

LES MISERABLES DU XXe SIÈCLE

Dir: Claude Lelouch. Phot: Pavans de Ceccatty. Players: Jean-Paul Belmondo, Michel Boujenah, Alessandra Martines, Annie Girardot, Philippe Léotard. Prod: Les Films 13.

LE MOULIN DE DAUDET

Script and Dir: Samy Pavel. Phot: Nino Céleste. Players: Jean-Pierre Lorit, Irène Jacob. Prod: Anna Films/Uderzo Prods.

LE PARFUM D'YVONNE

Script and Dir: Patrice Leconte. Phot: Eduardo Serra. Players: Jean-Pierre Marielle, Hippolyte Girardot, Richard Bohringer, Sandra Majani. Prod: Lambart Productions/Zoulou Films.

LES PATRIOTES

Script and Dir: Eric Rochant. Phot: Pierre Novion. Players: Yvan Banai, Richard Masur, Nancy

The versatile Jean Rochefort in WILD TARGET (CIBLE EMOUVANTE)

Allen. Prod: Les Productions Lazennec /Gaumont/ SFP Cinéma.

LA POUDRE AUX YEUX

Script: Jacques and Maurice Dugowson, Odile Barski. Dir: Maurice Dugowson. Phot: Jacques Guerin. Players: Robin Renussi, Maryline Canto, Marc Jolivet, Pierre-Loup Rajot. Prod: SFP Cinéma.

REGARD LES HOMMES TOMBER

Script: Jacques Audiard, Alain le Henry. Dir: Jacques Audiard. Players: Jean Yanne, Jean-Louis Trintignant, Mathieu Kassovitz, Bulle Ogier. Prod: Bloody Mary Productions/FR3 Cinema/CEC Rhone-Alpes.

LA REINE MARGOT

Script: Danièle Thompson, Patrice Chéreau. Dir: Patrice Chéreau. Phot: Philippe Rousselot. Players: Isabelle Adjani, Daniel Auteuil, Jean-Hugues Anglade, Vincent Perez, Virna Lisi, Dominique Blanc. Prod: Renn Productions/France 2 Cinema.

RIEN QUE POUR VOUS

Script and Dir: Philippe Triboit. Players: Isabelle Huppert, Serge Castellito. Prod: Les Films de l'Écluse.

LES ROSEAUX SAUVAGES

Script: André Téchiné, Gilles Taurand, Olivier Massart. Dir: André Téchiné. Phot: Jean Lapoirie. Players: Elodie Bouchez, Gael Morel, Stephane Gorny, Michele Moretti. Prod: IMA Films.

SANG D'ENCRE

Dir: Véra Cais. Players: Phillipe Noiret, Jean-Claude Dreyfus, Jiří Menzel. Prod: Triplan et Cipa Prods.

LA SEPARATION

Script and Dir: Christian Vincent. Phot: Denis Lenoir. Players: Daniel Auteuil, Isabelle Huppert, Karine Viard. Prod: Renn Productions.

TOUS LES JOURS DIMANCHE

Script and Dir: Jean-Charles Tacchella. Phot: Martial Thuri. Players: Thierry Lhermitte, Maurizio Nichetti, Marie-France Pisier, Molly Ringwald, Rod Steiger, Susan Blakely. Prod: Erato Films.

TROIS COULEURS: ROUGE

Script: Krzysztof Kieślowski, Krzysztof Piesiewicz. Dir: Krzysztof Kieślowski. Phot: Piotr

Sobocinski. Players: Irène Jacob, Jean-Louis Trintignant, Jean-Pierre Lorit, Frédérique Feder. Prod: MK2 Productions/CAB Prods./TOR Films, Warsaw.

UN ÉTÉ INOUBLIABLE

Script and Dir: Lucian Pintilié. Phot: Calin Ghibu. Players: Kristin Scott-Thomas, Claudiu Bléont, George Constantin. Prod: MK2/Filmex (Romania).

UN INDIEN DANS LA VILLE

Script: Hervé Palud, Igor Aptekmann, Thierry Lhermitte, Philippe Brunneau. Dir: Hervé Palud. Players: Thierry Lhermitte, Patrick Timsit, Miou-Miou, Ludwig Briand. Prod: Ice Films.

UNE FEMME FRANÇAISE

Dir: Régis Wargnier. Players: Emmanuelle Béart, Daniel Auteuil, Gabriel Barylli. Prod: UGC Images.

Producers

Argos Films
4 rue Edouard Nortier
92200 Neuilly sur Seine
Tel: 47 22 91 26
Fax: 46 40 02 05

BVF
77 rue Château
BP 409
91203 Boulogne
Tel: 41 10 12 00
Fax: 46 04 20 20

CIBY 2000
90 avenue des Champs Elysées
75008 Paris
Tel: 44 21 64 00
Fax: 40 76 02 75

DEAL
22 rue Beffroy
92200 Neuilly sur Seine
Tel: 47 47 95 95
Fax: 46 41 00 50

Films Christian Fechner
39 rue des Tilleuls

92100 Boulogne
Tel: 46 99 02 02
Fax: 46 99 03 43

Films du Losange
22 avenue Pierre 1er de Serbie
75116 Paris
Tel: 44 43 87 15
Fax: 49 52 06 40

Flach Film
47 rue de la Colonie
75013 paris
Tel: 44 16 40 00
Fax: 45 80 40 00

France 2 Cinema
22 avenue Montaigne
75008 Paris
Tel: 44 21 56 13
Fax: 44 21 57 84

Gaumont
30 avenue Charles de Gaulle
92200 Neuilly
Tel: 46 43 20 00
Fax: 46 43 21 68

Gemini Films
14 rue de la Cossonnerie
75001 Paris
Tel: 40 39 03 75
Fax: 42 33 12 13

Hachette Première
10 rue de Marignan
75008 Paris
Tel: 42 25 19 70
Fax: 42 56 00 81

IMA Productions
11 rue Christiane
75018 Paris
Tel: 42 23 01 01
Fax: 42 62 57 07

Lazennec Productions
36 rue René Boulanger
75011 Paris
Tel: 42 40 51 51
Fax: 42 40 92 10

MK2 Productions
55 rue Traversière
75012 Paris
Tel: 43 07 92 74
Fax: 43 41 32 30

Renn Productions
10 rue Lincoln

75008 Paris
Tel: 40 76 91 00
Fax: 42 25 12 89

Telé Image
64 rue Pierre Charron
75008 Paris
Tel: 44 35 17 00
Fax: 42 25 77 56

Téléma
26 rue Danton
92300 Levallois
Tel: 47 58 67 30
Fax: 45 61 90 78

UGC Images
24 avenue de Charles de Gaulle
92200 Neuilly
Tel: 46 40 44 00
Fax: 46 24 37 28

Distributors

A.A.A.
12 bis, rue Keppler
75016 Paris
Tel: 47 23 50 68
Fax: 47 20 45 54

Acasias/Cinéaudience
122 rue de la Boétie
75008 Paris
Tel: 42 56 49 03

A.F.M.D.
18 rue Troyon
75017 Paris
Tel: 44 09 08 08
Fax: 47 64 14 27

A.M.L.F.
10 rue Lincoln
75008 Paris
Tel: 40 76 91 00
Fax: 42 25 12 89

B.A.C.
5 rue Pelouze
75008 Paris
Tel: 44 70 92 80
Fax: 44 70 90 70

Ciné Classic
6 rue de l'Ecole-de-Médecine
75006 Paris
Tel: 46 34 75 74
Fax: 46 33 97 60

Columbia Tri-Star Films France S.A.
131 avenue de Wagram
75017 Paris
Tel: 44 40 60 00
Fax: 44 40 62 01

Diaphana
60 rue de Paradis
75010 Paris
Tel: 44 79 92 92
Fax: 42 56 54 48

Les Films Ariane
15 rue du Colonel Pierre Avia
75015 Paris
Tel: 46 62 17 77
Fax: 46 62 17 97

Films du Losange
22 avenue Pierre 1er de Serbie
75116 Paris
Tel: 44 43 87 15
Fax: 49 52 06 40

G.B.V.I.
5 rue du Colisée
75008 Paris
Tel: 46 43 24 53
Fax: 46 43 20 51

Mercure
47 rue de la Colonie
75013 Paris
Tel: 45 89 80 00
Fax: 45 65 07 47

MGM/UA Telecommunications France
25 rue de Marignan
75008 Paris
Tel: 42 89 32 32
Fax: 45 62 62 04

M.K.L.
55 rue Traversière
75012 Paris
Tel: 43 07 15 10
Fax: 43 44 20 18

Pan Européenne
107 boulevard Péreire
75017 Paris
Tel: 44 15 66 66
Fax: 47 64 36 38

Pyramide Film
6 rue Calulle Mendes
75017 Paris
Tel: 42 67 44 11
Fax: 42 67 80 08

Twentieth Century Fox
8 Rue Bellini
75782 Paris 16
Tel: 44 34 60 66
Fax: 44 34 61 01

U.G.C.
24 avenue Charles de Gaulle
92200 Neuilly sur Seine
Tel: 46 40 44 00
Fax: 46 37 61 82

U.I.P.
1 rue Meyerbeer
75009 Paris
Tel: 40 07 38 38
Fax: 47 42 57 16

Warner Brothers
BP 2116
75826 Paris Cedex 17
Tel: 44 01 49 99
Fax: 40 54 71 92

Useful Addresses

Centre National du Cinéma (CNC)
12 rue de Lubeck
75016 Paris
Tel: 44 34 34 40
Fax: 47 55 04 91

Unifrance Films International
4 Villa Bosquet
75007 Paris
Tel: 47 53 95 80
Fax: 47 05 96 55

Association Française des Cinémas d'Art et d'Essai (A.F.C.A.E.)
22 rue d'Artois
75008 Paris
Tel: 45 63 45 64
Fax: 45 61 13 66

Fédération Nationale des Cinémas Français
10 rue de Marignan
75008 Paris
Tel: 43 59 16 76
Fax: 40 74 08 64

Association Française des Producteurs de Films (A.F.P.F.)
50 avenue Marceau
75008 Paris
Tel: 47 23 79 10
Fax: 47 20 91 57

Chambre Syndicale des Producteurs et Exportateurs de Films Français
5 rue du Cirque
75008 Paris
Tel: 42 25 70 63
Fax: 42 25 94 27

Union des Producteurs de Films (U.P.F.)
1 place des Deux Ecus
75001 Paris
Tel: 40 28 01 38
Fax: 42 21 17 00

Fédération Nationale des Distributeurs de Films
43 Boulevard Malesherbes
75008 Paris
Tel: 42 66 05 32
Fax: 92 16 96 92

Fédération Nationale des Cinémas Français
10 rue de Marignan
75008 Paris
Tel: 43 59 16 76
Fax: 40 74 08 64

Fédération Internationale des Associations de Producteurs de Films (F.I.A.P.F.)
33 Champs-Elysées
75008 Paris
Tel: 42 25 62 14

Société des Réalisateurs de Films (S.R.F.)
215 rue de Faubourg Saint-Honoré
75008 Paris
Tel: 45 63 96 30
Fax: 40 74 07 96

Ministère de la Culture et de la Francophonie
3 rue du Valois
75042 Paris Cedex 01
Tel: 40 15 80 00
Fax: 42 61 35 77

Institut de Formation et d'Enseignement pour les Métiers de l'Image et du Son (F.E.M.I.S.)
Palais de Tokyo
13 avenue du Président Wilson
75116 Paris
Tel: 47 23 36 53
Fax: 40 70 17 03

GEORGIA — Rashmi Doraiswamy

In Georgia, film-makers are referring either directly or indirectly to the war in the Republic. Eldar Shengalaya's *Express Information* (1993) plays on the theme of the two faces of contemporary life: the woman protagonist at the end of the film gives birth to twins – when one of them laughs the other cries. The characters are presented as masks; everyone changes as the situations change, in just the same way that the protagonist changes the face of the political leader he owes allegiance to by turning the huge photograph-frame in his office around in accordance with the kind of people who are visiting him. But in the rapidly changing political situation, the same visitors take on a different "business" and a different visage every time!

In this as in Tsintssdze's *On the Verge* (1993) the television is present like a mirror, creating a farcical "truth" of the events, with tele-personalities facilely probing and passing judgement. *On the Verge* is, however, very different in mood; it is a sombre tale of the alienation of a young couple. The man quite by accident becomes a terrorist. Violence is part of life in the city in this film as well as in Levan Zakarieshvili's **They** (1993). This deals with a group of disoriented youngsters who have taken to drugs and crime. On the threshold of adulthood, one of them dies of an overdose, one of them is jailed and emerges from it as a hardened criminal and don; the others continue to live on the margins. **The Son of the Wakeful** (1993) by Babluani is a more optimistic film about a young boy who has taken to hooliganism. His father, a scientist who tests mice in a laboratory, is looking for a cure for cancer. The mice are named after philosophers. The father dies because he carries out an operation on himself with an unsterilised instrument. The boy, who is very attached to his father, must now take care of his family, and rethink the life he will lead, the path he will take. This is Babluani's fourth feature and has won the Silver Bear at Berlin and two Nika Awards this year – for the script and the Best Actor. (The Nika Awards are considered to be the Russian equivalent of the Oscars.) His first feature *Pokhishenie* (1979), a film about love, was banned and not shown anywhere; *Perelyot Vorobei* (1980) also met with trouble; *Brother* (1983), an historical film about the revolution, was tampered with by the censors to an extent that it was completely different from the way he had conceived it. His latest is semi-autobiographical; Babluani in his youth had led the life, in his own words, of a bandit. He is even today actively involved in the internal war.

The Chosen One (1992), by Mikhail Kalatozishvili, based on Prosper Merimée's *Mathew Falconet* and **Only Death Comes for Sure** (1993) based on Marquez's *No One Writes to the Colonel*, are more introspective in their mood and in their comment on the current state of affairs. The latter film follows the literary text closely but the transposition of the story from one land to another does not detract from the original story. The desolation of a strife-torn city, of the aged couple waiting for decades for their pension papers to be cleared as history changes tracks rapidly, and the youth who live both in and out of the political situation they are in ... all are captured sensitively in the visual, in the soundtrack and in the pacing by the director Marina Tsurumia.

Despite the turmoil, nearly a dozen films on an average are made every year in the Republic. The very strong roots and tradition of film-making in Georgia and a pronouncedly distinct style of image-making have no doubt helped cinema to survive, but it is a somewhat different one from the poetic and intellectual cinema of the past.

RASHMI DORAISWAMY is deputy editor of Cinemaya, the Asian Film Quarterly. She also teaches Russian at the University of Jamia Milia Islamia, New Delhi.

Still from Elder Shengalaya's EXPRESS-INFORMATION

GERMANY
Jack Kindred

Another bad year for German film. So what else is new? But it wasn't as if the industry wasn't trying. Supported largely by state and federal subsidies, 112 features were cranked out, many of which never found a distributor. And of the 67 German films released, 17 were international co-productions. At year's end, only one quasi-German production, producer Bernd Eichinger's **The House of the Spirits**, shot in English with an international cast, had reached the top ten in admissions, ranking eighth among the American majors on the ladder. And only one mother movie, the war epic **Stalingrad**, had lured more than one million Germans away from their TV and video sets and into the cinema. Time was when movies from the New German Cinema from such auteur directors as Rainer Werner Fassbinder, Werner Herzog or Volker Schlöndorff, received festival kudos. But at the 1994 Berlinale, the three German entries in the competition, Reinhard Munster's *Back to Square One (Alles auf Anfang)*, Michael Gwisdek's *Farewell to Angels*, and *The Blue One (Der Blaue)* from Lienhard Wawrzyn, failed to impress the jury. And at Cannes, no German movies were in the competition at all and only one, Jan Schütte's *Auf Widersehen Amerika*, was selected for the Directors' Fortnight.

For the most part, a flawed subsidy system was blamed, although a number of diehard director-producers like Wim Wenders and Peter Fleischmann claimed that Hollywood was the culprit, the octopus whose megabuck, crassly commercial productions were strangling German cinematic creativity. Wenders, whose adroit ability to obtain subsidy funds is matched only by Fleischmann, has turned out a number of spectacular flops, the latest being **Faraway, So Close**, drawing only 80,000 patrons during a fortnight's run.

Ignoring Realities

It is a fact, however, that the production side of the industry would have collapsed long ago had it not been for the subsidy system, largely financed by a 3% surcharge on admissions, meaning that, in effect, the popularity of American movies indirectly supports German flops. Up to now, committees have meted out support on the basis of a film project's cultural value, ignoring the vital commercial realities of the business.

However, observers of the scene have detected a change of attitude among critics and art-for-art's sake directors, ever since the new and disappointing Film Support

Two of German's leading producers, Hanno Huth (left), and Günter Rohrbach

Law FFG went into effect in 1993. Even Wenders remarked that it was high time German film-makers took a more commercial approach, something that Erich "Billy" Kocian, co-founder and editor emeritus of the trade publication *Blickpunkt Film*, had been preaching for years.

While the commerce versus culture debate goes on, no long-term solution is in sight. Producers face the dilemma of a domestic market too small to support high budget films, without which, however, their projects can hardly compete at home with the likes of Spielberg and company. The biggest hit among German exhibitors in 1993 was of course **Jurassic Park**, whose admission figures climbed to the ten million mark. Only a few producers like Eichinger and Dieter Geissler, who put the finishing touches on the fantasy picture **The Neverending Story III** late in 1993, take the risk of making high budget films, with the hope of being able to compensate on the world market with the U.S. majors. And for them, it is essential to shoot in English with an internationally known cast. Otherwise, they'll fail to recoup their production and promotion costs, even if the ancillary video and TV markets go well.

Academy Award for Germany

Despite all the problems, it wasn't all gloom. Lo and behold, a German film actually captured an Oscar at the 1994 Academy Awards, producer Alexander van Dülmen's short film **Clandestine Passenger** (*Schwarzfahrer*) directed by Pepe

Danquart. And a new talent emerged with Katja von Garnier, whose low budget (DM800,000) graduation opus, **Makin' Up** (*Abgeschminkt*) at the Munich Film Academy was a sleeper hit among moviegoers. The long-running, 55-minute comedy attracted more than one million patrons, received a nomination for the German Film Awards, and was among the five titles up for the Academy's "Student Oscar" in Los Angeles. Some critics think that von Garnier is the biggest female directing talent to appear since Doris Dörrie surprised the industry with the comedy *Men*. Watch for Dörrie's next project, *Nobody Loves Me (Keiner liebt mich)*.

Director Ralf Huettner's romantic western comedy, **Texas – Doc Snyder**, starring popular comedian Helge Schneider, also topped the one million admissions mark since its release in November, 1993, evidence that entertainment-hungry movie fans prefer the light touch. Hence, there are high hopes for the amusing romantic comedy **Tafelspitz** produced and directed by Xaver Schwarzenberger, although this release, with a New York setting, drew only 4,000 customers in its first weekend in May. A plus is Schwarzenberger's camerawork and his pastiche views of life in Gotham.

Another potential crowd pleaser is Reinhard Munster's *Alles auf Anfang*. Although it failed to score in the Berlinale, this comedy spoofing Germany's film scene with all the cliché's of moviemaking, including a rivalry between two actresses à la *All About Eve*, is another one worth waiting for.

Director Joseph Vilsmaier, whose credits include the 1988 sleeper *Herbstmilch*, the less successful *Rama Dama* (1992) and *Stalingrad*, came up with **Charlie and Louise**, a family comedy shot in Hamburg, Scotland, and Berlin. The antics revolve around twin sisters who perplex their divorced parents (who live in different cities) by switching identities in order to get Mom and Pop back together. The movie drew 542,000 spectators in a ten-week run, nicely over the half million mark success barrier. Vilsmaier is also working on his next project, the DM14 million *Sleepy Brothers (Schlafes Bruder)*, based on the internationally best-selling novel.

Peter Sehr's **Kaspar Hauser**, originally a three-part TV mini-series scaled down to 137 minutes, still had wobbly legs after fifteen weeks. The strange story of a boy kept isolated in a Bavarian dungeon for twelve years, who could hardly speak and had no idea of the outside world, drew 337,000 patrons, not bad considering its excessive length and depressing story.

August's Film a Hit Locally

Although nearly four million Germans went to see **The House of the Spirits**, adapted from Isabel Allende's novel, the movie flopped in the U.S. Success in Germany is no assurance a film will run well in America and Eichinger's English-language production was no exception. Director Bille August's star cast (Jeremy Irons, Meryl Streep, Glenn Close, Winona Ryder, Antonio Banderas, Vanessa Redgrave) evidently irritated Americans because of differing accents and acting styles. The dubbed German version had no such problem.

The "event" film of 1994 was Steven Spielberg's **Schindler's List**, the true life story of German industrialist Oskar Schindler, who saved 1,200 Jews from Nazi death camps. The dubbed version had a gala premiere at Frankfurt's ornate old opera house, attending by some 1,000 VIP invitees including President Richard von Weizsäcker. Some critics said it was a shame that the German film industry itself had failed to deal with the Schindler story. And the dean of Berlin producers, Artur Brauner, caused a minor flap when he accused the Federal Film Board FFA of turning down support for his 1984 project titled *An Angel in Hell*, the script of which was based on Oskar Schindler's life.

Although German films captured less than 10% of the market in 1993, exhibitors were more than satisfied. Bolstered by blockbusters from the U.S. majors like *Jurassic Park, The Bodyguard* and *Hot Shots: Part Deux*, a total of 130,487,000 visitors attended German theatres, an encouraging increase of 23.2% over the previous year. The box-office take at the unified nation's 3,700 houses rose 31.2% to DM1.17 billion ($705 million), the first year since the 1950's that grosses had topped one billion deutschmarks. Features released dropped from 309 in 1992 to 291, the lowest number in the postwar period. Besides the 67 German films, France had 21 releases, Britain 14 and Italy only one. All others were from the U.S.

JACK KINDRED, former University of Puerto Rico professor, ex-Variety bureau chief, and horse player, covers Germany's film and TV scene from Munich for U.S. trade publications.

TOP TEN GROSSING FILMS IN GERMANY: 1993

	Admissions
Jurassic Park	9,124,260
The Bodyguard	6,269,388
Aladdin	4,666,345
Hot Shots: Part Deux	4,360,603
The Jungle Book (re-release)	4,153,013
Dennis the Menace	3,969,190
Indecent Proposal	3,689,155
The House of the Spirits	3,070,472
Sommersby	3,012,944
The Firm	2,451,325

Recent and Forthcoming Films

AUFWIEDERSEHEN AMERIKA

Script: Thomas Strittmatter/Jan Schütte. Dir: Jan Schütte. Phot: Thomas Mauch. Players: Shmoul Segal, Martin Priest, Ryzsarda Hanin, Helena Stepiu. Prod: Novoskop Film, Zero Film, Good Machine, Wega Film.

ASTERIX IN AMERICA

Script: Thomas Platt, Pierre Tchernia. Dir: Gerhad Hahn. Prod: Extrafilm. *(Full-length animation feature)*

DER BEWEGTE MANN (The Moved Man)

Script and Dir: Söhnke Wortmann. Phot: Gernot Roll. Players: Til Schwaiger, Joachim Krol, Katja Riemann, Armin Rhode. Prod: Neue Constantin/ Olga Film.

HIGH CRUSADE

Script: Jürgen Egger, Robert Gerad Brown. Dir: H. Neuhäuser and K. Knösel. Players: Catherine Punch, John Rhys Davies. Prod: Clausse and Wöbke/Centropolis FP.

KEINER LIEBT MICH (Nobody Loves Me)

Script and Dir: Doris Dörrie. Phot: Helge Weindler. Prod: Cobra Film.

KILLING MOM

Script and Dir: Carl Andersen. Phot: Albert Kittler. Players: Stephanie Hofmeister, Dorothea Moritz, Lother Lambert. Prod: Carl Andersen.

LENI

Script and Dir: Leo Hiemer. Phot: Marian Czura. Players: Johannes Thanheiser, Johanna Thanheiser, Christa Berndl, N. Woerner. Prod: Daniel Zute FP.

NEBEN DER ZEIT (Next to Time)

Script and Dir: Andreas Kleiner. Phot: Sebastian Richter. Players: Rosel Zech, Julia Jäger, Sylvester Groth, Michael Poretchenkov. Prod: Ö-Film FP.

THE NEVERENDING STORY III

Script: Jeff Lieberman. Dir: Peter Macdonald. Player: Jason James Richter. Prod: CineVox. *(Partly animation.)*

DER OLYMPISCHE SOMMER (The Olympic Summer)

Script and Dir: Gordian Maugg. Phot: Andreas Giesecke. Players: Jost Gerstein, Verena Plangger, Otto Ruck, Johanna Maugg. Prod: Gordian Maugg Film and TV Productions.

DIE STURZFLIEGER (Heaven or Bust)

Script: Matthias Seelig. Dir: Peter Bringmann. Phot: Frank Brühne. Players: Götz George, Anja Kling, Ingo Naujoks, Michael Markfort. Prod: Bavaria Film.

TRANSATLANTIS

Script and Dir: Christian. Phot: Thomas Mauch. Players: Daniel Olbrychski, Birgit Aurell, Malgosche Gebel, Jörg Hube. Prod: Christian Wagner FP.

ZÄRTLICHKEIT DES TIGERS (The Tender Tiger)

Script and Dir: Paul Vecchiali. Phot: Georges Strouvé. Players: Fabienne Babe, Sam Djob, Jacques Martial, Rüdiger Vogler. Prod: Kristian Kühn FP, Ultra Marine Sarl.

Producers

Allianz Filmproduktion GmbH
Leibnitzstr. 60
10625 Berlin
Tel: (30) 323 9011
Fax: (30) 323 1693

Anthea Film GmbH
Widenmayerstr. 4
80538 Munich
Tel: (89) 226 194
Fax: (89) 221 251

Bavaria Film GmbH
Bavariafilmplatz 7
80336 Geiselgasteig/Munich
Tel: (89) 6499 2389
Fax: (89) 649 2507

BioSkop-Film GmbH
Türkenstr. 91/111
80799 Munich
Tel: (89) 394 987
Fax: (89) 396 820

Capitol Film + TV International GmbH & Co. Vertriebs KG
Harvestehuder Weg 43
20149 Hamburg 13
Tel: (40) 411 79-0
Fax: (40) 411 70-199

Connexion-Film Vertriebs & Produktions GmbH & Co.
Harvestehuder Weg 45
20149 Hamburg
Tel: (40) 411 79 300
Fax: (40) 411 79 399

Franz Seitz Produktions GmbH
Beichstr. 8
80802 Munich
Tel: (89) 391 1123
Fax: (89) 340 1291

Willy Bogner Film GmbH
Sankt Veitstr. 4
81673 Munich
Tel: (89) 436 06-0
Fax: (89) 436 06 429

CCC Filmkunst GmbH
Verlangerie Daumstr. 16
13599 Berlin
Tel: (30) 334 200-1
Fax: (30) 334 0418

CineVox Film GmbH
Bavaria Filmplatz 7
80336 Geiselgasteig
Tel: (89) 649 541
Fax: (89) 791 2164

Delta Film GmbH
Otto Suhr-Allee 59
10585 Berlin
Tel: (30) 342 4075
Fax: (30) 342 5082

Manfred Durniok Produktion
Hausotterstr. 36
13409 Berlin
Tel: (30) 491 8045
Fax: (30) 491 4065

Impuls Film
Grazestr. 20
30519 Hanover
Tel: (511) 835 001
Fax: (511) 838 6253

Hermes Film GmbH
Kaiserplatz 7
47441 Munich
Tel: (89) 394 368
Fax: (89) 344 363

Lisa Film GmbH
Widenmayerstr. 48
80538 Munich
Tel: (89) 227 195
Fax: (89) 291 156

Mondada Film
Klausenerstr. 19
8154 Munich
Tel: (89) 692 5884
Fax: (89) 691 6709

Neue Constantin Film GmbH
Kaiserstr. 39
47441 Munich
Tel: (89) 3860 9221/2
Fax: (89) 3860 9242

Oko-Film GmbH
Mauerkircherstr. 3
81679 Munich
Tel: (89) 987 666
Fax: (89) 987 602

Olga Film GmbH
Tengstr. 16
80798 Munich
Tel: (89) 271 2635
Fax: (89) 272 5768

Studio Hamburg
Tonndorfer Hauptstr. 90
22045 Hamburg
Tel: (40) 6688-0
Fax: (40) 665 601
(40) 6688 4370

Rialto Film GmbH
Bismarckstr. 108
13469 Berlin
Tel: (30) 310-000-0
Fax: (30) 310 00 559

Roxy-Film GmbH
Schützenstr. 1
80335 Munich 2
Tel: (89) 555 341
Fax: (89) 594 510

Tele-München GmbH
Kaufingerstr. 25
80331 Munich
Tel: (89) 296 661
Fax: (89) 227 875

Vision Film GmbH
Kurfürstenplatz 4
80796 Munich
Tel: (89) 390 025
Fax: (89) 395 569

Von Vietinghoff Filmproduktion
Potsdamerstr. 199
10783 Berlin
Tel: (30) 216 8931
Fax: (30) 215 8219

Regina Ziegler Filmproduktion
Budapesterstr. 35
10789 Berlin
Tel: (30) 261 8071
Fax: (30) 262 8213

Distributors

Ascot Filmverleih GmbH
St. Annastr. 16
80538 Munich
Tel: (89) 29 69 95
Fax: (89) 33 18 39

Columbia Tri-Star Filmgesellschaft mbH
Ickstattstr. 1
80469 Munich
Tel: (89) 23 69-0
Fax: (89) 26 43 80

Concorde Filmverleih GmbH
Widenmayerstr. 5/6
80538 Munich
Tel: (89) 22 07 44
Fax: (89) 29 64 50

Delta Filmverleih GmbH & Co KG
Rosenheimerstr. 2
81667 Munich
Tel: (89) 48 30 35-7
Fax: (89) 48 36 52

FIFIGE Hamburgische Filmeinkaufsgesellschaft GmbH-AG Kino
Allendeplatz 3
20146 Hamburg
Tel: (40) 44 40 06
Fax: (89) 41 85 71

Futura/Filmverlag GmbH
Rambergstr. 5
80799 Munich
Tel: (89) 38 170-1
Fax: (89) 38 17 00 20

Highlight Film Verleih GmbH
Herkomerplatz 2
81679 Munich
Tel: (89) 92 69 66 02
Fax: (89) 98 15 43

Impuls Film
Grazerstr. 10
30519 Hanover
Tel: (0511) 83 50 01
Fax: (0511) 838 6253

Jugend Film Verleih GmbH
Reichsstrasse 15
14052 Berlin
Tel: (30) 300 6970
Fax: (30) 300 697 11

Metropol Filmverleih GmbH
Viktoriastr. 34
80803 Munich
Tel: (89) 39 30 96
Fax: (89) 39 63 03

NEF 2 Filmverleih GmbH
Erhardstr. 8
80469 Munich
Tel: (89) 201 1747
Fax: (89) 201 1634

**Neue Constantin Film GmbH &
Co. Verleih KG**
Kaiserstr. 39
80801 Munich
Tel: (89) 38 60 90
Fax: (89) 38 60 92 42

**Scotia International Filmverleih
GmbH Deutschland**
Possartstr. 14
81679 Munich
Tel: (89) 41 30 90
Fax: (89) 470 6320

Senator Film Verleih GmbH
Kaiserstr. 35
80801 Munich
Tel: (89) 381 9030
Fax: (89) 3819 0325/0326

Tobis Film Verleih GmbH
Bismarckstr. 108
13469 Berlin
Tel: (30) 310 0050
Fax: (30) 3100 0559

Transit Film GmbH
Dachauer Str. 35
80335 Munich
Tel: (89) 55 52 61
Fax: (89) 59 61 22

**20th Century Fox of Germany
GmbH**
Hainer Weg 37-53
60599 Frankfurt
Tel: (69) 60 90 20
Fax: (69) 62 77 16

Warner Bros. Film GmbH
Rosenheimerstr. 143b
81671 Munich
Tel: (89) 418 0090
Fax: (89) 4180 0945

Useful Addresses

**Verband der Filmverleiher e.V
(VDI)**
(Assn. of Distributors)
Kreuzberger Ring 56
65205 Wiesbaden
Tel: (611) 77892-0
Fax: (611) 7789212

**Hauptverband Deutscher
Filmtheater e.V (HDF)**
(Assn. of German Exhibitors)

Langenbeckstr. 9
Postfach 2927
65189 Wiesbaden
Tel: (611) 30 66 60
Fax: (611) 37 64 05

Export Union
Türkenstr. 9
80333 Munich
Tel: (89) 39 00 95
Fax: (89) 39 52 23

Filmförderungsanstalt (FFA)
(Federal Film Board)
Postfach 301808
10787 Berlin
Tel: (30) 254090-0
Fax: (30) 262 8976

**Spitzenorganisation der
Filmwirtschaft e.V (SP10)**
(Film Industry Trade Organisation)
Kreuzberger Ring 56
65205 Wiesbaden
Tel: (611) 1727-0
Fax: (611) 17 27 39

GREECE

Yannis
Bacoyannopoulos

Greece is also living in the whirlwind of the audiovisual crisis in Europe. The demand for and consumption of audiovisual product has been increasing at an ever faster pace but it is covered largely by the American film industry, while European production seems to have lost its functional relationship with audiences. This phenomenon has assumed explosive dimensions in the field of television which still remains institutionally chaotic and out of control. More than 200 television stations, both national and local broadcasters, are bombarding viewers with extremely low quality programming. The best of these are feature films that are transmitted countless times yearly.

The fact that this crisis is now so acute, however, has fortunately led to some forms of reaction. Despite the lack of reliable statistics there has been a trend for a return to audiences to movie theatres, particularly those that have been renovated. The increase in admissions together with the fact that the price of a movie ticket has gone up more than the average rate of inflation, has improved the general financial situation of the film industry and has sparked the interest of investors. Of greater importance, however, has been the upgrading of cinema in the consciousness and habits of the most dynamic elements of social life. As opposed to the inert masses that sit glued in front of a ceaseless flow of television programming, movie audiences have begun to be selective as regards the product they will see.

Of course, *Jurassic Park* was a hit at the box-office. But thrillers showing raw violence and destruction attracted smaller audiences. Stallone's films found themselves fairly low on box-office charts and his cheap imitators disappeared altogether. Fine films such as *The Fugitive*, for example, were extremely successful.

Even more important is the fact that artistic films from Europe and the rest of the world attracted larger audiences and claimed the top places on box-office charts. It was not only the "miracle" of Jane Campion's *The Piano* that found itself in the top ten but also films by Sheridan, Kieślowski, Chen Kaige and Almodóvar.

Low Attendances for Local Films

Unfortunately, Greek films as a whole were not particularly successful in winning movie audiences. Most had an admissions figure of under 10,000 tickets each. A lively social satire by Nikos Zervos (*Poisonous Women*) managed to reach the 50,000 mark. But an encouraging element has been the success among discriminating audiences of a pair of "twins": the films of two new young film-makers Pericles Hoursoglou and Sotiris Goritsas who shared the Best Film Award at the National Thessaloniki Film Festival. Their *Lefteris* and *From the Snow* respectively made moviegoers aware that a new spirit prevails in Greek cinema as regards production and artistic direction. Both films have won awards at international festivals.

Furthermore, both films were made within the framework of the Greek Film Centre's new production programme involving low budget films called "New Perspectives". This optimistic note, however, should not be overrated nor is there any assurance that the trend will continue either as regards success with movie audiences or as a breakthrough in the production stalemate. The Greek Film Centre remains as the only organisation

producing and promoting Greek films. The private sector has been reluctant, in essence, to take the risk and state television lacks the capital. The law that provides that 1½% of the television channels' gross revenues be made available for film production has not yet been effectively activated.

Serious Crisis

The Greek Film Centre went through a serious crisis during the second half of 1993. With insufficient funding and with no board of directors, it continued its work only thanks to the dedication of its president and staff, until Mr. Papandreou's new socialist government could appoint a new board of directors and grant the necessary funds in order to revive production as well as the promotion of the national cinema. The death of Minister of Culture, Melina Mercouri, a figure of enormous international radiance, was a serious blow but her successor, Thanos Mikroutsikos, has proceeded with the study of the institutional as well as the organisational framework in order to formulate a long-term film policy.

At any rate the Greek cinema travels to the far corners of the world with systematic group screenings and with the "Cinemythology" retrospective, while an enormous programme of a similar nature involving 100 films is being prepared for the Centre Georges Pompidou in the spring of 1995.

But let us take a closer look at this year's films.

With **From the Snow**, Sotiris Goritsas moved Greeks and Europeans alike (winning awards at the Troia Film Festival in Portugal and the International Thessaloniki Film Festival) with the direct, sincere and powerful handling of a subject that deals with a burning issue in the Balkans today: the desperate migration in search of jobs and survival. The three heroes are members of Albania's Greek minority. Two men and an orphaned boy, they flee across the border but in essence

Discover the Greek Cinema

GREEK FILM CENTRE

10, PANEPISTIMIOU AVENUE 106 71 ATHENS
TEL. (01) 3631733 / 3634586 FAX (01) 3614 336 TELEX 222614 GFC

their flight does not end in Greece where they continue to be hunted down. They also come face to face with exploitation, rejection. They are innocents and their innocent gaze defines their bewildered clash with harsh reality. With the economy of a former documentary film-maker, Goritsas weaves a convincing story about heart-rending people and their surroundings, even though the film would benefit from a tighter script.

Pericles Hoursoglou's **Lefteris** (40,000 admissions) traces the course of a bright country boy from adolescent innocence and integrity to male maturity, which entails successive compromises and resignations. A classic rite of passage involving social adaptation as well as male egoism. Hoursoglou tells his story with a flashback from the festive New Year's Eve and a successful marriage and career for which, however, he has had to pay a price. A time of reckoning and the sense of a "death". The director constantly enriches his scenes with unexpected elements as well as conflicts which keep the film from being a rectilinear piece of psychology.

Classic Generation

A member of the classic generation of Greek cinema, Nikos Panayotopoulos offers us four moments in a painful passage between memory and reality: **I Dream of My Friends**, which won an award at Sanremo. Timely and timeless phases the span of twenty-five years with the hero different and yet unchanged. A gradual descent into loneliness, rapacity, and despair with the dramatic stylisation and the brilliant virtuoso style of a master craftsman.

In **A Starry Dome**, Costas Aristopoulos also dreams of the myth of Oedipus. In a free association, Antigone, Oedipus, Jocaste, Eteocles and Polyneices traverse the countries and the centuries but mainly the sky of our collective artistic memory, with millions of stars, from the theatre, poetry, architecture and dance. Against the background of stage scenery, under circular Venetian colonnades, in the tents

Still from Nikos Panayotopoulos's I DREAM OF MY FRIENDS

of circus people, in rocky sea-shores and abandoned factories, to the sounds of excerpts from Seferis, Pound, Dostoievsky and Shakespeare, music and arias, he weaves a ritualistic current into a highly aesthetic audiovisual ensemble.

Vassilis Vafeas' **The Cosmic Dissecting-Room Show** is also experimental cinema. Yet here the observation of the real stands out. The director persuades an avant-garde artist, Grigoris Semitecolo, to present his show-happening (with giant-sized, white, naked dolls which he, dressed as a surgeon, then proceeds to cut up) to a naïve audience of islanders in Samos. He follows the spectacle and their reaction but also interposes his own images in a new rhythmic and visual universe of cinema.

Film Noir in Greek Setting

New film-makers Nikos Grammatikos and Marcos Holevas have transferred the familiar models of the American film noir to Greece – a move that is only natural since modern life and its artistic expression tends to become a boundless, common "theatre" of experiences. **A Time to Kill** and **Eyewitness** skilfully bring to life games of life and death, with mysterious orders to kill in return for a lot of money or with dream-revelations, somewhere between the imaginary and the real.

Thanssis Rakitzis's **Ariadne Lives in Leros** conveys us to the field of the imaginary. Dark oedipal roads lead a daughter to seek her father, her mother's murderer, in the Leros mental institution

Still from Sotiris Goritsas's FROM THE SNOW

where ancient rituals, memories of the Minotaur, are performed.

The triptych by Menios Ditsas, Costas Zyrinis and Thanassis Scroubelos, **The Yard with the Rubbish**, also falls within the category of the imaginary but through the sharpening of the naturalistic boundary. A theatre of rawness, the belly, the guts of the city, crazy instincts as the symbolic in the tradition of "Mabuse" and Arabal.

Patrice Vivancos's **A Charmed Life** is a journey into the chimera, a leap into the paradise of people who have suffered hardship and humiliation. A group of senior citizens set off to meet their wealthy friend at the other end of the world, in Colombia. Yannis Papdakis's **White-Red** is

a little drama about card-sharpers and fraud, with the fast life of the hunted hare in the squares and streets of the city.

Dimitris Collatos's **A Red Rose for You** is about his autobiographical struggle after his wife commits suicide as he fights to rehabilitate his autistic son Alkis.

Finally, **The Little Dolphins** by Dinos Demopoulos is a children's film with children as its heroes.

An interesting series of full-length documentaries completed this year's production. Stella Theodorakis's **From the Unique to the Multiple** is a study on the authentic and the eternal as opposed to the mass-produced and ephemeral as we approach the year 2000 AD. In Lena Voudouris's **Just and Unjust Cause** two characters from Aristophanes's *Clouds* clash with everything that is being said for and against the Greek positions in the Macedonian problem providing the material. Yanna Triantafylli's **Will I Get Out?** follows three handicapped youngsters in their struggle to survive the poor conditions that exist in the institutions-ghettoes. Finally, Nikos Anagnostopoulos's **Time Sleeps in the Orient** is a question for the meeting of Alexander the Great with the peoples of the Orient in modern Turkmenistan.

Still from Costas Aristopoulos's THE STARRY DOME

Recent and Forthcoming Films

ARIADNE LIVES IN LEROS

Script: Thanassis Scroubelos (based on an idea by Thanassis Rakitzis). Dir: Thanassis Rakitzis. Prod: Greek Film Centre, Alekos Papageorgiou.

Ariadne leaves in search of answers to the questions that are tormenting her. The ball of thread will begin to unravel. Little by little her anguish will begin to take shape. Like some magical image the other people in the riddles she must solve will emerge. Riddles that are a legacy of parental sin. The circle will close and reopen and will bring the solution to the drama or a deadlock?

BORDERLINE

Script and Dir: Panayiotis Karkanevatos. Players: A.L. Lembessopoulos, N. Karydis, Ch. Kalavrouzos, M. Kyriaki. Prod: Greek Film Centre, Channel 4, ZDF.

Two brothers set off on their journey into the world from a mining village in the bowels of the earth. At the age of 25, the younger brother is a police sergeant, while the eldest disappears, fakes his own death, changes names. There comes a time when he finds his brother and discovers the multiple versions of his own self.

A CHARMED LIFE

Script: M. Karali, A. Theron, P. Vivancos. Dir: Patrice Vivancos. Players: Thanassis Vengos, Eva Kotamanidou, Giorgos Moschidis. Prod: Greek Film Centre, Ekas Film, Prooptiki (Greece, AGAT Films (France), A.D.C. Imatges (Spain), Pinto Producciones, Foto Club 76 (Colombia).

A bunch of senior citizens living out their remaining days on the sidelines, decide to make their great dream come true and become shipping magnates. But the ship they are looking for lies at anchor somewhere in the jungles of Colombia. They embark on their last crazy voyage in pursuit of the dream and a "charmed life".

THE COSMIC DISSECTING-ROOM SHOW

Dir: Vassilis Vafeas. Prod: Greek Film Centre, Vassilis Vafeas.

Avant-garde artist Grigoris Semitecolo presents his show-happening (with giant-sized, white, naked dolls which he, dressed as a surgeon, then proceeds to cut up to a naïve audience of islanders in Samos.

A DARING STORY

Script: Dimitris Makris, S. Makri. Dir: D. Makris. Players: Andras Vlachokyriakos, Regina Stani, Joaquin Blanco Calvache, Tanya Celaya Salvador, Constantinos Manos, Manos Cranidiotis, Simona Faj, Ramon Cajorla Hernandez. Prod: Greek Film Centre, D.M. Film Prod. (Athens), Movies (Athens), New Mark Films (Milan), Este Films (Barcelona), Artimm (Rome).

The writer allows his thoughts to wander in the only paradise he knows – the earthly paradise of the senses where ecstasy is law and order.

I DREAM OF MY FRIENDS

Script: Nikos Payanotopoulos, Dimitris Nollas. Dir: N. Payanotopoulos. Prod: Greek Film Centre.

The film covers a period of 25 years (1965-1990) and is in a way a brief history of the generation that is today in its fifties. It is a film based on four short stories by Dimitris Nollas.

THE LITTLE DOLPHINS

Script and Dir: Dinos Demopoulos. Players: Savros Doyakos, Constantina Alevra, Spyros Pantazis, Nikitas Chronis, Constantina Andriopoulous, Alexandros Rigas, Christos Zorbas, Haris Panayotou, Dimitris Papayannis. Prod: Greek Film Centre, Angelos Sideratos.

In a small seaside village in Greece two children discover the miracle of the world that surrounds them as well as the dark side of life. With the endless power of love they break down the barriers of convention and fear and open bright pathways to life that are quite inconceivable to grown-ups.

FROM THE SNOW

Script and Dir: Sotiris Goritsas. Players: Gerassimos Skiade-ressis, Vassilis Elefteriadis, Antonis Manolas, Mania Papadimitriou, Sofia Olympiou, Lazaros Andreou. Prod: Greek Film Centre, Hyperiod Productions, S. Goritsas.

The flight of three young refugees, members of the Greek minority of Albania and their acquaintance with contemporary Greek society.

LEFTERIS

Dir: Pericles Hoursoglou. Players: Nikos Georgakis, Maria Skoula, Nikos Orphanos, Manolis Mavromatakis. Prod: Greek Film Centre, Ciak Film, Stefil Film, Attika (Pantelis Mitropoulos), Pericles Hoursoglou.

Thirteen years in the life of a "bright" young man. They are the years during which he changes, loses his values, loses his youth. And the New Year's Eve during which he becomes aware of it all, when he throws his hands up in the air now that he knows he sacrificed one life for the right to acquire yet another.

POISONOUS WOMEN

Script: H. Romas, A. Hadzisofia. Dir: Nokos Zervos. Players: Spyros Papadopoulos, Ilias Logothetis, Costas Rigoloulos, Athena Tsilyra, Nadia Mourouzi, Anna Kyriakou. Prod: Greek Film Centre, Kineton S.A., G. Spentzos, N. Zervos.

Constantine Sebekos has it all. A famous psychiatrist, he is wealthy, has good friends, patients who adore him and an ideal relationship with a beautiful and high-powered businesswoman. On the night he is giving an important lecture, he is bombarded by a barrage of events that turn his life upside down.

THE STARRY SKY

Script: Costas Aristopoulos, Achilleas Kyriakides. Dir: C. Aristopoulos. Players: Sophocles Peppas, Irene Inglessi, Dimitris Lignardis, Smaragda Karydi, Kostas Zacharoff. Prod: Greek Film Centre, Stefi Films, Costas Aristopoulos.

The story begins with Oedipus who leaves Greece with Antigone and journeys to foreign lands and more specifically Germany. There they meet a group of artists. Some of them re-enact scenes from plays by well-known European writers such as Thomas Mann, Shakespeare, Goethe. At the same time in the group there are also some lyrical works such as Mozart's Apollo and Jacinth, Strauss's Electra, Oedipus Rex, etc. Oedipus and Antigone participate in this group and through a magical projector tell the story of the trilogy, Oedipus Rex, Oedipus at Colonus and Antigone.

A TIME TO KILL

Script: Nikos Grammatikos, Thanassis Scroubelos. Dir. N. Grammatikos. Players: M. Hadzisavvas, Betty Livanou, G. Yannopoulos, A. Sakellariou. Prod: Greek Film Centre, Hyperion Productions.

An existential thriller about male friendship, love and the moral value of murder.

WHITE-RED

Script and Dir: Yannis Papadakis. Players: Dimitris Alexandris, Takis Moschos, Lazaros Andreou, Gerassimos Skiadaressis, Dimitra Papadima, Vassilis Lagos, Fotis Polichronopoulos, Stelios Pavlou, Stavros Xenidis. Prod: Greek Film Centre, Yannis Papadakis.

The film describes the sidewalk world of cardsharpers through the story of Boy, the young "dealers" and traces the fine line between good guys and bad guys.

ENIOCHOS (THE CHARIOTEER)

Dir: Alexis Damianos. Prod: Greek Film Centre.

This is an attempt at a poetic approach to the journey of one man from 1940 to the present day and describes the effects of historical events on him and his circle.

THE GARDEN OF GOD

Script and Dir: Takis Spyridakis. Players: Vangelis Mourikis, Dinos Makris, Costas Markopoulos, Ilias Pakas, Nick Kalamo. Prod: Greek Film Centre, Takis Spyridakis.

The short guy, the beanpole, Alekos and Sinoue, everyday people gathered together with several other familiar types in the Garden of God. They spend their time going to church, working out in the yard, learning how to dance in the cafeteria, reciting poetry. They play ball. They lose their friends. They strike their enemies and they promise themselves that come Christmas they will make their way down to the sea.

THE SLAUGHTER OF THE COCK.

Dir: Andreas Pantzis.

TERRA INCOGNITA

Script: Yannis Typaldos, Giorgos Bramos, Dinos Hadzigiorgis. Dir: Y. Typaldos. Players: Oleg Jankovski, Piotr Mamonov, Liusin Stanislav, Tatiana Liutaiva. Prod: Greek Film Centre, Joint Stock Akvo Corp.

In a society in the not too distant future, a writer comes out of his voluntary isolation as soon as he learns of the death of a close friend. In his final attempt to find out the cause of this death he comes face to face with his personal decline.

TRANSIT

Script: Alexandros Kotzias and Stelios Pavlidis. Dir: S. Pavlidis. Players: Amalia Moutousi, Alexandra Pavlidou, Ilias Logothetis, Giorgos Constas, Giorgos Kentros. Prod: Greek Film Centre, Attica Films, ETI Production.

The pressure of the military junta pushes the dregs of society to the surface: a burglar, a small-time crook, taking advantage of the social solidarity and common frustration against the regime of the colonels, manages to worm his way among the resistance groups and climb the social ladder. With the fall of the junta, however, his support falls too; solidarity and camaraderie give way to individual efforts for survival. Life returns to its pre-junta pace. People go back to

their "places", but what about him? Go back where? To the streets? and the disintegration of social recognition? His fall is much swifter than his rise.

ACROPOLE

Script and Dir: Pantelis Voulgaris. Players: Spyros Papadopoulos, Themis Bazaka, Giorgos Moschidis, Constantinos Tzoumas, Manos Vakoussis, Despo Diamantidou, Alexia Bouloukou. Prod: Greek Film Centre, Alco Film Productions.

They say that when you go through the door into the ACROPOLE you've made it. That's what my hero Lakis Loizos was thinking when he set foot on its stage. All this happened in the winter of 1960.

JAGUAR

Script: Katerina Evangelakou, R. Georgakopoulou. Dir: K. Evangelakou. Players: N. Vosniakou, Y. Maltezou, D. Katalifos. Prod: Greek Film Centre, Katerina Evangelakou.

The story of the meeting of two women in their forties who have lived through the same historic events (German occupation, civil war, discord) and have experienced the same family situations (persecution, sacrifices, love affairs, deaths) but who have no common memory of these events. The past is alive. History is absent.

BLACK OUT

Script and Dir: M. Karamagiolis. Players: G. Horafas, K. Karbet. Prod: Greek Film Centre, M. Karamagiolis.

Mysterious tapes with the voice of the dead pilot Christou recall his love story with Maria in colour, while in the black-and-white present the patient role of the photographer Stavrou prevails.

CAFAVY

Script and Dir: Ianis Smaragdis. Players: Vassilis Diamantopoulos, Dimitris Katalifos, Dimitris Papadimitriou. Prod: Greek Film Centre, ET1, Lumiere LTT Cyprus, Alexandros Film.

A film on the life and work of the great Alexandrian poet, focusing on the relationship of the dying Cavafy and a young writer and student of his work who comes to read him a biography he has written of the poet.

THE DAWN

Script and Dir: Alexis Bistikas. Players. S. Zalmas, K. Kouka. Prod: Greek Film Centre, A. Bistikas.

The story of a woman who discovers herself and fights for her dignity, with songs and feelings as her guides ...

THE DEEP ABOVE

Screenplay: George Panoussopoulos, M. Zoumboulaki. Dir: G. Panoussopoulos. Players: K; Karabeti, A. Sissovitis, V. Christodoulidou. Prod: Greek Film Centre, G. Panoussopoulos, Filmiki Co., ELKE.

Every love affair seeks a vindication or an ending. Passion asks for nothing, has no memory, no "future". It is a fire that cleanses everything. It is an untrodden deep.

HAWAII

Script and Dir: Th. Scoubelos. Players: M. Vakoussis, L. Tsangas, G. Constas. Prod: Greek Film Centre, Fasma Ltd.

In a male brothel two lovers, Vassilis and Conchina, tear each other to pieces over who will be "queen" of the night.

THE HOUSE IN THE COUNTRY

Script and Dir: Layia Giourgou. Prod: G. Constas, E. Vlachakou, S. Smyrnaiou, T. Dimitriou, G. Karatzoyiannis, E. Poulikakos.

A writer isolates himself in order to write. Without wanting to, he is responsible for the fact that suspicion over a man's disappearance falls on a pair of illicit lovers. As the case is cleared up it will shed light on unknown aspects of the heroes' lives and will settle long-pending scores.

MOON RUNAWAY

Script and Dir: Thanassis Marangos. Players: V. Mourikis, A. Ladikou, I. Logothetis, Ch. Calavrouzos, N. Gerasimidou, K. Kafassis. T. Kapsali, V.

Diamantopoulos. Prod: Greek Film Centre, Prosechos Film, T. Marangos.

A police sleuth, Achilles Karafotias, undertakes a very difficult assignment and descends into a deep well. He discovers that the petrified fingers of the body he discovers at the bottom tightly conceal his childhood story.

LAIR OF THE OCTOPUS

Script and Dir: Nikos Nikolaidis. Prod: Greek Film Centre, N. Nikolaidis.

The last hours of a terrorist who has been wounded. Cut off from his contacts, he tries to give his pursuers the slip and get out of the city.

ORPHEUS DESCENDING

Script: N. Markakis, G. Zervoulakos. Dir: G. Zervoulakos. Players: Vana Barba, A. Collatos, A. Antoniou, Ch. Tsangas. Prod: Greek Film Centre, G. Zervoulakos.

Greece on its one-way course towards urban transformation as seen through the adventures of a band of travelling musicians performing in country fairs.

QUARTET IN FOUR MOVEMENTS

Script: G. Notaras, E. Soner, N. Papandreou. Dir: Lucia Rikaki. Players: G. Horafas, Themis Bazaka, C. Constantopoulos, Gioni. Prod: Greek Film Centre, Orama Film.

The outwardly peaceful married life of a couple is shattered with the sudden appearance of two newcomers in their life. A film on human relationships and erotic behaviour.

THE SECOND DEATH OF MARIA

Script and Dir: Giorgos Karypidis. Players: V. Yioulielmaki, D. Martinopoulou, G. Michalakopoulos, T. Stathopoulou, G. Constas, S. Kaloyirou. Prod: Greek Film Centre, P. Filipou.

Sofia, a young girl from Athens, slowly and painfully discovers the secret hidden by their household help, an orphan girl from the village.

SUITABLE GROUNDS

Script and Dir: F. Siskopoulou. Players: M. Hadzisavvas, D. Hatoupi.

The film looks through the eyes of a man in the process of seeking and capturing artistic form and at the same time the relationships and conditions that he creates out of the living reality that provides him with his subjects, his heroes and his material.

THIRD GRADE IN HIGH SCHOOL

Script and Dir: A. Kokkinos. Prod: Greek Film Centre, A. Kokkinos.

Athens. End of the decade of the decade of the 1960's. A group of adolescents try to understand the world as well as their own individual selves.

ULYSSES' GAZE

Script: Theo Angelopoulos, T. Guerra, P. Margaris. Dir: T. Angelopoulos. Players: Harvey Keitel, Majia Morgenstern, Wojtek Pszoniak, Giorgos Michalakopoulos, Thanassis Vengos. Prod: Theo Angelopoulos, Paradis Films, Basic Cinematografica, Greek Film Centre.

A film director wanders in the Balkan countries in search of a lost gaze.

THE WING OF THE FLY

Script: C. Shiopahas, Christos Poulos. Dir: C. Poulos. Prod: Greek Film Centre, C. Shiopahas, Plus Ltd.

THE WOMAN WHO RETURNS

Script and Dir: Maritina Passari, Nikos Savvatis. Players: Ch. Papamichou, K. Apostolidis, M. Passari, Ch. Voupouras. Prod: Greek Film Centre, Nikos Savvatis, Maritina Passari.

A contemporary love story – a tragic love triangle whose lives are driven by passion and chance.

THE RITES OF SPRING

Script: M. Vlachoyanni. Dir: G. Kourmouzas. Prod: Greek Film Centre, ET-1, G. Kourmouzas.

A documentary film on the mating habits of herons, among the most beautiful birds in Greece, from courtship to the final stage when the eggs are hatched. The delicacy and finesse of the ritual show that these birds have made an art of love.

IDAEAN MYTHS

Script and Dir: L. Haronitis. Prod: Greek Film Centre, L. Haronitis.

A documentary film covering ten years of archaeological excavations by G. Sakellarakis in the "IDAEAN CAVE".

SO THIS IS TRAGEDY

Script and Dir: S. Ioannou. Prod: Greek Film Centre, Filmode Ltd. Narration: Irene Papas, Ch. Sozos.

A documentary on the creation of the ancient drama, of tragedy and comedy, through Dionysiac worship.

STUTTGART 1978

Script: T. Hadzopoulos, L. Papasthatis. Dir: T. Hadzopoulos. Prod: Greek Film Centre, Cinetic.

A documentary on the course of Greek immigrants in Germany from 1978 to the present.

UNSMILING STONE

Script and Dir: P. Coutsaftis. Prod: Greek Film Centre, P. Coutsaftis.

A documentary that tells the story of a city. A ramble in the great and lowly places of the sacred landscape of Eleusis.

BALKAN BIOSCOPE

Script and Dir: Fotos Lambrinos. Prod: Greek Film Centre, Fotos Lambrinos.

YANNIS BACOYANNOPOULOS is one of the most well-known Greek film critics. He has worked for many newspapers and magazines beginning in 1960. For the past twenty years he has been the film critic of the Athens daily *Kathimerini* and Greek State Television ET-1.

A documentary on the period of the silent movies in all the Balkan countries.

ALL THE LATE AFTERNOONS

Script and Dir: M; Yiamalakis. Prod: Greek Film Centre, M. Yiamalakis.

A documentary on a sacred island. Shiploads of tourists in summer and fierce loneliness in winter. There are many here who cash in on piety for financial gain. Shut up in her own Olympian world, a nun paints saints without haloes.

HONGKONG — Derek Elley

Hongkong went through one of its periodic crises of confidence in the latter half of 1993, as a whole series of factors conspired to rattle the industry's cage. The main blow was more symbolic than anything else – for the first time in ten years a foreign movie occupied the top-grossing spot.

Jurassic Park beat off competition from works by favourite local comic Stephen Chiau (*Flirting Scholar, King of Beggars*) to attract HK$61.99 million. The previous time a U.S. movie had been the year's number one was in 1983 with *E.T. – The Extra-Terrestrial* (HK$16.74 million), and prior to that several James Bond movies during the 1970's.

The fact that the rest of 1993's top ten was solidly local seemed of little importance to an industry more than ever living off its nerves. The territory's handover to mainland China on July 1, 1997, is no longer a distant reality, as was shown when a delegation of 40 industry members journeyed to Peking in 1993 to seek reassurances about the future. All they basically got was an undertaking that Hongkong films could compete at international festivals under the title, "Hongkong, China".

Peking also made itself felt at the 1994 Hongkong Film Festival, withdrawing several titles in protest at the festival screening two independent mainland productions (*The Days* and *Red Beads*).

Under pressure, the Hongkong distributor of Tian Zhuangzhuang's controversial *The Blue Kite* also refused to let the film take part.

More of a Gamble

Escalating budgets (driven by stars' huge fees) are now making financial success more and more of a gamble; the recent craze for the costume martial arts spectacular is generally reckoned to be over, but no genre has since appeared to replace it; lucrative foreign territories like Taiwan, Singapore and Indonesia have started to resist producers' high demands and impose protectionist measures; and, since the start of 1994 China has imposed draconian rulings on co-productions (see China section).

The *Jurassic* news – though hardly unexpected, given the film's worldwide success – could not have come at a worse time. Hongkong's dollar-driven, genre-reliant film-makers have traditionally panicked whenever a fad has played itself out, but in the grab-it-while-you-can business ethic in the run-up to 1997 such an event took on symbolic proportions.

In reality, the box-office position of foreign movies has changed little. Apart from *Jurassic*, of the 157 non-Chinese films released during 1993 (up from 124 in 1992) none got even close to the top ten, apart from *Cliffhanger* (HK$23.50 million). Next biggest were *Last Action Hero* (HK$18.90 million), *Indecent Proposal* (HK$15.36 million), and *Aladdin* (HK$13.37 million).

Some 154 Hongkong movies were released during the year (only fractionally down from 1992's 160), plus the normal scattering of mainland (9) and Taiwan (5) productions, all of which grossed traditionally paltry amounts apart from Taiwan's *The Wedding Banquet* (HK$15.47 million).

There are, however, real fears – especially in the face of other markets' protectionism – whether Hongkong can sustain such a high output. The majority

Still from Stephen Shin's THE GREAT CONQUEROR'S CONCUBINE

lose money on paper, and the stakes are increasing daily. Only the fact that a large slice of the industry is little more than a money-laundering operation for shady businesses (including triads) seems to keep it going. At the end of 1993, the police finally set up a task force to investigate triad connections after a further spate of killings.

The move by Taiwan distributors followed the lacklustre performance of a string of expensive, big-budget Hongkong films there. Following talks with Hongkong industry reps that led nowhere, Taiwan distributors drew a line at HK$1.5 million a title for rights to all media. Though the figure is negotiable for blockbusters, the decision has panicked Hongkong producers, faced nowadays with budgets of over HK$30 million for starry, effects-heavy movies. In Taiwan, U.S. movies immediately filled the gap traditionally occupied by Hongkong product (see Taiwan section).

A further worry is that if, post-1997, Taiwan's government imposes official import restrictions on Hongkong product (as technically coming from China), the latter could lose what little it has of that market at present.

Continued Vitality

Despite the above problems, Hongkong film-making still retains a vitality that's out of all proportion to the territory's size. The

7-22 April, 1995

THE *19* th
HONG KONG
INTERNATIONAL
• • • F I L M • • • •
F E S T I V A L

Information:

Hong Kong International Film Festival,

Level 7, Administration Building,

Hong Kong Cultural Centre,

10 Salisbury Road,

Tsim Sha Tsui, Kowloon,

Hong Kong

Tel: (852) 734 2900-6

Fax: (852) 366 5206

Telex: 38484 USDHK HX

Cable: FESTUSD HK

Presented by
the Urban Council, Hong Kong

ENRICHING CITY LIFE

1993-94 season produced a rich and diverse crop of movies. Jackie Chan, after a year or so of career dithering, bounced back in New Year 1994 with **Drunken Master II**, an assured comedy action-adventure (bearing little relation to the 1978 original that launched his career into the big time) set in the early Republic, with Chan as the young Wong Fei-hung, veteran Ti Lung as his stern father, and singer/actress Anita Mui stealing every one of her scenes as Chan's relative. The film grossed a massive, face-saving HK$41 million, Chan's biggest to date, and did well all over East Asia.

Though the martial arts spectacular (invariably shot on the mainland) is reckoned to have peaked commercially, the genre still came up with some memorable examples during 1993-94. Ronny Yu's **The Bride with White Hair** (aka *Jiang Hu: Between Love and Glory*) teamed Brigitte Lin and Leslie Cheung in a magnificently shot, operatic tale of warring clans and doomed love; the rapid follow-up, David Wu's **The Bride with White Hair 2**, was more consciously exotic (including designer lesbianism) and more thinly plotted but provided a fine showcase for Lin.

As of summer 1994, Yu was set to direct the English-language *Slayer* in the U.S., his second English-language movie following the Amsterdam-set drugs thriller *China White* in 1990. John Woo, after the success of *Hard Target*, announced a string of stateside projects in the first half of 1994, including action movie *Shadow Warrior* (with Bruce Willis), youth drama *Dirty Boulevard* (exec produced by Martin Scorsese), *Ring of Blood* (with Chow Yun-fat making his English-language debut), plus a project to be written by Quentin Tarantino. As of summer 1994, he looked set to direct *Tears of the Sun*, a US$40 million drama to shoot in Brazil and Australia.

Other quality costume pictures included Stephen Shin's big-budget **The Great Conqueror's Concubine**, a three-hour historical extravaganza, shot on the mainland with stars Gong Li, Ray Lui and Zhang Fengyi, that recalled Shaw Bros. spectacles of the 1960's; veteran Yuen Woo-ping's **The Iron Monkey** and **The Tai-Chi Master**, the latter effectively teaming action stars Michelle Yeoh and Jet Li; and Benny Chan's **The Magic Crane**, a highly entertaining slice of fantastique sword-and-chivalry teaming Anita Mui and Tony Leung Chiu-wai.

Fresh Variation

Clara Law, best known overseas for delicate relationship movies like *Autumn Moon*, came up with a fresh variation on the costume genre in **Temptation of a Monk**, a sparely shot drama, almost Japanese in flavour, about a general-turned-monk (Taiwan actor Wu Hsing-kuo) and a vengeful princess disguised as a nun (Joan Chen) that starts impressively but later becomes tiresomely posey.

For Tsui Hark, it was not the best of years. A major disappointment, both financially and artistically, was **Green Snake**, his extravagant, Bava-esque version of Lilian Lee's retelling of the legend about two beautiful snake spirits (Maggie Cheung, Joey Wang) wreaking emotional havoc on earth. Yuen Woo-ping's Taiwan co-production, **Wing Chun**, was also a disappointing showcase for martial arts star Michelle Yeoh, often scrappily made.

Jeff Lau's **Treasure Hunt**, which marked the return of matinee idol Chow Yun-fat to the screen after a year's break, amassed a mega HK$37 million over Chinese New Year 1994 but was an unconvincing mix of action and whimsy, with Chow as a U.S. undercover agent sent to a Shaolin monastery in China. It was, however, more of a piece than **Executioners**, a loose sequel to the neo-modernist *The Heroic Trio* (a cult hit in the West) teaming the same big-names (Anita Mui, Maggie Cheung, Michelle Yeoh) but lacking the previous film's verve, despite being directed by the experienced Ching Siu-tung and Johnny To.

One small shift of the past year has been a sizable number of well-crafted modern relationship movies, recalling Taiwan *wen-yi pian* of the 1970's as well as local mandarin melodramas of the 1950's. Tony Au's **A Roof with a View**, a charming love story between a policeman (Tony Leung Kar-fai) and a young abandoned wife (Veronica Yip), was another quality offering from the director-cum-production designer, one of Hongkong's most underrated talents. Jacob Cheung's **Always on My Mind**, a black comedy about a TV presenter dying of terminal cancer, produced fine, moving performances from two veterans, Michael Hui and Josephine Hsiao. And Peter Chan and Lee Chi-ngai followed their well-observed ensemble films *Alan and Eric* (1991) and *Tom, Dick & Hairy* (1993) with the equally likable **He Ain't Heavy, He's My Father**.

Flashier, but with meaty parts for its lead actresses, was **Remains of a Woman**, reteaming director Clarence Fok Yiu-leung and actress Carrie Ng (after their high-gloss lesbian thriller *Naked Killer*) in a juicy story of sex, murder and dark passions. The film, made on deferred salaries, won Ng best actress award at Taiwan's Golden Horse Awards in late 1993.

Also worth noting (though uneven stylistically) is the portmanteau Taiwan co-production **Conjugal Affair**, grouping three connected short stories of modern relationships, Hongkong style, directed by Yang Fan, Sylvia Chang and promising newcomer Chao Liang-chün.

Michael Hui and Josephine Hsiao in Jacob Cheung's ALWAYS ON MY MIND

TOP TEN GROSSING FILMS IN HONGKONG: 1993	
	(HK$ million)
Jurassic Park	61.99
Flirting Scholar	40.17
King of Beggars	38.62
All's Well Ends Well Too	35.48
C'est la vie, mon chéri*	30.85
City Hunter	30.75
Fong Sai Yuk	30.66
Once Upon a Time in China III	27.54
Crime Story	27.45
Fight Back to School III	25.77
*including 1994 gross	
Apart from *Jurassic Park*, all the above are Hongkong productions.	

The year's biggest critical success (and a strong performer at the box-office) was actor-director Derek Yee Tung-shing's **C'est la vie, mon chéri**, which won almost all the major prizes at the 13th Hongkong Film Awards and made a star of actress Anita Yuen, as the girl was a heart of gold who falls for a poor jazz musican. Though the film skirts very close to a disease-of-the-week weepie, it is remarkable for its lack of cynicism and crowd-pleasing elements – a demonstration that, in Hongkong's industry, nothing can ever be taken for granted.

DEREK ELLEY has been associated with IFG for more than 20 years, during which time he has written extensively on East Asian cinema. An associate editor of Variety, he is also editor of the annual Variety Movie Guide. He is currently completing A Handbook of Chinese Cinema.

13th Hongkong Film Awards

The following prizes were awarded at the 13th Hongkong Film Awards on April 22, 1994:

Best Picture: *C'est la vie, mon chéri.*

Best Director: Derek Yee Tung-shing *(C'est la vie, mon chéri).*

Best Script: Derek Yee Tung-shing *(C'est la vie, mon chéri).*

Best Actor: Anthony Wong *(The Untold Story).*

Best Actress: Anita Yuen *(C'est la vie, mon chéri).*

Best Supporting Actor: Cheun Pui *(C'est la vie, mon chéri).*

Best Supporting Actress: Feng Bo-bo *(C'est la vie, mon chéri).*

Best Newcomer: Wu Hsing-kuo *(Temptation of a Monk).*

Best Costume Design: Emi Wada, Cheung Sin-yiu *(The Bride with White Hair).*

Best Editing: Peter Cheung *(Crime Story).*

Best Music: Tats Lau, Wai Kai-leung *(Temptation of a Monk).*

Best Art Direction: Eddie Ma *(The Bride with White Hair).*

Best Action Direction: Cory Yuen, Yuen Tak *(Fong Sai Yuk).*

Best Photography: Peter Pau *(The Bride with White Hair).*

Best Song: *The Heroic Trio.*

Still from Derek Yee Tung-shing's C'EST LA VIE, MON CHÉRI

Recent and Forthcoming Films

HUNG MUIGWAI YU PAK MUIGWAI

Dir: Stanley Kwan. Players: Joan Chen, Wu Hsing-kuo, Veronica Yip.

NAMGINGDIK GEIDUK

Dir: Tony Au, from the short story by Toru Akutagawa. Players: Nobuko Tomita. Prod: Golden Harvest (H.K.)/Amuse (Japan).

DUNGCHE SAIDUK (Ashes of Time)

Dir: Wong Kar-wai. Players:

Brigitte Lin, Carina Liu, Maggie Cheung, Jacky Cheung, Leslie Cheung, Tony Leung Kar-fai, Tony Leung Chiu-wai. Prod: Scholar Films (H.K.).

CHONGHING SAMLAM (Chung King)

Dir: Wong Kar-wai. Players: Brigitte Lin, Tony Leung, Chiu-wai, TAkeshi Kanershiro, Faye Wang, Valerie Chowe.

SUNG GA WONG CHIU

Dir: Mabel Cheung. Players:

Michelle Yeoh, Joan Chen.

FOSIU HUNG LIN TSI (Burning Paradise)

Script: Nam Yen. Dir: Ringo Lam. Exec. Prod: Tsui Hark.

HUNG FAN KUI

Dir: Stanley Tong. Players: Jackie Chan. Prod: Golden Way, Golden Harvest.

GWAI TOU

Dir: Raymond Leung.

HUNGARY ——— Derek Elley

The Socialist Party's majority in the May 1994 elections is generally seen as a good thing by Hungary's film community, with the Socialists perceived as naturally more sympathetic towards cultural activities. Blatant media manipulation (including wholesale sacking of journalists) prior to the election was the last straw for many Hungarians, disaffected by prime minister József Antall's fumbling market reforms that since spring 1990 had led to a growing gap between rich and poor, and increasing social tensions.

The voters' massive swing towards the reformed Communists, led by Gyula Horn, who now share power with former dissidents the Alliance of Free Democrats, is seen as a reaction against pure free-marketism and a hankering for some of the old certainties of a state-run system. But how the new government (largely composed of ex-Communists who gently steered the country to democracy in the late 1980's) will fare in practice is another matter.

Horn and his colleagues have to take some tough decisions if Hungary is to aspire to full EU membership in 5-6 years (it became an associate member on February 1, 1994). Hungary's film world, already split between those who have embraced the commercial market and those who hanker for the days of subsidised art, may see few changes in the short term. But at least the new government has brought fresh hope to a country whose confidence has been battered every which way during the past four years.

Production Drifts Downward

A total of 20 local features was released during 1993, down from 25 the previous year, though they attracted more admissions (293,000, up from 284,000). The rise was largely thanks to the massive box-office success of Róbert Koltai's comedy *We Never Die* (see IFG 1994), which drew almost 210,000 admissions from its release in mid-January 1993. However, Koltai's film is still the exception that proves the

FOR CLASSIC AND RECENT HUNGARIAN FILMS

contact

CINEMAGYAR
H-1054 Budapest
Báthori u. 10
Telex: 22 - 5768
Phone: (36 - 1) 111 - 4614
Telefax: (36 - 1) 153 1317

rule: despite talk of a need for movies that Hungarians actually want to see (rather than those that please foreign critics or go to festivals), few have been forthcoming during the country's shift to market principles.

The next most popular Hungarian film was Géza Bereményi's comedy *On Tour* (28,358 admissions), followed by György Molnár's glossy light comedy *Anna's Film* (12,631). The top ten for the year was dominated by U.S. movies, led by *Jurassic Park* (897,000), *The Bodyguard* (557,000), *Cliffhanger* (469,000), *Sister Act* (385,000), and *Last Action Hero* (373,000). Koltai's film aside, Hungarian films even competed poorly with foreign "arthouse" fare, like *1492: Conquest of Paradise* (87,000), *Twin Peaks: Fire Walk with Me* (67,000), *Baraka* (55,000), and *Indochine* (36,000).

Hungarian films made up some 10% of the 178 movies released in the country during 1993, second only to the U.S. (109 titles) and followed by the U.K. (15) and France (11). In terms of receipts, however,

Hungarian films captured only 2% of the Ft1.38 billion ($138 million) total, with the U.S. taking 91.4%, the U.K. 2.2% and France 1.8%. On the distribution side, Intercom (grouping Warners, MGM-UA, Carolco, Columbia/TriStar, and Buena Vista) had a 57.9% share of the box-office, followed by UIP-Dunafilm (22.7%) and indie Flamex (5.9%). Guild, which had a 2.3% share in 1993, has since withdrawn from the whole of Central Europe.

With a new government in place, Hungary finally looks like sorting out its Broadcast Law during 1994. After that, attention will turn to the long-planned Film Law. Meanwhile, the system of partial state subsidies, through the Hungarian Motion Picture Foundation, has continued, with an annual dispensation of some $8 million (of which feature films get about half). HMPF money generally forms one leg of a budget drawn from local sources (Hungarian TV, local producers, finance companies), European companies, and Eurimages.

However, in a production that looks like setting a new high in Hungarian feature film budgets, not one forint of HMPF money is involved. With *The Conquest*, to star Franco Nero and Anthony Quinn, director-producer Gábor Koltay (*Stephen, the King; Julianus*) is planning a $6 million drama-adventure celebrating the millenium of the Magyars settling in Central Europe. The movie, aimed at the international market, is scheduled to be ready for Expo '96 in Budapest.

Silver Jubilee for Film Week

The 25th Hungarian Film Week celebrated its silver anniversary in February 1994 amid a period of pre-election unease. However, the lineup of new films produced at least five high-quality works (*Woyzeck, Children of Cast-Iron Gods, Satan's Tango, Why Wasn't He There?, On Tour*), even if the bulk of the films on display still showed old tensions between art-for-art's sake and more accessible fare still in place.

Artistic champion of the year was without doubt János Szász's **Woyzeck**, a

Lajos Kovács in János Szász's WOYZECK

stark but beautifully played transposition of Georg Büchner's play to a railway yard, where the main character (played by sweat-stained verisimilitude by Lajos Kovács) is subject to daily humiliations from his sexy young wife (Diana Vacaru) and disciplinarian boss (Aleksandr Porokhovchikov). The film's beautiful monochrome photography, and heightened visual style, gives a poetic, cinematic feel to the drama, which is far more engrossing than it sounds.

Tamás Tóth's **Children of Cast-Iron Gods** (*Vasisten gyermekei*), co-produced with Mosfilm and shot in Russia(n), has a much more flamboyant feel in look and tone. The story of a group of tough steelworkers in a remote Siberian factory, the film has a *Mad Max*-like post-nuclear hardness with a flair for action that is only cramped by its lack of widescreen ratio. Tóth, who lived in Russia for several years, could well be a talent to watch.

András Jeles, one of the country's most maverick and impenetrable talents, sprang a major surprise with **Why Wasn't He There** (*Senkiföldje*), a portrait of anti-semitism in 1944 provincial Hungary through the eyes of a 13-year-old Jewish girl (Cora Fischer). Stunningly shot and emotionally engaging, the film mixes dream and reality without falling prey to the needless obscurities of some of Jeles's earlier works (*Dream Brigade; The Annunciation*). It deservedly enjoyed success on the festival circuit during 1993-94.

Free of any great ambitions, but spirited and enjoyable nonetheless, Géza Bereményi's **On Tour** (*A turné*) follows a small troupe of actors as they travel across the country on summer tour, quarrelling, making up, partying, and confessing their deepest desires. As in his previous *The Midas Touch*, Bereményi never stints either on emotion or visual coups, but the film is a fine showcase of a terrific cast (led by

Still from Béla Tarr's seven-hours-plus feature, SATAN'S TANGO

Károly Eperjes) let loose on a rich and funny script.

Over Seven Hours Long

At the other end of the spectrum lay Béla Tarr's 7½-hour **Satan's Tango** (*Sátántangó*), a stylised, hypnotic parable (from a novel by László Krasznahorkai) set in a remote community given new hope by a Messiah-cum-conman who enters their midst. Divided into chapters (some of which observe the same events from different perspectives), and beautifully shot in black-and-white by Gábor Medvigy, Tarr's "event movie" has much the same feel as his 1987 *Damnation* but on a grander scale.

None of the past year's other offerings measured up to these films in ambition or entertainment, but several were of more than passing interest. János Rózsa's **Good Night, Prince** (*Jó éjt, királyfi*), about a group of kids obsessed with amateur film-making, is a loose but pleasant divertissement, with lively playing by its young leads and an overall feel similar to his previous *Brats*. Robert-Adrian Pejo's **Lipstick** (*Rúzs*) is a likeable portrait of a young Yugoslav woman's emotional odyssey during a New Year's Eve in Budapest, and her friendship with a dour Hungarian (Péter Andorai) and boisterous Russian (János Bán).

Hungarian-American Péter Reich's **A Girl Has Never Had This Effect On Me** (*Rám csaj még nem volt ilyen hatással*) is a free-wheeling portrait of a group of young people that, in grainy black-and-white, has

the feel of an American independent feature transposed to Budapest. More structured, and made with the director's usual visual finesse, is János Zsombolyai's hour-long **Wedding Service** (*Székelykapu*), based on a true story of a Romanian woman (Eszter Nagy-Kálóczy) and an arranged marriage to a Hungarian (József Tóth).

Of two new films by Pál Erdőss, **A Light-Sensitive Story** (*Fényérzékeny történet*) is the more successful, a gentle, well-observed tale of a thirty-ish photographer (Erika Ozsda), her love affair with a younger student, and her struggles to bring up her young son in the New Hungary. Far from his usual territory of social-set stories, Erdőss' subsequent **Bloodline** (*Vérvonal*), shot in Lisbon, is an unconvincing melodrama about two teenage girls who bond in an orphanage and later set out to find one of their fathers.

Established Names Disappoint

Several films from well-established names failed to live up to expectations. Gyula Maár's **Balkans! Balkans!** (*Balkán! Balkán!*) is a flat, dully-directed reworking of two stories by novelist Panait Istrati set in a small town near the Danube late last century that has none of the twinkling humour and irony of his previous *Whoops*. Sándor Sára's **The Watchers** (*Vigyázók*) fails to bring off an interesting idea – one of the guests at a private gathering is a government spy but no one knows who – through uninteresting direction and an over-talky script; and Ferenc Grunwalksky's video-transferred **Utrius** is an only occasionally successful try at drawing parallels with the current Balkan situation through a love story set during the First World War.

Also disappointing was Krisztina Deák's **Mist, or Moonlight Shadow over Levebu** (*Köd, avagy holdárnyék Levebu fölött*), a pretentious drama about two beautiful sisters haunted by family ghosts and a destructive curse that is a big step down from her earlier *The Book of Esther*. Imre Gyöngyössy and Barna Kabay's **Death in Shallow Water** (*Halál a sekély vízben*), a

Still from Pál Erdőss's A LIGHT-SENSITIVE STORY
photo: Jósef Eisenmann

Still from MIST, directed by Krisztina Deák

political thriller based on a true story about a disappearing scientist and his family's attempts to find him, is fatally undermined by soap-opera scripting and over-loose direction – sadly the last by Gyöngyössy, who died in May 1994.

The year's biggest disappointment, however, was veteran Márta Mészáros' **Foetus** (*A magzat*), an unconvincing yarn about a young woman (Adél Kováts) who sells her unwanted pregnancy to a rich, childless businesswoman (Russian actress, Aliona Antonova). Despite a radiant performance by Kováts, the elements fail to gell, and the movie's often soapy images

seem a long, long way from Mészáros' great 1970's films on motherhood and female subjects (*Adoption, Nine Months,* etc.).

Mészáros was one of the few older-generation "names" (like Szabó, Jancsó, Bacsó, Makk) with a new work during the past year. In summer 1994, István Szabó was announced to direct *Histoire de ma femme* (*Story of My Wife*), a tale of marital jealousy set in the 1930's with Gérard Depardieu in the lead, in a production for France's UGC by Véra Belmont. The film is expected to be ready by 1996.

TOP TEN GROSSING FILMS IN HUNGARY: 1993

	*(million forints)**
Jurassic Park	103.4
The Bodyguard	59.1
Cliffhanger	52.8
Sister Act	41.8
Last Action Hero	43.4
Loaded Weapon	35.3
Nowhere to Run	29.6
Aladdin	32.4
Hot Shots! Part Deux	36.8
Honey, I Blew Up the Kid	25.4

*US$1=Ft100
Highest grossing Hungarian film was Robert Koltai's *We Never Die* (Ft 19.5 million), followed by Geza Bereményi's *On Tour* (Ft3.6 million).

Forthcoming Films

ESTI KORNEL (The Wondrous Voyage of Kornel Esti)
Dir: József Pacskovszky. Players: József S. Tóth, Kathleen Gati. Prod. Hunnia.

A TORVENYTELEN (The Bastard)
Dir: Ferenc András. Players: Daniel Olbrychski, György Cserhalmi, Ference Bacs. Prod: Dialog (Hungary)/Transfilm Berlin (Germany)/Domfilmowe (Poland).

MAGIC HUNTER
Dir: Ildikó Enyédi. Players: Gary Kemp, Sadie Frost, Aleksandr Kaidanovsky. Prod: Budapest

(Hungary), Accent (Canada)/UGC Images (France)/Panorama (Germany).

RESZLEG (The Section)
Dir: Péter Gothár. Players: József Szarvás, Marian Nagy. Prod: Hunnia.

A BROOKLYNI TESTVER (The Brooklyn Brothers)
Dir: Péter Gardos. Players: Károly Eperkes, Dezsö Garas, Judit Hernádi, Grulla Marcus. Prod: Hunnia.

EBREDESEK (Awakenings)
Dir: Judit Elek. Players: Petra Koves, Judit Hernádi, Fruszina Eszes. Prod: Budapest.

VOROS COLIBRI (Red Colibri)
Dir: Zsuzsas Böszörményi. Players: Barbara De Rossi, Branislav Tesanovic. Prod: Cinema Film Director Foundation (Hungary(/VIDI (Italy).

A HETEDIK TESTVER (The Seventh Little Brother)
Prod: InterPannonia Film. *Feature-length animation.*

Producers

InterPannonia
(animation, also distribution)
Gyarmat utca 36
1145 Budapest
Tel: 267-6514, 267-6515
Fax: 267-6516

Béla Balázs Studio/Toldi Cinema
Bajcsy-Zsilinszky ut 36-38
1057 Budapest
Tel/Fax: 111-2809, 131-8129

Budapest Film Studio
Róna utca 174
1145 Budapest
Tel: 251-8568
Fax: 251-0478

Focus Film
Pasaréti ut 122
1026 Budapest
Tel: 176-7484
Fax: 176-7493

Forum Film
Könyves Kálmán körút 13-15
1097 Budapest
Tel/Fax: 134-3745

Hétföi Mühely Studio
Róna utca 174
1145 Budapest
Tel/Fax: 251-0087

Hunnia Studio
Róna utca 174
1145 Budapest
Tel: 252-3170
Fax: 251-6269

Magic Media
Róna utca 174
1145 Budapest
Tel/Fax: 163-3479

Movie Innovation Partnership (MIP)
Kinizsi utca 28
1092 Budapest
Tel: 218-3600, 218-0983
Fax: 216-3601

Novofilm
(also services)
Városmajor utca 20
1121 Budapest
Tel: 155-5440, 155-2621
Fax: 155-9177

Objektiv Film Studio
Róna utca 174
1145 Budapest
Tel: 252-5359
Fax: 251-7269

Pannonia Film
(animation)
Hüvösvölgyi ut 64
1021 Budapest

Tel: 176-3333
Fax: 176-7092, 176-3409

Transatlantic Media Associates (TMA)
(also services)
Táltos utca 4
1123 Budapest
Tel: 155-3200, 201-2299
Fax: 175-2444

SuperPlan
Róna utca 174
1145 Budapest
Tel/Fax: 252-5168

Satellit-Film/Europe 2000
(also services)
Finkenstrasse 48
8130 Starnberg
Germany
Tel: 8151-3551
Fax: 8151-28544
Róna utca 174
1145 Budapest
Tel/Fax: 183-5930

Varga Studio
(animation, F/X)
PF 394
1536 Budapest
Tel: 202-3984
Fax: 175-6026

Distributors

Budapest Film
Báthori utca 10
1054 Budapest
Tel: 123-8198, 111-2492
Fax: 111-2687, 131-5946

Flamex
Vaci ut 14
1132 Budapest
Tel: 131-8771
Fax: 112-5038

Hungarofilm
(also production services)
Báthori utca 10
1054 Budapest
Tel: 111-0020, 131-4746
Fax: 153-1850

Intercom
Karolina ut 65
1113 Budapest
Tel: 209-0933
Fax: 209-0930

Useful Addresses

Cinemagyar
(foreign sales)
Báthori utca 10

1054 Budapest
Tel: 111-4614, 132-8729
Fax: 153-1317

Hungarian Film Union
(festivals, foreign promo)
Városligeti fasor 38
1068 Budapest
Tel: 269-7760, 269-7761
Fax: 268-0070, 269-7766

Hungarian Film Institute
Budakeszi ú 51 B
1012 Budapest
Tel: 176-1018, 176-1322
Fax: 176-7106

Assoc. of Hungarian Film & TV Makers
Városligeti fasor 38
1068 Budapest
Tel/Fax: 142-4760

Assoc. of Hungarian Film Distributors
Frangepán utca 50-56
1135 Budapest
Tel/Fax: 140-2922

Assoc. of Hungarian Video Publishers
Tárogató utca 2-4

1021 Budapest
Tel/Fax: 176-7291

Hungarian Federation of Film Societies
Róna utca 174
1145 Budapest
Tel: 184-3337, 251-5666
Fax: 251-2896

Motion Picture Foundation of Hungary (MMA)
Városligeti fasor 38
1068 Budapest
Tel: 269-7696
Fax: 268-0070

MOVI
(studio facils)
Könyves Kálmán körút 13-15
1097 Budapest
Tel: 215-7550, 215-6300
Fax: 215-3410

Mafilm Corp.
(studio complex)
Róna utca 174
1145 Budapest
Tel: 251-5666, 252-2870
Fax: 251-1080

Gísli
Einarsson

Iceland boasts a plethora of natural scenery which has few parallels in the world but high prices and the unavailability of trained film crew and equipment discouraged American and European film companies for years from filming here. Lately a steady stream of schooled talent has arrived from film centres abroad, changing this situation, and film producers are beginning to take notice.

One would imagine Iceland as a natural backdrop to New Line-financed **Kjartan's Saga**, produced by Paul Gurian, and directed by Michael Chapman (*Clan of the Cave Bear*). While the film, shot here in early 1994, can scarcely be categorised as

more than a low-budget Viking-exploitation film, its cast, including the female lead (Ingibjörg Stefánsdóttir from *Wallpaper*), was largely made up of local actors.

Also some second unit footage for the first film adaptation of the long running British comic, **Judge Dredd**, was shot here in July 1994, as Iceland certainly does have an abundance of the stark sci-fi wastelands the Judge Dredd mythos require.

If this influence of foreign productions becomes a trend it will be a much needed boost for the local talent and technical pool which competes for jobs on two-three local features a year.

Two New Films Open

Two new films premiered between July 1993 and June 1994, Hrafn Gunnlaugsson's **The Sacred Mound** (*Hin helgu vé*) and Friðrik Thór Friðriksson's **Movie Days** (*Bíódagar*).

The Sacred Mound tells of a little city boy's crush on a country girl much older than him, and the unusual path his attraction takes him on. This semi-auto-biographical film is uncharacteristic for Gunnlaugsson, who has made a reputation for unflinching psycho-dramas and Viking-actionners. It does bare some of Gunnlaugsson's trademarks in his honest depiction of the lad's budding sexual fantasies, but on the whole the film is too superficial and unfocused. *The Sacred Mound* got a lukewarm reception from the local press and audiences, but helped steer Gunnlaugsson out of the Viking mould which was starting to restrict him.

Movie Days is Friðrik Thór Friðriksson's third feature to date, and the first one after his Oscar-nominated *Children of Nature*. Although it is doubtful that *Movie Days*

will receive the same accolades as *Children of Nature* (see review) it will be Iceland's widest overseas commercial release yet.

Friðriksson already has his next film in the can, **Cold Fever**, an American-financed film about the misadventures of a young Japanese man on a pilgrimage to the remote site of his parent's death in Iceland. *Cold Fever* was shot in Japan and Iceland with Masatoshi Nagose (*Mystery Train*) in the lead and including American actors Fischer Stevens (*Super Mario Bros.*) and Lili Taylor (*Short Cuts*) in smaller parts.

Films on the Horizon

Rarely seen in Icelandic films, special visual effects and animation will play a part in **Sky Palace** (*Skýjáhöllin*), based on a popular children's book about a boy who saves all his money, so he can buy a puppy his father has promised him. When his father reneges on his promise, he buys it anyway and runs away with it. Adapted and directed by Thorsteinn Jónsson (*The Atomic Station, Dot Dot Comma Dash*) the film will also be shown in Danish- and German-language versions, in each country respectively.

Jóhann Sigmarsson (co-scripter of *Wallpaper*) goes solo with a guaranteed unusual look at modern relationships in **One Big Family** (*Ein stór fjölskylda*). The film is serio-comic and tells the story of a young man who is socially abused by his girlfriend and her parents.

Tears of Stone from Hilmar Oddsson promises to be a major film, shot both in Iceland and Germany. The story is based on fact and tells of a crucial period in Icelandic composer Jón Leifs's life, when he was living and working in prewar Berlin, married to a Jewish woman. Oddsson showed promise for handling emotional material in *The Beast* (1986) and his new film is one of Iceland's most ambitious to date.

GÍSLI EINARSSON is a film critic in Reykjavík currently suing theatres who refuse to admit him.

There was a slight decline in box-office sales (5%) in 1993, possibly due to a rare glut of film festivals (whose admissions are tallied separately), including the Nordic Film Festival. As in the previous year, local films took an impressive 8% slice of the Icelandic box-office.

Still from MOVIE DAYS

BÍÓDAGAR (Movie Days)

Script: Einar Már Guðmundsson, Friðrik Thór Friðriksson. Direction: Friðrik Thór Friðriksson. Photography: Ari Kristinsson. Music: Hilmar Örn Hilmarsson. Players: Örvar Jens Arnarsson, Rúrik Haraldsson, Sigrún Hjálmtýrsdóttir. Production: Icelandic Film Corporation, Peter Rommel Film Production, Zentropa Entertainment.

For *Movie Days*, director Friðrik Thór Friðriksson and co-screenwriter, novelist Einar Már Guðmundsson, focus upon little incidents from Friðriksson's childhood and barely thread them together to tell the tale of a little boy who spends his summer running around, first in the city, then in the countryside.

Movie Days is a somewhat charming film, with its rose-tinted view of the past (which is lavishly re-created). However, the structure does not allow for much drama, and there is no storyline to speak of. Altogether the episodes paint a nostalgic picture of Reykjavík in 1964, the city still reeling from the effect of British and American occupation during the Second World War. The years following were turbulent and in the blink of a generation the old suddenly gave way to the new. In Reykjavík's east and west ends, gangs of youngsters tussle between football and Sunday movie matinees, American soldiers from the nearby airbase dally with local girls, smuggled luxury goods entice the middle-class, and television emerges in a city that still hasn't quite lost all its innocence.

Out in the country things are more rustic and traditional and once there, the film turns quirky and somewhat confused. These episodes don't quite gel. The epi-sodic structure of *Movie Days* is too loose for its own good; there is little to push the movie forward, and no resolution to speak of.

Technically the film is top-notch on every level; Ari Kristinsson's (*Children of Nature*) lush cinematography is simply out-standing, yet again.   Gísli Einarsson

TOP TEN GROSSING FILMS IN ICELAND: 1993

	Attendance
Jurassic Park	78,000
Hekla, the Men's Choir (Iceland)	54,000
Home Alone 2	45,000
The Fugitive	37,000
The Bodyguard	36,000
Behind Schedule (Iceland)	35,000
Cliffhanger	33,000
Indecent Proposal	30,000
Hot Shots: Part Deux	25,000
The Firm	23,000

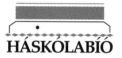
Distributors

Association of Film Distributors in Iceland
Stjörnubíó
Laugavegi 110
101 Reykjavík
Tel: 354-1-611212
Fax: 354-1-627135

Sam-Film
Álfabakka 8
Tel: 354-1-878900
Fax: 354-1-878930

Bergvík Film Distribution
Ármúli 44
P.O. Box 8534
108 Reykjavík
Tel: 354-1-677966
Fax: 354-1-670288

Useful Addresses

Icelandic Film Fund
Laugavegur 24
P.O. Box 320
121 Reykjavík

Tel: 354-1-623580
Fax: 354-1-627171

Association of Icelandic Film Producers
Pósthússtræti 13
P.O. Box 476
121 Reykjavík
Tel: 354-1-628188
Fax: 354-1-623424

Association of Icelandic Film-makers
Tel: 354-1-623225
Fax: 354-1-627171

Ministry of Culture and Education
Sölvhólsgötu 4
105 Reykjavík
Tel: 354-1-609500
Fax: 354-1-623068

Alda Sigurdardóttir in Hrafn Gunnlaugsson's THE SACRED MOUND   *photo: Per Källberg*

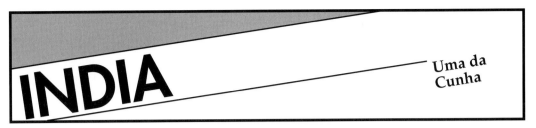

INDIA — Uma da Cunha

Life continued to write some lousy scripts for the industry in 1994. Sympathy might have been in order were the troubles less self-induced. Crass wooing of low common denominators, near obscenity in song and dance, obligatory violence, disunity in professional and business settings, poor government relations and even worse handling of cable and video interests, a still unbridled star system matched only by some hefty egos among producers – all of this was bound to come to a head. And it did, like the thousand heads of Ravana, India's villain of the epic *Ramayana*.

The film industry noted that liberalisation of the Indian economy promised new prosperity in most business areas except their own. Internationalisation and proliferation in the broadcast media as well as in home video and cable began to take place at the expense of cinema audiences and income.

The first half of 1994 saw fitful and contrary attempts within the film industry to unite and negotiate with government. The studio greats, dictators in the entertainment arena for decades, had trouble dealing on rights over their own films with the new-rich video/cable operators.

In fact, intellectual property rights, so far negligently respected, became a key matter. Parliament passed the 1993 Copyright Amended Bill which spelt out heavy penalties for infringement. Parliament also seemed likely to approve the 1993 Cable Television Network Bill to aid copyright protection. Both measures meant that video and other piracies were now upfront issues. But the regulations face one formidable challenge: effective enforcement.

Prolonged differences on simultaneous release of film and video led to a month-long withdrawal of new films. The Film-Makers' Combine (FMC) and the Film Distributors' Council finally reached agreement. Not so the video people and free-wheeling cable operators. The triangular film-video-cable confrontation was still a sullen stalemate in mid-year. At stake is potentially one of the world's largest country markets in film and electronic media.

The FMC faced opposition from within its own ranks. The previous year it had restricted film stars to acting in no more than a dozen films at a time. Reasonable enough, some felt. Former star Asha Parekh, new President of the Cine Artistes Association (CAA), announced that CAA would monitor star behaviour. CAA's treasurer, current star Dimple Kapadia, had been penalised by FMC for refusing to play mother-in-law to top star Juhi Chawla in the film *Kartavya* (Kapadia had no objections when the role was played by budding actress Divya Bharti, who died in a tragic accident). CAA undermined the FMC by absolving Kapadia of the offence.

Mid-year, the FMC forbade producer Subhash Rai to shoot *Trimurti* with Sanjay Dutt because the actor had exceeded his quota. Rai went ahead, obtaining CAA's okay who argued that Dutt had less than twelve on-going assignments. By the time FMC called for a punitive meeting, Rai's shooting with Dutt was complete. Problems there are but, by and large, the effort at self-discipline has all-round support.

Production Harvest Declines

Film production, highest in the world, declined for the third consecutive year. In 1993, 812 films were certified as against 838

Still from THE CLOUD DOOR

in 1992 and 910 in 1991. Hindi films led with 183 (289/215 in 1992/1991 respectively). South India followed with 168 in Tamil, 148 in Telugu, 78 in Kannada, 71 in Malayalam, all four showing a drop from the previous two years. Indian language films that registered a rise were Bengali, with 57 against 42 in 1992, along with Oriya (20 against 13), Assamese (9 against 4), Punjabi (14 against 12).

The number of films imported was 174 – a 50% increase, with 130 from the U.S.A., eight from Hongkong, six from the U.K., four from Canada, three each from France and Australia, two each from Italy, Spain, Netherlnds and Germany, and one each from Yugoslavia and Indonesia. Known box-office hits were coming in quickly; films such as *A Perfect World, The Pelican Brief* and *Bad Girls*, some getting away with free TV spots on Fox/Turner-connected Star TV and CNN.

One foreign release created box-office history. *Jurassic Park* was the first film to be released simultaneously in English and Hindi-dubbed prints, and that on a massive scale. It is a thundering success. By mid-year it had earned US$3 million, a record for a Hindi film. The Film Federation of India issued fierce protests against the Hindi dubbing of foreign films on the grounds that dubbed American blockbusters would further damage their interests. The American studios were cautiously examining the new-found Hindi-language territory. It seems fairly certain that at least two such would be released every year.

The Hindi film was roundly denounced by government and elements of the public for its deteriorating standards, especially its risqué songs and senseless violence. One film set up shock waves with over-gyrating Karishma Kapoor dancing to "Sexy, sexy, sexy." It was ultimately censored to "Baby, baby, baby," by which time it had been aired enough over radio and TV to make little difference. The film *Khal-Nayak* featured a dance number which had bosoms heaving to the words "What lies behind my tight blouse?" Box-office returns soared and imitation followed fast, lyrics with suggestive *double-entendres* on what lies behind what. A new film's giant billboard boasted of its eleven murders.

New Licence and Spice

The hypocrisies of Hindi movie definitions, of hero/villain and wife/vamp permit much straying. The hero-villain played by super-star Sharukh Khan in three successful films set a style: demented hero out to kill. Adoring teenagers loved the ambiguity. Film violence enjoys a new licence and spice.

A barrage of protests from women's groups and in Parliament provoked the Central Board of Film Certification. It censored film songs before their telecast and was assessing whether lyrics and dances could be censored at the time of shooting. A sigh of relief rose to the skies when Vinod Chopra's blockbuster *1942 – A Love Story* had old-fashioned lyrical songs. They topped the charts.

A modest film from the south, Mani Ratnam's **Roja**, reinforcing patriotism and the devoted wife set topically in Kashmir, stole a march over other highly touted productions. The film had lilting music (by newcomer A.R. Rahman) that audiences could, for a change, relish without guilt or controversy.

Sensing that the future at home may be dicey, the film industry took stock of the international market. The success of Shekhar Kapur's well-crafted, ruggedly Indian **The Bandit Queen** in Cannes was an eye-opener.

Seema Biswas in Shekhar Kapur's BANDIT QUEEN

Kapoor is now the sought-after director with enough funds to start his next project, *Nine O'Clock War*, about a Third World War that is taken over by a TV station.

Veteran producer G.P. Sippy announced a $200 million Indo-American production. Mahesh Bhatt was reportedly offered a $6 million deal with Star TV to make 40 Hindi films. Paramount Studios approached Subhash Ghai to direct a film and Warner Bros. has a proposal for producer F.C. Mehra. The government-owned National Film Development Corporation has three co-productions in hand: *Story Teller*, an Indo-American film written and directed by Gustad Kaizad, another French co-production written and directed by Paris-based Vijay Singh, and an Indo-South African saga on Gandhi's formative years as a London-trained lawyer, to be directed by Shyam Benegal.

Ismail Merchant, following the acclaim accorded to *In Custody*, has plans to direct another film in India and produce one more that marks the directorial debut of actress Madhur Jaffrey. Merchant grows from strength to strength in India-based ambitions. Shekhar Kapur and Bombay studio giants do not lag far behind in wanting to make it big in North America and Western Europe. Too long has the field been left open to Los Angeles operators Jagmohan Mundhra and Ashok Amritaj's Indo-American capers.

Mira Nair and Deepa Sahi, now in the international league, are directing North American scripts. The Indian immigrant scene continues to attract fresh talent. Kenya-born Gurinder Chadha settled in Britain, came up with the delightfully incisive caper **Bhaji on the Beach** about a bunch of London-based Indian women shedding their inhibitions while on a Blackpool binge. Another film, **Wild West**, scripted by young British-Indian writer Harwant Bains, dwelt with amusing perception on British-Indian youth leaving hearth and home for western pop culture.

In India there is a move to dub indigenous films in English for the world market, starting with highly regarded producer-director Yash Chopra's film **Lamhe**. Two directors, Basu Bhattacharya in Bombay and Kamalahasan in Madras, are each shooting their next film in two versions, English and the local language. That Americans are eyeing India's market and entertainment potential is a factor that the wily Bombay film player is weighing to see how he can gain from it.

India was back too as a choice location for the international big-budget movie. A major chunk of Disney's action film, *The Jungle Book*, was shot in Jodhpur and Bombay, with Kenya-based producer Sharad Patel's involvement and Bombay producer Yash Johar handling its production.

But the country lost two great film personalities. The foremost star of the 1930's and 1940's, Devika Rani, passed away in Bangalore a year after her Russian husband, the renowned painter Nicholas Roerich. V. Prasad, the errand boy turned actor-director-producer and finally owner of India's largest film studio and laboratory located in Madras, died in June. Their inspired achievement is a consoling thought during this tangled phase in India's film world.

Still from Garin Nugroho's LETTER TO AN ANGEL

Mohan Agashe and Anjan Srivastava in Sandip Ray's TARGET

UMA DA CUNHA heads Medius-India Services Pvt Ltd, a company that provides promotional and executive services for films and film shooting in India. She is a free-lance film journalist and a consultant on Indian film programming for festivals in India and abroad.

TOP TEN GROSSING FILMS IN INDIA: 1993

Ankhen
Baazighar
Darr
Anari
Tiranga
Khal-Nayak
Damini
Hum Hai Rahee Pyar Ke
Roja
Gardish
Sangram

Recent and Forthcoming Films

TARGET

Lang: Hindi. Script: Satyajit Ray, based on Prafula Roy's novel. Dir/Music: Sandip Ray. Phot: Barun Raha. Players: Om Puri, Mohan Agashe, Champa, Anjan Srivastav. Prod: OEG Worldwide, Bangalore.

An ageing landowner and avid huntsman uses machiavellian ways to pursue his decadent pleasures until he crosses the line between hunter and the hunted.

MAMMO

Lang: Hindi. Script: Shama Zaidi. Dir: Shyam Benegal. Story: Khalid Mohammad. Phot: Piyush Shah. Music: Vanraj Bhatia. Players: under selection. Prod: NFDC.

A film that conveys the arbitrary and illogical context in which national borders operate thereby affecting human lives and family ties.

MAKING OF THE MAHATMA

Script: Shama Zaidi, based on Fatima Meer's book. Dir: Shyam Benegal. Phot: Piyush Shah. Music: Vanraj Bhatia. Players: under selection. Prod: Echo Prods/South African Broad-casting Corp/Govt of India.

A film on Mohandas Karamchand Gandhi's crucial and formative 23-year-stay in South Africa starting with his arrival in 1893 as a London-trained barrister.

PONTHAN MADA

Script and Dir: T.V. Chandran, based on C.V. Sreeraman's short stories. Phot: Venu. Music: Johnson. Players: Mammootty, Naseerudin Shah, Labani Sarkar, Reshmi. Prod: Horizon Cinema, Trivandrum.

A strange bond links a low-caste labourer and his aristocratic landlord who has returned after a stint with the IRA in England during the 1940's, leaving behind an English wife and daughter. Five 1993 National Awards.

PHOOLAN DEVI (The Bandit Queen)

Lang: Hindi. Script: Mala Sen. Dir: Shekhar Kapur. Phot: Ashok Mehta. Music: Nasrat Fattehally Khan. Players: Seema Biswas, Nirmal Pandey, Manoj Bijpai. Prod: Channel 4.

The extreme oppression of Indian women is reflected in the exploits of low-caste Phoolen Devi who became one of India's most feared bandits. She surrendered in 1983. Her release in 1994 was joyously greeted by the lower classes.

PRATIMURTI (Image)

Lang: Hindi. Script and Dir: Bimal Dutt. Phot: K.K. Mahajan. Music: Bupen Hazarika. Players: Suresh Oberoi, Rakhee, Rajen Gupta. Prod: NFDC.

An engineer, now retired, settles down to a quiet small-town life with his poetess wife. He is manipulated by a friend to assume the mantle of an activist in a tribal area. His family is intrigued by the change in him.

TUNNU KI TINA (Tunnu's Tina)

Lang: Hindi. Script and Dir: Paresh Kamdar. Phot: K.K. Mahajan. Music: Rajat Dholakia. Players: Rohini Hattangadi, Nandita Thakur, Sunil Bharve, Rajeswari. Prod: NFDC.

A stylistic collage representatively presents a low-income family, each with a dream image of themselves. The youthful son loves a plain girl but chances on a liaison with a rich one. For him the fusion of fact and fantasy pose problems.

THE DAY OF REMEMBRANCES

Lang: Bengali; Script and Dir: Mrinal Sen.

Three generations meet in a forest bungalow and reminisce about a phenomenal woman they know. An octagenerian recalls an incident that destroys her reputation.

ASTHA IN THE PRISON OF SPRING

Lang: Hindi/English. Script and Dir: Basu Bhattacharya. Phot: Santosh Sivan. Music: Sharang Dev. Players: Rekha, Om Puri, Taboo. Prod: Aarohi Films.

Man-woman relationships are seen in the context of the growing consumerism that has overtaken Bombay, India's commercial centre.

1942 – A LOVE STORY

Lang: Hindi. Dir: Vidhu Vinod Chopra. Phot: Vinod Pradhan. Music: R.D. Burman. Players: Anil Kapoor, Manisha Koirala, Jackie Shroff, Anupam Kher, Danny Denzgoppa, Pran. Prod: Vinod Chopra Films.

The trials of a couple in love, set in 1942, during the turbulence of the Quit India movement.

AMODINI

Lang: Bengali. Script and Dir: Chidananda Dasgupta. Phot: Venu. Music: C.R. Chowdhury. Players: Aparna Sen, Ranjit Mallick, Rajeshgwari Sachdev. Prod: NFDC.

Life among the landed gentry aristocracy of Eighteenth-century Bengal – a time when the Mughal order was giving way to British rule.

THE CLOUD DOOR

Script and Dir: Mani Kaul. Story: adapted from three Indian literary classics. Phot: Anil Mehta. Music: Ustad Zia Foriduddin Dagar. Players: Anu Arya Agarwal, Murad Ali. Prod: Regina Zeigler; "Contes de la Séduction" (six directors with 30 min. individual versions of erotic tales).

A parrot whispers erotic tales to Princess Kurangi. Later, when freed from its prison-cage by the Princess's suitor, Ratnasen, the parrot leads him through a secret passage to her bed-chamber.

MARUDANAYAGAM

Lang: Tamil and English versions.

Script and Dir: Kamalahasan. Phot: Santosh Sivan. Player: Kamalahasan. Prod: Rajkamal Films International.

Based on the true story of a Seventeenth-century hero who fought the British much before the Sepoy Mutiny.

CHARACHAR (Shelter of the Wings)

Lang: Bengali. Dir: Budhadeb Dasgupta. Story: Prafula Roy. Music: Biswadeb Dasgupta. Players: Rajit Kapoor, Laboni Sarkar, Indrani Haldar, Sadhu Meher.

Repercussions are extreme when a young man who catches birds for a bird seller is sensitive to the job. 1994 Berlin competitive entry; National Award for Best Film, 1993.

Useful Addresses

Film Makers Combine (FMC)/ Indian Motion Pictures Producers Association (IMPPA)
IMPPA House
Unit No 11
Dr Ambedkar Road
Bandra
Bombay 400034
Tel: 4946477

Theatre Owners Association (TOA)
G 11 Everest Building
Tardeo Road
Bombay 400034
Tel: 4942012

Indian Film Exporters Association
5 C Everest Building
Tardeo Road
Tardeo
Bombay 400050
Tel: 494 9480

Indian Documentary Producers Association (IDPA)
223 Famous Cine Building
Mahalaxmi
Bombay 400011
Tel: 492 0757

South Indian Film Chamber
Film Chamber Building
T R Sunderam Avenue
605 Anna Salai
Cathedral Post
Madras 6000006
Tel: 872 9175/872 5628/872 5642
Fax: (91-44) 872 5870

Karnataka Film Chamber
28 1st Main Crescent Road
High Grounds
Bangalore 560001

Kerala Film Chamber
Post Box No: 3577
M G Road
Ernakulam
Cochin 682 035
Tel: 351546

Eastern India Motion Pictures Association
98E B N Sircar Square
Calcutta 700072
Tel: 274040/274041/274042

National Film Development Corporation (NFDC)
Discovery of India Building
Nehru Centre
Worli
Dr Annie Besant Road
Bombay 400018
Tel: 495 2262
Fax: 495 0591

Doordarshan Film Chamber
Doordarshan Bhavan
Mandi House
Copernicus Marg
New Delhi 110001
Tel: 387786/382021/382488
Fax: 386507

INDONESIA

Marselli Sumarno

Not much happened in Indonesian film affairs last year. In recent years the level of production has continued to drop. In 1993 only 24 titles were produced. As only a few of them had any quality, the 1993 Indonesian Film Festival failed to see the light of day.

In the meantime, five private TV channels which are relatively new but have a national reach, are now competing in Indonesia. These private TV stations spare no time in posing as rivals to the state-owned TV station, TVRI, which prior to the emergence of the private TV stations had been dominant. In the last few years advertisement spending at these private TV stations has been soaring and this has been a great support to them. In 1992 this spending amounted to 287.79 million US dollars but in 1993 it rose to 383.93 million US dollars, which accounted for 49.1% of advertisement spending in Indonesia.

The flourishing of private TV stations in the past three years has kept film people really busy. Among those involved in the making of serials or mini-series are leading directors such as Teguh Karya, Slamet Rahardjo, Ami Priyono, Wim Umboh, Arifin C. Noor and Chaerul Umam.

As is the general trend in Asia, local TV products win popularity among domestic viewers. However, considering the high demand while the manpower is not ready, there is apprehension as to whether or not the TV film boom will only repeat the debacle in Indonesian film production.

According to a fairly successful production house owner, in realistic terms some 60 production houses are enough to supply the needs of the TV programmes. This statement takes into account the fact that there are hundreds of production houses in operation now, even if most are amateurish. He also mentioned that there is now a greater demand for experts and creative workers in television.

Output Sluggish

While the television industry is in its heyday, sluggishness in film production is still greatly felt. To revive the enthusiasm for production, national film circles organised last March a "film month" programme, one of whose items was the screening in one day of only Indonesian films in all cinema halls in Jakarta, about 300 in number. National films, produced recently or some two years back, were screened. What happened was that all cinema halls in Jakarta were inevitably empty that day. This proves that the challenge confronting Indonesian film-makers is to recoup the public's confidence in their capacity for making good films.

Two new films widely spotlighted by observers are **Letter to an Angel** (*Surat untuk Bidadari*) and **Clowns of the City** (*Badut-Badut Kota*). Garin Nugroho's *Letter to an Angel* has aspirations to becoming an artistic film. Ucik Supra, who has served as assistant film director many times, presents *Clowns of the City* in an "innocent" style. This is a comedy film that satirises the hypocrisy of city people.

Another person considered still young is Gotot Prakosa. He is now about to make **Mr. Salam** (*Sinyo Salam*). This is a unique story about a child suffering from albino and searching for his identity within Javanese culture. Leading actress Christine Hakim will be cast in this first film by Prakosa, who has previously been actively making experimental shorts.

Another concrete step has also been taken by the National Film Council to bolster national film production. It is sponsoring a number of film-makers to make new films. Slamet Rahardjo, one of Indonesia's leading directors, tends to reject the offer on the grounds of limited funds, while Garin Nugroho is one of those accepting it. Under the scheme Garin will soon make his third film **Bulan and Ilalang** (*Bulan Tertusuk Ilalang*).

Considering the sluggishness of film production here, a "realistic" measure has also been taken by film producers. They are making films liberally sprinkled with sex scenes. Now we have such "sex shops" as *Nocturnal Desire, The Stained Bed, Night Girl, Woman at the Crossroads* and the like. According to statistics, some of these "sex shop" films sell well commercially but at the same time they attract criticism from the public. With this tendency, it is estimated that 1994 film production will double compared with 1993 output.

However, the presence of films teeming with exotic sequences, just as happened in the past, serves only as a temporary cure for the malady affecting the Indonesian film world. Expectations about the revival of the national film industry should properly be pinned on the implementation of the government's new laws, originating in the new Law on Film (ratified in 1993).

With regard to film import, there is the problem with *Schindler's List* and the mushrooming of laser discs. In previous years, Oscar-winning best films would immediately find their way into the cinema halls here. *Schindler's List* has sparked a controversy, namely being considered Jewish propaganda or not. Finally Indonesian censors have banned

Schindler's List, saying that the film contains too much violence and nudity. According to Soekanto, Executive Director of the Film Censorship Board, the board did not judge the film in terms of whether or not this can be considered as a Jewish propaganda. "It's purely because of the nudity and sadistic actions," he said.

The granting of licences for laser disc imports to Indonesia has boosted the number of rental shops in large cities. Most of the laser discs rented are those released by U.S. producers. This has provoked the anger of the American majors because of the absence of agreements with the Indonesian side regarding the import of laser discs for rental purposes.

MARSELLI SUMARNO, film and television critic, writes regularly for the leading daily *Kompas*. He also acts as a researcher for film books.

SURAT UNTUK BIDADARI (Letter to an Angel)

Script: Garin Nugroho and Armatono. Direction: Garin Nugroho. Photography: Winaldha Melalatoa. Editing: Arturo G. Pradjawisastra. Music: Tony Prabowo. Players: Windy, Nurul Arifin, Adi Kurdi, Viva Westi. Produced by Prasidi Teta Film and PT Gema Tondoi Barito.

After his debut with *Love in a Slice of Bread* (1991), Garin Nugroho is now ready to launch his latest work, *Letter to an Angel*.

The central character in this film is a young boy named Lewa. He is always strongly driven to question truth. His desire has often led to trouble as he lives in a seemingly traditional rural environment. His biggest problem occurs when he has to face a village thug called Kuda Liar (or wild horse) played by Adi Kurdi. When he is cornered, Lewa "reports" his trouble to the Angel, who he believes is the guardian of this world, as in the fairy tales he has heard from his lady teacher (Viva Westi). The method is sending a letter to the Angel.

In his narration, Garin resorts largely to long shots and uses dialogue with considerable economy. Will everything then become poetic? If a comparison may be taken, Japanese film-maker Yasujiro Ozu shows through his works that "a little is a lot". Garin in his film, however, shows "a lot but not enough". In other words it entails the focus of ideas.

Nevertheless, exoticism in this film (traditional rites, slaughtering of animals) has its own attraction. Another attraction is that some members of the cast play their role excellently, particularly Windy as Lewa and Nurul Arigin as Berlian Merah (or the red diamond).

Marselli Sumarno

TOP TEN GROSSING FILMS IN INDONESIA: 1993

Jurassic Park
The Bodyguard
Indecent Proposal
The Firm
The Fugitive
Hard Target
Sleepless in Seattle
Kungfu Master III (Mandarin)
Taichi Master (Mandarin)
Lupa Aturan Main (Indonesian)

Recent and Forthcoming Films

SI KABAYAN MENCARI JODOH (Kabayan Finds His Lover)

Script: Eddy D. Iskandar. Dir: Maman Firmansyah. Phot: Suryo Susanto. Players: Didi Petet, Desy Ratnasari, Rachmat Hidayat. Prod: PT Kharisma Jabar Film.

BADUT-BADUT KOTA (Clowns of the City)

Script and Dir: Uci Supra. Phot: Adrian Susanto. Players: Dede Yusuf, Ayu Azhari. Prod: Prasidi Teta Film.

SESAL (Regret)

Script and Dir: Sophan Sophiaan. Phot: Herman Susanto. Players: Ami Priyono, Widya-wati, Rima Melati, Frans Tumbuan. Prod: PT. Sinemasakini.

SINYO SALAM (Mr. Salam)

Script: Gotot Prakosa and Seno Gumira Ajidarma. Dir: Gotot Prakosa. Phot: Bambang Supriadi. Player: Christine Hakim. Prod: PT. Eka Praya Film.

BULAN TERTUSUK ILALANG (Bulan and Ilalang)

Script and Dir: Garin Nugroho. Prod: Dewan Film Nasional.

Producers

PT Elang Perkasa Film
Jalan Kayu Putih 4/48
Jakarta Timur
Tel: 4700801

PT Prasidi Teta Film
Jalan Dr. Sahardjo 149 J
Jakarta Selatan
Tel: 8282740, 8281324

PT Rapi Film
Jalan Cikini II/7
Jakarta Pusat
Tel: 357135, 332860

PT Eka Praya Film
Jalan Walet Raya
Blok K-8/12, Nintaro Jaya
Jakarta 12330
Tel: 7360835

PT Kanta Film
Jalan Kayu Putih VI B/ 28
Jakarta Timur
Tel: 4896434

PT Bola Dunia Film
Jalan Pintu Air 51 C
Jakarta Pusat
Tel: 3843983, 3848721

PT Sepakat Bahagia Film
Jalan Mangga Besar Raya 107
Blok D-7
Jakarta Pusat
Tel: 6496657, 6496657

PT Raviman Film
Jalan Pangeran Jayakarta 68
Blok B-27
Jakarta
Tel: 6595042, 6499086

PT Virgo Putra Film
Jalan KH Hasim Ashari Dalam 111
Jakarta Pusat
Tel: 363308

PT Cipta Permai Indah Film
Jalan Gunung Sahari Raya no. 1
Blok B no. 16
Jakarta
Tel: 6296363 6299694

PT Parkit Film
Roxi Mas
Blok C-2 no. 31-34
Jakarta
Tel: 3867315, 3867316
Note: PT is a short form for Limited Company.

Distributors

PT Perfin
(*domestic distribution of Indonesian films*)
Jalan Menteng Raya 62
Jakarta Pusat
Tel: 341207

PT Satrya Perkasa Estetika
(*European/American films*)
Subentra Building
Jalan Gatot Subroto Kav.21
7th floor
Jakarta
Tel: 5220022

PT Suptan Film
(*Mandarin films*)
Subentra Building
Jalan Gatot Subroto Kav. 21
7th floor
Jakarta
Tel: 5220022

PT Buanavista Indan Film
(*Asia non-Mandarin films*)
Jalan Pintu Air 51 C
Jakarta
Tel: 3843983, 3848721

Useful Addresses

Directorate for Film and Video Development
Ministry of Information
Jalan Merdeka Barat 9
Jakarta
Tel: 377408

Perum Produksi Film Negara
(*State Film Production Centre*)
Jalan Otto Iskandardinata 125-127
Jakarta Timur
Tel: 8192508

Fakultas Film dan Televisi – Institut Kesenian Jakarta
(*Faculty of Film and Television – The Jakarta Institute of the Arts*)
Jalan Cikini Raya 73
Jakarta Pusat
Tel & Fax: 323603

Dewan Film Nasional
(*National Film Council*)
Jalan Menteng Raya 62
Jakarta Pusat
Tel: 320773, 336106

PT Surya Citra Televisi (SCTV)
Jalan Raya Darmo Permai III
Surabaya 60018
Tel: (0631) 714567, 714003

ANTEVE
Mulia Centre Building
7th floor Suite 711
Jalan HR Rasuna Said
Jakarta 12940

**Persatuan Producer Film
Indonesia**
(*Indonesian Film Producers
Association*)
Pusat Perfilman H. Usmar Ismail

Jalan Rasuna Said
Jakarta 12940
Tel: 5254076, 5250558

Karyawan Film dan Televisi
(*Association of Film and TV
Technicians*)
Pusat Perfilman H. Usmar Ismail
Jalan Rasuna Said
Jakarta 12940
Tel: 525091, 5251992

Sinematek Indonesia
Pusat Perfilman H. Usmar Ismail
Jalan Rasuna Said
Jakarta 12940

Tel: 5256891
Fax: 5255027

TVRI
(*State-owned TV network*)
Jalan Gerbang Pemuda
Senayan
Jakarta
Tel: 5704732

**PT Rajawali Citra Televisi
Indonesia (RCTI)**
Jalan Raya Perjuangan
Kebon Jeruk
Jakarta 11530
Tel: 5303540, 5493852

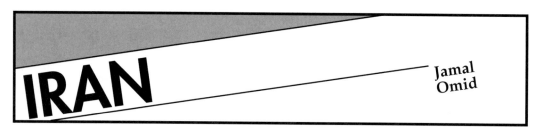

IRAN

Jamal
Omid

Since 1983, when the rehabilitation of the Iranian cinema started, it had always been believed that film production in the country faced no essential problem. Directors were mostly preoccupied with restrictions that they imagined they would have to encounter during the lengthy procedure from the approval of the script to the issuance of a screening licence. There were also debates concerning the effectiveness of government policies for the advancement of film art.

But all such preoccupations and debates receded into the background in the first months of the Iranian year 1372 (March 21, 1993 – March 20, 1994) when the adoption of a single parity rate for foreign exchange upset film producers' calculations. Prior to that date producers could buy film stocks and equipment at an official rate of hard currency which was far below the free market rate. Under the new scheme, production costs more than doubled, and the current box-office revenues were not at all sufficient to cover production costs.

This was the beginning of a serious crisis, and the majority of film-makers lost all hope of ever surmounting the new crisis. Very few producers were ready to put their trust in the ability of government authorities who had until then weathered previous difficulties.

The financial crisis was intensified by the lifting of the ban on video, which had always been feared as a formidable rival for the cinema, while the imminent arrival of satellite was expected to deliver the *coup de grâce*. Consequently most producers were wary of risking investment in film projects. Under the circumstances a special scheme of offering government financial support to the film industry (explained in detail in last year's report) was prepared and put into execution. Nevertheless film production came virtually to a halt during the first half of the year.

Violence and Fistfights

The implementation of the scheme of government financial support produced a positive result during the second half of the year, and the more experienced directors were persuaded to engage cautiously in film production. To ensure the box-office success of the pictures, the producers relied heavily on scenes of violence and fistfights. A second group of producers, who launched their film projects later in the year, tried to work with directors whose professional background ensured the film's success. And finally the spectacle of a revived film industry encouraged the remainder of the film-makers to try their luck under the new conditions.

As a result, at the time of the 12th Fajr International Film Festival – the usual deadline for presentation of Iranian cinema's annual production – 58 producers announced films for the Festival. At the same time more than 40 other titles were being shot or were in post-production stage and obviously could not meet the Festival deadline. Seven of the films submitted to the Festival were rejected because of their over-indulgence in violence, and will be considered for public

screening after their violent scenes have been toned down. Some 44 films were finally selected for screening in the Festival, and this would have seemed an incredible annual output by the most optimistic estimates at the beginning of the year. But apparently the momentum created by the crisis was harnessed and put at the service of the industry. All the same it has to be admitted that last year's crop includes either debut efforts by fledgling directors, or mediocre films with no remarkable qualities, and unlike the previous year's top-grade pictures by Iran's first-rate directors are rather rare.

Ironically, the Iranian cinema enjoyed one of its most successful and active years at world film festivals (179 Iranian films were screened at 125 festivals and won 34 prizes). The latest and perhaps the most noteworthy international success for Iranian cinema has been the participation of Abbas Kiarostami's *Under the Olive Trees* in the competition at Cannes, while *Zinat*, a debut film by Ebrahim Mokhtari, was presented in the Critics' Week at the same event.

Building New Screens

Another measure adopted in the past year to strengthen the economic foundation of the film industry was the allocation of 20 billion rials of credit facilities for the construction of inexpensive screening halls all over the country. Another factor which is bound to have some effect on film production is the eagerness of the national television to engage in film production after Dr. Larijani, the ex-minister of culture and Islamic guidance, took over as the head of the Islamic Republic of Iran Broadcasting.

Abbas Kiarostami

The films released in the Iranian year 1372 could be classified as follows: a limited number of superior pictures (*Under the Olive Trees, Bread and Poem, Tick Tack, The Spouse*), the avowedly mystic films (*Zero Heights, The Fall, Seven Candles*), substandard films from major film-makers (*Green Ashes, Day of the Angel, The Legend of Domrol*), a few well-made films on Iran's

FARABI

Promoting Iranian Cinema All Over The World

PRODUCTION

PROMOTION

IMPORT

CO.PRODUCTION

DISTRIBUTION

EXPORT

Farabi Cinema Foundation
No.55 SIE.TIR AVE. TEHRAN 11358/I.R. IRAN
TELEX: 214283FCF TEL:671010/678156
FAX:678155

Still from THE SPOUSE

eight-year war *(The Last Reconnaissance, War of the Oil Tankers, The Epic of Majoun, Altar of Fire),* and surprises from lesser-known directors *(The End of Childhood, Zinat* and *The Devil's Eye).*

In the wake of recent changes in the Ministry of Culture and Islamic Guidance, S.M. Beheshti, the managing director of the Farabi Cinema Foundation and Fakhraddin Anvar, deputy for cinematographic affairs of the Ministry of Culture resigned after 12 years of work in their respective positions. Although the successors to Beheshti and Anvar have emerged from among their colleagues of recent years, the absence of the two outgoing executives from the film scene will no doubt bring about further bureaucratic shufflings.

UNDER THE OLIVE TREES

Script and Direction: Abbas Kiarostami. Photography: Hossein Jafarian. Editing: A. Kiarostami. Players: Hossein Rezai, M.A. Keshavarz, Zarifeh Shiva. Produced by A. Kiarostami. 103 mins.

Kiarostami had already been following his own sincere and unadorned style of film-making with an exemplary steadfastness for 17 years before the exceptional success of *Where Is the Friend's Home?* brought him international recognition in 1986. Since then he has created two more films – *And Life Goes On ...* and *Under the Olive Trees* –

which together with *Where Is the Friend's Home?* make up his "trilogy of friendship".

The third title in the trilogy is as effective in its honest treatment of details of life as the two previous pictures. *Under the Olive Trees* is a film about film-making, which tells the story of a simple worker who asks for the hand of a girl, and is turned down because he doesn't own a house of his own. When the earthquake destroys all houses in the village and the boy and the girl he loves are cast as principal players in a film about the catastrophe, the boy proposes again. In a final extreme long-shot, lasting four minutes, the boy receives a positive response.

Kiarostami's admirers believe that *Under the Olive Trees* is a perfect film. The Cannes Film Festival presented it as the first Iranian movie in that Festival's competition. And Werner Herzog, who viewed the film in Tehran, said, "After seeing this picture I do not feel I was in an alien land. Now I feel I have a brother in Tehran, named Kiarostami." Jamal Omid

Still from UNDER THE OLIVE TREES, screened to much acclaim at Cannes in 1994

ZINAT, shown at the Critics' Week in Cannes in 1994

Recent Films

ZINAT

Script and Dir: Ebrahim Mokhtari. Phot: Homayun Pievar. Players: Atefeh Razavi, Mehdi Fat'hi, Shahin Alizadeh. Prod: Bahman Farhangsara.

This debut picture by Ebrahim Mokhtari, who had previously directed only documentaries, is characterised by a strong and confident use of the film medium. *Zinat* presents thought-provoking images with unusual characters as well as unfamiliar rites and traditions. The film is especially notable for its treatment of the woman's position in a closed community dominated by masculine rule and harsh traditions. As a result Mokhtari's cool, slow and detached tone is admirably suited to the film's overall strategy. *Zinat* was among the seven titles presented at the Critics' Week at Cannes.

THE SPOUSE

Script and Dir: Mehdi Fakhimzadeh. Phot: Mahmud Klari. Players: Fatemeh Motamed-Aria, Mehdi Hashemi. Prod: Sina Film Organisation.

This intelligently-made comedy challenges the traditional notion of male superiority in Iranian society. Mehdi Fakhimzadeh is a film-maker of the last generation whose greatest concern is to attract the audience and convey a meaningful social comment. His latest picture provides opportunities for the manifestation of feminine capabilities in humorous situations, and is expected to be one of the year's box-office hits.

The Spouse was a great surprise particularly for the foreign guests of the Fajr Festival in February. Tadao Sato, the prominent Japanese critic and historian, said that he was surprised by the film. Like many outsiders, he believed that Iranian society was characterised by male superiority, and *The Spouse* dispelled that misconception.

TICK TACK

Script: Hushang Moradi Kermani, Mohammad Ali Talebi. Dir: M.A. Talebi. Phot: Farhad Saba. Players: Saeed Ghorai, Hassan Ghasemkhani, Shirin Bina. Prod: Shahed Television Group.

Mohammed Ali Talebi, who grew up working with 8mm cameras in the libraries of the Institute for the Intellectual Development of Children and Young Adults, is now determined to devote his career to the creation of films for children. *Tick Tack* tells the story of a small boy who is awarded a prize in school. His friend feels that he too could have received a prize if his family had been more attentive to his work.

Tick Tack is in the vein of Talebi's previous picture, *The Boots*, which has had a great deal of success at international festivals. It is a candid tale of the childhood world with excellent performances by young actors.

BREAD AND POEM

Script and Dir: Kiumars Poorahmad. Phot: Parviz Malekzadeh. Players: Mehdi Bagherbeigi, Parvindokht Yazdanian. Prod: The House Art and Literature for Children and Young Adults.

Kiumars Poorahmad's latest film, which was praised by UNICEF at the 1994 Berlinale, will mark the final appearance of his teenage character named Majid who became popular through a number of TV movies. In the course of his growth from adolescence to youth, the hero of the series has lost his fine humour although he is still as perky as before. And that is perhaps why Poorahmad's treatment in *Bread and Poem* is much more bitter than previously. All the same, Poorahmad's skilful use of pictorial language and his satirical treatment are almost as effective.

DAY OF THE ANGEL

Script: M.R. Honarmand, B. Dayyani, B. Afkhami. Dir: Behruz Afkhami. Phot: N. Haghighi, A. Javanruh. Players: E. Entezami, M.R. Honormand, Mina Lakani. Prod: Mahab Film.

Behruz Afkhami's efforts in *Day of the Angel* – loosely inspired by *Ghost* – remain largely ineffectual in spite of the director's obvious mastery of cinematic language. In fact, Afkhami fails to come up to the expectations that were raised by his previous and highly successful picture, *The Bride*.

THE GREEN ASHES

Script and Dir: Ebrahim Hatamikia. Phot: Lasto Cross. Players: Attila Pasiani, Barbara Bobolova. Prod: Islamic Propagation Organisation, Centre for the Promotion of Experimental Film-making.

Ebrahim Hatamikia, the young film-maker who reached the height of his career with the brilliant war epic *The Immigrant*, has been treating themes that are indirectly related to war after the cessation of hostilities, and his previous film, *From Karkheh to Rhein*, was a beautiful and effective picture. In his latest film he relates the adventures of an Iranian director who travels to Bosnia to select locations for his next film project.

With *The Green Ashes*, Hatamikia has started to explore new ground, but apart from his usual mastery of the film medium, he seems to be abandoning his former attitudes and ideals.

THE ALTAR OF FIRE

Script: Ali Shah-Hatami, A. Moradpoor. Dir: Ahmad Moradpoor. Phot: M.T. Paksima. Players: M.R. Iranmanesh, Ali Burian, H. Haddad. Prod: Farabi Cinema Foundation, Islamic Propagation Organisation.

This first feature by Ahmad Moradpoor is an exception among films on war that have become a regular feature of the Iranian cinema. The director exhibits remarkable understanding of the psychology of characters and a rare appreciation of dramatic situations. The picture's pictorial quality is greatly enhanced by meticulously executed special effects.

THE DEVIL'S EYE

Script and Dir: Hassan Hedayat. Phot: Hassan Puya. Players: Alireza Khamseh, Mohammad Barsuzian. Prod: Hamrah Film Production Group.

The Devil's Eye is an adventure romp, in the vein of Spielberg's films, that could provide entertainment for the entire family. Set in the historial city of Isfahan, the picture tells the story of a treasure hunt without falling prey to inordinate exaggerations. Hedayat, however, took a great risk by casting a comedian in a serious role. It has to be admitted that Hedayat has secured an excellent contribution from the special effects department, make-up as well as fine performances.

Forthcoming Films

In the second month of the year, 61 projects were in shooting or post-production stages, and it was estimated that 30 more projects would be under way by the end of September, the last date to start shooting if the films are to reached the Fajr Festival deadline in February.

THE FAIRY AND THE GREEN BOOK

Script and Dir: Daruish Mahrjut. Phot: Alireza Zarrindast. Players: Niki Karimi, Khostro Shakibai, Turan Mahrzad, Ali Mossaffa.

MAHARAJA

Script and Dir: Mohsen Makhmalbaf. Phot: Mahmud Klari. Players: local people in Bombay where it is scheduled to be shot.

THE FATEFUL DAY

Script: Bahram Beizai. Dir: Shahram Asadi. Phot: Maziar Partov. Players: Alireza Shoja Noori, Ezzatollah Entezami, Jamshid Mashayekhi, Moham-mad Ali Keshvarz. Prod: Farabi Cinema Foundation.

THE HEART AND THE DAGGER

Script and Dir: Masud Jafari Jozani. Phot: Turaj Mansuri. Players: Mohammad Motavas-selani, Ferdows Kaviani, Turan Mehrzad. Prod: Dadgu, Golkar, Jafari.

THE COMMERCE

Script and Dir: Masud Kimia'ie. Phot: Mahmud Klari. Players: Framarz Gharibian, Bita Farrahi. Prod: Morteza Shayesteh.

THE HEAVENLY EARTH

Script: Mohammad Ali Najafi, Mohammad Reza Sharifi. Dir: M.A. Najafi. Phot: Asghar Rafi'ie-Jam. Players: Mahnaz Afzali, Dariush Arjomand, Roghiyeh Chehreh-Azad. Prod: Farabi Cinema Foundation.

DAY OF THE DEVIL

Script and Dir: Behruz Afkhami. Phot: Mahmud Klari. Players: Attila Pasiani, Hamid Ta'ati, Ezzatollah Entezami. Prod: Seyyed Zia Hashemi.

STARS IN THE DUST

Script and Dir: Azizollah Hamidnezhad. Phot: Farhad

Still from THE GREEN ASHES

Saba. Player: Mehdi Gholipoor. Prod: Centre for the promotion of Experimental Film-making.

FLIGHT FROM THE CAMP

Script: Mohammad Reza Alipiam. Dir: Hassan Karbakhsh. Phot: Azim Javanruh. Players: Jamshid Hashempoor, Tajaddod, Freydun Maleki, Alireza Alipiam. Prod: Minafilm.

I WANT TO LIVE

Script: Rasul Sadr-Ameli. Dir: Iraj Ghaderi. Phot: Faraj Heidari. Players: Framarz Gharibian, Fatemeh Gudarzi, Jalal Moghaddam, Mahnaz Ansarian. Prod: Morteza Shayesteh.

THE LONG AUTUMN

Script: Hassan Hedayat, Manuchehr Asgarinassab. Dir: M. Asgarinassab. Phot: Reza Banki. Players: Framarz Seddigh, Saeed Poorsamimi, Mahvash Afsharpanah. Prod: Islamic Propagation Organisation.

DISARMAMENT

Script and Dir: Alireza Davudnezhad. Phot: Albert Yavarian. Players: Mohammad Reza Davudnezhad. Victor Annanin, Hossein Miraghai, Zohreh Miraghai. Prod: Mahvash Jazayeri (Iran-Armenia co-production).

PATH OF GLORY

Script: Dehghn. Dir: Dariush Farhag. Phot: Farhad Saba. Players: Jamshid Mashayekhi, Davud Rashidi, Hamid Delshakib. Prod: National Iranian Oil Company.

SUN MIRROR THIEVES

Script and Dir: Marzieh Borumand. Phot: Azia Sa'ati. Players: Mehdi Hashemi, Roghiyeh Chehreh-Azad, Hassan Rezai. Prod: Film Emruz Cinema Company.

NAFTGAN

Script: Esmail Abbasi. Dir: Majid Javanmard. Phot: Hossein Maleki. Players: Framarz Gharibian, Morteza Ahmadi, Hassan Rezai, Manuchehr Hamedi. Prod: Yaran Film.

THE ENTOMOLOGIST

Script: Hossein Amiri, Mohammad Reza Safavi. Dir: Mohammad Reza Zehtabi. Phot: Alireza Zarrindast. Players: Akbar Abdi, Leyla Mosaddeghi, Morteza Ahmadi. Prod: Puya Film.

THE LEGION

Script and Dir: Seyyed Zia-addin Dari. Phot: Mehrdad Fakhimi. Players: Homa Rusta, Mohammad Ali Keshavarz, Fat'hali Oveisi, Khosro Shakibai. Prod: Mir Valiyollah Madani.

IN COLD BLOOD

Script: Freydun Jairani, Asghar Abdollahi. Dir: Siamak Shayeghi. Phot: Hassan Gholizadeh. Players: Abolfazi Poorarab, Ateneh Faghih Nasiri, Mahtaj Nojumi, Attila Pasiani. Prod: Milan Film.

GREAT EXPECTATIONS

Script: Bahram Ruzbehani. Dir: Khosro Shojai. Phot: Parviz Malekzadeh. Players: Amin Tarokh, Akbar Abdi, Amir Hossein Khanshahri. Prod: Abbas Jahanbakhshi.

ALCHEMY

Script and Dir: Ahmad Reza Darvish. Phot: Mahmud Klari. Players: Khosro Shakibai, Bita Farrahi, Reza Kianian. Prod: Harun Yeshayai.

CROCODILE'S JOURNEY

Script: Mon'em Saeedipoor, Mehdi Vadadi. Dir: M. Vadadi. Phot: Mahmud Klari. Players: Abolfazi Poorarab, Niki Karimi. Prod: Jahanbakhsh Soltani.

THE VISIT

Script: Jamshid Malekpoor. Dir: Mohammad Reza Honarmand. Phot: Mehrdad Fakhimi. Players: Mina Lakani, Mehran Modiri, Jamshid Shah-Mohammadi. Prod: Mahab Film, Islamic Art and Thought Bureau.

THE BLUE SCARF

Script and Dir: Rakhshan Bani-etemad. Phot: Aziz Sa'ati. Players: Ezzatollah Entezami.

Producers, Distributors

Arman Film
No. 126 Razi St
Jomhuri Ave
Tehran
Tel: 675418

Iranmilad Cinema Organisation
No. 186 Bahar-e Shiraz St
Tehran
Tel: 7505674

Abgun Cinema Organisation
No. 401 Shariati Ave
Tehran
Tel: 763047

Atlas Film
No. 26 Jomhuri Ave
Tehran
Tel: 6466131

Avishan Film
No. 5 Parvin Etesami St
Dr. Fatami Ave
Tehran
Tel: 654415-6

Mostazafan Foundation Cinema Organisation and Film Distribution
Abbasabad Ave (corner of Vali-e Asr)
Tehran
Tel: 623536

Pakhshiran Cinema Organisation
Somayeh St, Bahar St
Tehran
Tel: 8824052, 57

Purika Film
No. 119 Forsat St
Taleghani Ave
Tehran
Tel: 8828442

Puya Film Organisation
Tavakol Bldg., Jomhuri Ave
Tehran
Tel: 673574

**Arts Bureau, Islamic
Propagation Organisation**
213 Somayeh St
Hafez Ave
Tehran
Tel: 6464037, 6401366

Tasvir-e Zendagi Company
No. 2 Shahid Shokrabi Alley
Tehran
Tel: 840359

Jozan Film
No. 5 Ghaffari Alley, Jam St
Motahari Ave
Tehran
Tel: 8822117

Jahan Film
No. 1313 Vali-e Asr Ave
Tehran
Tel: 8882893

Khane-ye Film Iran
Tavakol Bldg
Jomhuri Ave
Tehran
Tel: 671247

Khane-ye Film Sabz
No. 89 Mirdamad Ave
Tehran
Tel: 8089919, 2225960

Children's Literature Mansion
No. 135 Kashef (Noor) St
Hedayat Ave
Tehran
Tel: 7532181

Roshan Film
No. 97 Arbab Jamshid Alley
Kushk St, Ferdowsi Ave
Tehran
Tel: 6452975

Sina Film
Varavini Soleiman Khater (Amir
Atabak) St
Motahari Ave
Tehran
Tel: 837732, 8837471

Sobhan Film
No. 45 Noori Alley
Vali-e Asr Ave
Tehran
Tel: 6401807

Sepahan Cinema Organisation
No. 126 Razi St
Jomhuri Ave
Tehran
Tel: 673047, 676268

Shiraz Film Organisation
No. 1/56 Neaufle le Chateau St
Tehran
Tel: 672958, 677952

Shahed Television Group
No. 8 Shahid Tehrani Alley
Maghsudbeik St
Tehran
Tel: 276676

Filmiran Cinema Organisation
No. 101 Bahar Mastan St
Haft Tir Sq
Tehran
Tel: 8824432

Fajr Cinema Organisation
No. 52 Shariati St
Farahani Ave
Tehran
Tel: 8837991, 8825650

Filmsazan Cinema Organisation
No. 7 Ghaffari Alley,
Bahar Mastan St
Haft Tir Sq
Tehran
Tel: 830676

Film Emruz Cinema Company
No. 27 Sohrevardi Ave
Tehran
Tel: 862621, 862583

**Sahra Cultural and Cinema
Institute**
No. 39 Nilufar Alley, Apadana St
Abbasabad Ave
Tehran
Tel: 865392, 866110

Laleh Cinema Organisation
Lalezarno St
Tehran
Tel: 6452954

Milad Cinema Organisation
Jami St (corner of Estakhr)
Tehran
Tel: 679865

Mahab Film Organisation
No. 91 Bakhtiar Alley
Haft Tir Sq
Tehran
Tel: 837547

Mina Film Organisation
No. 1317, Vanak Sq
Tehran
Tel: 689314

Athar Institute
No. 3 Hamid Seddigh Alley
Somayeh Junction, Shariati Ave
Tehran
Tel: 7500679

Novin Film Organisation
No. 15, Passage 48
Jomhuri Ave (Serah Jomhuri)
Tehran
Tel: 6403697

Hedayat Film Organisation
No. 10 4th Alley
Farahani Ave
Tehran
Tel: 623687

**Hamrah Film Production Co-
operative**
No. 64 Aljavad Mosque Alley
Haft Tir Sq
Tehran
Tel: 8846140

IRELAND — Michael Dwyer

The years 1991 and 1992 were lean times for film production in Ireland with just *Into the West, High Boot Benny* and *The Snapper* going into production, to the relief of the Irish actors and crew who were signed to work on them. Last year told a very different story, with a total of ten movies in production here, six of them by Irish directors. The prospects for 1994 are even better with the likelihood of at least a dozen and possibly as many as 16 features filmed in Ireland before the end of the year, along with a number of large-scale TV mini-series such as *Shannongate, Scarlett* and *The Old Curiosity Shop.*

"There's so much going on that everyone's very far-stretched," comments leading Irish entertainment lawyer James Hickey of Matheson Ormsby Prentice. "But by any terms this is an extraordinarily vibrant time, and Ireland is reaping the rewards enormously."

He credits the upswing in production here to "a whole confluence of factors" – the high-profile image of Irish films abroad in recent years, making Ireland a popular and fashionable location; the financial incentives available under Section 35 of the Finance Act, which have attracted substantial investment; the wealth of activity by the ever-growing number of Irish production companies; and the re-establishment of the Irish Film Board.

Although the board was only re-activated by the arts and culture minister, Michael D. Higgins, as recently as the spring of 1993 it already has become involved in a wide range of projects. "When we started up last year some people said we would only assist pointy-headed art movies and others said we would merely go downmarket and sell out to the most commercial projects," said Rod Stoneman, the board's chief executive.

"But we're moving right across the range from art-house to hopefully commercial material."

Even though quite a few of the features filmed in Ireland during 1994 emanated from Irish production companies, very few are the work of Irish directors. "It's most important that we have continuity of production," says film board chairwoman Lelia Doolan. "I'm very encouraged by the talent that's around. But we can't ignore the fact that we're in Europe and that there will be many co-productions. That is the reality of film-making today, but I am confident that in the years ahead we will see more Irish people writing, producing and directing."

Huge Battle Scenes

Meanwhile, there was dismay in the British film industry when Mel Gibson, director and star of the Scottish historical drama, *Braveheart*, decided to shoot eleven weeks of the high-budget epic in Ireland, and just five weeks in Scotland. Gibson's decision was influenced not just by the Section 35 tax incentives available in Ireland, but by the offer of culture minister Higgins of access to ten Irish castles for location purposes and the provision of 1,600 members of the reserve defence forces for the film's huge battle scenes.

Braveheart is not the only British-set film to be shot in Ireland in 1994 – others include Mike Newell's feature, *An Awfully Big Adventure*, shot entirely in Dublin though set in 1950's Liverpool, and producer Greg Smith's mini-series, *The Old Curiosity Shop*, which recreated Dickensian London at Ardmore Studios near Dublin.

And there is more excitement in Irish

film industry circles at the time of going to press with strong speculation that the ingenious and highly prolific Hollywood producer, Roger Corman, is planning to open a studio in Dublin and to produce up to six low-budget features a year. Corman visited Ireland in May and had discussions with all the relevant government departments.

Attendances Climbing Again

Parallel to the upswing in Irish film production, cinema attendances continued to climb – increasing by 14% in 1993 to reach over 9.3 million admissions, the highest since 1980, and certain to increase again when the 1994 figures are in. As an instance of quite how lucrative the relatively small Irish market can be, the record set by Alan Parker's *The Commitments* in 1992 – of being the first film to take over £2 million at the Irish box-office – was broken in 1993 by the new champion, *Jurassic Park*, which took just under £3 million, and again in the early months of 1994 by Jim Sheridan's *In the Name of the Father* (£2.5 million) and Chris Columbus's *Mrs. Doubtfire* (£2.3 million). Sheridan's controversial film, which had its world premiere in Dublin, attracted a huge amount of media and audience interest, and built on that when it received seven Oscar nominations, including best picture, director and actor. The other big hits in the first half of 1994, each of which has taken over £1 million, have included *Schindler's List*, *Philadelphia* and *Four Weddings and a Funeral*.

On the art-house circuit, the twin Light House cinema in Dublin had a very successful 1993 with hits such as *Orlando*, *Un Cœur en Hiver* and *Three Colours: Blue*, and a strong start to 1994 with *Farewell My Concubine*. The Irish Film Centre marked its first birthday in September 1993, having attracted 15,000 members – the biggest hits at the two-screen venue were led by Spanish imports *Jamón Jamón* and *Belle Epoque*.

On the Irish film festival circuit, the Galway Festival turned five in the summer of 1993 and drew an impressive guest list

which included directors Paolo Taviani and Stephen Frears, actors Stephen Rea and Rutger Hauer, and two-time Oscar winner, Irish make-up artist Michele Burke.

Although few international film-makers visited the Cork Film Festival in October, the organisers compensated with a strong programme of screenings. The event opened with *Three Colours: Blue* and closed with Irish director Joe Comerford's *High Boot Benny*. The festival's principal award, for best European short film, went to the Irish entry, *After '68*, directed by Stephen Bourke.

In the spring of 1994, the ninth Dublin Film Festival fielded a packed programme of international cinema, opening with Bille August's *The House of the Spirits* and closing with the world premiere of a new Irish film, Maurice O'Callaghan's *Broken Harvest*. The subjects of the festival retrospectives were actor Jeremy Irons and Russian director Alexander Rogozkhin, both of whom were in Dublin for the event.

And in June the Film Society of Lincoln Center in New York launched a major four-week programme of Irish cinema spanning 84 years from the silent period to the world premieres of two new Irish films, Paddy Breathnach's *Ailsa* and Mary McGuckian's Yeats adaptation, *Words Upon the Window Pane*. It is clear that anyone planning a similar retrospective in the future will have many more recent Irish films to screen.

IN THE NAME OF THE FATHER

Script: Jim Sheridan and Terry George. Direction: Jim Sheridan. Photography: Peter Biziou. Editing: Gerry Hambling. Music: Trevor Jones. Production Design: Caroline Amies. Players: Daniel Day-Lewis, Pete Postlethwaite, Emma Thompson, John Lynch. Produced by Hell's Kitchen/Gabriel Byrne for Universal Pictures. 133 mins.

On one level, Jim Sheridan's *In the Name of the Father* is charged with the power and urgency of such searing factually based political thrillers as *Z*, *All the President's*

Daniel Day-Lewis and Emma Thompson in IN THE NAME OF THE FATHER

Men, The Battle of Algiers and *Missing*; on another, it is a tender and deeply moving picture of a father and son finally growing to know and understand each other under the most adverse circumstances.

Sheridan's film is crowned by the achievements of an exemplary, impeccably chosen cast headed by Daniel Day-Lewis in an astonishing performance, a vivid and complex portrayal of Gerry Conlon, one of the four people who spent almost 15 years in jail when they were wrongly accused of the pub bombings which killed five people and maimed many more in Guildford, Surrey, on October 5, 1974.

As the film opens, the screen fills abruptly with a huge explosion that destroys a Guildford bar. Establishing its flashback structure, the film cuts to the solicitor, Gareth Peirce, listening in her car to a cassette on which Gerry Conlon tells his story. That story begins in Belfast where Conlon, a petty thief, is saved from a Provisional IRA knee-capping only by the intervention of his father, Giuseppe, a morally upright working-class man

ashamed of his son's activities. Moving to London, Gerry and his friend, Paul Hill, move into a hippy commune; having come from Belfast, they are almost oblivious to the bombs which are going off in London.

Two days after the Guildford bombings, Conlon and Hill were arrested, and by the end of seven days in detention, both men bowed to pressure and signed confessions admitting to the pub bombings; together with Carole Richardson and Paddy Armstrong, who also lived in the hippy commune, they were convicted on October 22, 1975 and sentenced to life imprisonment.

Contrary to misassumptions expressed before the film was released, *In the Name of the Father* cannot be interpreted, however remotely, as an apologist for the Provos. In fact, the sole substantial Provo character in the film is depicted as sinister, unscrupulous and fundamentally evil. That character is a fictitious creation, and one example of the dramatic licence taken by the film which has been employed to criticise it.

TOP TEN GROSSING FILMS IN IRELAND: 1993

Jurassic Park
The Fugitive
The Bodyguard
Sleepless in Seattle
Indecent Proposal
A Few Good Men
Cliffhanger
Bram Stoker's Dracula
The Firm
In the Line of Fire
(Compiled by Michael Dwyer)

But *In the Name of the Father* is not a documentary and it is far from uncommon for dramatisations of factually based stories to make changes of necessity, to telescope events, to create composite characters. What matters is that the film proves true to the nature of the events depicted and in that respect, Jim Sheridan's powerful film emerges with integrity and conviction.

Michael Dwyer

MICHAEL DWYER is Film Correspondent of *The Irish Times*. He co-founded the Dublin Film Festival in 1985 and acted as its Programme Director until 1991. He is working on his first book, the authorised biography of Alan Parker.

Still from BROKEN HARVEST

Recent and Forthcoming Films

AILSA

Script: Joe O'Connor. Dir: Paddy Breathnach. Phot: Cian De Buitlear. Players: Brendan Coyle, Andrea Irvine, Gary Lydon, Juliette Gruber. Prod: Temple Films.

ALL OUR FAULT

Script: Daniel Mornin. Dir: Thaddeus O'Sullivan. Players: Tim Roth, Ian Hart. Prod: Little Bird.

AN AWFULLY BIG ADVENTURE

Dir: Mike Newell. Phot: Dick Pope. Players: Hugh Grant, Alan Rickman, Georgina Cates, Peter Firth. Prod: Portman Productions/Wolfhound Films.

BROKEN HARVEST

Script: Maurice O'Callaghan, Kate O'Callaghan. Dir: Maurice O'Callaghan. Phot: Jack Conroy. Players: Colin Lane, Marian Quinn, Niall O'Brien. Prod: Destiny Films.

CIRCLE OF FRIENDS

Script: Andrew Davies. Dir: Pat O'Connor. Phot: Ken MacMillan. Players: Chris O'Donnell, Minnie Driver, Geraldine O'Rawe, Saffron Burrows. Prod: Price Entertainment/Lantana for Savoy Pictures.

HIGH BOOT BENNY

Script and Dir: Joe Comerford. Phot: Donal Gilligan. Players: Marc O'Shea, Frances Tomelty, Alan Devlin. Prod: Sandy Films.

MOONDANCE

Script: Bert Weinshanker and Mark Watters. Dir: Dagmar Hirtz. Phot: Steve Bernstein. Players: Ian Shaw, Ruaidhri Conroy, Julia Brendler, Marianne Faithfull. Prod: Little Bird.

THE SECRET OF ROAN INISH

Script and Dir: John Sayles. Phot: Haskell Wexler. Players: Mick Lally, John Lynch, Eileen Colgan. Prod: Skerry Movies.

THUMBELINA

Script: Don Bluth, Gary Goldman. Dir: Don Bluth. Voices: Jodi Benson, John Hurt, Carol Channing. Prod: Don Bluth Entertainment. *Animated feature.*

THE WAR OF THE BUTTONS

Script: Colin Welland. Dir: John Roberts. Phot: Bruno De Keyser. Players: Colm Meaney, Gregg Fitzgerald, Gerard Kearney, Darragh Naughton. Prod: Enigma.

WORDS UPON THE WINDOW PANE

Script and Dir: Mary McGuckian. Phot: William Diver. Players: Geraldine Chaplin, Geraldine James, Jim Sheridan, Ian Richardson, Donal Donnelly, John Lynch. Prod: Pembridge Productions.

Producers

Crescendo Concepts
88 Leinster Road
Dublin 6
Tel: 497 4676
Fax: 497 4799

Ferndale Films
4 Harcourt Terrace
Dublin 2
Tel: 676 8890
Fax: 676 8874

The Good Film Company
15 Vesey Place
Monkstown
Co Dublin
Tel: 284 4881
Fax: 284 4882

Little Bird Productions
122 Lower Baggot Street
Dublin 2
Tel: 661 4245
Fax: 660 0351

Merlin Films International
41 Fitzwilliam Place
Dublin 2
Tel: 676 4460
Fax: 676 4368

Temple Films
4 Windmill Lane
Dublin 2
Tel: 671 9313
Fax: 671 9323

Distributors

Abbey Films
35 Upper Abbey Street
Dublin 1
Tel: 472 3422
Fax: 472 3687

Columbia TriStar Films
Merchant's Court
24 Merchant's Quay
Dublin 8
Tel: 679 8234
Fax: 679 8237

Light House Cinema
12 Anglesea Street
Dublin 2
Tel: 679 9585
Fax: 679 9586

Warner Bros.
Russell House
Stokes Place
St Stephen's Green
Dublin 2
Tel: 478 4000
Fax: 478 4572

United International Pictures
D'Olier Chambers
D'Olier Street
Dublin 2
Tel: 679 2433
Fax: 679 8801

Useful Addresses

Ardmore Studios
Herbert Road
Bray
Co Wicklow
Tel: 286 2971
Fax: 286 1894

The Arts Council
70 Merrion Square
Dublin 2
Tel: 661 1840
Fax: 676 0436

Espace Video Européen (EVE)
6 Eustace Street
Dublin 2
Tel: 4679 5744
Fax: 679 9657

Film Institute of Ireland
6 Eustace Street
Dublin 2
Tel: 4679 5744
Fax: 679 9657

Film Makers Ireland
6 Eustace Street
Dublin 2
Tel: 679 6716
Fax: 679 6717

Irish Film Board
The Halls
Quay Street
Galway
Co Galway
Tel: 091 61398
Fax: 091 61405

Irish Film Centre
6 Eustace Street
Dublin 2
Tel: 679 5744
Fax: 679 9657

Irish Trade Board
Merrion Hall
Strand Road
Dublin 4
Tel: 269 5011
Fax: 269 5820

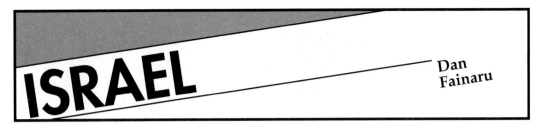

ISRAEL — Dan Fainaru

ilm-making in Israel hasn't been this hectic for years: ten new feature films released in the course of the last twelve months, another ten in the can, and at least five more in various stages of production. The Second Channel, which has finally emerged as a commercial broadcaster after years of preparation, may be excessively studio-oriented, but has nevertheless contributed significantly to the volume of available jobs on the market. Foreign units and co-production deals are keeping free-lancers busy, paying them better than ever before. Three official film schools (the film department at the Tel Aviv University, the School of Film and Television in Jerusalem and Camera Obscura in Tel Aviv), not to mention several fly-by-night operations, are churning out new professionals and they all seem to find employment as soon as they get out, some of them grabbed while still wet behind the ears. In a sense, it is finally possible to talk about an active film industry working on more than a day by day basis, which was not the case in the past.

From this perspective, things couldn't be better. And if it is indeed true that quantity leads to quality, as some people tend to believe, the first masterpiece of the Israeli cinema must be hiding just around the corner. But, from this year's output, that corner is still some distance away. Neither the films already released commercially nor the eight new ones unveiled at the Jerusalem Film Festival in July 1994, were truly encouraging, and it was with a great sense of relief that film critics saw the main Festival award go to veteran Dan Wolman for his latest effort, *The Distance*. A small, intimate production, observing its char-acters in close-ups, but still the most satisfying picture of the year, it was made on a shoestring budget and encountered difficulties all through its production, from those who are supposed to assist Israeli cinema but chose to think Wolman's effort isn't worth the trouble.

Improved Quality of Production

As for the rest of this year's crop, if there was one distinguishing feature most of them shared, it was the improved quality of the production, a trait to be expected from an industry striking its first solid roots. Israeli producers, mainly well-intentioned amateurs in recent past, seem to realise the importance and be in a position to satisfy, of course within the boundaries of the limited resources at their disposal, most of their directors' requests. What they have to learn now, is to be far more challenging in the demands they make on these directors and make sure that the production values, such as they are (considerable for this country, non-existent on a Hollywood scale) should not be wasted in vain.

Marek Rosenbaum, still the busiest producer around, had no less than four films to his credit in the last year, a remarkable performance for any producer, anywhere. The most expensive and the least successful of them was Amnon Rubinstein's historical pageant **The Heritage**, shot partly in Spain, an uninter-esting love story going back and forth between the present and the Spanish Inquisition, whose only purpose seems to be the exhibition of costumes and sets the Israeli cinema has never indulged in before. **Max and Maurice**, a broad crime comedy involving some of the clumsiest safe breakers on record, directed by Yankul Goldwasser, was Rosenbaum's conscious contribution to the commercial cinema relying on the talents of the largely overexposed Moshe Ivgi, present nowa-days in every second film made here, and

Uri Gavriel, both of them hamming it up with a vengeance.

In a different register, **Dreams of Innocence**, unveiled at the Berlin Children's Film Festival and due for a summer release here, has first time director Dina Zvi-Riklis in a reflective but not very exciting mood, following a boy who learns the bitter truth about the mythomaniac father (once again Ivgi) he idolised. **The Flying Camel**, a fantasy by another beginner, Rami Ne'eman, while lacking some of the imagination necessary for the genre, shows at least lots of sympathy for the three protagonists involved in an allegory about Jews, Arabs and Christians joining forces to rekindle the ancient spirit of the country.

Another producer who has come to the fore lately is Haim Sharir. He started the year with Aner Preminger's **Blindman's Buff**, winner of last year's top award in Jerusalem, a pleasant, adequate but pedestrian melodrama about a young pianist who has to come to terms with her maturity and sever the umbilical cord which ties her to her family. A nicely balanced performance by Hagit Dassberg compensated for the picture's numerous clichés and helped put it on the festival map, winning prizes in Montevideo and Montpellier. Much was expected of his other production, **New Land,** premiered at the Jerusalem Festival, one year later, which turned out to be an ambitious but sadly unfocused film about two young orphans who survive the Holocaust and about early immigration to Israel in the 1950's. Poor script and hesitant direction by Orna Ben Dor-Niv cannot disguise, however, the effort invested by the producer to recreate the period.

Exploiting Russian Talent

An interesting effort, on the production level, was **Coffee with Lemon**, a calculated attempt to exploit the cinematic talents of the massive Russian immigration. Producer Zwi Shapira, previously involved in television work only, commissioned Leonid Gorovetz, four years in the country, to

Still from Dina Zvi-Riklis's DREAMS OF INNOCENCE

direct his own story of a Russian actor and his family who come to Israel and have to face inevitable obstacles posed by a new land, a new language and a totally different mentality. Never more than a string of incidents poorly tied together by a tentative script, the picture nevertheless manages to touch several sensitive points and proves, in the process, that Gorovetz may not be a great writer but he certainly can direct.

This is more than one could say for **Black Box**, Yaud Levanon's adaptation of an Amos Oz bestseller which failed to deliver either the characters or the plot of the original novel dealing with a marriage gone sour; **Snow in August**. Hagai Levi's underbudgeted, limp romantic thriller taking place in Jerusalem's orthodox community; **In the Name of Love**, Irith Schori's pseudo-psychological drama about a destructive mother-daughter relationship; or **On the Edge**, directed again by Amnon Rubinstein from another highly respected

novel about a family falling apart in the 1930's, a film devoid of any of the qualities to be found in the writing of author Yehoshua Knaz.

Two films which delivered, at least commercially, were **Zohar** and **The Revenge of Itzik Finkelstein**. The first was Israel's only contribution to the top twenty box-office hits of 1993, a shrewd exploitation of a mythical image, that of Zohar Argov, singer, composer, idol, drug addict and convicted rapist, who died of an overdose while still in his early thirties. A far cry from the typical "pop star movie", requiring production values beyond the means available here, and more than accommodating, considering the controversial nature of the character, Eran Riklis's film, helped along by the dedicated performance of Shaul Mizrahi as Argov, drew over 200,000 admissions, an enviable record at the present time. *The Revenge of Itzik Finkelstein*, a Latin-American satire fitting rather uneasily in the context of Israeli reality, is the first directorial effort by Enrique Rottenberg, a successful building contractor who decided to take the plunge after financing and producing other directors, such as Amos Guttman and Daniel Waxman. Rottenberg may still need to hone his talents but he certainly has won the sympathy of his peers, who awarded his film most of the Israeli Film Academy prizes, creating the kind of expectations it couldn't hope to satisfy. Still, it certainly helped through the first weeks of the film's release.

Vital Role of Quality Fund

Whether the pace set by this year's film production will continue in future, depends almost exclusively on the government's film supporting policies. For, as time goes by, it becomes painfully evident that no Israeli production has much of a chance to materialise without the participation of the Fund for the Promotion of Israeli Quality Films. All credit should be given to civil rights leader Shulamit Aloni, who moved from the head of the Ministry of Education and Culture to the Ministry of the Arts, which was created specially for her, and who took cinema along as part of her dowry. She has been stretching the resources of her new office to the limit, practically doubling the sums allotted to cinema, but her partner, the Ministry of Industry and Commerce, originally supposed to share half of the Fund's burden, is gradually divesting itself of any financial responsibility, while still insisting that its authority in the management of the Fund should remain unimpaired.

The result of this uneasy partnership being a series of decisions which lead to most of the aforementioned films, destined to satisfy all sides, and falling short of expectations in most cases. The rejection of several veteran film-makers, who could not persuade the Fund to participate in their projects, resulted in the absurd situation of Wolman's *The Distance* being made by the director himself from a small subsidy, usually given for short films. Even

completed, the film met with the Fund's cold shoulder, finally managing to obtain participation for print costs, but not more. No wonder vast policy and personal changes, which might improve the operation of this all-important organism, are in store now and it only remains to be seen whether they will be implemented over the head of the more conservative elements among the Fund's directors.

Several new initiatives may help expand the horizons of the local industry in the immediate future. The Fund's willingness to enter co-production deals, even when films are not entirely shot in this country and not necessarily in Hebrew, may encourage investors abroad to dip their feet on this side of the Mediterranean waters. Minister Aloni has pledged yet again to bring Israel, at least partially, into the European community film funds, and is trying to raise the necessary financial and political backing in order to do so. She is also responsible for creating a second Film Fund, whose purpose is to support very low budget productions, mostly documentaries, a genre whose prestige has gone up in the last year. Such a Fund may help young students who are eager enough to go independent and hungry and who, until now, had to bide their time until they were neither young nor eager any more, to embark on their first project with their enthusiasm still intact.

Distribution

Home video may be languishing, as a result of aggressive cable penetration into some 70% of Israeli homes, but theatrical attendance has been stable for the second year in a row (approximately 10 million), the significant change being in the percentage of American films distributed, climbing sharply from 62% to 80%. The predilection of local audiences for family fare has been reconfirmed once more with films such as *Aladdin* and *Scent of a Woman* raking in over two million dollars each, while world champion *Jurassic Park* was relegated to only fifth place, lagging far behind both in admissions and popularity.

TOP TEN GROSSING FILMS IN ISRAEL: 1993

	Admissions
Aladdin	590,196
Scent of a Woman	438,671
The Fugitive	432,875
Indecent Proposal	379,926
Jurassic Park	376,542
The Bodyguard	366,000
Fried Green Tomatoes	302,000
The Crying Game	250,000
A Few Good Men	240,000
The Firm	233,433

Life is becoming increasingly more complicated for independents, not only because the two leading exhibition chains, Globus Group and Israeli Theatres, control over 50% of the screens (usually the best located and the most lucrative ones in the country), but also because both these chains prefer to exploit predominantly American material they either represent or secure through long-term contracts. The competitors, companies such as Shani, Shapira and Gelfand, are trying to get along the best they can through their own, smaller circuits, but their potential for profits is evidently more modest. As for Israeli films, no wonder the three that did go somewhere, *Zohar* (the only domestic product in the top 20), *The Revenge of Itzik Finkelstein* and *Max and Maurice*, were all handled by the Globus Group distribution branch.

HAMERHAK (The Distance)

Script, Direction and Production: Dan Wolman. Photography: Victor Bielokopitov. Editing: Shoshi Wolman. Music: Slava Ganelin. Players: Haim Hadaya, Ghenia Chernik, Ruth Farchi, Michael Shilo, Miriam Nevo, Bat Sheva Nevo. A Lonely Spy production. 85 mins.

There is very little veteran director Dan Wolman hasn't done in his career just because he insisted on making films at any cost. Anything, from adaptations of suc- cessful novels to softcore (and sometimes not so soft) commercial items to TV dramas. But he is still best known and respected for his intimate, close obser- vation of Israeli society, from a very personal point of view, in films whose qualities belie their minimal budgets.

His new feature film, the first in nine years, shows him in top form, as he follows a young Israeli architect based in the United States, visiting his parents in a Tel Aviv suburb, and checking an offer to relocate back home after several years abroad. In a minor tone, mostly implying and never forcing himself on his char- acters, he observes the relations between his parents and a young Russian woman who lives in his old room, helping take care of his ailing father; he encounters old friends; he faces the emotional collapse of his old Nanny, the woman dearest to him in his childhood; he meets the people who wish to employ him and those who may eventually be his future colleagues.

During the one week of his stay, he is torn between affection and concern for his parents who need his presence, and his fear of abandoning the comfortable posi- tion he has secured for himself abroad. He also cannot help being jealous of the Russian woman who is taking his place, to a certain degree, in the heart and life of his genitors, and who may, or may not round up her income by moonlighting at night on Tel Aviv's pavements.

Haim Hadaya and Ruth Farchi in Dan Wolman's THE DISTANCE

His camera close to every one of the characters, observing everything from the son's point of view, Wolman does wonders within his limitations (the film was entirely shot in his parents' home and neighbourhood) and displays the kind of human warmth and understanding that is so often absent from other Israeli films. Ghenia Chernik is perfect as the frank, handsome, sympathetic Russian, a new immigrant who wants a life of her own and is out to get it, difficult as this may be. Accurate, well moulded and restrained performances by the rest of the cast (some may find them too restrained) help Wolman round up one of his most successful films yet.

Dan Fainaru

DAN FAINARU is an Israeli film critic and journalist who is Editor in Chief of the European Film Review, and has been correspondent for I.F.G. for several years. A former director of the Israeli Film Institute, he is a familiar face at the world's major and minor festivals alike.

HAGAMAL HA'MEOFEF (The Flying Camel)

Script and Direction: Rami Ne'eman. Photography: Yoav Kosh. Editing: Tova Asher. Music: Shem-Tov Levi. Players: Gideon Singer, Salim Daw, Laurence Bouvard, Gabi Amrani. Produced by Marek Rosenbaum for Transfax Productions. 93 mins.

This project went for a while into Hollywood turnaround before landing back home to be made on a modest scale adequate for Israeli productions. A gentle, pleasant and at times terribly naïve allegory, it has a Jew who is a former history professor encountering an Arab garbage collector who dreams of replanting his father's orange grove, and an Italian missionary coming to the Holy Land to repent some of the not-so-holy things she did in her past.

It so happens that the professor lives in a shack, surrounded by all the antiques he could collect to preserve the past alive. This shack and the junkyard around it are located on the land once belonging to the Arab's family, and the missionary parks her van there just as the two men are arguing about their respective rights on the territory. Once human nature and mutual sympathy vanquishes the inevitable enmity between the rivals, the trio decide to join forces in order to find and reconstruct the Flying Camel, once the emblem of the Tel Aviv Fair and the symbol of every dream nurtured in this country.

The metaphor is obvious, and so are all the observations on the destruction of traditional customs and values and on the greed motivating modern life. Going for a kind of fantastic, poetical approach, which is not always sustained by the images he

Gideon Zinger, Salim Daw and Laurence Bouvard in THE FLYING CAMEL

can affort to put on screen, Ne'eman's film obviously tries to achieve something similar to neorealistic film lyricism (i.e. *Miracle in Milan*). Gideon Singer, Salim Daw and Laurence Bouvard soulfully try to help him along.

Dan Fainaru

Distributors

Globus Group
(UIP, MGM Pathe, Cannon,
Warner)
10 Glinkson St.
Tel Aviv
Tel: 972-3-200221
Fax: 972-3-283187

A.D. Matalon & Co.
(Columbia, TriStar, Twentieth
Century Fox, Orion, Carolco)
15 Hess St.
Tel Aviv
Tel: 972-3-29625, 296251
Fax: 972-3-292977

Forum/Israeli Theatres
91 Medinath Hayehudim St.
P.O. Box 12598
Herzlyia Pituakh 46766
Tel: (09) 562111
Fax: (09) 561581

Shapira Films
34 Allenby St.
Tel Aviv
Tel: 972-3-5102530
Fax: 972-3-5101370

Golfand Films
34 Allenby St.
Tel Aviv
Tel: 972-3-657010
Fax: 972-3-657994

Shani Films
Dizengoff Centre
Tel Aviv
Tel: 972-3-5288282
Fax: 972-3-204749

Erez Films
32 Allenby St.
Tel Aviv
Tel: 972-3-658654
Fax: 972-3-659874

Nachshon Films
22 Harakevet St.
Tel Aviv
Tel: 972-3-5660015
Fax: 972-3-615112

Shoval Films
32 Allenby St.
Tel Aviv
Tel: 972-3-659288
Fax: 972-3-659289

Tamuz Films
5 Pinsker St.
Tel Aviv
Tel: 972-3-201512

Useful Addresses

Israel Film Institute
13 Sa'adia Gaon St.
Tel Aviv 67135
Tel: 972-3-562 6098
Fax: 972-3-561 1658

Israel Film & TV Producers
Association
Attn: Katriel Schory
26 Ruppin St.
Tel Aviv 63457
Tel: 972-3-226116
Fax: 972-3-235821

Israel Film Centre
Ministry of Industry & Trade
P.O. Box 299
94190 Jerusalem
Tel: 972-2-750433, 750297
Fax: 972-2-245110

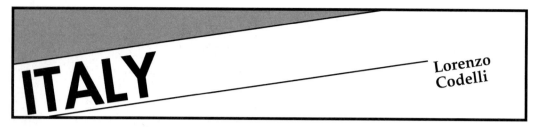

ITALY

Lorenzo
Codelli

A transitional season in Italy, going from Federico Fellini's sad disappearance to his arch-enemy Silvio Berlusconi's rise to omnipotence as Prime Minister-cum-networks. A new film law, approved at the last second by the former parliament, which imposed stricter rules on state grants, failed to improve a constantly declining output: barely 50 Italian pictures were released (–20%), attracting 11.8% of the gross (– 4.2%), none of them in the top ten list – excluding, of course, Bernardo Bertolucci's foreign hit, *Little Buddha*.

Not even foolproof shlock farces, like *Anni 90 parte II*, a portmanteau follow-up starring familiar TV clowns, or Paolo Villaggio's umpteenth instalment as *Fantozzi in Paradiso*, Carlo Verdone's bittersweet vehicle *Perdiamoci di vista*, Ezio Greggio's misconceived send-up of *The Silence of the Lambs*, entitled *Il silenzio dei prosciutti*, could appeal to a wide number of their fans.

Bible and Code

Diego Abatantuono scored as Joseph, Jesus Christ's forgotten father, in *Per amore solo per amore*, Giovanni Veronesi's feeble adaptation of the late film-maker Pasquale Festa Campanile's bestseller. Abatantuono's former partner Gabriele Salvatores directed **Sud**, about a band of angry Sicilian jobless demonstrating against local politicians. Tricky jump cutting, plus rough raps by hip rockers enlivened this inert release.

The "judicial movie" trend – nourished by daily reports about trials of leaders, mafiosi, managers, etc – continued with **Giovanni Falcone**, a biography of a celebrated magistrate killed by the Mafia, plotted by Giuseppe Ferrara as a sort of

Wax Museum. Alessandro di Robilant's **Il giudice ragazzino** denounced in anonymous TV-style the murder of yet another anti-Mafia judge.

Farewell Old Glories

A sudden loss, that of Mario Cecchi Gori, Italy's most powerful film mogul, who had produced the best comedies of the 1960's, as well as Fellini's final work (*La voce della luna*). At the Venice Mostra he attended the premiere of **Mille bolle blu**, Leone Pompucci's breezy first work evoking some of the 1960's mythical *topoi*. Cecchi Gori could not fail to ignore the unfortunate commercial career of his ambitious production, **Cari fottutissimi amici**, a picaresque end-of-war satire directed by his old chum Mario Monicelli, a Tuscan like himself. Was its star Paolo Villaggio responsible also for the box-office disaster of Ermanno Olmi's academic if visually gorgeous reworking of Dino Buzzati's **Il segreto del bosco vecchio**? Audiences seem to be weary of all our veteran talents. This also harmed Alberto Sordi's spottily released **Nestore**, an almost unbearably sincere self-portrait by the once extraordinary comedian, playing a derelict coachman who must eliminate his dear horse.

Established film-makers tend to be repeating themselves. Take, for instance, Franco Zeffirelli's **Storia di una capinera**, a pretentious melodrama upgraded by nice lighting and costumes. Or the emotionless **Il sogno della farfalla**, the ultimate revenge by vampiristic psychoanalyst/scriptwriter Massimo Fagioli on his patient/director Marco Bellocchio. Or Liliana Cavani's **Dove siete? Il sono qui**, a cliché-ridden romance involving deaf youngsters. Oscar-winner Giuseppe Tornatore earned a mixed reaction in Cannes for **Una pura formalità**,

Paolo Villaggio in Ermanno Olmi's IL SEGRETO DEL BOSCO VECCHIO

an overblown conflict between a suspect writer (hammy Gérard Depardieu) and a police officer (witty Roman Polanski). Tinto Brass revelled in his customary dose of bourgeois hardcore, **L'uomo che guarda**, vaguely inspired by Alberto Moravia's novel.

Mavericks and Newcomers

Three idiosyncratic features emerged from three permanent outsiders. Mario Brenta's **Barnabo delle montagne**, an Olmian, ecstatic, but boring version of Dino Buzzati's mountain novel. Protean, genial Sabina Guzzanti – she pokes fun on TV at Berlusconi and other personalities – played a dozen foolish characters in Giuseppe Bertolucci's **Troppo sole**. A countryside family intrigue with a French flavour was at the core of Fabio Carpi's uneven **La prossima volta il fuoco**.

The younger generation, frequently acclaimed at festivals, has to fight hard against growing opposition from distrib-

utors and exhibitors alike. A group of film-makers founded a reformist movement called Maddalena '93, which is publishing a polemic magazine, *Script* (via dei Banchi Vecchi 50, Rome). Another bunch, linked by Nanni Moretti's vision, produced a collective propaganda short, *L'unico paese al mondo (The Only Country in the World*, allowing a media-mogul to run for government), in a vain attempt to curb Berlusconi's power.

Revolution Again?

The New Right's rule will definitely enhance the dissenting tone of many sophomore film-makers. Silvio Soldini's **Un'anima divisa in due** attacks the racist treatment of gypsy immigrants. Maurizio Zaccaro's **L'articolo 2** does the same for Arab immigrants. Pasquale Pozzessere's **Padre e figlio** investigates a clash between father and son in working-class milieu. Alessandro D'Alatri's **Senza pelle** deals with a case of psychiatric solidarity in a Roman neighbourhood.

Gérard Depardieu and Roman Polanski in UNA PURA FORMALITÀ

With his populist dramas **La ribelle** – starring the exciting Spanish teenager Penelope Cruz – and **Le buttane** – starring a gang of expansive ladies as 20 buck whores – Sicilian novelist-director-school-teacher Aurelio Grimaldi would like to be at the forefront of the neo-Rossellinian movement, which was successfully launched in 1989 by Marco Risi's *Mery per sempre*, scripted by Grimaldi himself.

Debutante Simona Izzo – Ricky Tognazzi's partner – served up **Maniaci sentimentali**, a talkative film about love. Actor Giulio Base directed **Lest**, a very original romance in the Lubitsch vein, about a driver and an heiress leisurely visiting some remnants of Mitteleuropa. Spaghetti horror traditions were restored by Michele Soavi's **Dellamorte Dellamore**, comic-strip author Tiziano Sclavi's fable about a private eye exterminating a thousand zombies in a surrealistic cemetery. Mario Martone, following his masterful *Morte di un matematico napoletano* (1992), filmed one of his avantgarde Neopolitan stage shows, **Rasoi**.

A surprise at the Venice Festival, **Portagli i miei saluti-Avanzi di galera**, revealed Gianna Maria Garbelli's many talents. A blonde, sexy graduate from Lee Strasberg's Actors Studio, she wrote, produced, directed, and starred in a steamy dope and jail saga, worthy of the 1950's most extravagant weepies.

The most interesting publications include the memoirs of producer Mario Cecchi Gori, *Una pasta d'uomo* (Mondadori); a posthumous 1944 journal by great comedy craftsman Steno, *Sotto le stelle del '44* (Sellerio); and Monica Vitti's brief autobiography, *Sette sottane* (Sperling & Kupfer). The prolific Gremese Editore printed *Dizionario del cinema italiano, I registi*, a database of 1,300 Italian directors, plus a well-illustrated monograph on *Bernardo Bertolucci*. Historian Gian Piero Brunetta revised and updated his essential *Storia del cinema italiano* (Editori Riuniti). The fascinating pictorial roots of Italian movies were tracked down by Roberto Campari's *Il fantasma del bello* (Marsilio Editori). Luchino Visconti came back into fashion, thanks to a welcome restorationn of *La terra trema* (1948) – with a companion catalogue edited by Lino Miccichè for Centro Sperimentale di Cinematografia – and to his rediscovered 1930's novel, *Angelo*.

LORENZO CODELLI has written for many books and periodicals, including *Positif*. He is a member of the board of the Pordenone Silent Film Festival, and of the Trieste Cappella Underground film society.

L'AMICO D'INFANZIA (Childhood Friend)

Script and Direction: Pupi Avati. Photography: Cesare Bastelli. Music: Stefano Caprioli. Editing: Amedeo Salfa. Production Designer: Thomas Beall. Players: Jason Robards III, Amy Galper, Lee R. Sellars, Richard Grubbs, Jim Mullins, Joe Ryan, Robert Swan, Jim Ortlieb. Produced by Antonio Avati and Aurelio De Laurentiis for Duea Film, Filmauro. 100 mins.

An acclaimed Chicago anchorman is getting threatening calls from a stranger. On the track of the mysterious killer, he digs up some misdeeds from his past. Unpredictable, bloody twists, and an atmosphere of decadence, distinguished *L'amico d'infanzia* from Pupi Avati's recent, more spiritual works. He seems to be gazing back at his early Po Valley metaphysical horrors.

Shooting on location all around Chicago, Avati blends à la Aldrich an angry denunciation of the power of television and a reappraisal of noir conventions – including an icy editing style. From Jason Robards

Pupi Avati (left) directing Jason Robards III in L'AMICO D'INFANZIA

III, a lookalike of his father, ambiguous and perverted, to all minor freaks of the cast, this slice of life in a "naked city" is alive with villains.

This, the fourth Avati brothers' picture made from their Davenport, Iowa, permanent base since 1990, was produced in English back-to-back with Fabrizio Laurenti's *La stanza accanto*, soon followed by Avati's autobiographical instalment, *Dichiarazioni d'amore*, filmed in Bologna – both yet to be released. Who is busier than Pupi?

Lorenzo Codelli

CARO DIARIO (Dear Diary)

Script and Direction: Nanni Moretti. Photography: Giuseppe Lanci. Music: Nicola Piovani. Editing: Mirco Garrone. Production Design: Marta Maffucci. Players: Nanni Moretti, Renato Carpentieri, Jennifer Beals, Renato Neiwiller, Conchita Airoldi, Valerio Magrelli, Raffaella Lebboroni, Marco Paolini, Giulio Base. Produced by Nanni Moretti, Angelo Barbagallo, Nella Banfi for Sacher Film, Raiuno (Rome)/Banfilm, La Sept Cinéma, Studio Canal Plus (Paris). 96 mins.

Three extracts from an extremely intimate diary, handwritten by Nanni Moretti. In the first one, *In Vespa*, the film-maker – no longer hidden beneath fictional pseudonym – confesses his greatest pleasure: biking alone on his Vespa through the empty avenues of Rome. A white helmet on his head, favourite songs on the soundtrack, he wanders and wanders, from old downtown to the newest developments, while the camera follows him in an endless, forward perspective that Kubrick would enjoy. A few casual meetings, funny or embarrassing, pepper the fugitive's perpetual quest. At the end of what could be defined as the greatest, most lyrical "documentary" on Capet Mundi, he goes biking towards a dirty Ostia beach where Pier Paolo Pasolini was murdered. Keith Jarrett's *The Köln Concert* on the soundtrack makes this abrupt, understated trip incredibly moving.

In the second chapter, *Isole (Islands)* – echoing some of Moretti's former satires – he sails around various Sicilian small islands to meet an old friend. This pure philosopher who rejects civilisation will, in a matter of days, become a TV addict. In the third chapter, *Medici (Doctors)*, Nanni exposes, prescription by prescription, the long, useless cures from mindless doctors he underwent before discovering he was really suffering from cancer. The rushed operation was successful; so Nanni, looking wide-eyed at the camera, invites the audience to follow his example and drink a prophylactic glass of water every morning, right before coffee. Notwithstanding a happy epilogue, and numerous ironic punches, Moretti's final experience leaves us devastated, but hopeful of a better beginning. Utopia after Hell, after all.

Lorenzo Codelli

Nanni Moretti in his CARO DIARIO

Recent Films

ANNI 90 PARTE II (The Nineties, Part II)

Script and Dir: Enrico Oldoini. Phot: Giuseppe Ruzzolini. Players: Massimo Boldi, Nino Frassica, Andrea Roncato, Christian De Sica. Prod: Filmauro. *Farce.*

L'ARTICOLO 2 (Article 2)

Script and Dir: Maurizio Zaccaro. Phot: Pasquale Rachini. Players: Mohamed Miftah, Rabia Ben Abdallah, Susanna Marcomeni. Prod: Bambù Cinema e TV, Produzione SI. RE. *Drama.*

BARNABO DELLE MONTAGNE (Barnabo from the Mountains)

Script: Angelo Pasquini, Mario Brenta from Dino Buzzati's novel. Dir: Mario Brenta. Phot: Vincenzo Marano. Players: Marco Pauletti, Duilio Fontana, Alessandra Milan. Prod: Nautilus Film, Raiuno, Istituto Luce, Direzione Generale dello Spettacolo (Rome) – Les Films Number One, Flach Film (Paris) – T & C Film AG, SSR/TSI, Ufficio Federale della Cultura (Switzerland). *Drama.*

LE BUTTANE (The Whores)

Script: Aurelio Grimaldi from his novel. Dir: Aurelio Grimaldi. Phot (b & w): Maurizio Calvesi. Players: Ida Di Benedetto, Guia Jelo, Lucia Sardo. Prod: Trio Cinema e TV. *Drama.*

CARI FOTTUTISSIMI AMICI (Dear Fucked Friends)

Script: Suso Cecchi d'Amico, Mario Monicelli, Leo Benvenuti, Piero De Bernardi from Rodolfo Angelico's story. Dir: Mario Monicelli. Phot: Antonio Nardi. Players: Paolo Villaggio, Massimo Ceccherini, Antonella Ponziani, Vittorio Benedetti. Prod: Penta Film, Officina Cinematografica. *Comedy.*

CONDANNATO A NOZZE (Condemned to Marry)

Script: Giuseppe Piccioni, Franco Bernini, Fabrizio Bettelli. Dir: Giuseppe Piccioni. Phot: Roberto Meddi. Players: Sergio Rubini, Margherita Buy, Valeria Bruni Tedeschi. Prod: Penta Film, Esterno Mediterraneo Film. *Comedy.*

DELLAMORTE DELLAMORE

Script: Gianni Romoli from Tiziano Sclavi's novel. Dir: Michele Soavi. Phot: Mauro Marchetti. Players: Rupert Everett, Anna Falchi. Prod: Audifilm, Urania Film, Kgp, Bibo Film, Reteitalia. *Horror.*

DOVE SIETE? IO SONO QUI (Where Are You? I Am Here)

Script: Liliana Cavani, Italo Moscati. Dir: Liliana Cavani. Phot: Armando Nannuzzi. Players: Chiara Caselli, Gaetano Carotenuto, Anna Bonaiuto. Prod: San Francisco Film, Raiuno, Sacis. *Drama.*

FANTOZZI IN PARADISO (Fantozzi in Heaven)

Script: Leo Benvenuti, Piero De Bernardi, Alessandro Bencivenni, Domenico Saverni, Paolo Villaggio, Neri Parenti. Dir: Neri Parenti. Phot: Alessandro D'Eva. Players: Paolo Villaggio, Milena Vukotic, Gigi Reder. Prod: Cecchi Gori Group Tiger Cinematografica, Maura International Film. *Farce.*

GIOVANNI FALCONE

Script: Armednia Balducci, Giuseppe Ferrara. Dir: Giuseppe Ferrara. Phot: Claudio Cirillo. Players: Michele Placido, Anna Bonaiuto, Massimo Bonetti. Prod: Clemi Cinematografica. *Drama.*

IL GIUDICE RAGAZZINO (The Boy-Judge)

Script: Andrea Purgatori, Ugo Pirro, Alessandro di Robilant from Nando Dalla Chiesa's book. Dir: Alessandro di Robilant. Phot: David Scott. Players: Giulio Scarpati, Sabrina Ferrilli, Leopoldo Trieste. *Drama.*

LEST (The East)

Script and Dir: Giulio Base. Phot: Dante Della Torre. Players: Giulio Base, Valentina Emeri, Gianmarco Tognazzi. Prod: Claudio Bonivento Production. *Comedy.*

MANIACI SENTIMENTALI (Sentimental Maniacs)

Script: Simona Izzo, Graziano Diana, Giuseppe Manfridi. Dir: Simona Izzo. Phot: Alessio Gelsini Torresi. Players: Ricky Tognazzi, Barbara De Rossi, Alessandro Benvenuti. Prod: Dir International Film, Union P.N. *Comedy.*

MILLE BOLLE BLU (Thousand Blue Bubbles)

Script: Filippo Pichi, Leone Pompucci, Paolo Rossi. Dir: Leone Pompucci. Phot: Massimo Pau. Players: Stefano Masciarelli, Paolo Bonacelli, Stefania Montorsi. Prod: Sorpasso Film. *Comedy.*

I MITICI – COLPO GOBBO A MILANO (The Mythical Ones – The Big Milan Robbery)

Script: Enrico Vanzina, Carlo Vanzina. Dir: Carlo Vanzina. Phot: Luigi Kuveiller. Players: Claudio Amendola, Monica Bellucci, Ricky Memphis. Prod: Video 80, Dean Film. *Comedy.*

NESTORE – L'ULTIMA CORSA (Nestor – The Last Ride)

Script: Rodolfo Sonego, Alberto

Still from LE BUTTANE, directed by Aurelio Grimaldi

Sordi. Dir: Alberto Sordi. Phot: Armando Nannuzzi. Players: Alberto Sordi, Matteo Ripaldi, Cinzia Cannorozzo. Prod: Aurelia Cinematografica, Silvio Berlusconi Communications – Florida Movies (Paris). *Comedy.*

PADRE E FIGLIO (Father and Son)

Script: Pasquale Pozzessere, Roberto Tiraboschi. Dir: Pasquale Pozzessere. Phot: Bruno Cascio. Players: Michele Placido, Stefano Dionisi, Enrica Origo. Prod: Angelo Rizzoli for Erre Cinematografica, Reteitalia – Flach Film (Paris). *Drama.*

PER AMORE SOLO PER AMORE (For Love, Only for Love)

Script: Ugo Chiti. Giovanni Veronesi from Pasquale Festa Campanile's novel. Phot: Giuseppe Ruzzolini. Players: Diego Abatanuono, Penelope Cruz, Alessandro Haber. Prod: Filmauro. *Drama.*

PERDIAMOCI DI VISTA (Let's Lose Sight of Each Other)

Script: Carlo Verdone, Francesca Marciano. Dir: Carlo Verdone. Phot: Danilo Desideri. Players: Carlo Verdone, Asia Argento, Aldo Maccione. Prod: Cecchi Gori Group Tiger Cinematografica, Penta Film. *Comedy.*

PICCOLO GRANDE AMORE (Little Big Love)

Script: Enrico Vanzina, Cesare Frugoni, Carlo Vanzina. Dir: Carlo Vanzina. Phot: Luigi Kuveiller. Players: Barbara Snellenburg, Raoul Bova, Susannah York. Prod: Video 80, Reteitalia. *Romance.*

PORTAGLI I MIEI SALUTI – AVANZI DI GALERA (Give Him My Kind Regards – Jailbirds)

Script and Dir: Gianna Maria Garbelli. Phot: Blasco Giurato. Players: Gianna Maria Garbelli, Annie Girardot, Stéphane Ferrara. Prod: M Film Produzioni, Ministero Turismo e Spettacolo. *Drama.*

LA PROSSIMA VOLTA IL FUOCO (Next Time the Fire)

Script: Fabio Carpi, Luigi Malerba. Dir: Fabio Carpi. Phot: Renato Berta. Players: Jean Rochefort, Marie Christine Barrault, Lila Kedrova. Prod: Gam Film, Ministero Turismo e Spettacolo, Italnoleggio Cinematografico – Erato Film (Paris) – Frama Film International (Switzerland). *Drama.*

UNA PURA FORMALITA' (A Simple Formality)

Script and Dir: Giuseppe Tornatore. Phot: Blasco Giurato. Players: Gérard Depardieu, Roman Polanski, Sergio Rubini. Prod: Cecchi Gori Group Tiger Cinematografica (Rome) – Film Par Film (Paris). *Drama.*

RASOI (Razors)

Script: Mario Martone, Tony

Servillo from Enzo Moscato's play. Phot: Pasquale Mari. Players: Gino Curcione, Isacco Esposito, Iaia Forte. Prod: Teatri Uniti. *Drama*.

LA RIBELLE (The Rebel)

Script and Dir: Aurelio Grimaldi. Phot: Maurizio Calvesi. Players: Penelope Cruz, Stefano Dionisi, Laura Betti. Prod: Taodue Film, Banda Magnetica, Reteitalia. *Drama*.

IL SEGRETO DEL BOSCO VECCHIO (The Secret of the Old Wood)

Script: Ermanno Olmi from Dino Buzzati's novel. Dir: Ermanno Olmi. Phot: Dante Spinotti. Players: Paolo Villaggio, Omero Antonutti, Giulio Brogi, Riccardo Zannantonio. Prod: Penta Film, Aura Film. *Drama*.

SENZA PELLE (No Skin)

Script and Dir: Alessandro D'Alatri. Phot: Claudio Collepiccolo. Players: Anna Galiena, Massimo Ghini, Kim Rossi Stuart. Prod: Rodeo Drive. *Drama*.

IL SILENZIO DEI PROSCIUTTI (The Silence of the Hams)

Script and Dir: Ezio Greggio. Phot: Jacques Haytkin. Players: Ezio Greggio, Dom Deluise, Joanna Pacula. Prod: Thirtieth Century Wolf Ltd. *Farce*.

IL SOGNO DELLA FARFALLA (The Butterfly's Dream)

Script: Massimo Fagioli. Dir: Marco Bellocchio. Phot: Yorgos Arvanitis. Players: Thierry Blanc, Simona Cavallari, Bibi Andersson. Prod: Filmalbatros, Raidue, Istituto Luce (Rome) – Pierre Grise Productions (Paris) – Waka Films, SSR/TSI, Ufficio Federale della Cultura (Switzerland) – Happy Valley Films (England).

STORIA DI UNA CAPINERA (Story of a Blackcap)

Script: Allan Baker, Franco Zeffirelli from Giovanni Verga's novel. Dir: Franco Zeffirelli. Phot: Ennio Guarnieri. Players: Angela Bettis, Jonathan Schaech, Sinead Cusack. Prod: Tiger Cinematografica, Officina Cinematografica, Penta Film. *Drama*.

SUD (South)

Script: Franco Bernini, Angelo Pasquini, Gabriele Salvatores. Dir: Gabriele Salvatores. Phot: Italo Petriccione. Players: Silvio Orlando, Francesca Neri, Antonio Catania. Prod: Colorado Film, Penta Film. *Drama*.

TROPPO SOLE (Too Much Sun)

Script: Giuseppe Bertolucci, Sabina Guzzanti, David Riondino. Dir: Giuseppe Bertolucci. Phot: Fabio Cianchetti. Player: Sabina Guzzanti. Prod: La Banda Magnetica, Navert Film, Reteitalia. *Comedy*.

IL TUFFO (The Dive)

Script: Roberto De Francesco, Massimo Martella, Maurizio Fiume. Dir: Massimo Martella. Phot: Paolo Ferrari. Players: Carlotta Natoli, Vincenzo Salemme, Arturo Paglia. Prod: River Film, Centro Sperimentale di Cinematografia. *Drama*.

L'UOMO CHE GUARDA (The Man Who Watches)

Script: Tinto Brass from Alberto Moravia's novel. Dir: Tinto Bras. Phot: Massimo Di Venanzo. Players: Katerina Vassilissa, Cristina Garavaglia, Francesco Casale. Prod: Angelo Rizzoli for Erre Cinematografica, Rodeo Drive. *Drama*.

Useful Addresses

Agis
Via di Villa Patrizi, 10
00161 Roma
Tel: 884731
Fax: 8848079

Anica
Viale Regina Margherita, 286
00198 Roma
Tel: 8841272
Fax: 8848789

Banca Nazionale del Lavoro
Piazza San Bernardo, 101
00100 Roma
Tel: 47021
Fax: 47025179

Carol Levy Company
Via G. Carducci, 10
00100 Roma
Tel: 486961

Cinecittà
Via Tuscolana, 1055
00173 Roma
Tel: 74641, 722931
Fax: 7222155

Cecchi Gori Group
Via B. Oriani 91
00197 Roma
Tel: 8088861
Fax: 8088378

Cinema 5
Via Aurelia Antica, 422
00100 Roma
Tel: 663901

Ente Gestione Cinema
Via Tuscolana, 1055
00173 Roma
Tel: 722221/722861
Fax: 7221883

RCS
Via Mecente 91
20138 Milano
Tel: 580811
Fax: 58011890

Film Export Group
Via Polonia, 9
00198 Roma
Tel: 8554266, 8444187
Fax: 8550248

Fininvest
Largo del Nazareno, 3/8
00100 Roma
Tel: 25141
Fax: 67386044

TOP TEN GROSSING FILMS IN ITALY: 1993/94

Jurassic Park
Aladdin
Mrs. Doubtfire
The Fugitive
Schindler's List
The Son of the Pink Panther
Philadelphia
Little Buddha
A Perfect World
The Firm
(Source: Gionale dello Spettacolo)

Filmauro
Via della Vasca Navale, 58
00146 Roma
Tel: 5577611/5560788
Fax: 5590670

International Recording
Via Urbana, 172
00184 Roma
Tel: 4821066, 4819006, 4827970
Fax: 4745246

Istituto Luce
Via Tuscolana, 1055
00173 Roma
Tel: 722931
Fax: 7222090

Loeb and Loeb
Piazza Digione, 1
00197 Roma
Tel: 874557

MGM Pathe Studio
Via Pontina KM 23
00100 Roma
Tel: 5050242

Penta Film
Via Aurelia Antica, 422
00165 Roma
Tel: 66390
Fax: 66390

Direzione Generale dello Spettacolo
Via della Ferratella in
Laterano, 45-51
00184 Roma
Tel: 7732

Rai – Radiotelevisione Italiana
Viale Mazzini, 14
00195 Roma
Tel: 38718

Sacis
Via Teulada 28
00195 Roma
Tel: 374981
Fax: 3723492

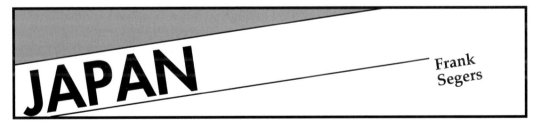

JAPAN — Frank Segers

The events of the last year in this lucrative market – the second largest in the world for American films – generally confirm the cautious assessment that Japan is slowly pulling out of a painful and surprisingly long-lasting recession. General business confidence is improving for the first time in five years, a view that is beginning to permeate the cinema industry. While no one is standing up and cheering, a slight ray of optimism is tempering the dark pronouncements issued by film business figures.

In his annual "Film Day" address last December, Toho topper Isao Matsuoka declared 1993 a period of "violent concussion". He noted that Japan's fundamental economic, political and international changes left "no possibility that the film industry could remain stable". Matsuoka, a hard-nosed businessman who hails from Osaka, Japan's commercial-industrial capital, also took a swipe at a proposed government consumption tax to be tacked onto Japan's theatre admission fees, already the highest in the world.

It cost on average 1,252 yen per person to catch the evening show in a Japanese hardtop (that's nearly $US13 a pop at the exchange rate of 98 yen to each U.S. dollar). Box-office admission prices rose sharply over the last five years as attendances and Japan's number of theatres fell. Matsuoka and others put much of the blame for the latter on the former. While admission prices continued to climb in 1993, three other key statistics happily kept pace.

For the first time since 1990, theatrical admissions increased from the year before. Ditto for total box-office. Overall revenues from theatrical distribution (film rentals) jumped 16% over 1992's total. And perhaps most important of all, the depressing decline of the number of screens in Japan – about 2,200 ten years ago, 1,744 in 1992 – appears to have abated. Toho's Matsuoka notes that 1993 experienced a net loss of 10 screens, as opposed to the year before, which saw nearly ten times that number shutter. In 1993, 78 theatres closed but 68, including video theatres and drive-ins, opened. Matsuoka's point: increase in total

theatrical earnings is inducing the creation of new screens.

American Lock on Market

Not mentioned is that 1993's upbeat results stem from the lock American films exert on this market. For the first time ever, the American majors (UIP, Warners, Disney, Col-TriStar and Fox) earned more in theatrical revenues than did the three big Japanese majors (Toho, Toei and Shochiku). Since the latter are powerhouse exhibitors as well as producer-distributors, the moans from the Japanese side were muffled. But the fact that 1993 film rentals for the American majors totalled 35.6 billion yen – rising 62.3% from 1992 – while at the same time the Japanese majors earned rentals of 23.8 billion yen – down 10% from 1992 – cast suspicion on the "business is bad because of the recession" plaint.

The Americans dominated the top 10 chart with *Jurassic Park, The Bodyguard, Aladdin* and *Home Alone 2*, among other titles. The best the Japanese side could offer was Shochiku's distribution of producer Haruki Kadokawa's *Rex: Kyoryu Monogatari*, a cleverly-packaged dinosaur-themed fluff designed to cash in on the subject matter of the Steven Spielberg blockbuster. Ironically, given its box-office appeal, *Rex* might be producer Kadokawa's last hurrah, at least for a while. Japan's most successful independent producer ran foul of authorities on several drug-related charges in 1993, and has all but vanished from the Japan film world.

Popular Japanese cinema in 1993 can be summarised by reptiles (**Godzilla** and **Rex**), animation and **Tora-san**. The latter is the seemingly never-ending series of films from director Yoji Yamada and Shochiku about Japan's most famous itinerant peddler, Mr. Tora, portrayed with relish by actor Kyoshi Atsumi. The 45th in the series made the Top Ten list in 1993, indicating that critic Ian Buruma is correct in observing that filmgoers regard Mr. Tora's world with great nostalgia, a simpler, much-desired Japan that is no more.

Yamada, Shochiku's blue-ribbon director, also came up with **School** (*Gakko*), a gentle reminiscence of life in a rural secondary school, and walked away from the 17th Japan Academy Awards with no less than six citations including ones for best picture, best director and best screenplay. The "best film" award was the versatile Yamada's third from the Academy, Japan's rough equivalent of the U.S. Oscars, following *Sons* (1992) and *The Yellow Handkerchief* (1978). Yamada at the end of 1993 was engaged in making the 46th sequel in the Tora-san series, dedicating the film to the venerable Chishu Ryu, who died in 1993. Born in 1906, and a mainstay of director Yasujiro Ozu's films (*The Flavour of Green Tea Over Rice* and *Tokyo Story*), Ryu was the son of a Buddhist priest, and indeed portrayed a Buddhist priest in the first 45 Tora-san films.

Film Figure of Consequence

One of Japan's most energetic figures, Takeshi "Beat" Kitano (known as "Beat" Takeshi), emerged during the year as a film figure of consequence. The ubiquitous Takeshi (he is all over Japanese television in everything from game and quiz shows to sports commentary, even beer commercials) is probably best known for his role as the tough Japanese sergeant in Nagisa Oshima's Second World War POW drama, *Merry Christmas, Mr. Lawrence*. Takeshi is rapidly establishing himself as an auteur, a director-writer-lead actor to be taken seriously. His **Sonatine**, a bristling melodrama about a hit man who himself is set up to be killed, while not a smash hit, was received respectfully by critics in Japan and abroad.

The dominance of American films in the market, along with the effects of the recession, had several curious effects on key Japanese importers. Ascii Pictures, part of the computer conglomerate, all but bowed entirely out of foreign film distribution. Toho-Towa, the premier importer, expressed fears of the American majors shutting out independent local distributors altogether. Harumasa Shirasu, Toho-Towa president, voiced concern that the majors

Still from Kazuyoshi Okuyama's RAMPO, produced for Shochiku

are keen on buying worldwide rights to big-budget, independently-made features. With the American company's financial power, indies such as Toho-Towa would have rough sledding competing for big pictures for Japan playoff. Nonetheless, Toho-Towa had success distributing Carolco's *Cliffhanger* – pushing the Japanese company into substantial profit – and in 1994, is racking up healthy returns from Morgan Creek's *Major League II*.

Nippon Herald Films, another of Japan's stronger importer-distributors, started off 1993 aggressively then took a low profile stance for the rest of the year. It shelled out a considerable sum to import and promote the video-game-inspired *Super Mario Bros.*, which failed to achieve the company's expectations. Perhaps most interestingly, Nippon Herald's twelve-year-old art and classic films wing, Herald Ace, announced a renewed push for producing and distributing Japanese titles. The company is linking with several independent producers, among them Algo Pictures, and working on several projects: director Takeshi Ishii's *Nights of the Nude*, Junji Sakamoto's *Tokalev*, and *The Friends*, from one of Japan's best regarded younger helmers, Shinji Somai.

Kuzui Enterprises, a scrappy independent producer-distributor (run by husband-wife team, Kaz and Fran Rubel Kuzui) upped its operations a notch by joining Nissho Iwai, a leading trading house, and Sogei, a big ad agency, in a partnership designed to snare Japan rights to major European and U.S. titles. Separately, Fran Rubel Kuzui is carving out for herself a career as a director bringing an American perspective to Japanese subjects, as in the American-girl-falls-for-Japanese-boy story, *Tokyo Pop* (1988). The remaining half of the erstwhile husband-wife team of Kazuko and Hayao Shibata of France Eiga Sha distributed Sally Potter's *Orlando* to solid results.

Much-loved Personalities Pass Away

Hayao Shibata's late wife, Kuzuko Kawakita-Shibata, the daughter of the founder of Toho-Towa, died last June, and was commemorated by her husband via a series of Tokyo screenings of her favourite foreign films from a wide range of directors. Kawakita-Shibata's 85-year-old mother, Madame Kashiko Kawakita, also died in 1993, shortly after the sudden death of her 53-year-old daughter. Both were memorialised at the 1994 Cannes Film Festival – Cannes through the years was a regular stop for mother and daughter – with a special "homage" screening of Jean Renoir's *Rules of the Game*. It was the first time such a "homage" was held in honour of a film distributor. A memorial series of screenings of Japanese films was also held just before the Cannes Festival at the Cinémathèque Française in Paris.

The 1993 Tokyo International Film Festival was considered a popular success – more than 150,000 admissions (up 25% from the 1992 turnout) were recorded the sixth edition, Sept. 24-Oct. 3, concurrent with the Tokyo Film Market. For the first time, spectators lined the streets of Tokyo's Shikuya section the night before the screening of Hongkong director Joe Chan's *92 Legendary La Rose Noire*, the hit of the Best Asian Film section.

Although it may sound oxymoronic, the 1994 Tokyo International Film Festival was held (Sept. 24-Oct. 2) in Kyoto, Japan's old capital city about two hours south (by speedtrain) from Tokyo. The event is part of the 1,200th anniversary celebration of Kyoto. Perhaps the shift in locales is a convenient way to draw from local prefectural officials new funding for a festival that has been hard hit by drop-offs in corporate sponsorship due to Japan's stubborn economic recession. In 1995, however, the Tokyo Festival will return to home base. The 1994 edition of the Tokyo Film Festival Market, meanwhile, remained in Tokyo.

Continued Internal Changes

The big majors are engaged in some aesthetic transformation and continued internal change. Toei, renowned for a generation of action-packed gangster or "yakuza" films, surprised the local industry with the announcement that *The Man Who Killed a Don* (1994) will be the company's last of the genre. For some 30 years, Toei has ground out yakuza titles such as *Abashiri Bangaichi*, *Jinginaki Tatakai* and *Hibotan Bakuto* creating stars (Ken Takakura, among others) and making healthy profits. The profits have diminished over time, if not disappeared. Three genre titles in 1993 bombed, prompting Toei to wash its hands of yakuza films, or at least one variety of them. Since a female yakuza series from the company, *Cokudono Onnatachi* starring Shima Iwashita, continues to make money, it will carry on, said Toei.

Meanwhile, Kazuyoshi Okuyama, son of Shochiku chairman Toru Okuyama, created a stir in 1994 with the production of **Rampo**, a romantic drama about the life, loves and books of Edogawa Rampo, a popular turn-of-the-century mystery writer considered the Japanese Edgar Allan Poe. The film is largely fantasy about the writer's new novel in which a woman is accused of murdering her husband by suffocation – replaying itself in reality with the writer becoming involved with the wife. The film was screened by Shochiku at the last Cannes Festival to raves from the critics, and bowed in in Japan in June to strong public response.

So far, so good. The background of *Rampo* is more complicated. The original version of the film was directed by Rentaro Mayuzumi, who has helmed TV films for

TOP TEN GROSSING FILMS IN JAPAN: 1993

	Film Rental (millions of yen)
Jurassic Park	8,400
The Bodyguard	4,100
Aladdin	2,600
Home Alone 2	2,500
Rex: Kyoryku Monogatari	2,300
Godzilla vs. Mothra	2,250
The Fugitive	2,200
Samurai Kids	2,050
Doraemon	1,650
Indecent Proposal	1,500

NHK, Japan's public broadcaster. Kazuyoshi Okuyama was the producer. However, he was deeply dissatisfied with Mayuzumi's handling of the subject matter. Following a carefully worked out compromise, Okuyama, a veteran producer of 17 titles but a novice director, took over, reshooting about 80% of the picture using the same leading actors. To appease Mayuzumi (and, by extension, NHK), Okuyama prevailed upon Shochiku to release both versions of *Rampo*. The version seen at Cannes as well as the version playing to strong box-office in Japan's is Okuyama's. In all, a peculiarly Japanese solution to the age-old "creative differences" problem.

Takeo Endo, a savvy Shochiku executive who was formerly general manager of the company's international department, has been appointed secretary-general of UniJapan Film, formerly known as the Association for The Diffusion of Japanese Films Abroad. Endo succeeds Toyoji Kuroda, who held the secretary-general post for 38 years. UniJapan is now planning a 1995 retrospective of films from Shochiku directors to mark the 100th anniversary of the birth of the late Shiro Kido, former Shochiku chairman and seminal figure in the world of Japanese cinema, who hired a host of Shochiku signature directors – including Yasujiro Ozu, Keisuke Kinoshita and Yoji Yamada. The "Shiro Kido Retrospective" will tour film libraries and institutes throughout Europe.

FRANK SEGERS writes for *Variety* and specialises in Far Eastern entertainment issues.

Statistics
Figures for the period, January-December 1993, with previous year's figures in brackets.

Number of cinemas
total	1,734	(1,744)
for domestic films only	530	(560)
for foreign films exclusively	682	(697)
for both categories	552	(487)

Included in the total are 20 drive-in theatres (5 more than in 1992) and 62 (14 more than in 1992) video theatres, small (generally 100-seat) venues playing films and other programming transferred to videotape.

Number of films distributed
total	590	(617)
domestic films	238	(240)
foreign films	352	(377)

Box-office
annual attendance	130,720,000	(125,600,000)
gross theatre receipts (million yen)	163,700	(152,000)
average admission fee (yen without tax)	1,252	(1,210)

Useful Addresses

Assn. for the Diffusion of Japanese Films Abroad
(UniJapan Film)
Ginza 5-9-13
Tokyo

Cine Saison
Asako Kyobashi Bldg. 2F
6-13 Kyobashi, 1-Chome
Chuo-ku
Tokyo

Comstock Ltd.
Akasaka Omotemachi Bldg.
4-18-19 Akasaka
Minato-ku
Tokyo

Daiei Co., Ltd.
1-18-21 Shimbashi
Minato-ku
Tokyo

Dela Corp.
Razan Bldg. 813
7-15-13 Roppongi
Minato-ku
Tokyo

Gaga Communications
East Roppongi Bldg.
3-16-35 Roppongi
Minato-ku
Tokyo

Humax Pictures
13-19 Tomihisa-cho
Shinkuju-ku
Tokyo

Kuzui Enterprises
Jingumae-Otowa Heights 201
5-50-3 Jingumae
Shibuya-ku
Tokyo

Japan Cinema Associates
LSP Hanzomon 513
1-5-4 Kojimachi
Chiyoda-ku
Tokyo

Japan Audio Visual Network
Wako 32 Bldg.
2-11-10 Tsukiji
Chuo-ku
Tokyo

**Japan Satellite Broadcasting
WOWOW**
4th Floor
Sumitomo-Irifune Bldg.
2-1-1 Irifune
Chuo-ku
Tokyo 104

Media International Corp.
2-14-5 Akasaka
Minato-ku
Tokyo

Mitsubishi Corp.
6-3 Marunouchi
2-Chome
Chiyoda-ku
Tokyo

New Century Producers Co
Kyodo Bldg. 313
4-3-1 Akasaka
Minato-ku
Tokyo

New Select Co.
Nakamura Bldg.
5-9-13 Ginza
Chuo-ku
Tokyo

**Nippon Film Development and
Finance, Inc.**
1-22-3-2503 Nishi-Waseda
Shinjyuku-ku
Tokyo 169 Japan

Nippon Herald Films
11-1, 5-Chome
Ginza
Chuo-ku
Tokyo 104 Japan

Pioniwa Film Co.
(Tokyo Pioneer Film)
3-1-3 Kyobashi
Chuo-ku
Tokyo

Shibata Organisation
(France Eigasha)
2-10-8 Ginza
Chuo-ku
Tokyo

Shochiku Co.
13-5 Tsukiji 1-chome
Chuo-ku
Tokyo

Shochiku-Fuji Co.
13-5 Tsukiji, 1-chome

Chuo-ku
Tokyo

Toei Co.
2-17. 3-chome
Ginza
Chuo-ku
Tokyo

Toei Astro Inc.
2-17, 3-chome
Ginza
Chuo-ku
Tokyo

Toho International Co.
Hibiya Park Bldg.
8-1 Yurakucho, 1-chome
Chiyoda-ku
Tokyo

Toho-Towa Co.
6-4 Ginza
2-chome
Chuo-ku
Tokyo

Tohokushinsha Film Co.
17-7 Akasake, 4-chome
Minato-ku
Tokyo

SOUTH KOREA — Frank Segers

A curious paradox emerged in South Korean cinema in 1993, the culmination of commercial and artistic trends established years earlier. While the confluence of artistic and box-office success was happily a more than occasional occurrence, the prevailing mood among business practitioners was doom and gloom.

The growing strength of foreign films in South Korea, particularly those from the ever-more-firmly entrenched American majors, had both literally and figuratively a depressing effect on the local industry. This market, the second largest in Asia, is awash in foreign product. There were 341 foreign films released in South Korea in 1993, more than five times the number of domestic films (65).

The number of Korean features produced in 1993 dropped yet again, to about 70 titles – compared with 96 in 1992 and 109 the year before. More production companies disappeared from the scene. The lower number of features from the pipeline is even threatening the nation's sacrosanct screen quota system. There are simply not enough titles to fill screentimes mandated under the system, set up to assure minimal levels of exhibition of home-grown product.

TOP TEN GROSSING DOMESTIC FILMS IN SOUTH KOREA: 1993

	Attendance
Sopyonje	*1,035,741
The Woman and the Man	217,605
Blue in You	153,184
The Man with Breasts	128,334
Two Cops	90,736
The 101st Proposition	82,913
A Woman for Love and A Woman for Marriage	69,743
Hwaomkyoung	65,403
I Will Survive	40,229
When Adam Is Awakened	31,267

*Broke all existing attendance records for a domestic feature film.
NOTE: 1993 theatrical attendance in South Korea totalled 48,230,788 for a total box-office of 178,971,074,542 Wan (U.S.$223,714,000), according to statistics released by the Korean Motion Picture Corp.

Easier access to the market afforded the American majors – UIP, Twentieth Century Fox, Columbia-TriStar, Warner Bros. and Buena Vista all have direct distribution offices in Seoul – is rolling the domestic industry. Restrictions on the number of prints of imported films have been eased considerably or scuttled entirely. (Only about ten prints per picture was the rule before.) The predictable has occurred. American-made features from the majors are taking increasing shares of the market; the tenth most popular Yank title in 1993, Disney's *Sister Act*, outdrew the second largest earner on the Korean side, Kim Ui-suk's *The Woman and the Man*.

"The state of affairs of the Korean film industry in 1993 was more than just a depression," observed *Korean Cinema*, a trade journal. Its slump was so serious that the industry might have collapsed completely. The industry was in great danger." But despite the apocalyptic tones emanating from the Seoul film world, Korean cinema marked several achievements during the year and worked hard to bolster its position at home and increase visibility abroad.

Adventurous Allegory

The event of the year without question was director Im Kwon-taek's **Sopyonje**, an adventurous, almost experimental allegory for the struggles of the Korean people as well as an illumination of the obscure *pansori*, a genre of traditional Korean folk songs vocalised in gentle and mournful style by common people living in the peninsula's southwest. (It is said to take more than ten years of difficult training to be a master singer of *Sopyonje*.)

Im, by now a familiar name on the international festival circuit, proved he has a Midas touch. *Sopyonje* emerged as the top-grossing Korean film ever, very nearly outdrawing in the market Steven Spielberg's worldwide blockbuster, *Jurassic Park*. That feat is all the more impressive because *Sopyonje* tests its audiences in ways unthinkable for standard popular palliatives. Through a series of flashbacks, it tells of a vagabond musician family in which the father cruelly blinds his adopted daughter so that she can more intensely master the folksinging art. Another scene, demonstrating Chung Il-sing's superb pastoral photography, captures the family descending a hill singing "Jin-do Arirang", a *Sopyonje* song in its entirety. The long take lasts nearly 5¼ minutes.

Korean audiences were often moved to tears by Im's exploration of the nation's rural past, and repeat business was strong, propelling *Sopyonje* past one million admissions. The 58-year-old Im, with more than 80 films to his credit, is now established as Korea's pre-eminent director, as important to the domestic film world as Fellini, Kurosawa, and Bergman were to theirs. He is currently working on a longstanding project, *Taeback Mountains*, based on Cho Chong-rae's bestselling novel about the North-South division of the peninsula. Im's film is said to be big-budget, by local standards, involving mob scenes charging across huge sets. It is expected to be, typically given its director, controversial.

More Cause for Celebration

Another cause for celebration is Yoon Sam-Yook's costume period drama, **I Will Survive**, set in Korea's feudal period and dealing with a romance between a slave-butcher and a nobleman's daughter. Portraying the commoner is Lee Duk-hwa, who for his efforts won the Best Actor award at Moscow International Film Festival held last year. The trade here regards costume dramas like parts of the West regard satire – something that closes on Saturday night. Nonetheless, *I Will Survive* proved to be the seventh most popular film in Korea last year.

Anyone who has been paying attention to the festival world knows that Korean cinema is increasingly being recognised at prize-awarding time. *Sopyonje* won Im a best director citation at the 1993 Shanghai International Film Festival. Chang Sun-woo's *Hwaom kyung* came away from the last Berlin Film Festival with the Alfred Bauer Prize. Baek Il-seong's *In the Handful of Time* ran off with the Grand Prix at the 1993 Salerno International Film Festival.

For its part, the government's Motion Picture Promotion Corp. is strenuously pursuing foreign exhibition of Korean features both for the usual "cultural exchange" purposes as well as to create new markets abroad. Last year's Pesaro Film Festival screened some 30 Korean titles in a sidebar section. Perhaps the biggest coup was the October 1993-February 1994 unspooling of more than 85 titles, spanning Korea's seventy-year film history, at the Georges Pompidou Centre in Paris. The Promotion Corporation intends to mount similar exhibitions in London, New York, Sydney and Beijing. Chicago's adventurous Film Centre at the School of the Art Institute mounted under the rubric "A Korean Film Renaissance" a six-film series in July exposing the works of such directors as Im and Lee Do-yong to popular audiences in the American midwest.

Back in Seoul the central government, which took control last year, is apparently heeding the persistent film trade complaints. Films have been included under a new five-year plan, classifying their production and distribution as a "manufacturing" rather than "service" industry, and thus making production funds more easily obtainable. The Ministry of Culture and Sports is revising the Korean Motion Picture Act in an effort to make domestic product more competitive with foreign films – and therefore more exportable. More concretely, the Motion Picture Promotion Corp. is supervising the construction of the Seoul Cinema Complex and Film Studio, actually located on a 325-acre site Namyangju-gun, Kyonggi-do, an hour's drive from the capital. By the time it opens in 1996, the complex will boast four big sound stages plus an array of ultra-modern post-production facilities. First stage of the construction will be ready late next year, with film-making already underway on an open set unveiled November 17, 1993.

Korean audiences have a preference for erotic melodramas that often tackle sensitive social topics and themes. At the 32nd edition of the Grand Bell Awards – Korea's rough equivalent of the Oscars – 38-year-old director Lee Chong-kuk's **Story of Two Women** walked off with the best film, best director, best screenplay and best cinematographer citations. The story line revolves the alternately joshing and jealous relationship between two women vying for the affections of the same man. *Story* is a departure for the 38-year-old *wunderkind* Lee. His last film, *Song of*

Resurrection (1990) concerns the 1980 Kwangju civil uprising. A whiff of controversy arose at the April Grend Bell ceremonies, sponsored by the Samsung conglomerate, when *The Vanished* was nominated in three key categories. The English-language Korea Times wrote that the nominations "tarnished" the Grend Bell ceremony because the plot of *The Vanished* revolves about the mysterious disappearance of a former intelligence chief under the late president Park Chung-hee, whose regime many Koreans prefer to forget.

FRANK SEGERS is a *Variety* staffer who has long specialised in Asian cinema.

Useful Addresses

Da Moa Films Co. Ltd.
164-7, Nonhyun-dong
Kangnam-gu
Seoul

Dong-A-Exports Co. Ltd
120-1, 1-ga, Changchung-dong
Chung-gu
Seoul

Dong Bo Film Corp.
Bong Wo Bldg., 2nd Floor F
203, 31-7, Changchung-dong
1-ga, Chung-gu
Seoul

Han Jin Enterprises Co. Ltd.
62-15, 3-ga. Pil-dong, Chung-gu
Seoul

Hap Dong Film Co. Ltd.
59-7, Kwansoo-dong, Chongno-gu
Seoul

Hwajin Film Co.
52-111, Chongun-dong
Chongno-gu
Seoul

Hyunjin Film
5th Floor, Chiam Bldg.
73-1, 5-ga, Chungmuro
Chung-gu
Seoul

Jimi Films Co. Ltd.
151-11, Ssanglim-dong
Chung-gu
Seoul

Motion Picture Promotion Corp. of Korea
34-5, 3-Ka, Namsan-Dong
Chung-ku
Seoul

Tae Hung Production Co. Ltd.
16-6, 2-ga, Pildong
Chung-gu
Seoul

LATVIA — Andris Rozenbergs

From the Middle Ages until the Nineteenth Century there stood on the bank of the River Daugava a stream which traverses Riga, a wooden statue of a bulky man with an oar in his right hand and a little girl sitting on his left shoulder. Legend has it that Lielais Kristaps (the Great Christoph) had saved her from the torrent and carried her ashore. Now a copy of this statue is used to award the winner of the national film competition. This year it was conferred for the sixteenth time, but never before have we needed somebody who could bring the Latvian cinema across the whirlpools of the market economy as Lielais Kristaps (the Great Christoph) did the little girl a couple of centuries ago.

It is really remarkable that this time the award was given to a film which was conceived some fifteen years ago by a well-known documentary film-makers, Ansis Epners. **The Cage** is his debut in the genre of fiction film. It conveys the history of his generation in a very personal, non-story-telling, non-fictional way by using a large range of symbols.

Curiously enough, perhaps the most interesting film of the last two years was finished some days after the festival had ended. It is a full-length documentary, **Come Down, Pale Moon** by Ivars Seleckis (the Felix prizewinner, 1989) who tells the tragic stories of people who have regained their land. The land, the soil has never been for a Latvian farmer only a means of agricultural production. For generations of farm labourers it was a cherished dream; they attributed the highest moral and spiritual values to those notions as the cradle of the nation, as to something very essential, basic to every individual. Now these almost eternal values are confronted with the harsh realities of the market economy combined with the confused legislation of an endless transition period and the lack of clear-cut state policies.

Almost the same may be said about the situation in Latvian cinema. The collapse of the party and state-ruled system also put an end to a certain hierarchy of values, habits and stratagems of behaviour. While some were hesitating whom to ask permission to do what they were free to do, others, the former location managers, administrators who had some experience in handling cash, realised that in these times of dawning economic and even moral liberalisation they did not need to hide the nefarious practices they had picked up during previous years. So more than 30 film and video studios were registered as independent enterprises.

Years of painful experience have shown that we are all sitting in this mess. It has also made clear that raising money for new productions by applying to the state or visiting rich people's offices with an outstretched hand, of course, is very important, but might not be the only concern. We discovered with a kind of

astonishment that films don't sell not only in Latvia but also in other small countries, such as the U.K., for instance, and that there is an urgent need to protect our very limited market against expansion of American videos (most of them procurred illegally).

Since October 1993 the Latvian National Film Centre has begun the licensing of film and video distributors in order to avoid piracy. The Latvian National Film Centre is a small state institution modelled after the film foundations of Scandinavian countries and exercises similar functions. The Latvian Producers' Association has also been created and its first important move is to initiate the Law on Cinema covering all issues from funding to the social protection of cinematographers.

So, preparing to celebrate the centenary of the cinema which will commence this September with the international film festival "Arsenals", little by little we arrive at the conclusion, maybe not very consoling for my generation, that none but providence knows whether it will yet be able to conceive works that will amaze the world; but we may, and we must, create a solid and efficient social, legal, and managerial infrastructure where such works might be produced.

ANDRIS ROZENBERGS graduated in 1969 from the State Institute of Cinematography in Moscow. He has made seven fiction films and a dozen documentaries. He is also responsible for the foreign relations of the Latvian National Film Centre.

Recent and Forthcoming Films

SODS PAR SAPNI (Punishment for a Dream)

Script: Inta Geile, Andris Rozenbergs. Dir: Andris Rozenbergs. Phot: Kalvis Zalcmanis. Music: Martin Brauns. Prod: Riga Documentary Film Studio. 52 mins.

Documentary. In 1951 a group of Latvian intellectuals – poets, artists, actors, translators of French literature – were arrested and accused of betraying their motherland only by virtue of their interest in Western culture.

NACLEJA, BALAIS MENES! (Come Down, Pale Moon)

Script: Andris Vanadzins. Dir. and Phot: Ivars Seleckis. Music: Ivars Vigners. Prod: Riga Documentary Film Studio. 90 mins.

Documentary. How does a Latvian peasant feel, having regained his land after fifty years of Soviet rule? What is his legacy from the time of collective farming, and what are his prospects for the future?

DROSME NOGALINAT (Courage to Kill)

Dir: Igors Linga, Aigars Grauba. Players: Armands Reinfelds, Uldis Norenbergs. Prod: From Europe to Hongkong Productions. 90 mins.

First Latvian film in Dolby Stereo!

LITHUANIA — Grazina Arlickaite

The general picture of the new (or young) Lithuanian feature film remains pretty colourless. All attempts to make a new film neglecting the requirements of professionalism, and sometimes inventing an old thing, failed.

It would be naïve to expect the Lithuanian feature film after four years of rebellion (known widely as "perestroika") to have a new face. It will take time to carry out a new change in quality. On the other hand, there are productive as well as creative changes. Film-makers have been looking for new methods of production. There are first films made in co-operation with foreign companies, and the small independent studios try to do their best, too. There is a rather clear division between

Still from AND HE BID YOU FAREWELL
photo: Valius Níkolenka

intellectual films and film for public audience. The following films are the most representative of this kind of cinema: **Three Days** (1991), directed by Šarúnas Bartas, and **And He Bid You Farewell** (1993), by Andrius Šiuša.

For the first time in the history of Lithuanian film-making there have been co-productions with directors from other countries. Film production gradually splits into works for the intellectual elite and those for the masses. All these processes are taking place under the influence of the American movie invasion that has hit Lithuanian cinemas and TV screens. TV programmes devote more time and give more information on Hollywood movies, actors and directors, while the average American film supplants Lithuanian and other European titles in the cinemas.

The choice made by young Lithuanian directors determined their initial success. *Three Days* (1991) by Šarúnas Bartas and *And He Bid You Farewell* (1993) by Andrius Šiuša have won international recognition. *Three Days* was highly appreciated at the Berlin Forum. *And He Bid You Farewell* won the main prize at the Nordic Film Festival in Lübeck. The best Lithuanian films made in the 1960's and 1970's (*Feelings, Nobody Wanted to Die, Herkus Mantas, A Woman and Her Four Men*) were based on "story" structures, but the new· films are abandoning this approach.

Three Days starts with the arrival of two Lithuanian guys in Kaliningrad (now Königsberg), where they are planning to stay for a few days. They meet some local girls, then get involved in a scuffle. The film ends with the boys' return to Lithuania.

Andrius Šiuša, the director of *And He Bid You Farewell*, was inspired by Eduardas Cinzas's (a Belgian of Lithuanian origin) *The Note of Maurice Bred*. The story begins with an accident; then a man, Marius, loses his memory and starts living in a world of his own visions. His world is either in a hospital or mental home, and sometimes it turns into a dream. The doctor does his best to help the patient. His friends are waiting for his recovery and "return" to the real world. However, Marius bids them farewell and stays on to live in that strange space.

Each of the directors in their own way neglects the dictate of dramatic composition, understressing the plot and putting more stress on atmosphere as well as on a language of symbols and metaphors. More than that, both of them change the image of a typical character. However, each of the heroes in *Three Days* has his own dramatic biography and a tragic sense of life and loneliness. The picture of a dilapidating city emphasises the meaninglessness of existence. In this context the heroes have no names, and the spare dialogue is drowned by the urban sounds that flow into a modern symphony of today's world degradation.

With this film, Bartas displayed his visual thinking at a high level. This quality is considered to be one of the most significant in Lithuanian cinema.

Andrius Šiuša's *And He Bid You Farewell* also exemplifies modern film aesthetics and a rather frequent fondness for a language of symbols in Lithuanian film. More than that, Šiuša continues dealing with man's existential problems. The director, together with the film's composer and cameraman, creates a strange world of faded colours that is far away from modern reality, but very close to a modern man's soul with his loss of orientation and confusion. The main character does not struggle for his memory to be restored and comes to a sad and final conclusion. Better oblivion than memory when you like a fake life. Moreover, the strangers in this "story" remain unknown; we do know whether Marius's partners at a hospital are real or imaginary; did he really make the decision to stay in oblivion or did he fail to recover? or ... ? It is left for the audience to find the solution.

DR. GRAŽINA ARLICKAITE graduated from the Historical and Philological Faculty, Vilnius University, in 1970. Served on a number of magazines as a journalist or film and theatre critic. Since 1981 chief editor of the screenplay editorial board of the Lithuanian Film Studio. Since 1991 took over the Department of International and Commercial Relations in the Studio. Represents Lithuania in the European Film Defence Organisation (EFDO).

LUXEMBOURG

Jean-Pierre Thilges

Despite the fact that the Grand-Duchy of Luxembourg has been elected European Cultural Capital of the Year in 1995, it doesn't look as if film will provide many of that year's highlights. As a matter of fact, at press-time, not a single Luxembourgish film was in production, although two rather attractive projects were struggling to get beyond their year-long pre-production schedules. Cameras were expected to roll several times already on the comedy *Black Dju*, which after many a rewrite was to be directed by Andy Bausch. Creative differences with the producers (Samsa Films) on his last film *Three Shake-a-leg Steps to Heaven*, which subsequently bombed at the box-office, led to Bausch's replacement with young director Pol Cruchten, whose *Hochzaitsneucht (Wedding Night)* won the Max Ophüls Prize in 1993. After yet another time-consuming rewrite, Cruchten was supposed to start shooting *Black Dju* in December 1994, hoping for a Christmas 1995 release date.

Meanwhile, Andy Bausch has been totally absorbed by German television, where he recently worked on several productions for state-owned ZDF and ARD, as well as for the ever expanding private web RTL Television. Apart from the ill-fated *Three Shake-a-leg Steps to Heaven*, his only other film released in Luxembourg during 1993/1994, was *Thes Dansants*, a quirky 1960's featurette on local rock-musicians, which went into oblivion after a one-time-showing on local television. Bausch did submit several projects to the Luxembourg Film Fund, but none of these were retained by the fund's committee. While it might be a pity that the offbeat director of *Troublemaker* cannot work in Luxembourg, his future in (German) television seems to be more than assured.

America's world-famous photographer Edward Steichen (he had been appointed Director of Photography at New York's MOMA in the 1950's), was born in Luxembourg in 1882. After an extensive restoration period, Steichen's renowned "Family of Man" Collection found a permanent exhibition site in Clervaux, a small city in the Luxembourg Ardennes. Despite the fact that Steichen's work has influenced still photographers around the world, his life has never been documented on film. To coincide with the restoration of "Family of Man", and after a two-year research period, director Claude Waringo of Samsa Films has started shooting his ambitious 52-minute documentary **Steichen** in the United States and Luxembourg, where he is trying to retrace the itinerary and work of the famous photographer, whose parents had emigrated to the States in 1882. Budgeted at 21 million francs (US$650,000), the docu is co-produced by television webs FR3, RTBF and RTL and supported by Media 95, Eurimages Documentary and the Luxembourg Film Fund, with a 1995 release date in mind.

Obvious Visual Flair

Young director Christian Delcourt was the only new local talent to emerge in 1994. Although his 40-minute short **D'Sandauer** (*The Hour Glass*; a Filmkessel Production) suffers from an over-indulgent, sugary screenplay and some all too obvious non-professional acting, the film's retelling of a "lost opportunity" love-story sports an obvious visual flair, some gorgeous photography and several first-rate performances by lead actresses Nicole Max and Alexandra Ley, whose charm and screen presence should lead to better parts in the future. With this sometimes stunning work, novice director Christian Delcourt

*Alexandra Ley and Nicole Max in D'SANDAUER,
directed by Christian Delcourt*

positions himself as a hopeful candidate for more ambitious productions, though he will have to search for better screenplays in the future.

Although deluged with an ever increasing amount of film and documentary projects, the Luxembourg Film Fund, whose annual budget has been boosted to over US$2 million, is experiencing difficulty in awarding its funds, as many of the projects, though ambitious in scope and budget, lack proper funding, co-production commitments and, of course, decent screenplays. Apart from *Black Dju* and *Steichen*, which were both generously supported by the Fund in 1993, subsidies were only awarded to several short subjects and documentaries, all to be shot in 1994 and early 1995. These projects were: *Dialogue*, an eight-minute fiction by Paul Cruchten (for Samsa Films); *Letzebuerg*, an experience in time-lapse photography by Bady Minck (for Samsa Films); *Roger*, a fiction by Geneviève Mersch (for Samsa Films); *Siggy*, a cartoon by Roger Leiner (for AFO Films); *Gehaansbierg*, a documentary by Carlo Thiel (for Ni-Films) and *Oak Tree Rap*, a puppet film by Pit Winandy (for Golden Screen). Several documentaries by fledgling Lynx Productions were also promised subsidies, pending co-produc-

tion agreements. Several of these short subjects, when finished, will be released in 1995, as a showcase programme for the country's young film-makers.

In order to take advantage of Luxembourg's tax-shelter opportunities, foreign productions are compelled to shoot inside a studio, as exterior permits are only granted reluctantly. Though there are still no state-of-the-art film studios around, Delux Productions, who are operating the country's two sound stages, are fully booked the year round, mostly with sitcoms, but also with the odd TV mini-series and feature film. Over the last twelve months, Delux-Studios have seen the likes of Timothy Dalton, Marg Helgenberger, Nigel Havers and Omar Sharif stalk their stages for the Ken Follett mini-series *Red Eagle*; have offered shelter to Geraldine Chaplin and Jim Sheridan in Mary McGuckian's *Words Upon the Window Pane* and have seen Joan Collins actually ride Steven Berkoff piggyback for the latter's screen adaptation of his play *Decadence*.

The other Luxembourg sector which is definitely booming is cinema exhibition. While attendance figures have been constantly on the rise over the last four years, construction of the long-delayed ten-screen multiplex Utopolis has finally been approved. Utopolis is co-financed by Luxembourg-based Utopia S.A. and Luxempart Fund as well as the Kinepolis Group of Brussels/Belgium. It is scheduled to open for business in the autumn of 1995.

JEAN-PIERRE THILGES is 41. After working in banking for 20 years and doubling up as a film critic, he has been actively involved in the restructuring of Luxembourg's Cinema business and is currently developing a 10-screen multiplex together with equally movie-struck friends.

Useful Addresses

Mediaport Luxembourg
Maison de Cassal
5, rue Large
L-1917 Luxembourg
Tel: (352) 47 82 160
Fax: (352) 47 56 62

**Centre National de
L'Audiovisuel**
5, route de Zoufftgen
L-3598 Luxembourg
Tel: (352) 52 24 24 1
Fax: (352) 52 06 55

Delux Productions
(Studios/Co-production)
2, rue Nicolas Bové
L-1253 Luxembourg
Tel: (352) 25 42 83
Fax: (352) 44 06 40

TOP TEN GROSSING FILMS IN LUXEMBOURG: 1993

Jurassic Park

The Bodyguard

Aladdin

The Fugitive

Dennis the Menace

Sister Act

Bram Stoker's Dracula

The Piano

Accidental Hero

A Few Good Men

Lynx Productions
(Production/Co-Production)
34, avenue Victor Hugo
L-1750 Luxembourg
Tel: (352) 22 06 36
Fax: (352) 22 10 38

**Monipoly/Paul Thiltges
Distributions**
(Animation/Distribution)
1, rue de Nassau
L-2213 Luxembourg
Tel: (352) 45 19 60 – 206
Fax: (352) 44 24 29

352 Production
(Animation Studios)
459, route de Longwy
L-1941 Luxembourg
Tel: (352) 25 17 17
Fax: (352) 25 18 95

Samsa Film
(Production/Co-Production)
1, rue de Nassau
L-2213 Luxembourg
Tel: (352) 45 19 60 1
Fax: (352) 44 24 29

Utopia S.A.
(Exhibition/Cinema)
16, avenue de la Faïencerie
L-1510 Luxembourg
Tel: (352) 46 49 02
Fax: (352) 22 46 12

MALAYSIA
Baharudin A. Latif

The past 1993-94 season can be said to be the year of Sofea Jane, whose presence in two films that dominated the scene for various reasons has at one go escalated her to superstar status. This has afforded her the rarely heard luxury of choosing roles of her own choice. So far she has selected wisely.

The First and Last Lover (*Kekasih Awal Dan Akhir*) showed Sofea in a frothy Cinderella-type soap opera about forbidden love that went on to gross RM2.400 (US$900,000), a record for domestic films. *Azura* was the previous champion, earning RM2.2 million

(US$850,000) back in 1984. Coincidentally Jamal Abdillah, a top singer over the past decade, was the male star in both films. Also, both films catered to the under-25's. There must be a message in this.

Sofea's **Woman, Wife & ...** (the last title was censored by the Film Censorship Board, making it a first) stirred a furore culminating in hysteria such as has never been seen locally. Suddenly everybody, including the intelligentsia, was eulogising its artistic leanings as if they really understood what essentially is a complex film about a nympho's journey into degradation and self-destruction. Some

Tiara Jacquelina in RINGGIT KASORRGA

quarters were calling it the ultimate Malay film. Talks and seminars were held at various levels and the normally tacit and unassuming director U-Wei had a problem explaining why the film was so good and he so brilliant.

The film grossed RM1.4 million (US$500,000) which probably surprised the producer too. Sofea Jane was the key to the film's success and under U-Wei's astute direction, she gave a flawless performance which will be remembered for a very long time. Sales of the video cassette have reportedly been good as it is a sure bet it will be banned on television.

Equalling WWW's media print notoriety was the banning of Steven Spielberg's *Schindler's List*, reaching proportions never heard of before. Five reasons were given by the Film Censorship Board for the ban, the main one being the film's over-zealous sympathy towards the victimised Jews. It was rather unfortunate that at that juncture the Jews were no longer the oppressed but the oppressor, with the Hebron incident an ugly reminder of the harsh realities of contemporary politics. With Malaysia's anti-Zionist stance all too well known, the Board thought it was doing the country a big favour by banning the film.

The controversy picked up added mileage when Deputy Prime Minister Datuk Seri Anwar Ibrahim announced after one weekly Cabinet meeting that the original reason for the ban was nullified. This was the first time ever that a film's ban had been discussed at the highest level of government. Only a film-maker of

Spielberg's stature could have merited it. The film, however, still had to survive normal censorship guidelines.

It did not. The Board decided that seven scenes amounting to no more than five minutes were no good for the delicate Malaysian mentality and had to go. The scenes depicted sex and nudity, taboo under any circumstances since colonial days, and no one was about to change censorship laws just to please Spielberg, who had ordained that the film be shown intact or not at all. Spielberg fans, despairing of ever seeing the film, rushed down to Singapore where it was shown intact to above-25 crowds. Well, people will remember him for *Jurassic Park* which did a 77-day stint and broke all records.

Early in 1992 a special committee was set up to draft what was hopefully The National Film Policy: its terms of reference included identifying weaknesses in national film-making, steps to correct them and to put the industry on an international footing. The bulky report has been finished and submitted to the Cabinet. What happens next is anybody's guess. Nobody's hoping for much.

It is already common knowledge that the committee, at its many lengthy meetings and dissertations, had repeatedly taken the National Film Development Corporation (FINAS) to task for its failure to implement effective measures to rejuvenate an ailing industry. Accusations of rampant licensing malpractices hurled at FINAS prompted the Anti-Corruption Agency (ACA) to step in: the department's officers were thoroughly grilled and even the Director General, Dato Zain Haji Hamzah, was not spared the whole day question-and-answer routine. He has been forced to resign seven months before his current contract expired. His hurried and premature departure has caught most people by surprise and raised more questions.

Among forthcoming films, U-Wei's second effort, entitled **The Black Widow** (*Mas Ayu*) is definitely the film to watch for: it is the second in a trilogy of films about women. Aziz M. Osman's banned **Fantasy** *(Fantasi)* was finally released after two years but it failed to ignite the box-office – which proves again that the public has a short memory.

As expected, U-Wei's *Woman, Wife & ...* took the Best Film and Best Director awards at the recent 11th Malaysian Film Festival, and three other main awards. Sofea Jane, tipped to win the Best Actress award, lost out to Erma Fatima, whose second win this is. Earlier, Sofea was named the Most Popular Artiste in a competition conducted by RTM, the government-owned television station, and a newspaper group.

BAHARUDIN A. LATIF is a veteran writer on Malaysian cinema, contributes to numerous world publications including *Variety* and *Movie/TV Marketing*, and is now working on a book for the World Cinema series.

Elaine Kang in THE RED-HAIRED TUMBLER OF MALAYA

Recent and Forthcoming Films

RINGGIT KESORRGA (High Society)

Script, Dir. and Prod: Shuhaim Baba. Phot: Badaruddin Azmi. Music: Razman. Players: Deanna Yusoff, Tiara Jacquelina, Hans Isaac, Zaidi Omar, Sara Wang Abdullah, Shazleen Shabhi, Hani Mohsin. A Persona Pictures Presentation in association with Mural Productions & Design.

THE BLACK WIDOW WAJAH AYU (The Black Widow)

Script and Dir: U-Wei Haji Shaari. Phot: Azman Razali. Music: M. Nazir. Players: Hashimah Yon, Nurul Jasmine, Misbun Sidak, Mohd. Rodzi, Puteri Salbiah, Zaidi Omar, Rubiah Suparman, Aziz Jaafar, JD Khalid. Prod: Raja Azmi Raja Sulaiman.

PENYU (Turtle)

Dir: Z. Lokman. Script: Z. Lokman & Ariz M. Osman. Phot: Ng Ah Tai. Music: Azman Abu Hassan. Players: Susan Menon, Yantzen,

Jaafar Onn, R. Jaafar, A. Aida, Wendy Lee, Helmy Salleh. Prod: Abdul Raof Abdul Rahman.

PANGGILAN PULAU (Call of the Island)

Script, Dir. and Prod: Ahmad Fauzee. Phot: Johan Ibrahim. Players: Ahmad Fauzee, Sharmaine Farouk, Raissudin Hamzah, Lyana Sulaiman, Jalaludin Hassan, Sulaiman Yassin.

PESONA CINTA (Love's Dilemma)

Script: Anwar Idris. Dir. and Prod: Arief Karmahani. Phot: Johan Ibrahim. Music: Shuhaimi Mohd. Zain. Players: Shaharuddin Thamby, Ida Narrina, Azlinda Rafar, Suhana Yahya, Shukery Hashim, Nasir Bilal Khan, Rambo Chin.

THE RED-HAIRED TUMBLER OF MALAYA

Script: H.K. Ho, M.W. Tan, Y.K.

Lai. Dir: Eddie Pak. Phot: Omar Ismail. Music: Peter Lim. Players: Elaine Kang, Ahmad Fauzee, Ong Soo Han, Os, Correy Felino, Wilson Ting, Carol Low, Johan Abdullah. Prod: Nancie Foo, Wendy Wong.

CINTA KITA (Our Love)

Script and Dir: Kamal Ishak. Phot: Jamal Maarif. Players: Sofea Jane, Arma Baharom Chik, Fawzi Kamaruddin, Sharifah Shahira, Yanti Abdul Jalil, Nazatus Shima Kamaruddin. Prod: Pansha.

Useful Addresses

FINAS
(The National Film Development Corporation of Malaysia)
Studio Merdeka Complex
Lot 1662, Hulu Klang
68000 Ampang
Selangor DE
Tel: (603) 408-5722
Fax: (603) 407-5216

PFM
(Association of Malaysian Film Producers)
Studio Merdeka Complex
Lot 1662, Hulu Klang
68000 Ampang
Selangor DE
Tel: (603) 408-4660
Fax: (603) 407-2291

SENIMAN
(Artistes Association of Malaysia)
Studio Merdeka Complex
Lot 1662, Hulu Klang
68000 Ampang
Selangor DE
Tel: (603) 408-0008
Fax: (603) 407-5216

Producers/ Distributors

Mural Productions & Designs Sdn. Bhd.
159A Jalan Aminuddin Baki,
Taman Tun Dr. Ismail
60000 Kuala Lumpur
Tel: (603) 719-1602
Fax: (603) 719-1586

HW Entertainment Design & Production Sdn. Bhd.
15-1 & 2, Jalan 2/27A
Section 1, Bandar Wangsa Maju
53300 Kuala Lumpur
Tel: (603) 412-2888
Fax: (603) 411-9459

Production Seni 2020 Sdn. Bhd.
48C, Jalan Rawa
off Jalan Imbi
55100 Kuala Lumpur
Tel: (603) 981-2020

Sunny Lim Corporation Sdn. Bhd.
60-B, Faber Plaza
Jalan Desa Bakti
Taman Desa
58100 Kuala Lumpur
Tel: (603) 783-9018/781-3881
Fax: (603) 238-4724

Televisual Sdn. Bhd.
64 Burhanuddin Helmi
Taman Tun Dr. Ismail
60000 Kuala Lumpur
Tel: (603) 718-9766
Fax: (603) 717-3192

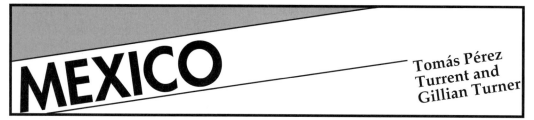

MEXICO

Tomás Pérez Turrent and Gillian Turner

Production in 1993 consisted of 39 films, plus two foreign films made in Mexico: not really very different from previous years, with the variation that in 1993 very few fiction videos (home videos) were made because the market has dropped completely. There are actually only two organisations with a consistent production level: Televicine, a subsidiary of the enormous television conglomerate called Televisa, producing 21 films, or over 50% of total production; and the Instituto Mexicano de Cinematografia (Imcine – the Mexican Film Institute), which co-produced a total of eight films with film-makers becoming their own producers and small production companies.

1993 was not a good year for Mexican cinema. It is fair to say that almost all national production of certain artistic and expressive pretensions has been left without exhibition outlets, and a cinema without a public is a cinema condemned. The situation has been made worse by the privatisation of the Compañia Operadora de Teatros (COTSA, the state distribution chain) which is now in the hands of an entrepreneur heavily involved in selling furniture and electrical gadgets. The conditions offered to Imcine by the new management were not at all favourable and very few films were shown successfully.

Cronos, which has been very successful outside the country both in film festivals and commercially, was shown in Mexico for the first time in December 1993 (two months after its successful screening in Spain) and then only because UIP distributed it. The results were good: it was shown for several weeks in various cinemas with, however, less success than was expected although it has been doing better outside Mexico City. Televicine (and its distributing subsidiary Videocine) has managed to maintain continuous exhibition activity although only two films have had good box-office results: **The Stork Made a Mistake** (*Se equivoco la cigueña*) starring a popular comic actress (the biggest box-office draw for two decades) and **Old Shoes** (*Zapatos viejos*) starring Gloria Trevi, a popular young singer who owes her success to her uninhibited and provocative manner. All others have been resounding flops, the majority of the films being shown for one week only and then disappearing completely from the circuits.

The situation is made worse by the fact that 1994 is the last year of the actual Presidential regime and the ensuing instability, outbreaks of social unrest provoked by the economic situation, the assassination of the official presidential candidate as well as difficulties germane to the film industry itself, are not conducive to investment. Mexican film-makers are emigrating to Hollywood, as in the case of Alfonso Arau and Alfonso Cuaron, as well as the photographer Emmanuel Lubezki. There exists, nonetheless, the paradox that in 1994 two Mexican films were shown in Cannes, one in the official section being **The Queen of the Night** (*La reina de la noche*) by Arturo Ripstein; the other in La Quinzaine des Réalisateurs: **The Garden of Eden** (*El jardin del Eden*) by Maria Novaro.

1993 also marks the destruction of the Churubusco Film Studios, leaving a mere mini-studio, the rest having been made over to the new Centro de las Artes (Arts Centre), a megalomaniac project supposed to unite under one roof schools of theatre, dance, graphic arts and music as well as cinema, this last in the Centro de Capacitacion Cinematografica which has been operating within the grounds of the Churubusco Studios for about twenty years now.

Distribution and Exhibition

Now that Operadora de Teatros has been sold to private enterprise, the most important distribution chains (Operadora de Teatros itself, Organizacion Ramirez, Real) share the same films, these being for the greater part Hollywood box-office hits. The arrival of the U.S. company Cinemark, programmed to build a multiplex of 12 small cinemas at the back of what used to be the Churubusco Studios (the company

has promised to devote four of its movie theatres exclusively to Mexican cinema) will now, however, drastically change the situation. The panorama in 1993 was very similar to that of previous years: U.S. films dominating the scene completely. Of the 274 films screened 166 (or 61%) were from the United States. Only 47 Mexican films were shown (16%) and the remaining 23% was distributed among 14 nationalities. Not a very promising outlook for Mexican cinema.

PRINCIPIO Y FIN (Beginning and End)

Script: Paz Alicia Garcia Diego, based on the novel by Naguib Mahfouz. Direction: Arturo Ripstein. Photography: Claudio Rocha. Music: Lucia Alvarez, Rafael Castanedo. Art Direction: Marisa Pecanins. Editing: Rafael Castanedo. Players: Julieta Egurrola, Ernesto Laguardia, Lucia Muñoz, Blanca Guerra, Bruno Bichir, Alberto Estrella, Veronica Merchant, Luisa Huertas, Luis Felipe Tovar. Produced by Alfredo Ripstein, Jr. for Alameda Films, Imcine, FFCC, Universidad de Guadalajara.

For this, his twentieth film, Arturo Ripstein uses a novel by the Egyptian Nobel Prize winner Naguib Mahfouz, deftly accommodating the action to Mexico City which in the novel occurs in Cairo, to narrate the misfortunes of the Botero family following upon the death of the father. The mother takes over and decides coldly and remorselessly the fate of her children: three must sacrifice themselves for the sake of the fourth who alone will be able to solve the family's economic difficulties.

Still from Arturo Ripstein's PRINCIPIO Y FIN

The city itself and the places where the characters live are closed, suffocating spaces. Ripstein instills into this atmosphere the drama of the family, unashamedly making a melodrama of his film, in exaltation of the historical drama of Mexican cinema constructed always around the matriarch. However, at the end of *Principio y Fin* there is a subtle change of tone: the melodramatic fate becomes a tragic one.

The film is not only a reflection on the melodrama and the society from whence it comes, as well as on relationships between individuals, family and society in general, but is also a Christ-like parable: the death of Man to save mankind, becomes the death of Man resulting in the ruin of mankind.

Tomás Pérez Turrent

HASTA MORIR (To the Death)

Script: Marcela Fuentes Berain. Direction: Fernando Sarinana. Photography: Guillermo Granillo. Music: Eduardo Gamboa. Art Direction: Gloria Carrasco. Editing: Carlos Bolado. Players: Demian Bichir, Veronica Merchant, Juan Manuel Bernal, Vanessa Bauche, Dolores Beristain, Maru Dueñas. Produced by Imcine, Vida Films, S.A., de C.V., FFCC, Ocixem, S.A. de C.V.

Fernando Sarinana has previously worked mainly in production although he has also directed three shorts. *Hasta morir* is his first feature film. Using an excellent script by Marcela Fuentes Berain, he narrates a story of a friendship between two young men: one living in Tijuana on the northern frontier with the United States, the other in Mexico City. They are planning an important business deal which will hopefully enable them to open a school for dogs in the States.

The film portrays the world of those living precariously on the outskirts of the monstrous metropolitan Mexico area, and their counterparts on the border, the so-called "cholos", and the various charac-

teristics of each of these worlds. Friendship, treachery, violence, companionship, the discovery of love, are the themes of a plot rich in adventures and full of subtleties. Although at time the filmmaker resorts to complicated takes and editing tricks, the film displays great authenticity both in the behaviour and in the dialogues of the characters, which are complex and grow, evolve, change as the plot unfolds; and the actors are all excellent!

Tomás Pérez Turrent

EN MEDIO DE LA NADA (In the Back of Beyond)

Script: Hugo Rodriguez, Marina Stavenhagen. Direction: Hugo Rodriguez. Photography: Guillermo Granillo. Music: Eduardo Gamboa. Editing: Hugo Rodriguez. Art Direction: Gloria Carrasco. Players: Manuel Ojeda, Blanca Guerra, Gabriela Roel, Ignacio Guadalupe, Alonso Echanove, Emilio Cortes, Guillermo Garcia Cantu, Daniel Gimenez Cacho. Produced by Jorge Ramirez Suarez, Hugo Rodriguez for Imcine, Ladron de Besos, S.A. de C.V.

A promising debut by another director graduated from the CCC (Centro de Capacitacion Cinematografica) is this first feature-length film by Hugo Rodriguez, whose career so far includes having co-directed a series of animated cartoons in Nicaragua, having been the sound engineer on several occasions and having made various television programmes and documentary shorts. The film in question narrates the clash between three runaways (one of them a woman) and the owner of a lonely café *cum* service station on a bleak highway, his wife, his adolescent son and two friends.

The location is the desert-like area of Northern Mexico. The film has a good sense of rhythm thanks to agile, imaginative editing, makes the most of its rather meagre resources and by way of an efficient use of cinematographic timing creates an excellent mood of suspense. Unexpected changes and reactions towards the end weaken the impact somewhat but

Blanca Guerra in EN MEDIO DE LA NADA

nonetheless *En medio de la nada* is a good film without great pretensions or solemnities which leaves one waiting with interest for Rodriguez's next production.

Tomás Pérez Turrent

TOMÁS PÉREZ TURRENT has published several books on the cinema since 1963. He has also written numerous film scripts. He is a graduate of UNAM (National Autonomous University of Mexico) in Philosophy.

TOP TEN GROSSING FILMS IN MEXICO: 1993(*)

	Pesos
Jurassic Park	51,889,155.00
The Bodyguard	32,608,560.00
Cliffhanger	27,614,502.00
Indecent Proposal	24,998,588.00
Aladdin	24,771,008.00
Demolition Man	23,280,216.00
Under Siege	20,508,900.00
Se Equivoco la Cigueña	18,522,406.00
Zapatos Viejos	17,346,683.00
Hard Target	14,274,436.00

*New Pesos, average exchange rate 1993, 3.21 new pesos per U.S. dollar.

Recent and Forthcoming Films

AMBAR (Amber)

Script: Hugo Iriart, Jaime Sampietro, Luis Estrada, based on the play by Hugo Iriart. Dir: Luis Estrada. Phot: Emmanuel Lubezki. Players: Hector Bonilla, Jorge Russek, Alfredo Sevilla, Muni Lubezki, Angelica Aragon. Prod: Sebastian Avila, Emilia Arau for Imcine, Bandidos Films S.A. de C.V.

AMOROSOS FANTASMAS (Loving Ghosts)

Script: Paco Ignacio Taibo II, based on his novel. Dir: Carlos Garcia Agraz. Phot: Xavier Perez Grobet. Players: Sergio Goyri, Mariana Levy, Manuel Ojeda, Salvador Sanchez, Bruno Bichir, Mercedes Olea. Prod: Ignacio Sada Nadero for Televicine.

BIENVENIDO (Welcome)

Script: Gabriel Retes, Maria del Pozo. Dir: Gabriel Retes. Phot: Chuy. Players: Lourdes Elizarraras, Luis Felipe Tovar, Juan Claudio Retes, Fernando Arau, Maria Fernanda Garcia, Gabriel Retes, Lucia Balzaretti. Prod: Gonzalo Lora for Cooperativa Rio Mixcoac, Cooperative Conexion, Universidad de Guadalajara, Trata Films S.A. de C.V.

DESIERTOS MARES (Empty Seas)

Script: José Luis Garcia Agraz, Ignacio Ortiz. Dir: José Luis Garcia Agraz. Phot: Carlos Marcovich. Players: Arturo Rio, Dolores Heredia, Juan Carlos Colombo, Lisa Owen, Veronica Merchant, Javier de la Piedra. Prod: Gonzalo Infante, Tita Lombardo for Imcine, Desiertos Films, Resonancia, Gobierno del estado de Sonora, Effecine.

DOLLAR MAMBO

Script: Paul Leduc, Jose Joaquin Blanco, Jaime Aviles, Hector Ortega, Juan Tovar. Dir: Paul Leduc. Players: Roberto Sosa, Dolores Pedro, Raul Medina, Kandido Uranga, Gabino Diego, Eduardo Lopez Rojas, Tito Vasconcelos. Prod: Arturo Walley, Berta Navarro, Angel Amigo for Programa Doble S.A. de C.V., Igeldo Zine Produkzionak S.A., Euskal Media, Channel Four.

GUERRERO NEGRO (Black Warrior)

Script: Raul Araiza, Franciso Sanchez. Dir: Raul Araiza. Players: Alejandro Camacho, Helena Rojo, Padro Armendariz Jr., Bruno Rey, Norma Herrera, Monica Dionne. Prod: Ignacio Sada Madero for Televicine.

LA ULTIMA BATALLA (The Last Battle)

Script: Fernando Galiana, Ramon Obon. Dir: Juan Antonio de la Riva. Phot: Arturo de la Rosa. Players: Jorge Russek, Margarita Isabel, Arcelia Ramirez, Alonso Echanove, Alberto Pedret. Prod:

Ignacio Sada Madero for Televicine.

VAGABUNDA (Tramp)

Script: Lola Madrid, based on the novel by Luis Spota. Dir: Alfonso Rosas Priego II. Phot: Xavier Pérez Grobet. Players: Dolores Heredia, Eric del Castillo, Guillermo Garcia Cantu, Claudia Ramirez, Victor Carpinteiro, Ernesto Gomez Cruz. Prod: Alfonso Rosas Priego II, Angelo Giacomo for Cineproducciones Internacionales, S.A. de C.V., Imcine, FFCC.

LOS VUELCOS DEL CORAZON (The Lurchings of the Heart)

Script: Mitl Valdes, based on the short story by Jose Revueltas. Dir: Mitl Valdes. Phot: Marco Antonio Ruiz. Players: Maria Rojo, Arturo Beristain, Ernesto Gomez Cruz, Dobrina Liubomirova, Martin Barraza, Luisa Huertas, Ignacio Guadalupe. Prod: Mitl Valdes for Producciones Carlos Salgado S.A. de C.V., Imcine, FFCC, DGAC-UNAM. Gecisa Internacional S.A. de C.V., Seccion 49 del STIC.

Eric del Castillo and Dolores Heredia in VAGABUNDA

NETHERLANDS

Pieter van Lierop

A difficult operation has been completed at last as the two Dutch film funds merged. In December 1993, the first management board of the Nederlands Fonds voor de Film (Dutch Film Fund) was installed under the chairmanship of Ryclef Rienstra, who had spent the previous four years as executive secretary of Eurimages in Strasbourg. The new fund has an annual budget of about 17 million guilders (about 9 million dollars). That is 2.5 million guilders more than the two former funds received together from the Ministry of Welfare, Public Health and Cultural Affairs. But it remains a scandalously low contribution for a developed Western European nation with a population of 14 million.

The Fund chairman aims to spend more money on fewer films. Grant applications in the future can only be submitted by producers and it is intended that these producers also take a financial risk themselves. In the past, skilful producers often managed to create a set-up in which all the costs were covered by various funds and broadcasting companies also receiving government money. This even included an attractive fee for the producer so he didn't need to suffer a single sleepless night even if his film failed to survive a week in the cinemas.

Rienstra now wants to force film-makers to take more interest in whether their productions can make a profit, so the award of the various grants will be in phases. The financial support for the developmental phases of a film will be greater than in the past, but the selection will be more stringent. Support for a project in the development phase does not mean that it will continue to receive help later.

The board of the Fund is able to award a maximum of 85,000 guilders for the development of a full-length feature project, up to 30,000 for a long documentary, 15,000 for a short documentary, 10,000 for a short drama production and 25,000 guilders for an animation film. The maximum contribution to meet production costs are 1,000,000 guilders for a full-length feature, 300,000 for a long documentary, 200,000 for a short drama or animation film and 150,000 for a short documentary.

In principle, all requests for a financial contribution are submitted to an advisory board comprising nine permanent members and about 25 ad hoc advisors. In early 1994, the Dutch Film Fund was able to start work. And with the sociologist Rob

Elliott Gould in Leon de Winter's HOFFMAN'S HUNGER   *photo: Max de Winter*

Renée Soutendik in Ben Verbong's HOUSE CALL

Boonzaijer Flaes as director and a budget to be finalised, it will soon also be possible to shape the new Filmwerkplaats (Film Workshop) that aims to make it possible for recent graduates from film schools to complete their first projects.

Too Much TV Influence

It looks as if the innovative measures taken are also an improvement, yet one can only regard with concern the development now affecting the Dutch film industry. The best Dutch directors no longer concentrate exclusively on films for the cinema screens, but on short TV series, from which a shorter film version may be cut if things work out right. Frans Weisz, Ben Sombogaart and Alejandro Agresti did that as early as 1993 with, respectively, *The Betrayed (Op Afbetaling)*, *The Penknife (Het Zakmes)* and *The Act in Question (El acto in cuestion)*. Their example has been followed by Léon de Winter with *Hoffman's Hunger*, Pieter Verhoeff with *The Lighthouse (Het Vuurtoren)* and Gerardjan Reinders with *Oude Tongen*.

This last production was screened as a cinema film before broadcast on TV, but was dead on arrival. It was an eccentric exercise by theatre director Rijnders with members of Toneelgroep Amsterdam and was inspired by a child-pornography scare in a small town in the north of the Netherlands. Numerous children were alleged to have been enticed and abused by adults dressed as clowns. However no one was ever arrested and it has never been established whether criminal acts ever actually took place or whether it was all just a case of mass hysteria. Rijnders employed black humour and typical big-city disdain of the backward provinces to adapt the affair into a very confusing patchwork film with much "borrowing" from *Twin Peaks*.

The talented Ben Verbong also turned to the TV medium with the project *Charlotte Sophie Bentinck*, shooting of which was recently completed. In the spring of 1994 the same director premièred **House Call** *(De Flat)* in the cinemas. This erotic thriller was widely compared with *Sliver* because it is also about a woman living on her own in an ominous apartment building; about sexual lust, voyeurism, murder and a lover who is recognised as a baddy from the very first by everyone except the heroine of the story. She is played by Renée Soutendijk, who has built up a solid reputation in Holland and abroad since her wonderful performance in Verbong's début *The Girl with the Red Hair* (1981). This eminent actress and the thriller elements sketched above put a box-office hit on the cards. But the critics could hardly spare a single compliment for this psychologically weak crime film in which two murders and a shooting all take place off camera, while Verbong focuses all his attention on Soutendijk's sexual escapades to little effect. Audiences also were not very interested.

A week earlier the cinemas also failed to fill when Frouke Fokkema's second feature **It Will Never Be Spring** *(Wildgroei)* was first screened. The story, with leading roles for Hilde van Mieghem and Thom Hoffman, is about the "amour fou" between a cosmopolitan woman with literary aspirations and a young and haughty lord of the manor in Holland's lush river landscape. The film looks like a gushing illustration of the idea that love is basically war. Many critics were especially unhappy

Hilde van Mieghem, Thom Hoffman and Ellen ten Damme in IT WILL NEVER BE SPRING

with the artificial-sounding dialogue, but what was said is often sharp and astute. The real problem of the film is that Fokkema expended too much effort trying to make an "art film" with an unnecessarily complex narrative structure and gratuitous changes from colour to black and white and back. And what is one supposed to expect from a cold lover who tries to confront all women and the whole world with chilling calculation and cutting sarcasm, but who lets the tears flow free when in the cinema watching *India Song* by Marguerite Duras? At one stage the script said it should be *Cinema Paradiso*, but that was finally deemed too common. In any case, several French critics were impressed by *It Will Never Be Spring* and selected the film for the Semaine de la Critique at Cannes.

The failure of these three films in a row in April 1994 was even more painful because it happened at a time when the cinema industry as a whole was picking up.

Two Million Tickets Ahead!

After the disastrous year 1992 (13,683,380 tickets sold in a country with more than 14 million inhabitants), attendances rose in 1993 to more than 16 million. The circuit of film houses run on a non-commercial basis

attracted 702,000 visitors compared with 676,000 in 1992. The increase has continued in the first five months of 1994, while the first Dutch Megaplexes still have to open their doors; the first are expected in Scheveningen (The Hague), Maastricht and Groningen.

The distributors and cinema owners are optimistic enough, but not about the chances for Dutch film. In late 1993 two other commercial thrillers flopped miserably in the cinemas: **Angie** by Martin Lagestee and **Unknown Time** (*Tussentijd*) by Marianne Dikker. In that same period there was respect and some success for **Love Hurts** (*Hartverscheurend*) by Mijke de Jong and for Digna Sinke's film **Belle van Zuylen**. *Love Hurts* sketches the shipwrecked relationship between the girl Loe, who lives an uncompromising life among Amsterdam's urban nomads, and her friend Bob who is a young lawyer succumbing to increasingly middle-class behaviour and views. Excellent dialogue and notable acting by Marieke Heebink and Mark Rietman bring the personal drama convincingly to life. The film also provides a striking picture of a subculture where anarchists and squatters, drop-outs, illegal immigrants support each other in the face of decreasing tolerance from society. The film was awarded the audience prize at the Locarno Festival and was given the Critics' Prize during the Dutch Film Days.

At this national festival, *Belle van Zuylen* seemed to be the jury favourite. Ms Sinke's film collected the most nominations for Golden Calves, but in the end it did not receive a single prize. However it was by far the best Dutch feature film to have been made in 1993 and was more ambitious than all the prize winners put together. Sinke has provided a fascinating portrait of the eighteenth-century Dutch writer and composer Belle van Zuylen, better known abroad as Madame de Charrière. Based largely on surviving correspondence, Digna Sinke manages to bring to life the brief love affair that the intelligent and sensitive Belle van Zuylen (a perfect role by Will van Kralingen) had with the young

Nino Manfredi in Jos Stelling's forthcoming THE FLYING DUTCHMAN

Benjamin Constant (Laus Steenbeke). In the end she lost this passionate correspondent and fleeting lover to Madame de Staël (Carla Hardy). The film is subtle and restrained and wonderfully captures the mood as the Englightenment makes way for Romanticism. Much of the charm is evoked by the inspired photography of Goert Giltay. This very talented professional was given a Golden Calf, but for his complete oeuvre.

Giltay is also sure to be a major influence on the film production that everyone hopes will be eligible for competition in a major festival in 1995: **The Flying Dutchman** *(De Vliegende Hollander)*. Shooting for this film directed by Jos Stelling lasted eight months in fantastic sets, the most pastoral landscapes and the most appalling conditions that the Dutch climate has to offer. With a budget of fourteen million guilders and an international cast (Nino Manfredi plays one of the leading roles) the result is expected to be an historic epic very loosely based on the most internationally famous legend in Dutch culture. Before shooting was completed in May 1994, the international rights had already been sold to UGC.

In the field of documentaries, quantity won from quality, with the exception of three films for which the makers returned to their roots. Film critic Jos de Putter made his début with **It Has Been A Lovely Day** *(Het is een Schone Dag Geweest)*. He went back to the farm where he was born and followed in a sober yet riveting way the last year that his father plodded through

the clay as a small farmer who eventually had to make way for the modern agriculture industry. Hedy Honigman, born in Peru, made the impressive *Metal and Melancholy* about taxi drivers in her native Lima. Sonia Herman Dolz (Spanish mother, Peruvian father) made a very elegant study of bull-fighting under the title *Romance de Valencia, Only the Brave*, in which she spiritedly refused to condemn this bloody mixture of art and sport.

A Welcome for Outsiders

While the new Dutch Film Fund has announced it will focus on film projects in Dutch, Holland remains a hospitable country for film-makers from abroad. This is best illustrated by the Hubert Bals Fund that, as part of the International Film Festival Rotterdam, provides encouragement grants to film-makers from developing countries. Thanks to an additional grant from the Ministry of Development Aid (450,000 guilders), this fund's annual budget has been doubled.

Rotterdam itself is becoming increasingly important via the CineMart, an international meeting place where non-commercial co-productions are put together. The festival itself grew in 1994 to welcome 155,000 seats sold, making it the largest cultural event in the Netherlands. The extensive programme of Chinese films, many of them not authorised, caused a major clash with the People's Republic and put six film-makers on the "blacklist". The FIPRESCI Prize was awarded to *Red Beads* by the Chinese He Yi. The organisation of Dutch critics rewarded the Russian film *Living* by Alexander Rogozhkin.

A Russian film also won a prize during Amsterdam's International Documentary Film Festival. The Joris Ivens Award was given to *The Beloved* by Victor Kossakovsky. The Dutch Film Days, renamed in 1994 as the Dutch Film Festival, managed to attract 36,000 visitors and clear its debts despite a sober week. The Golden Calf for the best feature was given to *Little Blond Death (De Kleine Blonde Dood)* by Jean van der Velde and Rob Houwer. The Special Jury Prize went to *The Forbidden Quest* by Peter Delpeut. Best director: Ben Sombogaart for the children's film *The Penknife (Het Zakmes)*. Best actor: Rik Launspach in *Going Home (Oeroeg)*. Best actress: Els Dottermans in *Beck*. Best full-length documentary: *Child in Two Worlds (Kind in Twee Werelden)* by Willy Lindwer. Best short documentary: *Isingiro Hospital* by Hillie Molenaar and Joop van Wijk. Best short film: *World of Marionettes (De Marionettenwereld)* by Elbert van Strien. Technical prize (photography): Goert Giltay.

PIETER VAN LIEROP is film editor of the *Utrechts Nieuwsblad* since 1974, also serving the 18 daily papers syndicated in the Netherlands Press Association (GPD). He has been correspondent of the International Film Guide since 1981.

Will van Kralingen in the title role, in Digna Sinke's
BELLE VAN ZUYLEN

TOP TEN GROSSING FILMS IN THE NETHERLANDS: 1993

	H.Fl.
Jurassic Park	21,831,743
The Bodyguard	7,840,987
Indecent Proposal	7,619,843
The Fugitive	7,397,810
The Firm	6,399,632
Aladdin	6,284,777
Cliffhanger	6,186,785
Home Alone 2	5,905,316
Hot Shots: Part Deux	5,276,898
A Few Good Men	4,325,926

(*In Dutch guilders. One dollar is about 1.9 guilders*)

Recent and Forthcoming Films

BELLE VAN ZUYLEN, MADAME DE CHARRIÈRE

Script and Dir: Digna Sinke. Phot: Goert Giltaij. Players: Will van Kralingen, Laus Steenbeke, Kees Hulst, Patty Pontier, Carla Hardy, Kitty Courbois. Prod: René Scholten for Studio Nieuwe Gronden.

HARTVERSCHEUREND (Love Hurts)

Script: Mijke de Jong and Jan Eilander. Dir: Mijke de Jong. Phot: Joost van Starrenburg. Players: Marieke Heebink, Mark Rietman, Andre-Arend van Noord, Mientja Kleijer, Tanar Catalpinar, Roef Ragas. Prod:

René Goossens and René Scholten for Studio Nieuwe Gronden.

WILDGROEI (It Will Never Be Spring)

Script and Dir: Frouke Fokkema. Phot: Gerard Vandenberg. Players: Hilde van Mieghem,

Thom Hoffman, Ellen ten Damme, Julien Schoenaerts, Hans Croiset, Fiet Dekker, Pim Lambeau, René Eljon, Ger Thijs. Prod: Matthijs van Heijningen for Sigma Filmproductions.

DE FLAT (House Call)

Script: Jean van de Velde. Dir: Ben Verbong. Phot: Theo Bierkens. Players: Renée Soutendijk, Victor Löw, Hans Hoes, Jaimy Siebel, Mirjam de Rooij, Leslie de Gruyter, Jacques Commandeur. Prod: Chris Brouwer and Haig Balian for Movies Film Productions.

CURFEW

Script and Dir: Rashid Masharawi. Phot: Klaus Juliusburger. Players: Salim Daw, Na'ila Zayaad, Mahmoud Qadah, Younis Younis, Assem Zoabi, Salwa Naqara Haddad. Prod: Nahy Abu-Assad and Samir Hamed for Ayloul Film Produc-tions, Henri Kuipers and Peter van Vogelpoel for Argus Film Produkties.

DE ZWIJGENDE REIZIGER (The Silent Traveller)

Script and Dir: Ibrahim Selman. Phot: Peter Brugman. Players: Abdulkadir Yousif, Walid Hadji, Halima Sadik, Umet Ali, Sakik Abdullah. Prod: Rolf Orthel for DNU Film BV.

DUIZEND ROZEN (One Thousand Roses)

Script: Gustav Ernst and Theu Boermans. Dir: Theu Boermans. Phot: Theo Bierkens. Players: Marieke Heebink, Bert Geurink. Prod: Matthijs van Heijningen for Sigma Film Productions.

RIT OVER DE GRENS (Ride Across The Border)

Script and Dir: Rosemarie Blank. Photo: Martin Gressmann. Players: Christien Vroegop, Ursula Geyer-Hopfe, Ange van't Hof, Mady van't Hof, Nele Paul. Prod: Casa Film/Wüste Film.

KLADBOEKSCENES (Waste Book Scenes)

Script: Frans van de Staak and Hanneke Stark. Dir: Frans van de Staak. Phot: Jan Wich. Players: Rik van Uffelen, Michiel Nooter, Marlies Heuer. Prod: Van de Staak Filmprodukties.

VENUS IN FURS

Script and Dir: Maartje Seyferth and Victor Nieuwenhuijs. Phot: Victor Nieuwenhuijs. Players: Anne van der Ven, André Arend van Noord, Raymond Thiry, Hilt de Vos. Prod: Victor Nieuwenhuijs for Moskito Films.

OUDE TONGEN

Script and Dir: Gerardjan Rijnders. Phot: Maarten Kramer. Players: Jasper Kraaij, Fred Goessens, Kitty Courbois, Lineke Le Roux, Hanna Rassalada, Peter Oosthoek, Catherine ten Bruggencate, Pierre Bokma. Prod: Hans de Weers and Hans de Wolf for Bergen.

DAGBOEK VAN EEN ZWAKKE YOGI (Diary of a Weak Yogi)

Script and Dir: Ronald da Silva. Phot: Emil Busurca. Players: Kamaran Abdalla, Manouk van der Meulen, Robert C. Smit, Dela Maria Vaags, Saskia van Engeland, Marline Williams. Prod: Margot Barel and Pim de la Parra for Weak Yogi Productions.

HOFFMAN'S HUNGER

Script: Léon de Winter and Ton van Nieuwenhuyzen. Dir: Léon de Winter. Photo: Jean François Robin. Players: Elliott Gould, Jacqueline Bisset, Marie Trintignant, Huub Stapel, Johan Leysen, Gerard Thoolen, Thom Hoffman, Gwen Eckhaus, Jules Croiset. Prod: Ludi Boeken. Belbo Nederland.

DE VUURTOREN (The Lighthouse)

Script and Dir: Pieter Verhoeff.

Phot: Paul van den Bos. Players: Hans Heerschop, Jaron de Paauw, Jacky Lok, Peter Tuinman, Joke Tjalsma, Annet Malherbe, Marije Nieuwen-huijse, Rense Westra. Prod: Hans de Weers and Hans de Wolf for Bergen.

DE VLIEGENDE HOLLANDER (The Flying Dutchman)

Script: Jos Stelling and Hans Heesen. Phot: Goert Giltaij. Players: René Groothof, Nino Manfredi, Willy Vandermeulen, Eugene Vervoets, Veerle Dobbelare, Daniel Emilfork, Ingrid de Vos, Gerard Thoolen, Bert André, Josse de Pauw. Prod: Jos Stelling, Eddy Wijngaarde, Christoph Hahnheiser, Frank Henschke and Alain Keytsman for Jos Stelling Film Produkties.

HOOGSTE TIJD (Last Call)

Script: Jan Blokker. Dir: Frans Weisz. Phot: Robbie Mueller. Players: Rijk de Gooijer, Kitty Courbois, Camilla Siegertsz, Josse de Pauw, Wil van Kralingen, Joop Doderer, Willem Nijholt. Prod: Jos van der Linden and René Seegers for Hoogste Tijd C.V.

DE VLINDER TILT DE KAT OP

Script: Carel Donck, Willeke van Ammelrooy and Sander Vos. Dir: Willeke van Ammelrooy. Phot: Eduard van der Enden. Players: Arjan Kindermans, Marolein Beumer, Rik Launspach, Karla Wierenga, Jules Croiset, Josee Ruiter. Prod: Jos van der Linden and Willeke van Ammelrooy.

ALL MEN ARE MORTAL

Script: Ate de Jong, Steven Gaydos and Olwen Wymark from the novel by Simone de Beauvoir. Dir: Ate de Jong. Phot: Bruno de Keyzer. Players: Irène Jacob, Stephen Rea, Marianne Sägebrecht, Chiara Mastroianni, Derek de Lint. Prod: Mattijs van Heijningen, Rudolf Wichman,

Jean Gontier for Nova/Sigma/Rio Filmproduction.

Producers

AFI/Added Films International
Paul Voorthuysen
Lange Muiderweg 616
1398 PB Muiden
Tel: +31 2942 63277
Fax: +31 2942 64868

Argus Film BV
Rob Langestraat
P.O. Box 18269
1001 ZD Amsterdam
Tel: +31 20 6254585
Fax: +31 20 6268978
Telex: 11084 argus nl

Ariel Film Produkties
Suzanne van Voorst
Prinsengracht 770
1017 LE Amsterdam
Tel: +31 20 6388199
Fax: +31 20 6380149

Belbo Film Productions BV
Mrs. I. Lochem
Sarphatikade 11
1071 WV Amsterdam
Tel: +31 20 6387999
Fax: +31 20 6388209

Bergen
Hans de Wolf/Hans de Weers
Haarlemmerstraat 124 a
1013 EX Amsterdam
Tel: +31 20 6269991
Fax: +31 20 6262070

CinéTé Film Prods.
Willem Thijssen
Elisabeth Wolffstraat 45
1053 TR Amsterdam
Tel: +31 20 6855339
Fax: +31 20 6891954

Cine Ventura
Ruud den Drijver/
Dorna van Rouveroy
Hudsonstraat 52
1057 SN Amsterdam
Tel: +31 20 6837439
Fax: +31 20 6160500

Nico Crama Films

Nico Crama
Stevinstraat 261
2587 EJ The Hague
Tel: +31 70 3544964

First Floor Features
Laurens Geels/Dick Maas
P.O. Box 30086
1303 AB Almere
Tel: +31 36 5327003
Fax: +31 36 5327940

Flying Dutchman Productions Inc.
Ate de Jong
2016, Navy Street
Santa Monica, Los Angeles
90405 USA
Tel: +1 310 4501040
Fax: +1 310 4505793

Bert Haanstra Films BV
Bert Haanstra
Verlengde Engweg 5
1251 GM Laren
Tel: +31 2153 82428
Fax: +31 2153 82428

Stichting Jura Filmprodukties
Ruud Monster/Jan Heijs
Korte Leidsedwarsstraat 12
1017 RC Amsterdam
Tel: +31 20 6255442
Fax: +31 20 6202426

Roeland Kerbosch Film Prods. BV
Roeland Kerbosch
Keizersgracht 678
1017 ET Amsterdam
Tel: +31 20 6230390
Fax: +31 20 6279879

Linden Film BV
Jos van der Linden
Chopinstraat 25
1077 GM Amsterdam
Tel: +31 20 6793128
Fax: +31 20 6641046

Lowland Productions
Rene Seegers
Duivendrechtsekade 82
1096 AJ Amsterdam
Tel: +31 20 6680492
Fax: +31 20 6941018

Lucid Eye Productions
Johan van der Keuken
Oude Schans 69 A

1011 KW Amsterdam
Tel: +31 20 6230354
Fax: +31 20 6382968

MGS Film Amsterdam BV Golden Egg Film
George Sluizer/Anne Lordon
Singel 64
1015 AC Amsterdam
Tel: +31 20 6231593/6629960
Fax: +31 20 6243181

Molenwick Film Productions
Hillie Molenaar/Joop van Wijk
Tuinstraat 64-66
1015 PG Amsterdam
Tel: +31 20 6248805
Fax: +31 20 6386384
ext. 0005/6252296

Moskito Film
Victor Nieuwenhuis/Maartje Seyferth
Oostelijke Handelskade 12
1019 BM Amsterdam
Tel: +31 20 6381924
Fax: +31 20 6381855

Movies Film Productions BV
Chris Brouwer /Haig Balian
Postbus 432
1200 AK Hilversum
Tel: +31 35 261500
Fax: +31 35 248418

Odusseia Films
Stadhouderskade 6
1054 ES Amsterdam
Tel: +31 20 6181821
Fax: +31 20 6163284

Rolf Orthel Film Prods.
Rolf Orthel/Evelyn Voortman
Zoutkeetsgracht 1161
1013 LC Amsterdam
Tel: +31 20 6220255
Fax: +31 20 6261885

Praxino Pictures BV
René Solleveld
Onstein 190
1082 KN Amsterdam
Tel: +31 20 6466121
Fax: +31 20 6613411

Fons Rademakers Prods. BV
Fons Rademakers
Prinsengracht 685
1017 JT Amsterdam
Tel: +31 20 6221298

Red Dog Productions
Olivier Koning
Valeriusstraat 111
1075 ER Amsterdam
Tel: +31 20 6625747
Fax: +31 20 6756901

Scorpio Verstappen Films BV
Wim Verstappen
P.O. Box 245
1000 AE Amsterdam
Tel: +31 20 6225552
Fax: +31 20 6208660

Shooting Star Filmcompany BV
Hans Pos/Dave Schram/
Maria Peters/José Steen
Prinsengracht 546
1017 KK Amsterdam
Tel: +31 20 6247272
Fax: +31 20 6268533

Sigma Film Productions BV
Matthijs van Heijningen
Bolensteinseweg 3
3603 CP Maarssen
Tel: +31 3465 70430/70431
Fax: +31 3465 69764

Van de Staak Film Prods.
Frans van de Staak
Jacob Oliepad 2
1013 DP Amsterdam
Tel: +31 20 6260634

Jos Stelling Film Prods. BV
Jos Stelling
Springweg 50-52
3511 VS Utrecht
Tel: +31 30 313789
Fax: +31 30 310968

Studio Nieuwe Gronden
René Scholten
Van Hallstraat 52
1051 HH Amsterdam
Tel: +31 20 6867837
Fax: +31 20 6824367
Telex: 12682 sngfp

Distributors

Argus Film BV
Rob Langestraat
P.O. Box 18269
1001 ZD Amsterdam
Tel: +31 20 6254585
Fax: +31 20 6268978
Telex: 11084 argus nl

Cinemien
Entrepotdok 66
1018 AD Amsterdam
Tel: +31 20
6279501/6238152/6258357
Fax: +31 20 6209857
Telex: 18995 Cinem

**Columbia/Tri-Star Films
(Holland) BV**
P.O. Box 533
1000 AM Amsterdam
Tel: +31 20 5737655
Fax: +31 20 5737656

Concorde Film
Robbert Wijsmuller
Lange Voorhout 35
2514 EC The Hague
Tel: +31 70 3605810/3924571
Fax: +31 70 3604925
Telex: 34568 cofil nl

Contact Film Conematheek
Gerard Huisman
P.O. Box 3100
6802 DC Arnhem
Tel: +31 85 434949
Fax: +31 85 511316

Cor Koppies Filmdistribution BV
P.O. Box 75242
1070 AE Amsterdam
Tel: +31 20 6767841
Fax: +31 20 6714968

Express Film
Heemraadschapslaan 13
1181 TZ Amstelveen
Tel: +31 20 6412331

Filmtrust BV
Molenkade 57A
1115 AC Duivendrecht
Tel: +31 20 6957719/6955503
Fax: +31 20 6956625

Holland Film Releasing BV
De Lairessestraat 111-115
1075 HH Amsterdam
Tel: +31 20 5751751
Fax: +31 20 6622085

Hungry Eye Pictures BV
Krijn Meerburg
Duivendrechtsekade 82
1096 AJ Amsterdam
Tel: +31 20 6686126
Fax: +31 20 6683452

International Art Film
Rieks Hadders
Vondelpark 3
1071 AA Amsterdam
Tel: +31 20 5891418/5891426
Fax: +31 20 6833401

Melior Films BV
Steynlaan 8
1217 JS Hilversum
Tel: +31 35 245542
Fax: +31 35 235906

Meteor Film BV
Postbus 432
1200 AK Hilversum
Tel: +31 35 261500
Fax: +31 35 248418

The Movies BV
Postbus 432
1200 AK Hilversum
Tel: +31 35 261500
Fax: +31 35 248418

Useful Addresses

**Ministry of Welfare, Health and
Cultural Affairs
Department of Film**
P.O. Box 3009
2280 ML Rijswijk
Tel: +31 70 3406148
Fax: +31 70 3405742

COBO Fund
Jeanine Hagen
Postbus 26444 (NOS TV)
1202 JJ Hilversum
Tel: +31 35 775348

**Dutch Film and Television
Academy**
(Nederlandse Film en Televisie
Academie)
Ite Boeremastraat 1
1054 PP Amsterdam
Tel: +31 20 6830206
Fax: +31 20 6126266

Dutch Film Fund
(Stichting Nederlands Fonds voor de
Film)
Jan Luykenstraat 2
1071 CM Amsterdam
Tel: +31 20 6643368
Fax: +31 20 6750398

Dutch Film Museum

Vondelpark 3
1071 AA Amsterdam
Tel: +31 20 5891400
Fax: +31 20 6833401

Holland Film Promotion
Jan Luykenstraat 2
1071 CM Amsterdam
Tel: +31 20 6644649
Fax: +31 20 6649171

MEDIA Desk/AV Platvorm
Renske Heddema
P.O. Box 256
1200 AG Hilversum
Tel: +31 35 238641
Fax: +31 35 218541

**Netherlands Institute for
Animation Film**
Ton Crone
Bachlaan 640
5011 BN Tilburg
Tel: +31 13 562925
Fax: +31 13 562428

Sources
(Stimulating Outstanding Resources
for Creative European
Screenwriting)
Dick Willemsen/Margot Knijn
Jan Luykenstraat 92
1071 CT Amsterdam
Tel: +31 20 6720801
Fax: +31 20 6720399

**Association of Dutch Film
Theatres. (Associated with the
Netherlands Cinematographic
Assn.)**
(Associate van Nederlandse Film
Theatres)
Prinsengracht 770
1017 LE Amsterdam
Tel: +31 20 6267602
Fax: +31 20 6275923

Europe Cinema Nederland
Henk Camping
P.O. Box 75242
1070 AE Amsterdam

GNS
(The Filmmakers Society of the
Netherlands)
P.O. Box 581
1000 AN Amsterdam
Tel: +31 20 6765088
Fax: +31 20 6765837

KNF
(Circle of Dutch Film Critics)
Snelliuslaan 78
1222 TG Hilversum
Tel: +31 35 856115

**The Netherlands
Cinematographic Foundation**
(Nederlandse Federatie van
Cinematografie)
Jan Luykenstraat 2
1071 CM Amsterdam
Tel: +31 20 6799261
Fax: +31 20 6750398

NBF
(The Association for Film and
TV Directors)
Jan Luykenstraat 2
1071 CM Amsterdam
Tel: +31 20 6646588
Fax: +31 20 6643707

NEW ZEALAND — Phil Wakefield

After years of having only the occasional flutter, the Kiwi film industry is soaring to new and sustained heights. The volume of feature film production is low but its visibility has never been higher, and the box-office is booming because of a multiplexing blitzkrieg. Admissions for the year were tipped to top a record 13.5 million, with figures for the first six months showing a 42% jump on the previous year. That came on top of a 50% rise during the 1993 calendar year, and means New Zealand's cinema revival is outpacing any other country's.

Motion Pictures Distributors (N.Z.) chief Tim Ord, who also heads UIP (N.Z.), says the annual per capita admissions is exceeded only by the far more densely populated Hongkong and Singapore. New Zealand, which has a population of only 3.3 million, now has more screens than in the so-called "heyday" of cinema before the advent of TV in the 1960's. Since 1992, the number has leapt from 142 to 220 but will level off with the construction of new cinemas reaching saturation point.

The dominant players are Hoyts Cinemas N.Z. and a joint venture between Australia's Village Roadshow and property developer, Force Corporation. During the past year both increased their market share markedly by striking deals in separate cities to buy the last of the screens

Haka performers in Lee Tamahori's ONCE WERE WARRIORS, winner of the Grand Prix at Montréal

owned by Everard Cinemas. Barrie Everard, the country's biggest independent distributor, overreached himself by buying the remnants of the Pacer Kerridge circuit after it went into receivership. The screens turned out to be dinosaurs in an age when multiplexes were doing the *Jurassic Park* business.

One of the biggest contributors to the box-office was the surprise Kiwi block-buster, **Once Were Warriors**, a searing, urban drama about marital mayhem which took only six weeks to become the highest-grossing N.Z. pic in domestic release. Whereas N.Z.'s previous most popular Kiwi release, *Footrot Flats: A Dog's Tale*, notched up $NZ2.3 million, *Once Were Warriors* exceeded this in 42 days. At the time of writing it had topped $NZ3 million after only two months and seemed *Jurassic Park*-bound as it overtook the made-in-N.Z. but not N.Z.-made Oscar-nominee, *The Piano*, which grossed $NZ3.8 million in 40 weeks. What's more, *Warriors* has earned $NZ3 million in sales, and returned its investors well over $NZ1 million in

rentals – the highest ever achieved for a N.Z. film. Film Commission marketing chief Lindsay Shelton reports: "It's the biggest surprise in New Zealand cinema for many years, all the more so because it has an untried director (Lee Tamahori) and is a tough subject."

The irony of *Warriors'* success is it occurred when feature production was in the doldrums. The year's only other releases were **Heavenly Creatures**, splatter king Peter (*Braindead*) Jackson's highly-acclaimed mainstream dramatisation of a 1954 murder case, and John Reid's **The Last Tattoo**, a romantic thriller with a Second World War setting, starring Kerry Fox and Rod Steiger. (The N.Z./Australia co-production, *Cops and Robbers*, was in release limbo and seems destined for a straight-to-video debut.)

Compare this to 1993 when the Kiwi release schedule boasted *The Piano, Desperate Remedies, Jack Be Nimble, Absent without Leave, Crush, Alex* and made-for-TV *Bread and Roses.*

Peter Jackson on the set of HEAVENLY CREATURES

Projects Fall Through

The lull was due to several factors. A couple of projects fell over although one, the comedy, *Jack Brown, Genius*, which Peter Jackson produced, was resurrected and is in post-production. (The second production shot in 1994 was a teenage romance called *Bonjour Timothy* from Moonrise producer Murray Newey; it's a co-production between Tucker Films and Canada's Cinar Films.) Another reason for the standstill was that some of the country's most active film producers took a break after making projects back-to-back – to wit, Bridget Ikin (*Angel at My Table*, *Crush* and *Loaded*) and Robin Laing (*Ruby & Rata, Absent without Leave*, and *Bread and Roses*). Not only were they tired but they needed time to focus on development.

A tougher Film Commission stance on the proper packaging of projects also made it harder to win funding – the Commission still is the principal backer of New Zealand film – and at the same time there was a decline in applications. The latter was partly due to producers being more TV-focused, with the medium's deregulation creating new opportunities for local production. To kick-start more features, the Commission initiated some of its most radical policies yet and appointed its first chief executive officer, Richard Stewart, who replaced executive director Judith McCann. Previously director of Film Queensland, Stewart is developing a strategy whereby the Commission can invest in eight features a year instead of four using the same $N.Z6.2 million production budget.

The extra money would be brought to the table by producers through pre-sales and other initiatives. For instance, an industry group called Project Blue Sky has been pushing banks to lend on distribution guarantees and steps have been taken to set up a film location office to better promote New Zealand as not only a location – four Hercules telefeatures were shot here in 1994 – but also a co-production partner.

The Commission already has co-production treaties with Canada, France, Australia and, more recently, the U.K. (the first project to result from the latter was the thriller *Loaded*, helmed by Jane Campion's sister, Anna). It is pursuing such treaties with other major territories, focusing more on Asia as a market and a source of funding, and is beefing up its marketing in Europe.

But its biggest gamble has been to axe its sales arm in the hope international sales agents will provide sales advances to producers. It's part of the NZFC's bid to secure more investment for feature funding from a wider variety of sources. "Such increased investment will allow New Zealand film-makers to build upon the recent surge of international interest in New Zealand films," says Commission chair Phil Pryke.

The jury is still out on whether the move is in the best interests of N.Z. film. Even after six months of being canvassed by the Commission, the industry remained split on sales options.

Smaller Films Neglected

Veteran producers like John Barnett, who's now production chief for TVNZ subsidiary South Pacific Pictures, has long argued films should be sold according to genre, not geography, while director Gaylene Preston (*Bread and Roses, Ruby and Rata*) says one reason N.Z.'s profile is so high is because of the Commission's dedicated sales and marketing efforts.

Concern has also been voiced that smaller films will be neglected by overseas sales agents, that N.Z. films could lose their Kiwi identity because of pressure to homogenise them for the international market, and that projects by unknown first-time directors will not draw offshore funds.

These issues aside, the timing of the decision couldn't have been better. Stewart has brought with him a vast range of international contacts, the industry is maturing and becoming more entrepreneurial, and the success of *Warriors, The Piano* and the largely German-financed *Heavenly Creatures* (for which Miramax International snapped up the worldwide rights) have given N.Z. film an unprecedented profile and market premium.

This has been reflected in the increased North American interest in this part of the world and the signing of all the major new directors – Jackson, Tamahori, Stewart Main and Peter Wells (*Desperate Remedies*) – by top talent agencies. But one of the healthiest signs for the industry is that these directors, in spite of the U.S. overtures, want to keep shooting features in New Zealand. Jackson, for instance, treasures the creative freedom he has here. He and U.S. film-maker Bob Zemeckis have developed a dark comedy thriller as his next picture, and were planning a 1995 N.Z. shoot with Zemeckis acting as executive producer.

Also in the pipeline are a colonial drama from Tamahori called *I Shall Not Die*; a contemporary, sexually ambiguous spin on *Romeo and Juliet* from Stewart Main entitled *You're My Venus*; *The Last Beat of My Heart*, an epic love story from *Jack Be Nimble* director Garth Maxwell; and Preston's documentary feature, *What Did You Do in the War, Mummy?*

Producers like Jonathan Dowling and Kelly Rogers (*Jack Be Nimble*), James Wallace (*Desperate Remedies*), Robin Scholes (*Once Were Warriors*) and John O'Shea (*Ngati*) have projects in the works while international distributor UIP (N.Z.) has already committed to a family drama

Alexis Arquette in JACK BE NIMBLE

called *Bow Down Shadrach*, from Kiwi Films, whose first feature it will be.

"UIP is actively looking to pick up features and guaranteeing what we perceive as commercial films distribution before they go into production," says UIP's Ord. "After *The Piano* and *Once Were Warriors*, the film industry has a wonderful opportunity to cash in on the local and international market. ... But the industry must make more commercial films. ... It has to make pictures that return more money, not for the sake of profit but so there is additional money to make more films."

Lee Tamahori, director of ONCE WERE WARRIORS

Recent and Forthcoming Films

BONJOUR TIMOTHY

Script: David Parry and David Preston. Phot: Matt Bowkett. Players: Unknown. Prod: Tucker Films and Cinar Films.

COPS AND ROBBERS

Script: Timothy Bean. Dir: Murray Reece. Phot: Steve Arnold. Players: Rima Te Wiata, Mark Wright, Grant Dodwell, Melissa Kounas, Gosia Dobrowolska. Prod: Isambard Productions/ Total Film and Television.

HEAVENLY CREATURES

Script: Peter Jackson, Frances Walsh. Dir: Peter Jackson. Phot: Alun Bollinger. Players: Melanie Lynskey, Kate Winslet, Sarah Pierse, Diana Kent, Clive Merrison. Prod: Wingnut Films.

JACK BROWN, GENIUS

Script and Dir: Tony Hiles. Phot: Allen Guilford. Players: Tim Balme, Eddie Campbell, Lisa Chappell. Prod: Wingnut Films.

THE LAST TATTOO

Script: Keith Aberdein, John Reid. Prod: John Reid. Phot: John Blick. Players: Kerry Fox, Tony Goldwyn, Robert Loggia, Rod Steiger, John Bach. Prod: Plumb Productions.

ONCE WERE WARRIORS

Script: Riwai Brown. Dir: Lee Tamahori. Phot: Stuart Dryburgh. Players: Temuera Morrison, Rena Owen, Cliff Curtis, Mamaengaroa Kerr-Bell, Tauronga Emile. Prod: Communicado Communications.

Useful Addresses

N.Z. Film Commission
PO Box 11546
Wellington
Tel: (04) 385-9754
Fax: (04) 384-9719

N.Z. On Air
PO Box 9744
Wellington
Tel: (04) 382-9524
Fax: (04) 382-9546

N.Z. Film Archive
Cnr Jervois Quay/Cable St
Wellington
Tel: (04) 384-7647
Fax: (04) 382-9595

Independent Producers and Directors Guild
PO Box 3969
Wellington
Tel/Fax: (04) 385-8055

Project Blue Sky
PO Box 6619
Auckland
Tel: (09) 358-7104
Fax: (09) 483-3528

Avalon Studios
PO Box 31-444
Lower Hutt
Tel: (04) 619-0600
Fax: (04) 619-0464

Communicado Communications
PO Box 5779
Auckland
Tel: (09) 379-3734
Fax: (09) 307-8885

Endeavour Productions
PO Box 68445
Auckland
Tel: (09) 378-1900
Fax: (09) 378-1905

The Gibson Group
119 Taranaki Street
Wellington
Tel: (04) 384-7789
Fax: (04) 384-4727

Hibiscus Films/John Maynard Productions
PO Box 1852
Auckland
Tel: (09) 309-8388
Fax: (09) 373-4722

Isambard Productions
PO Box 41066
St Lukes
Auckland
Tel: (09) 849-7772
Fax: (09) 849-7755

Kiwi Film Productions
PO Box 6698
Wellington
Tel: (04) 384-4060
Fax: (04) 384-3774

Pacific Film
PO Box 9625
Wellington
Tel: (04) 387-2191
Fax: (04) 382-9916

Pinflicks Productions
PO Box 9438
Wellington
Tel: (04) 387-8741
Fax: (04) 387-8794

Plumb Productions
PO Box 2070
Wellington
Tel: (04) 385-1283
Fax: (04) 382-8787

Preston-Laing Productions
PO Box 9175
Wellington
Tel: (04) 384-6405
Fax: (04) 384-7406

South Pacific Pictures
PO Box 35656
Auckland
Tel: (09) 444-3000
Fax: (09) 443-5900

Tucker Films
562 Richmond Road
Grey Lynn
Auckland
Tel: (09) 360-1312
Fax: (09) 376-2295

James Wallace Productions
PO Box 67057
Auckland
Tel: (09) 302-5271
Fax: (09) 302-5272

Wingnut Films
PO Box 9101
Wellington
Tel: (04) 382-8364
Fax: (04) 801-6920

Everard Films
PO Box 3664
Auckland
Tel: (09) 302-1193
Fax: (09) 302-1192

Hoyts Entertainment (NZ)
PO Box 6923
Auckland
Tel: (09) 309-0955

Roadshow Film Distributors
PO Box 68246
Auckland
Tel: (09) 377-9669
Fax: (09) 377-9449

United International Pictures (NZ)
PO Box 105263
Auckland
Tel: (09) 379-6269
Fax: (09) 379-6271

NORWAY

Trond Olav Svendsen

Since January 1, 1993 the all-important system of film subsidies in Norway has included a so-called consultant, a person with enough power and funds to get a specific project going – or to stop it.

The consultant represented an improvement, but who should have the job? Most people who know one or two things about cinema in a small country (Norway has four million people) wants to direct or produce films. The first consultant, the former director Oddvar Bull Tuhus, has already left for the fiction department of Norway's major TV-corporation, the government-controlled NRK.

One of Norway's problems in producing quality films is the low rate of production, five to seven pictures a year. With as many as 25-30 experienced film directors who have all made a film or two in the last ten years, and with several young aspiring directors making themselves felt with excellent short films, the problem is a real one and a matter of concern to bureaucrats and film-makers alike.

In the last two to three years some solutions to these problems have been offered. There is more money available than ever before, costs no longer rise as quickly as they did in the 1980's, and there are closer and more fruitful links between the government money (the aforementioned film consultant) and the film-makers. And it's easier to make films on a smaller scale, from low-budget to no-budget, giving young directors some alternatives.

A Good Average Year

The best news of the 1993-94 season was perhaps that cinema attendance was on the rise, and that the Norwegian producers came forward with several quality films.

Expectations were high before the premiere of the war story **The Last Lieutenant** at the 1993 Haugesund Festival. It marked the directorial debut of Hans Petter Moland, a well-known director of commercials, and gave centre stage to Norway's favourite actor of his generation, Espen Skjønberg.

representing

NORWAY

worldwide

festivals-

markets-

film weeks-

archives-

Cinemateque

and

feature film

Production

RECENT FILMS at
RECENT FESTIVALS
STELLA POLARIS
Karlovy Vary,
San Sebastian

DADDY BLUE
Best film at Rouen Festival;
Giffoni, Edinburgh

HEAD ABOVE THE WATER
Norway´s entry for the
Nordic Amanda Award

THE TELEGRAPHIST
Berlin

BAT WINGS
Best direction, Moscow

BEYOND THE SKY
Telluride, Giffoni, London

DREAM PLAY
Un certain Regard, Cannes;
Montreal, Edinburgh

THE LAST LIEUTENANT
Gothenburgh,
Mill Valley, London, New York

CARL AND THE ANGELS
Berlin, Giffoni

FILM MUSEUM AND ARCHIVES DEPARTMENT &
DEPARTMENT OF PRODUCTION AND
INTERNATIONAL RELATIONS:

Grev Wedels plass

P.O.Box 482, Sentrum

N-0105 Oslo

Tel. + 47 22 42 87 40

fax. + 47 22 33 22 77

ADMINISTRATION & DEPARTMENT
OF ACQUISITIONS AND DISTRIBUTION:

Schwensensgt. 6,

P.O.Box: 2655, St. Hanshaugen

N-0131 Oslo

Tel. + 47 22 60 20 90

Fax. + 47 22 60 92 00

The Last Lieutenant takes place during the weeks immediately following the German attack on Norway on April 9, 1940. Outnumbered and intimidated by German air superiority, the commanding officers of a regiment plan to surrender. An elderly second-lieutenant, recently retired as captain of a merchant vessel, steps forward, organises his own unit and fights on from a base in the mountains. For a couple of weeks the Germans' progress is halted.

The film is handsomely shot and directed, but there is a significant problem connected to the development of the action itself. The script tends to go off in ever new directions, exploiting too many themes. Despite the true story behind it and the focus on one strong-willed character, the film does not emerge as the fresh, subjective look at war that was hoped for.

The Blue Wolves is the third and probably final instalment in the story of two very popular teenage detectives cribbed from a series of books. This time the production looks handsome enough, the cinematography of Pål Bugge Haagenrud being a major asset and the direction of Morten Kolstad a definite improvement on the previous film, the disappointing *Poisonous Lies*. Unfortunately, the plot dissolves into thin air and instead the young Sherlocks get nosey about Dad's possible affair with a young woman. A very sad development indeed in the career of a detective!

Beyond the Sky is the kind of movie that offers enjoyment both through the realistic setting and some off-beat and not very believable situations. Mari is a twelve-year-old girl who quarrels incessantly with her parents and with her little boy scout brother. She finally finds a friend in Miss Kjær, a retired teacher. Miss Kjær (played by that wonderful icon of Swedish cinema, Harriet Andersson) is such a bad-tempered, unsentimental old hag that she quits the teaching profession not, it seems, because of the ill-behaved children, but because of all the well-behaved ones who she can't stand. When Mari offends her, a lasting friendship begins.

Still from DADDY BLUE

Later Miss Kjær reveals that she cherishes the memory of an old flame, last seen 41 years ago. Rather incredibly the man is found on a nearby island, the two women go off to visit him, and find that true love never dies.

The experienced TV-director Berit Nesheim and the playwright and actor Klaus Hagerup are the brains behind this lively picture aimed at a young audience. Nesheim is a good film director despite the fact that her TV background is often noticeable. She makes the film carry weight through its humorous tone, and she makes one forget the sometimes unlikely turns of the story.

Only One Real Surprise

The films of the 1993-94 season had only one real surprise among them, but so soft-voiced as to escape the attention of the audiences. This was **Daddy Blue**, the first feature of René Bjerke who has been making short films for more than twenty years. *Daddy Blue* tells the simple story of a sixteen-year-old boy who is fed up with his parents and runs away from home in a stolen sailing boat. Cruising in the Oslo fjord, he meets a young woman who has left her boyfriend, though the break-up has not left any scars. The father comes looking for his son, however, and the three of them travel on, relating rather uneasily to each other.

Bjerke has a gift for naturalness, his two young leads give unforced, seemingly carefree performances and the film is

TOP TEN GROSSING FILMS IN NORWAY: 1993

Jurassic Park	361,345
The Bodyguard	340,590
Cliffhanger	290,547
The Fugitive	258,550
Dennis the Menace	200,696
The Telegraphist (Norw.)	199,825
The Jungle Book	147,548
Home Alone 2	145,886
The Firm	131,588
Head Above Water (Norw.)	94,460

simply and smoothly staged in and around the boat. Bjerke is anything but a pretentious film-maker; he goes for the simple, human truth of every situation without making any of it banal. His inspiration, subliminally, is the early New Wave, with its fresh use of actors and lightweight directorial and cinematic style.

All in all the films of the 1993-94 season maintained a fair level in terms of relevance and production values. But it is towards the future that all eyes are turned. The new season will see the changes in Norwegian cinema pay off with a sharp rise in the number of cinema-released films. It is the fruit of a revived interest for Norwegian cinema in the government, some rethinking and reorganisation of old institutions, and a lot of new directors with a better education behind them than the preceding generation. It looks exciting.

TROND OLAV SVENDSEN holds a degree in history from the University of Oslo, and works for a publisher in Oslo besides being a film critic and film historian. In 1991 he published a Theatre and Film Encyclopedia.

Recent and Forthcoming Films

SECONDLØITNANTEN (The Last Lieutenant)

Script: Axel Hellstenius. Dir: Hans Petter Moland. Phot: Harald Paalgard. Players: Espen Skjønberg, Lars Andreas Larsen, Gard B. Eidsvold, Bjørn Sundquist. Prod: Norsk Film (Esben Høilund Carlsen and Harald Ohrvik).

DE BLÅ ULVENE (The Blue Wolves)

Script: Axel Hellstenius, based on a novel by Ingvar Ambjørnsen. Dir: Morten Kolstad. Phot: Pål Bugge Haagenrud. Players: Håvard Bakke, Tommy Karlsen, Viggo Jønsberg. Prod: Filmkameratene (John M. Jacobsen).

KOLOSS (Colossus)

Script and Dir: Witold Leszcynski based on the novel by Finn Alnæs. Phot: Grzegorz Kedzierski. Players: Ove Christian Owe, Sverre Anker Ousdal, Leon Niemczyk, Karolina Rosinska. Prod: Regionalfilm (Inge Tenvik and Trond G. Lockertsen).

KALLE OG ENGLENE (Carl and the Angels)

Script and Dir: Ole Bjørn Salvesen. Phot: Erling Thurmann-Andersen. Players: Tom Beck Letessier, Karl Sundby. Prod: Mekano Film (Anders Birkeland).

HODET OVER VANNET (Head Above Water)

Script: Erik Ildahl and Geir Eriksen. Dir: Nils Gaup. Phot: Erling Thurmann-Andersen. Players: Lene Elise Bergum, Svein Karlsen. Prod: Filmkameratene (John M. Jacobsen).

HØYERE ENN HIMMELEN (Beyond the Sky)

Script: Klaus Hagerup, based on his own novel. Dir: Berit Nesheim. Phot: Philip Øgaard. Players: Inger Lise Winjevoll, Harriet Andersson. Prod: Northern Lights (Axel Helgeland).

DU, PAPPA (Daddy Blue)

Script and Dir: René Bjerke. Phot: Peter Mocrosinski. Players: Håkon Bolstad, Benedikte

Lindbeck, Nils Ole Oftebro. Prod: Norsk Film A/S.

HODIAK

Script: Hans Petter Blad, Thure Erik Lund. Dir: Hans Petter Blad. Phot: Thure Erik Lund. Players: Håkan Islinger, Guandaline Sagliocco. Prod: Uwaga Film.

DRAUMSPEL (Dreamplay)

Script and Dir: Unni Straume, based on the play by August Strindberg. Players: Ingvild Holm, Bjørn Willberg Andersen, Lars Erik Berenett, Liv Ullmann, Bibi Andersson. Prod: Unni Straume Filmproduksjon (Petter Bøe).

TROLLSYN (Second Sight)

Script: Anja Breien. Dir: Ola Solum. Phot: Harald Paalgard. Players: Julia Onsager Steen, Liv Bernhoft Osa, Bjørn Willberg Andersen, Bjørn Sundquist. Prod: Northern Lights (Hilde Berg).

TI KNIVER I HJERTET (Cross My Heart and Hope to Die)

Script: Lars Saabye Christensen. Dir: Marius Holst. Phot: Philip Øgaard. Players: Martin Garfalk, Devo, Kjersti Holmen, Reidar Sørensen. Prod: Nordic Screen Development.

VILLHESTEN (The Wild Horse)

Script: Morten Kolstad and Lars Borg. Dir: Morten Kolstad. Phot: Bål Bugge Haagenrud. Players: Linda Digernes, Susanna Nilsen. Prod: ViPro (Jørn Brente and Lars Borg).

BIKINISESONGEN (The Bikini Season)

Script: Morten Barth. Dir: Runar Jarle Wiik. Phot: Peder Norlund. Players: Thor-Ivar Forslund, Eduardo Verdu, Ole Paus, Sverre Anker Ousdal. Prod: Norsk Film A/S.

DET VAR EN GANG (Once Upon a Time)

Script: Ketil Jakobsen and Beate Krumpska. Dir: Ketil Jakobsen. Prod: Norsk Film and Ketil Jakobsen. *Animated feature.*

LYKKE, LYKKE

Script: Axel Hellstenius. Dir: Eva Isaksen. Phot: Kjell Vassdal. Players: Anneke von der Lippe, Johannes Joner. Prod: MovieMakers A/S.

KRISTIN LAVRANSDATTER

Script and Dir: Liv Ullmann, based on the novel by Sigrid Undset. Phot: Sven Nykvist. Players: Elisabeth Matheson, Bjørn Skagestad, Rut Tellefsen. Prod: Norsk Film A/S.

Producers

Aprilfilm A/S
Box 88
N-1321 Stabekk
Tel: 22 20 60 68
Fax: 22 36 05 52

Atomfilm A/S
Thomesheivn. 2
N-3770 Kragerø
Tel: 35 98 11 98
Fax: 35 98 06 27

Caprino Filmcentre A/S
Mario Caprinos vei 3
N-1335 Snarøya
Tel: 67 53 31 95
Fax: 67 58 14 70

Favola Film A/S
Kløvervn. 13 C
N-1450 Nesoddtangen
Tel: 66 91 53 10

Filmhuset A/S
Schübelers gt. 7
N-0577 Oslo
Tel: 22 68 16 02
Fax: 22 67 12 15

Filmkameratene A/S
Box 6868
St. Olavs pl.
N-0130 Oslo
Tel: 22 33 47 50
Fax: 22 33 27 97

Infofilm Production A/S
Box 8256
Hammersborg
N-0129 Oslo
Tel: 22 50 56 00
Fax: 22 41 06 73

Lars Berg Filmproduksjon
Sørbyhaugen 48
N-0377 Oslo
Tel: 22 49 01 27
Fax: 22 49 08 22

Magdalena Film A/S
c/o Bente Erichsen
Kirkevn. 147 E
N-0361 Oslo
Tel: 22 56 44 81
Fax: 22 56 44 51

Mefistofilm A/S
Gyldenløves gt. 41
N-0260 Oslo
Tel: 22 43 82 60
Fax: 22 55 77 77

Motlys A/S
Islandsgt. 6
N-0658 Oslo
Tel: 22 68 60 63
Fax: 22 68 21 91

MovieMakers A/S
Box 6858
St. Olavs pl.
N-0130 Oslo
Tel: 22 36 09 90
Fax: 22 36 41 28

Nordic Screen Development A/S
Box 4
N-1342 Jar
Tel: 67 58 04 20
Fax: 67 59 12 44

Nordnorsk Filmsenter A/S
Box 94
N-9751 Honningsvåg
Tel: 78 47 30 11
Fax: 78 47 36 90

Norsk Film A/S
Box 4
N-1342 Jar
Tel: 67 52 53 00
Fax: 67 12 51 08

Northern Lights Film & TV Produksjon A/S
Box 104

N-1342 Jar
Tel: 67 52 53 00/67 52 53 30
Fax: 67 52 53 40

Penelope Film A/S
Box 618
N-4601 Kristiansand
Tel: 38 02 60 59

Regional Film A/S
Nydalsvn. 33E
N-0483 Oslo
Tel: 22 95 20 69
Fax: 22 95 20 49

Svekon Film
Seiersbjerget 5
N-5018 Bergen
Tel: 55 31 02 25
Fax: 55 31 81 80

Teamfilm A/S
Keysers gt. 1
N-0165 Oslo
Tel: 22 20 70 72
Fax: 22 20 64 81

ViPro A/S
Box 4316 Torshov
N-0402 Oslo
Tel: 22 35 20 40
Fax: 22 35 20 42

Viscom A/S
Parkvn. 28
N-5007 Bergen
Tel: 55 31 34 31
Fax: 55 32 25 64

Åsfilm A/S
Sentralvn. 35
N-1430 Ås
Tel: 64 94 29 38
Fax: 64 94 10 61

Distributors

Action Film A/S
Box 9343 Vålerenga
N-0610 Oslo
Tel: 22 67 31 31
Fax: 22 67 30 05

Arthaus
Teatergt. 3
N-0180 Oslo
Tel: 22 11 26 12
Fax: 22 20 79 81

BV-Film
Nedre Slottsgt. 5
N-0157 Oslo
Tel: 22 42 55 90
Fax: 22 42 77 77

Europafilm A/S
Stortingsgt. 30
N-0161 Oslo
Tel: 22 83 42 90
Fax: 22 83 41 51

A/S Fidalgo Filmdistribusjon
Box 2054 Posebyen
N-4602 Kristiansand
Tel: 38 02 40 04
Fax: 38 02 23 54

Kommunenes Filmcentral A/S
Nedre Vollgt. 9
N-0158 Oslo
Tel: 22 41 43 25
Fax: 22 42 14 69

Norsk FilmDistribusjon A/S
Stortingsgt. 12
N-0161 Oslo
Tel: 22 42 36 00
Fax: 22 42 23 13

SF Norge A/S
Box 6868
St. Olavs pl.
N-0130 Oslo
Tel: 22 33 47 50
Fax: 22 42 72 93

United International Pictures A/S
Box 7134 Homansbyen
N-0307 Oslo
Tel: 22 56 61 15
Fax: 22 56 71 81

Warner Bros. (Norway) A/S
Box 7053 Homansbyen
N-0306 Oslo
Tel: 22 43 18 00
Fax: 22 55 46 83

Useful Addresses

The National Association of Municipal Cinemas
Kongens gt. 23
N-0153 Oslo
Tel: 22 33 05 30
Fax: 22 42 89 49

The Norwegian Cinema and Film Foundation
Kongens gt. 23
N-0153 Oslo 1
Tel: 22 33 05 30
Fax: 22 42 89 49

Norwegian Film and Video Producers' Association
Storengvn. 8 B
N-1342 Jar
Tel: 67 53 74 98
Fax: 67 12 48 65

Norwegian Film Distributors' Association
Nedre Vollgt. 9
N-0158 Oslo
Tel: 22 42 48 44
Fax: 22 42 30 93

The Norwegian Film Institute
Box 482 Sentrum
N-0105 Oslo
Tel: 22 42 87 40
Fax: 22 33 22 77

Espen Skjønberg in THE LAST LIEUTENANT

PAKISTAN
Aijaz
Gul

The death of Pakistan's most imaginative, ambitious and creative film director Nazrul Islam left the film industry shattered in January 1994. We also lost director Luqman, Aslam Irani and Agha Hussaini. Actress Rani, still in her forties, also died. Composer Kamal Ahmad, creator of many popular film songs, left in his prime.

Turning back to 1993, 88 feature films were released (65 in Punjabi-Urdu, 23 in Pushto). No new trends emerged. Violence and lawlessness continued to be favourite themes of the film-makers where the hero's mother also took up the assault rifles for a showdown either in the Punjab fields or in the traditional gaudily painted mansion of the landlord. As many as three films were rejected by the Central Board of Film Censors in April 1994 for too much violence and brutality (all the three films were all set to open on the festivities of Eid).

Pervaiz Kaleem was the discovery of 1993, not as an actor but as a director. Kaleem had earlier established himself as a scriptwriter, excelling in titles like *The Market*. He made his directorial debut with the low-budgeter Urdu film, **The Sin**, the story of a young man who is married to an older woman. The man is actually after the woman's voluptuous daughter and this is enough for the woman to commit suicide. With a new cast, *The Sin* played extremely well all over Pakistan.

Syed Noor, a screenwriter with hundreds of Urdu and Punjabi films to his credit (and discredit), also made an entry as a director with **The Vow**, an action-ridden vengeance drama with the final shootout in a cemetery. *The Vow* played moderately well.

Actor-producer-director Omar Sharif gave us his third film, **Miss Troublesome**. It was a work without the competence and professional skill displayed so well in Sharif's earlier *Mr. 420* and *Mr. Charlie*. But now in 1994, Sharif was minting gold on the Lahore stage and he took the backseat. The film was practically completed and released in 25 days with the comedian's starlet Shakila Qureshi in the limelight. Filmgoers rejected this makeshift quickie, devoid of expensive and impressive production values, good script and popular melodies. Omar Sharif had to learn his lesson the hard way with heavy losses to the exhibitors and sub-distributors.

Best Film Proves a Loser

Director Iqbal Kashmiri is a calculated commercial film-maker who is at his best only with a rich and resourceful producer. His social film **The Heaven** (1993) played well.

The best film of 1993 was not a winner but a loser. Director Nazrul Islam's **The Wish**, scripted by Asghar Nadeem Syed with Sameena Peerzada and producer Moin-ur-Rehman in the leading roles, was a powerful comment on rape, moral decay and corruption of the politicians and their spoiled rich brats. Unlike a regular film with six to eight songs, *The Wish* contains only two songs, with no comedy and no dances. It turned out to be the disaster of the year but a critical success. The film was chosen by Woman Action Groups for special screenings. *The Wish* was technically a first-rate film with prints processed and printed in London. The film was recently shown at the Commonwealth Film Festival in London.

Actress-producer-director Shamim Ara, who won box-office glory in the 1980's

Kubra Khanum in GUNAH (THE SIN)

with the "Miss" series (*Miss Hongkong, Miss Colombo*), made a comeback after almost five years with **The Elephant Walk**, a co-production between Pakistan and Sri Lanka. The film had absolutely no script but was loaded with time-tested cheap gimmicks, romance, suspense and third-rate comedy. Shamim Ara and the distributor hit the jackpot with a pop song and scenes of a temple with Adam's footprints (only starved audiences would believe in such far-fetched fantasies).

Shamim Ara is now repeating the same cast (Reema, Mohsin Khan) with same picture postcard locations of Sri Lanka in her new film **The Son**. Shamim Ara is still remembered as a serious actress from the 1960's but she is totally devoid of any serious directorial style, cinematic sense and artistic sensibilities. Director Masood Butt's **Witness** played well. Husnain's **Humanity** also did fair business. Husnain's **Lady, King** and Hassan Askari's **Fame** opened poorly.

In terms of sheer quantity, Husnain directed eight features, followed by Masood Butt with five. Hassan Askari, Altaf Hussain, Iqbal Kashmiri and Zahoor Hussain were the other notable directors. Sultan Rahi, Nadeem, Omar Sharif, Izhar Qazi, Mohsin Khan, Saima and Anjuman proved to be bankable stars. The three most popular composers, Zulfiqar Ali, Wajahat Attrey and M. Ashraf, came up with 13 films each in 1993.

During the first six months of 1994, the only notable film was producer-director Saeed Rizvi's **The Headless**, a science-fiction movie with TV commercial-like laser effects, undertaken by Rizvi at his own special-effects laboratory, Novitas. Former superstar Shabnam made a comeback this year in a melodramatic young-to-old role in **Daughter**, with Reema, Sultan Rahi and Omar Sharif. The film is playing on the sentiments of female filmgoers, particularly at Lahore. Infamous model-actress Aneeta Ayub, who had earlier left no stone unturned in Bombay with Dev Anand's **Love Song** returned to her soil at Karachi and came out with two disasters: **The Swifters** in 1993 and **The Fast Ones** in 1994. This may be beginning of the end for Aneeta Ayub's film career.

Cliffhanger on Top in 1993

Among imports, *Cliffhanger* was the biggest hit of 1993, notwithstanding the business of local films. People were wildly attracted to Stallone, action and special effects, and special promo reels of the making of *Cliffhanger* were prominent on TV. The other hits of 1993 included *Hard Target, Dragon – The Bruce Lee Story, Showdown in Little Tokyo* and *Lionheart*. Van Damme had suddenly become the most popular hero for the young crowd.

Jurassic Park bowed in April in English and Urdu-dubbed versions. This was the first time in the last forty-five years that a major American film opened with 30 prints and Urdu dubbing. More children saw *Jurassic Park* in Pakistan than all the films put together from the last forty-five years. Special school and college shows were held. Gift shops in the cinema lobbies also did roaring business with JP bedsheets, badges, tee-shirts and stationery items. Of course the film industry was not happy with JP and they first went to the Government and then to the Central Board of Film Censors to stop the film. When nothing worked, they tried to go to the court and eventually warned the 13 cinemas to discontinue the film or be black-listed. These American megahits have managed to bring back the lost film fans (from their homes watching movies on TV networks, video and dish) to the cinema. Thanks to Stallone, Van Damme and Spielberg for reviving the cinema in Pakistan during 1993-94.

The National Film Development Corporation arranged film festivals from South Korea, Finland, Japan in 1993 and a festival of Hungarian films in April 1994.

AIJAZ GUL was born in 1947, and earned his B.A. and M.A. in Cinema from USC, Los Angeles. He has written three books and numerous articles on film, and presently works for the National Film Development Corporation.

TOP TEN GROSSING FILMS IN PAKISTAN: 1993

Cliffhanger
Hard Target
Hathi Merey Sathi (Elephant Walk)
Mr. Charlie
Gunah (The Sin)
Insaniat (Humanity)
Jannat (The Heaven)
Qasam (The Vow)
Behrupia (Double-cross)
Khuda Gawah (Witness)

NAZRUL ISLAM (1939-1994)

Pakistan's most polished and sophisticated film director Nazrul Islam died on January 11, 1994. He began his career in Dhaka as an editor and made his directorial debut with *Kajal (Eyes)* in 1963. He later shifted to Lahore and made some of our best films including *Aina (Mirror), Bandish (The Bar), Nahi Abhi Nahi (Sweet Sixteen)* and *Kaley Chor (Thieves)*. His last film *Khawhish (The Wish)* came out in December 1993 and was acclaimed by selected audiences. Nazrul Islam would always be remembered for good taste, intelligence, colour sense and cinematic imagination.

Recent and Forthcoming Films

KHAWHISH (The Wish)

Script: Asghar Nadeem Syed. Dir: Nazrul Islam. Phot: Waqar Bokhari. Music: Javed Allah Ditta, Robin Ghosh. Players: Sameena Peerzada, Moin-ur-Rehman, Babra Sharif.

A young widow is raped but, with the prevailing corruption and lawlessness, she does not get justice.

KHAZANA (The Treasure)

Dir: Hassan Askari. Players: Nadeem, Izhar Qazi, Sahiba.

The dramatic if very sentimental story of a family.

QASAM (The Vow)

Script and Dir: Syed Noor. Music: Amjad Bobby. Phot: Babar Bilal. Players: Nadeem, Imran Hassan, Saleem Sheikh, Kanwal.

A standard vehicle which played well due to strong emotions and climactic action.

JANNAT (The Heaven)

Script: Tanveer Kazmi. Dir: Iqbal Kashmiri. Music: Wajahat Attrey. Phot: Saleem Butt.

The story of three friends and their problems with their parents, with the final reunion taking place at a saint's tomb. The film also comments on adult illiteracy in Pakistan.

SAR KATA INSAN (The Headless)

Script: Mahmood Rizvi. Dir and Phot: Saaed Rizvi. Music: Kamal Ahmad. Players: Ghulam Mohiuddin, Babra Sharif, Izhar Qazi.

A human head from a fresh grave is given to a scientist for macabre experiments.

GUNAH (The Sin)

Script and Dir: Pervaiz Kaleem. Music: Altaf Hussain. Players:

Kubra Khanam, Saud, Simi.

The story of a young man who gets married to a rich woman old enough to be his mother. He later falls for her daughter and the rich woman commits suicide.

Useful Addresses

National Film Development Corporation Limited
56-F, Blue Area,
P.O. Box No. 1204
Islamabad
Tel: 092 051 823148
Fax: 092 051 221863

Ministry of Culture
Block-D,
Pak Secretariat
Islamabad
Fax: 092 051 221863
092 051 211790 & 213121

Central Board of Film Censors
St. No. 55,
Sector f-6/4
Islamabad
Tel: 092 051 824939
Fax: 092 051 221863

Pakistan Film Producers Association
Regal Cinema Building
Shahrah-e-Quaid-e-Azam
Lahore
Tel: 092 042 322904

Eveready Pictures (Pvt) Limited
18 Mowlai Mansion
M.A. Jinnah Road
Karachi
Tel: 092 021 2621775 & 2621293
Fax: 092 021 2627843 (Karachi)
Fax: 092 042 323435 (Lahore)

Evernew Pictures
2 Abbot Road
Lahore
Tel: 092 042 7226929 & 7227063
Telex: 44960 EVNEW PK

Imran Films
Royal Park
Lahore
Tel: 6363310

Meeran Al-Bachal Production
Jora Building
Royal Park
Lahore

Mandviwalla Entertainment
Nishat Cinema Building
M.A. Jinnah Road
Karachi
Fax: 092 021 7227259
Telex: 23323 HAKIM PK

PHILIPPINES
Agustin
Sotto

resident Fidel V. Ramos's reversal of his censors' decision to cut scenes from *Schindler's List* was, at least, an unexpected triumph for the anti-censorship forces who were despairing at a dangerous slide towards moral hypocrisy and intolerance. The administration's courtship of the powerful religious lobbies had resulted in the placement in the Board of many Christian fundamentalists bent on cleaning up the movies and re-instituting an ultra-conservative sensibility. To the surprise of the local cinema artists, who saw their freedom curbed, even passionate kissing was removed and low voltage curse words blipped out. Scenes deemed offensive to a puritan morality – like the suicide in Steven Soderbergh's *King of the Hill* were also ordered to be cut.

Steven Spielberg's decision not to allow cuts on his film had the support of the local journalists who thought it the opportune time to challenge the moral tyrants. The brouhaha was subsequently picked up by the international press, and the negative reaction abroad finally prevailed upon the administration to review the censorship policies. The censors were instructed not to cut films but to strictly implement a ratings system ("GP", "PG-15", "R", "X") as mandated in the Marcos law.

But just as the liberals were about to toast their victory, the board struck again by giving an "X" rating to *The Piano* and *Belle Epoque*. The catch here is that "X" means the film could not be shown at all. In order to stave off another controversy, the board was quietly allowed to reverse itself and consent to the screening of the uncut versions. Unfortunately, other films with less credentials could not be accorded the same treatment and have to be sanitised by their distributors to earn an acceptable rating. For now, only Oscar winners could command a certain degree of epidermal exposure.

With the censorship code again under review in Congress, Cirio Santiago, chairman of the Film Foundation of the Philippines, the government agency that replaced the Experimental Cinema of the Philippines, announced a line-up of activities that would lift it off its moribund status. Foremost is his solicitation of twelve foreign productions to be filmed in Manila. These are mainly action films with stars Jean-Claude van Damme, Gary Busey, Fernando Lamas and Michael Dudikoff. Under a government plan, these productions would be allowed tax incentives, low-cost production services, below-the-line financing, and access to military hardware. With the former American bases as the production centres, Cirio hopes to turn Manila into a world cinema capital.

Film Ratings Board Review

Another pet project of his is the revival of the Film Ratings Board, the Marcos film agency that gave out rebates to quality films. However, this has been most difficult to re-instate due to the resistance from city and municipal treasurers in remitting the cash.

All this is happy news for the film industry that is seeing more government involvement in film activities. Another national project in the works is the mounting of a mammoth Lino Brocka retrospective at Nantes and the Cinémathèque Française at the end of 1994. This is a segment of the Philippine year in France. Many of these films have never been shown abroad, and some have been critically acclaimed by visiting French critics.

Another important development is the growing cable demand for film titles. This has made producers aware of the value of their old films. Unfortunately, many of them are lost forever due to the harsh tropical weather and a general lack of understanding regarding film preservation. In order to remedy this situation,

Still from Ucik Supra's CLOWNS OF THE CITY

several film archivists have banded together to form the Society of Film Archivists (SOFIA). Its first task is to form a viable archival system that would cut across the politics and lack of hardware. It has been getting a lot of sound advice from visiting FIAF archivists who would like to see honest-to-goodness archives not only in the Philippines but also in the East Asian region.

Film year 1993 saw 123 local films produced – an average that the industry has been maintaining for several years now. The bad news is that, due to stiff censorship, it is losing its competitive edge to Hollywood. In 1993, at least three Hollywood films would be considered certifiable hits: *Jurassic Park, Cliffhanger* and *The Bodyguard*, but the absence of gross figures makes this rather inconclusive. The top local films at the box-office were, as usual, superstar-oriented with Sharon Cuneta and Robin Padilla as the top attractions.

Bizarre Crime of Passion

Still the hottest genre is the *sub judice* film – material based on screaming headliners and peppered with innuendo, neighbourhood gossip, hysteria and political grandstanding. It became so white-hot at the box-office that two companies vied for the screen rights of a bizarre crime passionel in which a pretty secretary was chopped up by her American lover. Two versions were produced – one based on the estranged husband's (*The Chop-Chop Lady*) and the other on the mother's (*The Elsa Castillo Story*). The conflicting portrayals, at least, brought out the residual irony of the situation, and not a few commentators thought that the two should be viewed as a diptych. After a few weeks run, both films were considered inimical to the court interest as the case is still *sub judice* and were ordered removed from public view. But not after amassing huge profits.

The year turned out to be a vindication for scriptwriter-turned-director, Jose Javier Reyes. Although small in scale, his films are rich in poignant observations on the human condition. **Paana Kita Mililimutan**, about an illiterate migrating to the city to take care of his scholar sister and younger brother, brings out the pathos and tragedy of the untutored trying to adhere to time-worn family values. **May Minamahal** goes against the grain of the highly popular convoluted melodramas by keeping to a simple storyline. A scion of the upper crust falls in love with a girl not of the same social status. The conflicting views results in a sprightly comedy of manners that is spiced with affable comic turns and engaging romantic gestures. **Makati Av. Office Girls** takes on an even bigger canvas by relating very concisely the lives of its female office workers. The deft control over the material, despite the many characters, and the superior acting of its principals combine to produce what the local critics considered as the best film of the year.

Useful Addresses

Film Department
College of Mass Communications
University of the Philippines
Diliman
Quezon City

Film Department
De La Salle University
Taft Avenue
Manila

Film School Board of the Philippines
23 Maginhawa
U.P. Village
Quezon City

Society of Film Archivists
C63A Gueventville II
Libertad,
Mandaluyong

Manunuri ng Pelikulang Pilipino
(Film Critics' Association)
C63A Gueventville II
Libertad
Mandaluyong

Film Academy of the Philippines
Sampaguita Compound
Gilmore
Quezon City

Mowelfund
66 Rosario Drive
Cubao
Quezon City

Film Commission
National Commission for Culture
and the Arts
Intramuros
Manila

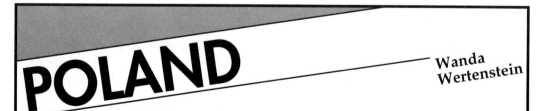

POLAND — Wanda Wertenstein

This year began surprisingly well: admissions in the first six months were 20% higher than in 1993, with three Polish films among the top ten. First on the list was Spielberg's *Schlindler's List*, but a Polish film was third. The title is an easy guess: *Last Blood (Ostatnia krew)*, Pasikowski's sequel to his *Pigs* and generally referred to as *Pigs 2*. Of the three Kieślowski "colours", *Blue* opened in October 1993, *White* in March 1994 and *Red* in May. After four months in release *White* was sixth on the list.

Among new films, **Aquarium** (*Akwarium*), directed by Antoni Krauze and based on the book by the Soviet spy Viktor Sokurov, is not yet on release but said to be interesting; and **Miss Wet-Head** (*Panną z mokrą głową*, adapted from Kornel Makussyński's novel and directed by first-time director Kazimierz Tarnas, enjoyed moderate success with its teenager public.

Dorota Kędzierzawska's **Crows** (*Wrony*) was noticed in Cannes and confirmed hopes for her future achievements. J.J. Kolski's **Miraculous Place** (*Cudowne miejsce*) continues his lovingly satirical way of portraying Polish rural life.

There was success of the younger generation. Cezary Harasimowicz, the scriptwriter for Maciej Dejczer's *300 Miles to Heaven*, won the Hartley-Merrill award for his script **Hoodlum**, which they play to film with Dejczer as soon as they find enough financial backing. Other films written by Harasimowicz were: Bogusław Linda's *Seychelles* (*Seszele*), Janusz Kijowski's *State of Terror* (*Stan strachu*) and Waldemar Dziki's *Lazarus*. Let us hope that the second half of the year will be as good as the first. An old Warsaw joke declares: "the situation is good but not hopeless." Maybe it is even better ...

WANDA WERTENSTEIN is a veteran Polish film critic on the staff of *Kino*. She is secretary of the Film Critics' Section of the Polish Film-makers' Association. She has translated English and Italian film books and published two Polish books, about Wajda and his famous Group "X".

TOP TEN GROSSING FILMS IN POLAND: 1993

	Admissions
Jurassic Park	2,727,096
Home Alone 2: Lost in New York	911,841
The Bodyguard	586,328
Hot Shots 2	525,690
Bram Stoker's Dracula	480,213
Beauty and the Beast	356,122
Bitter Moon	276,055
Scent of a Woman	258,534
Sliver	243,441
The Fugitive	225,194

Recent and Forthcoming Films

AKWARIUM (Aquarium)

Script: Jan Purzycki and Antoni Krauze, based on the book by Victor Suvorov. Dir: Antoni Krauze. Phot: Tomasz Tarasin. Players: Janusz Gajos, Juri Olennikov. Prod: Studio Dom, Polish Television, WFDiF (Warsaw), Manfred Durniok Prod. (Berlin), Ukrtelefilm (Kiev).

BALANGA (Bash)

Script and Dir: Tomasz Wylężałel. Phot: Krzysztof Tusiewicz.

Players: Jacek Palucha, Paweł Fesołowicz, Jan Tesarz, Sława Kwaśniewska, Maciej Kozłowski. Prod: Karol Irzykowski Film Studio (Warsaw), Polish Television.

CUDOWNE MIEJSCE (Miraculous Place)

Script and Dir: Jan Jakub Kolski. Phot: Piotr Lenar. Players: Grażyna Błęcka-Kolska, Adam Kamień, Krzysztof Majchrzak, Elżbieta Dębska, Mariusz Saniternik. Prod: Karol

Irzykowski Film Studio, Polish Television (Warsaw), WFF2 (Wrocław).

CYRKOWA PUŁAPKA (Circus Trap)

Script: Martin Ward and Andrzej Jasiewicz. Dir: Andrzej Jaasiewicz. Phot: Tomasz Tarasin. Players: Nigel Davenport, Jack McKenzie, Mathias Zimmermann, Sally Spencer, Marie-Louise McKenzie, Greg Sanders. Prod: Amber Corporation (Poland),

Luna Production (Switzerland), Jar Film (United Kingdom).

DWA KSIĘŻYCE (Two Moons)

Script and Dir: Andrzej Barański. Phot: Ryszard Lenczowski. Players: Bożena Adamek, Artur Barciś, Henryk Bista, Jerzy Bończak, Stanisława Celińska, Bożyena Dykiel. Prod: Scorpion Film for Polish Television.

KOMEDIA MAŁŻEŃSKA (Marital Comedy)

Script: Ilona Łepkowska, Roman Załuski. Dir: Roman Załuski. Phot: Maciej Kijowski. Players: Ewa Kacprzyk, Jan Englert. Prod: Fenix-Film (Warsaw).

LATO MIŁOŚCI (Summer of Love)

Script and Dir: Feliks Falk. Phot: Krzystof Tusiewicz. Players: Serguey Shnyriev, Daria Poviriennova. Ewa Bukowska, Ernest Romanow. Prod: Focus Film, WFDiF, Studio Perspektywa (Warsaw), PHF Akorn, Studio 1 (Minsk).

LAGENDA TATR (The Legend of the Tatra Mountains)

Script and Dir: Wojciech Solarz. Phot: Zbibniew Wichłacz. Players: Rafał Królikowski, Ryszard Sobolewski, Jerzy Binczycki, Jerzy Trela, Krzysztof Jasiński, Edward Linde-Lubaszenko. Prod: Filmcontract (Warsaw).

LES MILLES

Script and Dir: Sebastien Grall. Phot: Andrzej Jaroszewicz. Players: Jean-Pierre Marielle, Philippe Noiret, Henryk Bista, Marek Walczewski, Jan Peszek. Prod: Studio Tor (Warsaw), Blue Films (Paris), Studio Babelsberg-Schlöndorff (Berlin).

ŁOWCA (Hunter)

Script: Jerzy Łukaszewicz, Ryszard Zatorski. Dir: Jerzy

Łukaszewicz. Phot: Zdzisław Najda. Players: Mateusz Damięcki, Joanna Trzepiecińska, Wojciech Malajkat, Jacek Wójcicki, Tomasz Sapryk, Sławomir Orzechowski. Prod: MTL Maxfilm for Polish Television.

MIASTO PRYWATNE (Private Town)

Script and Dir: Jacek Skalski. Phot: Andrzej Adamczak. Players: Maciej Pawłowski, Bogusław Linda, Maria Gładkowska, Mirosław Baka, Dariusz Gnatowski. Prod: Film Studio, Polish Television (Warsaw), IFDF Odra Film, WFF2 (Wrocław).

NASTAZAJA (Nastassia)

Script: Andrzej Wajda and Maciej Karpiński, from Dostoyevsky's *The Idiot*. Dir: Andrzej Wajda. Phot: Paweł Edelman. Players: Tamasaburo Bando, Toshiyuki Nagashima. Prod: Say-To-Workshop Inc. (Tokyo)/Heritage Film (Warsaw).

OSTATNIA KREW (Last Blood, also known as Pigs 2)

Script and Dir: Władysław Pasikowski. Phot: Paweł Edelman. Players: Bogusław Linda, Cezary Pazura, Artur Żmijewski, Magdalena Dandourian, Jan Machulski, Jerzy Zelnik, Edward Linde-Lubaszenko. Prod: Visa Film International Ltd (Warsaw).

PANNA Z MOKRĄGŁOWĄ (Miss Wet-Head)

Script: Tomasz Piotrowski, Kazimierz Tarnas, based on the novel by Kornel Makuszyński. Dir: Kazimierz Tarnas. Phot: Grzegorz Kędzierski. Players: Paulina Tworzyńska, Anna Nehrebecka, Marek Kondrat, Hanna Stankówna, Iga Cembrzyńska. Prod: MAF (Warsaw) and Polish Television.

POLSKA ŚMIERĆ (Polish Death)

Script and Dir: Waldemar Krzystek. Phot: Dariusz Kuc. Players: Cezary Pazura, Agnieszka Pilaszewska. Prod: Skorpion Film and Polish Television (Warsaw).

PORA NA CZAROWNICE (Time for Witches)

Script and Dir: Piotr Łazarkiewicz. Phot: Artur Reinhardt. Players: Jolanta Fraszyńska, Andrzej Mastalerz, Bogusław Linda, Henryk Bista, Mariiusz Czajka. Prod: Casting Service Ltd, Polish Television.

POŻEGNANIE Z MARIĄ (Farewell to Maria)

Script: Maciej Maciejewski and Filip Zylber, based on Tadeusz Borowski's short story. Dir: Filip Zylber. Phot: Dariusz Kuc. Players: Marek Bukowski, Agnieszka Wagner, Katarzyna Jamróz, Danuta Szaflarska, Jan Frycz, Sławomir Orzechowski. Prod: Polish Television.

PRZYGODA JOANNY (Joanna's Adventure)

Script: Anna Sokołowska and Jacek Korcelli. Dir: Anna Sokołowska. Phot: Jacek Korcelli. Players: Leonard Pietraszak, Janusz Michałowski and children. Prod: Skorpion Film for Polish Television.

ROZMOWA Z CZŁOWIEKIEM Z SZAFY (Conversation with a Cupboard Man)

Script and Dir: Mariusz Grzegorzek, based on a story by Ian McEwan. Phot: Jolanta Dylewska. Players: Bożena Adamek, Rafał Olbrychski, Stanisława Celińska, Marek Walczewski, Adam Ferency, Leon Niemczyk, Marek Siudym, Piotr Pawłowski. Prod: Film Studio Indeks (Łódz), Polish Television (Warsaw).

SIÓDMY POKÓJ (The Seventh Room)

Script and Dir: Marta Mészáros. Phot: Piotr Sobociński. Players: Fanny Ardant, Jan Nowicki, Evy Pataki. Prod: Studio Tor (Warsaw), Morgan Film Srl (Rome), Baccara Prod. (Paris), Budapest Film (Budapest).

SKUTKI NOSZENIA KAPELUSZAW MAJU (The Consequences of Wearing a Hat in May)

Script and Dir: Katarzyna Krupska-Wysocka. Phot: Grzegorz Kędzierski. Players: Wiesław Michnikowski, Barbara Krafftówna, Sławomira Łozińska, Katarzyna Chrzanowska, Marek Kondrat, Piotr Skarga, Piotr Grabowski. Prod: Studio Pespektywa for Polish Television.

SPIS CUDZOŁOŻNIC (List of Adulteresses)

Script and Dir: Jerzy Stuhr, from the novel by Jerzy Pilch. Phot: Witold Adamek. Players: Jerzy Stuhr, Proeben Østerfelt, Dorota Pomykała, Stanisława Celińska, Jan Frycz, Agnieszka Wagner. Prod: Close-up Prod. (Warsaw) for Polish Television.

STRASZNY SEN DZIDZIUSIA GÓRKIEWICZA (The Terrible Dream of Babyface Górkiewicz)

Script: Jerzy Stefan Stwiński. Dir: Kazimierz Kutz. Phot: Wiesław Zdort. Players: Edward Dziewoński, Katarzyna Skrzynecka, Stanisława Celińska, Janusz Gajos, Jan Peszek, Artur Barciś, Marek Kondrat. Prod: Polish Television.

SZACH CESARZOWI (Check to the Emperor)

Script: Andrzej Kostenko, Gilles Adrien, Gerald McDonald, John Hewlett. Dir: Andrzej Kostenko. Phot: Jarosław Żamojda. Players: Peter O'Toole, Sandrine Dumas, Steven Berkoff. Prod:

Film Studio Tor (Warsaw), Made in Europe Prod. (Paris), Portman Prods. (U.K.), Videal (Hamburg).

SZCZUR (Rat)

Script: Jan Englert and Jan Łomnicki. Dir: Jan Łomnicki. Phot: Bogdan Stachurski. Players: Jan Englert, Mariusz Benoit, Marek Kondrat, Marzena Trybała, Ewa Szykulska. Prod: Film Studio Kadr (Warsaw).

TARANTHRILLER

Script: Wojciech Lepianka. Dir: Mirosław Dembiński. Phot: Paweł Edelman. Players: Hanna Mikuć, Marek Kondrat, Iga Mayr, Dorota Segda, Anna Ciepielewska, Bartek Topa, Henryk Bista. Prod: Opus Film for Polish Television.

TRZY KOLORY: BIAŁY (Three Colours: White)

Script: Krzysztof Piesiewicz, Krzysztof Kieślowski. Dir: Krzysztof Kieślowski. Phot: Edward Kłosiński. Players: Zbigniew Zamachowski, Julie Delpy, Jerzy Stuhr. Prod: Film Studio Tor (Warsaw), Marin Karmitz MK2 Productions (Paris), CAB Productions (Lausanne).

TRZY KOLORY: NIEBIESKI (Three Colours: Blue)

Script: Krzysztof Piesiewicz, Krzysztof Kieślowski. Dir: Krzysztof Kieślowski. Phot: Sławomir Idziak. Players: Juliette Binoche, Benoît Regent, Florence Pernel, Charlotte Very. Prod: Marin Karmitz MK2 Productions (Paris), CAB Productions (Lausanne), Film Studio Tor (Warsaw).

TRZY KOLORY: CZERWONY (Three Colours: Red)

Script: Krzysztof Piesiewicz, Krzysztof Kieślowski. Dir: Krzysztof Kieślowski. Phot: Piotr Sobociński. Players: Irène Jacob, Jean-Louis Trintignant, Jean-Pierre Lorit, Frédérique Feder.

Prod: Marin Karmitz MK2 Production (Paris), CAP Productions (Lausanne), Film Studio Tor (Warsaw).

TYLKO STRACH (Fear)

Script and Dir: Barbara Sass. Phot: Wiesław Zdort. Players: Anna Dymna, Dorota Segda, Dorota Pomykała, Krzysztof Globisz, Cezary Pazura. Prod: Polish Television.

WRONY (Crows)

Script and Dir: Dorota Kędzierzawska. Phot: Artur Reinhardt. Players: Karolina Ostrożna, Katarzyna Szczepanik, Małgorzata Hajewska, Anna Prucnal. Prod: Film Studio Oko and Polish Television.

WYNAJMĘ POKÓJ (Room to Rent)

Script and Dir: Andrzej Titkow. Phot: Jacek Knop. Players: Igor Przegrodzki, Beata Scibak, Michał Żebrowski, Elżbieta Jarosik, Renata Dancewicz, Barbara Brylska, Elżbieta Dębska. Prod: Marek Nowowiejski Film Productions Ltd. for Polish Television.

ZŁOTE DNO (Golden Depth)

Script: Ivan Biriukov and Marek Nowicki. Dir: Marek Nowicki. Phot: Lomer Achwedianii. Players: Tomasz Stockinger, Cezary Pazura. Prod: Film Studio Perspektywa (Warsaw), Studio 12 (Moscow).

ZAWRÓCONY (Reverted)

Script and Dir: Kazimierz Kutz. Phot: Wiesław Zdort. Players: Zbigniew Zamachowski, Henryk Bista, Anna Waszczyk, Krzysztof Janczar, Waldemar Kownacki. Prod: Polish Television.

PORTUGAL

Peter Besas

After several years of internal bickering and bureaucratic confusion, the Portuguese Film Institute has emerged from its long tunnel under its new name, the Portuguese Institute of Cinematographic and Audiovisual Art, better known by its acronym IPACA, ready to boost the production and promotion of Portuguese cinema at home and abroad. The new entity is directed by Salvato Manezes, who formerly ran the Troia Film Festival, under the presidency of Zita Seabra.

The move ahead coincided with Lisbon being designated "cultural capital of Europe" in 1994 by the Economic Union and the production of half a dozen feature films.

Even though the new roster of features still fails to draw much attention at the local box-office, three of the films were chosen for competing sections in Cannes this year. This, allied to the IPACA's higher international profile, helped put Portugal back on the filmic map again.

In 1994, the IPACA partly financed four features, for a total of about $5 million. The funds are obtained from a 4% tax on all television commercials on all stations in Portugal. An additional four features were partly bankrolled by the "Lisbon 1994"

organisation, sponsored by national and municipal authorities, totalling around $2 million. The average cost of a film is somewhat over $1 million, with the maximum subsidy given by the government being $800,000.

Over the past year there has been a boom in exhibition as well, with new screens opening and old hardtops being converted and refurbished. The largest exhibitor and distributor by far continues to be Luis Silva's Luso-Mundo organisation, which is partnered with Warner Bros. in Portugal and Spain. Also increasingly important as an exhibitor is Paulo Branco, heretofore mainly known as a producer of arthouse fare, usually in co-production with France. In all, Portugal has 268 screens.

Portugal's most famous director, Manoel de Oliveira, despite his advanced age, made **Blind Man's Buff** (*La caixa*), shown in Cannes, produced by Branco. Also screened in Cannes was **Down to Earth** (*Casa de Lava*), directed by Pedro Costa, produced by Branco, who also made **Three Palm Trees** (*Tres Palmeiras*), directed by João Botelho.

Among other films in 1994 were Leao Lopes's **The Island of Content** (*Ilheu de Contenda*), Luis Alvaraes's **The Thief's Gold** (*O Oiro do Bandido*), Teresa Villaverde's **Three Brothers** (*Tres Irmaos*), and Eduardo Goedes's 60-minute **Angry Shoes** (*De Pe Em Pe*). On the more commercial track was **Passage to Lisbon** (*Passagem Por Lisboa*), directed by Eduardo Geada, using Anglo thesps and Fernando Matos Silva's **Southbound** (*Ao Sul*).

Isabel de Castro and Jean-Pierre Cassel in HOT LEMON TEA, directed by António de Macedo

PETER BESAS has lived in Madrid since the 1960's and is chief of Variety's bureau there. He has written various books, including a history of Spanish cinema.

Useful Addresses

IPACA
Rua S. Pedro de Alcantra, 45
Lisbon 1200
Tel: (3511) 346-6634
Fax: 347-2777

Filmoteca Portuguesa
Rua Bernardo Lima 35
Lisbon 1000
Tel: (3511) 570965
Fax: 570667

Filmes Luso Mundo
(Distributor/exhibitor)
Praca de Alegria 22
Lisbon 1294
Tel: (3511) 347-0964
Fax: 346-5349

Madragoa Films
*(Paulo Branco –
producer/distributor/exhibitor)*
Av. D. Carlos I, 72D
Lisbon 1200
Tel: (3511) 397-0220
Fax: 397-4723

Animatografo
*(Antonio da Cunha Telles –
producer)*
Rua de Rosa, 252
Lisbon 1200
Tel: 347-4593
Fax: 347-3562

Still from Manoel de Oliveira's NON OU A VÃ GLÓRIA DE MANDAR

PUERTO RICO

José Artemio
Torres

We've said it before in these pages: Puerto Rican film goes in cycles of dry and rainy seasons. After a dry spell of three years, in the second half of 1993, the rain started again with the release of **The Air Bus** (*La guagua aerea*), the second feature by Luis Molina. This comedy about Puerto Rican emigration to New York city during the 1960's owes to local TV not only most of its actors but also its situations, the jokes, the sets and the lighting. Not a hit with the critics but a hit with the audience. A clever marketing scheme involving special excursion trips with the film to New York and Chicago has helped the production to travel. But that's as far as it will go because of the film's mostly local appeal.

The end of the year saw the filming of **Shortcut to Paradise**, a Spanish-Puerto Rican co-production starring Charles Dance, Assumpta Serna and a group of American and Puerto Rican actors. This thriller shot in the city of Ponce but set in the U.S.A., was co-produced and directed by the Spaniard, Gerardo Herrero. Local producers, Juan González and Letvia Arza, raised half the budget through a limited partnership organised by the local branch of Clark Melvin Securities. The English-language feature, due out in the autumn of 1994, was the first film in a plan to establish a 20-million dollars film fund.

Rice, Beans and Ketchup, another English-language local production, was shot at the beginning of 1994. This film about a Dominican who goes to New York via Puerto Rica to pursue a career in the theatre, was in development for several years by its producer Juan Carlos Codazzi. Another limited partnership created through Clark Melvin Securities brought the last sum needed for the film to go into production under the direction of New Yorker Joseph Vázquez.

Another film that was in development for a long time, Jacobo Morales's **Beautiful Sara** (*Linda Sara*), got its go-ahead with a pre-sale to the government's TV station and a loan from Banco Popular, the island's largest commercial bank. Morales is Puerto Rico's leading feature director; his previous film *Lo que le pasó a Santiago* having been nominated for an Oscar. The new one has the beautiful Sara as the centre of a family that loses its wealth as time goes by. It was shot in Spanish.

Dayanara Torres and Chayanne in Jacobo Morales's LINDA SARA

Still another feature film went into production in the first half of 1994. *The Power of the Shatki* will be a martial arts film produced and directed by Joseph Landó. Financing for this film has been private.

More Local Films in the Pipeline

It seems that at last the financial community is taking notice of the possibilities of film production based on the tax-incentive laws approved in the previous years. More local films and co-productions are in the pipeline. Their fate will depend on the success of the first group of films recently produced.

In other areas of local film production, Paco López continued his string of inventive animation shorts with the **Ecological Filminutes**, a series of messages to make the public aware of the importance of environmental conservation. Among the documentaries, perhaps the most ambitious (although flawed) was Sonia Fritz's *Luisa Capetillo: Passion for Justice*, a docudrama about our first feminist.

Other documentaries, mostly on video, were: *El barrio, la historia de todos* by José Orraca, *Sementerlo de Antonio Martorell*, by José Estrada, *Raíces indígenas* by Ginnette Grant and Edgardo Pratts, *Adombe* by Edwin Reyes, *Un impulso insurreccional* by Ramón Almodóvar and Emilio Rodríguez, *La composta* by Dennis Martínez and

Laboratorio de ideas by Emilio Rodríguez.

There were two fiction shorts: *Lucid* by Jorge Oliver and *Monica* by Roberto Busó, to round up a busy Puerto Rican film year.

As for production from outside, it was also a good year. The NBC soap *One Life to Live* and the German TV sitcom *Happy Journey* did a couple of chapters. Spanish director Pedro Massó returned to our shores for a TV mini-series called *Dressed and without a Boyfriend*. Mira Nair shot three days of her *The Pérez Family* for Goldwyn with Marisa Tomei. And O.J. Simpson starred on *Frogmen*, a pilot for NBC, just before his troubles with the law.

TOP TEN GROSSING FILMS IN PUERTO RICO: 1993

Jurassic Park
Dennis the Menace
Free Willy
Home Alone 2
The Bodyguard
Cliffhanger
Demolition Man
The Fugitive
Hot Shots: Part Deux
Indecent Proposal

1994 (until June)
Mrs. Doubtfire
Philadelphia
On Deadly Ground
Naked Gun

Useful Addresses

Commonwealth of Puerto Rico
Economic Development Administration
P.O. Box 362350
San Juan
Puerto Rico 00936-2350
Tel: (809) 758-4747
Fax: (809) 756-5706

San Juan Cinemafest
P.O. Box 4543
San Juan
Puerto Rico 00902-0769
Tel: (809) 721-6145
Fax: (809) 723-6412

Puerto Rico International Film Festival
17 Mayagüez Street
Suite B-1
Hato Rey
Puerto Rico 00918
Tel: (809) 763-4997
Fax: (809) 753-5367

Clark Melvin Securities
1414 Banco Popular Center
Hato Rey
Puerto Rico 00918
Tel: (809) 759-8080

RUSSIA

Andrew
Horton &
Michael
Brashinsky

Current Russian cinema resembles an iceberg without a tip: it's virtually invisible, but it's there indeed. While daily life in Russia appears more and more like a badly written exploitation flick, fewer customers line up to buy tickets at the decaying movie theatres. In 1991 there were 2,757 cinemas; in 1993 only 1,337. There are even fewer this year (some rent their lounges to car dealers) with no sign of change. For 1993, American films (that sell 5 to 10 times cheaper to a distributor than Russian films) captured 55% of the ticket sales while Russian films brought in only 14% of the home audience. As the state donated 7 billion roubles (less than $5 million) to finance (in full or in part) more than 70 features in 1993, film production fell 50% as compared to 1991. Most movies get completed only with foreign (primarily French) investment. And with even the most successful box-office sales covering only 20% of a film's budget today, "There is almost no incentive in Russia to make a movie now," laments Dr. Kirill Razlogov, head of the Institute for Cultural Research.

And yet nothing can prevent movies from being made. Film culture here oscillates in the high voltage between the increasing alienation of the auteurs and ever more desperate attempts to cook up an edible cine-*borscht*. Auteurs, such as Alexei Gherman, shooting his fourth feature for the second year in a row, and Alexander Sokurov who refuses to show his recent films, including the latest, *Quiet Pages*, to any audience but a festival one, maintain their reputation as the untouchables. Meanwhile, *Beethoven 2*, *Home Alone 2*, and several Jean-Claude Van Damme vehicles are the box-office favourites here this season.

The New Wave?

Those who were able to catch a glimpse of current domestic (non)releases look hopefully in the direction of what young critics call "the second wave": directors such as Valery Todorovsky, Dmitry Meskhiev, Sergei Debizhev, Sergei Livnev, Alexei Balabanov, and Yevgeny Yufit who have completed their second features this year. Others assert that the genuine new wave is yet to come from commercial television where young talent is breeding, shielded from the hardships of the day by

Still from PETTY PASSIONS

ANDREW HORTON is a professor of film and literature at Loyola University in New Orleans. MICHAEL BRASHINSKY teaches film studies at the School of Visual Arts in New York City. Their forthcoming book together is *Russian Critics on the Cinema of Glasnost* (Cambridge University Press).

small format, low costs, sophisticated equipment, and social disengagement. In any case, everybody agrees, the raw Russian culture is germinating. What it will bring forth is anybody's guess.

The most enigmatic of remaining Soviet auteurs, Kira Muratova, flies high above the current political battle in **Petty Passions** (*Uvlechenya*), a film whose only message is that horses are better than men. In Muratova's comically absurd and latently tragic universe the only value left is beauty, as amoral, nonpolitical, and anti-psychological as horses are. Ergo, horses make sense. People don't.

In the space of the film situated between the racetrack and the circus, six characters wander around in search of an author, a story, a genre, a relationship, and find none. Those characters whom Muratova likes are filmed so that they become "centaurs": their human legs are matched in motion with equine torsos. So much for matching. The film defines itself in defying the notion of congruity: people's gestures mismatch their words that, in turn, mismatch their meaning, just as characters miss a story that could happen with them but does not.

The film is most genuine when nothing at all happens in it but the horses' unstaged promenades. It is as pure and transparent as it is mystifying. And it is as gorgeous and mesmerising as it is almost unbearable to watch.

Vladimir Khotinenko, whose credits include the much admired 1987 *Mirror for A Hero* and last year's dark satire, *Patriotic Comedy*, turned out **Makarov**, voted by critics the Best Russian Film of 1993. This is a riveting contemporary morality tale of a renowned poet, named Makarov, who buys another "Makarov", a brand of handgun. From that moment on until the predictably tragic ending, Makarov's life turns upside down. The weapon which was supposed to make him feel safe in the "new Russia" of muggings, contract killings, and Mafia politicians in limos, leads instead to increased fear including

the problem of where to hide the damn thing (he opts for inside the toilet water tank). Wife, children, friends, lovers all fall away as the poet's final "friend" remains the cold steel of his gun.

Khotinenko and screenwriter Valery Zolotukha have etched a level-headed but strangely affecting meditation that points no easy way out of the current dilemma that will seem very pertinent to many around the world today: to arm or not to arm? Simply shot, well acted, and memorable in many of its moments. At one point Makarov, who shares his name and patronymic with Pushkin, carves out a thick volume of the great poet's verse in order to hide his gun and then proceeds to carry it everywhere. In another brief moment, we see him eating soup while watching Mel Gibson in *Lethal Weapon* on TV.

Most Appealing Film of the Year

Winner of the Best Debut Prize of 1993, and certainly the most appealing film of the year, **Russian Ragtime** is the latest despatch from the pop-film front as well as a sample of production from the young TTL Studio that seems to determine the filmic weather in the Moscow of the 1990's.

This is a story of a young Russian-Jewish "John Doe" who, in the frigid Brezhnevist 1970's, wants to emigrate to America, comes to Moscow and gets stuck there because his estranged father, an apparatchik, won't sign a release for him to

Still from RUSSIAN RAGTIME

leave. He falls in love, makes friends, and finally gets into trouble with the KGB which blackmails him into signing a report against his buddies in exchange for a one-way ticket to New York.

The story, which the director claims to be true, is in fact the least of what the film has to offer. It is contrived and often didactic, and only the film-maker's self-irony keeps it afloat. *Russian Ragtime* is more fun when it's about the myths from the 1970's, when the KGB's popular status equalled that of disco music and the "American dream". What makes this film, superbly acted and shot with obvious joy, a winner is the tone, mixing nostalgic naïveté of a warm period melodrama with alienation of a clever pastiche that alludes to everything from Capra to Konchalovsky, and from Antonioni to Sergio Leone.

First Post-Soviet Cult Film

Nicotine should have been titled *Ultimately Breathless*, and not only because it could use a gulp of fresh air, but also because it is yet another remake of a Jean-Luc Godard 1959 classic. Released last autumn, it threatens to become the first post-Soviet cult film, as fashionable and largely unseen as any cult film should be.

"Every generation makes it own *A bout de souffle*," says screenwriter Sergei Dobrotvorsky, a culture critic and leader of the late Russian film underground. "Every generation gets an *A bout de souffle* it deserves." If so, this generation deserves nothing but endless references to other movies (in one, to *Un chien andalou*, an eye from a newspaper photo is cut with a razor; in another, the local femme fatale hums "Blue Velvet"). What in the Godard original was quirky here is drowsy, what was impassioned is now mechanical. This is an empty film about emptiness in which even black-and-white is grey; a film so tenaciously esoteric and claustrophobic that, in a nearly perfect match between form and contents, it erases the border between ennui and satisfaction.

Recent and Forthcoming Films

KHRUSTALYOV, MASHINU! (The Car, Khrustalyov!)

Script: Svetlana Karmalita, Alexei Gherman. Dir: Alexei Gherman. Phot: Vladimir Svetozarov. Players: Yuri Tsurillo, Misha Dementyev, Yuri Yarvet, Jr. Prod: First and Experimental Film Studio. *Historical drama.*

KUROCHKA RYABA (Ryaba my Chicken)

Script: Andrei Konchalovsky, Victor Merezhko. Dir: Konchalovsky. Phot: Yevgeny Guslinsky. Players: Inna Churikova, Alexander Surin, Gennady Egorychev. Prod: Arc-Film/Russian Roulette/Parimedia (France).

PODMOSKOVNYE VECHERA (Moscow Nights)

Script: Maria Sheptunova,

Stanislav Govorukhin, Alyona Krinitsyna. Dir: Valery Todorosvky. Phot: Sergei Kozlov. Players: Ingeborga Dapkunaite, Vladimir Mashkov, Alisa Freindlich, Alexander Feklistov. Prod: TTL Studio/Le Film du Rivage (France).

GOD SOBAKI (The Year of the Dog)

Script: Semyon Aranovich, Albina Shulgina, Vadim Mikhailov in collaboration with Zoya Kudrya. Dir: Semen Aranovich. Phot: Yuri Shaigardanov. Players: Inna Churikova, Ogor Sklyar, Alexander Feklistov. Prod: Kinodocument Studio/Lenfilm/Sodaperaga (France). 135 mins.

Useful Addresses

Double D Agency
(sociological research, publishing)

7 Maly Gnezdnikovsky per., room 604,
103877 Moscow
Tel: (095) 229-7921
Fax: (095) 151-0272

Gorky Film Studios
8 Eisenstein St
129226 Moscow
Fax: (095) 188-9871
Telex: 411941

Intercinema Agency
(distribution, production)
Contact: Raissa Fomina at Kinocentre *(see below)*

Kinocentre
(programmes, publishing, museum, information, production)
15 Druzhinnikovskaya St
123242 Moscow
Tel: (095) 255-9489 or 255-9087
Fax: (095) 973-2029
Telex: 411070 CENTRE

Lenfilm Concern
10 Kamenbnoostrovsky Ave
197101 St Petersburg
Tel: (812) 232-8374
Fax: (812) 232-8881 or 233-2174
Telex: 121534 FILM SU

Mosfilm Concern
1 Mosfilmovskaya St
119858 Moscow
Tel: (095) 143-9100
Fax: (095) 938-2083
Telex: 411293 MSFILM SU

TTI Studio
8 Eisenstein St
129226 Moscow
Tel: (095) 181-6052
Fax: (095) 188-9287

SERBIA & MONTENEGRO

Goran
Gocić

A "film industry" (in the Hollywood sense) vanished in Yugoslavia with the death of the studio system in the late 1950's. However, until recently, the majority of film projects have been state-sponsored. Today, it seems that independent producers in Serbia are strong enough to make between five and ten films a year. Bearing in mind a state of country's sanctions-strapped economy this is quite a feat! A minor miracle in fact, bearing in mind that many wealthier countries with richer cinematic traditions, manage to make less.

Miroslav Lekić's **Better Than Escape** (*Bolje od bekstva*) deservedly swept all the major prizes of the newly established Yugoslav Film Academy for Arts and Sciences, whose ceremony is spitefully set just days before the American Academy Awards. Alas, its numerous nominations had to be shared between only six films.

Full Moon over Belgrade (*Pun mesec nad Beogradom*), one of our few domestic horror films, was technically ambitious considering its tight budget and won a special jury prize at the Festival of Fantasy & Science Fiction in Brussels. However, some retrograde inadequacies could be spotted, both in terms of genre (vampire's house featuring large cross) and real (confusing witchcraft with exorcism). **Byzantine Blue** (*Vizantijsko plavo* aka *Matematika druge vrste*) ran a close second. It aspired to bring together Eastern "fundamentalism" and Western "postmodernism". The result was a failure, not because of the incompatibility

of East and West, but because the film's more or less talented contributors somehow managed to cancel each other's energies out.

Tell Me, Why Did You Leave? (*Kaži zašto me ostavi*) in spite of a somewhat thin war-time story, is a promising directorial debut by Oleg Novković, whose talent is yet to be proven.

Makavejev Re-works Favourite Themes

It seems that Dušan Makavejev, along with his famous contemporaries, feels that this is the time to summarise or "reconstruct" what he has already done, rather than enrich his opus. Consequently, his latest film **Gorilla Bathes at Noon** (*Gorila se kupa u podne*) – similarly to Altman's *Short Cuts* – inherits motifs from his previous works. Stalin and Lenin are special guest stars from *WR: Mysteries of the Organism*, a cyclist peddles in from *Sweet Movie*, and a gang of suburban outcasts arrives from *Montenegro*. An old movie also finds its way into *Gorilla* as in *Innocence Unprotected*, and the film also features lots of Slav accented bad English as in *Montenegro*.

Gorilla's sole striking innovation is that it is uncharacteristically chaste by Makavejev's standards. As a rule, Makavejev's disrobed actresses look even better in his films than in others (for example, Eva Ras in *Switchboard Operator* or Greta Scacchi in *Coca Cola Kid*). His own discoveries look pretty good too (Camilla Soeberg in *Manifesto*). This film, also

Still from Makavejev's GORILLA BATHES AT NOON

known as *For the Night of Love*, is even billed as softcore porn in New Delhi which, when one forgets Makavejev's political reputation, is probably the most accurate generic description. Alas, there is not a glimpse of female flesh or even a hint of eroticism in *Gorilla*, unless one finds the sight of Russian soldiers kissing each other (and even the bodies of their dead comrades) exciting, as happens in Chiaureli's *Battle for Berlin*.

Gorilla was shot on location, mostly in Berlin; up to 80% of its funding and cast came from Serbia. The title derives from a sign in Berlin's Zoo. The original scene where the gorilla actually bathes has not survived, but a totally unrelated title remains. The real hero of *Gorilla* – and the one who does bathe at noon – is Lenin. The fall of the Berlin Wall – at least in the CNN trailer – was bound for glory. On the other hand, deposing Lenin and emptying Soviet army barracks – at least in *Gorilla* – gives off a whiff of nostalgia. Stalin, as in *WR*, remained a grotesque clown, but Lenin, on the contrary, is still pompously mighty and heroic, even though his statue in Berlin is

temporarily decapitated and put away in a closet.

Fully-fledged Melodrama

While *Gorilla*'s "reality" (the Soviet take-over of Berlin) became historic fiction, and "historic fiction" (German domination in Europe) turned into reality, *Better than Escape* contains more complex intertextual links. Firstly, the film shared the destiny of many individuals. Processed in Croatia, it remained blocked there until it was surreptitiously spirited out after a year and a half. (Nikola Stojanović's *Belle Epoque*, left behind in Sarajevo, is unlikely ever to be finished.) Secondly, the principal actor (Žarko Laušević) is in jail charged with murder, just like his character in the film who finds himself behind bars after accidentally killing a woman in a car crash.

Finally, it is the first fully-fledged Serbian melodrama in years, and the best film of the season especially in terms of storyline and craftsmanship (screenplay, directing, acting, editing). At the same time it is interwoven with perceptive responses to Serbian contemporary issues: proliferation of *kitsch*, re-defining of tradition, relationship between artists, audience and regime.

As the budget for the average Serbian movie still ranges between $200,000 and $650,000, Aleksandar Petrović's $11.5 million production **Migrations** (a film and TV series) considerably surpasses the cost of the country's entire annual cultural output. Besides its epic scope and brilliant cinematography by Oscar-winning Igor Luther (*The Tin Drum*), *Migrations* unfortunately proves to be just another abortive Serbian *retro* project. The $3m film and uncompleted $8m TV series (the most expensive project in the history of Yugoslav television), are based on Miloš Crnjanski's novel. Considered by some the most prominent work of national literature, *Migrations* is a kind of Serbian *War and Peace*, dealing with the tragic destiny of the Serbs in the wars of the eighteenth century.

Despite its origins, apparently heroic and tragic overtones of this adaptation are drenched into darkest nihilism. *La guerre* is there, but *la glorieuse* never appears. Aleksandar Petrović, despite his international reputation, is probably the last person who should be behind projects of national myth-making. Ironically, though, he double-codes it. Through a thin layer of tragedy appears the masochistic stupidity of characters who deserve their misfortunes. Serbian military successes give way to the barbarism of the troops and a sentimental dilemma hides sickness and infidelity.

Aided by a wooden, disinterested and badly dubbed international cast (Isabelle Huppert, Richard Berry), Petrović largely ignores his characters' destinies. The most dramatic moments are not when somebody confesses love, leaves for war or dies, but rather when minor characters get drunk, beaten up or fall from their horses. Above all *Migrations* is a film about horses and their suffering in past wars as well as in contemporary costumed spectaculars about them!

TOP TEN GROSSING FILMS IN BELGRADE: 1993

	Attendances
Bolje od Bekstva (Better than Escape)	53,110
Arizona Dream	50,398
Basic Instinct	33,031
Kaži Zašto me Ostavi (Tell Me why did you Leave?)	26,041
Vizantijsko Plavo (Byzantine Blue)	25,791
Atame! (Tie Me Up! Tie Me Down!)	22,215
Tri Karte za Holivud (Three Tickets to Hollywood)	21,890
Mediterraneo	20,927
Strictly Ballroom	18,626
Universal Soldier	16,514

Recent and Forthcoming Films

BIĆE BOLJE (It's Gonna Be Better)

Script: Stevan Koprivica. Dir: Milan Živković. Phot: Radoslav Vladić. Players: Dragan Nikolić, Maja Sabljić. Prod: Gama, Beograd.

DNEVNIK UVREDA (A Diary of Insults)

Script: Gordan Mihić. Dir: Zdravko Šotra. Phot: Veselko Krčmar. Players: Vera Čukić, Marko Nikolić. Prod: RTV Srbija – TV Beograd.

LJUBAV U VUKOVARU (A Love in Vukovar)

Script: Maja/Boro Drašković. Dir: Boro Drašković. Phot: Aleksandar Petković. Players: Mirjana Joković, Boris Isaković. Prod: Kapital Plus, Beograd, Dan Film Production, Limassol, Cyprus.

NI NA NEBU NI NA ZEMLJI (Castles in Spain)

Script: Dušan Jelić and Ivan Panić. Dir: Miloć Radivojević. Phot: Radoslav Vladić. Players: Svetozar Cvetković, Bojana Maljević. Prod: TRZ Viktorija/RTV

Srbija – TV Beograd/Smart Egg Pictures (London)/MVA (Beograd).

PAKET ARANŽMAN (Package Tour)

Script: Đorđe Milosavljević. Dir: Ivan Stefanivić, Srđan Golubović, Dejan Zečević. Phot: Miloš Kresoja. Players: Milica Mihajlović, Bojana Žirović, Bogdan Diklić.

RAJ (Heaven)

Script and Dir: Petar Zec. Phot: Miloš Spasojević. Players:

Tihomir Stanić, Nebojša Glogovac. Prod: RTV Srbije – TV Beograd. *(Video release only.)*

SLATKO OD SNOVA (Sweets out of Dreams)

Script: Aleksandar Barišić and Srđan Dragojević. Dir: Vladimir Živković. Phot: Fatmir Nusi. Players: Dragana Mirković, Nebojša Bakočević. Prod: D.P. FIVET, Beograd; RTV Srbija – TV Beograd.

TITO PO DRUGI PUT MEĐU SRBIMA (Tito for the Second Time Amongst Serbs)

Script and Dir: Želimir Žilnik. Phot: Miodrag Milošević. Player: Dragoljub Ljubičić-Mićko. Prod: Radio B'92. *(Video release only.)*

Useful Addresses

Institut za film
(Yugoslav Film Institute)
Čika Ljubina 15
11000 Beograd
Tel: (38111) 62 51 31
Fax: (38111) 63 42 53

Vans
(Independent Producer & Distributor)
Njegoševa 84
1100 Beograd
Tel: (38111) 43 24 92
Fax: (38111) 41 80 70

Avala Film International DD
(Production Company & Studio Facilities)
Kneza Višeslava 88
11030 Beograd
Tel: (38111) 55 73 31
Fax: (38111) 55 94 74

Beograd film
(Theatre chain)
Terazije 40
11000 Beograd
Tel: (38111) 68 89 40
Fax: (38111) 68 79 52

GORAN GOCIĆ is a freelance film and art critic. He has written for numerous magazines and is co-author of a book on the Hollywood of the 1970's and 1980's. He is preparing a study of the work of Andy Warhol.

SLOVAKIA   Hana Cielová

Nothing new on the Eastern Front: this sums up the current situation of the Slovak cinema. In the last year almost no change has taken place in the area of the cinema: the situation in the newly independent Slovakia, suffering political, economical and social problems typical for the post-Communist countries and characterised by the lack of finances, has not exactly been favourable to the development of the film industry. The new Film Laws, in preparation already since the 1989 Czechoslovak "velvet revolution", still do not exist. Therefore, to set aside one crown from every film ticket sold in favour of the Fund of the Cinematography, as is being done in the neighbouring Czech Republic, is impossible in Slovakia as such a fund simply does not exist yet.

The Czech Republic became a member of Eurimages in 1994, but Slovakia unfortunately has not succeeded in joining the European structures and initiatives so quickly, mainly because of its constantly changing legislation and political situation. In spring 1994 the new Czech Film Promotion was established in the Czech Republic – nothing like this exists in Slovakia yet either. The Slovak Film Institute/National Cinematographic Centre is trying to gather all information about the new films, but there is no law which obliges the new private producers to disclose any information about their production. What is more, after the politically motivated replacement of the director of the Centre, not all of the producers are willing to co-operate with this institution.

Koliba, the only Slovak film studio in the capital Bratislava, five years after the "velvet revolution", still is not privatised and it is anyone's guess when and especially *how* this might happen. The only sure thing is that the state wants to keep the majority of Koliba's future shares so as not to lose its control completely.

However, there is not really all that much going on at Koliba. Instead of new Slovak feature films there are from time to time some commercials being produced or the studio provides services for some cheap international productions.

In spite of this rather depressing general situation there is reason for some optimism: the young directors. One of them is Martin Šulík, whose film *Everything I Like* (see IFG 1994) represented Slovakia last year at various film festivals and won several international prizes among them the special prize in Strasbourg, Angers, Cottbus and Porto. This unexpected positive reaction abroad surprised even Martin Šulík himself who thought he was making just a "small, local" film. He is now already preparing, together with the producer Rudo Biermann, his third feature film **The Garden** (*Záhrada*), which will be most likely a Slovak-French co-production.

Another young director, Štefan Semjan, shot his first feature last year. **On the Wonderful Blue Danube** (*Na krásnom modrom Dunaji*) is a story situated in contemporary Bratislava about three friends who help to steal a picture of Andy Warhol from the local gallery. Another first feature **Bašt'ovanský and Son-in-law** (*Bašt'ovanský a zat'*), written by the young writer Dušan Taragel, is a black satire about a contemporary Slovak village. It was directed by Tomáš Krnáč and was produced originally for television, but it will hopefully also be distributed in the cinemas. And there are still some other first features in preparation. Miro Šindelka will direct his first film **A Kiss** (*Bozk*), a contemporary love story in which he wants to cast not only Slovak, but also some popular Czech actors. And Ivo Solan, the son of the former Slovak director Peter Solan, will come back to Slovakia from Canada to shoot his first feature **Lady Elisabeth**, an historical film about the legendary figure from Slovak history. Both films will be produced by the most prolific Slovak producer, Rudolf Biermann and his company Charlie's.

Vlado Hajdu and Juraj Johanides in ON THE WONDERFUL BLUE DANUBE

Historical Epic

There is also another film which was produced mostly thanks to the financial support of Slovak television and which became the first Slovak-Czech co-production since the split of Czechoslovakia. It is the historical film **Angel of Mercy** (*Anjel milosrdenstva*), based on the book by the well-known Czech writer and scriptwriter Vladimír Körner. *Angel of Mercy* was directed by the prolific Slovak television director Miloslav Luther, and takes place during the First World War. The young wife of an Austrian officer comes to the army hospital to visit her dying husband. His suffering is ended before her eyes by a mysterious prisoner-of-war. From that moment they stand next to each other as well as opposite each other. Bound together by their passion they fight for happiness against an era that has lost all feelings or hope. Let's hope that Slovak Television will support more similar non-commercial projects in the future.

Among the projects that received financial support from the state art foundation Pro Slovakia, worth mentioning is the sequel to the successful box-office hit of the 1970's, *She Grazed Horses on Concrete* (*Pásla kone na betóne*), directed by recently deceased Štefan Uher. This popular but also quality film was based on the idea and acting of the actress Milka Zimková, who wrote the synopsis for the sequel as well and who should be again the main actress. The director Štefan Uher will be replaced by the television director

TOP TEN GROSSING FILMS IN SLOVAKIA: 1993

	Admissions
Jurassic Park	387,524
Fontána pre Zuzanu 2	335,701
The Bodyguard	275,555
Sister Act	236,398
Home Alone 2	230,835
Hot Shots: Part Deux	226,010
Show White and the Seven Dwarfs	174,311
Le comiche 2	166,468
Bram Stoker's Dracula	148,510
Dědictví aneb Kurvahošigutntag	147,292

Ingrid Timková in ANGEL OF MERCY

Stanislav Párnický and the film will be produced by the promising new company JMB Film and TV Production Ltd, which also produced Štefan Semjan's *On the Beautiful Blue Danube*.

Among documentary films, it is worth mentioning most of all the long-awaited, but still unfinished film *Paper Heads*, again partially financed by the French and directed by Dušan Hanák.

Another reason for cautious optimism is the fact that the Slovak film **Fountain for Susanna** (*Fontána pre Zuzanu*) reached an incredible second place in last year's Top Ten with 335,701 admissions. So it seems that the Slovak film, in spite of all unfavourable conditions, is still alive and well.

HANA CIELOVÁ is a freelance film critic and scriptwriter as well as programme adviser to various international film festivals.

Recent and Forthcoming Films

NA KRÁSNOM MODROM DUNAJI (On the Wonderful Blue Danube)

Script: Martin Hečko, Štefan Semjan. Dir: Štefan Semjan. Phot: Martin Štrba. Players: Adi Hajdu, Juraj Johanides, Maroš Kramár. Prod: JMB Film and TV Production.

ANJEL MILOSRDENSTVA (Angel of Mercy)

Script: Vladimír Körner, Marián Puobiš, Miloslav Luther. Dir: Miloslav Luther. Phot: Vladimír Holloš. Players: Ingrid Timková, Juraj Šimko, Jozef Vajnar, Peter Šimun, Marta Sládečková. Prod: Slovak Television, Czech Television, Ars Media.

PÁSLA KONE NA BETÓNE II (She Grazed Horses on Concrete)

Script: Milka Zimková, Stanislav Párnický. Dir: Stanislav Párnický. Phot: Stanislav Szomolányi. Players: Mirka Zimková, Lubomír Paulovič, Veronika Jeníková, Peter Staník. Prod: JMB Film and TV Production.

BAŠĆOVANSKÝ A ZAŤ
(Baščovanský and Son-in-Law)

Script: Dušan Taragel, Tomáš Krnáč. Phot: Asen Šopov. Players: Ferdinand Macurák, Gejza Benko. Prod: Slovak Television.

BOZK (A Kiss)

Script: Miro Šindelka, Ondrej Šulaj. Dir: Miro Šindelka. Phot: Marek Jícha. Players: Ivana Chýlková, Jiří Bartoška, Jozef Króner, Roman Luknár, Sidi Tobias. Prod: Charlie's.

ZÁHRADA (The Garden)

Script: Martin Šulík, Marek Leščák. Dir: Martin Šulik. Prod: Charlie's.

LADY ELISABETH

Script: Tibor Vichta, Ondrej Šulaj. Dir: Ivo Solan. Prod: Charlie's, Lady Elisabeth Prod.

Distributors

Attack
Karpatská 2
811 02 Bratislava
Tel: (7) 498 788, 492 520

Gemini Film
Štefánikova 47, P.O. 124
811 04 Bratislava
Tel: (7) 491 127, 491 084
Fax: (7) 496 361

Royal Film Distribution
Karpatská 2
811 05 Bratislava

Tatra Film
Miletičova 1
821 08 Bratislava
Tel: (7) 611 40
Fax: (7) 630 44

Bioscop
Hviezdoslavovo nám. 17
811 02 Bratislava
Tel: (7) 335 049
Fax: (7) 335 815

Slovenska Požičovňa Filmov
Priemyselná 1
821 09 Bratislava
Tel: (7) 211 301

Intersonic Taunus Productions
Staré Grunty 36
842 25 Bratislava
Tel & Fax: (7) 722 070

Q Film
Priemyselná 1
821 09 Bratislava
Tel: (7) 211 301, line 284

Producers

ALEF
Brečtanová 1
833 14 Bratislava
Tel & Fax: (7) 374 601

Ars Media
Brečtanová 1
833 14 Bratislava
Tel & Fax: (7) 373 758

Barok Film
Brečtanová 1
833 14 Bratislava
Tel & Fax: (7) 371 426

HQ Agency
Nevädzová 2
821 08 Bratislava
Tel & Fax: (7) 236 606

JMB Film and TV Production
Koreničova 12
811 03 Bratislava
Tel & Fax: (7) 315 778

SFT-Koliba Film Studios
Brečtanová 1
833 14 Bratislava
Tel: (7) 377 303, 371 921
Fax: (7) 372 224

Atan Studio
Mliekárenská 10
824 95 Bratislava
Tel & Fax: (7) 212 803

ARTTEP
Hlavná 30
900 31 Stupava
Tel: (7) 935 349
Fax: (7) 935 452

B.M.A.
Drieňová 3
821 02 Bratislava
Tel & Fax: (7) 230 408

In Film
Špitálska 4
811 09 Bratislava
Tel: (7) 36 34 30, 36 33 96
Fax: (7) 32 36 78

Mirofilm
Brečtanová 1
833 14 Bratislava
Tel: (7) 371 966
Fax: (7) 371 126

Useful Addresses

Slovak Film Archive – National Cinematographic Centre
Grösslingova 32
811 09 Bratislava
Tel: (7) 517 89, 572 32
Fax: (7) 594 61

Slovak Television
(*Foreign Department*)
Mlynská Dolina
845 35 Bratislava
Tel: (7) 729 440
Fax: (7) 727 448

SLOVENIA

Milan
Ljubić

Over the three years since 1991 when the new country of Slovenia has existed as an independent state, there has been a fall in Slovene film productions. The reason for this should be sought primarily in lack of money, a problem that affects all former communist Eastern European countries. As part of the former Yugoslavia, Slovenia once had behind it a larger market, greater opportunities for screening films and, above all, certain international contacts which were organised at the former Yugoslav level. The war in Bosnia and Hercegovina, which has transformed the Balkans into an unstable region, has added its contribution to the collapse of the relatively strong former Yugoslav market. This is reflected not only in Slovene, but also in Croatian, Macedonian and other film industries in the former Yugoslavia. If one could speak in the former ideal years of an annual production rate of five feature films and twenty shorts (in 1988, for example, Slovenia made some nine drama films which, in the circumstances, was a unique record); the current production rate has slipped to two or three title per year. The slump in film productions, of course, does not mean that Slovenia is inactive in film-making.

After the collapse of the former Yugoslavia, social changes and moves towards a market economy, Slovenia found itself facing a pile of tasks including, among others, new legislation based on modern European standards. In the past year (1994) the Slovene parliament ratified a law on film-making and a law about the formation of the Slovene Film Production Fund. According to the models of cultural associations in other spheres such as the National Gallery, Philharmonic and National Theatre, the government has created the Slovene national technical film base and studios, Viba Film, the Slovene Film Production Fund and Slovene Film Archives.

In the meantime, the Museum of Film has been in existence for twenty years and the Film Department of the National Archives of Slovenia for a somewhat longer period. All these institutions have the role on the one hand, to preserve the film heritage of Slovenia, and on the other (similar to other European countries) to enable the operation of national film-making. This should be made financially feasible; first, by a film production fund, and second, the technical film base or studios which would be in charge of the technical production of films while not assuming the role of producer. Film-making would be entrusted to individual independent producers who would apply for a project through a competition announced by the Ministry of Culture and open for entry till the year end 1994. Thereafter, this role is going to be performed by the film production fund. In short, despite the apparent stagnation or at least considerably reduced number of Slovene film productions, something is stirring in the area of film-making.

Among the new films made in Slovenia it is worth mentioning one by Andrej Mlakar entitled **Halgato**. The screenplay was written by the director himself together with his colleague Feri Lainšček. The films of Andrej Mlakar include around 30 documentaries and short dramas as well as films for television. However, the film-maker has remained famous chiefly for his feature film premiere *Christophorus*, screened at a whole series of film festivals and awarded first prize at the International Film Festival in Strasbourg on the theme of human rights. After graduating in film and television direction at the Ljubljana

Academy of Theatre, Radio, Film and Television Arts, Andrej Mlakar (born in 1952) did his post-graduate studies at the drama department under Professor Wolfgang Langsfeld at the Munich Film School (HFF). The events in *Halgato* are set among gypsies in the Slovene part of the Pannonian plains in close proximity to the Hungarian border, and his main actors come from remote regions. The film-makers say that it is "chiefly a film about love and friendship, offering reminiscences of two principal characters who have been branded by their gypsy ethics and ethos since their childhood."

Entering Eureka ...

Slovenia has become a member of Audiovisual Eureka and in this context this European link has triggered several proposals for international co-operation, but these projects are still in the planning phase. As for international co-operation, the reaction from various countries has been favourable, although Slovenia will obviously have financial problems in making film productions for some time.

In the new social and economic conditions, distributors and cinemas have managed to find their feet the fastest. The data that shows cinema attendance figures have begun to grow is encouraging. This is on account of the faster supply of the latest American and other foreign hits, as the film releases shown in Slovenia are on a par with Berlin, Vienna, Rome, Paris and other major European cities. All foreign films in Slovenia are screened in their original versions with subtitles in Slovene. Slovenia possesses one of the best laboratories in Central Europe for subtitling 35mm film.

Among the innovations in television legislation it is necessary to mention the new law on public information which obliges national television to produce a share of its programme output in collaboration with foreign and independent producers, as has been the practice for years in Western European countries. Mainly film directors and

Still from Tugo Stiglić's A SMILE UNDER THE VEIL

producers have responded to this measure. In collaboration with the television station they see it as an opportunity to compensate for the slump in film productions in the conventional sense.

For Slovenia the same assertions hold true as for other European countries: critics blame film programmes for being "Americanised", and bemoan the fact that American films predominate in cinemas. That is true for commercial distribution, but as regards T.V., non-commercial film distribution and chiefly the only Slovene international film festival, Film Art Fest, provide a balance. Therefore, apart from American films, viewers have the opportunity to become acquainted with films from Australia, New Zealand, European countries and occasionally also Africa. As a matter of fact, the film image of Slovenia is not as black as it would seem at first sight.

A proverb states: "When someone beholds the dawn, another experiences the dusk." That also applies to film producers and distributors, for whom a brighter future is approaching, while video pirates will be groping in the dark. New legislation about copyright has fundamentally strained conditions in the market-place for copyright; video pirates are awaiting sentences not worth risking. Not only legal standards that enable a considerable increase in claims for damages have been raised, but the provisions of the new penal law includes punishments for copyright law offences, which could also send offenders to jail.

If Slovenia cannot find firm ground with its own larger film productions, it can at least be involved in several other activities which are occasionally required for film. Few directors and even professional film critics are aware that the entire classic car fleet in Spielberg's *Schindler's List* is Slovene. The classic pre-Second World War vehicles that were also driven during the war were all Slovene. Employing specialist Slovene mechanics for servicing the old vehicles, they were taken from Ljubljana to the shooting location in Kraków, Poland. Slovenia is one of the rare countries which has available old steam engines and coaches from the times before the First World War, freight cars and passenger coaches from the inter-war period (those were the days when wooden carriages still ran on rails), and trains which transported German and other soldiers along various European lines from one front to another.

Useful Addresses

The country code for phone and fax calls to Slovenia is +386 and for Ljubljana 61.

Slovenia Archives
Film Dept.
61000 Ljubljana
Zvezdarska 1
Tel: 125 12 22, 125 12 66, 125 13 08
Fax: 216 551

Slovene Film Museum
61000 Ljubljana
Mestni trg 17
Tel: 212 728
Tel/Fax: 210 142

Slovenia Television
61000 Ljubljana
Kolodvorska 2-4
Tel: 13 11 333
Fax: 317 479

Academy of Theatre, Radio, Film and Television
61000 Ljubljana
Nazorjeva 3
Tel: 210 412, 210 503, 219 518, 126 43 16
Fax: 210 450

Infomedia 3 Filming d.o.o.
Film production, distribution and other film services
61104 Ljubljana
P.O. Box 53
Tel/Fax: 61 13 13 261
Tel/Fax: 61 331 954

Pegaz Film d.o.o.
Film and video productions
61117 Ljubljana
Pržanjska 10b
Tel/Fax: 61 159 17 32

E-motion Film d.o.o.
61000 Ljubljana
Kersnikova 4
Tel: 61 132 91 12
Fax: 61 329 185

Filmal Pro d.o.o.
68000 Novo mesto
Nad mlini 26
Tel: 68 22 601

Studio 37 d.o.o.
ICT – Peska
61234 Mengeš
Tel/Fax: 61 714 837

Viba Film p.o.
61000 Ljubljana
Zrinskega 9
Tel: 61 325 971
Fax: 61 329 179

Subtitling Laboratory Film Plus d.o.o.
61000 Ljubljana
Kvedrova c. 9
Tel: 61 444 352
Fax: 61 444 880

SOUTH AFRICA — Martin Botha

The past twelve months will be remembered for a mixture of positive and negative developments regarding South African cinema. On the positive side unity was at last established within the film industry by the joining of eight prominent film bodies (African Film and Television Collective, Association of Community Arts Centres, Black Film and Television Foundation, Film and Allied Workers' Organisation, National Television and Video Association, Performing Arts Workers Equity, SA Film and Television Institute, and the SA Scriptwriters Association). This unification resulted in the Film and Broadcasting Steering Committee.

Recommendations on ways to transform the local film subsidy scheme (which is simply based on box-office earnings) were presented at two major forums: the ANC's Culture and Development Conference and the National Arts Initiative's congress. The French Centre National de la Cinématographie (CNC) was recognised by both forums to be an important model for a future South African Film Foundation (SAFF). The SAFF will be an independent statutory body, headed by a Board of Governors appointed from leaders in the South African society and in communications and the media. Its composition will be such that it cannot be used to further the commercial interest of any one company or sector of the local film industry. Funding procedures by the SAFF should apply to different branches of the industry and should encourage films of all types, including non-commercial and short films. The SAFF could be financed by a levy on cinema tickets and TV licences, but wide-ranging, ongoing research needs to be undertaken in order to guide the changes that need to be brought about in the industry.

The historic elections during April 1994 during which a democratic Government of National Unity was established, focused the attention of the world community on South Africa. It is expected that this government of National Unity will create a positive climate in which the above-mentioned proposals for an indigenous, non-racial film industry will be favourably considered.

Personally one feels optimistic about the future of South Africa and the local film industry, but the development of a post-apartheid film industry will be difficult. During 1993 for example the South African film world reacted very angrily to a deal made between Dr Wally Serote of the African National Congress' Department of Arts and Culture (DAC) and Elmo de Witt Films. This deal, which has resulted in the establishment of the jointly-controlled National Film Trust of Southern Africa (Naftsa), was seen as a case of the DAC forging a privileged relationship with one private film company, and thus a direct contradiction of the abovementioned film proposals. Naftsa was also accused of disrupting other industry-wide training and development initiatives. Severe criticism came from members of the Film and Broadcasting Steering Committee, which has been painstakingly working on the proposals for a national film trust for more than a year. According to two progressive members of the Steering Committee, the Film and Allied Workers' Organisation (FAWO) and the African Film and Television Collective, the DAC would receive 25% of all funds and profits generated by the trust. The Naftsa initiative has not only disrupted plans for the SAFF, but also the research process which needs to guide necessary changes to the current subsidy scheme by the new government.

Although the previous government announced during February 1994 the establishment of an interim South African film trust to help budding television and film producers, one would be cautious to see how the Naftsa initiative is going to affect this trust (which is to be financed jointly by the state and private enterprise). On the positive side, the trust can grant bursaries, help the development of scripts and sponsor young, promising directors to enable them to produce short films. Young film-makers could get a subsidy of up to R300,000 for production and laboratory costs.

Links with Foreign Companies

During the months before the elections, some of our most important film directors either made films in foreign countries such as the U.S.A. (Darrell James Roodt, **Father Hood**) or the Netherlands (Ian Kerkhof, **The Mozart Bird**), or they made locally-based movies with foreign currency like Elaine Proctor with **Friends**. Proctor's drama about the friendship between three South African women is set against the political turmoil of the 1980's. Although ambitious the film is ultimately dis-appointing. The main focus of the film remains with the white political activist (played by Kerry Fox) and Proctor never analyses the unique interaction between the three women. Maybe a longer director's cut will fill the numerous gaps in the narrative and characterisation. It took Proctor one whole year simply to raise money for her film – from Channel Four; the French equivalent, Canal Plus; and British Screen, a state-funded film body.

The South African film industry has exceptionally talented individuals: actress Embeth Davidtz, for example, received an important part in Spielberg's masterful *Schindler's List*. Trevor de Kock's wildlife BBC documentary **Springbok of the Kalahari** is a stunning piece of film-making. These achievements do distract one's attention from the less successful examples of local cinema: poorly made farces such as **There's a Zulu on My Stoep**, and vulgar slapstick comedy about inter-racial relationships in this country, and yet

another television spin-off entitled **Orkney Snork Nie (Nog 'n movie).** **Zulu** grossed 4.5 million rands at the SA box-office in 1993. Other features were bad examples of Hollywood genre films: a hideous Americanisation of the hit stage musical **Ipi Tombi** and two routine thrillers, **Cyborg Cop** and **Woman of Desire**.

The saddest aspect of 1993 was the suicide of our most prominent film director, Manie van Rensburg, a director who has painstakingly chronicled the Afrikaner past over a period of more than two decades, especially in a film like **The Fourth Reich**. The 48-year-old director was always an outsider to the South African film community. He never became part of those so-called film-makers who made a fast buck from various ludicrous tax payback and subsidy schemes which were created during the 1980's. He also never sold his artistic soul as other contemporary Afrikaans directors have done. His steadfast unwillingness to compromise his artistry was responsible for the unique, distinctive voice of his films and television dramas/series, ranging from revisionist portrayals of the history and psyche of the Afrikaner in *Lost Springtime* and *Heroes* to a film adaptation of Nadine Gordimer's *Country Lovers*, an across-the-colour-line love story during a time when the subject was taboo.

Shorts Offer Hope for Future

A real hope for a new, post-apartheid South African cinema lies within local short film production which is presented to the public every year at the Annual *Weekly Mail/Guardian Weekly* Film Festival's Short Film Competition. In the past such films as *Sales Talk* and the animation films by William Kentridge; *Sacrifice*, about the disintegration of an Afrikaner family and Guy Spiller's *The Boxer*, about white working-class fears regarding political change in South Africa, stunned audiences. Last year Catherine Meyburgh's **The Clay Ox**, about white South Africans trying to redefine their role in an apartheid society and to come to terms with their heritage, gave one new hope for another revival in innovative local film making.

The local pay-television network M-Net has provided funding for the making of 30-minute films in their project *New Directions: The Rhythm of our Lives*. Kenneth Kaplan's **The Children and I**, Rozelle Vogelman's **The Apology**, Lance Gewer and Zahariah Rapola's **Come see the Bioscope** and Peni Flascas's **Learning the Hard Way** were broadcast on the network in February 1994. The project is a showcase for new talent in this country and especially **The Apology** about pupils' reactions to an abortion case at school, and the evocative **Come See the Bioscope** about ANC member Soi Plaatje's attempts to educate rural blacks (see *review*, are worthwhile short films.

Other good news are that Darrell Roodt again will direct a feature in South Africa after his rather unfortunate *Father Hood* which was made in the United States. The film, **Cry the Beloved Country**, is being made by local producer Anant Singh's Distant Horizon. The film will be a 15-million dollar production and it is based on Alan Paton's famous novel about two families in the 1950's – one black, one white – who come together during the worst apartheid era because they see humanity in each other. This message of reconciliation is very important for a post-apartheid South Africa.

Still from COME SEE THE BIOSCOPE

Gewer is at the moment the most promising new director to emerge from local cinema. His previous short film, *Sacrifice*, concerns an Afrikaans family in the process of disintegration. The film narrates the extremes of human behaviour with a sombre skill. The result is a chamber work with a brilliant eye for detail that looks at the pessimistic side of transition and upheaval in contemporary South Africa.

With *Come See the Bioscope*, another model for future "chamber" works in South African cinema, Gewer deals with the past. The film is set in a small rural community in the Western Transvaal, Driefontein, during the 1920's. Sol Plaatje travels from town to town with his bioscope to educate rural blacks politically. During this visit to Driefontein he meets with a small boy and the encounter leads to an enriching process for the boy. In a gentle and evocative way Gewer, Rapola and scriptwriter Weinek explore a significant moment of popular memory in the lives of this rural community: the effects of the Land Acts on blacks and the efforts by one South African to create a political awareness by means of cinema among this

COME SEE THE BIOSCOPE

Script: Catharina Weinek. Direction: Lance Gewer, Zacharia Rapola. Editing: Micki Stroucken. Photography: Lance Gewer. Music: Lloyd Ross and Didi Kriel. Art Direction: Leon van der Merwe. Players: Ernest Ndlovu, Simanga Nhlapo, Deborah Ramokagdi, Abdul Sadek. Produced by Phakathi Films in association with Richard Green and Associates. Executive Producers for M-NET: Michael Cheze, Tania Jenkins: The M-NET Project: *New Directions: The Rhythm of Our Lives.* 30 mins.

Among the 37 short films at the *7th Mail and Guardian* Film Festival, as well as the four short films commissioned by the pay-television M-NET, Lance Gewer's *Come See the Bioscope* clearly stood out.

community. Again the eye for detail is remarkable. The film is a prime example of the rise in short film-making in this country.   Martin Botha

MARTIN BOTHA is a research specialist on South African cinema and television, as well as a film lecturer. He is co-author of *Images of South Africa: The Rise of the Alternative Film,* co-editor of *Movies Moguls Mavericks: South African Cinema 1979-1991* and is working on a new book: *Gays in African, Asian and Latin American cinema.*

TOP TEN GROSSING FILMS IN SOUTH AFRICA: 1993

There are effectively two SA Top 10 lists: distributor UIP's, comprising films released at Ster-Kinekor and Nu Metro cinemas and distributor/exhibitor Ster-Kinekor's, made up of figures from cinemas on its circuit only.

	Gross in rands
UIP's list:	
Jurassic Park	12 million
The Bodyguard	6.6 million
The Fugitive	5.6 million
Indecent Proposal	5.5 million
Dennis the Menace	5 million
Scent of a Woman	3.6 million
Under Siege	3.5 million
The Firm	3.5 million
Sommersby	2.7 million
Sliver	2.5 million
Ster-Kinekor's list:	
Aladdin	10.8 million
Jurassic Park	6.4 million
There's a Zulu on my Stoep	4.5 million
Cliffhanger	4 million
The Lover	3.5 million
The Fugitive	3.3 million
Indecent Proposal	3.1 million
Last Action Hero	2.9 million
Hot Shots 2	2.9 million

Recent and Forthcoming Films

THE CLAY OX

Script: Damon Galgut. Dir: Catherine Mayburgh. Phot: Dewald Aukema. Players: Vincent Meyburgh, Marina Coetzee.

COME SEE THE BIOSCOPE

Script: Catharina Weinek. Dir: Lance Gewer and Zacharia Rapola. Editing: Micki Stroucken. Players: Ernest Ndlovu, Simanga Nhlapo, Deborah Ramokagdi, Abdul Sadek. Prod: Phakathi Films in association with Richard Green and Associates.

DUST DEVIL

Script and Dir: Richard Stanley. Players: Robert Burke, Chelsea Field, Marianne Sagebrecht, Zakes Mokae, John Matshikiza.

FRIENDS

Script and Dir: Elaine Proctor. Editing: Tony Lawson. Players: Michelle Burgers, Kerry Fox, Dambisa Kente, Marius Weyers. Prod: British Screen, Channel Four and Chrysalide Films.

IN DARKEST HOLLYWOOD

Script, Dir, Editing and Prod: Daniel Riesenfeld and Peter Davis. Interviews with: Lewis Nkosi, Arthur Maimane, Erica Rutherford, Lionel Ngakane and Jamie Uys. *Documentary*.

IPI TOMBI

Dir: Donald Hulette and Tommie Meyer. Players: Jan-Michael Vincent, Maxwell Caulfield, Henry Cele, Nana Moloi, Ernest Ndlovu.

A LEGITIMATE BUSINESS

Script: Malcolm Purkey. Dir: Roberto Bangura. Players: David Calder, Oke Wambe, Sydney Cole. Prod: Ben Barker for the National Film and Television School in Britain.

LIVING IN SOUTH AFRICA

Dir: Mark Newman. Editing: Lois Davis. Prod: Robyn Hofmeyr. *Documentary*.

MAYIBUYE AFRIKA

Dir: Charlotte Owen, Peter Corbett. Interviews with: Nelson Mandela, Oliver Tambo, Walter Sisulu and Mangosuthu Buthelezi. *Documentary*.

ORKNEY SNORK NIE! (NOG 'N MOVIE) (Orkney Doesn't Snore) (Another Movie)

Script & Dir: Willie Esterhuizen. Players: Zack du Plessis, Annette Engelbrecht. Prod: Philo Pieterse for WESTEL Productions and Philo Pieterse Productions.

SENZENI NA?

Script and Dir: Bernard Joffa. Editing: Alex Olivares. Players: Sam Phillips, Duduzile Mkhize, Ivan Berold. Prod: Anthony E. Nicholas (U.S.A.).

SGUDI SNAYSI

Script: Richard Beynon. Dir: Roberta Durrant. Editing: Rene Engelbrecht. Players: Joe Mafela, Daphne Hlomuka, Gloria Mudau, Theembi Mtchali. Prod: Roberta Durrant for Penguin Films and Toron International.

SOUL

Script and Dir: Marcus Kadalie. Editing: Lotue Mehnart. Players: Marcus Kadalie, Tiger Haynes, Mirjam Thate.

SPRINGBOK OF THE KALAHARI

Script: Barry Paine. Dir: Trevor de Kock. Prod: Pelican Pictures for BBC-TV and the National Geographic Society. *Documentary*.

THERE'S A ZULU ON MY STOEP

Script: Leon Schuster, Gray Hofmeyr. Dir: Gray Hofmeyr. Editing: Johan Lategan, Alastair Henderson. Players: Leon Schuster, John Matshikiza, Wilson Dunster and Terri Treas. Prod: Edgar Bold for Toron Koukus-Troika.

A TRAVELLING SONG

Dir: Lindy Wilson. Editing: Cathy Meyburgh. Players: Gcina Mhlope, Patrick Shai. Prod: Lindy Wilson. *Documentary*.

TREKKING TO UTOPIA

Script, Dir and Phot: Michael Hammon. Editing: Mona Bauer. *Documentary*.

WOMAN OF DESIRE

Script and Dir: Robert Ginty. Players: Jeff Fahey, Bo Derek, Robert Mitchum, Steven Bauer.

Producers

Video Vision Enterprises
134 Essenwood Road
Berea
Durban 4001
Tel: (27-31) 224000
Fax: (27-31) 222444

Toron Studios
2 Johannesburg Road
Gresswold
Johannesburg 2000
Tel: (27-11) 7862360
Fax: (27-11) 4405132

L & O Leisureco Ltd
TV Park
Sysie Road
Randpark Ridge Ext. 39
Randburg 2156
Tel: (27-11) 7953781
Fax: (27-11) 7952603

Mimosa Films
28 Harley Street
Ferndale
Randburg 2156
Tel: (27-11) 7871075

M-NET (Multichoice Kaleidoscope)
New Directions: The Rhythm of our Lives
P.O. Box 4950
Randburg 2125

Philo Pieterse Productions
231 Old Pretoria Road
Midrand 1685
Tel: (27-11) 3142080
Fax: 27-11) 3142265

Scy Productions
P.O. Box 2980
Randburg 2125
Tel: (27-11) 7891353
Fax: (27-11) 7891376

Combined Artists
109 Central Street
Houghton 2198
Johannesburg
Tel: (27-11) 4831532
Fax: (27-11) 7286157

Distributors

Nu Metro
6 Hood Avenue
Rosebank 2196
Tel: (27-11) 8807040
Fax: (27-11) 4427030

Ster-Kinekor
158 Main Street
Johannesburg 2000
Tel: (27-11) 3314944
Fax: (27-11) 3319885

UIP Warner
7 Junction Avenue
Castrol House
Parktown
Johannesburg 2000
Tel: (27-11) 4844215
Fax: (27-11) 4843339

Useful Addresses

African Film and Television Collective
Rapitse Montsho
Tel: (27-11) 296811
Fax: (27-11) 296812

Black Film and Television Foundation
Joyce Ndamase
Tel: (27-11) 6424183
Fax: (27-11) 8343336

The Film and Broadcasting Steering Committee
Karen Thorne
P.O. Box 16939
Doornfontein 2028
Tel: (27-11) 4024570
Fax: (27-11) 4020777

Film Resource Unit
Training, Distribution and Resource Centre
Gate 2, Newtown Cultural Precinct
1 President Street
Newtown
Johannesburg 2001
Tel: (27-11) 8384280/1/2
Fax: (27-11) 8384451

Human Sciences Research Council
Dr. Martin Botha
Social Dynamics
Private Bag x41
Pretoria 0001
Tel: (27-12) 2022308
Fax: (27-12) 3265362

Newtown Film and Television School
Clarence Hamilton
1 President Street
Newtown
Johannesburg 2001
Tel: (27-11) 8387462/3/5/6
Fax: (27-11) 8381043

Screen Africa
Helen Grau
Sun Circle Publishers
P.O. Box 706
Strathavon 2031
Sandton
Tel: (27-11) 7820283

Showdata
Johan Blignaut
P.O. Box 15756
Vlaeberg
Cape Town 8018
Tel: (21-21) 245483/e-mail:
Showdata @ worknet.alt.za

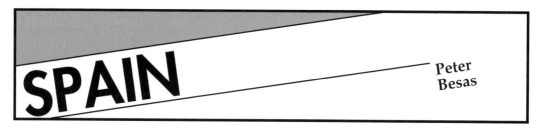

SPAIN

Peter Besas

If films were bottled and corked, the 1993 vintage in Spain would certainly not go down in history as in any way memorable. Nonetheless, last year *was* distinguished by Fernando Trueba winning the country's second Oscar for *Belle Epoque*, made in 1992; on the same gala show, Spanish actor Antonio Banderas consolidated his claim to internationality, by being chosen by the Academy to host one of its other prizes.

The "night of the Spaniards" unfortunately was not symptomatic of the scene back home where, two months earlier, Spain's own Goya awards, modelled on the Oscars, were doled out to such limp and undistinguished fare as Luis García Berlanga's **All Off to Jail** (*Todos a la carcel*), Francisco Regueiro's **Madregilda** and **Banderas, the Tyrant** (*Tirano Banderas*). The

ceremony was the poorest since the inception of the Goyas, eight years hence.

The Berlanga film almost seemed like a parody of his earlier (1978) *National Shotgun*; *Madregilda* was one, long, hermetic, political "in" joke, with Juan Echanove hamming up the part of General Franco; and José Luis García Sánchez's *Banderas, the Tyrant*, vaguely based on the classic by Ramón del Valle Inclán, seemed like a disjointed synopsis of a teleseries. It had earlier been savaged by most critics at the Valladolid Film Festival and then died a quick death at the box-office.

Released with a great deal of fanfare, films such as Vicente Aranda's **Intruso** and Bigas Luna's **Golden Balls** (*Huevos de oro*) failed to live up to expectations, and drew attendances well below those directors'

LA MADRE MUERTA, with director Juanma Bajo Ulloa flanked by the two actors

earlier films, *Jamón, Jamón* and *El Amante*, respectively.

Madcap Spoof from Almodóvar

Even Spain's *wunderkind*, Pedro Almodóvar, failed to enthuse critics or audiences with **Kika**, which starts as a madcap spoof of the media, and then trails off into self-conscious melodrama. Its main saving graces were the costume and set designs and a wonderful performance by Verónica Forqué.

There was, nonetheless, one film which won a minor Goya for special effects, and is perhaps the most innovative and startling film to come out of Spain last year. Directed by Juanma Bajo Ulloa, **The Dead Mother** (*La Madre Muerta*), the film is a strange, violent, evocative, idiosyncratic tale of a criminal in the Basque area and his obsession with a mentally retarded girl, who had earlier been his victim. Bajo Ulloa's earlier *Butterfly Wings* had already been heralded by local critics as a discovery, but *The Dead Mother*

consolidates his position as one of the most daring and promising of the new directors.

Otherwise, the few remaining Spanish producers have turned to grinding out local comedies which are relatively cheap to make and are fairly sure of a good return, but, of course, don't "travel". Among such "youth" fare were **How To Be Unhappy and Enjoy It** (*Como ser infeliz y disfrutarlo*) by Enrique Urbizu, **You Men Are All the Same** (*Todos los hombres sois iguales*), and **Tales of the Stinking Military Service** (*Historias de la puta muli*) by Manel Esteban.

Thanks largely to these, Spain still managed to corner 8.52% of its own market in 1993, slightly less than the previous year. Meanwhile, the perennial talk of "filmic crisis" persists. Producers pressured the government to try to pass a restrictive new film law, which would limit the activities of the majors, but at press time, amid the worst political scandals since the advent of the Socialist government a decade ago, the law seemed doomed to failure. Opposition

TOP TEN GROSSING FILMS IN SPAIN: 1993

(Dollar equivalent figured at 125 pesetas to the dollar)

Jurassic Park	$20,628,000
Bram Stoker's Dracula	10,281,000
Aladdin	9,767,000
Indecent Proposal	9,521,000
The Fugitive	9.361,000
The Bodyguard	9,072,000
Beauty and the Beast	8,515,000
Cliffhanger	6,825,000
Sommersby	5,784,000
Scent of a Woman	5,592,000

from exhibitors and distributors was so fierce that a one-day strike protesting the legislation shuttered all cinemas in Spain on December 20.

Hopes for the Future

Although no film was selected in any official section in Cannes (1994), Spanish producers nonetheless have their hopes pinned on various films in the offing.

Among the contenders for success are: Gonzalo Suárez's *Death and the Detective*, a "surreal thriller", currently ready for release. Bigas Luna's *The Tit and the Moon*, described as "a Mediterranean love story about three men madly in love with one woman", is another hopeful. Vicente Aranda started shooting *Turkish Passion* on locations in Istanbul in mid-May and a quirky eye-opener may be the result. Enrique Urbizu's *Woman's Horns* is also ready for an autumn release. All of the above are being made by Spain's biggest producer, Iberoamericana Films.

Producer Elías Querejeta is preparing *Historia del Kronen*, to be directed by Montxo Armendariz, set to roll in August. Querejeta will also co-produce *The City of Lost Children*. In early 1995 he also expects to make *All Souls* on location in Oxford, directed by his daughter, Gracia, who made *Passing Season* in 1992.

Perhaps the most ambitious project in the works is Fernando Trueba's *Two Much*, with Andy Garcia set to star, due to roll in Miami in September for Iberoamericana.

Among films already completed are Imanol Uribe's *Numbered Days* and Mario Camus's *Self Esteem*, produced by Sogepaq. On the erotic tack, there's *Fire My Passion*, with Miguel Bosé and Emma Suárez, about a fetish-minded botanist, directed by José Miguel Ganga. Other directors such as Manuel Gutiérrez Aragón, Gerardo Vera, Mariano Barroso, Cecilia Bartolomé, Juanma Bajo Ulloa, Alex de la Iglesia, Rafael Moleón and Felipe Vega are all preparing films.

Over in Barcelona the film scene has been very quiet, and those films produced there rarely get released outside Cataluña. Since politically the Catalans held the power balance in Spain, they were able to increase demands for subsidies and at one point a decree was considered that would have enabled them to set their own exhibition and distribution quotas. But the best of Catalan talent, such as directors Bigas Luna, Vicente Aranda and actors Juanjo Puigcorbé, Assumpta Serna, etc, have long since migrated to Madrid.

Substantial Subsidies to Producers

The Culture Ministry has been virtually comatose over the past two years in promoting Spanish cinema, though it still feeds substantial subsidies to producers. The biggest change certainly has come in the exhibition sector, where Warner

Brothers, AMC (American Multi Cinemas), CINESA, the French company UGC, and other non-Spanish groups are already building or are planning to build multiplex cinemas. The arthouse sector is also booming, with the rapid expansion of the Renoir Cinema group, captained by Enrique González Macho, who already has two complexes in Madrid and is now planning houses in Barcelona, Guenca and other cities.

Miguel Bosé in FIRE MY PASSION

Since late 1993, a running battle has been waged among the different film sectors in Spain. The feuding started when a group of key producers convinced Culture Minister Carmen Alborch to pass a decree favouring the producers, but detrimental to independent distributors and exhibitors. The warring continued at mid-year 1994, with the GATT and Economic Union controversies about audiovisual matters in the background. Meanwhile, the clout of the U.S. majors continues to grow, sweeping before it the various efforts by the Spaniards and the Media Programme to stop the multinational juggernaut via restrictive decrees.

In fact, the controversial government decree was violently opposed by the remaining independent distributors such as Antonio Llorens, Francisco Hoyos, Enrique González Macho and others, who fear that the change in legislation would force the majors to snap up all potentially commercial independent European films.

PETER BESAS has lived in Madrid since the mid-1960's and is chief of Variety's bureau there. He has written various books, including a history of Spanish cinema.

Recent and Forthcoming Films

TIRANO BANDERAS (Banderas, the Tyrant)

Script: José Luis García Sánchez and Rafael Aszcona based on the novel of Ramón del Valle-Inclán. Dir: García Sánchez. Phot: Fernando Arribas. Players: Gian Maria Volonté, Ana Belén, Juan Diego, Ignacio López Tarso, Fernando Guillén. Prod: Ion Films in association with Ibero-americana Films, Atrium Producciones, Promociones Audiovisuales Reunidas, in collaboration with Luz Directa, ICAIC (Cuba) and Cinematográfica del Prado (Mexico).

Period piece shot in Cuba about a fictitious dictator.

INTRUSO (Intruder)

Script: Alvaro del Amo and Vicente Aranda, based on story by Pedro Costa. Dir: Vicente Aranda. Phot: José Luis Alcaine. Players: Victoria Abril, Imanol Arias, Antonio Velero. Prod: Pedro Costa P.C., Atrium Productions, Promociones Audiovisuales Reunidas, in collaboration with Antena 3 TV.

Morbid love triangle set in northern Spain.

TODOS A LA CARCEL (Everyone Off To Jail)

Script: Jorge and Luis G. Berlanga. Dir: Luis García Berlanga. Phot: Alfredo Mayo. Players: José Sazatornil, José Luis López Vázquez, José Sacristán, Antonio Resines. Prod: Sogetel S.A., Central de Producciones Audiovisuales, Antea Films.

Madcap modern comedy with political overtones shot in the Valencia penitentiary.

HEUVOS DE ORO (Golden Balls)

Script: Bigas Luna and Cuca Canals. Dir: Bigas Luna. Phot: José Luis Alcaine. Players: Javier Bardem, Maribel Verdú, María de Medeiros. Prod: Lolafilms, Iberoamericana Films, Ovideo TV, Film Auto.

Sexy story about a construction worker who tries to rise to rule the real estate roost.

KIKA

Script and Dir: Pedro Almodóvar. Phot: Alfredo Mayo. Players: Verónica Forqué, Peter Coyote, Victoria Abril, Alex Casanovas, Rossy de Palma. Prod: El Deseo S.A. and Ciby 2000.

The zany goings-on of a hairdresser, Kika, as she gets involved with a homicidal American writers, a reality-show TV reporter and other loony characters.

MADREGILDA

Script: Francisco Regueiro and Angel Fernández-Santos. Dir: Regueiro. Phot: José L. López Linares. Players: José Sacristán, Juan Echanove, Barbara Auer, Kamel Cherif, Fernando Rey. Prod: Tornasol and Marea Films, in co-production with Road Movies Dritte Produktionen (Germany) and Gemini Films (Paris).

Spoof about Franco and his fascist aides, laden with symbolism and ham acting.

ENCIENCE MI PASION (Fire My Passion)

Script and Dir: José Luis Ganga. Players: Miguel Bosé, Juan Luis Galiardo, Emma Suárez. Prod: Penelope Films.

EL DETECTIVE Y LA MUERTE (The Detective and Death)

Script and Dir: Gonzalo Suárez. Phot: Carlo Suárez. Players: Héctor Alterio, Javier Bardem, María de Madeiros. Prod: Ditirambo Films and Lola Films.

LA TETA Y LA LUNA (The Tit and the Moon)

Script: Bigas Luna and Cuca Canals. Dir: Bigas Luna. Phot: José Luis Alcaine. Players: Methilde May, Gerard Darmon, Biel Duran and Miguel Poveda. Prod: Lola Films.

LA MADRE MUERTA (The Dead Mother)

Script: Juanma and Eduardo Bajo Ulloa. Dir: Juanma Bajo Ulloa. Phot: Javier Aguirre-sarobe. Players: Karra Elejalde, Ana Alvarez, Lio. Prod: Gasteizko Zinema.

Violent burglar and killer falls in love with former victim, who's now mentally deficient.

Producers

Iberoamericana Films
Velázquez 12
Madrid 28001
Tel: 4314246
Fax: 4355994

El Deseo S.A.
Ruiz Perelló 15
Madrid 28028
Tel: 7250285
Fax: 3557467

Elias Querejeta
Maestro Lasalle 21
28016 Madrid
Tel: 345 7139
Fax: 345 2811

Cartel
Orense 33
Madrid 28020
Tel: 5970772
Fax: 5970766

Avanti Films
Ronda de San Pedro 46
Barcelona 08010
Tel: 268-1233
Fax: 268-1617

Sogepaq
Caídos de la División Azul 1
Madrid 28016
Tel: 522-0529
Fax: 350-3033

ESICMA
Maestro Lasalle 24-26
Madrid 28016
Tel: 345-8708
Fax: 359-6683

Ditirambo Films
Glorieta López de Hoyos, 5
Madrid 28006
Tel: 411-3249
Fax: 562-8166

Atrium Films
Fernán González 28
Madrid 28009
Tel: 431-4790
Fax: 431-7555

Lola Films
Pintor Gimeno 12
Barcelona 08022

Tel: 418-4044
Fax: 418-4748

Distributors

Disney/Buenavista
José Bardasano
Baos 9, Madrid 28016
Tel: 383-0312
Fax: 766-9241

United International Pictures
Plaza del Callao 4
Madrid 28013
Tel: 5227261
Fax: 532-2384

Warner Bros
Manuel Montilla 1
Madrid 28016
Tel: 3506200
Fax: 3451948

Lauren Films
Balmes 87
Barcelona 08008
(In Madrid: Tetuán 29
Madrid 28013)
Tel: 3235400 (Barcelona)
5218285 (Madrid)
Fax: 323-6155 (Barcelona)

Araba Films
San Prudencio 13
Vitoria 01005
Tel: 140126
Fax: 143156

Musidora Films
Princesa 17
Madrid 28008
Tel: 541-6869
Fax: 541-5482

20th Century-Fox
Avda de Burgos 8A
Madrid 28036
Tel: 302-4481
Fax: 383-8081

Prime Films
Clara del Rey 17
Madrid 28002
Tel: 5190181
Fax: 413-0772

Alta Films
Martin de los Heros 12
Madrid 28008

Tel: 5422702
Fax: 542-8777

Columbia Pictures
ed. Piovera Azul
Peonias 2
Madrid 28042
Tel: 320-0744
Fax: 320-6105

Wanda Films
Avda. Europe 9
Pozuelo 28224
Tel: 352-8376
Fax: 352-8371

Golem Distribution S.A.
Avda. de Bayona 52
Pamplona 31008
Tel: 260243
Fax: 171058

Cine Company
Zurbano 74
Madrid 28010
Tel: 4422944
Fax: 441-0098

Ivex Films
Paseo San Gervasio 16
Barcelona 08022
Tel: 418-4858
Fax: 418-5070

Filmayer
Ed. Bronce. Avda. Burgos 8-A,
planta 10-1
Madrid 28036
Tel: 383-1572
Fax: 383-0845

Useful Addresses

Federación de Productores de Cine (FAPAE), Producers' Assoc.
Sagasta 20
Madrid 28004
Tel: 448-2289
Fax: 593-4648

Spanish Culture Ministry (Film Institute)
San Marcos 40
Madrid 28004
Tel: 532-5089
Fax: 531-9212

Fedicine (Distributors' Association)
Velázquez 10
Madrid 28001
Tel: 576-9511
Fax: 578-0028

Federación de Exhibidores (Exhibitors' Association)
Velázquez 10
Madrid 28001
Tel: 576-9913

PROCINES (Producers' Association)
Ayala 20
Madrid 28001
Tel: 576-6066
Fax: 578-1915

Catalan Film & TV
Diputació 279
Barcelona 08007
Tel: 4881038
Fax: 4874192

Basque Film Producers Association
República Argentina 2
San Sebastian 20004
Tel: 422944
Fax: 428782

Academia de las Artes y las Ciencas Cinematograficas de España
General Oraa 68
Madrid 28006
Tel: 5633341

SRI LANKA

Amarnatha Jayatilaka

An event of far-reaching significance in the promotion of the national cinema began with the dawn of the new year. When the Sinhala Cinema reached its 47th year on January 21, 1994, the government announced the setting up of the National Film Development Fund (NFDF). This is the second most important contribution that the government of Sri Lanka has made for the development of the national cinema, since the formation of the National Film Corporation in 1972.

It is pertinent to look back into the way in which the NFDF came into being. With the assassination of President Premadasa on May 1, 1993, the then Prime Minister D.B. Wijetunga was unanimously elected by the parliament to be the Head of State and Chief Executive. President Wijetunga farsightedly appointed Tyronne Fernando as the new Minister of Information and Broadcasting. For the first time in 15 years the new minister was allocated the functions only of mass communication with specific reference to film, television, radio and print media. Newly appointed Minister Fernando is well-known as a straightforward and able politician with a distinguished background. Moreover, Fernando has produced two Sinhala movies, one of which is a biographical feature directed by the veteran Lester James Peries on the national hero and martyr, Puran Appu, who is a direct ancestor of the minister.

The first task the minister undertook was to persuade the government to release an annual grant of 15 million rupees for the setting up of the NFDF. Having thus laid the foundation for the development of the film industry, the minister got down to the task of removing the many problems that face us owing to the misdemeanours of previous administrations at the National Film Corporation (NFC). The basic action plan of the NFDF boils down to three primary aims: to assist the production of outstanding movies; to assist the improve-ment and modernisation of movie theatres; to assist the advancement of technical skills among film technicians.

In order to derive maximum benefit from the NFDF, it has been decided to release loan facilities at a very nominal rate of 5% interest to the above three categories.

Fight Against Ticket Corruption

In streamlining the film industry another very important decision taken by the minister was implemented on the occasion of the 47th anniversary of the Sinhala cinema. Admission tickets to all cinemas here are now printed and released by the NFC. This unique method was imple-mented to safeguard the interests of local producers, and to ensure that the income goes to the NFC as the sole and exclusive distributor of domestic films. This action became necessary owing to the protests of the Film Producers Association against the cheating on admission rates by unscrupu-lous theatre owners.

The next major problem encountered by the film industry in Sri Lanka is the lack of

cinemas. In 1983 there were 350 screens. Owing to the ethnic riots and the subsequent terrorist actions almost a hundred were destroyed. However, during the last year 18 new cinemas have begun construction and three new ones have already opened. The first multiplex is now under construction in the capital city of Colombo.

When the country returned to normal after the siege of '89-'91 period due to terrorist actions, there was a spurt in film production. The number of completed films came up to almost 100 and the release of these films required another new circuit. Thus the new minister had to intervene on this matter and order the formation of a new circuit in addition to the existing five circuits allocated for the release of new Sinhala films.

Outstanding New Film

Meanwhile, an outstanding Sinhala film, written and directed by the leading Sri Lankan actor Gamini Fonseka, was completed. This is the first time that a Sinhala film was made on the theme of Tamil terrorism which has persisted for the last decade in the northern part of Sri Lanka. Having considered its pioneering effort of dealing with a very crucially important theme about the war of the state army versus the northern terrorists, the government ordered the release of this film, **The Immortals**, on a priority basis. This decision stirred a section of the film industry and for the first time ever a picketing movement was organised by a hurriedly arranged *ad hoc* body of film workers – in front of the offices of the NFC in protest against the release of this film on February 4, 1994 – which happens to be Independence Day. Thus *The Immortals* gained enormous publicity and became not only a very big commercial success but was also critically acclaimed as an outstanding movie, highlighting the importance of national unity among the two leading ethnic groups in Sri Lanka.

Twenty-five Sinhala films were released in the year 1993 through our five circuits – each circuit comprising 12 opening centres.

An equal number of Indian films was imported. Some 60 English films were released and 99% of these were American productions.

AMARNATH JAYATILAKA is a filmologist and one of Sri Lanka's leading film-makers. He periodically lives in Hollywood where he is a vice-president of Amerilanka Entertainment Inc.

NOMIYENA MINISUN
(The Immortals)

Script and Direction: Gamini Fonseka. Photography: V. Vamadevan. Sound: Lionel Gunaratna. Editing: D.B. Nihalsingha. Players: Gamini Fonseka, Shanta Saparamadu, Damith Fonseka, Sangeetha Weeraratna. Production: Bernard Gunasekara. World Sales: Sardonyx Films, 293 Jampettah St, Kotahena, Colombo 13 Sri Lanka.

Superstar Gamini Fonseka's latest film is a blockbuster. It stands strikingly as one of the best photographed colour movies of the Sri Lankan cinema. The creative vision of its director – who also plays the lead – could not have been realised without the great contribution made by its producer – Bernard Gunasekara – who deserves kudos for its spectacular achievement. Thus this film heralds the emergence of true professionalism in the Sri Lankan cinema, where a majority of mediocre films masquerade as art. Writing on this film, the internationally-known veteran film-maker Lester James Peries has this to say: "*Nomiyena Minisun* is a vastly ambitious film epic in its scope, daring in the complex themes it orchestrates, and powerful in its impact on the viewer. Dealing as it does with the most crucial national problem of our time – the ongoing war between the

Confrontation between Gamini Fonseka and Shanta Saparamadu in THE IMMORTALS

army and its confrontations with the Tiger terrorists in the north, in their ruthless pursuit of a Tamil homeland."

A brief synopsis can do no justice to the many strands, themes and subplots in this extremely rich film. But the most moving scenes are between the senior officer (played by Gamini) and the younger commando (played by Damith Fonseka) involving the gradual revelation of the senior officer's past – married to an Indian woman forced by the ethnic carnage of 1983 to return to India with their son. The theme of a father in search of a lost son is poignantly underlined.

An integral part of the film is its multi-national characters. Indian and local artistes, Sinhala, Tamil and English dialogue add to the complexity of the film. Apart from the fact that this is Gamini Fonseka's tribute to the army and specifically to the young men who are sacrificing their lives to preserve the unity of our country, *The Immortals* is as topical as today's headlines – the "Killing Fields of Sri Lanka".   Amarnath Jayatilaka

SWEDEN — Jannike
Åhlund

The best Swedish film last year was made in Hollywood (well, Texas, actually). The next best Swedish film didn't quite make it to Hollywood – and the Oscars. And yet there is a certain kinship between directors Lasse Hallström and Åke Sandgren, recipient of last year's Gold Bug for best film, **The Sling Shot**. The world depicted in *The Sling Shot* is considerably darker and more menacing than that of the now legendary *My Life As A Dog*. *The Sling Shot* (the Swedish title *Kådisbellan* literally means condom-slingshot) was undoubtedly the best film of the year with its smooth rendering of a rather troubled and dramatic childhood during the 1930's, that of author Roland Schütt. Stellan Skarsgård plays the seductively charming, but viciously diabolic father, terrorising the family with his unpredictable moods as well as his socialistic fervour. Sandgren's directorial talent is indisputable as is his artistic integrity and ingenuity.

Strangely enough, the bug for best direction at the annual Gold Bug event, was not awarded to Åke Sandgren, but to Clas Lindberg for his third feature film, **The Ferris Wheel**, an adroit but rather unengaging adventure involving some small-time crooks.

The Gold Bug gala where, to cite Ingmar Bergman, "the pimps and the butchers of the business celebrate themselves and their gifted, courageous and loyal colla-borators", was an occasion marked by "a little something for everyone" – collective jury cowardice rather than a search for originality or outstanding talent. It can, of course, be argued that there isn't always enough talent to go around each and every year in a country where the annual output is roughly twenty feature films per year, and that, ultimately, these events are

always a matter of taste – be it consensual or not.

Helena Bergström, a brightly shining star in Swedish films during the last four years, finally got rewarded – for her roles in *The Ferris Wheel* and *The Last Dance*, husband/director Colin Nutley's tale about dance, love and sudden death. The cinematographer, Jens Fischer, received a prize for his exquisite work in the film. **The Last Dance**, however, is a somewhat unbalanced composite of crime mystery, everyday drama and comedy of errors – failing to be one or the other. It couldn't repeat the huge success that *House of Angels* scored with the audience (1.2 million saw the film in Sweden), but half a million spectators is still a respectable total for Swedish conditions.

Marika Lagercrantz has emerged as the most charismatic and interesting actress in Sweden, since the temporary departure of Lena Olin. Marika played in two films, *Grandpa's Journey* and *Dreaming of Rita* (both premiered during the first half of 1993) and by now has a succession of roles to her credit.

Veteran Sven Lindberg was awarded a Gold Bug for his role as a suddenly widowed father in **Spring of Joy**, an enchanting low-key drama about crumpling family relations with outstanding performances from Lindberg, Göran Stangertz as hopelessly failed wanna-be rock star and Camilla Lundén as his patient girlfriend.

Ambitious Project

Director Richard Hobert had a second undertaking during the year, **The Hands**, a thriller featuring a slightly deranged Sven-Bertil Taube as yet another social misfit.

The two films are part of an ambitious project aiming a making a series of films relating to the Seven Deadly Sins, much in the same vein as Kieślowski treated the Ten Commandments in his *Decalogue*. Just as in Kieślowski's case, Hobert chooses a less than obvious approach to his theme, and leaves the viewer guessing.

Jonas Cornell and newcomer Daniel Alfredson shared script credits – and a Gold Bug – for **The Man on the Balcony**, one of no less than six films produced during the year based on legendary crime writers Maj Sjöwall and Per Wahlöö's compelling stories. Three of the films, co-produced with German Rialto Film, premiered in the cinema, three were released directly on video. Most of the social and critical edge of these highly popular books, however, was lost in the process of turning them into films.

The Swedish box-office hit of the year, only topped by *Aladdin* and *Jurassic Park*, was **Sune's Summer**, a family comedy directed with impressive brio and a Tatiesque touch by debutant Stephan Apelgren. The story is based on a popular children's book character and is about the Andersson family's cancelled holiday trip to Greece. Sune has to make do with a caravan holiday at home – and there is simply no end to how things can go astray, especially with a well-meaning but absentminded father around. Peter Haber inhabits this role in a fashion that makes him the pretender to Gösta Ekman in the farce department.

If Tati sprinkled his inspiration over *Sune's Summer*, Fellini lent some of his magic to Agneta Fagerström-Olsson's *Magic Stronger than Life*. There are certainly strokes of genius in this *opera buffo* set in northern Sweden. On the director's artistic map, anything can happen – and happens! – when people come together for a country wedding, where a lot of hearts are broken and dreams evaporate into thin air.

Chamber Music of Punk Concert

During a season that seemed to be

Fun and games in MAGIC STRONGER THAN LIFE

dominated by mainstream crime and comedy, *Magic Stronger than Life*, along with Suzanne Osten's *Just You and Me* certainly contributed originality and a refreshingly "anti-conceptual" approach to the repertoire.

Suzanne Osten, who last year made a film – *Speak Up! It's So Dark* – about racism, chose the same theme for her new feature *Just You and Me*. But the two films compare to one another like a piece of chamber music to a punk concert, full blast. This is a tale about contemporary, multicultural Sweden, where a black 25-year-old woman becomes Minister of Youth. Osten has a lot to say not only about xenophobia and racism, but about immigration policies, school politics, new family patterns, the generation gap and the war between the sexes. And – oh! – a modern woman's futile efforts to lead a life where love, children and work are possible to combine. There is a lot on Osten's agenda, too much, and the film describes life in that it can be described as mildly controlled chaos.

The disparate group of film-makers who, during the 1960's once again made Swedish films fly around the world, were active during the year: Bo Widerberg finishing work on **All Things Fair**, returning to the streets of his childhood Malmö, and the scene for his international breakthrough film, *Raven's End*. Vilgot Sjöman is preparing a biopic on Swedish chemist and industrialist, Alfred Nobel, the first Swedish film to be sponsored by a large corporation, in this case Volvo. Jan Troell is preparing a feature film on Knut

Hamsun, the Norwegian Nobel laureate, who was dragged to court for Nazi sympathies during the war.

The death of director Mai Zetterling in March struck a sad chord in Swedish film life, especially considering that there didn't really seem to be any possibilities for her to make films in her native country. Ever since her comeback from French exile with *Amorosa* in 1986, she had tried to get different projects off the ground. It is rather amazing to consider that her career ranged from starring in Ingmar Bergman's debut as a scriptwriter, *Frenzy*, to her own debut as first Swedish female talkie-director to a number of very good films to her directorial credit. Her talent equalled her ambition and her energy.

Fifth Anniversary for Fund

More than one in two Swedish films produced today are the result of Nordic co-production, not least since the existence of Nordic Film- and TV-fund, now in its fifth year of operation. During the years, however, the fund has had to be cautious more than once, because of shortage of funds. The Nordic Council of Ministers is now pondering whether to make the fund a permanent institution and whether to increase the 60 million kronor in the fund, provided equally by the Nordic TV-companies, cultural ministeries and film institutes. Nevertheless, many current projects are truly pan-Nordic, like Lars von Trier's *Breaking the Waves*, Jesper Nielsen's

Columbia TriStar bought world rights for Åke Sandgren's THE SLINGSHOT, *with Stellan Skarsgård (left) and Jesper Salen*

The Last Viking, Liv Ullmann's *Kristin Lavransdatter* and Henning Carlsen's *Pan*. One producer qualifies the Nordic production situation as "a Hollywood in clogs".

Although last year marked an all-time low in cinema attendance, it hasn't deterred Svensk Filmindustri, owner of 85% of cinemas in Sweden, from expanding and building new complexes. In the regions, cinema attendance has sometimes doubled as a result, while in Stockholm figures have been plummeting for many years. In spite of this negative trend, SF will inaugurate SF-Filmstaden by August next year, a "film city" in the heart of the capital, offering 14 screens and 2,800 seats.

In Gothenburg. distributor Conny Plånborg has teamed up with the French giant, Gaumont, for a grand scale project, *Bergakungens salar* – "The Halls of the

TOP TEN GROSSING FILMS IN SWEDEN: June 1993 – June 1994

	Attendance
Aladdin	1,045,591
Jurassic Park	1,017,621
Sune's Summer (Swedish)	932,677
The Fugitive	703,356
The Dream House (Swedish)	572,580
The Last Dance (Swedish)	504,377
The Three Musketeers	457,355
Hot Shots 2	419,798
Schindler's List	416,038
Cliffhanger	391,396

Mountain King". This magnificent cinema dome with 18 screens and 3,100 seats would actually be carved out of a mountain in central Gothenburg.

In May Ingrid Edström, head of the Swedish Film Institute, resigned. Her decision was in part influenced by the substantial government cuts imposed on the Film Institute. Seven million Swedish kronor were stripped from the budget, a blow primarily to SFI's cultural activities, i.e. the Cinémathèque, film archives, film restoration programme and film magazine *Chaplin*. Edström failed to impress politicians with reassurances of the importance of these activities, and newly installed managing director, ex-politician and newspaper man Lars Engqvist, sees it

as his most urgent mission to retrieve the money and set the record straight with politicians. "My job is to bring Swedish film into the centre of the cultural debate. It has dwelled too long on the periphery," he said in an interview shortly before his appointment in September, and added: "Let's show some fighting spirit and let's teach the politicians something about the significance Swedish films have for Swedish culture!"

Many of us Swedes prayed that he would be successful in his venture.

JANNIKE ÅHLUND is Editor of Sweden's leading film magazine, *Chaplin*. This year she received a special diploma at the Gold Bugs gala.

Recent and Forthcoming Films

DOCKPOJKEN (Boy Doll)

Script and Dir: Hilda Hellwig. Phot: Bertil Wiktorsson. Players: Sven Wollter, Lena Granhagen, Hampus Petterson. Prod: Swedish Film Institute/Sveriges SVT1.

DRÖMKÅKEN (The Dream House)

Script: Peter Dalle, Bengt Palmers. Dir: Dalle. Phot: Esa Vuorinen. Players: Björn Skifs, Suzanne Reuter, Zara Zetterqvist, Mikael Haack. Prod: Cinema Art Promotions/Svensk Filmindustri/Piscon.

DRÖMMEN OM RITA (Dreaming of Rita)

Script: Rita Holst, Jon Lindström. Dir: Lindström. Phot: Kjell Lagerros. Players: Per Oscarsson, Marika Lagercrantz, Philip Zandén, Yaba Holst. Prod: FilmLance Intl./Swedish Film Institute/Sveriges TV2, Film Teknik/Svensk Filmindustri/Finnish Film Foundation/Nordic Film & TV-Fund.

PARISERHJULET (The Ferris Wheel)

Script and Dir: Clas Lindberg. Phot: Andra Lasmanis. Players: Helena Bergström, Claes Malmberg, Jakob Bergström. Prod: Cinetofon, Joson, Lindberg & Landoff Film/Sandrews/Sveriges TV2.

BRANDBILEN SOM FÖRSVANN (The Fire Engine That Disappeared)

Script: Rainer Berg, Beate Langmaack. Dir: Hajo Gies. Phot: Achim Poulheim. Players: Gösta Ekman, Kjell Bergqvist, Rolf Lassgård. Prod: Victoria Film/Sveriges SVT1 Drama/Rialto Film Berlin/Nordic Film & TV-Fund/Svensk Filmindustri.

HÄRIFRÅN TILL KIM (From Here to Kim)

Script: Sten Holmberg. Dir: Lars Egler. Phot: Sten Holmberg. Players: Jonas Karlsson, Aida Jercović, Kristian Almgren. Prod: Kraakbacken Film & Television/Nordic Film & TV-Fund/FilmTeknik.

SISTA DANSEN (The Last Dance)

Script and Dir: Colin Nutley. Phot: Jens Fischer, Jan Pehrson. Players: Helena Bergström, Reine Brynolfsson, Ewa Fröling, Peter Andersson. Prod: Sandrews/Sveriges TV2/Metronome-Denmark.

LOTTA FLYTTAR HEMIFRÅN (Lotta Leaves Home)

Script and Dir: Johanna Hald. Phot: Olof Johnson. Players: Grete Havnessköld, Linn Gloppestad, Martin Andersson. Prod: Svensk Filmindustri.

KÄRLEKENS HIMMELSKA HELVETE (Magic Stronger Than Life)

Script: Staffan Göthe. Dir: Agneta Fagerström-Olsson. Phot: John O. Olsson. Players: Agneta Ahlin, Krister Henriksson, Marita Nordberg, Rea Mauranen. Prod: Giraff Film for Sveriges TV2/Swedish Film Institut/Film pool Nord/OY Filmfotograferna/Nordic Film & TV-Fund.

MANNEN PÅ BALKONGEN (The Man on the Balcony)

Script: Jonas Cornell, Daniel Alfredson. Dir: Alfredson. Phot: Peter Mokrosinski. Players: Gösta Ekman, Kjell Bergqvist, Rolf Lassgård, Niklas Hjulström. Prod: Victorifilm/Sveriges SVT1 Drama/Svensk Filmindustri/ Nordic Film & TV-Fund.

DEN ANDRA STRANDEN (The Other Shore)

Scrip: Mikael Wiström, Lars Palmgren. Dir: Wiström. Phot: Peter Östlund. Prod: Månharen/ Film Film/Sveriges SVT1.

SÖKARNA (The Searchers)

Script: Daniel Fridell-Holmsten. Dir: Fridell-Holmsten, Peter Cartriers. Phot: Yngvar Lande. Players: Liam Norberg, Ray Jones, Malou Bergman, Thorsten Flinck. Prod: Sökarna/Svensk Filmindustri.

GLÄDJEKÄLLAN (Spring of Joy)

Script and Dir: Richard Hobert. Phot: Lars Crépin. Players: Sven Lindberg, Göran Stangertz, Camilla Lundén. Prod: Sveriges TV2 Malmö.

SUNES SOMMAR (Sune's Summer)

Script: Stephan Apelgren, Anders Jacobsson, Sören Olsson. Dir: Stephan Apelgren. Phot: Andra Lasmanis. Players: Peter Haber, Carina Lidbom, Andreas Hoffer. Prod: Svensk Filmindustri/Sveriges SVT1 Drama.

TRYGGARE KAN INGEN VARA (Winter in Paradise)

Script and Dir: Thomas Samuelson. Phot: Mats Olofsson. Players: Jacqueline Ramel, Fredrik Dolk, Mats Huddén. Prod: Omega Film & Television, Douglas film/Filmteknik.

DANSAREN (The Dancer)

Script and Dir: Donya Feuer. Phot: Gunnar Källström. Players: Katja Björner, Anneli Alhanko, Erland Josephson. Prod: Swedish Film Institute/Sveriges TV2.

LUST (Desire)

Script and Dir: Janne Wallin. Phot: Lennart Peters. Players: Cia Berg, Gerhard Hobertstorfer, Kjell Bergqvist. Prod: Facta Fiction/ Sandrews/Swedish Film Institute.

FRIHETSLIGAN (The Freedom Gang)

Script: Layla Assaf-Tengroth, Bo Bjelfvenstam. Dir: Assaf-Tengroth. Phot: Roland Lundin. Players: Rim Al Hamad, Elie Laii, Walid Takriti. Prod: Cadmos Film/Sveriges SVT1 Drama/ Swedish Film Institute.

HÄNDERNA (The Hands)

Script and Dir: Richard Hobert. Phot: Lars Crépin. Players: Boman Oscarsson, Sven-Bertil Taube, Camilla Lundén. Prod: Sveriges TV2 Malmö.

ILLUSIONER (Illusions)

Script and Dir: Lars Mullback. Phot: Jan Weincke. Players: Anders Ekborg, Reine Brynolfsson, Jonna Järnefeldt. Prod: Omega Film/Svensk Film-industri/Swedish Film Institute.

HIMMEL ÖVER MALMÖ (A Malmoe Suite)

Script and Dir: Torgny Schunnesson, Jean Hermanson. Phot: Hermanson. Prod: Swedish Film Institute/Kulturbryggarna/ Sveriges TV2.

PILLER TRILLAREN (Piller Trillaren)

Script and Dir: Björn Gunnarsson. Phot: Olof Johnson. Players: Jacob Eklund, Kayo, Kent Andersson. Prod: Svensk Filmindustri.

SIXTEN (Sixten)

Script: Ulf Stark. Dir: Catti Edfeldt. Phot: Rolf Lindström. Players: Peter Viitanen, Hans Henriksson, Jonas Magnusson. Prod: Svensk Filmindustri/Swedish Film Institute.

STOCKHOLM MARATON (Stockholm Marathon)

Script: Rainer Berg, Beate Langmaack. Dir: Peter Keglević. Phot: Wolfgang Dickmann. Players: Gösta Ekman, Kjell Bergqvist, Rolf Lassgård. Prod: Victoriafilm / Sveriges SVT1 Drama/Rialto Film/Svensk Film-industri.

SOMMARMORD (Summer Murder)

Script and Dir: Lars Molin. Phot: Jan-Hugo Norman. Players: Peter Haber, Lena T. Hansson, Ulrika Hansson, Thomas Pontén. Prod: Sveriges SVT1 Drama/ Swedish Film Institute.

ZORN (Zorn)

Script and Dir: Gunnar Hellström. Phot: Jörgen Persson. Players: Hellström, Liv Ullmann, Stig Grybe, Jarl Kulle. Prod: Sveriges SVT1 Drama/Nordic Film & TV-Fund.

Distributors

Atlantic Film
Box 920
S-120 07 Stockholm
Tel: +46-8 642 53 86
Fax: +46-8 702 98 45

Capitol Film Distribution
Södra vägen 12
S-392 33 Kalmar
Tel: +46-480 122 15
Fax: +46-480 240 85

Columbia Tri-Star Films
Box 9501
S-102 74 Stockholm
Tel: +46-8 658 11 40
Fax: +46-8 84 12 04

Egmont Film
Box 507
183 25 Täby
Tel: +46-762 100 50
Fax: +46-762 120 46

Film AB Corona
Brantingsgatan 35
S-115 35 Stockholm
Tel: +46-8 661 05 09
Fax: +46-8 702 98 45

Filmkompaniet Distribution
Box 16
131 06 Nacka
Tel: +46-8 718 33 20
Fax: +46-8 718 08 97

Filmo
Skulptörvägen 25
S-121 43 Stockholm
Tel: +46-8 722 95 10
Fax: +46-8 722 99 66

Folkets Bio
Box 2068
S-103 12 Stockholm
Tel: +46-8 20 30 59
Fax: +46-8 20 40 23

Fox Film
117 88 Stockholm
Tel: +46-8 658 75 00
Fax: +46-8 668 50 70

Plånborg Film
Granhällsvägen 23
S-182 75 Stocksund
Tel: +46-8 85 71 92
Fax: +46-8 665 03 40

Polfilm
Östra Rönneholmsvägen 4
S-211 47 Malmö
Tel: +46-40 12 40 44

Rifilm
Sturegatan 18
S-114 36 Stockholm
Tel: +46-8 666 00 83

Rosenbergs Filmbyrå
Linnégatan 82 nb
S-115 23 Stockholm
Tel: +46-8 660 53 44

Fax: +46-8 660 90 22

Sandrew Film & Teater
Box 5612
S-114 86 Stockholm
Tel: +46-8 23 47 00
Fax: +46-8 10 38 50

Sonet Film
Box 20105
S-161 02 Bromma
Tel: +46-8 764 77 00
Fax: +46-8 29 90 91, +46-8 28 58 34

Succéfilm
Klippvägen 3
S-181 31 Lidingö
Tel: +46-8 765 26 10
Fax: +46-8 767 61 40

Svensk Filmindustri
S-117 88 Stockholm
Tel: +46-8 658 75 00
Fax: +46-8 658 37 04

Swedish Film
Luntmakargatan 52
S-113 58 Stockholm
Tel: +46-8 16 05 25
Fax: +46-8 34 59 00

Swedish Film Institute
Box 27126
S-102 52 Stockholm
Tel: +46-8 665 11 00
Fax: +46-8 661 18 20

Triangelfilm
Box 17156
S-200 10 Malmö
Tel: +46-40 12 55 47
Fax: +46-40 12 90 99

United International Pictures
Box 9502
S-102 74 Stockholm
Tel: +46-8 658 10 40
Fax: +46-8 84 38 70

Walt Disney Production
Sweden
Box 9503
S-102 74 Stockholm
Tel: +46-8 658 10 50
Fax: +46-8 658 64 82

Warner Bros Sweden
Box 9503
S-102 74 Stockholm
Tel: +46-8 658 10 50
Fax: +46-8 658 64 82

Örnfilm
Östgötagatan 67
S-116 64 Stockholm
Tel: +46-8 714 48 90
Fax: +46-8 97 23 38

Useful Addresses

Swedish Film and Video Organization
Box 49084
S-100 28 Stockholm
Tel: +46-8 785 04 00
Fax: +46-8 653 24 25

The Swedish Institute
Cultural Film Events
Box 7434
S-103 91 Stockholm
Tel: +46-8 789 20 00
Fax: +46-8 20 72 48

The Swedish Film Distributors' Association
Box 49084
100 28 Stockholm
Tel: +46-8 785 04 00
Fax: +46-8 653 24 25

Swedish Exhibitors' Association
Box 49084
100 28 Stockholm
Tel: +46-8 785 04 00
Fax: +46-8 653 24 25

SWITZERLAND

Christoph
Egger

Swiss films are becoming more and more international. Or should we say "global"? For his feature-length documentary **The Congress of the Penguins** (*Der Kongress der Pinguine*) Zurich-based documentarist Hans-Ulrich Schlumpf has travelled far. All the way, in fact, to Antarctica, definitely the southernmost destination of all his films which have always been southward bound. The result is an impressive, beautifully filmed piece of work, its material gathered on four trips. Essentially documentary, the film nevertheless transcends the limitations of its genre. Inventing the character of a dreamer telling his dream, Schlumpf and his co-writer, the author Franz Hohler, have no difficulties in having him understand the language of the penguins and thus transmitting their message which is an urgent lamentation on the state of Planet Earth. With more than 70,000 spectators in the German-speaking part of Switzerland alone, *The Congress of the Penguins* represents the most successful documentary in the history of Swiss cinema, a film easily accessible abroad.

As to the rest of Swiss film production, however, there aren't many success stories to be reported. One exception is the amusing *début* by Denis Rabaglia, **Grossesse nerveuse**, a satire on parenthood desired and refused which won this year's Max Ophüls Prize at Saarbrücken and was also shown at the festivals of Los Angeles and Karlovy Vary. A début of a kind is also **Ludwig 1881** by Fosco and Donatello Dubini, the first full-length feature film of the two brothers who in the past years were working on portraits of prominent scientists and their links to politics. In strikingly beautiful tableaux their portrayal of Bavaria's Ludwig II – a convincing performance by Helmut Berger, Visconti's Ludwig twenty years ago – tells the story of a trip to Lake Lucerne which the unhappy king made in 1881 together with his favourite actor Josef Kainz in order to re-enact Schiller's *Wilhelm Tell* in its "original" setting.

As to the public it still doesn't seem to be too enthusiastic about Swiss films. Of the 15.9 million moviegoers in 1993 only a tiny fraction chose Swiss films. As usual the Top Fifteen included almost only American films. The two exceptions were *The Piano* and *Les visiteurs*, the 300,000 spectators of the latter almost exclusively due to its success in the French-speaking part of Switzerland.

SWISS FILMS

The Swiss Film Center
is a non-profit making organization which supports all aspects of professional independent film-making by means of specific promotions and by providing information in Switzerland and abroad.

Swiss Film Center / Schweizerisches Filmzentrum
Münstergasse 18, P.O. Box, CH-8025 Zürich
Tel: +41 1 261 28 60, Fax: +41 1 262 11 32

Thibault de Montalembert and Florence Darel in GREEN HENRY

Different Kinds of Love Stories

A big disappointment was **Green Henry**, Thomas Koerfer's ambitious 8.8 million franc adaptation of Gottfried Keller's novel *Der grüne Heinrich*. The director succeeded neither in catching the spirit of the novel, a landmark in Nineteenth-Century German literature, nor in his attempt to adapt the text to present-day manners. What resulted is a crude succession of sex scenes deprived of all vitality. It had to be Alain Tanner, the Grand Old Man of "Young Swiss Cinema", to show how to deal with sex on screen. Together with Myriam Mézières, already his collaborator and main actress in *Une flamme dans mon cœur*, he made **Le journal de Lady M.**, the intense and deep-probing study of the ecstasies and desperations of love.

Love as a comedy of errors, attainable only by a series of complicated detours, has been the subject of Jean-François Amiguet's films. But unlike its predecessor *La Méridienne*, a subtle and elegant drama, his third feature film **L'érivain public**

Patrick Braoude in Denis Rabaglia's GROSSESSE NERVEUSE

mainly attempts to be charming and witty. If it succeeds in this task at all then only in the dialogue but not in the images which appear flat without any atmosphere. The story of an impossible love gives way to a grim look at society in Silvio Soldini's **Un'anima divisa in due**. A detective in a Milanese department store who falls in love with a shop-lifting gypsy woman eventually comes to realise that there are boundaries between "ordinary" citizens and outcasts that are insurmountable even with the best of intentions.

New Approaches in the Documentary Field

As (almost) always there is good news from the documentaries' side. Born in 1955 in Baghdad, raised in a Zurich suburb, Samir has created a reflection of his biography in **Babylon 2**. Retracing the author's personal history as well as addressing the situation of young people in Switzerland whose parents have immigrated from Mediterranean or third world countries, the film tackles questions of immigration as

Helmut Berger in LUDWIG 1881
photo: Felix von Muralt

Still from DER KONGRESS DER PINGUINE

well as of urbanisation. Genuinely inventive as usual, Samir operates with a variety of electronic means that, however, are not there for their own sake but manage to catch the spirit of these young people very well. Thomas Imbach's third film is also quite an achievement. In a similar way but obviously inspired less by video than by underground or avant-garde film techniques, **Well Done** through its imagery offers an analysis of a high-tech company that works in a classical Swiss domain: money. It does so not in the traditional way, i.e. by meticulously collecting and combining facts and situations, but by assembling them in an almost associative montage.

Less avant-garde than his earlier works, **Picture of Light** by Peter Mettler transcends the limitations of the documentary genre by its sheer subject. The northern lights, the *aurora borealis* that eventually appears in all its magic, casts a spell of enchantment over the whole trip to the north and its odd inhabitants that the author who lives in Canada undertakes in search for it. A particular blend between *Volkskunde*, folk-lore in the true sense of the word, and an almost mythical reality is **Ur-Musig** (i.e. very ancient music), Cyrill Schläpfer's first film. Probably too long yet beautifully photographed, it fulfils an important task in collecting a great variety of all musical styles still to be found in some Swiss alps. **L'homme des casernes** by Jacqueline Veuve depicts a quite different but equally important part of traditional Switzerland. The grand old lady of Swiss documentary follows the tracks of an essentially male duty, namely military service. There are no interviews with the young man doing their 17 weeks of basic training; no commentaries to blur the exact registration of a system that reveals the shifting boundaries between a civil, almost familiar tone with an army that has never had to face the threat of war and disorder.

TOP TEN GROSSING FILMS IN SWITZERLAND: 1993

	Attendance
Sister Act	785,873
Jurassic Park	755,914
Aladdin	601,407
The Fugitive	428,861
The Jungle Book	404,116
The Bodyguard	370,653
Sommersby	344,287
Sliver	342,583
Made in America	321,855
Hot Shots: Part Deux	320,815

Recent and Forthcoming Films

Anna annA

Script: Greti Kläy, Jürgen Brauer, Lukas Hartmann. Dir: Greti Kläy, Jürgen Brauer. Phot: Jürgen Brauer. Players: Lea and Wanda Hürlimann, Ilona Schulze, Steve Karier. Prod: Fama Film/Rhewes Film/Samsa Film/DEFA.

BABYLON 2

Script and Dir: Samir. Phot: Samir, Pierre Mennel. Players: Michel Hüttner. Prod: Samir. *Documentary.*

L'ÉCRIVAIN PUBLIC

Script: Anne Gonthier. Dir: Jean-François Amiguet. Phot: Hugues Ryffel, Robert Alazraki. Players: Anna Galiena, Robin Renucci. Prod: Erato Films/Zagora Films/Narcissus Film.

ERNESTO "CHE" GUEVARA – THE BOLIVIAN DIARY

Script and Dir: Richard Dindo. Phot: Pio Corradi. Prod: Ciné Manufacture. *Documentary.*

GROSSESSE NERVEUSE

Script and Dir: Denis Rabaglia. Phot: Pierluigi Zaretti. Players: Tom Novembre, Sabine Haudepin, Isabelle Townsend, Catherine Samie. Prod: Bloody Mary Productions/Les Productions Crittin & Thiébaud.

DER GRÜNE HEINRICH (Green Henry)

Script: Thomas Koerfer, Peter Müller, Barbara Jago. Dir: Thomas Koerfer. Phot: Gérard Vandenberg. Players: Thibault de Montalembert, Assumpta Serna, Florence Darel, Dominique Sanda, Mathias Gnädinger. Prod: Condor Productions/Toro Film/Osby Films.

HÉLAS POUR MOI

Script and Dir: Jean-Luc Godard. Phot: Caroline Champetier. Players: Gérard Depardieu, Laurence Masliah. Prod: Vega Film/Les Films Alain Sarde.

L'HOMME DES CASERNES

Script and Dir: Jacqueline Veuve. Phot: Hugues Ryffel. Prod: J.M.H. Productions/Aquarius Film. *Documentary.*

JAZZ (working title)

Script: Walter Bretscher, Christine Madsen-Julen. Dir: Daniel Helfer. Phot: Michi Riebl. Players: Pasquale Aleardi, Kaspar Weiss, Marie-Louise Hauser, Karl Spoerri, Imanuel Humm. Prod: Catpics/Dor Film/Calypso.

JOE & MARIE

Script: Tania Stöcklin, Cyrille Rey-Coquais. Dir: Tania Stöcklin. Phot: Ciro Cappellari. Players: Estelle Vincent, Gay Etgar, Mathias Gnädinger, Viktor Lazlo. Prod: Artimage/Interimages/Galla Film.

DER KONGRESS DER PINGUINE (The Congress of the Penguins)

Script and Dir: Hans-Ulrich Schlumpf. Phot: Pio Corradi, Patrick Lindenmaier, Luc Jacquet. Prod: Ariane Film. *Documentary feature.*

LE LIVRE DE CRISTAL (The Book of Crystal)

Script: Patricia Plattner, Seth Linder, Didier Haudepin. Dir: Patricia Plattner. Phot: Matthias Kaelin, Milivoy Ivoković. Players: Jean-François Balmer, Valeria Bruni Tedeschi. Prod: Light Night Production/Gemini Films/Madragoa Filmes.

LOU N'A PAS DIT NON

Script and Dir: Anne Marie Miéville. Phot: Jean-Paul Rosa de Costa. Players: Marie Bunel, Manuel Blanc, Métilde Weyergans, Caroline Micla. Prod: Vega Film/Sara Films/Peripheria.

LUDWIG 1881

Script and Dir: Fosco and Donatello Dubini. Phot: Matthias Kälin. Players: Helmut Berger, Max Tidof. Prod: Filmproduktion F. + D. Dubini.

PICTURE OF LIGHT

Script, Dir and Phot: Peter Mettler. Prod: Grimethorpe Film. *Documentary.*

UN'ANIMA DIVISA IN DUE

Script: Silvio Soldini, Roberto Tiraboschi. Dir: Silvio Soldini. Phot: Luca Bigazzi. Players: Fabrizio Bentivoglio, Maria Bako. Prod: Pic Film/Aran/JSSK.

UR-MUSIG (Primal Music)

Script and Dir: Cyrill Schläpfer. Phot: Thomas Kremke, Pio Corradi, Jürg Hassler, Cyrill Schläpfer, Otmar Schmid. Prod: CSR Film/Records. *Documentary.*

VATER LIEBER VATER

Script: Leopold Huber, Hansjörg Schneider, Milan Dor. Dir: Leopold Huber. Phot: Christian Reitz. Players: Dagny Giulami, Laszlo I. Kish, Astrid Keller, Michel Adatte, Hilde Ziegler, Jürgen Cziesla, Christian Kohlund. Prod: Carac Film.

WACHTMEISTER ZUMBÜHL (Constable Zumbühl)

Script and Dir: Urs Odermatt. Phot: Rainer Klausmann. Players: Michael Gwisdek, Anica Dobra, Jürgen Vogel, Rolf Hoppe,

Norbert Schwientek. Prod: Triluna/Nordwest Film/Sera Filmproduktion.

WELL DONE

Script: Thomas Imbach, Monika Gsell. Dir: Thomas Imbach. Phot: Jürg Hassler. Prod: Bachim Film/Filmkollektiv Zürich. *Documentary.*

Producers

Alhena Film
13, rue de Vollandes
CH-1207 Geneva
Tel: +41 22 700 06 90
Fax: +41 22 735 35 34

Artimage
19, rue de la Coulouvrenière,
P.O. Box
CH-1211 Geneva 11
Tel: +41 22 781 57 87
Fax: +41 22 321 16 09

Balzli & Cie Filmproduktion
Hauptstrasse 33
CH-2560 Nidau
Tel: +41 32 51 75 10
Fax: +41 32 51 28 10

CAB Productions SA
17, rue du Port-Franc
CH-1003 Lausanne
Tel: +41 21 312 80 56
Fax: +41 21 312 80 64

Cactus Film AG
Neugasse 6, P.O. Box
CH-8021 Zürich
Tel: +41 1 272 87 11
Fax: +41 1 271 26 16

Carac Film AG
Zinggstrasse 16
CH-3007 Berne
Tel: +41 31 372 00 40
Fax: +41 31 372 04 81

Catpics Coproductions AG
Steinstrasse 21
CH-8003 Zürich
Tel: +41 1 451 23 58
Fax: +41 1 462 01 12

Ciné Manufacture
8, Côtes-de-Montbenon
CH-1003 Lausanne
Tel: +41 21 311 58 58
Fax: +41 21 312 93 43

Condor Films AG
Restelbergstrasse 107
CH-8044 Zürich
Tel: +41 1 361 96 12
Fax: +41 1 361 95 75

Fama Film AG
(production and distribution)
Balthasarstrasse 11
CH-3027 Bern
Tel: +41 31 992 92 80
Fax: +41 31 992 64 04

J.M.H. Productions SA
70, av. de Beumont
CH-1010 Lausanne
Tel: +41 21 653 65 50
Fax: +41 21 653 65 53

Bernard Lang AG
(production and distribution)
Kirchgasse 26
CH-8001 Zürich
Tel: +41 1 252 64 44
Fax: +41 1 252 77 29

Les Productions Crittin & Thiébaud SA/Cinergie SA
12, rue Grenus
CH-1201 Geneva
Tel: +41 22 731 69 64
Fax: +41 22 738 27 25

S.F.P.C. SA
9, rue de la Fontaine
CH-1204 Geneva
Tel: +41 22 311 51 80
Fax: +41 22 311 32 23

T & C Film AG
Seestrasse 41A
CH-8002 Zürich
Tel: +41 1 202 36 22
Fax: +41 1 202 30 05

Thelma Film AG
Josefstrasse 106
CH-8031 Zürich
Tel: +41 1 271 81 24
Fax: +41 1 271 33 50

TriLuna Film AG
Neugasse 6, P.O. Box 299
CH-8021 Zürich
Tel: +41 1 273 00 53
Fax: +41 1 271 26 16

Vega Film AG
Sophienstrasse 2, P.O. Box
CH-8030 Zürich
Tel: +41 1 252 60 00
Fax: +41 1 252 66 35

Distributors

Alpha Films SA
4, place du Cirque
CH-1211 Geneva 11
Tel: +41 22 328 02 12
Fax: +41 22 781 06 76

Buena Vista Int. Ltd
Am Schanzengraben 27
CH-8002 Zürich
Tel: +41 1 201 66 55
Fax: +41 1 201 77 70

Columbus Film AG
Steinstrasse 21
CH-8036 Zürich
Tel: +41 1 462 73 66
Fax: +41 1 462 01 12

Elite Film AG
Molkenstrasse 21
CH-8026 Zürich
Tel: +41 1 242 88 22
Fax: +41 1 241 21 23

Filmcooperative
Fabrikstrasse 21, P.O. Box 172
CH-8031 Zürich
Tel: +41 1 271 88 00
Fax: +41 1 271 80 38

Focus Film AG
Seestrasse 73
CH-8008 Zürich
Tel & Fax: +41 1 383 50 73

Look now!
P.O. Box 3172
CH-8031 Zürich
Tel: +41 1 272 03 60
Fax: +41 1 272 39 36

Monopole Pathé Films
Neugasse 6, P.O. Box 299
CH-8031 Zürich
Tel: +41 1 271 10 03
Fax: +41 1 271 56 43

Praesens Film AG
Münchhaldenstrasse 10, P.O. Box
CH-8034 Zürich
Tel: +41 1 422 38 32
Fax: +41 1 422 37 93

Rialto Film AG
Heinrichstrasse 269, P.O. Box 102
CH-8037 Zürich
Tel: +41 1 271 42 00
Fax: +41 1 271 42 03

Sadfi SA
8, rue de Hesse, P.O. Box
CH-1211 Geneva 11
Tel: +41 22 311 77 67
Fax: +41 22 781 31 19

Stamm Film AG
Löwenstrasse 20, P.O. Box
CH-8023 Zürich
Tel: +41 1 211 66 15
Fax: +41 1 212 03 69

Trigon-Film, Filmverleih Dritte Welt
Rösmattstrasse 6
CH-4118 Rodersdorf
Tel: +41 61 731 15 15
Fax: +41 61 731 32 88

Twentieth-Century Fox
P.O. Box 1049
CH-1211 Geneva 26
Tel: +41 22 343 33 15
Fax: +41 22 343 92 55

CHRISTOPH EGGER is responsible for cinema in the media section of the *Neue Zürcher Zeitung* for which he has been writing since 1978. He is also a member of the Swiss Jury for quality awards and has taught film criticism at the University of Zürich.

UIP (Schweiz) GmbH
Signaustrasse 6, P.O. Box 295
CH-8032 Zürich
Tel: +41 1 383 85 50
Fax: +41 1 383 61 12

Warner Bros. Inc.
Studerweg 3, P.O. Box
CH-8802 Kilchberg
Tel: +41 1 715 50 11
Fax: +41 1 715 34 51

Useful Addresses

Swiss Film Centre
Münstergasse 18, P.O. Box
CH-8025 Zürich
Tel: +41 1 261 28 60
Fax: +41 1 262 11 32
Lausanne Office (for French-speaking countries)
33, rue St-Laurent
CH-1003 Lausanne
Tel: +41 21 311 03 23
Fax: +41 21 311 03 25

Federal Office of Culture (Film Department)
Hallwylstrasse 15
CH-3003 Berne
Tel: +41 31 322 92 71
Fax: +41 31 322 92 73

Pro Helvetia
Arts Council of Switzerland
Film Department
Hirschengraben 22
CH-8024 Zürich
Tel: +41 1 251 96 00
Fax: +41 1 251 96 06

Swiss Producers' Association for Feature and Documentary Film
Zinggstrasse 16
CH-3007 Berne
Tel: +41 31 372 40 01
Fax: +41 31 372 40 53

Procinema
Swiss Association of Exhibitors and Motion Picture Distributors
Effingerstrasse 11, P.O. Box 8175
CH-3001 Berne
Tel: +41 31 381 50 77
Fax: +41 31 382 03 73

Swiss Association of Industrial Film and Audiovision
Weinbergstrasse 31
CH-8006 Zürich
Tel: +41 1 262 27 71
Fax: +41 1 262 29 96

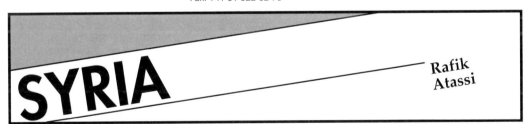

SYRIA — Rafik Atassi

Film production in Syria continued its slow crawl via the National Film Organisation while it came to a complete standstill in the private sector. Two more films were shot through the NFO. Both were postponed from the previous year's plan. **Oh Sea** by Moh'd Shaheen, based on the famous novel by Syrian writer Hanna Mineh called "El-Dakl", and **Year of Birds**, with script and direction by newcomer Riad

Shaya. Both of them talk about recent past history in the late 1940's and discuss the socio-political struggle among various classes of people. The first one, *Oh Sea*, takes place on the Syrian coast and shows the difficulties of life that poor fishermen faced some fifty years ago, while the other, *Year of Birds*, has its focus in the south in the area inhabited by the Druz minority of whom the director himself is a member.

Saad Bakdounes in YEAR OF BIRDS

Censorship still prevents the screening of Ossama Mohammad's *Stars of Midday*, produced five years ago and Moh's Mala's *The Night*, which was analysed in last year's IFG. Nevertheless, this latter film was shown in many festivals around the world. This means that no official statement has been issued concerning its screening, which is the same situation as its predecessor, and that certain sensitivities govern the timing of its public release, if ever!

Film audiences in Syria declined consistently in the past year because film theatres were shut for fifteen days all over the country mourning the sudden death of the President's eldest son on January 21, 1994, which affected the entertainment business as a whole, and still does. Thus many important films went unnoticed. The greatest flop was *Unforgiven*, the Oscar-winning film which lasted two weeks only in the capital, Damascus.

Damascus Film Festival

This regional festival was inaugurated in 1979 and takes place once each two years. Its motto "For a Progressive and Liberated Cinema" seems a childish ideology now. But at that time, the late 1970's, it attracted many young and enthusiastic film-makers who thought they would find a new window open for their creativity. But year after year the Festival became more and more traditional, showing government choices instead of encouraging courageous experiments in various film fields as was originally planned.

RAFIK ATASSI is a Syrian film critic. He has written many books on Arabic cinema and has served as a jury member at many international film festivals. He contributes to various Arabic and world journals. He has written several scripts for cinema and TV and has a weekly programme on cinema on Syrian TV.

Still from EXTRAS, directed by Nabil Maleh

TOP TEN GROSSING FILMS IN SYRIA: 1993

Sayyad the Workman (Egypt)

The Forgotten (Egypt)

Voice of Love (India)

No Way To Run

In the Line of Fire

Demolition Man

Double Impact

The Fugitive

Something Burning

Sky Commandos

Recent and Forthcoming Films

EXTRAS

Script and Dir: Nabil Maleh. Phot: Hanna Ward. Players: Samar Sami, Bassam Kousu.

Two young lovers meet in an apartment but they are unable to communicate because of strong social and political conflicts.

ECHOES OF SIDES

Script and Dir: Maher Keddo. Phot: George Khouri. Players: Mai Skaff, Ali Karim, Moh'd Hariri.

A group of bandits attack a village, kill the parents of a girl and rape her. She seeks vengeance, crossing different parts of Syria and meeting various kinds of people.

OH SEA

Script and Dir: Moh'd Shaheen. Phot: George Khouri. Players: Mono Wassef, Jamal Shamout, Adnan Barakat.

Poor fishermen in the western coast of Syria on the Mediterranean work in severe conditions to improve their lives.

YEAR OF BIRDS

Script and Dir: Riad Shaya. Phot: Abda Hamza. Players: Saad Bakdounes, Lina Bate, Fouad Rashed, Sana Depsi.

Based on a story by Mamdouh Azzam, this film concentrates on love in a conservative society, that forbidden fruit which everyone wants.

Producers

National Film Organisation
Rawda
Damascus
Tel: 3334200

Nadez Alassi
Fardous str
Damascus
Tel: 2216009

Tahseen Kawadri
Tigheez str
Damascus
Tel: 2230767

Abdulrazaq Ghanem
Tigheez str
Damascus
Tel: 3336279

Igraa Films
Khateeb str
Damascus
Tel: 441446

Raja Groub
PO Box 11905
Salheia
Damascus
Tel: 33245

Distributors

Tiba and Abboud
Fardous str
Damascus
Tel: 2221096

Mamoun Serri
Fardous str
Damascus
Tel: 2211888

Khaldoun Maleh
Mezza
Damascus
Tel: 6662812

Useful Addresses

Cham Cinema
Maysaloum str
Damascus
Tel: 223230

Boraq
Mazraa
Damascus
Tel: 449306

Haysam Hatahet
Salheia
Damascus
Tel: 2222212

Saad
Bagdad str
Damascus
Tel: 427153

Daoud Sheikjani
Rawda
Damascus
Tel: 333491

Abdul Masih Atia
Tijara
Damascus
Tel: 457532

Syndicate of Artists
Bagdad str
Damascus
Tel: 45809

Syrian TV
Omayad Square
Damascus
Tel: 720700

TADJIKISTAN — Rashmi Doraiswamy

In the last two years, due to the political turmoil, many film-makers from the Republic have emigrated. Davlat Khudonazarov, actively involved in the movement for democracy in Tadjikistan, and former Secretary of the Cinematographers' Union of U.S.S.R., it is said, now lives in the U.S. because it is dangerous for him to live in Moscow. Bakhtiar Khudoinazarov lives in Germany, Mariam Yusupova in Moscow, Margarita Kassy-mova in the Ukraine, Gulbakhor Mirzoeva in Paris. Those who have stayed on in Tadjikistan are finding it difficult to make films. Bako Sadykov, one of the few to have remained behind, has finished *The Island* (1993) and is currently working on a film entitled *Alambir Bukhari* which is being financed by independent organisations in several countries: Tadjikistan, Uzbekistan, Iran, the Islamic Centre in England, Saudi Arabia.

Despite the political situation, the Tadjik emigré film-makers have continued to make their presence felt. **The Well** (*Kolodets*, 1991) by Jamshed Usmanov is a small budget, black-and-white film. A young boy has to fetch water for his family from a well that is located at a distance. His tee-shirt has American idols on it and he wants his parents to sell their cows to buy him a foreign music-system. The alcoholic father who has been a violinist, now has only one dream – to strike water and to have a well. The mother, tired of the impasse, has an affair on the sly with a friend of the family. The space this quiet tragedy is inscribed in – the house the family lives in – is well conceived. Although stylistically uneven in places it is an impressive debut.

The documentary, too, has emerged as an important form of political comment with the Tadjik New Wave that was in the making before fighting in the Republic began. Mariam Yusupova's films are not directly interventionist. She has moved away from the centre in more senses than one, and has documented the life of "minorities" living in Tadjikistan. *Gilem* (1992) is about the women who weave beautiful carpets in a Turkish tribe that has lived in the Republic for centuries; *Remember Your Name* (1992) is about a mountain tribe in the Pamirs. Her latest film *Korean Man* (1993) concerns Koreans who have had to settle in Central Asia after being moved out by the order of Stalin from the Primorski Territory in 1937. In these and other films Yusopova captures the life of these people, their moments of work, their moments of joy and rest, the different languages they speak in, their rites and customs, dying art forms and the indifferent relationship of the State towards them not merely as an ethnographist, but also as an unobtrusive political statement about the contribution of the "others" to the cultural diversity in the Republic. She is currently working on a film entitled *Grecheskaya Vaza – Poslanie*, about myths on a Grecian vase. "The times we are living in lend themselves to be treated like myths," she says. Her film company "Rakurs" has also produced Gulbakhor Mirzoeva's interesting but little-known film *Sabbath* (1990) on the Jews living in Bukhara, the desire of some to emigrate to what they feel is a better life is Israel, and the will of the others to stay on, whatever the problems. In one memorable scene the people vote to the sounds of lashing carried over from the religious rite in the scene before.

Kosh ba Kosh by Bakhtiar Khudoinazarov (1993), one of the few features in recent times to be shot in Dushanbe, resolutely looks away from the war. Fighting is going on in the city (gunfire is heard only on the soundtrack) but life continues at its unhurried pace: card-players are completely involved in their gambling, a run-away girl and her boy friend – who saves her from the deal her gambler-father may be forced to make to pay off his debt – fight and make love in and out of the funicular; parents worry about them, and try to separate them ... it is life as usual. In his first film *Bratan*, the Tadjik countryside was captured sensitively; as the brothers travelled on the train the landscape opened up. In Bakhtiar Khudoinazarov's second film the landscape is seen from a funicular, but it lacks the rolling, unfolding quality of *Bratan*. Here the act of film-making is itself a gesture of defiance, and it draws its sustenance from the absent events that form its background rather than from the narrative itself: the story and script are slight.

In Tadjikistan not many directors are

Still from KOSH BA KOSH

taking up the recent political events as the subject of their films. The farce *All is Quiet in Baghdad* (1993) by Muhiuddin Muhammadiev is a rare exception. The documentary *Tadjik Café* (1993) on the turmoil in 1992-1993 and the plight of film-makers was made not by the Tadjiks themselves, but by Knut Ekström and Eric Stromdahl from Sweden for Amnesty.

Useful Addresses

Muhiuddin Muhammadiev
Chairman, Union of Young
Cinematographers of Tadjikistan
25 Behzod Str
Dushanbe 734013
Tadjikistan
Fax: 3772-210404

Mariam Yusupova
Director, Film Company "Rakurs"
10-25 Sverchcov Lane
Moscow 101000
Tel: 9259738

Bakhtiar Khudoinazarov
Eosanderstrasse 14
10587 Berlin
Germany

Tel: 030-3420651
Fax: 8854481

Bako Sadykov
Flat 10, Aine Str. 6
Dushanbe 734042
Tadjikistan
Tel: 3772-230791 (O)
3772-274515 (R)

TAIWAN — Derek Elley

Much the same as during the previous year, Taiwan has maintained its presence on the international stage with a small number of strong works, as well as providing the financial backing for a number of others carrying Hongkong or China labels. Locally, however, production is still in the doldrums, at 20-30 films a year, several of which owe their existence more to government subsidy (the *fudaojin* script fund) and video presales than to pure box-office income.

As well as Ch'iu Fu-sheng's Era International and Hsü Feng's Tomson Films, both of which have continued to invest in mainland-shot productions through their Hongkong affiliates, Wang Ying-hsiang's Long Sheng International has adopted a higher profile on the festival circuit with Huang Jianxin's *The Wooden Man's Bride* (see China section). As well as also funding co-productions with Hongkong, the well-established Taipei company has also co-produced Stan Lai's forthcoming *The Red Lotus Society* (aka: *Zen Jumping*). A portrait of modern Taipei through the story of a young man searching for a teacher to the legendary art of weightless "vaulting" (*qinggong*), the movie is theatre director Lai's second feature after his well-crafted, highly original *The Peach Blossom Land*.

Era's latest venture with mainland director Zhang Yimou, *To Live* (see China), premiered in competition at Cannes 1994 to a mixed reception, but the company remains committed to further projects with Zhang after his next film, *Shanghai Triad*, for France's UGC. Relations between Ch'iu and director Hou Hsaio-hsien (who together made *A City of Sadness* and *The Puppetmaster*) are reported to have cooled. There are also persistent rumours that Ch'iu intends to move away from production into the bigger arenas of theatrical distribution and satellite broadcasting in China, though the company has purchased a plot of land outside Peking with the stated intention of building a studio.

Tomson's Hsü Feng, after co-winning the Palme d'Or at Cannes 1993 and Golden Globe for *Farewell My Concubine*, failed to win the 1993 Best Foreign Film Oscar but is pursuing her relationship with director Chen Kaige on his next project, *Temptress Moon*, a melodrama in period Shanghai. Following China's new regulations on foreign-funded productions, Taiwan and Hongkong producers are more wary than ever of such investments.

Regulations Relaxed

Taiwan's own regulations on distribution of mainland-shot productions were relaxed in late '93 to allow the showing of *Concubine*, which finally opened on the island in early December, 1993. In addition, from October 1, 1994, the Government Information Office (GIO) is to end its import quota on Japanese films, following the total ban in 1972 (when Tokyo switched diplomatic recognition from Taiwan to China) and a partial relaxation in 1984. In practice, the market for Japanese films in Taiwan is small.

Following years of domination by Hongkong movies, Taiwan's theatrical market has been changed overnight by distributors' united boycott of Hongkong producers' prices (see Hongkong section). Almost overnight U.S. movies have filled the vacuum with not one Hongkong production making 1993's top ten (see table).

The sole Chinese-language movie to make the league table was Ang Lee's *The Wedding Banquet*, which failed to win the 1993 Foreign Film Oscar but whose success both at home and abroad has made Lee the first director since the emergence of New Taiwan Cinema over ten years ago to straddle the wall between commercial and critical acclaim.

Lee's latest film, the US$1.5 million **Eat Drink Man Woman** (*Yinshi nannu*), which opened the Directors' Fortnight at Cannes 1994, was his most accomplished yet, blending the humanity of his debut, *Pushing Hands*, with the technical and structural slickness of *Banquet* in a warm and funny tale of the less-then-tranquil home life of an ageing grand chef (Lee regular Sihung Lung) with his three grown daughters and an amorous widow next door. The film spins a tapesty of incidents and family relationships that builds into an engaging portrait of modern tensions in Chinese family life. Though Lee's films carefully play to western perceptions of the East, there's no denying his gift for dramatic construction and genial observation of humanity in all its colours.

Lee's easily digestible, politically safe films have made him the pin-up of the KMT-supported Central Motion Picture Corporation (CMPC), which has funded all his works to date. Spurred by Lee's successes, CMPC recently announced its intention to support a raft of films by newcomers, including Yin Ch'i's *In a*

Ni Shu-chün and Ch'en Hsiang-ch'i in Edward Yang's A CONFUCIAN CONFUSION

Strange City (*Zai moshengde chengshi*), Ch'en Yü-hsün's *Torrid Blood* (*Redai xue*), Yi Chih-yen's *Lonely Hearts Club* (*Jimo fangxin julebu*), and Liu Yi-ming's *Kangaroo Man* (*Daishu nanren*).

Yang Resurfaces

At the other end of the spectrum from Lee is Edward Yang, whose first film in three years, **A Confucian Confusion** (*Duli shidai*, literally *The Age of Independence*), competed at Cannes and showed he had lost none of his maverick qualities since *A Brighter Summer Day* (1991) and a detour into playwrighting (*Likely Consequence*, 1992; *Period of Growth*, 1993).

The independently financed movie, funded by local entrepreneur David Sun, is a rarefied look at a segment of modern Taiwanese society (and the East-West cultural battlefield) through the emotional ups-and-downs of a group of young Taipei professionals over a couple of days. The 133-minute, blackly comic film takes a while to come into focus as the web of relationships becomes clear; its underlying (anti-establishment) theme is that, to stand on its own legs, newly-affluent Asian societies like Taiwan need to rethink traditional moulds and break free of their limiting Confucian heritage.

Shot with Yang's customary precision, and illuminated by especially good playing from actresses Ni Shu-chün and Ch'en Hsiang-ch'i as former classmates, *A Confucian Confusion* is essentially a connoisseur item. But Yang remains Taiwan's most inventive, unpredictable and intellectually challenging film-maker, streets ahead of the competition.

The movie (since cut to 125 mins.) went out under the Warner Asia distribution banner, set up by the U.S. major for Mandarin-language markets like Taiwan, Singapore and (for the future) China.

Treasure Island (*Zhi yao wei ni huo yitian*), the second feature of former critic

TOP TEN GROSSING FILMS IN TAIPEI: 1993

	(NT$ million)
Jurassic Park	225.97
The Fugitive	91.47
Sliver	89.06
Cliffhanger	87.48
The Bodyguard	77.78
Sister Act	62.54
Indecent Proposal	52.63
Home Alone 2: Lost in New York	50.59
Honey, I Blew Up the Kid	48.92
The Wedding Banquet*	47.78

Apart from *The Wedding Banquet* (Taiwan), the highest grossing Chinese-language productions were all from Hongkong: *City Hunter* (NT$45.64m), *King of Beggars* (NT$41.88m, opened Xmas 1992), *Once Upon a Time in China III* (NT$39.27m, opened Xmas 1992), *The East is Red* (NT$33.63m), and *Fong Sai Yuk* (NT$31.67m).

Ch'en Kuo-fu, was a stylish, offbeat offering from Hou Hsiao-hsien and Chang Hua-k'un's City Films, a variation on the recent cycle of "urban youth alienation" movies (*Dust of Angels, Rebels of the Neon God*) lifted by a cleverly worked out script, careful direction, and some ironic pastiching of commercial genres. Like Yang's *Confusion*, it is essentially a connoisseur item but is in all ways more accomplished than Ch'en's debut, *High School Girls*.

Yü Wei-yen's **Moonlight Boy** (*Yueguang shaonian*) was a major disappointment after his impressive debut in 1989 with *Gang of Three Forever*. A frustratingly obscure reverie on local history and contemporary alienation, with the central character an ageless kid roaming the streets of Taipei, Yü's film is flatly directed and written, and pretentious at best.

Equally impenetrable is **Bodo** (*Baodao da meng*), the latest production from maverick independent Huang Ming-ch'uan, whose *The Man from Island West* (1990), set among the island's aboriginal population, heralded a quirky talent. *Bodo*, set in a remote military outpost, reprises many of the same themes, interweaved with Formosan ghost tales.

The biggest surprise of the past year was the re-emergence after a ten-year gap of veteran director/composer/singer Liu Chia-ch'ang (under the name Steven C.C. Liu) with the melodrama **May Jean** (*Mei Chen*), a kind of *Inn of the Sixth Happiness* tale of a brave Chinese woman leading a group of children to safety amid the Civil War chaos of 1947. Similar in tone to Liu's 1970's outings, including musical interludes, the handsomely-shot film's only point of interest is the lead performance from Chin Su-mei, better known as May Chin from *The Wedding Banquet*.

Still from EAT DRINK MAN WOMAN, directed by Ang Lee

Recent and Forthcoming Films

DOSAN (A Borrowed Life)

Script and Dir: Wu Nien-chen. Players: Ts'ai Chen-nan.

TAIBEI AIQING GUSHI

Dir: Chou T'an. Players: Carrie Ng, Wang Yü-wen.

GUODAO FENGBI (Motorola)

Dir: Ho P'ing. Players: Chang Shih, Ku Pao-ming. Prod: City Films.

FEIXIA ADA (The Red Lotus Society)

Dir: Stan Lai. Phot: Christopher Doyle. Players: Ying Chao-te, Li Tung-tsun, Joy Lo, Li Li-chün. Prod: Long Shong/Performance Workshop.

AIQING WANSUI (Vive l'Amour)

Dir: Ts'ai Ming-liang. Prod: CMPC.

30th Golden Horse Awards

The following 30th Golden Horse Awards were announced on December 4, 1993:
Best Film: *The Wedding Banquet.*
Best Director: Ang Lee (*The Wedding Banquet*).

Best Original Script: Ang Lee, Neil Feng, James Schamus (*The Wedding Banquet*).
Best Adapted Script: David Wu, Lam Kei-tou, Tseng Pik-yin, Ronny Yu (*The Bride with White Hair*).*

Best Actor: Jackie Chan (*Crime Story*).*
Best Actress: Carrie Ng (*Remains of a Woman*).*
Best Supporting Actor: Sihung Lung (*The Wedding Banquet*).
Best Supporting Actress: Ah-leh Gua (*The Wedding Banquet*).
Best Photography: Lee Pin-bing (*The Puppetmaster*).
Best Art Direction: Timmy Yip, Yang Zhanjia, William Lygratte (*Temptation of a Monk*).*
Best Costume Design: Juan Pei-yun, Chang Kuang-hui (*The Puppetmaster*).

Best Action Direction: Cory Yuen, Yuen Tak (*Fong Sai Yuk*).*
Best Music: Tats Lau, Wai Kai-leung (*Temptation of a Monk*).*
Best Song: Leslie Cheung, Lam Tsik (*The Bride with White Hair*).*
Best Editing: Peter Cheung (*Fong Sai Yuk*).*
Best Sound: Tu Tu-chih (*The Puppetmaster*).
Life Achievement Award: Huang Cho-han.
Mainland Film-maker Special Award: Michael Lee (*Temptation of a Monk*).*
Special Jury Prize: no award.
*Hongkong production.

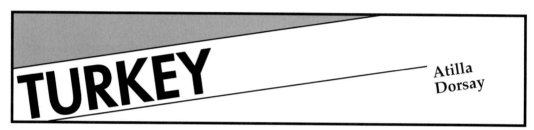

TURKEY

Atilla
Dorsay

After the economic boom which was inseparably associated with Turkey during the 1980's, recession seems to be the key word for the mid-1990's. Cultural and artistic activities, including cinema, which had largely benefitted during recent years, both from state subsidies and private sponsorship, are among the most seriously hit sectors. The subsidy provided by the Minstry of Culture and which made possible the making of practically all Turkish films since the late 1980's has been temporarily halted and the theatres, since 1994, have suffered a drastic loss (about one third) of their traditional customers.

But prior to this dramatic development, 1993 was in general a good year. Imports of features, thanks to the newly-opened multiplexes in big towns, climbed over 200 and local production was at a satisfactory level. About 40 films were produced and half could be theatrically released. One of them, **The American** (*Amerikali*) by the director of *Yol*, Serif Gören, was a box-office hit which sold about 500,000 tickets. **Berlin in Berlin** by Sinan Çetin, **Shadow Game** (*Gölge Oyunu*) by Yavuz Tuğrul, **Yellow Smile** (*Sar Tebessüm*) by the new-comer Seçkin Yasar, were also reasonably successful. Some other and eventually more interesting films, such as **The Blue Exile** (*Mavi Sürgün*) by Erden Kıral (winner of the Antalya national film festival in 1993, the Turkish entry for the Oscar and winner of the Golden Tulip award in Istanbul 1994) or **The Passenger** (*Yolcu*) by Başar Sabuncu, had to be satisfied with "prestige" audiences.

The Blue Exile was far from the most interesting piece of film-making on the domestic scene. The director of films such as *A Season in Hakkari*, *The Mirror* or *Dilan*, all shown in the past in Cannes, Berlin or Venice film festivals, Erden Kıral, made a successful attempt to revive one of the essential books of a very personal Turkish writer, Cevat Şakir, commonly known as **Fisherman of Halicarnasses** and beautifully recreating the 1920's. It is the story of a "search for the truth" and also a "road movie", half of which takes place in a train going from Istanbul towards the Egyan coast of Turkey. Can Togay, the Hungarian-born Turkish actor who was already seen in *Malina* by Werner Schroeter, and Hanna Schygulla are both excellent.

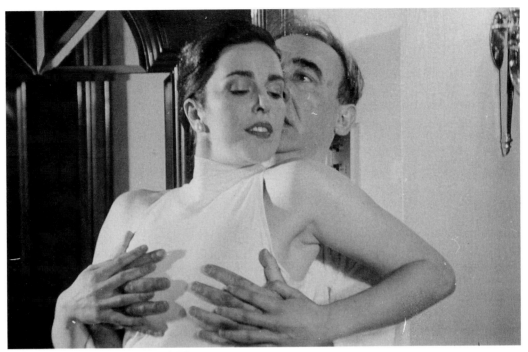

Still from Serif Gören's THE AMERICAN

Explicit Sexual Themes

Since censorship has been practically, although not theoretically abolished, one of the major trends in the current Turkish cinema is the explicit treatment of all kinds of sexual themes. Thus Orhan Oğuz, in his **Whistle if you Return** (*Dönersen Islık Çal*), depicts the night life of Istanbul and the pathetic friendship between a transvestite and a dwarf. The veteran Atıf Yımaz, after his much-discussed *Walking after Midnight*, an openly "lesbian love story", returns to the same waters and again takes the Beyoğlu-Pera district as a setting for his **The Night, Angel and Our Gang** (*Gece, Melek ve Bizim Çocuklar*) full of prostitutes, gays and transvestites again. And one of his ex-assistants, Seçkin Yasar, in her first feature **Yellow Smile** (*Sarı Tebessüm*), depicts a love triangle with much emphasis on sex.

Local directors are also concerned with the two million Turks in Germany. Two important films of this year bear witness to this: Tunç Okanis "our man in Geneva" (he lives there and his first – and successful – films, *The Bus* and *Saturday, Saturday*, were

made in Switzerland); in his first film in years, **Mercedes, my Love** (*Fikrimin Ince Gülü/Sarı Mercedes*), he makes a remarkable road movie and depicts the tragicomic journey of a Turkish worker from Munich to his native country. And Sinan Çetin in his **Berlin in Berlin**, shot in that city, emphasises the cultural shock of the two people through a complicated story of revenge.

The updating of old legends is fashionable, as suggested by **Sahmaran** by Zülfü Livaneli, a modern version of the well-known "snake-woman" legend and the **Hera and Leandro** (*Kızkulesi Aşıkları*) by İrfan Tözüm, from the old legend of the same name. The newly-established trend towards "İslamic films" **Hodja of İskilip** (*Iskilipli Atıf Hoca*) by Mesut Uçakan or **The Fifth Dimension** (*Beşinci Boyut*) by Ismail Güneş. Among other interesting releases are **The Passenger** (*Yolcu*) by Başar Sabuncu, a very sombre film adapted by the famous poet Nazim Hikmet, **The Nude** (*Çıplak*) by Ali Özgentürk, about two naked models from middle classes and their husbands shocked by the news, and **The Disintegration** (*Çözülmeler*) by Yusuf

Kurçenli, an honest attempt to depict the survival of leftist intellectuals after the military coup of 1980.

Huge Variety of Foreign Releases

Foreign films on the market, on the other hand, presented an unprecedented variety. The Ten Best Films list of the Turkish Critics' Association (SİYAD), which was officially refounded this year and joined FIPRESCİ, is as follows and proves this variety: *The Piano, Short Cuts, Kafka, Tous les matins du monde, Arizona Dream, Un Cœur en hiver, Schindler's List, The Remains of the Day, Farewell My Concubine, Husbands and Wives, Delicatessen, Waterland.*

The Antalya national festival, the İstanbul, Ankara and İzmir international festivals were again held with moderate success. In 1993, the İstanbul festival reached a peak of popularity wih 150,000 admissions, and a record number of 150 films. In April 1994 – due to the economic crisis, the festival could sell no more than 85,000 tickets. In the near future, cinema is likely to have some hard days ahead, as the recession is affecting even the existence of some important private TV channels. But the foreign co-production possibilities are still there and the Eurimages fund is still functioning well. And people in government, including the Minister of Culture himself, seem to be determined to continue, at any price, the state subsidy system to the cinema.

Still from Zeki Demirkubuz's C BLOCK

On the other hand, the non-stop devaluation of the Turkish currency is an advantage only to the foreign investor. This is perhaps one of the reasons (others can be breath-taking natural and historical sites and the existence of a reasonably good technical infrastructure and local craftsmanship) why recent co-productions and local shooting cases are increasing: *The Young Indiana Jones* by the Spielberg company, *The Turkish Passion*, a Spanish-Turkish co-production by the well-known director Vicente Aranda, and *Kodin* by Panait İstrati, a French-Turkish-Roumanian co-production are but a few examples.

ATILLÂ DORSAY has been a film critic since 1966, and is author of 15 books on cinema (in Turkish). President of SİYAD (Association of Movie Critics), member of the executive committee of the İstanbul International Film Festival since 1982.

TOP TEN GROSSING FILMS IN TURKEY: 1993

	Admissions
The Bodyguard	950,000
Home Alone	860,000
Jurassic Park	780,000
Basic Instinct	760,000
Hot Shots: Part Deux	550,000
The American (Turkish)	500,000
Indecent Proposal	450,000
Sliver	380,000
Scent of a Woman	350,000
Sister Act	320,000
Berlin in Berlin (Turkish)	290,000

Recent and Forthcoming Films

AĞRI'YA DÖNÜŞ (Return to Ararat Mountain)

Dir: Tunca Yönder. Script: Safa Önal, Tunca Yönder. Players: Haluk Kurdoğlu, Can Gürzap, Ayşegül Aldinc. Prod: Yeni Yapımlar.

AMERİKALI (The American)

Script: Ümit Ünal, Şerif Gören. Dir: Şerif Gören. Players: Şener Şen, Lale Mansur. Prod: Anadolu Filmcilik.

AY VAKTİ (Moon Time)

Script and Dir: Mahinur Ergun. Players: Zühal Olcay, Müşfik Kenter, Füsun Demirel. Prod: Mine Film.

BİR SONBAHAR HİKAYESİ (An Autumn Story)

Script and Dir: Yavuz Özkan. Players: Zühal Olcay, Can Togay, Kaan Girgin. Prod: Z Film.

C BLOK (Block C)

Script and Dir: Zeki Demirkubuz. Players: Serap Aksoy, Fikret Kuşkan. Prod: Mavi Filmcilik.

ÇÖZÜLMELER (The Disintegration)

Script: Yusuf Kurçenli, Cezmi Ersöz. Dir: Yusuf Kurçenli. Players: Tarık Akan, Nurseli İdiz. Prod: Film F.

GECE, MELEK VE BİZİM ÇOCUKLAR (The Night, Angel and Our Gang)

Script: Yıldırım Türker. Dir: Atıf Yılmaz. Players: Derya Arbaş, Deniz Türkali, Uzay Heparı. Prod: Yeşilçam Film.

HOŞÇAKAL UMUT (Goodbye Hope)

Script: Nuray Oğuz. Dir: Canan İçöz. Players: Serif Sezer, Kürşat Alnıaçık. Prod: T R T.

İZ (The Trace)

Script: Tayfun Pirselimoğlu. Dir:Yesim Ustaoğlu. Players: Aytaç Arman, Nur Sürer, Derya Alabora. Prod: Mine Film.

KARANLIK SULAR (Serpent's Tale)

Script and Dir: Kutluğ Ataman. Players: Gönen Bozbey, Daniel Chase. Prod: Kutluğ Ataman.

KIZKULESİ AŞIKLARI (Hera and Leandro)

Script: Macit Koper. Dir: Irfan Tözüm. Players: Nurseli Idiz, Beklan Algan. Prod: Muhteşm Film.

KIZILIRMAK-KARAKOYUN (Legend of Black Sheep)

Script: Tuncer Cücenoğlu, Şahin Gök. Dir: Şahin Gök. Players: Meral Oğuz, Berhan Şimşek. Prod: Dadaş Film.

MANISA TARZANI (Tarzan of Manisa)

Script: Nuray Oğuz. Dir: Orhan Oğuz. Players: Talat Bulut, Serap Sağlar. Prod: Promete Ltd.

ŞAHMARAN (Legend of Şahmaran)

Script: Zeynep Avcı, Zülfü Livaneli. Dir: Zülfü Livaneli. Players: Türkan Şoray, Mehmet Balkız, Faruk Peker. Prod: Inter Film.

TERSİNE DÜNYA (The World Upside-Down)

Script and Dir: Ersin Pertan. Players: Demet Akbağ, Rasim Öztekin. Prod: Özer Film.

YALANCI (The Liar)

Script and Dir: Osman Sınav. Players: Mehmet Aslantuğ, Fikret Hakan. Prod: T R T.

YAZ YAGMURU (A Summer Rain)

Script: T. Giritlioğlu, Ümit Ünal. Dir: Tomris Giritlioğlu. Players: Ahmet Leventoğlu, Pıtırcık Akkerman. Prod: T R T.

YOLCU (The Passenger/A Ship Anchored in the Desert)

Script and Dir: Başar Sabuncu. Players: Tarık Akan, Halil Ergün, Müjde Ar, Berhan Şimşek. Prod: Belge Film.

ZIKKIMIN KÖKÜ (Bullshit)

Script: Macit Koper, Memduh Ün. Dir: Memduh Ün. Players: Emre Akyıldız, Menderes Samancılar. Prod: Mine Film.

Useful Addresses

Çağdaş Sinema Oyunculari Derneği (ASOD)
(The Association of Actors)
İstiklal Caddesi, Atlas sineması pasajı, C Blok 53/3
Beyoğlu
İstanbul
Tel: (212) 251 97 75
Fax: (212) 251 97 79

Çizgi Filmciler Derneği
(The Association of Animated Film-makers)
P.K. 420 Galatasaray
İstanbul
Tel: (212) 244 34 99

Dünya Kitle İletişim Vakfi
(World Mass Communication Foundation)
Özveren Sokak No 3/8 Demirtepe
06570 Ankara
Tel: (312) 229 99 33-34
Fax: (312) 231 00 88

Film Yönetmenleri Derneği (FİLM-YÖN)
(The Association of Film Directors)
Ayhan Işık Sokak,

28/I Beyoğlu
80060 Beyoğlu, İstanbul
Tel: (212) 244 01 38
Fax: (212) 245 71 94

**Film Yapimcilari Derneği
(FİYAP)**
(The Association of Film Producers)
Gazeteci Erol Dernek Sokak No 8,
Beyoğlu, İstanbul
Tel: (212) 266 13 87
Fax: (212) 266 63 51

İstanbul Kültür ve Sanat Vakfi
*(The İstanbul Culture and Arts
Foundation)*
Yıldız Kültür ve Sanat Merkezi,
Beşiktaş 80746 İstanbul
Tel: (212) 258 32 12
Fax: (212) 261 88 23

**Sinema Yazarlari Derneği
(SİYAD)**
(The Association of Film Critics)
Gazeteci Erol Dernek Sokak,
No II/3 Beyoğlu, İstanbul
Tel: (212) 251 70 73
Fax: (212) 243 25 30

**Türkiye Sinema ve Audiovisuel
Kültür Vakfi (TÜRSAK)**
*(The Turkish Cinema and
Audiovisuel Culture Foundation)*
Gazeteci Erol Dernek Sokak No II/2
Hanif Han,
Beyoğlu, İstanbul
Tel: (212) 244 52 51
Fax: (212) 251 67 70

Alfa-Film
İstiklal Caddesi No 140
Beyoğlu, İstanbul
Tel: (212) 243 63 40
Fax: (212) 243 31 08

Asya-Film
Gazeteci Erol Dernek Sokak Erman
Han,
Kat I Beyoğlu, İstanbul
Tel: (212) 251 41 71
Fax: (212) 293 34 98

Still from AN AUTUMN STORY, directed by Yavuz Özkan

Erler Film
Kodaman Sokak No 106-108,
80220 Nişantaş,
İstanbul
Tel: (212) 224 06 09
Fax: (212) 224 06 05

Magnum Film
Pıtrak Sokak 7/4
34800 Yeşilyurt,
İstanbul
Tel: (212) 573 28 79
Fax: (212) 573 73 43

Mine Film
Ayhan Işık Sokak, Girik Han,
28/3, Beyoğlu, İstanbul
Tel: (212) 243 02 00
Fax: (212) 245 67 74

Özen Film
Sakızağacı Cad.
No 21 Beyoğlu,
İstanbul
Tel: (212) 245 58 54
Fax: (212) 244 58 51

Standart Film
Erol Dernek Sokak, Erman Hat
Kan 2,
Beyoğlu, İstanbul
Tel: (212) 243 33 97
Fax: (212) 252 98 50

UIP – Filmcivik ve Ticaret Ltd.
Eytam Cad. 16/16 80200 Maçka,
İstanbul
Tel: (212) 225 92 22
Fax: (212) 225 91 92

Umut Samut Ürünleri
Halaskargazi Cad. Gazi Ethem Paşa
Sitesi,
No 214/7 8022o Şişli,
İstanbul
Tel: (212) 230 40 41
Fax: (212) 232 35 83

İstanbul Film Ajansi – İFA
Gazeteci erol Dernek Sokak,
Hanif Han, II/5
Beyoğlu, İstanbul
Tel: (212) 245 56 02
Fax: (212) 245 54 17

Z Film
Valikonağı Caddesi, Akkirmanlı
Sokak,
Nayır Sitesi
D Blok No. 55 Nişantaşi, İstanbul
Tel: (212) 247 67 25
Fax: (212) 247 67 25

UNITED KINGDOM — George Perry

Could at long last there be signs of cheer in the habitually beleaguered British film industry? A new optimism is in the air, largely on the strength of one film. The international box-office success of **Four Weddings and a Funeral,** the highest grossing British comedy in the U.S. market since *A Fish Called Wanda* in 1988 ($50 million by mid-1994) was both unexpected and stimulating. The performance of the Polygram/Channel 4/Working Title production may be modest compared with the averagely successful Hollywood product, and has some distance to go to catch up with last year's standout in box-office returns, *The Crying Game,* but its achievement has been consistent in various territories, having reached the top chart position in Australia, France, Belgium, Ireland, the United Kingdom and the United States.

Given such confidence, Eric Fellner and Tim Bevan, the joint managing directors of Working Title, were able to announce the greenlighting of two major mainstream projects fusing U.K. and U.S. talent, for the latter quarter of the year, *Moonlight and Valentino* with Whoopi Goldberg and Kathleen Turner, directed by David Anspaugh, and *Loch Ness* with Ted Danson and Joely Richardson, directed by John Henderson.

British studios, bleak and empty a year ago, became so full that when the new James Bond film *Goldeneye* was announced (with Pierce Brosnan taking over the role from Timothy Dalton) it was discovered that Pinewood and the 007 stage were no longer available at the required dates. Filling Pinewood's stages was *Mary Reilly,* produced by Hyde Films for TriStar, with Stephen Frears directing a cast headed by Julia Roberts, John Malkovich and Glenn Close. Ealing Studios returned to business, using the closing weeks of the Government's Business Expansion Scheme to attract investment in production development. In mid-year, David Bill, Ealing's chairman, put in a bid for Elstree Studios which had languished in the hands of Brent Walker, with the intention of combining studio facilities with leisure and retail use. A sense of *déjà vu* was invoked by the announcement that the old Gainsborough Studios, a carpet warehouse for many years, were to be reopened.

Attendances Continue to Surge

On the exhibition side there were apprehensions that the steady growth in attendances from the mid-1980s which reached 114.4 million in 1993, a 10.3% rise on the previous year, could fall back slightly in view of the boost derived from Steven Spielberg's *Jurassic Park*. Exhibitors were heartened to note that attendances in the first quarter of 1994 were 23% up on the same period the previous year and that the figure of 33.5 million was the healthiest the industry had known since 1975. The increase in cinema screens is mainly responsible, and although the building of new multiplexes has slowed with most well-populated areas of Britain now within reasonable reach of at least one new development new screens are still averaging nearly 50 a year.

Warner opened their flagship complex in Leicester Square, a miracle of architectural ingenuity in that seven reasonably-sized cinemas have been inserted within the shell of the old Warner Theatre, with spacious lobby and mezzanine areas and minimum disturbance of the fine art-deco facade.

While multiplexes offer far more pleasant film-going conditions than those that British film-goers were inured to during the nadir years, a legitimate complaint concerns the monotony of programming, with standard Hollywood commercial product dominating all screens. Certain British films, particularly Ken Loach's *Raining Stones*, would have found a much larger audience given distribution at the same intensity of many mediocre American films. The arthouse front strengthened during the year with the merger of Artificial Eye and Mayfair, giving an inner London total of ten screens, but the enforced closure of the Camden Plaza for property development was a blow, leaving a busy focal point with no cinema. At Peckham a welcome reversal of trends occurred with the opening by Simon Perry of a six-screen multiplex to be programmed with the same independence as the nearby Greenwich Cinema, on the site of a former Sainsbury's supermarket. At Brixton, another inner London hub, the multi-screen development of the Ritzy continued, again with non-standard programming. Two miles to the west the Clapham Picture House concluded its first year, ensuring that South London was no longer a film-going desert.

An unwelcome resurgence of the censorship issue recurred during the year, following an appalling murder carried out by two Liverpool children. The judge in summing up referred to a video, *Child's Play 3*, although there had been no mention in evidence that the children concerned had seen it. Media pressure lashed the country into a lather of rage against so-called "video nasties" in spite of the fact that they had been outlawed for many years under the Video Recordings Act. David Alton, a Liberal Democrat Member of Parliament, proposed to introduce a bill that would effectively outlaw all 18-certificated videos for home consumption, with considerable cross-party support, but he was headed off when the Government conceded with tough new restrictions.

Shortly afterwards a British thriller called *Beyond Bedlam* opened in the cinemas to mild notices and poor attendances. James Ferman, director of the

British Board of Film Classification, announced that it would be banned from video release, rescinding its already granted 18 certificate. It joined a growing list of films that Britons are not allowed to see in their homes, regardless of whether or not they have impressionable children. Since the producers of *Beyond Bedlam* had based their expectations of a return from their investment on the video rentals (one had mortgaged his house and faced eviction) the capricious decision was clearly a publicity gesture. All the film members of the Critics' Circle noted that far more violent films have been released on video without a murmur. It can be seen that in the run-up to the super-highway, when even the BBFC will be unable to stem the floodtide, the spirit of Grundy is still alive in Britain.

GEORGE PERRY is Films Editor of The Sinday Times and author of several books on cinema. From 1991 to 1994 he was chairman of the Critics' Circle.

FOUR WEDDINGS AND A FUNERAL

Script: Richard Curtis. Direction: Mike Newell. Photography: Michael Coulter. Editing: Jon Gregory. Production Design: Maggie Grey. Music: Richard Rodney Bennett. Players: Hugh Grant, Andie MacDowell, Kristin Scott-Thomas, James Fleet, Simon Callow, John Hannah, David Bower, Charlotte Coleman, Corin Redgrave, Rowan Atkinson. Produced by Polygram Filmed Entertainment /Channel 4 Films, Working Title. 117 mins.

At last, a refreshingly bright British comedy, in which Hugh Grant excels as a charmingly vague fringe member of the London twiterati who is habitually unpunctual for his friends' weddings. He meets a beautiful American, Andie MacDowell, and their odd romantic relationship is conducted only on nuptial occasions, including her own. The screenwriter Richard Curtis has cleverly worked out the framework and Mike Newell, not previously noted for directing comedies, expertly marshals the large cast, including Kristin Scott-Thomas, James Fleet, Corin Redgrave, Sara Crowe and

Kristin Scott-Thomas and Hugh Grant in FOUR WEDDINGS AND A FUNERAL

Charlotte Coleman. The rich embarrassments and gaffes are shrewdly caught. Rowan Atkinson appears as a verbally dyslexic clergyman and Simon Callow is brilliant as a middle-aged queen who joyously exlaims on seeing the kilts fly at a Scottish baronial highland fling: "It's Brigadoon!"

George Perry

SHADOWLANDS

Script: William Nicholson. Direction: Richard Attenborough. Photography: Roger Pratt. Editing: Lesley Walker. Production Design: Stuart Craig. Music: George Fenton. Players: Anthony Hopkins, Debra Winger, John Wood, Edward Hardwicke, Joseph Mazzello, Julian Fellowes, Roddy Maude-Roxby, Michael Denison, Peter Firth, Andrew Seear, Tim McMullan, Andrew Hawkins, Peter Howell, Robert Flemyng. Produced by Shadowlands Productions/Spelling Films International in association with Price Entertainment/Savoy Pictures. 131 mins.

Anthony Hopkins as the Oxford bachelor don, C.S. Lewis, awakened to love in later life by a much younger American woman, is far better than in *The Remains of the Day* because his character is allowed to develop and change. Debra Winger is also marvellous as the strong-willed, sharply intelligent Joy Gresham who marries Lewis before God – they have already had a civil ceremony – on a hospital bed as cancer racks her body. William Nicholson's screenplay explores the effect of the New World on Lewis's reclusive imagination with much insight, humour and a positive, unmawkish tone, although it is hard to be unmoved. Richard Attenborough crowns his directing career, eliciting tender, affecting performances from his cast, and recreating the Morris Minor world of Oxford of the early 1950's with studied accuracy, with its dusty book-stacks, unheated bedrooms, unimaginative food, spiky common-room conversation and subtly observed details such as one of those flared BournVita mugs on a desk, an artefact that speaks eloquently of its time. It is a distinguished achievement for British cinema (even if the money was American.)

George Perry

TOP TEN GROSSING FILMS IN THE U.K.: 1993

	(millions)
Jurassic Park	46.4
The Bodyguard	16.8
Home Alone 2	13.7
The Fugitive	13.4
Indecent Proposal	11.8
Bram Stoker's Dracula	11.5
Cliffhanger	9.2
Sleepless in Seattle	9.0
A Few Good Men	8.4
The Jungle Book	7.4

Recent and Forthcoming Films

A BUSINESS AFFAIR

Script: William Stadiem. Dir: Charlotte Brandstrom. Phot: Willy Kurant. Players: Christopher Walken, Carole Bouquet, Jonathan Pryce, Sheila Hancock. Prod: Film & General Productions/Osby Films/ Connexion Films.

BACKBEAT

Script: Iain Softley, Michael Thomas, Stephen Ward. Dir: I. Softley. Phot: Ian Wilson. Players: Sheryl Lee, Stephen Dorff, Ian Hart, Gary Bakewell, Chris O'Neill. Prod: PolyGram/ Scala.

BEYOND BEDLAM

Script: Vadim Jean, Rob Walker. Dir: V. Jean. Phot: Gavin Finney. Players: Craig Fairbrass, Elizabeth Hurley, Keith Allen, Anita Dobson, Jesse Birdsall. Prod: Metrodome Films.

BHAJI ON THE BEACH

Script: Meera Syal. Dir: Gurinder Chadha. Phot: John Kenway. Players: Kim Vithana, Jimmi Harkishin, Sarita Khajuria, Mo

Sesay, Lalita Ahmen. Prod: Umbi Films/Channel Four.

BUTTERFLY KISS

Script: Frank Cottrell Boyce. Dir: Michael Winterbottom. Phot: Seamus McGarvey. Players: Amanda Plummer, Saskia Reeves, Paul Brown, Fine-Time Fontayne, Ricky Tomlinson. Prod: Dan Films/British Screen/Mida.

DEADLY ADVICE

Script: Glenn Chandler. Dir: Mandie Fletcher. Phot: Richard Greatrex. Players: Jane Horrocks, Brenda Fricker, Imelda Staunton, Edward Woodward. Prod: Zenith.

DECADENCE

Script and Dir: Steven Berkoff. Phot: Denis Lenoir. Players: Steven Berkoff, Joan Collins. Prod: Vendetta Films.

THE ENGLISHMAN WHO WENT UP A HILL BUT CAME DOWN A MOUNTAIN

Script and Dir: Christopher Monger. Phot: Vernon Layton. Players: Hugh Grant, Colm

Meaney, Ian McNeice, Ian Hart, Kenneth Griffiths. Prod: Parallax Productions.

FOUR WEDDINGS AND A FUNERAL

Script: Richard Curtis. Dir: Mike Newell. Phot: Michael Coulter. Players: Hugh Grant, Andie MacDowell, Kristin Scott Thomas, James Fleet, Simon Callow. Prod: PolyGram/Channel Four/Working Title.

FUNNY BONES

Script: Peter Flannery, Peter Chelsom. Dir: P. Chelsom. Phot: Eduardo Serra. Players: Oliver Platt, Jerry Lewis, Lee Evans, Richard Griffiths, Leslie Caron. Prod: Suntrust Films.

HALYCON DAYS

Script: Kerry Crabbe, Patrick Dewolf. Dir: P. Dewolf. Phot: Patrick Blossier. Players: Stephen Dorff, Gabrielle Anwar, Adrian Dunbar, Sophie Aubry, Joanna Lumley. Prod: PolyGram/ Red Umbrella/Septieme.

HEDD WYN

Script: Alun Llwyd, Paul Turner. Dir: P. Turner. Phot: Ray Orton. Players: Huw Garmon, Catrin Fychan, Ceri Cunnington, Lilo Silyn, Grey Evans. Prod: Pendefig/S4C.

THE HOUR OF THE PIG

Script and Dir: Leslie Megahey. Phot: John Hooper. Players: Colin Firth, Ian Holm, Donald Pleasence, Nicol Williamson, Justin Chadwick, Sophie Dix. Prod: BBC/Ciby 2000.

I.D.

Script: Vincent O'Connell. Dir: Philip Davis. Phot: Thomas Mauch. Players: Reece Dinsdale, Richard Graham, Claire Skinner, Sean Pertwee, Phil Glenister. Prod: BBC Films/The Sales Company/Parallax/Metropolis Filmproduktion.

IN CUSTODY

Script: Anita Desai, Shahrukh Husain. Dir: Ismail Merchant. Phot: Larry Pizer. Players: Shashi Kapoor, Sameer Mitha, Neena Gupta, Rupinder Kaur, Om Puri. Prod: Merchant Ivory/Channel Four.

THE INNOCENT

Script: Ian McEwan. Dir: John Schlesinger. Phot: Dietrich Lohmann. Players: Campbell Scott, Isabella Rossellini, Anthony Hopkins, Hart Bochner. Prod: Lakehart/Sievernich Film.

JEFFERSON IN PARIS

Script: Ruth Prawer Jhabvala. Dir: James Ivory. Phot: Piere Lhomme. Players: Nick Nolte, Greta Scacchi, Thandie Newton, Michael Lonsdale. Prod: Merchant Ivory.

LAND AND FREEDOM

Script: Jim Allen. Dir: Ken Loach. Players: Ian Hart, Rosana Pastor, Frederic Pierrot, Tom Gilroy.

Prod: Parallax Pictures, Messidor Films.

LEAVING LENIN

Script: Endarf Emlyn, Sion Eiri. Dir: E. Emlyn. Phot: Ray Orton. Players: Sharon Morgan, Wyn Bowen Harries, Ifan Huw Dafydd, Steffan Trevor. Prod: Gaucho/S4C.

LONDON

Script, Dir and Phot: Patrick Keiller. Narration: Paul Schofield. Prod: Konnick/BFI/Channel Four.

THE NEON BIBLE

Script and Dir: Terence Davies. Phot: Mick Coulter. Players: Gena Rowlands, Diana Scarwid, Denis Leary, Jacob Tierney, Leo Bermester, Peter McRobbie. Prod: Scala Productions.

SAVAGE HEARTS

Script and Dir: Mark Ezra. Phot: James Aspinall. Players: Richard Harris, Maryann D'Abo, Miriam Cyr, Jamie Harris, Dave Allmond. Prod: Savage Hearts Productions.

THE SECRET RAPTURE

Script: David Hare. Dir: Howard Davies. Phot: Ian Wilson. Players: Juliet Stevenson, Joanne Whalley-Kilmer, Penelope Wilton, Neil Pearson, Alan Howard, Robert Stephens. Prod: Greenpoint Films/NFTC.

SHADOWLANDS

Script: William Nicholson. Dir: Richard Attenborough. Phot: Roger Pratt. Players: Anthony Hopkins, Debra Winger, John Wood, Edward Hardwicke, Joseph Mazello. Prod: Shadowlands Prod/Spelling Films Int'l.

SHOPPING

Script and Dir: Paul Anderson. Phot: Tony Imi. Players: Sadie Frost, Jude Law, Sean Pertwee, Fraser James, Sean Bean, Marianne Faithful, Jonathan Pryce. Prod: Impact Pictures/Channel Four/PolyGram.

THREE STEPS TO HEAVEN

Script and Dir: Constantine Giannaris. Phot: James Welland. Players: Kartin Cartlidge, Frances Barber, James Fleet, Con O'Neil, Stuart Laing. Prod: Maya Vision/BFI/Channel Four.

TOM & VIV

Script: Michael Hastings, Adrian Hodges. Dir: Brian Gilbert. Phot: Martin Fuhrer. Players: Willem

Anthony Hopkins and Debra Winger in SHADOWLANDS

Dafoe, Miranda Richardson, Rosemary Harris, Tim Dutton, Nicholas Grace. Prod: New Era.

UFO

Script: Richard Hall, Simon Wright, Roy "Chubby" Brown. Dir: Tony Dow. Phot: Paul Wheeler. Players: Roy "Chubby" Brown, Sara Stockbridge, Roger Lloyd Pack. Prod: PolyGram.

WIDOWS PEAK

Script: Hugh Leonard. Dir: John Irvin. Phot: Ashley Rowe. Players: Mia Farrow, Joan Plowright, Natasha Richardson, Adrian Dunbar, Jim Broadbent. Prod: Jo Manuel Productions.

Producers

Allied Vision
3-4 Ashland Place
London W1M 3JH
Tel: (71) 224 1992
Fax: (71) 224 0111

British Film Institute Production
29 Rathbone Street
London W1P 1AG
Tel: (71) 636 5587
Fax: (71) 580 9456

British Lion
Pinewood Studios
Iver Heath
Bucks SL0 0NH
Tel: (753) 651 700
Fax: (753) 656 844

Enigma Productions
13-15 Queens Gate Place Mews
London SW7 5BG
Tel: (71) 581 0238
Fax: (71) 584 1799

Euston Films
Pinewood Studios
Iver Heath
Bucks SL0 0NH
Tel: (753) 650 222
Fax: (753) 654 321

Flamingo Pictures
47 Lonsdale Square
London N1 1EW

Tel: (71) 607 9958
Fax: (71) 609 7669

Mark Forstater Productions
Suite 66, Pall Mall Deposit
124-128 Barbley Road
London W10 6BL
Tel: (81) 964 1888
Fax: (81) 960 9819

Goldcrest Films and Television
36/44 Brewer Street
London W1R 3HP
Tel: (71) 437 8696
Fax: (71) 437 4448

Greenpoint Films
5A Noel Street
London W1V 3RB
Tel: (71) 437 6492
Fax: (71) 437 0644

HandMade Films
26 Cadogan Square
London SW1X 0JP
Fax: (71) 584 7338

Little Bird
91 Regent Street
London W1R 7TA
Tel: (71) 434 1131
Fax: (71) 434 1803

Merchant Ivory Productions
46 Lexington Street
London W1P 3LH
Tel: (71) 437 1200
Fax: (71) 734 1579

NFH
37 Ovington Square
London SW3 1LJ
Tel: (71) 584 7561
Fax: (71) 589 1863

Portobello Productions Ltd
42 Tavistock Road
London W11 1AW
Tel: (71) 379 5566
Fax: (71) 379 5599

Prominent Features
68A Delancey Street
London NW1 7RY
Tel: (71) 284 10242
Fax: (71) 284 1004

Recorded Picture Company
24-26 Manway Street
London W1

Red Rooster Films
29 Floral Street
London WC2E 9DP
Tel: (71) 379 7727
Fax: (71) 379 5756

Sands Films
119 Rotherhithe Street
London SE16 4NF
Tel: (71) 231 2209
Fax: (71) 231 2119

Skreba Films
5a Noel Street
London W1V 3RB
Tel: (71) 437 6492
Fax: (71) 437 0644

Michael White
13 Duke Street
London SW1Y 6DB
Tel: (71) 839 3971
Fax: (71) 839 3836

Working Title
1 Water Lane
London NW1 8NZ
Tel: (71) 911 6100
Fax: (71) 911 6150

Zenith Productions
43-45 Dorset Street
London W1H 4AB
Tel: (71) 224 2440
Fax: (71) 224 3194

Distributors

Majors

United International Pictures (U.IP.)
Mortimer House
37-41 Mortimer Street
London W1A 2JL
Tel: (71) 636 1655
Fax: (71) 636 4118

Warner Brothers
135 Wardour Street
London W1V 4AP
Tel: (71) 734 8400
Fax: (71) 437 2950

Columbia/TriStar Film Distributors
19-23 Wells Street
London W1P 3FP
Tel: (71) 580 2090
Fax: (71) 436 0323

Twentieth Century Fox
20th Century House
31-32 Soho Square
London W1V 6AP
Tel: (71) 437 7766
Fax: (71) 434 2170

Independents

Rank Film Distributors
127-133 Wardour Street
London W1V 4AD
Tel: (71) 437 9020
Fax: (71) 434 3689

Artificial Eye Mayfair UK
13 Soho Square
London W1V 5FB
Tel: (71) 437 2552
Fax: (71) 437 2992

Blue Dolphin Films
40 Langham Street
London W1N 5RG
Tel: (71) 255 2494
Fax: (71) 580 7670

British Film Institute
21 Stephen Street
London W1P 1PL
Tel: (71) 255 1444
Fax: (71) 436 7950

Contemporary Films
24 Southwood Lawn Road
London N6 5SF
Tel: (81) 340 5715
Fax: (81) 348 1238

Electric Pictures
15 Percy Street
London W1P 9FD
Tel: (71) 636 1231
Fax: (71) 636 1675

Entertainment Film Distributors
27 Soho Square
London W1V 5FL
Tel: (71) 439 1606
Fax: (71) 734 2483

First Independent Films
69 New Oxford Street
London WC1A 1DG
Tel: (71) 528 7767
Fax: (71) 528 7770/1/2

Gala Films
26 Danbury Street
London N1 8JU

Tel: (71) 226 5085
Fax: (71) 226 5897

Guild Film Distribution
Kent House
14-17 Market Place
Great Titchfield Street
London W1N 8AR
Tel: (71) 323 5151
Fax: (71) 631 3568

ICA Projects
12 Carlton House Terrace
London SW1Y 5AH
Tel: (71) 930 0493
Fax: (71) 873 0051

Mainline Pictures
37 Museum Street
London WC1A 1LP
Tel: (71) 242 5523
Fax: (71) 430 0170

Metro Tartan
79 Wardour Street
London W1V 3TH
Tel: (71) 734 8508
Fax: (71) 287 2112

Useful Addresses

**British Academy of Film and
Television Arts (BAFTA)**
195 Piccadilly
London W1V 9LG
Tel: (71) 734 0022
Fax: (71) 734 1792

**British Board of Film
Classification (BBFC)**
3 Soho Square
London W1V 5DE
Tel: (71) 439 7961
Fax: (71) 287 0141

British Actors Equity
Guild House
Upper St. Martins Lane
London WC2H 9EG
Tel: (71) 379 6000
Fax: (71) 379 7001

The British Council
11 Portland Place
London W1N 4EJ
Tel: (71) 389 3068
Fax: (71) 389 3041

British Screen Finance
14-17 Wells Mews
London W1P 3FL
Tel: (71) 323 9080
Fax: (71) 323 0092

**Cinema Exhibitors' Association
(CEA)**
22 Golden Square
London W1R 3PA
Tel: (71) 734 9551
Fax: (71) 734 6147

Directors' Guild of Great Britain
Suffolk House
Whitfield Place
London W1P 5SF
Tel: (71) 383 3858
Fax: (71) 383 5173

PACT
Gordon House
Greencoat Place
London SW1P 1PH
Tel: (71) 233 6000
Fax: (71) 233 8935

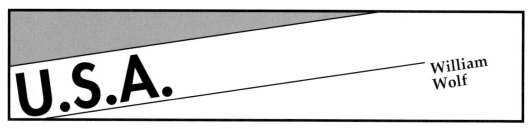

William Wolf

In the mainstream it was definitely the year of Steven Spielberg, but the breed taking pride in the term "independent film-maker" also unleashed a galaxy of work, sometimes with high-profile results. At the Cannes Festival controversial indie favourite Quentin Tarantino scored a triumph when his creative, pop-culture crime drama *Pulp Fiction*, a Miramax release, snared the Palme d'Or. An impressive measure of independent strength could be found at the Berlin International Film Festival, where no less than 41 new, American indie feature films and documentaries turned up either in official sections or in the busy marketplace.

Of course, nothing could outdo Spielberg, who scored a double coup. Not only did his **Jurassic Park** become the highest grosser of all time with an international take reaching $900 million, as well as the 1993 domestic champ with some $339 million. His **Schindler's List** finally earned him his long-sought best director Oscar and widespread acclaim for showing that he could excel with a major, ultra-serious work. This powerful film dealing with the Holocaust, which domestically grossed almost $100 million, took six other Academy Awards including one for best picture.

But apart from other selected Hollywood achievements, the main satisfaction for buffs could be derived from seeing many interesting offbeat films defy the blockbuster mentality gripping the mainstream industry. In fact, leading independent companies Miramax, Fine Line, and Goldwyn were developing so much clout that they were in effect becoming mini-majors. The best-known of American independent directors, perennial iconoclast Robert Altman, showed his versatility and ingenuity anew with the multi-character

Short Cuts (Fine Line), based on the writings of Raymond Carver, and Altman was honoured for his life's work in New York by the Film Society of Lincoln Center.

Low-Budget Films to Fore

The diversity of low-budget films was reflected by John Dahl's film noir **Red Rock West** (Roxie), Boaz Yakin's ghetto survival drama **Fresh** (Miramax), Henry Jaglom's childbirth talkfest **Babyfever** (Rainbow), Rose Troche's lesbian romantic comedy **Go Fish** (Goldwyn), which was a Panorama selection at the Berlin Festival, and novice Kevin Smith's ribald **Clerks** (Miramax), the winner of the Critics' Week Jury Prize at Cannes (see reviews).

Tom Noonan's **What Happened Was** (Goldwyn), a poignant, superbly acted two-character drama teaming Noonan and Karen Sillas, won both the Sundance Film Festival's Grand Jury Prize and Waldo Salt screenwriting award. **Fear of a Black Hat** (Goldwyn), directed by Rusty Cundieff, satirised rap. Whit Stillman, whose *Metropolitan* stirred previous interest, was back with **Barcelona** (Fine Line), about Americans in Spain. The very act of making independent films was satirised in **My Life's in Turnaround** (Arrow Releasing), a comic whine about the challenge, directed by fledglings Eric Schaeffer and Donal Lardner Ward, also the leads. Another newcomer, Dan Algrant, garnered the prestige of having Martin Scorsese present his film **Naked in New York** (Fine Line), about a young playwright trying to crack the New York theatre. Although the result was lukewarm, Algrant enlisted such stars as Kathleen Turner, Whoopi Goldberg, Eric Stolz, and Tony Curtis for the cast.

Kathleen Turner had her main star turn

in John Waters's **Serial Mom**, a Savoy Pictures release that spoofed the sanctity of motherhood and apple pie making by mom, delightfully played by Turner, a psycho killer. Once again the New Films/New Directors series in New York, sponsored by the Film Society of Lincoln Center and the Museum of Modern Art, was a prominent showcase. Among the presentations were Lodge H. Kerrigan's **Clean, Shaven**, a talented but gloomy and sometimes shocking portrait of a man's hallucinations as he falls apart, and the brighter, enjoyable **The Girl in the Watermelon**, Sergio M. Castilla's auto-biographically-inspired tale of a Brooklyn girl trying to discover who is her father.

Jay Craven made an impressive feature bow with **Where the Rivers Flow North** (Caledonia Pictures), shot in Vermont, with Rip Torn and Tantoo Cardinal starring in a backwoods drama with an ecological theme. David Russell's **Spanking the Monkey** (Fine Line), dealt with a college student, his ill mother and the subject of incest. One of the most popular off-beat films that captivated American audiences turned out to be an import; Mike Newell's *Four Weddings and a Funeral* (Gramercy), which grossed some $50 million.

Special Talent

Tom Hanks was riding high for his moving portrait of an AIDS-afflicted lawyer in Jonathan Demme's **Philadelphia** (TriStar), winning him a Silver Bear for best actor at Berlin and then the coveted Hollywood Oscar. He was also immensely popular co-starring with Meg Ryan in Nora Ephron's **Sleepless in Seattle** (TriStar), which topped $126 million as 1993's fourth highest grosser. (**The Fugitive** from Warner Bros. starring Harrison Ford, was second to *Jurassic Park* with $179 million, and **The Firm**, from Paramount, starring Tom Cruise, was third with $158 million.) Hanks had yet another triumph in Robert Zemeckis's alternately funny and touching **Forrest Gump** (Paramount) as a mildly retarded, naïve Southern nice guy, who stumbles to success as he navigates through America's turbulent times, including the Vietnam War.

Man of the Year: Steven Spielberg, with the double whammy of JURASSIC PARK and SCHINDLER'S LIST

It was a good year for rising star Rosie Perez, who received special mention at the Berlin Festival for her intensely dramatic performance in Peter Weir's **Fearless** (Warner Bros.), and then nabbed a featured actress Oscar nomination. Perez had another showy role as the funny, grasping wife in Andrew Bergman's entertaining comedy **It Could Happen to You** (Tri-Star), in which Nicolas Cage was perfect as her husband, the good-natured cop who shares his lottery winnings with a waitress (Bridget Fonda). In the previously mentioned *Red Rock West*, Cage was an ideal film noir hero, 1990's style.

Robert De Niro proved a point, too, revealing his ability as a director with **A Bronx Tale** (Savoy). Fans of Robin Williams were rewarded with his uproarious performance as the husband posing as a nanny in Chris Columbus's international hit **Mrs. Doubtfire**. Holly Hunter's Oscar for *The Piano* reflected her career climb. Score two for Debra Winger, who shone as a misfit in Stephen Gyllenhaal's **A Dangerous**

Jodie Foster in MAVERICK
photo: Andrew Cooper/Warners

Woman (Gramercy) and as the doomed woman who finds love in Richard Attenborough's moving *Shadowlands* (Savoy).

Summer Scramble

Name talent fuelled hopes among the majors for their 1994 summer battle of the box-office. The reputation of Keanu Reeves, popular with young audiences, soared with his performance as the action hero cop of Jan De Bont's **Speed**, Fox's surprise summer hit, cleverly scripted by Graham Yost with the gimmick of a bus that must go over 50 miles an hour or blow up with its passengers. *Speed* jump-started with $55 million within the first three weeks of its release. Jack Nicholson, as charismatic as ever, was teamed with beautiful Michelle Pfeiffer, in the urban horror tale, Mike Nichols's **Wolf** (Columbia; $37.7 million in the first two weeks). Mel Gibson and Jodie Foster, abetted by veteran James Garner, were the lure for Richard Donner's colourful **Maverick** (Warner Bros.; $80 million in less than six weeks). John Goodman was heavily promoted in Brian Levant's

mindless **The Flintstones**, Universal's quest for a bonanza and heavily marketed with commercial tie-ins (topping $100 million within five weeks).

Kevin Costner was the intended attraction for Lawrence Kasdan's **Wyatt Earp** (Warner Bros.), which emerged bloated and dull, save for a turn by Dennis Quaid as Doc Holliday, and limped to a modest life at the box-office.

Also in the action department, a big question was how James Cameron's *True Lies* (Fox), starring Arnold Schwarzenegger as the man of action, would do. It was reported to have cost more than $100 million. Harrison Ford was cast as a C.I.A. agent in Philip Noyce's *Clear and Present Danger* (Paramount). Jeff Bridges and Tommy Lee Jones starred in Stephen Hopkins's overblown, derivative bomb squad actioner *Blown Away* (MGM), and Alec Baldwin was counted on for box-office appeal in Russell Mulcahy's *The Shadow* (Universal), a reprise of the old radio serial which was slick, expertly crafted and brimming with sophisticated SFX and art direction. Susan Sarandon and Tommy Lee Jones starred in Joel Schumacher's version of the best-selling John Grisham novel *The Client* (Warner Bros.). Julia Roberts and Nick Nolte were paired for Charles Shyer's *I Love Trouble* (Touchstone), a comedy about Chicago newspaper reporters.

Woody Harrelson and Juliette Lewis headed the cast of Oliver Stone's awaited

Natural Born Killers (Warner Bros.), from a script by Quentin Tarantino, more promising than Stone's earlier and strangely uninvolving Vietnam tale *Heaven and Earth* (Warner Bros.). Billy Crystal returned as the lead in Paul Weiland's **City Slickers II** (Columbia, $30.5 million within three weeks), attempting to parlay the success of the original. The Disney Company's classy new animated **The Lion King**, aimed at family audiences, devoured $46 million in its wide-opening weekend, a Disney record.

Assorted Pleasures

An eclectic collection of American films merited appreciation, whether successful at the box-office or not. Woody Allen's **Manhattan Murder Mystery** (TriStar), teaming Allen and Diane Keaton once again, sparkled with fun and sophistication. Ron Howard's **The Paper** (Univer-sal) provided and slam-bang if sometimes sentimental look at putting out a New York tabloid. The Coen brothers, Joel and Ethan, did a mostly successful sendup of Capra-style movies with **The Hudsucker Proxy** (Warner Bros.).

Spike Lee directed a warm, gentle family drama, **Crooklyn** (Univer-sal), which showed a mellow side to his work.

Martin Scorsese's sumptuous **The Age of Innocence** (Columbia), his adaptation of Edith Wharton's novel, proved that he could trade mean streets for a stylish late-Nineteenth-century period setting. Wayne Wang's **The Joy Luck Club** (Buena Vista), based on Amy Tan's novel, proved to be a rare look at an Asian family in America. In Jessie Nelson's **Corrina, Corrina** (New Line), an inter-racial relationship drama enables Whoopi Goldberg and Ray Liotta to do some heartwarming, occasionally too much of it, was a picture-stealing performance by Tina Majorino as a child trying to get them together. Alex Proyas's **The Crow** (Miramax), a comic book tale about a resurrected avenger, aroused special interest as a result of star Brandon Lee being killed in a mysterious shooting on the set.

Industry News

The most dramatic business story was unquestionably the bitter, intensely personal battle for the acquisition of Paramount Communications, Inc. One suitor was Viacom, Inc., a power in cable television, the other QVC Network, Inc., the home shopping cable network headed by Barry Diller, who left his Paramount studio head post ten years before in a dispute with Paramount's chief executive Marvin S. Davis. Diller came close to upsetting Davis's deal with Viacom, but in the end Viacom defeated QVC and made the deal for some $9.8 billion. The takeover was yet another illustration of how corporate making movies in Hollywood has become.

Ted Turner's Turner Broadcasting System, Inc., bought Robert Shaye's independent New Line Cinema Corporation as well as Castle Rock Entertainment for some $700 million, with Shaye acquiring some $100 million in Turner company stock and continuing, along with partner Michael Lynne, to operate New Line and its culture boutique Fine Line, now with greater resources.

Ben Kingsley and Liam Neeson in SCHINDLER'S LIST

photo: David James

It was also the year in which moviegoing popcorn devotees were warned that oils used in theatre popping were surprisingly high in calories and cholesterol. The resulting furore prompted many exhibitors to find less frightening substitutes.

WILLIAM WOLF is an American film critic and journalist whose work has appear in Cue, New York Magazine, Gannett publications, and a variety of leading newspapers, magazines and journals. He teaches at New York University and is the author of *Landmark Films: The Cinema and Our Century*.

RED ROCK WEST

Script: John Dahl and Rick Dahl. Direction: John Dahl. Photography: Marc Reshovsky. Editing: Scott Chestnut. Music: William Olvis. Players: Nicolas Cage, Dennis Hopper, Lara Flynn Boyle, J.T. Walsh. Produced by Sigurjon Sighvatsson and Steve Golin for Propaganda Films. Released by Roxie Releasing. 98 mins.

Trying to make a *film noir* in the 1990's is no easy trick. But director John Dahl, co-

scripting with is brother Rick Dahl, has succeeded in recapturing the tone of 1940's grade-B *noirs* with style, tension, and irony. *Red Rock West* turns out to be a delightfully entertaining surprise that deserves to be seen and savoured internationally. No mere exercise in nostalgia, this hard-edged film drives ahead on its own oddball power and should amuse audiences who never even heard of the genre.

Nicolas Cage, perfectly cast in the part of Michael Williams, a loner dead broke and searching for an oil-rigging job in Wyoming, stops in the one-horse town of Red Rock. He is mistaken by a bar owner (J.T. Walsh) as the hitman due to fulfil the assignment of killing his wife. Cage takes the money offered, warns the wife, and is soon embroiled in trying to stay alive when the real hitman, menacingly played by Dennis Hopper, arrives and the bar owner, who also turns out to be the sheriff, seeks revenge for the double-cross.

The plot sizzles with the required twists and turns, and Laura Flynn Boyle portrays the wife Suzanne with a nifty combination of trouble and allure.

The tone is on target from the performances to the atmosphere, and the photography provides the dusty, small-town look that offers the perfect setting for the melodramatic events that unfold. Danger lurks incessantly and the hero, in over his head, is required to use his wits and plain dumb luck to extricate himself. The Dahl brothers show unmistakable talent for this sort of fun and merit wide attention.

William Wolf

Lara Flynn Boyle and Nicholas Cage in RED ROCK WEST

GO FISH

Script: Guinevere Turner and Rose Troche. Direction: Rose Troche. Photography: Ann T. Rossetti. Editing: Rose Troche. Music: Brenda Dolan, Jennifer Sharpe, and Scott Aldrich. Players: V.S. Brodie, Turner, T. Wendy McMillan, Migdalia Melendez, Anastasia Sharp. Producers: Troche and Turner. A Samuel Goldwyn release. 87 mins.

As a light-hearted, romantic comedy, the independently produced *Go Fish* has a particular distinction. It's about lesbians and there's no angst about "coming out". These lesbians living in Chicago are already in the open and struggling to find true love just as heterosexuals do. While in the Panorama section of the Berlin International Film Festival, *Go Fish* drew crowds precisely because of its jaunty, intimate glimpse into the daily romantic concerns of the heart, brightened by

humour and its taking-lesbianism-for-granted attitude.

The focal point is the evolving relationship between Max (Guinevere Turner), who longs for a steady companion, and Ely (V.S. Brodie), whose previous relationship is fading. Their mutual friends are determined to get Max and Ely together and match them as a happy couple. Another dimension is that Ely is not only shy but extremely plain-looking. Yet she's attractive to Max, much in the way the looks issue was passed over in the 1955 breakthrough heterosexual film *Marty*.

A drawback to *Go Fish* is not so much its crude, low-budget look under the direction of Rose Troche but the limitations of the script by Troche and Guinevere Turner. The assorted characters are not very interesting as people. Their sole function in the film is their lesbian identity, and one can quickly grow weary of them. Still, the film's breezy

Guinevere Turner and V. S. Brodie in GO FISH

treatment of these personaliies and their lives is likely to be greeted by partisan viewers as a giant step forward towards equal screen treatment and the film assumes importance on that level.

William Wolf

BABYFEVER

Script: Henry Jaglom and Victoria Foyt. Direction: Henry Jaglom. Photography: Hanania Baer. Editing: Henry Jaglom. Players: Victoria Foyt, Frances Fisher, Eric Roberts, Matt Salinger, Elaine Kagan, Dinah Lenney, Zack Norman. Produced by Judith Wolinsky. A Rainbow Film Company release. 110 mins.

The independent, very personal film-maker Henry Jaglom is at it again, this time with a provocative, wide-ranging exploration of what women think about having babies and measuring their attitudes against the ticking biological clock. Jaglom's method is by now familiar. As he did with *Eating*, his film about women and their relationship to food, he has assembled a marvellous group of actresses and put them on camera as a broad assortment of characters talking about their innermost feelings while attending a baby shower. Several personal stories provide a story thread.

One big plus is the casting of Victoria Foyt (Jaglom's wife), who co-authored the script. She has a great presence. The camera loves her face, and she is exceedingly good in the role of a woman who can't decide on being tied down in a relationship and is ambivalent

Victoria Foyt and Matt Salinger in BABYFEVER

about having a baby. Other directors should take note of her ability and looks. There are also pleasures provided by the rest of the lively cast, and Zack Norman is particularly good as a husband who is financially pressed and keeping his desperation from his wife.

Admittedly, some of the talk gets to be repetitious, but that's Jaglom's well-known style. Without the free-flowing form he enjoys there might not be the special impact. Although the lengthy dialogue provides a challenge for subtitlers or dubbers, the feelings and emotions of the women, here the Los Angeles set, should strike a note with many women in many countries, and with men as well.

William Wolf

FRESH

Script and Direction: Boaz Yakin. Photography: Adam Holender. Editing: Dorian Harris. Music: Stewart Copeland. Players: Sean Nelson, Giancarlo Esposito, Samuel L. Jackson, N'Bushe Wright. Produced by Lawrence Bender and Randy Ostrow. A Miramax release, in association with Lumière. 115 mins.

Writer-director Boaz Yakin, although helming his first feature, is experienced in the script department, having done various screenplays in Hollywood, including *The Rookie* for Clint Eastwood. *Fresh* reveals his capability as a sensitive director with a gritty touch and a feeling for the struggle of African-Americans trying to survive in a drug-infested environment. *Fresh*, wisely showcased in the New Directors/New Films series in New York presented by the Museum of Modern Art and the Film Society of Lincoln Center, is a compelling, tough film that is among the best of the year's independent features.

Yakin gets a terrific performance from young Sean Nelson in the title role of a 12-year-old black boy growing up in Brooklyn. His passive but fascinating face conjures up a wealth of inner emotion and wisdom beyond his years as he navigates the tricky course of survival. Instead of an opportunity to pursue a more constructive life in better surroundings, he deals in

Sean Nelson in Boaz Yakin's FRESH

drugs, faces grave danger, and uses his smarts to outfox the local villains.

There's an underlying terror to *Fresh*, thanks to the taut atmosphere Yakin creates through script and direction. The acting and action appear utterly real throughout, and one is quickly caught up in rooting for Fresh to win his battle for survival, and sympathy is created, too, for others trying to beat seemingly impossible odds. *Fresh* stands as a social document for the 1990's as well as an engrossing drama that does credit to Yakin as a talent to watch.

William Wolf

CLERKS

Script and Direction: Kevin Smith. Photography: David Klein. Editing: Smith and Scott Mosier. Music: Scott Angley. Players: Brian O'Halloran, Jeff Anderson, Marilyn Ghigliotti, Lisa Spoonauer. Produced by Mosier and Smith. A Miramax release. 103 mins.

This year's success story of a fledgling film-maker belongs to Kevin Smith, who at 23 teamed with co-producer Scott Mosier to make *Clerks* independently on a budget of about $27,000. The payoff came first with recognition at the Sundance Film Festival and the resulting pickup by Miramax, next with showcasing in the New Directors/New Films series in New York sponsored by the Museum of Modern Art and the Film Society of Lincoln Center, and then with the Critics' Week Jury Prize at Cannes.

Although the film has a primitive look, its raunchy humour, outrageous attitude, and offbeat performances by a small cast make *Clerks* very funny in a winsome, devilish way. Squares may be uncomfortable with much of the dialogue, but there is youthful in-your-face zest and freshness in the depiction of a day's misadventures for two male buddies.

Brian O'Halloran sympathetically plays decent but hapless Dante Hicks, who works in a New Jersey convenience store. Jeff Anderson portrays his friend Randall, who works at an adjacent video store and is the type of pal sure to get a buddy into trouble. Sex is uppermost in their minds, and as the day progresses problems increasingly surface, especially with Veronica (Marilyn Ghigliotti), and Caitlin (Lisa Spoonauer), the two young women in and out of Dante's life.

Smith, both as writer and director, has a wild sense of humour, typically exemplified by sexual confessions, racy dialogue, tripping over a casket at a wake, and even accidental necrophilia. The two pals facing an endless array of challenges are very funny guys in very funny situations. Young would-be film-makers have reason to envy Smith for his talent as well as his good fortune.

William Wolf

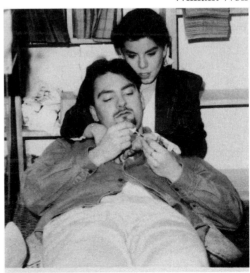

Brian O'Halloran and Marilyn Ghigliotti in Kevin Smith's CLERKS

Useful Addresses

Academy of Motion Picture Arts and Sciences
8949 Wilshire Boulevard
Beverly Hills
California 90211
Tel: (310) 247 3000

American Film Institute
John F. Kennedy Centre for the
Performing Arts
Washington D.C. 20566
Tel: (202) 828 4000
Fax: (202) 659 1970
West Coast Branch:
2021 N. Western Avenue
Los Angeles
California 90027
Tel: (213) 856 7600

Directors Guild of America
7920 Sunset Boulevard
Los Angeles
California 90046
Tel: (310) 289 2000

Independent Feature Project
104 W. 29th Street
New York
N.Y. 10001
Tel: (212) 465 8200
Fax: (212) 465 8525

Independent Feature Project/West
5550 Wilshire Boulevard
Suite 204
Los Angeles
California 90036
Tel: (213) 937 4379
Fax: (213) 937 4038

Motion Picture Association of America (MPAA)
1133 Avenue of the Americas
New York
N.Y. 10036
Tel: (212) 840 6161

Motion Picture Export Association of America
(same as MPAA)

National Association of Theatre Owners (NATO)
116 N. Robertson Boulevard
Suite F
Los Angeles
California

Tel: (310) 652 1093
Fax: (310) 657 4758

Distributors

110 Greene Street
Suite 1102
New York
N.Y. 10012

Buena Vista
(see production listing for Disney)

Castle Hill Productions
1414 Avenue of the Americas
New York
N.Y. 10019
Tel: (212) 888 0080
Fax: (212) 644 0956

Columbia
(see productionn listing)

Concorde New Horizons
(see production listing)

Samuel Goldwyn Company
10203 Santa Monica Boulevard
Los Angeles
California 90067
Tel: (310) 552 2255
Fax: (310) 284 8493

Hemdale
(see production listing)

Kino International
333 West 39th Street
Suite 503
New York
N.Y. 10018
Tel: (212) 629 6880
Fax: (212) 714 0871

MGM
(same address as production listing)

Miramax
375 Greenwich Street
New York
N.Y. 10013
Tel: (212) 941 3800
Fax: (212) 941 3949

New Line
(see production listing for California operations)
Also:
888 Seventh Avenue
New York

N.Y. 10106
Tel: (212) 649 4900
Fax: (212) 649 4966

Fine Line
(A New Line Co.)
(same address as New Line)
Tel: (212) 247 6110
Fax: (212) 956 1942

New Yorker Films
16 W. 61st Street
New York
N.Y. 10023
Tel: (212) 247 6110
Fax: (212) 307 7855

Orion Pictures
(see production listing)

Orion Classics
(same listing as Orion)

Paramount

(see production listing)

Sony Classics
550 Madison Avenue
New York
N.Y. 10022
Tel: (212) 833 8833

TriStar
(see production listing)

Twentieth Century Fox
(see production listing)

Universal
(see production listing)

Warner Bros.
(see production listing)

Producers

8912 Burton Way
Beverly Hills
California 90211
Tel: (310) 247 7800
Fax: (310) 247 7823

Avenue Pictures
11111 Santa Monica Boulevard
Suite 2110
Los Angeles
California 90025
Tel: (310) 996 6800
Fax: (310) 473 4376

Carolco Pictures
8800 Sunset Boulevard
Los Angeles
California 90069
Tel: (213) 850 8800

Castle Rock Pictures
335 North Maple Drive
Suite 135
Beverly Hills
California 90210
Tel: (310) 285 2300
Fax: (310) 285 2345

Columbia Pictures
10202 W. Washington Boulevard
Culver City
California 90232
Tel: (310) 8000
Fax: (310) 1300

Concorde New Horizons Inc.
11600 San Vicente Boulevard
Los Angeles
California 90049
Tel: (310) 820 6733
Fax: (310) 207 6816

Dino De Laurentiis Communications
8670 Wilshire Boulevard
Beverly Hills
California 90211
Tel: (310) 289 6100
Fax: (310) 855 0562

Walt Disney Company
(Walt Disney Pictures, Touchstone Pictures, Hollywood Pictures all released through Buena Vista)
500 South Buena Vista Street
Burbank
California 91521
Tel: (818) 560 1000
Fax: (818) 560 1930

Hemdale
7966 Beverly Boulevard
Los Angeles
California 90048
Tel: (213) 966 3700

Imagine
1925 Century Park East
Suite #2300
Los Angeles
California 90067
Tel: (310) 277 1665
Fax: (310) 785 0107

Woody Harrelson and Juliette Lewis in Oliver Stone's NATURAL BORN KILLERS   *photo: Warners / Sidney Baldwin*

Interscope
10900 Wilshire Boulevard
Suite 1400
Los Angeles
California 90024
Tel: (310) 208 8525
Fax: (310) 208 1764

Largo Entertainment
2029 Century Park E.
Suite 920
Los Angeles
California 90067
Tel: (310) 203 0055
Fax: (310) 203 0254

Metro-Goldwyn-Mayer Inc.
2500 Broadway
Santa Monica
California 90404
Tel: (310) 449 3000

Morgan Creek Productions
4000 Warner Boulevard
Bldg. 76
Burbank
California 91522
Tel: (818) 954 4800
Fax: (818) 954 4811

New Line Cinema
116 North Robertson Boulevard
Suite 200
Los Angeles
California 90048
Tel: (310) 854 5811
Fax: (310) 854 1824

New Regency Productions Inc.
4000 Warner Boulevard
Building 66
Burbank
California 91522
Tel: (818) 954 3044
Fax: (818) 954 3295

Orion Pictures
1888 Century Park East
Los Angeles
California 90067
Tel: (310) 282 0550

Paramount Pictures
5555 Melrose Avenue
Los Angeles
California 90038
Tel: (213) 956 5000
Fax: (213) 956 5555

TOP TEN GROSSING FILMS IN U.S.A. AND CANADA: 1993

	U.S.$
Jurassic Park	337,832,005
The Fugitive	179,257,409
The Firm	158,340,292
Sleepless in Seattle	126,490,134
Aladdin	117,898,051
Indecent Proposal	106,614,059
In the Line of Fire	102,314,283
Mrs. Doubtfire	89,199,899
Cliffhanger	84,049,211
A Few Good Men	78,211,341

Edward A. Pressman Film Corporation
445 North Bedford Drive, Penthouse
Beverly Hills
California 90210
Tel: (310) 271 8383
Fax: (310) 271 9497

TriStar Pictures
The TriStar Building
(A Sony Pictures Entertainment company with rest of address same as Columbia)
Tel: (310) 280 7700

Twentieth Century Fox
10201 West Pico Boulevard
Los Angeles
California 90035
Tel: (310) 277 2211

Universal Pictures
100 Universal City Plaza
Universal City
California 91608
Tel: (818) 777 1000

Warner Bros.
4000 Warner Boulevard
Burbank
California 91522
Tel: (818) 954 6000

Recent and Forthcoming Films

ABOVE THE RIM

Script: Barry Michael Cooper, Jeff Pollack from a story by Pollack, Benny Medina. Dir: Pollack. Phot: Tom Priestly Jr. Players: Duane Martin, Leon Tupac Shakur. Prod: New Line Cinema.

ACE VENTURA, PET DETECTIVE

Script: Jack Bernstein, Tom Shadyac, Jim Carrey, story by Bernstein. Dir: Shadyac. Phot: Julio Macat. Players: Jim Carrey, Courteney Cox, Sean Young, Dan Marino, Udo Kier. Prod: WB.

ACROSS THE MOON

Script: Stephen Schneck. Dir: Lisa Gottlieb. Phot: Andrzej Sekula. Players: Christina Applegate, Elizabeth Pena, James Remar. Prod: Hemdale.

THE AIR UP THERE

Script: Max Apple. Dir: Paul Michael Glaser. Phot: Dick Pope. Players: Kevin Bacon, Charles Gitonga Maina. Prod: Buena Vista.

AIRHEADS

Script: Rich Wilkes. Dir: Michael Lehmann. Phot: John Schwartz-man. Players: Brendan Fraser, Steve Buscemi, Adam Sandler, Chris Farley. Prod: Fox.

ALMA'S RAINBOW

Script and Dir: Ayoka Chenzira. Phot: Ronald K. Gray. Players: Kim Weston-Moran, Victoria Gabriella Platt, Mizan Nunes. Prod: Paradise Plum/Channel 4. (International Sales: Red Carnelian, N.Y.)

AMATEUR

Script and Dir: Hal Hartley. Phot: Michael Spiller. Players: Isabelle Huppert, Martin Donovan, Elina Lowensohn, Damian Young. Prod: UGC/American Playhouse Theatrical Films.

ANDRE

Script: Dana Baratta from the novel "A Field Called Andre" by Harry Goodridge and Lew Dietz. Dir: George Miller. Phot: Thomas Burstyn. Players: Keith Carradine, Tina Majorino, Keith Szarabajka, Chelsea Field. Prod: Paramount.

ANGELS IN THE OUTFIELD

Script: Dorothy Kingsley, George Wells, Holly Goldberg Sloan adapted from the 1951 film. Dir:

William Dear. Phot: Matthew F. Lionetti. Players: Danny Glover, Tony Danza, Brenda Fricker, Christopher Lloyd. Prod: Buena Vista.

ANGIE

Script: Tod Graff from Avra Wing's novel "Angie, I Says". Dir: Martha Coolidge. Phot. (Panavision widescreen): Johnny E. Jensen. Players: Geena Davis, Stephen Rea, James Gandolfini. Prod: Buena Vista/Hollywood Pictures.

APEX

Script: Philip J. Roth, Ronald Schmidt from story by Roth, Gian Carlo Scandiuzzi. Dir: Roth. Phot: Mark W. Gray. Players: Richard Keats, Mitchell Cox, Lisa Ann Russell, Marcus Aurelius. Prod: Republic Pictures.

BAD COMPANY *(tentative title)*

Script: Ros Thomas. Dir: Damian Harris. Phot: Ellen Barkin, Laurence Fishburne, Frank Langella, Michael Beach, David Ogden Stiers. Prod: Buena Vista/Touchstone.

BAD GIRLS

Script: Ken Friedman, Yolande Finch from story by Albert J. Ruddy, Charles Finch, Gray Frederickson. Dir: Jonathan Kaplan. Phot: Ralf Bode. Players: Madeleine Stowe, Mary Stuart Masterson, Andie MacDowell, Drew Barrymore, James LeGros. Prod: Fox.

BARCELONA

Script and Dir: Whit Stillman. Phot: John Thomas. Players: Taylor Nichols, Chris Eigman, Tushka Bergen, Mira Sorvino. Prod: Fine Line.

THE BEANS OF EGYPT, MAINE

Script: Bill Phillips from novel by Carolyn Chute. Dir: Jennifer Warren. Phot: Steven Larner.

Players: Martha Plimpton, Kelly Lynch, Rutger Hauer, Patrick McGraw. Prod: American Playhouse Theatrical Films.

BEING HUMAN

Script and Dir: Bill Forsyth. Phot: Michael Coulter. Players: Robin Williams, John Turturro, Anna Galiena, Vincent D'Onfrio. Prod: WB.

BEVERLY HILL COPS III

Script: Steve E. De Souza. Dir: John Landis. Phot: Mac Ahlberg. Players: Eddie Murphy, Judge Reinhold, Hector Elizondo, Alan Young. Prod: Paramount.

BLACK BEAUTY

Script: Caroline Thompson from Anna Sewell's novel. Dir: Thompson. Phot: Alex Thomson. Players: Sean Bean, David Thewlis, Jim Carter, John McEnery, Eleanor Bron, Peter Cook. Voice of Black Beauty: Alan Cumming. Prod: WB.

BLESSING

Script and Dir: Paul Zehrer. Phot: Stephen Kazmierski. Players: Melora Griffis, Carlin Glynn. Prod: Starr Valley Films production.

BLINK

Script: Dana Stevens. Dir: Michael Apted. Phot: Dante Spinotti. Players: Madeleine Stowe, Aidan Quinn. Prod: New Line Cinema.

BLOWN AWAY

Script: Joe Batteer, John Rice from story by Rice, Batteer, M. Jay Roach. Dir: Stephen Hopkins. Phot: Peter Levy. Players: Jeff Bridges, Tommy Lee Jones, Lloyd Bridges. Prod: MGM.

BLUE CHIPS

Script: Ron Shelton. Dir: William Friedkin. Phot: Tom Priestly Jr. Players: Nick Nolte, Mary

McDonnell, J.T. Walsh. Prod: Paramount.

BLUE TIGER

Script: Joel Soisson, story by Taka Ichise. Dir: Norberto Barba. Phot: Christopher Walling. Players: Virginia Madsen, Toru Nakamura. Prod: First Look Pictures.

A BRONX TALE

Script: Chazz Palminteri from his play. Dir: Robert De Niro. Phot: Reynaldo Villalobos. Players: De Niro, Palminteri. Prod: Savoy/ Penta/Tribeca. (Late 1993 release)

BULLETS OVER BROADWAY

Script: Woody Allen, Doug McGrath. Dir: Allen. Players: Jim Broadbent, John Cusack, Harvey Fierstein, Chazz Palminteri, Mary-Louise Parker, Bob Reiner, Jennifer Tilly, Tracey Ullman, Joe Viterelli, Jack Warden, Dianne Wiest. Prod: Miramax.

CAMILA

Script: Paul Quarrington. Dir: Deepa Mehta. Players: Jessica Tandy, Bridget Fonda, Hume Cronyn, Elias Koteas, Maury Chaykin, Graham Greene. Prod: Miramax.

CAMP NOWHERE

Script: Andrew Kurtzman, Eliot Wald. Dir: Jonathan Prince. Phot: Sandi Sissel. Players: Christopher Lloyd, Wendy Makkena, M. Emmet Walsh. Prod: Buena Vista/Hollywood Pictures.

CANADIAN BACON

Script and Dir: Michael Moore. Players: Rhea Perlman, Alan Alda, Rip Torn, Kevin Pollack, John Candy. Prod: MGM.

THE CHASE

Script and Dir: Adam Rifkin. Phot: Alan Jones. Players: Charlie Sheen, Kristy Swanson. Prod: Fox.

Lisa Bowman in RIVER OF GRASS, directed by Kelly Reichardt

Jennifer MacDonald in CLEAN, SHAVEN, directed by Lodge Kerrigan

CHASERS

Script: Joe Batteer, John Rice, Dan Gilroy from story by Batteer, Rice. Dir: Dennis Hopper. Phot: Uli Steiger. Players: Tom Berenger, Erika Eleniak, William McNamara. Prod: WB.

CITY SLICKERS II: THE LEGEND OF CURLY'S GOLD

Script: Billy Crystal, Lowell Ganz, Babaloo Mandell. Dir: Crystal. Phot: Adrian Biddle. Players: Crystal, Daniel Stern, Jon Lovitz, Jack Palance. Prod: Columbia.

CLEAN SLATE

Script: Robert King. Dir: Mick Jackson. Phot: Andrew Dunn. Players: Dana Carvey, Valeria Golino, James Earl Jones, Michael Gambon. Prod: MGM.

CLEAR AND PRESENT DANGER

Script: Donald Stewart, Steve Zaillian, John Milius from Tom Clancy's novel. Dir: Philip Noyce. Phot: Donald McAlpine. Players: Harrison Ford, Willem Dafoe, Anne Archer, James Earl Jones, Henry Czerny. Prod: Paramount.

THE CLIENT

Script: Akiva Goldsman, Robert Getchell from novel by John Grisham. Dir: Joel Schumacher. Phot: Tony Pierce-Roberts. Players: Susan Sarandon, Tommy Lee Jones, Mary Louise-Parker, Anthony LaPaglia, Brad Renfro. Prod: WB.

COBB

Script and Dir: Ron Shelton. Players: Tommy Lee Jones, Robert Wuhl. Prod: WB.

COLOR OF NIGHT

Script: Matthew Chapman, Billy Ray. Dir: Richard Rush. Players: Bruce Willis, Jane March, Ruben Blades, Lesley Ann Warren, Scott Bakula, Brad Dourif. Prod: Buena Vista/Hollywood Pictures.

COMING OUT UNDER FIRE

Script: Allan Berube, Arthur Dong from Berube's book. Dir: Dong. Phot: Stephen Lighthill. Narrator: Salome Jens. Prod: Deep Focus Prods./Zeitgeist Films. *(Documentary)*

CORRINA, CORRINA

Script and Dir: Jessie Nelson. Players: Whoopi Goldberg, Ray Liotta, Don Ameche, Jennifer Lewis, Tina Majorina. Prod: New Line Cinema.

CROOKLYN

Script: Joie Susannah Lee, Cinque Lee, Spike Lee from story by Joie Susannah Lee. Dir: Spike Lee. Phot. Arthur Jafa. Players: Alfre Woodard, Delroy Lindo, Zelda Harris, David Patrick Kelly, Carlton Williams. Prod: Universal.

THE CROSSING GUARD

Script and Dir: Sean Penn. Phot: Vilmos Zsigmond. Players: Jack Nicholson, Robin Wright, David Morse, Priscilla Barnes, Anjelica Huston. Prod: Miramax.

THE CROW

Script: David J. Schow, John Shirley based on the comic book and strip by James O'Barr. Dir: Alex Proyas. Phot: Dariusz Wolski. Players: Brandon Lee, Ernie Hudson, Michael Wincott. Prod: Miramax/Dimensions.

D2: THE MIGHTY DUCKS

Script: Steven Brill. Dir: Sam Weisman. Phot: Mark Irwin. Players: Emilio Estevez, Kathryn Erbe, Michael Tucker. Prod: Buena Vista.

DEATH AND THE MAIDEN

Script: Ariel Dorfman, Rafael Yglesias from Dorfman's play. Dir: Roman Polanski. Phot: Tonino delli Colli. Players: Sigourney Weaver, Ben Kingsley, Stuart Wilson. Prod: Fine Line/Capitol Films.

DISCLOSURE

Script: Paul Attansio from Michael Crichton's novel. Dir: Barry Levinson. Phot: Tony Pierce-Roberts. Players: Michael Douglas, Demi Moore, Donald Sutherland. Prod: WB.

DOC'S FULL SERVICE

Script: Henry Wideman jr., Eagle Pennell, Kim Henkel. Dir: Pennell. Phot: Jim Barham. Players: Kevin Wiggins, Christine McPeters, James Belcher. Prod: Brazos Film Prods.

DROP SQUAD

Script: David Johnson, Butch Robinson, David Taylor from a story by Taylor. Dir: Johnson. Phot: Ken Kelsch. Players: Eric LaSalle, Vondie Curtis Hall, Ving Rhanes, Vanessa Williams. Prod: Gramercy.

DROP ZONE

Script: Peter Barsocchini, John Bishop, Jeb Stuart. Dir: John Badham. Phot: Roy Wagner. Players: Wesley Snipes, Gary Busey, Yancy Butler, Michael Jeter. Prod: Paramount.

ED WOOD

Script: Scott Alexander, Larry Karaszewski. Dir: Tim Burton. Players: Johnny Depp, Martin Landau, Sarah Jessica Parker, Patricia Arquette, Jeffrey Jones, Bill Murray. Prod: Buena Vista/Touchstone.

EIGHT SECONDS

Script: Monte Merrick. Dir: John G. Alvidsen. Phot: Victor Hammer. Players: Luke Perry, Stephen Baldwin. Prod: New Line Cinema.

ENDLESS SUMMER II

Script: Bruce and Dana Brown. Dir: Bruce Brown. Phot: Mike

Hoover. Narrator: Bruce Brown. Prod: New Line Cinema. *(Documentary)*

EROTIQUE

Script: Lizzie Borden, Susie Bright, Monika Truet, Eddie Ling-Chinng Fong. Dir: Borden, Truet, Clara Law. Phot: Larry Banks, Elfi Mikesch, Arthur Wong. Players: Kamala Lopez-Dawson, Bryan Cranston, Priscilla Barnes, Camilla Soeberg, Tim Lounibos, Hayley Man. Prod: Beyond Films. *(Three-part anthology)*

EXIT TO EDEN

Script: Debra Anelon, Bob Bronner. Dir: Gary Marshall. Players: Dana Delaney, Paul Mercurio, Dan Aykroyd, Rosie O'Donnell. Prod: Savoy.

THE FAVOR

Script: Sara Parriott, Josann McGibbon. Dir: Donald Petrie. Phot: Tim Suhrstedt. Players: Harley Jane Kozak, Elizabeth McGovern, Bill Pullman, Brad Pitt. Prod: Orion.

FEAR OF A BLACK HAT

Script and Dir: Rusty Cundieff. Phot: John Demps, jr. Players: Cundieff, Larry B. Scott, Mark Christopher Lawrence. Prod: Samuel Goldwyn Co./ITC.

FEDERAL HILL

Script and Dir: Michael Corrente. Phot: Richard Crudo. Players: Nicholas Turturro, Anthony De Sando. Prod: Eagle Beach Prods.

THE FIRE THIS TIME

Script and Dir: Randy Holland. Phot: Jurg Walther, David May, Sal Paradise. Narrator: Brooke Adams. Prod: Blacktop Films. *(Documentary)*

THE FLINTSTONES

Script: Tom S. Parker, Jim Jennewein, Steve E. DeSouza from the Hanna-Barbera animated T.V. series. Dir: Brian Levant. Phot: Dean Cundey. Players: John Goodman, Elizabeth Perkins, Rick Moranis, Rosie O'Donnell, Kyle MacLachlan, Elizabeth Taylor. Prod: Universal.

FLOUNDERING

Script and Dir: Peter McCarthy. Phot: Denis Maloney. Players: James LeGros, John Cusack, Ethan Hawke, Liza Zane. Prod: Front Films Inc.

FOREIGN STUDENT

Script: Menno Meyhes. Dir: Eva Sereny. Phot: Franco DiGiacomo. Players: Robin Givens, Marco Hofschneider, Rick Johnson, Charlotte Ross. Prod: Gramercy.

FORREST GUMP

Script: Eric Roth from novel by Winston Groom. Dir: Robert Zemeckis. Phot: Dan Burgess. Players: Tom Hanks, Robin Wright, Gary Sinise, Mykelti Williamson, Sally Field. Prod: Paramount.

FREEDOM ON MY MIND

Script: Script: Michael Chandler. Dir: Connie Field, Marilyn Mulford. Phot: Michael Chinn, Steve Devita, Vicente Franco. Narrator: Ronnie Washington. Prod: Clarity Films Prod./Tara Release. *(Documentary)*

THE GETAWAY

Script: Walter Hill, Amy Jones from novel by Jim Thompson. Dir: Roger Donaldson. Phot: Peter Menzies, jr. Players: Alec Baldwin, Kim Basinger, Michael Madsen, James Woods. Prod: Universal.

A GIFT FROM HEAVEN

Script: David Steen. Dir: Jack Lucarelli. Phot: Steve Yaconellli. Players: Sharon Farrell, Gigi Rice, David Steen, Sarah Trigger. Prod: Hatchwell-Lucarelli Prods.

THE GLASS SHIELD

Script: Charles Burnett based partially on screenplay "One of Us" by Ned Welsh. Dir: Burnett. Phot: Elliot Davis. Players: Michael Boatman, Lori Petly, Ice Cube, Michael Ironside. Prod: Ciby 2000.

GOLDEN GATE

Script: David Henry Hwang. Dir: John Madden. Phot: Bobby Bukowski. Players: Matt Dillon, Joan Chen, Bruno Kirby. Prod: Samuel Goldwyn Co.

A GOOD MAN IN AFRICA

Script: William Boyd from his novel. Dir: Bruce Beresford. Phot: Andrzej Bartkowiak. Players: Colin Friels, Sean Connery, John Lithgow, Diana Rigg, Lou Gossett, jr, Joanne Whalley-Kilmer, Sarah-Jane Fenton. Prod: Gramercy.

GREEDY

Script: Lowell Ganz, Babaloo Mandel. Dir: Jonathan Lynn. Phot: Gabriel Beristain. Players: Michael J. Fox, Kirk Douglas, Nancy Travis, Olivia d'Abo. Prod: Universal.

GUARDING TESS

Script: Hugh Wilson, Peter Torokvei. Dir: Wilson. Phot: Brian Reynolds. Players: Shirley MacLaine, Nicolas Cage, Austin Pendleton, Edward Albert, Richard Griffiths. Prod: TriStar/Channel Prods.

GUNMEN

Script: Stephen Sommers. Dir: Deran Sarafian. Phot: Hiro Narita. Players: Christopher Lambert, Mario Van Peebles, Denis Leary, Patrick Stewart. Prod: Miramax/Dimension Films.

HANS CHRISTIAN ANDERSEN'S THUMBELINA

Script: Don Bluth. Dir: Bluth, Gary

Keanu Reeves in Jan De Bont's SPEED
photo: Fox/Richard Foreman

Tom Waits and Lily Tomlin in Robert Altman's SHORT
CUTS, Golden Lion Winner at Venice 1993

Goldman. Voices: Jodi Benson, Carol Channing, Charo, Gino Conforti, Barbara Cook, June Foray, Gilbert Gottfried, John Hurt. Prod: WB. *(Animated)*

HEAVEN'S PRISONERS

Script: Harley Peyton, Scott Frank. Dir: Phil Joanou. Players: Alec Baldwin, Mary Stuart Masterson, Kelly Lynch, Eric Roberts. Prod: Savoy.

HEAVYWEIGHTS

Script: Judd Apatow and Steven Brill. Dir: Brill. Players: Aaron Schwartz, Shaun Weiss. Prod: Buena Vista/Caravan Pic.

HIGH SCHOOL II

Dir: Frederick Wiseman. Phot: John Davey. Prod: Zipporah Films. *(Documentary)*

HOLY MATRIMONY

Script: David Weisberg, Douglas S. Cook. Dir: Leonard Nimoy. Phot: Bobby Bukowski. Players: Patricia Arquette, Joseph Gordon-Levitt, Armin Mueller-Stahl, Tate Donovan. Prod: Buena Vista/Hollywood Pictures.

HOUSE PARTY 3

Script: Takashi Bufford from a story by David Toney based on characters created by Reginald Hudlin. Dir: Eric Meza. Phot: Anghel Decca. Players: Christopher Reid, Christopher

Martin, David Edwards. Prod: New Line Cinema.

HOUSEHOLD SAINTS

Script: Nancy Savoca, Richard Guay from Francine Prise's novel. Dir: Savoca. Phot: Bobby Bukowski. Players: Tracey Ullman, Vincent D'Onfrio, Lili Taylor, Judith Malina. Prod: Fine Line. *(Late 1993 release)*

I LIKE IT LIKE THAT

Script and Dir: Darnell Martin. Phot: Alexander Gruszynski. Players: Lauren Velez, Jon Seda, Thomas Melly, Griffin Dunne, Rita Moreno. Prod: Columbia.

I.Q.

Script: Andy Breckman, Michael Leeson, Michael Goldenberg. Dir: Fred Schepisi. Phot: Ian Baker. Players: Meg Ryan, Tim Robbins, Walther Matthau. Prod: Paramount.

IMMORTAL BELOVED

Script and Dir: Bernard Rose. Phot: Peter Suschitzky. Players: Gary Oldman, Jeroen Krabbe, Valeria Golino, Isabella Rossellini, Johanna Ter Steege. Prod: Columbia.

THE INKWELL

Script: Tom Ricomstranza, Paris Qualles. Dir: Matty Rich. Phot: John L. Demps, jr. Players: Larenz Tate, Joe Morton, Suzanne

Douglas, Glynn Turman. Prod: Buena Vista.

INSIDE THE GOLDMINE

Script: Josh Evans, Uri Zignelboim. Dir: Evans. Phot: Fernando Aguilles. Players: Alan Marshall, Evans, Alicia Tully Jensen, Gary Chasen. Prod. Cineville.

IRON WILL

Script: John Michael Hayes, Djordje Millicević, Jeff Arch. Dir: Charles Haid. Phot: William Wages. Players: MacKenzie Astin, Kevin Spacey, David Ogden Stiers. Prod: Buena Vista.

IT COULD HAPPEN TO YOU

Script: Jane Anderson. Dir: Andrew Bergman. Phot: Caleb Deschanel. Players: Nicolas Cage, Bridget Fonda, Rosie Perez, Wendell Pierce. Prod: Tristar.

IT HAPPENED IN PARADISE

Script and Dir: George Gallo. Phot: Jack Green. Players: Nicolas Cage, Jon Lovitz, Dana Carvey. Prod: Fox.

IT RUNS IN THE FAMILY

Script: Jean Shepherd, Leigh Brown, Bob Clark. Dir: Clark. Players: Charles Crodin, Kieran Culkin, Mary Steenburgen. Prod: MGM.

IT'S PAT

Script: Jim Emerson, Stephen Hibbert, Julia Sweeney based on characters created by Sweeney. Dir: Adam Bernstein. Players: Sweeney, David Foley. Prod: Buena Vista/Touchstone Pictures.

JASON'S LYRIC

Script: Bobby Smith, jr. Dir: Doug McHenry. Players: Allen Payne, Forest Whitaker, Jada Pinkett, Bokeem Wood Pine. Prod: Grammercy.

JIMMY HOLLYWOOD

Script and Dir: Barry Levinson. Phot: Peter Sova. Players: Joe Pesci, Christian Slater, Victoria Abril. Prod: Paramount.

JUNIOR

Script: Chris Conrad, Kevin Wade. Dir: Ivan Reitman. Phot: Adam Greenberg. Players: Arnold Schwarzenegger, Danny De Vito, Emma Thompson, Pamela Reed, Frank Langella. Prod: Universal.

KILLER

Script: Gordon Melbourne based on Mark Malone's story. Dir: Malone. Phot: Tobias Schlissler. Players: Anthony LaPaglia, Mimi Rogers. Prod: Keystone Films/Worldvision.

KILLING ZOE

Script and Dir: Roger Avary. Phot: Tom Richmond. Players: Eric Stolz, Julie Delpy, Jean-Hugues Anglade, Gary Kemp. Prod: Davis Film Prods. (International Sales: PFG).

LASSIE

Script: Matthew Jacobs, Gary Ross, Elizabeth Anderson based upon the character created by Eric Knight. Dir: Daniel Petrie. Phot: Kenneth MacMillan. Players: Thomas Guiry, Helen Slater, Jon Tenney, Brittany Boyd, Frederic Forrest. Prod: Paramount.

THE LAST SEDUCTION

Script: Steve Barancik. Dir: John Dahl. Phot: Jeffrey Jur. Players: Linda Fiorentino, Peter Berg, Bill Pullman, J.T. Walsh, Bill Nunn. Prod: ITC Entertainment Group.

LEGENDS OF THE FALL

Script: Susan Shilliday, Bill Wittliff from a novella by Jim Harrison. Players: Brad Pitt, Anthony Hopkins, Aidan Quinn, Julia Ormond. Prod: TriStar.

LEON *(tentative title)*

Script and Dir: Luc Besson. Players: Jean Reno, Gary Oldman, Natalie Portman, Danny Aiello. Prod: Columbia.

LIFE SAVERS

Script: Nora Ephron, Delia Ephron from the French film "Le Père Noël est une Ordure". Dir: Nora Ephron. Players: Steve Martin, Kadeem Hardison. Prod: TriStar.

LIFE'S TOO GOOD

Script and Dir: Hilary Weisman. Phot: Frank Coleman. Players: Claudia Arenas, Michael Medico, Marjorie Burren. Prod: Kind Stranger Production.

THE LION KING

Script: Irene Mecchi, Jonathan Roberts, Linda Woodverton. Dir: Roger Allers, Rob Minkoff. Songs by Tim Rice (lyrics) and Elton John (music). Voices: Rowan Atkinson, Matthew Broderick, Niketa Calame, Jim Cummings, Whoopi Goldberg, Robert Guillaume, Jeremy Irons, James Earl Jones. Prod: Buena Vista. *(Animated)*.

LITTLE BUDDHA

Script: Mark Peploe, Rudy Wurlitzer from story by Bernardo Bertolucci. Dir: Bertolucci. Phot: Vittorio Storaro. Players: Keanu Reeves, Ying Ruocheng, Chris Isaak, Bridget Fonda. Prod: Miramax/Ciby 2000.

THE LITTLE RASCALS

Script: Paul Guay, Steve Mazur, Penelope Spheeris. Dir: Spheeris. Phot: Richard Bowan. Players: Travis Tedford, Bug Hall, Kevin Jamal Woods, Ross Bagley, Zachary Mabry. Prod: Universal.

LITTLE WOMEN

Script: Robin Swicord from Louisa May Alcott's novel. Dir: Gillian Armstrong. Phot: Geoffrey Simpson. Players: Winona Ryder, Gabriel Byrne, Trini Alvarado, Samantha Mathis, Kirsten Dunst, Claire Danes, John Neville, Susan Sarandon. Prod: Columbia.

LOSING ISIAH

Script: Naomi Foner from Seth Margolis's novel. Dir: Steve Gyllenhaal. Phot: Andrzej Bartkowiak. Players: Jessica Lange, Halle Berry. Prod: Paramount.

MARY SHELLEY'S FRANKENSTEIN

Script: Steph Lady, Frank Darabont from the novel. Dir: Kenneth Branagh. Players: Robert De Niro, Branagh, Helena Bonham Carter, Tom Hulce, Aidan Quinn, John Cleese, Ian Holm. Prod: TriStar.

THE MASK

Script: Mike Werb. Dir: Chuck Russell. Players: Jim Carrey, Cameron Diaz, Richard Jeni, Amy Yasbeck, Peter Riegert. Prod: New Line Cinema.

MAVERICK

Script: William Goldman from the T.V. show created by Roy Huggins. Dir: Richard Donner.

Phot: Vilmos Zsigmond. Players: Mel Gibson, Jodie Foster, James Garner, Graham Greene, James Coburn, Alfred Molina. Prod: WB.

MEN LIE

Script and Dir: John Andrew Gallagher. Phot: Bob Lechterman. Players: Doug DeLuca, Ellia Thompson, Frank Vincent. Prod: Lexington Pictures.

A MILLION TO JUAN

Script: Francisca Matos, Robert Grasmere based on a story by Mark Twain and characters inspired by Paul Rodriguez. Dir: Rodriguez. Phot: Bruce Johnson. Players: Rodriguez, Polly Draper, Pepe Serna. Prod: Samuel Goldwyn Co.

MILK MONEY

Dir: Richard Benjamin. Players: Melanie Griffith, Ed Harris, Malcolm McDowell. Prod: Paramount.

MINOTAUR

Script and Dir: Dan McCormack. Phot: Dan Gillham. Players: Michael Faella, Ricky Aiello, Holly Chant. Prod: RPFL Prod.

MIRACLE ON 34TH STREET

Script: John Hughes. Dir: Les Mayfield. Phot: Julio Macat. Players: Richard Attenborough, Elizabeth Perkins, Dylan McDermott. Prod: Fox.

MONKEY TROUBLE

Script: Franco Amurri, Stu Krieger. Dir: Amurri. Phot: Luciano Tavoli. Players: "Finster", Thora Birch, Harvey Keitel, Mimi Rogers. Prod: New Line Cinema.

MRS. PARKER AND THE VICIOUS CIRCLE

Script: Alan Rudolph, Randy Sue Coburn. Dir: Rudolph. Phot: Jan

Kiesser. Players: Jennifer Jason Leigh, Matthew Broderick, Campbell Scott, Peter Gallagher, Jennifer Beals, Andrew McCarthy, Wallace Shawn. Prod: Fine Line/Miramax.

MY FATHER, THE HERO

Script: Francis Veber, Charlie Peters from "Mon Père, ce héros" by Gerard Lauzier. Dir: Steve Miner. Phot: Daryn Okada. Players: Gérard Depardieu, Katherine Heigil, Dalton James, Lauren Hutton. Prod: Buena Vista/Touchstone.

MY GIRL 2

Script: Janet Kovalci based on characters created by Laurice Elehwany. Dir: Howard Zieff. Phot: Paul Elliott. Players: Dan Aykroyd, Jamie Lee Curtis, Anna Chlumsky, Austin O'Brien. Prod: Columbia.

NAKED GUN 33 1/3: THE FINAL INSULT

Script: Pat Proft, David Zucker, Robert LeCash. Dir: Peter Segal. Phot: Robert Stevens. Players: Leslie Nielsen, Priscilla Presley, George Kennedy, O.J. Simpson, Fred Ward, Ellen Greene. Prod: Paramount.

NATURAL BORN KILLERS

Script: David Veloz, Richard Rutarski, Oliver Stone. Dir: Stone. Phot: Robert Richardson. Players: Woody Harrelson, Juliette Lewis, Tommy Lee Jones, Robert Downey, jr. Prod: WB.

NELL

Script: Script: William Nicholson from the play "Idioglossia" by Mark Handley. Dir: Michael Apted. Phot: Dante Spinotti. Players: Jodie Foster, Liam Neeson, Natasha Richardson. Prod: Fox.

THE NEW AGE

Script and Dir: Michael Tolkin.

Players: Peter Weller, Judy Davis, Adam West. Prod: WB.

NIGHT OF THE DEMONS 2

Script: Joe Augustyn, story by James Penzi, Augustyn. Dir: Brian Trenchard-Smith. Phot: David Lewis. Players: Cristi Harris, Bobby Jacoby, Jennifer Rhodes. Prod: Republic.

NO ESCAPE

Script: Michael Gaylin, Joel Gross from Richard Harley's book "The Penal Colony". Dir: Martin Campbell. Phot: Phil Meheux. Players: Ray Liotta, Lance Henriksen, Stuart Wilson. Prod: Savoy Pictures.

NOBODY'S FOOL

Script: Robert Benton from John Russo's book. Dir: Benton. Players: Paul Newman, Melanie Griffith, Jessica Tandy. Prod: Paramount.

NORTH

Script: Alan Zweibel, Andrew Scheinman from novel by Zweibel. Dir: Rob Reiner. Phot: Adam Greenberg. Players: Elijah Wood, Julia Louis-Dreyfus, Jason Alexander. Prod: Columbia/New Line.

NOSTRADAMUS

Script: Knut Boeser, Piers Ashworth from story by Boeser, Roger Christian. Dir: Christian. Players: Tcheky Karyo, F. Murray Abraham, Rutger Hauer, Amanda Plummer, Julia Ormond. Prod: Orion Classics.

ON DEADLY GROUND

Script: Ed Horowitz, Robin U. Rossin. Dir: Steven Seagal. Phot: Ric Waite. Players: Seagal, Michael Caine. Prod: WB.

ONLY YOU

Script: Diane Drake. Dir: Norman Jewison. Players: Marisa Tomei,

Robert Downey, jr., Bonnie Hunt, Fisher Stevens. Prod: TriStar.

OUT OF SIGHT

Dir: David Sutherland. Phot: Joe Seamans, A.J. Dimaculangan. Prod: WGBH Educational Foundation. *(Documentary)*.

PCU

Script: Adam Leff, Zak Penn. Dir: Hart Bochner. Phot: Reynoldo Villalobos. Players: Jeremy Piven, Chris Young, Jon Faureau, David Spade. Prod: Fox.

THE PAGEMASTER

Script: David Kirschner, David Casci, Ernie Contreras. Dir: Maurice Hunt (animation), Joe Johnston (live action). Players: Macauley Culkin, Christopher Lloyd, Ed Begley, jr. Voices: Whoopi Goldberg, Patrick Stewart, Leonard Nimoy. Prod: Fox.

THE PAPER

Script: David Koepp, Stephen Koepp. Dir: Ron Howard. Phot: John Seale. Players: Michael Keaton, Robert Duvall, Glenn Close, Marisa Tomei, Randy Quaid, Jason Robards. Prod: Universal.

PAUL BOWLES: THE COMPLETE OUTSIDER

Dir: Catherine Warnow, Regina Weinreich. Phot: Burleigh Wartes. Music and Narration: Paul Bowles. Prod: First Run Features. *(Documentary)*.

THE PEREZ FAMILY

Script: Robin Swicord. Dir: Mira Nair. Players: Anjelica Huston, Marisa Tomei, Alfredo Molina, Chazz Palminteri. Prod: The Samuel Goldwyn Co.

PICTURE BRIDE

Script: Kayo Hatta, Mari Hatta, Diane Mark. Dir: Kayo Hatta. Phot: Claudio Rocha. Players:

Youki Kudoh, Akira Takayama, Tamlyn Tomita, Toshiro Mifune. Prod: Miramax/Cecile Co.

PONTIAC MAN

Dir: Peter Medak. Players: Ted Danson, Mary Steenburgen. Prod: Paramount.

PRET-A-PORTER

Script: Robert Altman, Barbara Shulgasser. Dir: Altman. Players: Danny Aiello, Anouk Aimée, Lauren Bacall, Michel Blanc, Anne Canovas, Jean-Pierre Cassel, Rossy De Palma, Richard E. Grant, Rupert Everett, Kasia Figura, Teri Garr, Linda Hunt, Sally Kellerman, Sophia Loren, Lyle Lovett, Marcello Mastroianni, Stephen Rea, Tim Robbins, Julia Roberts, Jean Rochefort, Lili Taylor, Forest Whitaker. Prod: Miramax.

PRINCESS CARABOO

Script: Michael Austin, John Wells. Dir: Austin. Players: Phoebe Cates, Wendy Hughes, Kevin Kline, John Lithgow, Stephen Rea. Prod: TriStar.

PULP FICTION

Script: Quentin Tarantino from stories by Tarantino, Roger Avary. Dir: Tarantino. Phot: Andrzej Sekula. Players: John Travolta, Samuel L. Jackson, Uma Thurman, Harvey Keitel, Tim Roth, Amanda Plummer, Ving Rhanes, Christopher Walken, Bruce Willis. Prod: Miramax. (International Sales: BAC Films, Paris).

QUIZ SHOW

Script: Paul Attanasio based on Richard N. Goodwin's book "Remembering America: A Voice from the Sixties". Dir: Robert Redford. Players: John Turturro, Rob Morrow, Ralph Fiennes, David Paymer, Paul Scofield. Prod: Buena Vista/Hollywood Pic.

RAPA NUI

Script: Kevin Reynolds, Tim Rose Price from a story by Reynolds. Dir: Reynolds. Phot: Stephen Windom. Players: Jason Scott Lee, Esai Morales, Sandrine Holt. Prod: WB/Hayden Films/Majestic Films.

THE RADIOLAND MURDERS

Dir: Mel Smith. Players: Brian Benben, Mary Stuart Masterson, Ned Beatty, Jeffrey Tambor, Bobcat Goldthwait. Prod: Universal.

RAVE REVIEW

Script and Dir: Jeff Seymour. Phot: Richard Crudo. Players: Seymour, Carmen Argenziano, Ed Begley, jr. Prod: Wildebeest Co.

REALITY BITES

Script: Helen Childress. Dir: Ben Stiller. Phot: Emmanuel Lubezki. Players: Winona Ryder, Ethan Hawke, Stiller. Prod: Universal.

THE REF

Script: Richard LaGravanese, Marie Weiss from story by Weiss. Dir: Ted Demme. Phot: Adam Kimmel. Players: Denis Leary, Judy Davis, Kevin Spacey, Robert J. Steinmiller, jr., Glynis Johns. Prod: Buena Vista/Touchstone.

RENAISSANCE MAN

Script: Jim Burnstein. Dir: Penny Marshall. Phot: Adam Greenberg. Players: Danny De Vito, Gregory Hines. Prod: Buena Vista.

RESTORATION

Script: Rupert Walters. Dir: Michael Hoffman. Players: Robert Downey, jr., Meg Ryan, Sam Neill, David Thewlis, Polly Walker, Ian McKellen, Hugh Grant. Prod: Miramax.

RICHIE RICH

Script: Tom S. Parker, Jim

Jennewein. Dir: Donald Petrie. Phot: Don Burgess. Players: Macaulay Culkin, John Larroquette. Prod: WB.

THE RIVER WILD

Script: Denis O'Neil. Dir: Curtis Hanson. Players: Meryl Streep, Kevin Bacon, David Straithairn, Joseph Mazzello, John C. Reilly. Prod: Universal.

ROBERT HEINLEIN'S THE PUPPET MASTERS

Script: Ted Elliott, Terry Rossio, David S. Goyer from the novel. Dir: Stuart Orme. Players: Donald Sutherland, Eric Thal, Julie Warner, Keith David, Will Paton. Prod: Buena Vista/Hollywood Pictures.

THE ROAD TO WELLVILLE

Script and Dir: Alan Parker. Phot: Peter Biziou. Players: Anthony Hopkins, Bridget Fonda, Matthew Broderick, John Cussack, Dana Carvey. Prod: Columbia.

S.F.W.

Script and Dir: Jeffery Levy. Phot: Peter Deming. Players: Stephen Dorff, Reese Wither-spoon, Jack Noseworthy, Jake Busey. Prod: Grammercy.

THE SANTA CLAUSE (tentative title)

Script: Len Benvenuti, Steve Rudnick, Janet Brownell. Dir: John Pasquin. Players: Tim Allen, Judge Reinhold, Wendy Crewson. Prod: Buena Vista/Hollywood Pictures.

THE SCOUT

Script: Andrew Bergman, Monica Johnson. Dir: Michael Ritchie. Phot: Laszlo Kovacs. Players: Albert Brooks, Brendan Fraser. Prod: Fox.

THE SECOND BEST

Script: David Cook. Dir: Chris

Menges. Players: William Hurt, John Hurt, Jane Horries, Keith Allen. Prod: WB.

SECOND COUSIN, ONCE REMOVED

Script: John Shorney, John McColpin, Pete Ellis, Dave Busan. Dir: Shorney. Phot: Roger Dean. Players: Ellis, Robyn Sands, Kevin Kildow, Kim Little. Prod: Intrepid Ventures Group.

THE SECRET OF ROAN INISH

Script: John Sayles from Rosalie K. Fry's novel "Secret of the Ron Mor Skerry". Dir: Sayles. Phot: Haskell Wexler. Players: Mick Lally, Eileen Colgan, Jeni Courtney. Prod: Jones Entertainment Group.

SERIAL MOM

Script and Dir: John Waters. Phot: Robert Stevens. Players: Kathleen Turner, Sam Waterston, Ricki Lane, Matthew Lillard, Mink Stole, Traci Lords, Patricia Hearst. Prod: Savoy.

THE SHADOW

Script: David Koepp based on Advance Magazine Publishers Inc's character. Dir: Russell Mulcahy. Phot: Stephen H. Burum. Players: Alec Baldwin, John Lone, Penelope Ann Miller, Peter Boyle, Ian McKellen, Tim Curry. Prod: Universal.

THE SHAWSHANK REDEMPTION

Script and Dir: Frank Darabont. Phot: Roger Deakins. Players: Tim Robbins, Morgan Freeman, Gil Bellows, James Whitmore, William Sadler. Prod: Columbia.

SILENT FALL

Script: Akiza Goldman. Dir: Bruce Beresford. Players: Richard Dreyfuss, Linda Hamilton, John Lithgow, J.T. Walsh. Prod: WB.

A SIMPLE TWIST OF FATE

Script: Steve Martin. Dir: Gillies MacKinnon. Players: Martin, Gabriel Byrne, Catherine O'Hara, Stephen Baldwin. Prod: Buena Vista/Touchstone Pictures.

SPANKING THE MONKEY

Script and Dir: David O. Russell. Phot: Michael Mayers. Players: Jeremy Davies, Alberta Watson, Benjamin Hendrickson, Carla Gallo. Prod: Fine Line/Buckeye Communications.

THE SPECIALIST

Script: Alexandra Seros. Dir: Luis Llosa. Players: Sylvester Stallone, Sharon Stone, James Woods, Eric Roberts. Prod: WB.

SPEECHLESS

Script: Robert King. Dir: Ron Underwood. Phot: Don Peterman. Players: Michael Keaton, Geena Davis, Christopher Reeve, Bonnie Bedelia, Ernie Hudson. Prod: MGM.

SPEED

Script: Graham Yost. Dir: Jan De Bont. Phot: Andzrej Bartkowiak. Players: Keanu Reeves, Dennis Hopper, Sandra Bullock, Joe Morton, Jeff Daniels. Prod: Fox.

SQUANTO: A WARRIOR'S TALE

Script: Darlene Craviotto. Dir: Xavier Koller. Players: Adam Beach, Eric Schweig, Michael Gambon, Nathaniel Parker, Alex Norton, Sheldon Peters Wolfchild, Stuart Pankin, Donal Donnelly, Mandy Patinkin. Prod: Buena Vista.

STAR TREK: GENERATIONS

Script: Ron Moore, Brannon Braga. Dir: David Carson. Phot: John Alonzo. Players: Patrick Stewart, William Shatner, Jonathan Frakes, Brent Spiner. Prod: Paramount.

STARGATE

Script: Roland Emmerich, Dean Devlin. Dir: Emmerich. Players: Kurt Russell, James Spader, Jaye Davidson. Prod: MGM.

STREET FIGHTER

Script and Dir: Stephen E. DeSouza. Players: Jean-Claude Van Damme, Raul Julia, Wes Studi. Prod: Universal.

TERMINAL VELOCITY

Script: David Twohy. Dir: Deran Sarafian. Phot: Oliver Wood. Players: Charlie Sheen, Nastassja Kinski, James Gandolfini, Christopher McDonald. Prod: Buena Vista/Touchstone Pictures.

THERE GOES MY BABY

Script and Dir: Floyd Mutrux. Phot: William A. Fraker. Players: Dermot Mulroney, Rick Schroeder, Kelli Williams. Prod: Orion.

THREESOME

Script and Dir: Andrew Fleming. Phot: Alexander Graszynski. Players: Lara Flynn Boyle, Stephen Baldwin, Josh Charles. Prod: TriStar.

TIMECOP

Script: Mark Verheiden. Dir: Peter Hyams. Players: Jean-Claude Van Damme, Ron Silver, Mia Sara, Gloria Reuben. Prod: Universal.

TOMBSTONE

Script: Kevin Jarre. Dir: George Cosmatos. Phot: William A. Fraker. Players: Kurt Russell, Val Kilmer, Sam Elliott, Powers Booth. Prod: Buena Vista/Hollywood Pictures.

TRIAL BY JURY

Script: Heywood Gould, Jordan Katz. Dir: Gould. Players: Joanne Whalley-Kilmer, William Hurt, Gabriel Byrne, Armand Assante. Prod: WB.

TRUE LIES

Script and Dir: James Cameron. Phot: Russell Carpenter. Players: Arnold Schwarzenegger, Jamie Lee Curtis, Tom Arnold, Bill Paxton. Prod: Fox.

UMBRELLAS

Dir: Henry Corra, Grahame Weinbren, Albert Maysles. Phot: Maysles, Robert Richman, Robert Leacock, Gary Stelle, Don Lenzer, Richard Pearce. Prod: Maysles Film Prods.

VANYA ON 42ND STREET

Script: David Mamet from Anton Chekhov's "Uncle Vanya". Dir: Louis Malle. Phot: Declan Quinn. Players: Juliane Moore, Brooke Smith, Wallace Shawn. Prod: Sony Classics.

THE WAR

Script: Kathy McWorter. Dir: Jon Avnet. Phot: Geoffrey Simpson. Players: Kevin Costner, Elijah Wood, Mare Winningham, Lexi Randall. Prod: Universal.

WES CRAVEN'S NEW NIGHTMARE

Script and Dir: Wes Craven. Players: Robert Englund, Heather Langenkamp, John Saxon, Miko Hughes. Prod: New Line Cinema.

WHAT HAPPENED WAS ...

Script: Tom Noonan from his play. Dir: Noonan. Phot: Joe DeSalvo. Players: Noonan, Karen Sillas. Prod: Samuel Goldwyn Co.

WHEN A MAN LOVES A WOMAN

Script: Ronald Bass, Al Franken. Dir: Luis Mandoki. Phot: Lajos Koltai. Players: Andy Garcia, Meg Ryan, Lauren Tom, Tina Majorino. Prod: Buena Vista/Touchstone.

WITH HONORS

Script: William Mastrosimone. Dir: Alex Keshishian. Phot: Sven Nykvist. Players: Joe Pesci, Brendan Fraiser, Moira Kelly. Prod: WB.

WOLF

Script: Jim Harrison, Wesley Strick. Dir: Mike Nichols. Phot: Giuseppe Rotunno. Players: Jack Nicholson, Michelle Pfeiffer, James Spader, Kate Nelligan, Christopher Plummer. Prod: Columbia.

WYATT EARP

Script: Dan Gordon, Lawrence Kasdan. Dir: Kasdan. Phot: Owen Roizman. Players: Kevin Costner, Dennis Quaid, Gene Hackman, Jeff Fahey, Bill Pullman, Isabella Rossellini. Prod: WB.

THE YELLOW DOG

Script and Dir: Phillip Borsos. Phot: James Gardner. Players: Bruce Davison, Mimi Rogers, Jesse Bradford, Tom Bower. Prod: Fox.

YOU SO CRAZY

Dir: Thomas Schlamme. Phot: Arthur Albert. Player: Martin Lawrence. Prod: Miramax/HBO Independent Prods. *(Concert comedy)*.

ZIMBABWE

Judy
Kendall

Zimbabwe is rapidly learning to hold its own in the African film industry. Until very recently, it was known in the film world only for its small but steady production of documentaries on music, culture and political issues – a situation forced on local film-makers because of the very real financial restrictions imposed on them.

Feature films, of which there were many, were always made by foreign film companies, lured to Zimbabwe by the stunning scenery, unequalled temperate weather, perfect light conditions and, not insignificantly, cheap labour costs in a country that was starved of hard currency. However, the Zimbabweans have learnt fast. In the past there was a great deal of frustration. Zimbabweans watched as leading black roles went to American actors, higher directorial positions were filled by overseas people, and even carpenters, who abound in Zimbabwe, were flown in from the U.K. Actors, directors, producers, set designers who hitherto had depended for their rather precarious livelihood on foreign film-makers, including such giants as Attenborough with *Cry Freedom* are now beginning to have more of a participatory role.

This change began with Michael Raeburn's locally made and cast feature film *JIT* in 1991. *JIT* is a musical comedy set in a Zimbabwean township with a very strong soundtrack replete with internationally known Zimbabwean musicians and acting by Oliver Mtukudzi, a popular Zimbabwean musician. It is a first for Zimbabwe and all credit is due to Raeburn for that. Raeburn managed to circumvent the perennial problem of persuading foreign investors to finance a totally Zimbabwean film that lacked any international names by raising the money locally. Although *JIT* was not as successful as Raeburn had hoped in the all-important overseas market, it was the first Zimbabwean-made film to break into the commercial cinema circuit in Zimbabwe, and heralded a new direction for Zimbabwean film-makers.

JIT was followed in 1992 by **Neria**, directed by Godwin Mawuru and John Riber, also starring Mtukudzi in a major acting role this time. *Neria* was scripted by Tsitsi Dangarembga (winner of the Commonwealth Writers award in 1989) and Mawuru. The story of a widow left destitute because of the abuse of a traditional custom by grasping relatives is earnest, and at times carries a heavy educational tone, but it carries forward the important step made by *JIT*. *Neria* was hugely successful in Zimbabwe, competing with *Rambo* at the box-office – and won the 1992 OAU award at the Carthage film festival in Algiers.

Inspired by *JIT*, UNESCO set up a talent search operation in Zimbabwe, offering a three-year directing and writing programme in an effort to encourage local film-making. The venture seems to be paying off. One can still trace the roots of a strong documentary background in Zimbabwean feature films, perhaps because this has traditionally been an easier route to obtaining finance. This at times makes the films rather heavy viewing. Inevitably, music plays an important role – hardly surprising when one considers that music has in the past been one of Zimbabwe's most successful artistic exports. And, as always, the eyes of Zimbabwean directors are firmly fixed on the foreign markets. The mood is optimistic. Isaac Mabhikwa, director of *More Time*, comments in the Zimbabwean magazine *Horizon* on the American market: "There is still not much information about African cinema, so that the new films they get are so fresh, appetising and appealing to them," and of other markets, "New markets are gradually opening up throughout Africa."

New Feature Films

More Time is a film about teenage love in the time of AIDS, and about growing up in an African township. It is scripted by UNESCO film course graduate Lazarus Fungurani in collaboration with Andrew Whalley. It was shot entirely on location in Mbare and Highfield townships of Harare in an old asbestos and brick township home, with the soundtrack played by popular Zimbabwean musician, Lovemore Majaivana. It has already won an award for Mabhikwa, its first-time director, from the Catholic Bishops Conference in Italy for a socially relevant film about "keeping death and disease at bay." It has run in a number of African countries and was the opening film in the New York African film festival in April 1994.

I **Am the Future** is the biggest locally produced feature film so far. It is directed by Godwin Mawuru and produced by Kubi Chaza-Indi, one of Zimbabwe's few women producers. Premiered at the end of May 1994 it was 18 months in the making. The script for *I Am the Future* is written by Charles Mungoshi, a beneficiary of UNESCO screenwriting training and joint winner of the NOMA award in 1992 and of the Commonwealth Writers Prize. The film tells the story of a young girl and her brother and sister. After their village home is torched by bandits they are left to survive refugee camps, inhospitable relatives and the unforgiving streets of the city. As with *Neria*, music is provided by Zimbabwe's top musician, Oliver Mtukudzi.

JUDY KENDALL is a freelance writer on Southern African film and music. She is also a playwright and currently working as a Writer in Residence with the Arts Council in the U.K.

Distributors

Libra Films
PO Box 855
Harare
Tel: 724841

Rainbow Organisations
PO Box 1219
Harare
Tel: 705901/3
Fax: 708561

Useful Addresses

Ministry of Information
Production Services
PO Box 8157
Harare
Tel: 707317/8, 796522

Ministry of Information
Film Section
PO Box 8150
Causeway
Harare
Tel: 707210, 703891

Producers

FilmAfrica (Pvt) Ltd
PO Box 5615
Harare
Tel: 734816/7/8
Fax: 735912

Media for Development Trust
135 Union Avenue
PO Box 6755
Harare
Tel: 729066

Zimmedia (Pvt) Ltd
42 East Road
Avondal
Harare
Tel: 733416
Fax: 723056

FESTIVALS

TRIBUTE:

International Film Festival of La Rochelle

The International Film Festival of La Rochelle brings to mind the finale of Jean Renoir's "La Règle du Jeu," when host Robert de la Chesnaye eulogises the accidentally killed air-ace André Jurieu: "...this exquisite friend, this companion of quality who knew so well how to make us forget that he was a famous man."

This non-competitive Festival too is exquisite and classy, and so enjoyable that it makes you forget that an affair of this magnitude and importance, ought, by all rights to be a gruelling endurance test.

Set by the Atlantic, in an engaging port-town of 75,000 people, the annual 10 day festival opens in late June or very early July. It began more than modestly in 1973, as an incidental side-event of the primarily music-orientated International Meetings of Contemporary Art.

Jean-Loup Passek, the progenitor of the cinema section, brought all the films (the entire festival!) from Paris, in his small car. That first programme consisted of a tribute to Georges Méliès and of "The World As It Is": 12 features (mostly 1971-72) from 12 countries, including Brazil, Egypt, Syria and Tunisia. Internationally, only some experts knew the work of directors like Ousmane Sembene, Nelson Pereira Dos

Krzysztof Kieślowski at the La Rochelle Festival in 1988
photo: Alain Le Hors

Santos, Theo Angelopoulos or the Taviani brothers. By and large the others were unknown.

Passek says that the first screening had an audience of three, who had wandered in by chance. Still, the programme caught on. By the following year there were 23 works from 16 countries. By 1975, with seven sections and 67 films—overwhelmingly rarities of value—the Film Festival was established as a force to be reckoned with. In a 1977 article I found, the late, great critic Jean-Louis Bory called La Rochelle "A Festival with a Human Face."

Retrospectives to the Fore

In 1982 (72 features plus shorts) came the Boris Barnet retrospective. It set the pattern for the three main sections of future

John Boorman, Michel Ciment and Jean Loup Passek at La Rochelle in 1978

photo: Alain Le Hors

Festivals: retrospectives devoted to the work of past film-makers; multi-film Tributes to contemporary directors, all present at the festival; "The World as it is," with recent unreleased films. The smaller sections include films for children—a relief from TV's stupid kid-vids; all-nighters; series selected by Cinémathèques and the like; "lost" or restored works; and other, ever-varying types of screenings.

1984 was the year of Victor Sjöström, Powell and Pressburger, Jan Troell, Reinhard Hauff, Matjaz Klopčić, Smila Patil, Claude Miller, Haile Gerima, and of African Cinema. It was also the last gasp of the International Meetings of Contemporary Art. Long before this, the Film Festival had become the belle of the ball. Now Jean-Loup Passek had to expand his never-ending struggle for subsidies.

The number of titles programmed kept rising in the 1980's. In 1987 for instance there were about 107 features. That was the year of the Lumière Brothers, Mauritz Stiller and Anna Magnani. Retrospectives of actors are unusual at La Rochelle. I can

think of only three others: the charming Indian Smita Patil (1984) who died two years later at age 31; the Italian vamp of silent films Francesca Bertini (1993); and—also in 1993—Michel Piccoli.

1987 was also the year of the Panorama of Georgian Cinema, of Kon Ichikawa, Jerzy Kawalerowicz, Adoor Gopalakrishnan, Ermanno Olmi, and a cult figure in France, John Cassavetes, who died in early 1989.

Dramatic Rise in Screenings

In the early 1990's film numbers rose spectacularly, to 140 on one occasion. By now, films from at least 75 countries have been to La Rochelle. But then, statistics are only part of the picture, as the Festival is not into the numbers racket. It is the interest and availability of films that determine the figures.

Most films are shown three times, staggered over ten days, in four theatres at the Dragon Multiplex and, a few yards away, in two big auditoriums in La

Peter Weir visited La Rochelle in 1991

photo: Régis d'Audeville

La Rochelle 1983: (from left to right) M. Chavier, Michel Deville, Michel Crépeau, Dr. Sabatier, Robert Aldrich, Xie Tieli, Xie Fang, Lu Yun, Zivojin Pavlović, Jean Loup Passek, Joel Boutteville   photo: Vimenet/Collectif

Class of 1985: (back row) Jacques Perrin, Robin Renucci, Alain Tanner: (front) Raoul Ruiz, Nicole Garcia, Christine Laurent, Ken Loach, Magali Noël

Coursive, a beautifully renovated historic building which also houses the Festival offices and meetings. All seating is most comfortable, projection is impeccable, electronic subtitling and simultaneous translation, excellent. The theatres have air conditioning—something still unknown in many major European festivals—and are generally not too crowded given the many (approx. 2,500) seats available.

The daily schedule begins at the civilised hour of 11 a.m. and continues at 2.30, 5.30, 8 and 10 p.m. The biggest dilemmas are posed by mid-afternoon projections which may overlap the "Rencontres" with directors.

The "grille," (printed schedule), is a tour-de-force of juggling titles, dates and times. The catalogue, better and better each year, is a model of its kind, practically free of publicity, exhaustively illustrated, with filmographies and substantial, first-rate articles on every director, written by specialists.

The only difficulty is obtaining enough still photographs, as the non-commercial, non-competitive nature of La Rochelle does not encourage distributors to send in press books. But this is a tiny price to pay for the absence of politics, hassles, troubles and artifice that can plague big and competitive festivals.

Human Scale

Even with 140 films, La Rochelle is not of Cannes, Berlin or Toronto size or nature. It's scale is human. There are no film-merchants, limousines or stars. It is not a dress-up occasion or a chic social event. The rules, regulations, hierarchies, privileges, colour coded passes and pecking order that afflict certain festivals simply do not exist here, nor does the rudeness or confusion that might be met elsewhere. All at La Rochelle—organisers, media people, guests and public—are on equal footing.

This happy state would make even a lesser Festival worthwhile. It makes La Rochelle blue-ribbon. Above all, La

Richard Brooks at the Festival in 1980

Rochelle's biggest asset is its maverick founder-director, Jean-Loup Passek, and his superb crew headed by Sylvie Pras and Prune Engler ("my two right arms," says Passek). Each year they engineer an event which aims strictly at film lovers and at the greater glory of world cinema.

Among the myriad activities of passion-ate Passek, his experience in organising mammoth film retrospectives at the Pompidou Centre (Paris) gives him a powerful edge in planning and implementing the Festival.

The programming strategy is "no strategy" but there seem to be two major guiding principles. One is horizontal: to roam far and wide among those films of our planet that have character and that open windows on the world. The other is vertical: to do justice to cinema's past by re-presenting it, discovering and re-discovering a heritage that, though far from dead, unlike other arts is mostly buried. Those are crucial credos at a time of too many fast-food, mass appeal movies,

Gleb Panfilov and Inna Tchourikova at La Rochelle in 1988   photo: Alain Le Hors

faceless co-productions and mainstream homogenisation; and a time when programming both on the big and the small screen is timorous, uncurious, and plays it safe.

From its inception, the Festival has rejected all mercantile or political connections, biases or partisanships. There is no *a priori* focus on specific themes or genres. Over-specificity can be intriguing, but also Procrustean, making the theory fit the practice. La Rochelle maintains flexibility in its selections. The result is eclecticism but not elitism, snobbery or false culture. It is variety, but without concessions to trendy, popular and ephemeral fashions.

Repeatedly, Passek has declared that there are no calculations in his planning, that it all comes from "coups de cœur," impulses from the heart. His point is well taken: the only special interest this Festival caters to is film as art and as document, not as a commodity.

If there is no strategy at La Rochelle, its basic principles do lead to a structure, one that inevitably stresses "auteurs," from acknowledged ones to new talents, but it does so without fanaticism. The unity and coherence of the offerings add to the Festival the dimension of a "teaching" festival. Tributes and retrospectives point to similarities and differences, continuities or breaks. The spectators can gain a concentrated and comprehensive knowledge of films and their makers.

It is at La Rochelle that most of us discovered, amongst a host of others: Australia's Fred Schepisi; Germany's Reinhard Hauff; Greece's Theo Angelopoulos; Hungary's Gyula Máar and Imre Gyöngyössy; India's Shyam Benegal; Italy's Pupi Avati; Russia's Elem Klimov and Aleksander Kaidanovski, and Aleksander Sokurov; Uzbekistan's Ali Khamraev; and Poland's Wojciech Has and Kazimierz Kutz. The list goes on and on. It includes many film-makers (e.g. Shohei Imamura, Manoel de Oliveira, Tenguiz

Jules Dassin enjoying the hospitality of La Rochelle in 1993   *photo: Régis d' Audeville*

Mrinal Sen and Xie Tian in conversation at La Rochelle (1982)   *photo: Alain Le Hors*

Dino Risi between screenings in 1994
          photo: Régis d'Audeville

Abuladze, Atom Egoyan) who, although not known world-wide before they were awarded a Golden Palm, Banana or Pterodactyl, had already been honoured at La Rochelle.

Wonders and Revelations

With its huge percentage of high quality films, although La Rochelle is no film market, its wonders and revelations do trickle down to programmers and distributors. There are no gold or silver medals, but one does strike precious metal with regularity. For instance, in 1991 there were retrospectives of Edmond T. Gréville (1906-1966) with ten films and of Vittorio De Sica (1901-1974) with 17. The showcasing rehabilitated both directors. It

Adoor Gopalakrishnan, Jerzy Kawalerowicz, Lana Gogoberidze, Revaz Esdadze, Nana Djordadze, Irakli Kvirikadze, Merab Kokotchachvili (with festival director, Jean Loup Passek, seated)

became clear that little-known Gréville, thought of (if at all) as a maker of mostly potboilers, had persistently brought to his (talking) pictures first-rate, original, silent-era techniques of composition, visual symbolism and filmic shorthand.

It was just as obvious that De Sica's work from the mid 1950's to the end of his life had been severely underrated, when not maligned. Those revealing retrospectives were major correctives to film history. Earlier that year, the excellent Pesaro Festival had proved that De Sica the actor had been the best Italian leading man of the 1930's. La Rochelle validated De Sica as a great director and corroborated the need for upgrading his place in books and doing away with many exaggerations about his decline.

The tributes are, of course, the most exciting, informative (and for the organisers, the most difficult) aspect of La Rochelle. The cumulative roster of guest film-makers—eight or nine in recent years—reads like a series of extracts from the *Larousse Dictionnaire du Cinéma* edited by none other than — J.-L. Passek!

The film-makers generally stay for most of the Festival, and, between the appeal of the Festival and the charm of the city—to quote the late Robert Aldrich—"they have a ball." Whether famous or local heroes, they do not come to sell themselves or do their social thing. Adapting to the Festival's spirit, they are accessible and in touch with the public in scheduled meetings and improvised get-togethers. Instead of the Cannes-type bedlam of massive press conferences, there is a daily, informal and informative "Rencontre" (meeting) with each director. These—with only a couple of notorious exceptions over the years—let their hair down and engage in straight, open talk with the audience.

The closest most filmgoers can approach film-makers in a mega-festival is 20 feet and across a barrage of flashes and func-tionaries. At La Rochelle it is not uncommon to find in a café John and Jane Doe (or Jean and Marie Dupont) sipping liquids with a director and chatting away. And the

directors are not encountered as Famous People but as cinephiles fascinated with their craft, the cinema of others and by films that they too are discovering at La Rochelle.

A few of them have been retired, like Jules Dassin (1993) or, nearing his 80th birthday, the late but then perfectly lucid Michael Powell (1984). Most however are active. All wax or waxed rhapsodic about the Festival, its quality, its warm and unpretentious atmosphere and hospitality.

Sometimes their gratitude is touching, as when a visibly moved Ukrainian director who had been in the business for 30 years publicly kept thanking Passek for having given him his first retrospective.

La Rochelle's Tumultuous History

The fiercely independent and stubborn Jean-Loup's festival takes place in a lovely city that used to be fiercely independent and stubborn. In its tumultuous history, La Rochelle became an English possession in 1152, reverted to France in 1226, to England again in 1360, and finally went back to France 12 years later. From the Fourteenth to the Seventeenth Century it was the main gate to the New World.

Fortified La Rochelle was once the hotbed of Protestantism. After a 15 month siege by Cardinal Richelieu, starvation forced the heroic defenders to surrender (1628). During the Occupation in the Second World War it was the main Atlantic base for Nazi submarines: you can see this in the movie *Das Boot.*

Jean Loup Passek with Polish animator, Jan Lenica, at La Rochelle in 1994 photo: *Régis d'Audeville*

The team behind the success of La Rochelle: (left to right) Jean Loup Passek, Prune Engler, Matilde Incerti, and Sylvie Pras

La Rochelle can look like a movie set. A marriage of stone and sea, it is intensively maintained and restored. It is a place of ancient buildings that go as far back as the Middle Ages, sidewalks under ancient, continuous arches and arcades, monumental towers watching over the Old Port, a pedestrian mall, and harmonious architecture wherever you look. It is also known for its seafood and fish restaurants.

Accessibility is a major attribute of the Festival. La Coursive and the Dragon theatres are in adjacent blocks that face the Old Port. The area also has a high concentration of hotels, restaurants, cafés and shops. The superb Restaurant La Marmite and its lower-priced annex are next to La Coursive.

More significant yet is the easy access to people. In spite of much increased programmes, audiences and media coverage, there are no barriers around the Festival director, the staff, their collaborators at La Coursive (manager Jackie Marchand and his team), and of course, the visiting film-makers. And in spite of its

international recognition, the Festival has not lost an inch of its homely atmosphere and the feel of a large family reunion.

The author of this article, the critic EDWIN JAHIEL, is Professor of French and of Cinema Studies as well as Director of the Unit for Cinema Studies at the University of Illinois in Urbana-Champaign, Illinois.

Ali Khamraev from Uzbekistan visited La Rochelle in 1990   *photo: Régis d'Audeville*

Guide to Leading Festivals

Annecy

May 30 - June 4, 1995

Long hailed as the first love of animators around the world, Annecy's idyllic setting makes for the perfect festival rendezvous, where animators can mingle and screen their latest works in congenial mood. There is a competitive section, as well as a Market for Animation. *Inquiries to:* Journées Internationales du Cinéma d'Animation, B.P. 399, 74013 Annecy Cedex, France. Tel: (33) 50 57 4172. Fax: (33) 50 67 8195.

Berlin

February 9-20, 1995

Berlin is generally recognised to be the most efficiently-organised of the world's major festivals. In addition to the competitive programme and information section, there is a Retrospective, screenings of all new German films, and of course the Forum of Young Cinema, directed by Ulrich Gregor, where many of the most imaginative films are screened. *Inquiries to:* Berlin International Film Festival, Budapester Strasse 50, 10787 Berlin. Tel: (30) 254890. Telex: 185255. Fax: (30) 25489249.

AWARDS 1994

Golden Bear: **In the Name of the Father** (U.K. /Ireland), Sheridan.
Special Jury Prize: **Strawberry and Chocolate** (Cuba/Mexico/Spain), Alea, Tabzo.
Best Director: Krzysztof Kieślowski for **Three Colours: White** (France/Poland/Switzerland).
Best Actor: Tom Hanks for **Philadelphia** (U.S.A.).
Best Actress: Crissy Rock for **Ladybird, Ladybird** (U.K.).
Silver Bears: Alain Resnais for **Smoking/No Smoking** (France); Rosie Perez for **Fearless** (U.S.A.).
FIPRESCI Award: **Ladybird, Ladybird** (U.K.), Loach.

Cambridge

July, 1995

A film festival in this historic university

annecy 95

International Animated Film Festival

ANNECY

30 mai - 4 juin

- International competition : short films, feature films, TV series, commissioned and advertising films
- International competition for student films and graduation films
- Poster competition «Jules Chéret prize»
- Film tributes, retrospectives and exhibitions
- International film projects competition

MIFA

1 juin - 4 juin

- International Animation film market
- International youth film pro grammes market : live drama, animation and documentaries
- Animation production and facilities market
- Computer-aided animation and new production technology market
- International encounter of multimedia and interactive audio-visual programmes
- Market for rights and patents for merchandizing

Contact : BP 399, 74013 Annecy - France - tel (33) 50.57.41.72 fax (33) 50 67 81 95

town can call on considerable local and student interest, and now deserves ranking alongside London and Edinburgh as the best festival in the U.K. Now in its 19th year the event is non-competitive and screens both shorts and feature films often in the presence of directors and actors. The 1994 event featured an impressive Kieślowski retrospective, as well as U.K. premieres of *Red* and Resnais' *Smoking/No Smoking*. *Inquiries to:* Tony Jones, Cambridge Film Festival, Cambridge Arts Cinema, 8 Market Passage, Cambridge, CB2 3PF, U.K. Tel: (223) 462666. Telex: 81574. Fax: (223) 462555.

Cannes

May 17-28, 1995

Cannes remains the world's top festival, attracting the American key independents and personalities as well as entries from the more obscure countries. Cannes includes three major sections: the Competition, "Un Certain Regard", and the Directors' Fortnight screenings. There

is also the Critics' Week, and innumerable other useful screenings (e.g. the Australian, New Zealand and Scandinavian films). The great advantage of Cannes is that everyone of importance attends the event. *Inquiries to:* 71-rue du Faubourg Saint-Honoré, 75008 Paris, France. Tel: (1) 42 66 92 20. Telex: 650765. Fax: (1) 42 66 68 85. Marché International du Film: Fax: (1) 42 66 68 85.

AWARDS 1994
Palme d'Or: **Pulp Fiction** (U.S.A.), Tarantino.
Grand Prix du Jury: (shared) **Burnt by the Sun**

(Russia/France), Mikhalkov; **To Live** (Hongkong /China), Yimou.
Best Director: Nanni Moretti for **Dear Diary** (Italy).
Best Actor: Ge You for **To Live** (Hongkong/China).
Best Actress: Virna Lisi for **La Reine Margot** (France).
Prix du Jury: **La Reine Margot** (France), Chereau.
Palme d'Or Short: **El Heroe** (Mexico).
Caméra d'Or: **Coming to Terms with the Dead** (France).

Cartagena

March 3-10, 1995

Cartagena is the oldest film festival in Latin America. In its 34th edition, in 1994, it showed 61 films from 18 Ibero-American countries. Cartagena is an old-world town and famous summer resort. President of the new Latin American Film Foundation, and Nobel Prize winner, Gabriel García Marquez, is one of the festival's sponsors. *Inquiries to;* Cartagena Film Festival, PO Box 1834, Cartagena, Colombia. Tel: (5753) 600 966. Fax: (5753) 600 970.

Chicago

October, 1995

Michael Kutza launched his festival more than a quarter of a century ago, which makes it the oldest competitive event in America. Always open to new ideas, especially from Europe and Asia, Chicago screens the best new films from Cannes and Venice, but also some wise and imaginative choices of its own. A "Gold Hugo" is a prize to be proud of. *Inquiries to:* Michael J. Kutza, Chicago International Film Festival, 415 North Dearborn, Chicago, Illinois 60610, U.S.A. Tel: (312) 644 3400. Fax (312) 644 0784.

Cel from Frédéric Back's LE FLEUVE AUX GRANDES EAUX, winner of the Grand Prix at Annecy in 1993

Clermont-Ferrand

January 27-February 4, 1995

The ideal destination for anyone who wants to explore over 200 of the best short films of the year, the volcanoes of the Auvergne and the exquisite cuisine of the region. This growing competitive event (46 countries in 1994, with 85,000 spectators) offers both national and international competitions alongside retrospectives, school programmes, debates and an accessible marketplace for shorts. *Inquiries to:* Clermont-Ferrand Short Film Festival, 26 rue des Jacobins, 63000 Clermont-Ferrand, France. Tel: (33) 73 91 65 73. Fax: (33) 73 92 11 93.

MAIN AWARDS 1994
International Festival:
Kisses on a Train (India/U.K.), Stafford.
Picc Mi (Senegal), Wade.
89 mm od Europy (Poland), Lozinski.
The Wrong Trousers (U.K.), Park.
National Festival:
Joyeux Noël, Marchand.
75 centilitres de prière, Maillot.

Dutch

Film

Festival

Annual screening of all new
Dutch features, shorts,
documentaries, tv-drama and
animations.

Retrospectives, seminars,
talkshows and the 'Cinema
Militans Lecture'.

Grand Prix for Dutch and
European Cinema:
The Golden Calf Awards.

**The Holland Film Meeting
22 - 25 September 1995.**

Information and contact:
Dutch Film Festival
Hoogt 4 -10
3512 GW Utrecht,
The Netherlands
tel: (31) 30 32 2684
fax: (31) 30 31 3200

Dimanche ou les fantômes, Archard.
Deus ex Machina, Mayrand.

Denver

October, 1995

More than 100 film programmes from
around the world make up the 18th Denver
International Film Festival for eight days in
October. New international features, documentaries, new American cinema and
critic's programmes are screened and more
than 40 film artists are due to attend the
event in Colorado's delightfully spacious
and friendly capital. Denver is non-
competitive, but presents an achievement
award. *Inquiries to:* DIFF, 999 18th Street,
Suite 1820, Denver, Colorado 80202, U.S.A.
Tel: (303) 298 8223. Fax: (303) 298 0209.

Dutch Film Festival

September, 1995

Long established as an important occasion
during which the entire output of Dutch
film-making may be assessed, in the
attractive old town of Utrecht. A selection
of Dutch features and shorts are screened
and judged, and there are Golden Calf
awards in eleven different categories (e.g.
Best Film and Best Director and best
foreign film). A special programme is the
Holland Film Meeting, the foreign section
of the festival. Useful for festival directors,
film buffs, distributors and critics, national
and international. *Inquiries to:* Stichting
Nederlands Film Festival, Hoogt 4, 3512
GW Utrecht, Holland. Tel: (31) 30 322684.
Fax: (31) 30 313200.

AWARDS 1993
Best Film: **De Kleine Blonde Dood**, Houwer, Velde.
Best Director: Ben Sombogaart for **Het Zakmes**.
Best Actor: Rik Launspach for **Oeroeg**.
Best Actress: Els Dottermans for **Beck.**
Best Short Film: **De Marionettenwereld**
Best Documentary Short: **Isingiro Hospital.**
Best Documentary Feature: **Kind In Twee Werelden.**
Special Jury Award: Peter Delpeut for **The Forbidden
Quest.**

Edinburgh

August 12-27, 1995

One of the world's oldest film festivals, 50

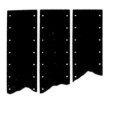

DENVER INTERNATIONAL FILM·FESTIVAL

18th Denver International Film Festival
October 12 - 19, 1995

ENQUIRIES TO:
Ron Henderson
Denver International Film Festival
999 18th Street, Suite 1820, Denver, CO 80202 USA

TEL: (303) 298 8223   FAX: (303) 298 0209

years old next year, Edinburgh is also one of the most accessible. Emphasis on U.K. films and young directors, with particularly well-chosen retrospectives and seminars. There's an offbeat sparkle to the Edinburgh selection which is reflected in the enthusiasm of local audiences. The 1994 event included a tribute to Derek Jarman and a retrospective of André de Toth. *Inquiries to:* The Drambuie Edinburgh Film Festival, 88 Lothian Road, Edinburgh, EH3 9BZ, Scotland. Tel: (31) 228 4051. Telex: 72166. Fax: (31) 229 5501.

Espoo Ciné
August 23-27, 1995

Held in the beautiful "garden city" of Tapiola and now in its sixth year, this event showcases a selection of new European cinema, highlights from other continents, and the latest Finnish output of quality. Outdoor screenings, special effects seminars, retrospectives, horror extravaganza, sneak previews and director guests make this a treat for film-fans. *Inquiries to:* Espoo Ciné, PO Box 95, FIN-02101 Espoo, Finland. Tel: (0) 466 599. Fax: (0) 466 458.

Fajr International Film Festival
January 21-February 1, 1995

The Fajr festival has flourished as a competitive event and is now the leading Iranian film festival, catering mainly for Iranian films, although screenings of international films are on the increase. The festival also plays host to foreign guests and industry figures. *Inquiries to:* Farhang Cinema, Dr. Shariati Ave., Gholhak, Tehran 19139, Iran. Tel: 265 086; 200 2088/89/90. Fax: 267 082. Telex: 216599 FAJR IR.

Fantasporto
February 3-11, 1995

The Oporto International Film Festival, now going into its 15th edition, specialises in fantasy and science-fiction films in its official competitive section. This festival also includes the 5th New Directors Week with an official competition, and a retrospective section dedicated to "100 Years Cinema" with a complete retrospective of George Méliès and Louis

Feuillade films. The Festival director is also preparing, with the help of the Portuguese Film Institute, a programme of Portuguese films for the benefit of foreign guests at Fantasporto. *Inquiries to:* Fantasporto, Oporto Film Festival, Rua da Constitucão 311, 4200 Porto, Portugal. Tel: (351-2) 550 8990/1/2. Fax: (351-2) 5508210.

AWARDS 1994

Best Film: **The Cronos Device** (Mexico), Toro.
Best Direction: Dave Borthwick for **The Secret Adventures of Tom Thumb** (U.K.).
Best Actor: Federico Luppi for **The Cronos Device** (Mexico).
Best Actress: Sarah Smuts-Kennedy for **Jack Be Nimble** (New Zealand).
Best Screenplay: Garth Maxwell for **Jack Be Nimble** (New Zealand).
Best Special Effects: **Necronomicon** (U.S.A.).
Best Short: **The Temptation of Sainthood** (U.K.), Pummel.
Jury's Special Award: **The Forbidden Quest** (Holland), Delpeut.

Fespaco

February, 1995

The Panafrican Film and Television Festival is held biannually in Ouagadougou and is the biggest and most important event in Africa. The festival features a competition for African features, a film and television market, and a seminar on *Cinema and History*. An invaluable event for African film-makers and a welcome showcase for smaller African countries, with huge local attendances, and around 60 nations participating. *Inquiries to:* Secrétariat Général Permanent du FESPACO, 01 BP 2505 Ouagadougou 01. Tel: (226) 30 75 38. Fax: (226) 31 25 09. Telex: 5255 BF/Burkina Faso.

Festival des 3 Continents

November, 1995

This is the only annual competitive festival in the world for films originating solely from Africa, Asia and Black and Latin America. Since 1979 the event has acquired great international prestige as well as a very large public audience. The retrospectives and the discovery of less well-known film-makers are also significant. The festival does not have a paternalistic view of third world countries; on the contrary, its aim is to present their cultural values in the best possible conditions. *Inquiries to:* Alain and Philippe Jalladeau, Director, Festival des 3 Continents, BP 3306, 44033 Nantes Cedex, France. Tel: (33) 40 69 74 14. Fax: (33) 40 73 55 22.

Festival Internazionale Cinema Giovani

November 10-18, 1995

This well-organised event takes place in Turin each autumn and focuses exclusively on films made by young directors. There is a competitive section for shorts, features and Italian independents, as well as a section for retrospectives. The festival has been recognised as a top-drawer showcase for hot new international talent and dubbed second only to Venice on the crowded Italian festival circuit. *Inquiries to:* Festival Internazionale Cinema Giovani, Piazza San Carlo 161, 10123 Torino, Italy. Tel: (11) 562 3309. Telex: 216803. Fax: (11) 562 9796.

AWARDS 1993
Best Film: **Rebels of the Neon God** (Taiwan), Ming-Liang.
Special Jury Award: **The Last Cold Days** (Kazakhstan), Kalymbetov, Iskakov.
Best Short: **Mama Said** (U.S.A.), Costanza.
FIPRESCI Award: **I'll Never Let You Go!** (Russia). Tonunc.

Film+arc.graz

October 8-12, 1995

The second edition of this bi-annual event, which celebrates and explores the relationship between film and architecture, takes place in the Austrian city of Graz, well known for its contemporary architecture. The extensive programme (Official Competitive Section, retrospectives and special screenings) features around 200 films, including fiction, documentary, animation and experimental. An international jury awards prizes to films in all categories which explore architecture or experiment with spacial structures. *Inquiries to:* FIlm+arc.graz, Rechbauerstrasse 38, 8010 Graz, Austria. Tel: (316) 84 24 87. Fax: (316) 82 95 11.

2nd international

festival

film + architecture

8.-12.nov.1995

for information:

rechbauerstraße 38

A-8010 graz

austria

phone: +(316)842487

fax : +(316)829511

13° FESTIVAL INTERNAZIONALE CINEMA GIOVANI TORINO-ITALIA

13th TURIN INTERNATIONAL FESTIVAL OF YOUNG CINEMA

NOVEMBER 10 - 18, 1995

OFFICIAL COMPETITION
Feature and short films

HORS CONCOURS SECTION

ITALIAN INDEPENDENTS

RETROSPECTIVE

SPECIAL EVENTS

Recognized by the International Federation of Film Producers Associations

FESTIVAL INTERNAZIONALE
CINEMA GIOVANI

Festival Internazionale Cinema Giovani
Piazza San Carlo, 161
10123 Torino, Italia
Phone + 39 - 11 - 5623309
Fax: + 39 - 11 - 5629796
Telex: 216803 FICG I

de Silva Associati

Flanders International Film Festival (Ghent)

October 10-21, 1995

Belgium's most prominent yearly film event attracts annual attendances of over 52,000 and focuses on "The Impact of Music on Film." The Ghent Festival is competitive (the Best Film receives US$ 120,000) and screens around 130 films, including those without a Belgium distributor. Outside the competitive section, screenings include Country Focus, a Film Spectrum of international titles receiving their Belgian premieres, as well a tribute to an important film-maker. Deadline for entry forms: mid August. Deadline for prints: October. *Inquiries to:* Flanders international Film Festival-Ghent, 1104 Kortrijksesteenweg, B-9051 Ghent, Belgium. Tel: (32) 9 221 89 46. Fax: (32) 9 221 90 74.

Robert Altman and actress Annie Ross came to Ghent to present SHORT CUTS

Fort Lauderdale

November, 1995

Fort Lauderdale is the largest festival in the Southeastern United States, attracting over 30,000 spectators in 1993. Fort Lauderdale screens international premieres as well as shorts, animation and documentaries. Director Gregory von Hausch attributes the success of the festival to its proximity to South America and convenience to Europe, plus the great weather in South Florida. The Festival features over 100 films, galas, award ceremonies, int'l student film competition international and over 24 Kodak seminars. *Inquiries to:* Fort Lauderdale Int'l Film Festival, 2633 East Sunrise Boulevard, Fort Lauderdale FL 33304, U.S.A. Tel: (305) 563 0500. Fax: (305) 564 1206.

AWARDS 1993

Best Film: **The Cement Garden** (U.K.).
Best Foreign Film: **The Last Lieutenant** (Norway),
Best Documentary: **Children of Fate: Life and Death in a Sicilian Family.**
Best Short: **Big Al.**
Golden Palm: **La ardilla roja** (Spain).
Lifetime Achievement Award: Roger Corman.

Giffoni International Film Festival

August, 1995

This popular annual event for children and young people celebrates its 25th anniversary this year. Giffoni is government funded and presents new, full length features aimed at 11-16 year olds. the films show in competition and are judged by a panel of over 150 youths from every part of Italy. Festival Director Claudio Gubitosi, who has been at the helm of the event began in 1971, hopes that Giffoni has played an active part in the campaign tp get cinema for the young taken seriously, and discussed without condescention. Inquires to: Giffoni International film Festival, Piazza Umberto 1, 84095 Giffoni Valle Piana (Salerno), Italy. Tel: (89) 868544. fax: (89) 866111. Telex: 721585.

AWARDS 1993

Grand Prix: **Marie** (Belgium/France/Portugal), Handwerker.

Special Jury prizes: **Calm in the East: Tango Argentino** (Serbia), Paskaljević; **Into the West** (Ireland), Newell. *Best Actor:* Alessandro Sogona **for Marie** (Belgium/France/Portugal). *Best Actress:* Marie Gillain **for Marie** (Belgium/France/Portugal).

Göteborg
February 3-12, 1995

A genuine success story. Now in its 18th year Göteborg has established itself as not only the best film festival in Norden but as one of the key events in Europe, with almost 92,000 eager and discriminating spectators who warm the cockles of a nervous director's heart with their spontaneous applause. Hotels and cinemas are close to one another. Swedish TV selects one film daily for simultaneous telecasting, a symbol of the prestige which the event carries in Sweden. *Inquiries to:* Göteborg Film Festival, PO Box 7079, S-402 32 Göteborg, Sweden. Tel: (31) 41 0546; Telex: 28674. Fax: (31) 410063.

Heartland Film Festival

October, 1995

The Festival was established in 1991 in Indianapolis, Indiana to affect change in the entertainment industry by honouring and rewarding film-makers whose work explores the human journey by artistically expressing hope and respect for positive aspects of life. Cash prizes of up to $20,000 for feature films and $5,000 for shorts are awrded to the winners each year. *Inquiries to:* Heartland Film Festival, 613 N. East Street, Indianapolis, Indiana 46202, U.S.A. Tel: (317) 464 9405. Fax: (317) 635 4201.

Helsinki Film Festival – Love and Anarchy

September, 1995

During its seven-year history, the Helsinki Film Festival has – according to the Finnish media – established itself as the most important Finnish feature-film festival, focussing on contemporary cinema. For one hectic week in late September, the festival is a showcase for visually powerful, uncompromising and controversial films from around the world. Over 100 screenings in the heart of Helsinki comprised of retrospectives (John Woo and Abel Ferrara in 1993), and a selection of new cinema full of surprises for those who thought they had seen it all. *Inquiries to:* Helsinki Film Festival, Unioninkatu 10 A 27, SF 00130 Helsinki, Finland. Tel: (358) 0 629 528/177 501. Fax: (358) 0 631 450.

Hongkong

April 7-22, 1995

The usual selection of Asian product is included among about 170 films on show at various venues in Kowloon and on the Hongkong island. The festival has been recognised as a "showcase" for Asian works and valuable for the West to discover the riches of Chinese cinema. *Inquiries to:* Senior Manager, Festivals Office, Urban Services Department, Level 7, Administration Building, Hongkong Cultural Centre, 10 Salisbury Road,

1993 guests at Helsinki included John Woo (right), with Jorg Buttgereit getting ready to fly in the background
photo: Matti Helariutta

Tsimshatsui, Kowloon, Hongkong. Tel. (852) 734 2903. Fax: (852) 3665206. Telex: 38484 USDHK HX. Cable: FESTUSD HK.

Independent Feature Film Market

September, 1995

The Independent Feature Film Market (IFFM) is the only market devoted to new, emerging American independent film talent. Since 1979, the IFFM has presented the industry with its first look at such landmark films as: *American Dream, Badlands, Blood Simple, Daughters of the Dust, El Norte, Let's Get Lost, Metropolitan, My Dinner with Andre, One False Move, Paris is Burning, Poison, Slacker, Stranger Than Paradise, Swoon, The Hours and Times, Roger & Me*, and many others. The IFFM screens over 250 film projects, including Works-in-Progress, and presents over 100 newly copyrighted scripts. *Inquiries to:* The Independent Feature Project, 104 West 29th Street, 12th Floor, New York, New York 10001-5310. Tel: (212) 465-8200.

India

January, 1995

The International Film Festival of India (IFFI) is held each year (Bombay in 1995) and is non-competitive (recognised by FIAPF). There is a substantial information section, and an annual focus on films from a particular geographical region or country (Asia, Africa or Latin America), foreign and Indian retrospectives, and a film market, as well as a most valuable panorama of the best Indian films of the

year, subtitled in English. *Inquiries to:* Mrs. Malti Sahai, Director, Directorate of Film Festivals, Ministry of Information and Broadcasting, Government of India, 4th Floor, Lok Nayak Bhavan, Khan Market, New Delhi 110003, India. Telex: (31) 62741 FEST IN. Cable: FILMOTSAV. Fax: (91) 11 694920. Tel: (91) 11 4615953/44 697167.

International Film Festival Mannheim – Heidelberg

October, 1995

The former Mannheim Film Festival has now been enlarged to become the International Film festival Mannheim-Heidelberg. For over 40 years it has been committed to discovering talented newcomers. The competition features new independent features, shorts and documentaries from all over the world. A Grand Prize of DM30,000 (as well as DM20,000 support for the German distributor) is offered for the best feature; DM10,000 for the most original film; DM10,000 plus the purchase of film rights by the SDR Broadcasting Company for the best documentary; and DM 2,000 for the best short. *Inquiries to:* Dr. Michael Koetz, International Filmfestival Mannheim-Heidelberg, Collini-Centre, Galerie, D-68161 Mannheim, Germany. Tel: (49) 621 10 29 43. Fax: (49) 621 29 15 64.

AWARDS 1993

Grand Prize: **The Forbidden Quest** (The Netherlands), Delpeut.
Special Fassbinder Prize: **Darkness in Tallinn** (Finland), Järvilaturi.
SDR Documentary Prize: **Le quattuor des possibles** (Switzerland), Politi.
Short Film Prize: **Reste** (France), Vermillard.

Internationale Hofer Filmtage

October, 1995

Dubbed "Home of Films" by Wim Wenders, Hof is famous for its thoughtful selection of some 40 features. Founded by the directors of the New German Cinema, Hof enjoys a high reputation among German film-makers and American cult figures like Roger Corman, Monte Hellman, John Sayles and Henry Jaglom, all of whom have attended retrospectives in their honour. The real

Please contact:
Heinz Badewitz, Director
Lothstraße 28
D-80335 München
FAX: -89 / 123 68 68
Telex: 5 212 042 flmw d

INTERNATIONAL HOF FILMDAYS

Every Last Week in October

THE HOF SOCCER DREAM TEAM:

THE HOF SOCCER DREAM TEAM:		
① ATOM EGOYAN	⑤ GEORGE A. ROMERO	
② JOHN SAYLES	⑥ TERENCE DAVIES	
③ VOLKER SCHLOENDORFF	⑦ ROBERTO BENIGNI	
④ HERBERT ACHTERNBUSCH	⑧ VINCENT WARD	

⑨ DAVID CRONENBERG	⑭ WERNER HERZOG
⑩ JIM JARMUSCH	⑮ WIM WENDERS
⑪ JOHN CARPENTER	⑯ PAUL COX
⑫ ROGER CORMAN	
⑬ NEIL JORDAN	COACH: SAM FULLER

SUBSTITUTES:
MONTE HELLMAN | PAUL BARTEL
MEHDI CHAREF | DETLEV BUCK
DORIS DÖRRIE | ALEX COX
BRIAN DE PALMA | SÖNKE WORTMANN
JOHN WATERS | PERCY ADLON

applause should go to the peripatetic Heinz Badewitz, who had the idea for the festival more than 25 years ago. A screening in Hof can often result in a distribution deal. *Inquiries to:* Postfach 1146, D-95010 Hof, Germany: or Heinz Badewitz, Lothstr. 28, D-80335 Munich 2, Germany. Tel: (89) 1297422. Fax: (89) 1236868. Telex: 5212042 FLMW D.

International Thessaloniki Film Festival

November, 1995

Now in its 36th year, this festival is the major international film event in Greece. Thessaloniki targets a new generation of film-makers, awarding a grand prize of US$ 50,000 in an international competition for first and second films by young directors. The event also includes tributes and retrospectives (Nagisha Oshima and Yorgos Tzavelas in 1994), a Greek Film Competition and "New Horizons," an information section with a large international selection of contemporary films, as well as a showcase of today's young cinema. *Inquiries to:*

International Thessaloniki Film Festival, 36 Sina Street, Athens 106 76, Greece. Tel: (30 1) 361 0418. Fax: (30 1) 362 1023. Telex: 4 10878 FEK.

AWARDS 1993
Golden Alexander: **From the Snow** (Greece), Goritsas.
Silver Alexander: (shared) **Lefteris** (Greece), Hoursoglou; **Darkness in Tallinn** (Finland), Järvilaturi.
Best Director: Ning Ying for **For Fun** (China).
FIPRESCI Award: **Eighteen** (Taiwan), Ho.

Gurinder Chadha, director of BHAJI ON THE BEACH, and main actress Kim Vithana, both attending the Hof Film Days

INTERNATIONAL THESSALONIKI FESTIVAL

A FORUM FOR THE YOUNG CINEMA
NOVEMBER 1995
TEL: (301) 3610418 - FAX: (301) 3621023

Encounters in İstanbul
1-16 April 1995

İSTANBUL FOUNDATION FOR CULTURE AND ARTS

14th INTERNATIONAL İSTANBUL FILM FESTIVAL

FILM

Istanbul
April 1-16, 1995

The only film festival which takes place in a city where two continents meet, the Istanbul International Film Festival, recognised as a specialised competitive event by FIAPF, acts as a valuable showcase for distributors – not just Turkish. Attendances reach 120,000 every year. Now in its 13th year, this dynamic event focuses on features dealing with arts (literature, music, cinema, dance, etc.) with other thematic sections such as Tributes, selections from World Festivals, "A Country – A Cinema", and a panorama of the Turkish cinema. A new regular section is devoted to films from the Asian Turkish Republics. *Inquiries to:* Ms Hülya Uçansu, Yildiz Kültür ve Sanat Merkezi, Beşiktaş 80746, Istanbul, Turkey. Tel: (90-212) 258 3212. Fax: (90-212) 261 8823. Telex: 26 678.

AWARDS 1993
Golden Tulip: **The Blue Exile** (Turkey/Germany/Greece), Kiral.
Special Jury Prize: **Trahir** (Romania/France), Mihaileanu.
Best Turkish Film: **An Autumn Story**, Özkan.

International Tournée of Animation

Now in production on the 27th edition, this feature-length touring showcase of international short animated films is exhibited in over 400 specialised theatres and art centres in the United States and Canada. Typically the Tournée includes 15 to 20 film selections including each year's Academy Award-winner, the prizewinners from the major festivals, and the best new work of independent animators. *Inquiries to:* Terry Thoren, 28024 Dorothy Drive, Agoura Hills, CA 91301, U.S.A. Tel: (818) 991 2884. Fax: (818) 991 3773. Telex: 247 770.

Jerusalem
July, 1995

Under the dedicated guidance of Mrs. Lia van Leer, who travels the world in search of films, the Jerusalem Festival has gained world recognition as a quality festival with a unique, intimate atmosphere, new films as well as retrospectives, and always a group of rewarding guests from abroad. *Inquiries to:* Jerusalem Film Festival, P.O. Box 8561, Jerusalem 91083, Israel. Tel: (972) 2 724131 Fax: (972) 2 733076.

Karlovy Vary
July, 1995

Now a yearly event, Karlovy Vary is the major competitive festival in Eastern Europe, with a strong emphasis on the latest Czech features. An international jury will award prizes for Best Film, Actor and Actress, as well as a Special Jury Award.

Outdoor screenings are a feature of the Jerusalem Film Festival

Inquiries to: Film Festival Karlovy Vary Foundation, Valdštejnsská 12, 118 11 Prague 1, Czech Republic. Tel: (42 2) 513 2473, 513 2412. Fax: (42 2) 530 542.

La Rochelle

June 30-July 10, 1995

Jean-Loup Passek builds a bright and enthusiastic bridge between past and future cinema with his popular and distinguished festival in this French resort, with some magnificent discoveries (the Francesca Bertini retrospective in 1993, for example), a profusion of new features and thematic programmes. At last year's festival, which was attended by over 56,000, audiences re-discovered the brilliance of early Lubitsch and Abram Room. Much more exciting than most competitive festivals! *Inquiries to:* Festival International du Film de La Rochelle, 16 rue du Saint Sabin, Paris 75011, France. Tel: (33-1) 48 06 16 66. Fax: (33-1) 48 06 15 40.

Local Heroes

March 12-18, 1995

Launched in 1984, the Local Heroes International Screen Festival brings some of the finest independent films from Canada and around the world, along with their creators, to Edmonton for five days every winter. The festival is non-competitive and comprises international screenings (recent guests have included Charles Burnett, Ken Loach and Bruce Beresford), daily debates and case studies on the current state of the Canadian film industry, and, in the Local Heroes section, a selection of the best of independent

Daniel Schmid, Freddy Buache and Jean-Loup Passek at a press conference at La Rochelle in 1994

XXIIIe FESTIVAL INTERNATIONAL DU FILM DE LA ROCHELLE

directed by jean-loup passek   **30 JUNE - 10 JULY, 1995**

100 FEATURE FILMS   300 SCREENINGS   NON COMPETITIVE

3 MAIN SECTIONS

- Retrospectives devoted to the work of past filmmakers

- Tributes to contemporary directors, in their presence

- Le Monde Tel Qu'il Est (The World As It Is), a selection of unreleased films from all over the world.

**Festival International du Film de la Rochelle
16, rue Saint Sabin, 75011 Paris
Phone: (1) 48 06 16 66 Fax: (1) 48 06 15 40**

Canadian film-making. *Inquiries to:* Local Heroes International Screen Festival, National Screen Institute - Canada, 3rd Floor, 10022 - 103 Street, Edmonton, Canada T5J 0X2. Tel: (403) 421 4084. Fax: (403) 425 8098.

Locarno
August, 1995

Under its director Marco Müller, Locarno is becoming a place where world and European premieres are regular occasions, and where serious buyers mingle with creative film-makers – not forgetting the local attendance of 150,000. Eurimages and the Council of Europe have been involved, as well as EFDO and the Foundation "Montecinemaverità" (with its annual budget of 300,000 Sfrs.). Müller can justifiably claim that Locarno is now one of the world's top half-dozen festivals. *Inquiries to:* Festival Internazionale del Film, Via della Posta 6, CH-6600 Locarno, Switzerland. Tel: (93) 31 02 32. Telex: 846565 FIFL. Fax: (93) 31 74 65.

London
November, 1995

The London Film Festival extends well beyond the National Film Theatre with screenings in major West End venues and around 180 features and documentaries shown. There are strong International selections including U.S. Indies (Europe's largest representation), France, Africa, Asia, and Latin America as well as of British productions supported by a British Feature Audience Award sponsored by the Post Office. *Inquiries to:* London Film Festival, South Bank, London SE1 8XT. Tel: (71) 815 1322/1323. Telex: 929220 NATFIL G. Fax: (71) 633 0786.

Los Angeles International Animation Celebration
April 1-10, 1995

This "festival of festivals" is a new concept for animation, and more than 400 films are showcased at the event. A panel of experts presents cash prizes and awards of more than $100,000 to the best in 15 categories. The festival is open to films in 16mm, 35mm, video (almost all standards), completed since January 1993. There are also retrospectives and artist tributes. *Inquiries to:* Terry Thoren, Chairman, Expanded Entertainment, 28024 Dorothy Drive, Agoura Hills, CA 91301, U.S.A. Tel: (818) 991 2884. Fax: (818) 991 3773. Telex: 247770 ANIM UR.

Los Angeles International Film Festival
June, 1995

Continuing the tradition started by Filmex, this event is the largest of its kind in the United States. Collaborating with over 30 film and arts organisations, the L.A. FilmFest is each year dedicated to different aspects of film-making. *Inquiries to:* Gary McVey, AFI Festivals, 2021 N. Western Avenue, Los Angeles, CA 90027. Tel: (213) 856 7707. Fax: (213) 462 4049.

Melbourne
June, 1995

Now flourishing again under the direction of Tait Brady, the Melbourne Festival is approaching its 44th year – making it the oldest festival in the Southern Hemisphere. Melbourne is respected for a broad and adventurous programme incorporating animation, experimental work, video and documentary alongside the principal feature film line-up, which features work from across the globe. *Inquiries to:* Melbourne International Film Festival, P.O. Box 296, Fitzroy 3065, Victoria, Australia. Tel: 03-417 2011. Fax: 03-417 3804.

MIFED (Milan)
October, 1995

Long established film market held in the expansive Milan Fair, particularly well attended by buyers and sellers from all over the world. Third (in calendar terms) of the year's big three film markets – preceded by the American Film Market and Cannes Film Festival – the atmosphere is all business, but Milan is still attractive, even in gloomy October. *Inquiries to:* Mrs Elena Lloyd, E.A. Fiera Internazionale di Milano, Largo Domodossola 1, 20145 Milano, Italy. Tel: (02)

Wim Wenders talking to members of the jury at the Giffoni children's film festival in Italy

49977267-7270. Telex: 331360. Fax: (02) 49977020.

Mill Valley

October 5-15, 1995

The Mill Valley Film Festival presents a wide variety of international programming that is shaped by a commitment to cultural and artistic excellence. This intimate event of unusually high calibre and dedication is set in a beautiful small town just north of San Francisco. The eleven-day, non-competitive festival includes the prestigious Videofest, as well as tributes, seminars and special events. *Inquiries to:* Mill Valley Film Festival, 38 Miller Avenue, Suite 6, Mill Valley, CA 94941, U.S.A. Tel: (415) 383 5256. Fax: (415) 383 8606.

Montpellier

October 26-November 5, 1995

The Montpellier Festival has a rich programme covering past and present productions from around the Mediterranean.

The event features competitive sections for features and shorts, and, with the help of the Commission of the European Union, awards at least two pre-production grants for full length features. The total value of the awards is in excess of $US 80,000. The 1994 Festival also included a full Pier Paolo Pasolini retrospective, coverage of "The Mediterranean, Baroque and Cinema," a retrospective of 30 years of Spanish Cinema, and a *carte blanche* for the Madrid cinémathèque. Deadline for the submission of films and projects: August 31. *Inquiries to:* Int'l Festival of Mediterranean, Film, 6 rue de la Vieille-Aiguillerie, 34000 Montpellier, France. Tel: (33) 67 66 3636. Fax: (33) 67 66 36 37.

AWARDS 1993
Features
Blind Man's Buff (Israel), Preminger.
Sundays On Leave (Romania), Caranfil.
Touchia (Algeria), Benhadj.
Shorts
The Bride (Egypt) Hetata.
The Little Man (Greece), Katsaboulas.
Quien mal andamaacaba (Spain), Sans.

Montréal World Film Festival
August, 1995

Serge Losique has established a major competitive festival in Montréal in late summer, and it is the only such event recognised by FIAPF in America. There are several categories, public attendance is extremely high, and the number of foreign personalities swells each year. Montréal is the ideal location for such an event, with its bilingual facilities and its proximity to all major North American outlets. *Inquiries to:* Serge Losique, World Film Festival, 1455 Boulevard de Maisonneuve Ouest, Montréal, Québec, Canada H3G 1M8. Tel: (514) 848 3883. Telex: 05-25472. Fax: (514) 848 3886.

AWARDS 1993
Grand Prix of the Americas: **Trahir** (Romania/France), Mihaileanu.
Special Grand Prix of the Jury: **And the Band Played On** (U.S.A.), Spottiswoode.
Best Director: (shared) **Tout ça pour ça** (France), Lelouch; **La madre muerta** (Spain), Ulloa.
Best Actor: (shared) Denis Mercier for **Le sexe des étoiles** (Canada); Johan Leysen for **Trahir** (Romania/France).
Best Actress: Carla Gravina for **Il lungo silenzio** (Italy/France).

Richard Fleischer (left) meets young spectators at the Mill Valley Film Festival in 1993

Best Screenplay: Richard Barrett, Michael Jenkins for **The Heartbreak Kid** (Australia).
Best Artistic Contribution: **Kalifornia** (U.S.A.), Sena.
Best Short Film: **Quien mal anda, mal acaba** (Spain), Sans.

Mystfest
June 25 – July 1, 1995

The International Mystery Film Festival aims to draw attention to and promote the distribution of films of the mystery, crime and detection genre. Prizes are awarded for the best direction and screenplay, and the event is well-attended by local talent (Scola, Verdone) as well as international directors. Last year's event screened a tribute to Orson Welles and a Lon Chaney retrospective. *Inquiries to:* Mystfest International Mystery Film Festival, Centro Culturale Polivalente, Piazza della Repubblica 31, 47033 Cattolica (RN), Italy. Tel: (541) 967802. Fax: (541) 967803.

MYSTFEST XVI, 1995

Festival Internazionale del Giallo e del Mistero cinema televisione letteratura

International Mystery Film Festival movies books and TV

Cattolica, Italy 25 giugno - 1 luglio 1995
Centro Culturale Polivalente
Tel: 0541/967802 - Fax 0541/967803

37. NORDIC FILM DAYS LÜBECK
2 – 5 November 1995

LARGEST SCREENING OF NORDIC FILMS IN GERMANY

THE BEST FILMS OF THE YEAR BIG SHOTS AND NEWCOMERS

Information:
NORDISCHE FILMTAGE LÜBECK
D-23539 Lübeck
Fax +49 451 7197

New York

October, 1995

Now in its 33rd year, the New York Film Festival has resisted the temptation to grow into a major market offering hundreds of films, remaining instead a small (under 30 total) selection of feature films and shorts culled from around the world. Attendance has been well over 95% for the past decade, and each selection receives extensive coverage in local, national and even international media. *Inquiries to:* Film Society of Lincoln Center, 70 Lincoln Center Plaza, New York, NY 10023, U.S.A. Tel: (212) 875 5610. Fax: (212) 875 5636.

Nordische Filmtage

November 2-5, 1995

This annual event held in the charming medieval town of Lübeck (north of Hamburg), throws a spotlight on the Scandinavian and Baltic cinema and enables members of the trade, critics, and other visitors to see the best of the new productions. *Inquiries to:* Nordische Filmtage Lübeck, D-23539 Lübeck, Germany. Tel: (451) 122 4105. Fax: (451) 451 7197.

Norwegian International Film Festival

August 25-September 1, 1995

Held in the west coast port of Haugesund every summer, the Norwegian film festival has now become the country's major film event attended by many international visitors along with more than 1,000 representatives from the Norwegian and Scandinavian film world. The festival is run by festival director Gunnar Johan Løvvik and programme director is Vigdis Lian. Honourable President is Liv Ullmann. The "Amanda Statuettes" are presented there. *Inquiries to:* PO Box 145, N-5501 Haugesund, Norway. Tel: (47) 52 734 430. Fax: (47) 52 734 420.

Nyon

September, 1995

For over 25 years, Nyon has been a focus for the world's documentaries to aim at. There are awards for the best entries and an indispensable retrospective section as well as informative screenings, all under the diligent stewardship of Erika de Hadeln. *Inquiries to:* Festival International du Film Documentaire – Nyon, Case postale 98, CH-1260 Nyon, Switzerland. Tel: (41) 22 361 60 60. Fax: (41) 22 361 70 71.

Oberhausen

April 27-May 3, 1995

Now in its 41st year, Oberhausen still has a just claim to be the world's premier short film festival. Not only is there a wider selection of shorts from all over the world (international and German competition), but also an opportunity to attend the Festival of Youth, an International Symposia and discussions about relevant questions in the media field. *Inquiries to:* Internationale Kurzfilmtage Oberhausen, Christian-Steger Strasse 10, D-46042 Oberhausen 1, Germany. Tel: (208) 807 088. Fax: (208) 852 591.

We look forward to greeting you again!

HAUGESUND
The NORWEGIAN INTERNATIONAL FILM FESTIVAL
AUG 25 - SEPT 1 1995

It is the aspiration of the Festival to maintain and enhance its particular blend of artistic ambition, business focus and conviviality. Our aim is to keep the Festival selective and of high artistic quality, with opportunities for both social and business contacts.

Gunnar Løvvik
Festival Director
Vigdis Lian
Programme Director

PO Box 145 N-5501
Haugesund, Norway
Tel: +47 52 73 44 30
Fax: +47 52 73 44 20

Honorary President:
Liv Ullmann

MAIN AWARDS 1994
Ara, Megobaro (Georgia), Mgeladze.
Mieso (Poland), Szulkin.
After '68 (Ireland), Burke.
Gbanga Tita (Belgium), Knauf.
Sorrow of the Black Gold (Romania), Dragin.
Satya: A Prayer for the Enemy (U.S.A.), Bruno.

Odense
August 1-6, 1995

Denmark's only international short film festival invites unusual films with an original and imaginative sense of creative delight – the sort of delight to be found in the works of Hans Christian Andersen. All 16mm and 35mm films can participate. Maximum length 60 minutes running time. *Inquiries to:* Odense Film Festival, Vindegade 18, DK-5000 Odense C, Denmark. Tel: (45) 66 131372, ext. 4044. Fax: (45) 65 914318.

MAIN AWARDS 1994
World of Glory (Sweden), Andersson.
Home Stories (Germany), Müller.
Franz Kafka (Poland), Dumala.

Oulu International Children's Film Festival
November 14-20, 1994

The only annual festival of full-length feature films for children in Scandinavia. Event is competitive and screens both recent films and retrospective seasons. *Inquiries to:* Oulu International Children's Film Festival, Torikatu 8, SF-90100 Oulu, Finland. Tel: (81) 314 1735. Fax: (81) 314 1730.

Palm Springs
January 5-15, 1995

Palm Springs International Film Festival is a glittering event, screening over 100 films from 25 countries, including U.S. and world premieres. Founded by Palm Springs' mayor, Sonny Bobo, the festival offers seminars on various aspects of film-making and presents awards to leading film-makers at a black-tie event. This year's event will pay tribute to Frederick Loewe, Alan Ladd and the Mary Pickford

**XIII
INTERNATIONAL
CHILDREN'S
FILM FESTIVAL
OULU**

14-20 NOV 1994

Torikatu 8,
SF-90100 Oulu, Finland
Tel: + 358 81 3141 732/3141 735
Fax: + 358 81 3141 730

Foundation. *Inquiries to:* Palm Springs International Film Festival, PO Box 2230, Palm Springs, California 92263, U.S.A. Tel: (619) 322 2930. Fax: (619) 320 8934.

Pesaro

June, 1995

The "Mostra Internazionale del Nuovo Cinema" (Pesaro Film Festival) is particularly concerned with the work of new directors and emergent cinemas – in other words, with innovation at every level of the film world. For the past 30 years this Mediterranean resort has been the centre for some lively screenings and debates, and in recent seasons the festival has been devoted to a specific country or culture. Pesaro also tries hard to arrange commercial distribution for films during the festival. *Inquiries to:* Mostra Internazionale del Nuovo Cinema, Via Villafranca 20, 00185 Rome, Italy. Tel: (39-6) 445 6643-491156. Fax: (39-6) 491163. Telex: 624596 NEWCINI.

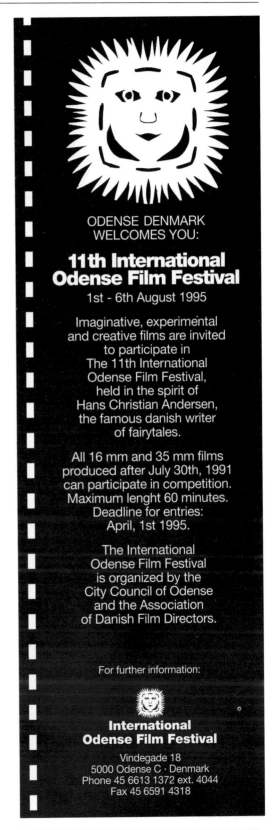

Winners of the 1993 Jean Mitry Award at Pordenone: Jonathan Dennis (founder of the New Zealand Film Archive), and David Shephard, of Film Preservation Associates, Los Angeles

Pordenone

October, 1995

Although, to quote Hemingway's *Farewell to Arms*, Pordenone is "not much of a place", for one week each autumn this small Italian town is visited by a devoted group of scholars, collectors, archivists and enthusiasts, who travel from Europe, America, and as far away as Japan or Australia to attend the "Giornate del Cinema Muto," a silent film festival held each year since 1982. In 1989 the festival presented a rare programme of Russian silents, while in 1992 the cartoons Walt Disney made before Mickey was invented were rediscovered. Pordenone 1994 hailed some of America's most underrated slapstick comedians, and explored Indian silent cinema. *Inquiries to:* La Cineteca del Friuli, Via Osoppo 26, 33013 Gemona (UD), Italy. Tel: (0432) 980458. Fax: (0432) 970542.

Portland

February 16 – March 5, 1995

The Portland International Film Festival is an invitational survey of over seventy films from thirty countries, screening features, shorts and documentaries. The event also includes tributes and retrospectives, with visiting directors, and a special showcase (the Pacific Rim in 1995). The festival is non-competitive and attracts around 30,000 spectators. *Inquiries to:* Portland International Film Festival, Northwest Film Center, 1219 S.W. Park Avenue, Portland, OR 97205, U.S.A. Tel: (503) 221 1156. Fax: (503) 226 4842.

Puerto Rico

November, 1995

The Puerto Rico International Film Festival started in 1991, an offshoot of the San Juan Cinemafest with a more international focus. The festival is non-competitive, but private sponsors back certain awards such as Best Film and a Youth Award. Between 85 and 100 films are acreened, with a Latin American section (which last year featured a focus on a new Chilean films), a Current Spanish Cinema Panorama, and a Women in Film section. *Inquiries to:* Juan Gerard Gonzalez, Puerto Rico International Film Festival, 70 Mayaguez Street, Suite B1, Hato Rey, Puerto Rico 00918, U.S.A. Tel: (809) 764 7044. Fax: (809) 753 5367.

18TH

PORTLAND

INTERNATIONAL

FILM

FESTIVAL

Northwest Film Center
1219 S.W. Park Avenue
Portland, OR 97205
(503) 221-1156 FAX 226-4842

FEBRUARY 16 - MARCH 5
1995

Programme:
Non-fiction?
Chinese cinema
Henry King
Max & Dave Fleischer

LE GIORNATE
DEL CINEMA
MUTO

14th
PORDENONE
SILENT
FILM
FESTIVAL
October 14-21,
1995

For information, contact the festival c/o
La Cineteca del Friuli, Via Osoppo 26
33013 Gemona (UD) Italia. Tel: (+39-432) 980458 Fax (+39-432) 970542

Riminicinema International Film Festival

September, 1995

The first festival in Italy to focus its attention on "displaced wandering film-makers and contaminated cinema", originating from the relationships and the exchanges between different cultures and peoples. Rimini-cinema takes place every year in Rimini, famous seaside holiday resort and native town of Federico Fellini. Besides the competition open to feature films, awarding the Golden "R" (plus fifteen million lire),and the Silver "R" (plus 5 million lire), the programme includes a competition open to film school students from all over the world, monographs, retrospectives, debates and special events. The Festival also selects a young film-maker for the Federico Fellini Award (20 million Lire). *Inquiries to:* Riminicinema, via Gambalunga 27, 47037 Rimini, Italy. Tel: (541) 26399-22627. Fax: (541) 24227. Telex: 550318.

San Francisco

April -May, 1995

The Western Hemisphere's oldest international film festival, now in its 38th year, continues to rise in importance and popularity – last year's attendance figures leapt up for the 12th year in a row. About 80 feature films were shown non-competitively, by invitation only, while the Golden Gate Awards sidebar (28 categories for documentaries, shorts, and work made for TV) attracted nearly 900 entries from all over the world. *Inquiries to:* San Francisco International Film Festival, 1521 Eddy Street, San Francisco, CA 94115-4102, U.S.A. Tel: (415) 567 4641. Fax: (415) 921 5032.

San Juan Cinemafest

October, 1995

With its Carribean Competition and World Cinema Section, the San Juan Cinemafest is an important and unique event on the Latin American circuit. The Carribean Competition accepts both film and video, and an international jury awards the Pitirre Prize in the categories of fiction, documentary and animation. The World Cinema Section has premiered in Puerto Rico such films as *The Crying Game, Farewell My Concubine* and *The Wedding Banquet. Inquiries to:* San Juan Cinemafest, PO Box 4543, San Juan, Puerto Rico 00902. Tel: (809) 721 6125, Fax (809) 723 64512.

Sanremo

April , 1995

This distinguished event exists to promote original cinema in all its forms, and also organises admirable retrospectives. The Gran Premio carries a substantial cash award. *Inquiries to:* Nino Zucchelli. Director, Mostra Internazionale del Film d'Autore, Rotonda dei Mille 1, 24100 Bergamo, Italy. Tel: (035) 243 566/162. Fax: (035) 240816.

Sophia Loren won the Desert Palm Award at the Palm Springs Festival in 1994

San Sebastian

September, 1995

Held in an elegant Basque seaside city, only 20 kilometres from the French border, San Sebastian remains the most important film festival in Spain in terms of budget, glitter, sections, facilities, attendance, competition, partying and number of films. The city is known for its superb gastronomy, beautiful beaches and quaint streets. The festival usually attracts a number of international celebrities, as well as a wide selection of national and international press, talent, and buffs. *Inquiries to:* San Sebastian International Film Festival, Plaza de Okendo s/n, Donostia - San Sebastian 20080, Spain. Tel: (43) 481-212. Telex: 38145 FCSS E. Fax: (43) 481-218.

AWARDS 1993
Golden Shell (shared): **Principio y Fin** (Mexico), Ripstein; **Sara** (Iran), Mehrjui.
Best Director: Philippe Loiret for **Tombés du ciel** (France).
Best Actor: Juan Echanove for **Madregilda** (Spain).
Best Actress: Niki Karimi for **Sara** (Iran)
Special Jury Prize: **Huevos de Oro** (Spain), Luna.

Stockholm

November 10-19, 1995

The Stockholm Film Festival offers a Competition for current feature films displaying new orientations in contemporary film-making, a focus on American Independents, a retrospective, a summary of the Swedish films released during the year, and a survey of new major features reflecting the world cinema of today. Around 100 films have their Swedish premiere during the festival. Stockholm is the only northern European festival with a FIPRESCI jury and is recognised by FIAPF. *Inquiries to:* Stockholm International Film Festival, P.O. Box 7673, 10395 Stockholm, Sweden. Tel: (46 8)20 05 50. Fax: (46 8) 20 05 90.

AWARDS 1993
Best Film: **Un deux trois soleil** (France), Blier.
Best First Film: (shared) **Mille Bolle Blu** (Italy), **Pompucci; Fear of a Black Hat** (U.S.A.) Cundieff.
Best Actor: Marcello Mastroianni for **Un deux trois soleil** (France).
Best Actress: Ana Alvarez for **La Madre Muerta** .
Best Script: Mike Leigh for **Naked** (U.K.).
Best Photography: Tamás Sas for **Child Murders** (Hungary).

Sundance Film Festival

January , 1995

The Sundance Film Festival (formerly the United States Film Festival) is widely recognised as one of America's most respected exhibition events of American independent cinema. The dramatic and documentary films presented in the Independent Feature Film Competition each year are indicators of the current trends prevalent in American independent cinema. *Inquiries to:* Sundance Film Festival, c/o

SAN SEBASTIAN
THE SEPTEMBER FESTIVAL

SAN SEBASTIAN INTERNATIONAL FILM FESTIVAL

Apartado de Correos, 397
Tel: 43 - 48 12 12
Fax: 43 - 48 12 18
Tx: 38145 FCSS E
20080 SAN SEBASTIAN • SPAIN

Art&Maña

Patrocinador Oficial
CANAL+

Stockholm International Film Festival
November 10-19,1995

Stockholm International Film Festival
Box 7673 S-103 95 Stockholm, Sweden
Phone: +46.8.20.05.50
Fax: +46.8.20.05.90

Columbia Pictures, 10202 West Washington Boulevard, Culver City, CA 90232, U.S.A. Tel: (310) 204 2901. Fax: (310) 204 3901.

AWARDS 1994

Grand Jury Prize (Feature): **What Happened Was**, Noonan.
Grand Jury Prize (Documentary): **Freedom on My Mind**, Field, Mulford.
Film-Makers Trophy (Feature): **Clerks**, Smith; **Fresh**, Yakin.
Film-Makers Trophy (Documentary): **Theremin: An Electronic Odyssey**, Martin.
Best Cinematography (Feature): Greg Gardiner for **Suture.**
Best Cinematography (Documentary): Morton Sandtroen for **Colorado Cowboy: The Bruce Ford Story**.
Waldo Salt Screenwriting Award: Tom Noonan for **What Happened Was**.

Sydney

June 9-24, 1995

Going into its 42nd year, Sydney remains a broad-based non-competitive festival with a loyal public following and a good reputation internationally. Current line-up, under director Paul Byrnes, is about 170 films, of which about 65 are new features. Festival is competitive for short Australian films only, and the event is well patronised by local distributors. *Inquiries to:* Paul Byrnes, PO Box 950, Glebe, NSW 2037, Australia. Tel: (2) 660 3844. Fax: (2) 692 8793.

Taipei

December, 1995

International Film Exhibition Taipei is run every year alongside Taiwan's Golden Horse Awards for offshore Chinese cinema, and is organised by the city's Film Library. *Inquiries to:* International Film Exhibition Taipei, Film Library, 4/F., 7 Ch'ingtao East Road, Taipei, Taiwan.

Tampere

March 8-12, 1995

The 25th year of one of the leading short film festivals in the world. This event attracts entries from 60 countries and has the tradition of offering an interesting collection from Eastern Europe. The International competition consists of categories for documentaries, animation, and fiction films. In addition, there is a full retrospective programme, tributes and a popular archive section, as well as open seminars and debates. In 1995 Festival will celebrate its Silver Anniversary and the Motion Picture Centenary on a major scale. *Inquiries to:* Tampere Film Festival, PO Box 305, FIN-33101 Tampere, Finland. Tel: (358) 31 213 0034. Fax: (358) 31 223 0121.

AWARDS 1993
Grand Prix: **The Wrong Trousers** (U.K.), Park.
Best Animation: **Not Without My Handbag** (U.K.), Kossmehl.
Best Documentary: **Whalesong** (UK), Valentine.
Best Fiction: **La Vis** (France), Flamand.
Special Jury Prize: **Oppressão** (Brazil), Martinelli.

Telluride

September, 1995

Over the past 20 years, this friendly gathering in a spectacular location in the mountains of Colorado has become one of the world's most influential festivals, with the town of Telluride virtually doubling in size as famous directors, players, and critics descend on the Sheridan Opera House and the other well-equipped theatres there. *Inquiries to:* The National Film Preserve Ltd., PO Box B1156, Hanover, New Hampshire 03755, U.S.A. Tel: (603) 643 1255. Fax: (603) 6435938.

Toronto International Film Festival

September 7-16, 1995

A rich diversity of world cinema is featured yearly with over 250 films in ten days during the Toronto International Film Festival. The event offers hundreds of films and film-makers, in a wide range of international programmes – Galas, Contemporary World Cinema, The Edge, First Cinema, Asian and Latin American Panoramas, Spotlight, Midnight Madness and Perspective Canada – to a large and eager audience. There is also a Sales Office and an industry Symposium. *Inquiries to:* Festival of Festivals, 70 Carlton St., Toronto, Ontario, Canada M5B 1L7. Tel: (416) 967-7371. Fax: (416) 967-9477.

Tromsø International Film Festival

January 25-29, 1995

Possibly the world's northernmost film event, far beyond the Arctic Circle – this "Winter Wonderland" festival is non-competitive and focuses on contemporary art films and young directors from all continents, as well as screening retro-

42ND
SYDNEY
FILM
FESTIVAL
JUNE 1995

fax
+61 2 692 8793
tel
+61 2 660 3844
address
PO Box 950
Glebe NSW 2037
Australia
Entries close
15 March 1995

spectives of Norwegian directors (Arne Skouen in 1994). The organisers co-operate informally with the Gothenburg Festival regarding programming. *Inquiries to:* Tromsø International Film Festival, Georgernes Verft 3, N-5011 Bergen, Norway. Tel:(47) 55 232 460. Fax: (47) 55 232 006.

Tyneside European Film Festival

November, 1995

The first Tyneside European Film Festival will be a competitive festival aiming to provide a major focus for European regional cinema through a wide range of screenings, debates, discussions and forums. The Festival will be inviting directors from all over Europe to present their work and to explore the cultural geography of European film production. *Inquiries to:* Tyneside European Film Festival, 10 Pilgrim Street, Newcastle upon Tyne, NE1 6QG, United Kingdom. Tel: (091) 232 8289. Fax: (091) 221 0535.

Canadian Math

5
years of
Cinematheque Ontario (1990 - 1995)

X

20
years of
Toronto International Film Festival (1976 - 1995)

=

100
years of CINEMA (1896 - 1995)

Celebrate these milestones:

Toronto International Film Festival
September 7 - 16, 1995

Cinematheque Ontario
all year long in 1995.

For more information, write to us at
2 Carlton Street, Suite 1600,
Toronto, ON Canada
M5B 1J3

CLASSIC
Wheat

AIR CANADA

40th VALLADOLID
INTL. FILM FESTIVAL (Spain)
20/28 OCT.'95

P.O. Box 646
Tel.: (34/83) 30 57 00/77/88
Fax: (34/83) 30 98 35
47003 VALLADOLID (SPAIN)

Umeå

September, 1995

Umeå is an annual, non-competitive event screening some 70 features, including a number of Swedish premieres from around the world. Director Stig Eriksson's lively programme includes a spotlight on women film-makers, a selection of sneak previews and films for children, as well as a focus on the contemporary cinema of a particular country or genre. The popular "Camera Obscura" section features restored or neglected classics. There are seminars and workshops for festival visitors. *Inquiries to:* Umeå Filmfestival, Box 43, 901 02 Umeå, Sweden. Tel: (46) 90 13 33 88/13 33 56. Fax: (46) 90 11 79 61. Telex: 54084 TELEUMB S.

Uppsala

October , 1995

The only International Short Film Festival in Sweden. Uppsala presents a wide range of film styles and topics. Awards in four categories – Short Fiction, Animation, Documentary, and Best Scandinavian Short. The festival also includes retrospectives, exhibits and seminars. Special section of international children's and youth films, with an award presented by a special children's jury. *Inquiries to:* Uppsala Short Film Festival, PO Box 1746, S-751 47 Uppsala, Sweden. Tel: (18) 12 00 25. Fax: (18) 12 13 50. Telex: 76020.

Valladolid

October , 1995

One of the best organised European fests and the year's most popular Spanish event, Valladolid offers an Official section with features and shorts in competition, special tributes, retrospectives and a competitive documentary section. The 1994 sidebars included a retro on Arthur Penn, a tribute to spanish actors Manuel Alexandre and Rafael Alonso, eleven features directed by Italian neo-realist Gianni Amelio, and a tribute to Canadian DP Jean-Claude Labrèque. *Inquiries to:* Semana Internacional de Cine de Valladolid, Spain. Tel: (34-83) 305700/77/88. Fax: (34-83) 309835. Telex: 26304 SEMINCI.

Jules Dassin awards the Golden Alexander to Sotiris Goritsas at the 1993 Thessaloniki Festival
photo: Popi Melliou

Vancouver

September 29 – October 15, 1995

Now in its fourteenth year, this festival has grown into an event of considerable stature. About 100,000 people attend more than 350 screenings, and the Canadian city's natural beauty adds to the hospitality offered guests. Areas of special focus are East Asia, Canada and Non-fiction Features. Overlapping events include the Annual Trade Forum, the Screenwriter's Art, international section and special showcase events. *Inquiries to:* Alan Franey, 410-1008 Homer Street, Vancouver, B.C., Canada V6B 2X1. Tel: (604) 685 0260. Fax: (604) 688 8221.

Venice

September, 1995

Gillo Pontecorvo's showy management of the Mostra del Cinema failed to encourage the innovations long needed for the whole Biennale d'Arte centenary body. Most of the pleasures of a costly visit to the aristocratic Lido (where "film market" still seems unheard-of expression) are coming from superb parallel art exhibits all around town. *Inquiries to:* Mostra Internazionale d'Arte Cinematografica, La Biennale, San Marco, Ca' Giustinian, 30124 Venice, Italy. Tel: (41) 5219711. Fax: (41) 5200569. Telex: 410685 BLE-VE-1.

10th Umeå International Film Festival 14-20 Sept

Features. Documentaries. Women Directors. Camera Obscura. Silent classics. Etcetera.

P.O. Box 43, S-901 02 Umeå, Sweden
Phone: +46-90-13 33 88, 13 33 56
Fax: +46-90-11 79 61

AWARDS 1993

Golden Lion: (shared) **Short Cuts** (U.S.A.), Altman; **Three Colours: Blue** (France), Kiéslowski.
Special Jury Prize: **Bad Boy Bubby** (Australia/Italy), De Heer.
Silver Lion: **Kosh ba Kosh** (Taadzhikstan),
Best Actor: Fabrizio Bentivoglio for **A Soul Torn in Two** (Italy).
Best Actress: Juliette Binoche for **Three colours: Blue** (France).
Best Ensemble Cast: **Short Cuts** (U.S.A.)

Viennale

October, 1995

A "Festival of Festivals", the Viennale presents a line-up of new international films; young cinema and a Children's Film Festival; a Twilight Zone section (midnight screenings); creative documentaries; world premieres and a selection of recent Austrian films; tribute programmes dedicated to "outsider" directors (Nanni Morretti and Mitsuo Yanagimachi in 1994); and a large thematic/ historic retrospective (*Hollywood 1960-1963: Pop and Politics* in 1994). *Inquiries to:* Viennale, Stiftgasse 6, A-1070 Vienna, Austria. Tel: (431) 526 59 47. Fax: (431) 93 41 72.

Vue sur les Docs

June 10-15, 1995

The Vue sur les Docs International Documentary Film Festival, along with the documentary film market *Sunny Side of the Docs*, takes place every summer in Marseille. 100 films are screened (20 in the International Competition), with priority being given to experimental films and those made with the spirit of freedom and discovery. As well as the competition, which awards prizes for shorts and features, there are retrospectives and a special "State of the World" section. *Inquiries to:* Vue sur les docs, 3 square Stalingrad, 13001 Marseille, France. Tel: (33) 91 84 40 17. Fax: (33) 91 84 38 34.

Warsaw

October 5-15, 1995

Annual audience-oriented event (in 1993 attended by 33,000) showing the cream of quality films from all over the world, along with a selection of new Polish productions. Non-competetive, by invitation only. Links with distributors and TV mean that over 50% of films shown open in Poland afterwards *Inquiries to:* Warsaw Film Festival, P.O. Box 816, 00-950 Warsaw 1, Poland. Tel/fax: (48-2) 635 7591.

Wellington

July, 1995

Screening an invited programme of 118 features and 70 shorts in 1994, this 23 year old Festival, along with its 26-year-old Auckland sibling, provides a non-competitive New Zealand premiere showcase for a striking diversity of film (and video) styles. An archival component, co-ordinated by Jonathan Dennis, also enjoys considerable prominence. Now in their second decade under the direction of the apparently tireless Bill Gosden, the latest editions played to audiences totalling 49,000 in Wellington and 80,000 in Auckland. *Inquiries to:* Wellington Film Festival, Box 9544, Te Aro, Wellington, New Zealand. Tel: (64) 4 385 0162. Fax: (64) 4 801 7304.

Wine Country Film Festival

July-August, 1995

Set in the heart of Northern California's premium wine country, this event accepts feature films, shorts, documentaries, animation, student films and videos. There are five categories including the independent features, international films, films that have a social comment, films about the arts and films about the environment. Non-competitive, but an award is given each year to to the film company of the year. Not surprisingly, the festival also presents special

Freddy Buache served as President of the International Jury at Vue sur les Docs in 1994

Twenty-Fourth Wellington Film Festival
Twenty-Seventh Auckland International Film Festival

★ JULY 1995 ★

Box 9544, Te Aro Wellington, Fax 64 4 801 7304. Phone 64 4 385 0162
Courier address: 3rd floor, 21-23 Cambridge Tce, Wellington, New Zealand

events featuring the culinary arts and the finest of wines. *Inquiries to:* PO Box 303, Glen Ellen, CA 95442, U.S.A. Tel: (707) 996 2536. Fax (707) 996 6964.

WorldFest-Charleston
November 8-12, 1995

This new annual festival, held in Charleston, South Carolina, offers premieres of independent and international features, shorts and documentaries. The five day event also offers in depth film and video production seminars, from screen-writing to independent feature production. Screenings are held in a restored Eighteenth-century opera house, and a select programme of 25 features are premiered. *Inquiries to:* WorldFest Charleston P.O. Box 838, Charleston, SC 29401, U.S.A. Fax: (713) 965 9960.

WorldFest-Houston
April 21-30, 1995

The Houston International Film Festival, 28 years old this year, offers competition for features, shorts, documentaries, student films, TV productions and commercials, music videos and screenplays. Worldfest-Houston is the largest film and video competition in the world in terms of the number of entries received (in 1994, over 4,100 entries from 38 countries). Festival director J. Hunter Todd now operates a new discovery festival programme which automatically enters all winners in more than 200 major international film festivals. They are then eligible for more than $2 million in cash awards. *Inquiries to:* WorldFest-Houston, P.O. Box 56566, Houston, TX 77256. Fax: (713) 965 9960.

Other Festivals and Markets of Note

Academic Film Olomouc, Křížkoveského 8, 771 47 Olomouc, Czech Republic. Tel: (68) 5508 277. Fax: (68) 26 476. (*International Festival of scientific and educational films – April.*)

Alexandria Film Festival, 9 Oraby Str., Cairo, Egypt Tel: 5780042. Fax: 768727. (*Competitive, mainly for Mediterranean countries-August/September.*)

American Film and Video Festival, 8050 Milwaukee Ave., PO Box 48659, Niles, IL 60714, U.S.A. (*Formerly in New York, this is the definitive round-up of documentaries and animated films in the States – May.*)

American Film Market, 12424 Wilshire Blvd, Suite 600, Los Angeles, CA 90025, U.S.A. (*Efficiently-run market primarily for English-language theatrical films. Buyers must be accredited – February.*)

American Independent Feature Film Market, 12th Floor, 104 West 29th, New York, NY10001, U.S.A. Tel: (212) 243 7777. Fax: (212) 243 3882. (*Showcase for independently produced American films – September.*)

Amiens, Marché International du Film, 36 rue de Noyon, 80000 Amiens, France. Tel: (22) 910 144. Fax: (22) 925 304. (*Film Market, with workshops and co-production finance deals being negotiated, plus competitive section – November.*)

Aspen Filmfest, PO Box 8910, Aspen, Colorado 81612, U.S.A. Tel: (303) 925 6882. Fax: (303) 925 1967. (*Features, documentaries and shorts – September. Short subject film competition – February.*)

Atlantic Film Festival, 2015 Gottingen Street, Halifax, Nova Scotia, Canada B3K 2E1. Tel: (902) 422 3456. Fax: (902) 422 4006.

This Fall discover the "Paris of the New World."

IF YOU'RE ACCUSTOMED TO GOING TO CANNES IN THE SPRING, YOU'LL REALLY FALL FOR CHARLESTON IN NOVEMBER.

Long regarded as one of the most romantic and European cities in America, Charleston is now host city to one of the industry's most exciting international film festivals.

World premiers. World class seminars and juried competitions. And an ambience reminiscent of the South of France. With graciously elegant hotels and inns, fabulous restaurants, pristine beaches, internationally ranked golf courses and enough history, mystery and romance to enthrall even the most jaded visitor.

This year's festival will include over 25 exciting premieres, plus a juried competition and generous cash awards in numerous catergories,

including features, shorts, medical, student, independent films, and screen plays. Winners are also eligible for up to two million in cash prizes through Worldfest's Discovery Festival Program, whereby all winners are submitted to the top 200 international festivals worldwide. There will be educational seminars conducted by world renowned film makers, a grand awards Gala, A lifetime Achievement Award to a major Hollywood star, complete 100 page program book and parties galore.

Please join us in our second year as we celebrate America's greatest art form in one of its most historic and beautiful cities-Worldfest Charleston.

WORLDFEST CHARLESTON
THE CHARLESTON INTERNATIONAL FILM FESTIVAL
FOR COMPLETE FESTIVAL/SEMINAR INFORMATION, AND ENTRY KIT, CONTACT:

J. HUNTER TODD, CHAIRMAN • WORLDFEST CHARLESTON • PO BOX 838, CHARLESTON, SC 29401-0868
1-800-501-0111 (713) 965-9955 FAX (713) 965-9960 TELEX: 317-876

(Features, documentaries, shorts and work-shops. Incorporates ScreenScene children's festival – September)

Banff Festival of Mountain Films, The Banff Centre, Box 1020, Stn. 38, Banff, AB, Canada T0L 0C0. Tel: (403) 762 6349. Fax: (403) 762 6277. *(International competition for all films and videos related to mountains and the spirit of adventure – November.)*

Banco Nacional International Film Showing, Rua Voluntarios de Patria 88, Rio de Janeiro, RJ 22270 Brazil. Tel: (21) 285 8505. Fax: (21) 286 4029. *(Screens over 50 American and European features – September.)*

Bergamo Film Meeting, Via Pascoli 3, 24121 Bergamo, Italy. Tel: (35) 23 40 11. Fax: (35) 23 31 29. *(Useful gathering aimed at the specialist distributors interested in buying quality films for Italy – competitive cash prizes – July.)*

Birmingham International Film and Television Festival, c/o Central TV, Central House, Broad Street, Birmingham B1 2JP, U.K. Tel: (21) 616 4213. Fax: (21) 616 4392. *(Growing provincial festival – October.)*

Brisbane International Film Festival, Level 3, Hoyts Regent Building, 167 Queen St. Mall, Brisbane, Queensland 4000, Australia. Tel: (7) 220 0333. Fax: (7) 2200400. *(New Australian event, aiming for a strong Asian input – August.)*

Cairo International Film Festival, 17 Kasr El Nil Street, Cairo, Egypt. Tel: 3923562/ 3923962. Telex: 21781 CIFFUN. Fax: 3938979. *(Competitive, aimed at showing major international films not usually available at local cinemas – December.)*

Cairo International Children's Film Festival, 17 Kasr El Nil Str., Cairo, Egypt. Tel: 3923 562. Fax: 3938 979. *(Competitive – September.)*

Camerimage, Foundation TUMULT, Rynek Nowomiojski 28, 87-100 Torun, Poland. Tel: (56) 248 79. Fax: (56) 275 95. *(International event celebrating the art of cinematography, with a competition and many top cinematographers in attendance – November-December.)*

Cape Town International Film Festival, Univ. of Cape Town, Private Bag, Rondes-bosch 7700, South Africa. Tel: (021) 23-8257. Fax: (021) 242355. *(Longest established such event in South Africa, non-competitive in structure, progressive in tone – April.)*

Cherbourg, Festival de Cinéma Franco-Britannique, Association Travelling, 1 rue du Fourdray, 50100 Cherbourg, France. *(Charming and enthusiastic small festival focusing on British film – October.)*

Chicago Latino Film Festival, 600 S. Michigan Ave, Chicago, IL 60605, U.S.A. Tel: (312) 431 1330. Fax: (312) 360 0629. *(Aims to promote awareness of Latino culture through film and video – April.)*

Cinequest, San Jose Film Festival, PO Box 720040, San Jose, California 95172, U.S.A. Tel: (408) 995 6305. Fax: (408) 277 3862. *(Showcase for independent films from around the world, grants awarded to indie-makers – November.)*

Cleveland International Film Festival, 1621 Euclid Ave., Cleveland, Ohio 44115, U.S.A. Tel: (216) 623 0400. Fax: (216) 623 0103. *(Round-up of new and classic films from all major countries – April.)*

Cork Film Festival, Festival Office, Tobin Street, Cork, Ireland. *(Annual competitive, for documentaries, animation, art films, fiction and sponsored shorts – October.)*

Cracow International Short Film Festival, c/o Apollo Film, ul. Pychowicka 7, 30-960 Kraków, Poland. Tel: (12) 671355. Fax: (12) 671552. *(Poland's oldest international film festival and respected short film showcase – May.)*

Damascus Film Festival, National Film Organisation, Rawa, Takriti, Damascus, Syria. *(Competitive event for third world cinema, aims to show films by young and experimental directors. Biannual – November.)*

Deauville Festival, c/o Promo–2000, 36 rue Pierret, 92200 Neuilly-sur-Seine, France. Tel: (1) 46 40 55 00 Fax: (1) 46 40 55 39. *(Feature films from the United States – September.)*

Dublin Film Festival, 1 Suffolk Street, Dublin 2, Eire. Tel: (353) 679 2937. Fax: (353) 679 2939. *(Amicable Irish festival focusing on world cinema with special emphasis on Irish film – March.)*

Duisburg Film Week, am König-Heinrich-Platz, D-47051 Duisburg, Germany. Tel: (203) 283-4187. Fax: (203) 2834-130. *(Dedicated to German documentaries – November.)*

Durban International Film Festival, University of Natal, King George V Avenue, Durban 4001, South Africa. Tel: (31) 811 3978. Fax: (31) 261 7107. *(Annual*

35 FESTIVAL INTERNACIONAL DE CINE DE CARTAGENA

(1960-1995) March 3-10

OFFICIAL COMPETITION (IBERO-LATIN-AMERICAN), FEATURE SHORT, OUT OF COMPETITION - INTERNATIONAL CINEMA - FRENCH AND ITALIAN CINEMA. MACLA FILM, TV, VIDEO AND CABLE MARKET.

THE ONLY FESTIVAL COMPETITIVE FOR IBERO-LATIN-AMERICAN FILMS RECOGNIZED BY THE F.I.A.P.F.

FESTIVAL INTERNACIONAL DE CINE DE CARTAGENA
Baluarte San Francisco Javier, Calle San Juan de Dios
Tels: (57-53) 600970-600966-642345
Fax: (57-53) 600970-601037
Apartado Aéreo 1834
Cartagena-Colombia

Avianca
La Aerolínea de Colombia
The Official Airline

festival devoted to a better understanding of international cinema. Arranges screenings in peri-urban Black areas of the city – July.)

Dylan Dog Horror Fest, Via M. Buonarroti 38, 20145 Milan, Italy. Tel: (2) 4800 2877. Fax: (2) 4819 5682. *(Promoted by Italy's number one horror comic, this event features previews and retrospectives, and an impressive line-up of special guests – June.)*

Emporium, Tenama Sdn. Bhd., 332a–15D, G.C.B. Plaza, Jalan Ampang, 68000, Kuala Lumpur, Malaysia. *(International exhibition of production and location co-ordination services for film and TV industries–November.)*

Europa Cinema, Via Giulia 66, 00186 Roma, Italy. *(Successor to the Rimini festival, concentrating on European product, now down near the heel of Italy at Bari – September.)*

Festival de Genève, Case Postale 561, CH–1211 Geneva 11, Switzerland. Tel: (22) 321 54 66. Fax: (22) 321 98 62. *(Previously known as Stars de Demain, this festival dedicates itself to seeking out future film-making talent – October.)*

Feminale, Luxemburger Str. 72, D-50674 Köln, Germany. *(International Films for women. Non-competitive-September/October.)*

Festival of French Cinema, Tel-Aviv Cinémathèque, 2 Sprintzak Street, Tel-Aviv, Israel. *(Screens new French fare, many Israeli premieres, with tributes and retrospectives – April.)*

Festival International du Film sur L'Art, 640 rue Saint-Paul Ouest, Bureau 406, Montréal, Québec H3C 1L9 Tel: (514) 874-1637. Fax: (514) 874-9929. *(Competition and retrospectives devoted to documentaries etc. on art – March)*

Festival dei Popoli, Via de Castalani 8, 50122 Florence, Italy. Tel: (55) 294 353. Fax: (55) 213 698. *(Documentaries on social issues,*

ACADEMIA FILM OLOMOUC

International festival of scientific and educational films, television and video programmes

The Festival is a contest open to programmes produced in the last two years, it gives awards in categories (humanities, medicine, natural sciences, theology, physical culture), for the best documentary work, the work on art and the educational work.
Held annually in April (2–5 April, 1995)
Deadline for entry: 31 January, 1995
Address of festival:
Academia Film Olomouc, Křižkového 8,
771 47 Olomouc, Czech Republic
tel. ++42 68 5508 277, fax: ++42 68 26 476

Daniel Schmid, Maddalena Fellini, and festival director Gianfranco Miro Gori at Riminicinema

films on history etc., in part competitive – November-December.)

Festival du Cinéma International en Abitibi-Témscamingue, 215 Avenue Mercier, Rouyn-Noranda, Québec J9X 5WB, Canada. Tel: (819) 762 6212. Fax: (819) 762 6762. *(Competitive for features and shorts held in northwestern Québec – October-November.)*

Festival International de Biarritz, Office de Tourisme, Square d'Ixelles, 64200 Biarritz, France. *(Films and cultural event on Spanish, Portuguese and South American countries – September.)*

Festival International Nouveau Cinéma et Vidéo, 3726 Boulevard Saint-Laurent, Montréal, Québec, Canada H2X 2V8. Telex: 5560074. *(Seeks to promote experimental films of outstanding quality as an alternative to the conventions of the commercial cinema – October.)*

Figueira da Foz, Apartado de Correios 5407, 1709 Lisbon Codex, Portugal. *(Competitive festival on the Portuguese coast – September.)*

Film Art Festival, Cankarjev Dom, Presernova 10, 61000 Ljubljana, Slovenia. Tel: (61) 125 8121. Fax: (61) 224 279.

(Presents work of young European writers and directors, U.S. Independents, documentaries and lesser known cinematography–October.)

Filmfest München, Kaiserstrasse 39, D-8000 Munich 40, Germany. Tel: (89) 381 9040. Fax: (89) 381 9042. *(Well attended, non-competitive event – June/July.)*

Florence Film Festival, c/o Assessorarto alla Cultura, Comune di Firenze, Diapartimento Arti Visive, Via Sant'Egidio 21, 50122 Florence, Italy. *(Review of independent cinema – features only – December.)*

Florida Film Festival, 1300 South Orlanda Avenue, Maitland, Florida 32751, U.S.A. *(Ten days of film premieres, seminars and galas. Competitive – June.)*

French Film Festival, 5555 North Tamiami Trl., Sarasota, Florida 34243, U.S.A. Tel: (813) 351 9010. *(Quality showcase for French cinema; a screening here could lead to national distribution – November.)*

Gay and Lesbian Film Festival, National Film Theatre, South Bank, London SE1 8XT. Tel: (71) 928 3535. Fax: (71) 633 9323. *(Films made by, or about, gays and lesbians – March.)*

Gijón International Festival for Young

People, Cerinterfilm, Paseo de Begoña, 24 entlo, Gijón 33205 Spain. Tel: (85) 343 739. Fax: (85) 354152. Telex: 87443 FICG E. *(Concentrates on films for young people, with competitive and non-competitive sections – July.)*

Gramado Film Festival, Av. des Hortensias 2029, Gramado 955670-000, Brazil. Tel: (5554) 286 2397. Fax: (5554) 286 2428. *(Latin language films–August.)*

Haifa International Film Festival, 142 Hanassi Avenue, Haifa 34633, Israel. Tel: (4) 386 246. Fax: (4) 384 327. *(A non-competitive event, including a broad spectrum of new films from around the world, special tributes, retrospectives and other events – September/October.)*

Hawaii International Film Festival, 700 Bishop Street, Honolulu, Hawaii 96813, U.S.A. Tel: (808) 528 1410. Fax: (808) 528 1410. *(Aims to bring East and West together through film; all screenings free – November-December.)*

Hiroshima Animation Festival, 4-17 Kako-machi, Naka-hu, Hiroshima 730, Japan. Tel: (82) 2450245. Fax: (82) 2450246. *(Competitive event for animation – August.)*

Holland Animation Film Festival, Hoogt 4, 3512 GW Utrecht, Holland. Tel: (30) 312 216. Fax: (30) 312 940. *(Unique biannual competitive survey of applied animation – November.)*

Indonesian Film Festival, National Film Council, Jalan Merdeka Barat No. 9, Jakarta, Indonesia. Tel: (21) 320 733. Fax: (21) 310 3560. *(Colourful annual survey of Indonesian cinema – November.)*

International Animated Film Festival – Cinanima, Rua 62, No. 251, 4501 Espinho Codex, Portugal. Tel: (2) 721 611. Fax: (2) 726 015. *(Animation – November.)*

International Cinema Week, Via S. Giacomo alla Pigna 6, 37121 Verona, Italy. Tel: (45) 800 6778. Fax: (45) 590 624. *(Offers a wide panorama of film-makers and genres from a particular country – April.)*

International Educational Film Festival of Roshd, No. 8 Semnan Lane, Bahar Ave., Tehran 15617, Iran. Tel: 762 280; Fax: 827 787. *(November.)*

International Festival of Films on Architecture and Town-Planning, Escaliers du Marché 19, CH-1003 Lausanne, Switzerland. Tel: (21) 312 17 35. Fax: (21) 23 78 42. *(Bi-annual event for films on theme of architecture – May.)*

Call for Entries

31st Chicago International Film Festival

5 – 22 October 1995

Competitive categories:
Feature film, short subject, television commercial, television production, documentary, animation

415 N. Dearborn St. Chicago, IL 60610
Phone: 312/644-3400
Fax: 312/644-0784

Deadline: July 1, 1995

International Festival of Films on Art, Escaliers du Marché 19, CH-1003 Lausanne, Switzerland. Tel. (21) 312 17 35. Fax: (21) 23 78 42. *(Bi-annual event – even years only – featuring films relating to painting, sculpture, design and architecture – October.)*

International Filmwochenende Würzburg, Filminitiative Würzberg, Gosbersteige 2, D-8700 Würzburg, Germany. Tel: (931) 414 098. Fax: (931) 416 279. *(Non-competitive event screening some 20-25 features, emphasis on dialogue between film-makers and audience – January.)*

Internationales Kinderfilmfestival im Frankfurt am Main, Kinder-und-Jugend-filmzentrum in der Bundesrepublik Deutschland, Kuppelstein 34, D-5630 Remsheid 1, Germany. Tel: (2191) 794 233. Fax: (2191) 71810. *(New films for, or featuring, children, judged by children and professionals. Plenty for parents too – September.)*

International Style, University Events Office, UC San Diego, 9500 Gilman Drive, La Jolla, California 92093-0078, U.S.A. Tel: (619) 534 0497. Fax: (619) 534 7860. *(Presents new films from the world's most talented film-makers, not necessarily the most well-known – January.)*

International Underwater Film and Photo Festival, Zeil 41, D-6000 Frankfurt am Main 1, Germany. Tel: (69) 28 18 81. Fax: (69) 28 22 66. *(Produced in association with Frankfurt's Filmmuseum, this unique festival presents films and exhibitions of underwater delights, with a focus on preservation of the environment – April/May.)*

International Wildlife Film Festival, 802 East Front Street, Missoula, Montana 59802, U.S.A. *(The worlds oldest wildlife film festival with an emphasis on children and learning–April)*

International Women Directors' Film Festival, Maison des Arts, Palace Salvador Allende, 94000 Créteil, France. Tel: (1) 49 80 38 98. Fax: (1) 43 99 04 10. *(Features, shorts, animated films all made by women. Annual spotlight on an actress – April.)*

Isfahan International Festival of Films for Children and Young Adults, Farhang Cinema, Dr. Shariati Ave., Gholbak, Tehran 19139, Iran. Tel: 265086. Fax: 267082. Telex: 214283 FCFIR. *(October.)*

Ismailia Festival for Documentary and Short Films, National Film Centre – Ministry of Culture, City of Arts Giza, Cairo, Egypt. Tel: 854 801. Fax: 854 701. *(National and international.)*

Leeds International Film Festival, 19 Wellington St, Leeds LS12 4DG, U.K. Tel: (532) 478 308. Fax: (532) 426 761. *(Retrospectives, premieres and director tributes with a yearly theme – October.)*

Leipzig Festival, Box 940, 04009 Leipzig, Germany. Tel: (347) 294660. Fax: (347) 294660. *(Documentaries and animation. Competitive – November.)*

Lille International Festival of Short and Documentary Films, 24-34 rue Washington, 75008 Paris, France. *(Competitive for shorts, with additional panorama of recent French production in the field – April.)*

London Jewish Film Festival, National Film Theatre, South Bank, London SE1 8XT, U.K. Tel: (71) 928 3535. Fax: (71) 633 9323. *(October.)*

Miami Festival, Film Society of Miami, 444 Brickell Road, Suite 229, Miami, FL 33131, U.S.A. Tel: (305) 377 3456. Telex: 264047. *(Non-competitive, with emphasis on Hispanic cinema – February.)*

Midnight Sun Film Festival, Malminkatu 36 B 102, 00100 Helsinki, Finland. Tel: (358–0) 685 2242. Fax: (358–0) 694 5560. *(Long weekend for film lovers in the Midsummer beauty of Finland, and above the Arctic Circle! – June.)*

Newark Black Film Festival, The Newark Museum, 49 Washington Street, PO Box 540, Newark, NJ 07101, U.S.A. *(Films by black independent film-makers or relevant to African-American experience and education – June).*

Nordisk Panorama, PB 259, SF-65101 Vaasa, Finland. Tel: (358) 6117-7748. Fax: (358) 6117-7749. *(Nordic shorts and documentaries – September.)*

Norwegian Short Film Festival, Storengveien 8b, N-1342 Jar, Norway. Tel: (67) 12 20 13. Fax: (67) 12 48 65. *(Local shorts in competition, plus selection of titles from other international festivals – held in Grimstad every June.)*

Norwich Festival of Women Film-Makers, Cinema City, St Andrews Street, Norwich NR2 4AD, U.K. *(Mixed programme of features, shorts, documentaries etc. made by women, with workshops and seminars –May.)*

Österreichische Filmtage, Columbusgasse 2, A-110 Vienna, Austria. Tel: 604 0126. Fax:

602 0795. (*Annual survey of new Austrian features, documentaries, TV, avant-garde, and video productions – June.*)

Polish Film Festival, Piwna 22, PO Box Nr. 192, 80-831 Gdańsk, Poland. Telex: 0512153. (*19th edition of the festival focusing on Polish film – November.*)

Potsdam Film Festival, Festivalbüro, am Bassinplatz 4/0-1560, Potsdam, Germany. Tel: (331) 42066. (*Spotlights young European independent film-makers – June.*)

Ragazzi Bellinzona, CH-6501 Bellinzona, Box 1419, Italy. (*Films for children – November*)

Rencontres Internationales de Musique à l'image, Office de Tourisme, Square d'Izelles, 64200 Biarritz, France. (*Music and sound tape film festival – October.*)

Riga Film Forum, ICNC "Arsenal", Marstalu Iela 14, Riga, LV, 1047 Latvia. Tel: (2) 221 620. Fax: (2) 882 0445. (*A non-competitive show of experimental, avant-garde film-making – September.*)

Rivertown (Minneapolis/St. Paul) International Film Festival, University Film Society, Minnesota Film Center, 425 Ontario Street SE, Minneapolis, MN 55414. Tel: (612) 627 4432. (*Event built up over 28 years by the reliable Al Milgrom. Scores of unusual foreign films on display – April-May.*)

Rotterdam Film Festival, PO Box 21696, 3001 AR Rotterdam, Netherlands. Tel: (31) 10 411 8080. Fax: (31) 10 413 5132. (*Largest annual cultural event in Holland, screens international premieres and houses a co-production market — January/February.*)

Rouen, Festival du Cinéma Nordique, 91 rue Crevier, 76000 Rouen, France. Tel: 35 98 28 46. Fax: 35 70 92 08. Telex: 771444. (*Competitive festival of Nordic cinema, including retrospective and information sections – March.*)

São Paulo International Film Festival, Alameda Lorena 937, 303-01 424 São Paulo, Brazil. Tel: (11) 883 5137. Fax: (11) 853 7936. (*Non-competitive event with features and shorts from around 30 countries. Emphasis on independents – October.*)

Santa Barbara International Film Festival, 1216 State Street, Suite 710, Santa Barbara, CA 93101, U.S.A. Tel: (805) 963 0023. (*Non-competitive, usually focusing on a single country – March.*)

Seattle International Film Festival, 801 East Pine Street, Seattle, Washington 98122,

---

30th Solothurn Film Festival
24-29 January 1995
The representative survey of all forms of independent Swiss film and video production of the preceeding year.
Phone +(65) 23 31 61   Fax +(65) 23 64 10
Telex 934 242 sofi ch

U.S.A. (*Unusual Northwest Pacific coast event that has done a great deal to establish Dutch cinema in the States – May-June.*)

Short and Documentary Film Festival, Farhang Cinema, Dr. Shariati Ave., Gholbak, Tehran 19139, Iran. Tel: 265 086. Fax: 678 155. (*July.*)

Shots in the Dark, Broadway, 14 Broad Street, Nottingham, NG1 3AL, U.K. Tel: (602) 526 600. (*Non-competitive festival of crime and mystery films – June.*)

Singapore International Film Festival, 11 Keppel Hill, Singapore 0409. Telex: 38283. Fax: 2722069. (*Biannual non-competitive event showcasing international films – January.*)

Sitges Festival, Paseo de Gracia 104, Barcelona, 08008, Spain. Tel: 237 3781. Fax: 237 0481. (*Decades-old science fiction and fantasy film festival, competitive, usually attended by celebrities and directors, set in charming seaside town – October.*)

Solothurn Film Festival, Postfach 1030, CH-4502 Solothurn, Switzerland. Tel: (65) 233161. Fax: (65) 236410. (*Screenings of all new Swiss films and video productions, Solothurn celebrates its 30th anniversary this year – January 24-29.*)

Southampton Film Festival, City Arts, Civic Centre, Southampton SO9 4XF, U.K. Tel: (703) 832 457. Fax: (703) 832 153. (*Different programme developed each year with workshops and other educational events – June.*)

Spoleto Festival of Two Worlds, Via Cesare Beccaria 18, Rome 00196, Italy. Tel: (6) 321 0288. Fax: (6) 320 0747. (*One of Italy's major cultural events, including music, theatre and dance as well as film – June.*)

St. Petersburg International Film Festival, 190 Kamennostrovsky Ave, St. Petersburg 197101, Russia. Tel: (812) 238 511. Fax: (812) 232 8881. (*Features international productions as well as local fare. Non-competitive – June.*)

Sunny Side of the Doc, 3 Square Stalingrad, Marseille, 13006, France. Tel: (33) 91 08 43 15. Fax: (33) 91 84 38 34. (*International documentary market – with international forums – June.*)

**PUERTO RICO
INTERNATIONAL
F I L M
F E S T I V A L**

NOVIEMBRE 8-19, 1995

Taormina International Film Festival, Palazzo Firneze, Via Pirandello 31, Taormina, Italy. Tel: (942) 21142. . Fax: (942) 23348. *(Competitive and non-competitive event in Sicily with stress on films by new directors, plus retrospectives and discussions – July.)*

Tokyo International Film Festival, 4th Floor, Landic Ginza, Bldg. II 1–6–5 Ginza, Chuo-ku, Tokyo 104, Japan. Tel: (813) 3563 6305. Fax: (813) 3563 6310. *(New mammoth event with competition and other sidebar events held in Kyoto in 1994 – September-October.)*

Troia Film Festival, 2902 Setúbal Codex, Troia, Portugal. Tel: (35165) 44121. Fax: (35165) 44123. *(Wide variety of categories in this competitive festival. Held in a summer recreational area on the tip of a peninsula – June.)*

USA Film Festival, 2917 Swiss Avenue, Dallas, Texas 75204, U.S.A. Tel: (214) 821 6300. Fax: (214) 8216364. *(Eight-day festival featuring new U.S. and foreign independents. Competition for U.S. shorts with cash prizes – April.)*

Valencia: Mostra of Mediterranean Cinema, Plaza Arzobispo, 2 acc. B., Valencia 46003, Spain. Tel: (96) 392 1506. Fax: (96) 391 5156. Telex: 63427. *(Major tributes for films made in and around the Mediterranean – October.)*

Viareggio Mystery Festival, Via dei Coronari 44, 00186 Rome, Italy. *(A festival for all genres and media covered by the term "mystery" – June.)*

Victoria Commonwealth Film Festival, Box 3035, Victoria B.C., Canada V8W 3P3. *(Focuses on films from commonwealth nations currently under-represented at most North American festivals – April/May.)*

Weekly Mail/Guardian Weekly Film Festival, PO Box 260425, Excom, 2023, South Africa. Tel: (27 11) 331 1712. Fax: (27 11) 331 3339. *(Screens local progressive films, with a short film competition – August/September.)*

Women in Cinema, International Festival of Films made by Women, Lavalle 1578 9 "B", Buenos Aires, Argentina. Tel: (541) 467 318. Fax: (541) 311 8964. *(September.)*

Women in Film Festival, 6464 Sunset Blvd., Suite 600, Los Angeles, California 90028, U.S.A. *(Dedicated to the improvement of women's image in film and TV. Various categories – November.)*

Zlín Festival, Film ateliéry, Zlín a.s., Filmová ul. 174, 761 79 Zlín, Czech Republic. *(Animated and feature films for children. Colourful and competetive – May.)*

FILM SCHOOLS

AUSTRALIA

Australian Film, Television and Radio School, PO Box 126, North Ryde, NSW 2113.

AUSTRIA

Hochschule für Musik und darstellende Kunst, Abteilung für Film und Fernsehen, Metternichgasse 12, A-1030 Vienna. Director: Prof. Mag. Robert Schöfer.

BELGIUM

Hogeschool voor Audiovisuele Communicatie (R.I.T.S.), Naamsestraat 54, 1000 Brussels. Tel: (32) 2 511 93 82. Fax: (32) 2 502 55 06

Institut des Arts de Diffusion, (I.A.D.), Rue des Wallons No. 77, B 1348 Louvain-la Neuve, Belgium.

Institut National des Arts du Spectacle et Techniques de diffusion (I.N.S.A.S.), Rue Thérésienne, 8, 1000 Bruxelles, Belgium.

Koninklijke Academie voor Schone Kunsten-Gent, Academiestraat 2, B-9000 Gent.

BRAZIL

Universidade de São Paulo, Escola de Comunicacões e Artes, Departamento de Cinema, Radio e Televisão, Av. Prof. Lúcio Martins Rodrigues 443, São Paulo 05508, Brazil. Tel: (5511) 813 3222. Fax: (5511) 8153083.

CANADA

Queen's University, 160 Stuart St, Kingston, Ont K7L 3N6. In its four-year B.A. (Honours) degree programme and three-year B.A. degree programme the Department of Film Studies provides an integrated approach to film criticism, history and production.

Sheridan College, Faculty of Visual Arts, 1430 Trafalgar Road, Oakville, Ontario, L6H 2L1, Canada. Dean: Donald Graves. The International Summer School of Animation is an intense three year diploma programme offered each year from the middle of May to the middle of August. For further information please call (416) 845 9430, ext. 2610.

Simon Fraser University, School for the Contemporary Arts, Burnaby, B.C. Canada V5A 1S6. Tel: (604) 291 3363. Fax: (604) 291 5907.

Vancouver Film School, 400-1168 Hamilton Street, Vancouver, British Columbia, V6B 2S2. Tel: (604) 685 5808. Fax: (604) 685 5830. President: James Griffin. VFS is a unique training centre that offers 5 immersion programmes in communication production: Film Production, Multimedia Production, Classical Animation, Computer Animation, and Acting for Film and Television. All programmes have been designed with industry consultation and are taught by industry professionals. Specialising in shorter (1 year) and intensive formats, students create their own graduate productions. For detailed information, please contact the Registrar.

Univ. of Manitoba, 450 University College, Winnipeg, Man R3T 2N2. Basic film-making, screenwriting.

University of Windsor, Ont. N9B 3P4. Film Radio TV.

York University, Faculty of Fine Arts, Film & Video Department, 4700 Keele Street, North York, Ontario M3J 1P3. Offers studies in Film, Video, Screenwriting, and Theory over a 4-year Honours BA or BFA programme. 2-year MFA.

CZECH REPUBLIC

FAMU Film and Television Faculty, Academy of Performing Arts, Smetanovo nábř. 2, CS 116 65 Prague 1. Tel: (42) 2 265623. Fax: (42) 2 268735. Dean: Josef Pecák.

DENMARK

European Film College, DK-8400 Ebeltoft. Tel: (45) 86 34 00 55. Fax: (45) 86 34 05 35. Headmaster: Bjørn Erichsen. Chairman of the Board: Morten Arnfred. Annual 32-week course starting September. No special qualifications required (although students must be over nineteen years of age, and must be able to speak and write in English).

The National Film School of Denmark, Store Søndervoldstræde 4, DK - 1419 Copenhagen K. Tel: (45) 31576500. Fax: (45) 31576510.

EGYPT

Higher Film Institute, Academy of Arts, Gamal EL Din El Afaghani Str., Pyramids Ave., Giza. Tel: 537703. Fax: 5601034.

FINLAND

Taideteollinen korkeakoulu, elokuvataiteenlaitos. University of Industrial Arts, Department of Cinema and TV, Pursimiehenkatu, 29-31, SF-00150 Helsinki.

FRANCE

Institut de Formation et d'Enseignement pour les Métiers de L'Image et du Son, Palais de Tokyo, 2 rue de la Manutention, 75116 Paris. Chairman: Jean-Claude Carrière. Director: Christine Juppé-Leblond.

Students at the European Film College in Ebeltoft (Denmark)   *photo: Henrik Saxgren*

Conservatoire Libre du Cinéma Français (C.I.C.F.), 16 rue de Delta, 75009 Paris.

GERMANY

Deutsche Film- and Fernsehakademie Berlin GmbH, DFFB, Pommernallee 1, 1000 Berlin 19. Director: Prof. Reinhard Hauff. Four-year course dealing with theories of film-making, film-history, and all aspects of practical film and television production; script-writing, direction, camerawork, editing and special effects. Students make films and videos and are encouraged to gain experience in as wide a variety of techniques as possible.

Hochschule für Fernsehen und Film, Frankenthaler Strasse 23, D-81539 München. President: Prof. Dr. Helmut Oeller. Approx. 200 students, 50 staff. Four-year course providing instruction in the theory and practice of film and television. Facilities provide for work in 16 and 35mm as well as video equipment. Studies are free. Two-step admission

process; ask for details in January each year. Studies begin each Autumn.

Hochschule für Film und Fernsehen "Konrad Wolf", Karl Marx Strasse 33/34, 14482 Potsdamm. Rector: Prof. Wolf-Dieter Panse.

HONGKONG

Hongkong Academy for Performing Arts, School of Technical Arts-TV/Film, 1 Gloucester Road, GPO Box 12288, Wanchai, Hongkong. Dean: Dr. Pat Elliot. Tel: (852) 584 1593. Fax: (852) 802 4372.

HUNGARY

Szinbáz-es Filmmiivészeti Föiskola, Vas u. 2/c, 1088 Budapest. Rector: Péter Huszti. General Secretary: Lászlo Vadäsz.

INDIA

Film and Television Institute of India, Law College Road, Pune 411 004, India. Director: John Shankaramangalam. Chairman: Adoor Gopalkrishnan. India's

premier film school is 34 years old, and imparts training in four disciplines: Film Direction, Motion Picture Photography, Sound Recording & Sound Engineering (3 year courses), and Film Editing (2 year course). All four courses include 1 year's integrated training. 40 students, including 8 from Afro-Asian countries, are admitted per year. The Institute publishes a technical journal, **Lenslight,** and also conducts short courses in Film Appreciation, Video Techniques, Lighting, Still Photography etc. The Television Wing gives in-service training to employees of Doordarshan, the Television Authority of India.

IRELAND

European School of Animation, Senior College, Ballyfermot, Dublin 10. Tel: (353) 1626 9421. Fax: (353) 1 626 6754.

ISRAEL

Department of Film and Television, Tel Aviv University, Tel Aviv.

The Jerusalem National Film and Television School, 4 Yad Harutzim St, Jerusalem. Director: Renen Schorr.

ITALY

Centro Sperimentale di Cinematografia (C.S.C.), Via Tuscolana 1524, Rome. Director: Angelo Libertini.

Instituto di Storia del Cinema e dello Spettacolo, Universitá di Torino Facoltá di Magistero, Via San'Ottavio 20, 10124 Torino.

JAPAN

Nihon University College of Art, Asahiganoka 2-42, Nerimaku, Tokyo, 176. Head of Film Department: Professor Toru Otake.

NETHERLANDS

Nederlandse Film en Televisie Academie, Ite Boeremastraat 1, 1054 PP Amsterdam. Managing Director: Richard Woolley. 260 students, 60 staff. Four years.

POLAND

Państwowa Wyższa Szkola Filmowa, Telewizyina c Teatralna, im Leona Schillera, ul. Targowa 61/63, 90 323 Lódz. Tel: (42) 743943. Fax: (42) 748 139.

ROMANIA

Academia de Teatru si Film, str. Matei-Volevod nr. 75-77 sect. 2 cod 73226, Bucharest. Dean: Stere Gulea.

RUSSIA

Vserossuyski Gosudarstvenni Institut Kinematografi (VGIK) (All-Union State Institute of Cinematography), ulitsa Vilgelma Pika 3, Moscow 129226. Fax: (95) 187 7174.

SERBIA

Fakultet dramskih umetnosti (pozorišta, filma, radija i televizije), Bulevar umetnosti 20, 11070 Belgrade. Tel: (381 11) 135 684. Fax: (38 11) 130 862.

SPAIN

University of Valladolid, Cátedra de Historia y Estética de la Cinematografica, Palacio de Sta. Cruz, Valladolid. Director: Sr. Dr. Francisco Javier de la Plaza.

SWEDEN

Department of Film Studies, University of Stockholm, Filmhuset, Borgvägen 1-5, Box 27062, S-102 51 Stockholm.

Dramatiska Institutet (College of Theatre, Film, Radio and Television), Borgvägen, Box 27090, S-102 51 Stockholm. Head of School: Kjell Grede. Formed in 1970, the Institute is intended to provide instruction in production techniques for theatre, film, radio and television. The Institute is equipped with film and TV studios, 10 editing rooms for 8, 16 and 35mm, and 4 video editing rooms with S-VHS, 2 video editing rooms with Light Work, 1 on-line editing room with M II, sound mixing studios and portable video equipment.

TURKEY

Sinema/TV Enstitüsü Kislaönü, Besiktas, Istanbul. Director: Sam Sekeroglu.

U.K.

Bristol University, Department of Drama, Film and Television Studies, Cantocks Close, Woodland Road, Bristol BS8 1UP.

University of Derby, Kedleston Road, Derby DE22 1GB. Director of Studies: John Fullerton. MA/FT/PT in Film with Television Studies. BA(Hons) – subject to validation.

University of Westminster, Harrow School of Design and Media, Northwick Park, Harrow, HA1 3TP.

London International Film School, 24 Shelton Street, London WC2H 9HP. Principal: Martin M. Amstell. The School offers a practical, two-year Diploma course to professional levels, accredited by the British film technicians' union – B.E.C.T.U. Approximately half each term is devoted to film production and half to practical and theoretical tuition. All students work on one or more films each term and are encouraged to interchange unit roles termly to experience different skill areas. Facilities include two cinemas, two shooting stages, two rehearsal stages and fifteen cutting rooms. Equipment includes 16mm and 35mm Panavision, Arriflex and rostrum cameras, Nagra recorders, Steenbeck editing machines and U-matic video. Tuition is by permanent and visiting professionals. Entrance requirements: a degree or an art or technical diploma. Lesser qualifications accepted in cases of special ability or experience. All applicants must submit examples of their work and be proficient in English. New courses commence each January, April and September.

Middlesex Polytechnic, Faculty of Art and Design, Cat Hill, Barnet, Herts EN4 8HT. Tel: (081) 368 1299.

National Film and Television School, Station Road, Beaconsfield, Bucks, HP90 1LG. Tel: (0494) 671234. Fax: (0494) 674042. Director: Henning Camre.

Newport Film School, Faculty of Art and Design, Gwent College of Higher Education, Clarence Place, Newport, Gwent NP9 0UW.

Northern School of Film and Television, Leeds Metropolitan University, 2-8 Merrion Way, Leeds LS2 8BT. Tel: (532) 833 193. Fax: (532) 833 194.

University of Westminster, School of Communication, 18/22 Riding House Street, London W1P 7PD. M.A. in Film and Television Studies; advanced level part-time course (evenings and weekends) concerned with theoretical aspects of film and TV. Modular credit accumulation and transfer scheme, with exemption for work previously

Still from ZAIL, directed by Britta Krause at the London International Film School

done. Postgraduate Certificate normally awarded after one year (40 credits), Postgraduate Diploma after two years (70 credits), M.A. after three years (120 credits, including research thesis). Modules offered: Authorship and Mise-en-Scène, Structuralism and Genre, Realism and Anti-Realism. The Film and TV Audience; Film, Culture and Society; Hollywood 1900-1940, British Cinema 1927-1947, British TV Drama, The Documentary Tradition, Public Service Broadcasting, TV Genres and Gender, Psychoanalysis and Cinema, Third World Cinema, Soviet Cinema of the 1920's and 1930's, Production Studies, Issues in British Film Culture, Modernism and Postmodernism, Women and Film Narrative, European Cinema since 1945, European Broadcasting Policy.

No practical component. Course leader: Dr Robert E. Peck.

Royal College of Art, Department of Film and Television, Kensington Gore, London SW72EU. 30 students.

The Surrey Institute of Art and Design, Farnham Campus, Falkner Road, Farnham, Surrey GU9 7DS. Tel: (0252) 722 441.

University of East Anglia, School of English and American Studies, Norwich NR4 7TJ.

University of Stirling, Film and Media Studies, Stirling FK9 4LA. Head of Department: Professor P.R. Schlesinger.

URUGUAY

Escuela de Cinematografia, 18 de Julio 1265 p.2, Montevideo. Director: Juan José Ravaioli.

U.S.A.

Information on the many thousands of U.S. film courses is contained in the *American Film Institute's Guide to College Courses in Film and Television* which can be ordered at Publications, The American Film Institute, 2021 North Western Avenue, Los Angeles, California 90027.

FILM ARCHIVES

Note: each year we write to all Archives listed in this section. Those who respond will usually find most of the data they submit included in their entry. We can no longer print suspect data year after year without confirmation from the appropriate archive.

ARGENTINA

Cinemateca Argentina, Corrientes 2092, 2nd floor, 1045 Buenos Aires. Tel: (54-1) 953 3755/953 7163. Fax: (54-1) 951.8558. Executive Director: Mrs. Paulina Fernandez Jurado. Established in 1949. Stock: 11,700 film titles, 6,100 books, collection offilm periodicals, 352,000 film stills, 6,600 film posters. The collection of micro-filmed clippings holds files on individual films, and on foreign and Argentine film personalities. The library is open to researchers and students. The Cinemateca operates one film theatre with daily screenings.

AUSTRALIA

National Film and Sound Archive, McCoy Circuit, Acton, Canberra A.C.T. 2601. Tel: (61-6) 2671711. Fax: (61-6) 2474651. Director: Ron Brent. Deputy Director: Ray Edmondson. Stock: 75,000 film and video titles, 425,000 stills, 68,500 scripts, 64,000 posters, 400,000 publicity items, 89,000 memorabilia items.

State Film Archives, Library and Information Service of Western Australia, Alexander Library Building, Perth Cultural Centre, Perth, WA 6,000. Tel: (619) 427 3310. Film Archivist: Robin Faulkner. Stock: 1,800 film titles.

AUSTRIA

Österreichisches Filmarchiv, A-1010 Vienna, Rauhensteingasse 5. Film stores and theatre; Laxenburg, Altes Schloss. Tel: 5129936. Fax: 513 5330.

Österreichisches Filmmuseum, A-1010 Vienna, Augustinerstr. 1. Tel: 533 70 54-0. Fax: 533 70 56 25. Directors: Peter Konlechner and Prof. Peter Kubelka. Stock: app. 10,000 film titles, and an extensive library.

BELGIUM

Cinémathèque Royale, 23 rue Ravenstein, 1000 Brussels. Tel: 5078370. Fax: 513 1272.

BRAZIL

Cinemateca Brasileira, Caixa Postal 12900, 04092 São Paulo. Tel: 577 4666. Fax: 577 7433. Director: Thomaz Farkaz.

Cinemateca do Museu de Arte Moderna, Caixa Postal 44, CEP 20021, Rio de Janeiro, RJ. Tel: (021) 2102188. Telex: 21-22084 FTVRBR. Director: João Luiz Vieira.

BULGARIA

Bulgarska Nacionalna Filmoteka, ul. Gourko 36,1000 Sofia. Tel: (359 2) 876004, 802749.

CANADA

La Cinémathèque Québécoise, 335 boul de Maisonneuve est. Montréal, Québec H2X 1K1.Tel: (514) 842 9763. Curator: Robert Daudelin. Stock: 28,000 film titles, 350,000 stills, 15,000 posters. The Cinémathèque specialises in preserving the work of animators and of Canadian film-makers and this collection is on show at thirteen screenings a week, together with other aspects of world cinema.

Conservatoire d'Art Cinématographique de Montréal, 1455 de Maisonneuve West, Montréal, Québec. Director: Serge Losique.

National Archives of Canada, Moving Image and Sound Archives, 395 Wellington Street, Ottawa, Ontario, K1A 0N3. Tel: (613) 9966009. Telex: 0533367. Director: Jana Vosikovska.

CHINA

Cinémathèque Chinoise, 25B rue Xin Wai, Beijing. Tel: 2014316. Telex: 22195.

CZECH REPUBLIC

Národní filmový archiv, Malešicka ul, CS-1300 00 Praha 3. Tel and Fax: 894501. Curator: Vladimir Opéla.

DENMARK

Det Danske Filmmuseum, Store Søndervoldstraede, DK-1419 Copenhagen K. Tel: (45) 31576500. Telex: 31465. Fax: (45) 31541312. Director: Ib Monty. Stock: 18,000 film titles, 48,000 books, 350 periodicals subscribed to, 1,950,000 film stills, 18,000 posters, 158-seat cinema used for three daily screenings and for researchers and students. The Museum also publishes a magazine, "Kosmorama", and a year book.

EGYPT

National Film Archive, c/o Egyptian Film Centre, City of Arts, Pyramids Road, Giza, Egypt. Tel: 854801/850897. Telex: 21863 EG-FICUN. Fax: 854701. Curator: Nagui Riad.

FINLAND

Suomen elokuva-arkisto, Pursimiehenkatu 29-31 A, P.O. Box 177, SF-00150 Helsinki. Tel: (358) 0 615400 Telex: 125960. Fax: (358).0.615 40 242. Director: Matti

SOUTH AFRICAN NATIONAL FILM, VIDEO AND SOUND ARCHIVE

The aims of this Archive are the acquisition, preservation, storage, adaptation and supply of available films, video and sound material of archival value, with specific reference to South Africa. Further, to provide an information service with regard to film, video, sound material and photographs.

It is a division of the State Archives of the Department of National Education.

Private Bag X236
PRETORIA
0001
South Africa

Fax +27 12 3445143

Lukkarila. Stock: 8,000 feature film titles, 20,000 shorts and advertising film (spots), 11,000 video cassettes, 16,000 books, 132 magazines (currently subscribed), 9,000 dialogue lists and scripts, 320,000 different stills, 110,000 posters and 40,000 documentation files. The archive arranges regular screenings in Helsinki and eight other cities.

FRANCE

Cinémathèque Française, 29 rue du Colisée, 75008 Paris. President: Jean Rouch.

Cinémathèque de Toulouse, rue de Faubourg Bonnefoy 12, 31500 Toulouse, France. Tel: (33)61 48 90 75. Fax: (33) 61 58 19 79. President/Curator: Guy-Claude Rochemont.

Cinémathèque Universitaire, UFR d'Art et d'Archéologie, 3 rue Michelet, 75006 Paris.

Institut Lumière, 25 rue du Premier-Film, 69008 Lyon. Tel:

78.00.86.68. President: Bertrand Tavernier.

Musée du Cinéma de Lyon, 69 rue Jean Jaurès. 69100 Villeurbanne. Tel: 7853 27 69. President: Paul Génard. Stock: 1,600 film titles, 1,000 film stills, 50 posters.

Service des Archives de Film du Centre National de la Cinématographie, 7 bis rue Alexandre Turpault, 78390 Bois d'Arcy. Tel: 34602050.

GERMANY

Arsenal Kino der Freunde der Deutschen Kinemathek, Welserstrasse 25, D-1000 Berlin 30. Tel: 213-6039. The nearest equivalent of Britain's NFT. Programming: Ulrich and Erika Gregor , Milena Gregor and Christiane Habich. The Freunde also run a non-commercial distribution of about 800 films, most of them from the International Forum of Young Cinema, the independent second main programme of the Berlin

Film Festival, organised by the Freunde.

Bundesarchiv-Filmarchiv, Fehrbelliner Platz 3, 10707 Berlin. Tel: (49-30) 86811. Fax: (49-30) 868 1310.

Deutsches Filmmuseum Frankfurt am Main, Schaumainkai 41, 60596 Frankfurt am Main 70. Tel: (069) 212 38830. Fax: 212 37881. Director: Prof Walter Schobert. Deputy Director: Claudia Dillmann. Film Archive: Rudolf Worschech.

Deutsches Institut für Filmkunde, Schaumainkai 41, 60596 Frankfurt am Main 70. Tel: (069) 617045. Telefax: (069) 620060. Director: Dr. Gerd Albrecht. Administrative Director: Peter Franz. Stock: 4,200 film titles, 54,000 books, 260 periodicals, 1,000,000 film stills, 30,000 posters, 16,000 dialogue lists, 5,000 scripts. Also programmes, newspaper clippings, advertising material.

Münchner Stadtmuseum/Filmmuseum, St.-Jakob-Platz 1, 8000 München 2. Tel: (49) 89233 22348. Fax: (49) 89 2333931. Curator: Enno Patalas.

Stiftung Deutsche Kinemathek, Pommernallee 1, 1000 Berlin 19. Tel: 30307234. Fax: 3029294. Director: Hans Helmut Prinzler. Stock: 8,000 film titles, 1,500,000 film stills, 15,000 posters, 60,000 film programmes, 10,000 scripts etc. The Kinemathek's library of books and periodicals is amalgamated with that of the Deutsche Film-und-Fernsehakademie-Berlin, in the same building.

HUNGARY

Magyar Filmintézet, Budakeszi ut 51b, 1021 Budapest. Tel: 17.67.106. Director: Vera Gyürey. Stock: 7,022 feature titles, 8,713 short films, 3,756 newsreels, 13,224 books, 3,710 periodicals, 2,708 scripts, 5,381 manuscripts, 143,159 stills, 15,365 posters. The institute, besides housing the archive, also does research into the history of the cinema, particularly the Hungarian cinema, and encourages the development of film culture in Hungary.

Szinház-és Filmmüvészeti Föiskola, Vas utca 2/c, Budapest 1088. Tel: (361) 1384 749. Fax: (361) 1294 790. Rector: Péter Huszti. General Secretary: Lajos Tiszeker.

ICELAND

Kvikmyndasafn Islands (Icelandic Film Archive), Laugavegur 24, 101 Reykjavik. (Postal: P.O. Box 320, 121 Reykjavik.) Tel: 10940. Fax: 627171. Nearly 400 titles in the collection, documentaries being the larger part of it. Numerous sources of information regarding Icelandic films and the national film history.

INDIA

National Film Archive of India, Ministry of Information and Broadcasting, Government of India, Law College Road, Poona 411 004, India. Tel: 331 559.

Director: Suresh Chabria. Stock: 12,922 films, 1069 video cassettes, 20,935 books, 152 periodicals, 21,403 scripts, 7,287 pamphlets/folders, 136,273 press clippings, 97,989 stills, 3,236 slides, 6,410 wall posters, 6,252 song booklets, 1,858 disc records, 153 audio tapes, 1,957 micro films, 42 microfiches, 209 pre-recorded cassettes.

IRAN

National Iranian Film Archive, Baharestan Square, Tehran. Tel: 324 1601. Director: Mohammad Hassan Khoshnevis.

ISRAEL

Israel Film Archive/Jerusalem Cinémathèque, PO Box 8561, Jerusalem 91083, Israel. Tel: (972) 2 724 131. Fax: (972) 2 733 076. Director: Lia van Leer. Stock: 18,000 prints – international, Israeli, Jewish film collections. Books, periodicals, stills, posters and scripts. Israeli and Jewish film documentation and educational programme for school children and adults. Permanent exhibition of early cinema apparatus and cinema memorabilia. Organisers of the Jerusalem Film Festival.

Tel Aviv Cinémathèque (The Doron Cinema Centre), 2 Sprintzak Street, Tel Aviv. PO Box 20370, Tel Aviv 61203. Tel: (03) 6917181-8. Fax: (03) 6962841. Director: Alon Garbuz. Stock: 12,000 video cassettes, 5,000 books, periodicals, stills, posters, scripts. 1,500 screenings yearly, various activities, lectures and seminars for the general public, and special morning educational programmes for schools.

ITALY

Cineteca del Friuli, 26 via Osoppo, 33013 Gemona del Friuli (Udine). Tel: (0432) 980458. Fax: (0432) 970 542. Established in 1977, this excellent Italian archive conceived the idea for the Pordenone Silent Film Festival, and organises regular

screenings. Stock: 2,000 film titles, 3,000 newsreels, 7,000 books.

Cineteca Italiana, Via Palestro 16, 20121 Milano. Tel: 799224. Sec. General: Gianni Comencini.

Cineteca Nazionale, Via Tuscolana n. 1524, 00173 Rome. Tel: 722941. Fax: 7211619. Interim Curator is presently the General Director of the Centro Sperimentale di Cinematografia: Avv. Angelo Libertini. Preservation Management Consultant: Dr. Guido Cincotti. Head of Archive/Preservation Section: Dr. Mario Musumeci. Head of Access/Screenings Section: Dr.ssa Irene Proietti.

Museo Internazionale del Cinema e dello Spettacolo, Casella Postale 6104, 00195 Rome. Tel: 370 0266. Fax: 397 33 297

JAPAN

Japan Film Library Council/ Kawakita Memorial Film Institute, Ginza-Hata Building, 4-5, 4-chome, Ginza, Chuo-ku, Tokyo. Director Masayo Okada.

National Filmcenter, 7-6, 3 chome, Kyobashi, Chuoku, Tokyo. Curator: Masaioshi Ohba.

LATVIA

Riga Film Museum, P.O. Box 391, Kraslavas str. 22. LV1047, Riga. Tel: (0132) 220282.

LUXEMBOURG

Cinémathèque Municipale de la Ville de Luxembourg, 19 rue de la Chapelle, L-1325 Luxembourg. Tel: (352) 4796-2644. Fax: (352) 4593 75. Curator: Fred Junck.

MEXICO

Cinemateca Luis Buñuel, Calle 5, Oriente 5, Apdo. Postal 255, Puebla, Pue. Curator: Fernando Osorio Alarcon.

Cinemateca Mexicana, Museo Nacional de Antropologia, Calzada M. Gandhi, México 6, D.F. Director: Galdino Gomez Gomez.

Cineteca Nacional, Av. Mexico-Coyocán 389, 03330 Mexico. Tel: 688 8814. Telex: 1760050 RTCME. Director: Mercedes Certucha. Mexico's main film archive, supported by the Federal government.

Direccion General de Actividades Cinematograficas UNAM, San Ildefonso 43 Centro, 06020 Mexico, D.F. Tel: (525 7) 02 64 32. Fax: (525 7) 02 45 03. General Director: Biol. Ivan Trujillo Bolio. Stock: 15,000 film titles, 150,000 stills, 5,000 posters, 83,000 lobby cards, 9,200 books, 2,100 original scripts, 49 subscriptions to film periodicals, 5 film theatres and 200 early *apparati* dating from 1880 to 1960.

NETHERLANDS

Stichting Nederlands Filmmuseum, Vondelpark 3, 1071 AA Amsterdam. Tel: (020) 5981 400. Fax: (020) 6833401. Director: Hoos Blotkamp. Deputy Director: Eric de Kuyper.

Audiovisual Archive of the Netherlands Government Information Service, PO Box 20.009, 2500 EA The Hague, Tel: (3170) 3564106/4110. Fax: (3170) 3647756. Head: Mr Robert Egeter-van Kuyk.

NEW ZEALAND

The New Zealand Film Archive, P.O. Box 11-449, cnr. Cable Street and Jervois Quay, Wellington. Tel: 3847647. Fax: 382 9595. Telex: 30386.

NORWAY

Henie-Onstad Art Centre, 1311

Hovikodden, Oslo. Director: Per Hovdenakk.

Det Norske FIlminstituttet, Militærhospitalet, Grev Wedels plass, Postboks 482, Sentrum, 0105 Oslo 1. Tel: 472 428740. Fax: 472 332277. Telex: 11619. Director: Per Morten Løchsen. Curator: Arne Pedersen. Head of Cinémathèque: Kjell Billing. Stock: 13,000 film titles, 15,000 books, 130 periodicals and a large collection of stills and posters. Also over five hundred pieces of early cinema apparatus and a fine theatre for screening films. The cinémathèque of the film institute is run in co-operation with the organisation "The Friends of the NFI".

PANAMA

Cinemateca del GECU, Apartado 6-1775, El Dorado, Panama. Fax: (507) 29 1066. Stock includes films, books, periodicals, film stills and posters. It has a small theatre in the University of Panama, with three daily screenings. Co-ordinator: Roberto Enrique King.

POLAND

Filmoteka Narodowa, ul. Pulawska 61, 00-975 Warszawa. Tel: 455074. Fax: 455074. Telex: 813640.

Muzeum Kinematografñ, Pl Zwyciestwa 1, 90312 Lódź. Tel: 740957.

PORTUGAL

Cinemateca Portuguesa, Rua Barata Salgueiro 39-1200 Lisboa. Tel: 546279/547732. Fax: 3523180.

Director: João Bénard da Costa.

RUSSIA

Gosfilmofond of Russia, Belye Stolby, Moskovskaia oblast. Tel: 546 05 16, 546 05 13.Telex: 411700 LASTI 007913.

SERBIA

Jugoslovenska Kinoteka, Knez Mihailova 19, 11000 Belgrade. Tel: 622 555, 550 471 (Archive). Fax: 622 587, 555 015 (Archive). Director: Radoslav Zelenović Head of Archive: Stevan Jovičić. Programme Director: Dinko Tucaković.

SOUTH AFRICA

South African National Film, Video and Sound Archives, Private Bag X236, Pretoria 0001. Director: J.H. de Lange. Enormous variety of 35mm and 16mm footage, video and sound material as well as stills, scripts, books, posters and other material. The Archive is a State controlled organisation, dedicated to the classification and preservation of all items relating to the film, video and sound industries.

SPAIN

Filmoteca Española, Carretera Dehesa de la Villa, s/n. 28040 Madrid. Tel: 549 00 11. Fax: 549 73 48. Director: José María Prado.

Filmoteca de la Generalit de Catalunya, Diputació 279-283, Barcelona 08007. Tel: 488 1038.

Fax: 487 4192. Director: Antoni Kirchner.

Biblioteca de Cinema "Delmiro de Caralt", Rambla de Catalunya, 81 pral. 08008 - Barcelona. Tel: (343) 215 1069. Fax: (343) 487 "50 76.

SWEDEN

Asta Nielsen Filmmuseum, Vapenkroken 29, S-226 47. Lund. Established in 1946 by G.D. Postén, Head of the Film History section at the Dept. of History, University of Lund. This is one of the biggest, private, non-commercial international collections of published, written materials on motion pictures and the film industry. Included in the collection are stills, programmes, books, magazines, posters, historical materials, etc. with the emphasis on the silent screen. Also the most complete collection of material on Asta Nielsen.

Cinemateket, Svenska Film institutet. Filmhuset, Box 27126, S-102 52 Stockholm. Tel: (46-8) 665 1100. Telex: 13326 FILMINS S. Fax: 08-6611820. Curator: Rolf Lindfors. Head of Documentation: Margareta Nordström. Stock: 13,700 film titles, 38,000 books, 250 subscriptions to periodicals, 1,500,000 film stills, 30,000 posters, and unpublished script material on 6,700 foreign films and 1,800 Swedish films.The collection of microfilmed clippings holds 51,500 jackets on individual films, 15,500 jackets on film personalities and jackets on general subjects classified by the FIAF scheme. Cinemateket has two theatres and four daily screenings in Stockholm. A selection of the yearly programme is also shown in Gothenburg and Malmö. There is also a film club for teenagers, *Filmögat,* with weekly screenings of film classics in the three cities.

SWITZERLAND

Cinémathèque Suisse, 3 Allée Ernest Ansermet, 1003 Lausanne. Tel: 237406. Fax: (021) 204 888.

Curator: Freddy Buache. Stock: 25,000 titles (300,000 reels), 260 apparati, 35,000 posters, 300,000 film references, 15,000 books, and 1,000,000 stills. Three projections each day.

THAILAND

The National Film Archive of Thailand, 4 Chao Fa Road, Bangkok 10200. Tel: 282 0170/282 1847. Director: Penpan Jarernport.

U.K.

Imperial War Museum, Lambeth Road, London SE1 6HZ. Tel: (071) 416 5000. Fax: (071) 4165379. Keeper of the Department of Film: Roger Smither. Deputy: Paul Sargent. Stock: over 40 million feet of actuality film relating to conflict in the Twentieth Century, from Britain and other countries. Viewing facilities for students and researchers *by appointment only*; public film screenings.

National Film Archive, 21 Stephen Street, London W1P 1PL. Tel: (071) 255 1444. Telex: 27624 BFILDNG. Fax: (071) 436 7950. Curator: Clyde Jeavons. Deputy Curator: Anne Fleming. Stock: 175,000 film and television titles, 6,500,000 black-and-white stills, 1,000,000 colour transparencies, 12,000 posters, 2,500 set-designs. Viewing service for students and researchers, production library for film-makers.

The Scottish Film Archive, Scottish Film Council, 74 Victoria Crescent Road, Dowanhill, Glasgow G12 9JN. Tel: (041) 334 4445. Fax: (041) 334 8132.

URUGUAY

Cinemateca Uruguaya, Lorenzo Carnelli 1311, Casilla de Correo 1170, Montevideo. Tel: 482460, 494 572. Fax: 494 572. Curator: M. Martinez Carril.

U.S.A.

Academy of Motion Picture Arts and Sciences, Centre for Motion Picture Study, Academy Film Archive, 333 South La Cienega

Blvd., Beverly Hills, California 90211. Director: Michael Friend. Curator: Daniel Woodruff.

American Cinematheque, 1717 N. Highland Ave. (at Hollywood Blvd.), Hollywood 90028. Executive Director: Barbara Zicka Smith. A viewer supported arts organisation dedicated *exclusively* to the public exhibition of film and video. State-of-the-art theatres, galeries and gathering places (including a café and bookstore) scheduled to open in 1995. Meanwhile, regular film and video programming for the public is underway now at the new Directors Guild theatre complex in Hollywood.

American Film Institute/National Center for Film and Video Preservation, John F. Kennedy Center for the Performing Arts, Washington, DC 20566. Archivist: Susan Dalton.

George Eastman House/ International Museum of Photography, 900 East Avenue, Rochester, N.Y. 14607. Tel: (716) 271 3361. Film Dept: Dr. Jan-Christopher Horak, Senior Curator of Film; Dr. Paolo Cherchi Usai, Assistant Curator.

Harvard Film Archive, Carpenter Center for the Visual Arts, Harvard Univ, 24 Quincy Street, Cambridge, MA 02138. Tel: (617) 4954700. Curator: Vlada Petric. Films (16mm and 35mm); 4,000 titles, including the Film Study Center collection (Robert Gardner, Producer/Director).

The Library of Congress, Motion Picture, Broadcasting and Recorded Sound Division, Washington, DC 20540. Tel: (202) 707 5840. Fax: (202) 707 2371. Telex: 64198. Chief: Devid Francis.

Museum of Modern Art, Department of Film, 11 West 53rd Street, New York, NY 10019. Tel:(212) 708 9602. Telex: 62370. Chief Curator: Mary Lea Bandy. Curators: Adrienne Mancia, Larry Kardish. Stock: 10,000 film titles, 2,500 books, 250 periodicals, 4,000,000 film stills. The excellent research and screening facilities of the department are available to serious students only by appointment with the supervisor, Charles Silver; 1,000 of its films are available for rental, sale, and lease. Stills Archive open by appointment with Mary Corliss.

National Museum of Natural History/Human Studies Film Archives, Rm E307 Smithsonian Institution, Washington DC 20560. Tel: (202)357-3349. Fax: (202) 357 2208. Director: John P. Homiak.

Pacific Film Archive, University Art Museum, 2625 Durant Avenue, Berkeley, California 94720.

UCLA Film and Television Archive, 302 East Melnitz Hall, University of California, 405 Hilgard Avenue, Los Angeles, CA 90024. Tel: (310) 206 8013. Fax: (310) 206 3129. Director: Robert Rosen. Stock: Over 200,000 film and television programmes, and 27 million feet of newsreel.

The Wisconsin Center for Film and Theater Research, 816 State Street, Madison, Wisconsin 53706. Tel: (608) 264 6466. Fax: (608) 2646472. Head of Archive: Maxine Fleckner Ducey.

Stock Footage Libraries

The following is a listing of the major U.S. independent stock footage libraries.

Archive Films, 530 West 25th Street, New York, NY 10001. Tel: (212) 620 3955. Fax: (212) 645 2137. Invaluable source of film extracts, newsreels, cartoons etc. Patrick Montgomery's archive contains a vast assortment of material from 1894 through the 1990's.

Producing everything from commercials to full-length documentaries, **Archive Films** specialises in the use of historical footage. Experts in the utilisation of existing films and tapes, the firm houses a vast collection of archival footage as well as maintaining exclusive arrangements throughout the world with other distributors, archives and libraries. All footage has been transferred to video cassettes for reference purposes and is available on all film and video formats for use.

By definition, historical or "archival" footage is any type of footage, film or videotape, colour or b&w, 16mm or 35mm shot as early as 1898 or as recently as yesterday. Archive Films locates its footage from a number of different origins – acquiring clips from newsreels, silent film comedies and dramas, home movies, Hollywood feature films (primarily those shot outside of the studio system), rare music footage, educational films and cartoons.

Film Bank, 425 South Victory Blvd, Burbank, CA 91502. Tel: (818) 841 9176. Fax: (818) 5674235. President: Paula Lumbard. Film and video stock footage library.

Producers Library Service, 1051 North Cole Avenue, Hollywood, CA 90038. Tel: (213) 4650572. Fax: (213) 465 1671. Houses more than 5 million feet of 35mm colour film from the 1950's to the present, 1 million feet of 16mm colour film from the 1940's and 1950's, and more than 1 million feet of 35mm black-and-white film from the 'teens through the 1940's; it represents stock footage from the productions of ABC Circle and Orion, specialises in Hollywood history and has direct access to stock footage from all Hollywood studios.

Sherman Grinberg Film Libraries, Inc., 630 Ninth Avenue, New York, NY 10036. Tel: (212) 765 5170. Fax: (212) 262 1532. Also, 1040 North McCadden Place, Hollywood, CA 90038. Tel: (213) 464 7491. Fax: (213) 462 5352.

FILM BOOKSHOPS POSTERS & RECORDS

Australia

Electric Shadows Bookshop,
Akuna Street, Canberra City, ACT 2601. Tel: (06) 2488342. Fax: (06) 2478924.
Readings Records and Books,
P.O. Box 482, South Yarra 3141. Tel: (03) 867-1885.
Soft Focus,
P.O. Box 508, Hawthorn, Victoria 3122.
Catalogue available listing movie books, magazines, posters, and memorabilia.

Canada

Theatrebooks,
11 St. Thomas Street, Toronto, M5S 2B7. Tel: (416) 922-7175. Fax: (416) 922 0739.
Founded first as a source of theatre, opera, and dance books. Theatrebooks has since 1982 also developed a first-class film book collection. Worldwide mail order is handled.
Lux,
5220 boul. St-Laurent, Montréal.
Large stock of European movie posters. Open daily 10 a.m. to 4 p.m.

France

Atmosphère, Librairie du Cinéma,
7-9 rue F. de Pressensé, 75014 Paris. Tel: 45.42.29.26.

Situated in a leisure complex that includes an art cinema and a café. Atmosphère offers a wide range of film publications, with a large stock of stills, postcards, posters of new and old movies, of all origins and sizes. Also back issues of magazines. Open every day except Sunday, from 2 p.m. to 8 p.m. Atmosphère sets up shop during the Cannes Festival, too.
Cinédoc,
45-53 Passage Jouffroy, 75009 Paris.
Posters, books, stills, pressbooks, magazines, etc.
Ciné-Folie,
14 rue des Frères-Pradignac, 06400 Cannes. Tel: 93.39.22.99.
Stills, books, posters, postcards.
Cinémagence,
12 rue Saulnier, 75009 Paris. Tel: 42.46.21.21. Fax: 42.46.20.20.
Stills, posters, magazines, books. Mail Order service.
Contacts Champs Elysées,
24 rue du Colisée, 75008 Paris. Tel: (1) 43.59.17.71. Fax: (1) 42.89.27.65.
Cinema bookshop established 35 years ago in the area of the Champs Elysées close to the film production companies. Amply stocked with French and foreign-language books on technique, theory, history, and director monographs. Also magazines. Reliable mail order

service. Free "new acquisitions" list. Open year round.
Le Réverbère,
4 rue Neuve, 69002 Lyon.

Germany

Buchhandlung Walther König,
Ehrenstr. 4, 50672 Köln. Tel: (221) 20 59 60.
Offers a comprehensive catalogue of international titles in the film department, also useful antiquarian section.
Buchhandlung Langenkamp,
Beckergrube 19, D-2400 Lübeck. Tel: (0541) 76479.
H. Lindemanns,
Nadlerstrasse 4-10, D-70173 Stuttgart 1. Tel. (711) 233 499. Fax: (711) 236 9672.
Photography and film.
Sautter & Lackmann,
Admiralitätstrasse 71/72, Postfach 110431, D-20404 Hamburg 11. Tel: (40) 37 31 96. Fax: (40) 36 54 79.
Marga Schöller Bücherstube,
Knesebeckstr. 33, D-10623 Berlin. Tel: (030) 8811122.
One of the fabled literary haunts of western Europe, Marga Schöller's shop is justly proud of its film book selection.
Verlag für Filmschriften Christian Unucka,
Am Kramerberg 7A, D-85241

Hebertshausen. Tel: (08131) 13922. Fax: (08131) 10075.
Books, posters, programmes, stills, postcards, videos, rare items, etc.

Italy
Libreria dello Spettacolo,
via Terraggio 11, 20123 Milan. Tel: (02) 864 51730.
"Il Leuto",
via Di Monte Brianzo 86, 00186 Rome. Tel: (06) 656 9269.
M.I.C.S./Museo del Cinema,
Casella Postale 6104-00195 Rome. Tel: (6) 370 0266. Fax: (6) 397 33297.
Mail order publishing company.

Spain
El Espectador,
Consejo de Ciento 475 bis, 08013 Barcelona. Tel: (93) 231 65 16.
Specialising in cinema and video books, magazines, etc.
Filmoteca Nacional, Cine Doré,
Santa Isabel 3, Madrid.
Well-stocked bookstore dealing with movie topics.
R. Seriña,
Calle Aribau 114, Barcelona 11.
A specialist collection of books, photos, magazines, press books, posters and programmes on sale to the public in Spain and abroad.

Switzerland
Filmbuchhandlung Hans Rohr,
Oberdorfstr. 3, CH-8024 Zurich. Tel: (01) 251 36 36. Fax: (01) 251 33 44.
In its long-established existence, Hans Rohr has offered an efficient and reliable service when it comes to dealing with mail order inquiries for literally any film book or magazine in print. Libraries and institutions rely on Rohr – even beyond Switzerland. Ask for quarterly film-bibliographic catalogue.
Librairie du Cinéma,
9 rue de la Terrassière, CH-1207 Genève. Tel: (022) 736.8888. Fax: (022) 736 6616.
Immaculate display of posters, books, stills, film postcards, soundtrack CD's, and videos. A veritable treasure trove for the movie buff. Closed Monday mornings.

U.K.
Arcadia Booksearch, 2 Kennilworth Court, Waungron Road, Fairwater, Cardiff CF5 3BB. Tel: (0222) 576 541. Fax: (0222) 397 392.
A comprehensive arts booksearch service, specialising in locating out of print books. Send s.a.e. for details.
The Cinema Bookshop,
13-14 Great Russell Street, London WC1. Tel: (071) 637.0206.
Fred Zentner's film bookshop close to the British Museum has succeeded by virtue of prompt and friendly service, and an eye for rare items.
Cox, A.E.,
21 Cecil Rd., Itchen, Southampton SO2 7HX. Tel: (0703) 447989.
This long-established dealer specialises in books, magazines, and ephemera on both theatre and cinema.
Film Magic,
The Business Centre, Colne Way, Watford, Herts.
Mail order service for colour and black-and-white stills of film and TV stars, plus books, magazines and posters.
Sylvia Edwards,
23 Marchmont Road, Edinburgh EH9 1HY, Scotland. Tel: (031) 229 5165.
Rare film posters and select ephemera. Send for an illustrated catalogue.
Greenroom Books
11 Bark Lane, Addingham, Ilkley, West Yorkshire LS29 0RA. Tel (0943) 830 497.
Mail order service for books on the performing arts. Write for a catalogue.
MOMI Shop,
Museum of the Moving Image, South Bank, London SE1. Tel: (071) 928 3535.
Visitors to the National Film Theatre now have a bookshop in the foyer, to complement the stock of posters, postcards, toys and videos available at the MOMI shop.
Anne FitzSimons,
62 Scotby Road, Scotby, Carlisle, Cumbria CA4 8BD. Tel: (0228) 513815.
A useful source for second-hand and out-of-print books on the cinema, as well as the theatre, puppeteering, etc.
58 Dean Street Records,
58 Dean Street, London W1V 5HH. Tel: (071) 437 4500, 734 8777.
Specialising in soundtracks, original cast shows (incl. imports), personalities, and nostalgia. Over 7,000 titles both current and deleted items; LP's, cassettes, and CD's. (Mail Order service).
David Henry,
36 Meon Road, London W3 8AN. Tel: (081) 993 2859.
Mail-order business – catalogues on request.

Ed Mason,
Shop 5, Chelsea Antique Market, 253 King's Road, London SW3. Tel: (071) 352 6338.
Large and carefully-assembled stock of memorabilia from the silents to the 1980s. Plus stills, pressbooks, posters. Customers served by post.

Movie Finds,
4 Ravenslea Road, Balham, London SW12 8SB. Tel: (081) 673 6534.
Teddy Green has built this small firm into a treasure trove of film stills and memorabilia. The range is huge, and the catalogue contains innumerable posters and movie scenes.

Dress Circle,
57-59 Monmouth Street, Upper St. Martin's Lane, London WC2H 9DG. Tel: (071) 240 2227, (071) 836 8279.

Flashbacks,
6 Silver Place, (Beak St.), London W1R 3LJ. Tel: (071) 437 8562.
Most impressively stocked establishment which, in London's West End, caters for those interested in movie ephemera – posters, stills, pressbooks – from many countries and every period of cinema history. Also extensive Mail Order service. Four catalogues per annum.

Zwemmer, A.,
80 Charing Cross Road, London WC2. Tel: (071) 379 7886.
Solid, professional approach to stocking, dealing efficiently with mail order inquiries. Location near Leicester Square is also handy.

Movie Boulevard,
3 Cherry Tree Walk, Leeds LS2 7EB. Tel: (0532) 422 888. Fax: (0532) 438 840.
Welcome north of England addition to the ranks of shops specialising in

soundtracks, videos. Headed by the enthusiastic Robert Wood.

U.S.A.
Applause,
211 West 71 Street, New York, NY10023. Tel: (212) 496 7511.
Now one of the few – and certainly the only uptown – film and showbiz bookstores in Manhattan. Hailed for its courageous publications (e.g. *The JFK Screenplay*).

Books of Latin America,
P.O. Box 1103, Redlands, California 92373. Tel: (909) 793-8423. Fax: (909) 335 9945.
Specialist in works on Latin American cinema, and Spanish and Portuguese cinema in general.

Cinema Books,
4753 Roosevelt Way NE, Seattle, Washington 98105. Tel: (206) 547-7667.
Fine selection of film books and magazines, with space also devoted to TV and theatre. Mail Orders welcome.

Cinemonde,
1932 Polk Street, San Francisco,
California 94109. Tel: (415) 776-9988.
Installed in a capacious, loft-like HQ on Polk Street, Cinemonde may well be the world's leading poster store for cinema buffs. Items are immaculately displayed and stored, and the colourful catalogue is a collectors' item ($8 inc. airmail costs).

Dwight Cleveland,
P.O. Box 10922, Chicago, Illinois 60610-0922. Tel: (312) 523 9152.
Buys and sells movie posters.

Collectors Book Store,
1708 N. Vine Street,Hollywood, California 90028. Tel: (213) 467-3296.
Offers a commendable range of posters, stills, lobby cards, TV and film scripts.Fax: (213) 467 4536

Samuel French's Theatre & Film Bookshop,
7623 Sunset Boulevard, Hollywood, California 90046. Tel: (213) 876-570.
The world's oldest and largest play publisher (est. 1830) operates a separate film bookshop. Complete range of new movie books available: directories, reference, writing,

acting, biography, screenplays, etc. 3,000 titles and growing! Worldwide mail order service. Note that French's also have a store at 11963 Ventura Blvd, Studio City, California 91604. Tel: (818) 762-535. Gwen Feldman prepares some meticulous catalogues that include more data than most similar efforts.

Gotham Book Mart,
41 West 47th St., New York, NY 10036. Tel: (212) 719 4448.
This famous literary bookshop in mid-Manhattan, established in 1920, is the only New York city bookstore offering new, used and out-of-print film and theatre books. Also an extensive stock of "quality" magazines dating from the 1950's to the present.

Larry Edmunds Bookshop,
6644 Hollywood Blvd., Hollywood,

California 90028. Tel: (213) 463 3273.
The stills collection alone is a goldmine for any film buff. Back numbers of movie annuals, posters, lobby cards and largest collection of new and used books in the world. Magazines always available.

Libros Latinos-Books of Latin America
P.O. Box 1103, Redlands, California 92373. Tel: (909) 793-8423. Fax: (909) 335 9945.
Specialist in works on Latin American cinema, and Spanish and Portuguese cinema in general.

Limelight Film and Theatre Bookstore,
1803 Market Street, San Francisco, California 94103. Tel: (415) 864-2265.
Roy A. Johnson runs this lively store

for film and theatre books. Collection includes plays, screenplays, biographies, history and criticism of films and film and television technique.

Movie Madness,
1222 Wisconsin Avenue NW, Washington DC 20007.
Posters, etc. available at this tiny store adjacent to the Key (one of Washington's best repertory cinemas).

Jerry Ohlinger's Movie Material Store Inc.,
242 West 14th Street, New York, NY 10011. Tel: (212) 989-869.
Jerry Ohlinger's emporium stocks a wealth of stills from the 1960's through the 1990's, specialising in colour material. Posters are also plentiful and there are some magazines as well.

MAGAZINES

The following list amounts to a selection only of the world's hundreds of film publications. Editors wishing to receive a free listing must send sample copies (preferably opening a sample subscription for us). Address: IFG, Variety, 34-35 Newman Street, London W1P 3PD, U.K.

NEW TITLES

DOX
PO Box 100534, 45405 Mulheim an der Ruhr, Germany. An independent magazine on documentary film, film-making and viewing. Interviews, international news, festival reports and industry profiles. Bi-monthly.

FILA 7 VIDEO
Avda. de la Sierra, 6. 2° D, Aptdo. de Correos 55, 28700 San Sebastian de los Reyes, Madrid, Spain. New sister publication to Fila 7, this colourful monthly deals with video and television, with features on new technology and video games.

FILM INTERNATIONAL
5th Floor, 12 Sam St. Hafez Avenue, Tehran, Iran. Quarterly publication which not only focuses on Iranian films and film-makers, but also on issues regarding third world cinema. In English.

FILMJOURNALEN
Finlandssvenskt filmcentrum, Nylands-gatan 1, 25700 Åbo, Finland. Well-printed Swedish-language quarterly focusing on Nordic and Finnish cinema.

FILMMAKER
132 West 21st Street, 6th Floor, New York, NY 10011-3203, U.S.A. Sponsored by the Independent Feature Project and IFP/West, this lively quarterly covers all aspects of independent film-making, with features, interviews, festival and technical news.

IMMAGINI & SUONI
FIAIS, Casella postale 6306, 00195 ROme, Italy. Published by the International Federa-tion of Film Archives. In French and Italian.

THE LIMITED EDITION
The Score Company, Linzer Str. 5, 53604 Bad Honnef, Germany. Quarterly devoted to soundtracks and the art of film scoring.

MEDIAFILM
Haachtsesteenweg 35, B-1030 Brussels, Belgium. Serious Belgian quarterly, with extensive reviews, analysis and focus on directors.

WELTWUNDER DER KINEMATOGRAPHIE
Postfach 100 274, D-10562 Berlin, Germany.

Fascinating, well-researched new title, with detailed articles on the past, present and future of cinematography and the technical art of film-making. Yearly.

REGULAR

AMERICAN CLASSIC SCREEN
P.O. Box 7150, Shawnee Mission, Kansas 66207, U.S.A. Bi-monthly devoted to the preservation of old films, filled with useful addresses.

AMERICAN PREMIERE
8421 Wilshire Blvd., Penthouse; Beverly Hills, CA 90211, U.S.A. Bi-monthly industry magazine, free to members of the Academy of Motion Picture Arts and Sciences.

ANIMATION MAGAZINE
5889 Kanan Road, Suite 317, Agoura Hills, California 91301, U.S.A. International guide to the animation industry in an eye-catching format. Bi-monthly.

ANIMATOR
Filmcraft Publications, 13 Ringway Road, Park Street, St. Albans, Herts, AL2 2RE, U.K. Entertaining and informative magazine for animators and animation buffs.

AUDIENCE

P.O. Box 7149, Van Nuys, CA91409-7149, U.S.A. Billed as an "informal commentary on film", this witty, well-informed bi-monthly features articles and reviews, both recent and retrospective.

AVANT PREMIERE

Case Postale 5615, 1211 Geneva 11, Switzerland. Colourful monthly with lengthy reviews of new releases, as well as updates on Swiss production and distribution.

BIANCO E NERO

1524 via Tuscolana, 00173 Rome, Italy. Italian quarterly that boasts a reputation for scholarship second to none in its country.

BRIGHT LIGHTS

PO Box 420987, San Francisco, CA 94142-0987, U.S.A. Resurrected from the late seventies, this monthly is a hybrid of academic and general film fan magazine, with great visuals and hand-tinted covers.

CAHIERS DU CINEMA

Editions de l'Etoile, 9 passage de la Boule Blanche, 75012 Paris, France. Celebrated French journal now enjoying a second lease of life after a long spell in the wilderness.

CHAPLIN

Box 27 126, S-102 52 Stockholm, Sweden. Sponsored by the Swedish Film Institute and covering world cinema in lively fashion. Now one of the most appealing film magazines in Europe. Bi-monthly.

CIAK SI GIRA

C. so I, Europa 5/7, 20122 Milan, Italy. Glossy Italian monthly, well established, full of lively articles. Similar to France's *Première*.

CINEASTE

Suite 1601 200 Park Avenue South, New York, NY 10003, U.S.A. Perhaps the finest anti-establishment movie magazine, never afraid to tackle controversial issues and never prone to Hollywood worship. Interviews are especially good in *Cineaste*.

CINE-BULLES

4545 avenue Pierre-de-Coubertin, CP 1000, Succursale M. Montréal, Canada H1V 3R2. Remarkable and informative Québécois quarterly that may just be the best in Canada.

CINE-BULLETIN

Swiss Film Centre, Münstergasse 18, CH-8025 Zürich, Switzerland. Serious Swiss monthly in French and German with box-office and films in production.

CINECRITICA

Via Yser, n.8-00198 Rome, Italy. Dense Italian quarterly focussing on world cinema.

CINE CUBANO

Calle 23, no. 1115 Apdo. 55, Havana, Cuba. Vital information on all Latin American cinema, unfortunately only in Spanish.

CINEFANTASTIQUE

P.O. Box 270, Oak Park, Ill. 60303, U.S.A. An enthusiastic, well-written, beautifully produced bi-monthly with a special emphasis on fantasy films.

CINE-FICHES DE GRAND ANGLE

Rue d'Arschot 29, B-5660 Mariembourg, Belgium. Monthly review of new films and videos.

CINEMA 2002

Adremans 64, Madrid 28, Spain. First-class Spanish monthly packed with pictures, serious articles and interviews, and a great many news items.

CINEMA & CINEMA

1 via Battibecco, 40123 Bologna, Italy. Respected quarterly.

CINEMA JOURNAL

University of Illinois Press, 54 E Gregory Drive, Champaign, IL 61820, U.S.A. A scholarly and respected American magazine, now published twice a year.

CINEMA NOVO

Apartado, 78, 4002 Porto Codex, Portugal. Bi-monthly Portuguese magazine dealing with international and Portuguese topics.

CINEMA NUOVO

PO Box 362, 70100 Bari, Italy. Polemical, academic Italian bi-monthly with excellent articles.

CINEMA PAPERS

43 Charles Street, Abbotsford, 3067, Australia. Excellent large-format Australian bi-monthly, packed with information and pictures, useful for anyone monitoring the industry in Oz.

CINEMATECA REVISTA

Lorenzo Carnelli 1311, Casilla de Correo 1170, Montevideo, Uruguay. Bright magazine with international slant published by Cinemateca Uruguaya. Ten times a year.

CINEMATHEQUE

P.O. Box 20370, Tel Aviv 61203, Israel. Fine monthly Israeli magazine (with summary in English) dwelling on seasons at the Tel-Aviv Cinémathèque but also reporting on world festivals etc.

CINEMAYA

B 90 Defence Colony, New Delhi 110 024, India. Informative, elegant magazine, published quarterly in English since 1988, on all aspects of the Asian film industry.

CINE SITH

142 Abeyratne Mawatha, Boralesgamuwa, Sri Lanka. Sri Lanka's only film publication, this serious quarterly focuses on local and other Asian cinema.

CLASSIC IMAGES

P.O. Box 809, Muscataine, IA52761, U.S.A. Formerly "Classic Film Collector," a good source for film buffs eager to enlarge their library of movies. Monthly.

CULTURE AND CINEMA

P.O. Box 11495-147, Tehran, Iran. Monthly magazine featuring Iranian cinema.

DIRIGIDO

Rbla de Cataluña, 108 3. 1, Barcelona 08008, Spain. This handsomely-produced Spanish monthly throws the spotlight each issue on a particular genre, studio or director of international renown.

EKRAN

c/o Slovene Film-makers Association, 6100. Ljubljana, Ulica Talcev 6, Slovenia. Provides critical evaluation and topical consideration of Slovene and foreign films.

EL REFUGIO

José Granda 460, Lima 27, Peru. South American monthly with reviews and features on world cinema.

EMPIRE

1st Floor, Mappin House, 4 Winsley Street, London W1N 7AR, U.K. Glossy magazine with American slant, heavy on reviews and behind-the-scenes. Monthly.

ENFOQUE

Publicaciones y Audiovisuales, Linterna Mágica Ltda., Casilla 15, Correo 34, Santiago, Chile. Occasional quarterly taking an in-depth look at the Chilean/Latin American markets and new-releases.

ENTERTAINMENT HERALD

Corrieres 2817 3-A 1015, Buenos Aires, Argentina.

FANTASTIC

Gran Via de les Corts Catalanes M° 133. 29, 0814 Barcelona, Spain. Monthly, dedicated to sci-films, with articles and photographs.

FARABI FILM QUARTERLY

55 Sie-Tir Ave., Tehran 11358, Iran. Quarterly periodical issued by the Farabi Cinema Foundation, with the aim of upgrading film culture in the country.

FATAL VISIONS

P.O. Box 133, Northcote 3070, Victoria, Australia. Lively bi-annual title covering horror, sci-fi, sexploitation and fantasy from all angles; cinema, laser, video and T.V.

FILA 7

Avda. de la Sierra 6. 2° D, Aptdo. de Correos 55, 28700 San Sebastian de los Reyes, Madrid, Spain. Monthly consumer-oriented, with features and photographs.

FILM

Pulawska 61, 02595 Warsaw, Poland. Popular Polish weekly with international slant.

FILM

(Yeonghwa), Motion Picture Promotion Corporation of Korea, 34-5, 3-ga, Namsan-dong, Junggu, Seoul. South Korea's only serious film magazine, packed with information. Bi-monthly.

FILMHÄFTET

Box 101 56, 100 55 Stockholm, Sweden. Egghead monthly with features on international directors, retrospectives, and Scandinavian television.

FILMKULTURA

Solymár u. 8, 1032 Budapest, Hungary. Essays and reviews on Hungarian and international cinema. Six times a year.

FILMMAKER MAGAZINE

Independent Feature Project, 104 West 29th Street, 12th Floor, New York, NY 10001, U.S.A. Aimed at independent film-makers, this quarterly offers interviews, news and sound advice.

FILMVILAG

Pozsonyi út 20, H-1137 Budapest, Hungary. Monthly with reviews and interviews.

FILMS IN REVIEW

P.O. Box 589, New York, NY 10021, U.S.A. Compact bi-monthly journal, reviewing notable new releases with interviews, retrospective articles and television/video reports.

FILM & DOBA

Halkova 1, 120 72 Prague 2, Czech Republic. The principal Czech film monthly.

FILM APPRECIATION

The National Film Archive of the R.O.C., 4th Floor, 7 Ching-tao East Road, Taipei, Taiwan R.O.C. Taiwan's premier serious film journal, published as a bi-monthly. Focus on the cinematic output of Taiwan, Hong Kong and mainland China, as well as from Chinese communities overseas.

FILM EN TELEVISIE + VIDEO

Haachtesteenweg, 35, 1030 Brussels, Belgium. Extensive reviews of major new film and video releases, profiles and interviews, festival news.

FILM BULLETIN

Postfach 137, Hard 4, CH-8408 Winterthur, Switzerland. Informative, straightforward look at international cinema, with useful Swiss material also. Bi-monthly.

FILM COMMENT

Film Society of Lincoln Center, 70 Lincoln Center Plaza, New York, NY 10023, U.S.A. Informative, feisty, and uncompromising articles as well as interviews on wide-ranging international topics. New video section. Still the best U.S. bi-monthly on the cinema.

FILM CRITICISM

Allegheny College, Box D, Meadville, PA 16335, U.S.A. Scholarly essays on film history, theory, and culture. Tri-quarterly.

FILM DOPE

74 Julian Road, Nottingham NG2 5AN. Not so much a magazine, more a part-work film dictionary, this irregular British quarterly is to be welcomed for its exhaustive research.

FILMIHULLU

c/o Suomen elokuvakethojen-litto, Annankatu 13 B 11, SF-00120 Helsinki 12. Finnish film and TV magazine with perverse, rather old-fashioned critical approach, appearing eight times a year.

FILM HISTORY

John Libbey and Co. Ltd., 13 Smiths Yard, Summerley Street, London SW18 4HR, U.K. Articles on the historical development of the motion picture, in a social, technological and economic context.

FILM INTERNATIONAL

5th Floor, 12 Sam ST., Hafez Ave., P.O. Box 11365-5875 Tehran, Iran. Informative look at world cinema, the first English language quarterly in Iran.

FILM LITERATURE INDEX

Film and Television Documentation Centre, State University of New York, 1400 Washington Avenue, Albany, NY 12222, U.S.A. Manuscripts invited for submission, reviews, interviews or analysis.

FILM MONTHLY

P.O. Box 11265-5875, Tehran, Iran. Reviews and features on the latest releases.

FILM NA SWIECIE

Polish Federation of Film Clubs, Plocka 16/34, 01138 Warsaw, Poland.

FILM QUARTERLY

University of California Press, 2120 Berkeley Way, Berkeley, California 94720. Now much improved visually, this magazine neatly straddles the barrier between the glossy journals and academic tomes.

FOTOGRAMAS

Gran Via de les Corts, Catalanes M° 133. 39, 08014 Barcelona, Spain. Glossy monthly, packed with colourful articles and photographs, also video reviews and television film listings.

GRIFFITHIANA

Cineteca del Friuli, 26 via Osoppo, 33013 Gemona del Friuli (Udine), Italy. Italian quarterly devoted exclusively to the study of silent cinema and animation. Each issue is a miracle of scholarship and devotion.

HOLLAND ANIMATION BULLETIN

Stevinstraat 261, 2587 EJ The Hague, Netherlands. Authoritative Dutch bulletin edited by Nico Crama.

IMAGEN

Casilla 1733, La Paz, Bolivia. Magazine of the Bolivian New Cinema Movement.

IMAGENES DE ACTUALIDAD

Rambla de Cataluña 108, 08008 Barcelona, Spain. Glossy, well presented international magazine with strong Hollywood bias. Monthly.

IMMAGINE

20 Via Villafranca, 00185 Rome, Italy. Much-admired quarterly, full of articles on world cinema from its origins to the fifties.

THE INDEPENDENT FILM/VIDEO GUIDE

EFLA, 45 John Street, New York, NY 10038, U.S.A. Quarterly index to the works exhibited by non-commercial film-video show-cases in New York City and New York State.

INTERFILMS

Valportillo Primera 16, Poligono Industrial Alcobendas, Alcobendas 28100, Madrid, Spain. Monthly film magazine for consumers.

INTERNATIONAL DOCUMENTARY

1551 South Robertson Boulevard, Suite 201, Los Angeles, CA 90035, U.S.A. The only publication to focus exclusively on non-fiction film and video. Presents new work and ideas in the documentary field with informative articles, reviews and interviews. Published ten times a year.

ISKUSSTVO KINO

9 ul. Usievicha, 125319 Moscow, Russia. Chunky, theoretical, most authoritative Russian film monthly.

JUMP CUT

P.O. Box 865, Berkeley, California 94701, U.S.A. Published only once or twice a year, this tabloid contains an extraordinary amount of closely-woven text.

KINEMA

Fine Arts (Film Studies), University of Waterloo, Waterloo, Ont. N2L 3G1, Canada. A journal of history, theory and aesthetics of world film and audiovisual media. Twice yearly.

KINO

c/o Holloway, Helgoländer Ufer 6, 10577, Berlin, Germany. Excellent quarterly devoted to both German cinema and international festival reports. Features reviews, interviews and credits.

KINO

Chelmska 19/21, 00-724 Warsaw, Poland. Culturally-inclined Polish magazine designed to promote European cinema, with interviews, reviews and essays.

KOSMORAMA

The Danish Film Museum, Store Søndervoldstræde, DK-1419 Copenhagen K, Denmark. One of the most beautifully-designed and lovingly-edited of Nordic film magazines. Quarterly.

LA STRADA

P.O. Box 432, 33101 Tampere, Finland. Finland's largest film magazine, this quarterly is provocative and entertaining, with lots of news and reviews. In Finnish.

MEDIUM

Postfach 50 05 50, Frankfurt am Main, Germany. Dense German publication covering film, radio, T.V., and the press. Bi-monthly.

MOVIELINE

1141 South Beverly Drive, Los Angeles, CA 90035, U.S.A. Intelligent, irreverent and refreshingly candid Hollywood monthly. Great interviews.

THE NIGHTINGALE REPORT

45 Barclay Road, Toronto, Ontario M3H 3EZ, Canada. Fortnightly newsletter aimed at Canadian film and television industry. News and comprehensive listings.

NUOVO CINEMA EUROPEO

Via delle Cinque Giornate 15, 50129, Florence, Italy. Chunky bi-monthly report on Italian film industry, in English with Italian summary. Includes industry news, such as box-office, markets and foreign sales.

NZ FILM

P.O. Box 11-546, Wellington, New Zealand. News from the New Zealand Film Commission, a twice yearly round-up of the country's film industry.

ONFILM

P.O. Box 6374, Wellington, New Zealand. A film, television and video magazine for New Zealand, with location reports and a production survey.

PHOTOGRAPH

No 20, 19th Alley, Gandhi Ave., Tehran, Iran. A monthly magazine by the Young Iranian Cinema Society.

PICTURE HOUSE

5 Coopers Close, Burgess Hill, W. Sussex RH15 8AN. Admirable quarterly devoted to the cinema buildings of the past.

POPULAR CINEMA

(Dazhong dianying), 22 Belsanhai Donglu, Peking, China. Leading mainland Chinese monthly, also carrying pieces on Hongkong, Taiwan and foreign cinema.

POSITIF

156 rue Oberkampf, 75011 Paris, France. In-depth interviews, articles, all immaculately researched and highly intelligent. Recently celebrated its 400th issue, and remains Europe's best film magazine.

PREMIERE

149 rue Anatole France, 92534 Levallois-Perret Cedex, France. France's biggest movie monthly, packed with information, reviews and filmographies.

PREMIERE

2 Park Avenue, New York, NY 10016, U.S.A. Diluted in size and scope since its launch six years ago, but still has its finger on the pulse of Hollywood and retains a huge circulation.

PREMIERE U.K.

Mappin House, 4 Winsley Street, London W1N 7AR, U.K. Glossy monthly with in-depth personality profiles and stylish photography. Ninety percent original editorial, ten percent taken from U.S. edition.

PRODUCER

162-170 Wardour Street, London, W1V 4LA, U.K. Welcome voice for the independent British producer.

QUADERNI DI CINEMA

Via Benedetto Varchi 57, 50132 Florence, Italy. Wide-ranging Italian bi-monthly, striving to match cultural politics with an enthusiastic appreciation of film.

RECTANGLE

CAC Voltaire, Rue Général-Dufour 16, 1204 Geneva, Switzerland. Only film magazine in the Suisse romande, and admirably poised between the theoretical and researchist approach to the cinema, with a fresh and lively layout.

RIVISTA DEL CINEMATOGRAFO

Via Giuseppe Palombini, 6-165 Rome, Italy. Important Italian monthly.

SEGNOCINEMA

Via G Prati 34, Vicenza. Italian bi-monthly, with particularly useful September issue that lists complete guide to all films released the previous season.

SIGHT AND SOUND

British Film Institute, 21 Stephen Street, London W1 1PL, U.K. Apart from its invaluable reference guide to every film released in the U.K., this once-celebrated magazine has improved during recent months, to include foreign films in its perspective.

SKRIEN

p/a Filmmuseum, Vondelpark 3, 1071 AA Amsterdam, The Netherlands. Excellent Dutch magazine that appears with regularity and enthusiasm. Bi-monthly.

SOUNDTRACK!

317 Skyline Lake Drive, Box 609, Ringwood, NJ 07456, U.S.A. Excellent quarterly for film music collectors.

SPECIAL EFFECT

B/4, Balgachia Villa, Calcutta 700 037, India. Formerly *Magic Lantern*, this Indian film quarterly mixes interviews and reviews with insightful comment, and surveys different trends in Indian cinema.

STARS

Rue d'Arschot 29, B-5660 Mariembourg, Belgium. Quarterly publication giving actors' biographies and filmographies.

STUDIO MAGAZINE

116 bis, avenue des Champs-Elysées, 75008 Paris, France. Glossy, beautifully designed monthly with reviews, articles and interviews.

TALKING PICTURES

Valis Books, 52A Lascotts Road, London N22 4JN, U.K. SLim quarterly with articles, reviews and interviews..

24 IMAGES

3781, rue Laval, Montréal, QC M2W 2M8, Canada. Exceptionally attractive French/Canadian quarterly, witty and well-informed.

VE CINEMA

Hil Yayinlari, Cagaloghi, Istanbul, Turkey. Quarterly published in Turkish.

VERTIGO

7-9 Earlham Street, London WC2H 9LL, U.K. New quarterly for independent British film-makers and audiences. A forum for critical debate.

VIDEO MAKER

Oasis Publishing, Media House, Boxwell Road, Berkhamsted, Herts, England. Film and video monthly that concentrates on the craft of making your own films.

VIDEO MARKT

Stahlgrubbering 11a, 81829 Munich, Germany. Glossy monthly for those in the video industry.

VIDEO PROFESSIANAL

Consell de Cent 83, 6ª planta, 08015 Barcelona, Spain. Monthly, dedicated exclusively to home-video, photos and articles.

WIDE ANGLE

The Johns Hopkins University Press, Baltimore, Maryland 212180, U.S.A. Scholarly thematically arranged journal. Wide range.

WORLD SCREEN

China Film Press, 22 Beisanhuandonglu, Beijng 100013, China. Monthly primarily devoted to new/classic features from around the world, with artist profiles and events.

Z FILMTIDSSKRIFT

Teatergt 3, 0180 Oslo 1, Norway. Enthusiastic quarterly with a focus on film theory and history, both Norwegian and international.

ZOOM

Bederstrasse 76, Postfach, 8027 Zürich, Switzerland. Slim Swiss monthly highlighting new releases, with good festival coverage. In German.

National Organs

AFC INFORMATION UPDATE

GPO Box 3984, Sydney NSW 2001, Australia. Monthly, with regular production slate, industry statistics, funding approvals and Australian films at international markets and festivals.

CHINA SCREEN

China Film Export and Import Corporation, Xinjiekovvwai Dajie 25, Beijing, China. Quarterly.

CINEMA, CINEMA

Ministère de la Culture Française, avenue de Cortenbur 158, 1040 Brussels, Belgium.

FEPACI NEWS

01 BP. 2524 Ouagadougou 01, Burkina Faso. Monthly newsletter of the Pan-African Federation of film-makers.

FILM CANADA YEARBOOK

Cine Communications, Box 152, Station R, Toronto, Ontario MAG 323, Canada. Comprehensive directory of the Canadian Film Industry.

ISRAEL FILM CENTRE INFORMATION BULLETIN

Ministry of Industry and Trade, 30 Agron Street, Jerusalem, Israel. Yearly review of Israeli film industry and catalogue of Israel films.

KINO

Türkenstrasse 93, 8000 München 40, Germany. Monthly.

Trade and Technical

AMERICAN CINEMATOGRAPHER

ASC Holding Corp., Box 2230, Los Angeles, CA 90078, U.S.A. Monthly.

IMAGE TECHNOLOGY – JOURNAL OF THE BKSTS

M6-M14 Victoria House, Vernon Place, London WC1B 4DF, U.K. Covers technologies of motion picture film, television and sound at professional level. Ten times yearly.

BLICKPUNKT-FILM

Stahlgruberring 11a, 81829 Munich, Germany. Strong on box-office returns and marketing, this German weekly also covers the video and T.V. market.

BOXOFFICE

6640 Sunset Blvd, Hollywood, California, 90028-7159, U.S.A. Business monthly for the Hollywood community.

CINE & TELE INFORME

Grand Via 64, 28013, Madrid, Spain. Monthly that covers Spanish and international film, video and TV development.

CINEMA D'OGGI

Viale Regina Margherita 286, 00198 Rome, Italy. Fortnightly. Interviews with producers.

ECOMONO PRESS ACTING NEWS

Via Belluno 1, 00161 Rome, Italy. Comprehensive weekly reports on Italian film starts. Four market issues have English translations.

LE FILM FRANÇAIS

90 rue de Flandre, 75947 Paris Cedex 19, France. Lightweight weekly with news, reviews, box-office and production schedules.

FILM-ECHO/FILMWOCHE

Marktplatz 13, 65183 Wiesbaden, Germany. Doyen of the German trade. Weekly.

FILM JOURNAL

Pubsun Corp., 244 West 49 Street, New York, NY 10019, U.S.A. Monthly magazine aimed at U.S. exhibitors.

FILM OG KINO

Stortingsgaten 16, 0161 Oslo 1, Norway. Wide-ranging and well illustrated, covering trade matters but often controversial issues too.

GIORNALE DELLO SPETTACOLO

Via di Villa Patrizi 10, 00161 Rome, Italy. Box-office data, legal requirements, technical information etc.

HOLLYWOOD REPORTER

5055 Wilshire Boulevard, Los Angeles, CA 90036-4396, U.S.A. Daily.

MONITEUR DU FILM

36 rue des Frambosiers, 1180 Brussels, Belgium. Monthly.

MOVIE/TV MARKETING

Box 30, Central Post Office, Tokyo, 100-91 Japan. Monthly from Japan – in English.

MOVING PICTURES INTERNATIONAL

151-153 Wardour Street, London W1V 3TB, U.K. European-orientated monthly trade paper published in London.

MÜNCHEN FILM NEWS

Kaiserstrasse 39, 80801 Munich, Germany. A bi-monthly put out by Munich's Informationbüro Film containing festival reports, films in production, personalities and other news concerning the Munich film scene. English version available.

SCREEN INTERNATIONAL

33-39 Bowling Green Lane, London, EC1R 0DA, U.K. Weekly. U.K.-oriented trade organ.

VARIETY

5700 Wilshire Boulevard, Suite 120, Los Angeles, CA 90036. The world's foremost newspaper (daily and weekly) of the entertainment business.